Modern Conflict in the Greater Middle East

Modern Conflict in the Greater Middle East

A Country-by-Country Guide

SPENCER C. TUCKER, EDITOR

 ABC-CLIO™

An Imprint of ABC-CLIO, LLC
Santa Barbara, California • Denver, Colorado

Copyright © 2017 by ABC-CLIO, LLC

Library of Congress Cataloging-in-Publication Data

Names: Tucker, Spencer, 1937- editor.
Title: Modern conflict in the greater Middle East : a country-by-country guide /
    Spencer C. Tucker, editor.
Description: Santa Barbara, Calif. : ABC-CLIO, [2017] | Includes bibliographical
    references and index.
Identifiers: LCCN 2016047938 (print) | LCCN 2016048879 (ebook) |
    ISBN 9781440843600 (alk. paper) | ISBN 9781440843617 (ebook)
Subjects: LCSH: Middle East—Politics and government—21st century. |
    Arab countries—Politics and government—21st century. | Arab Spring, 2010-
Classification: LCC DS63.123 .M63 2017 (print) | LCC DS63.123 (ebook) |
    DDC 956.04—dc23
LC record available at https://lccn.loc.gov/2016047938

ISBN: 978-1-4408-4360-0
EISBN: 978-1-4408-4361-7

21 20 19 18 17   1 2 3 4 5

This book is also available as an eBook.

ABC-CLIO
An Imprint of ABC-CLIO, LLC

ABC-CLIO, LLC
130 Cremona Drive, P.O. Box 1911
Santa Barbara, California 93116-1911
www.abc-clio.com

This book is printed on acid-free paper ∞

Manufactured in the United States of America

For our good friend Don Hasfurther, the master of Hickory Hill

Contents

Preface

Modern Conflict in the Greater Middle East: A Country-by-Country Guide includes entries on 22 countries, each consisting of a narrative history, a timeline, and a further reading list, as well as sidebars and documents. ABC-CLIO specified the inclusion of Afghanistan, Pakistan, and the Maghreb countries of North Africa—Morocco, Algeria, and Tunisia—since they are considered by most scholars to be part of the Greater Middle East. These five states are not normally thought of as belonging to the Middle East, but they are closely linked to it by religion and culture. The term "Greater Middle East" is a new one, advanced by the George W. Bush administration early in this century and specifically included the Maghreb, Turkey, Iran, Afghanistan, and Pakistan.

Readers are advised that the necessity to cover so much material has forced me to provide more of a summary of a particular war in the case of one belligerent while furnishing a more detailed explanation of events in that of another country. Thus, the Turkish invasion of Cyprus in 1974 is chiefly covered in the entry on Cyprus, and the most detail on the 1982 Lebanon War is found in the entry on Lebanon rather than in Israel. Finally, because of publishing deadlines this work covers events only through the end of June 2016.

In writing the essays, I was able to draw on work by other scholars in encyclopedias I have edited for ABC-CLIO. These individuals are credited at the end of the country narratives, but most of the work here is my own. I am grateful to my associate Paul G. Pierpaoli Jr. for assembling the documents.

I hope this work will lead to a greater understanding of the region, its history, and its many pressing issues—above all that of the relationship between the Arab states and Israel.

Spencer C. Tucker

Introduction

World War I is the great watershed in the history of the Greater Middle East. The decision of Ottoman leaders to enter that conflict on the German side was tumultuous, for it ended with a redrawn Middle East. Both Britain and Germany had courted the Ottomans well before the beginning of the war in August 1914, but the August 1, 1914, decision by the British to sequester two powerful battleships being built in British yards that had already been paid for by popular Ottoman subscription angered many Turks. The Germans also capitalized on traditional animosity felt by the Ottomans against Russia.

Still, the Ottoman Empire was undecided and on August 3 declared its neutrality in the war. German admiral Wilhelm Souchon's Mediterranean Squadron of the modern battle cruiser *Goeben* and the light cruiser *Breslau* dramatically changed the course of events. Souchon managed to avoid larger British and French warships and escape to Istanbul (Constantinople) on August 11. The presence of these two warships was of immense benefit to the pro-German faction in the government.

On August 16 Souchon arranged to sell both warships to the Ottomans as replacements for the two dreadnoughts sequestered by Britain. Although given Turkish names, the two warships retained their German crews, and Souchon became commander of the Ottoman Navy.

With the secret support of Ottoman minister of war Ismail Enver Pasha, the leading supporter of an alliance with Germany, Souchon set sail from Istanbul on October 27 under the guise of a training exercise in the Black Sea. Two days later his ships bombarded Russian bases and laid mines. The Ottoman cabinet had not been informed of the operation in advance, and Souchon falsely reported that the Russians had attacked him first.

Souchon's actions brought a formal declaration of war by Russia against the Ottoman Empire on November 4, 1914. Despite the resignation of four cabinet members in protest against what Enver and Souchon had engineered, the Ottoman Empire remained in the war on the side of the Central Powers. This had great impact. It created a new theater of war in the Middle East and caused the Western Allies and Russia to divert important resources to the Transcaucasian and Middle Eastern fronts, perhaps enabling Germany to prolong the war. It also cut French and British access to Russia transiting from the Mediterranean into the Black Sea. The loss to the Entente of this important shipping lane greatly increased the difficulty of getting needed military supplies to Russia. It also denied Russia a means of exporting its goods to the West, greatly adding to its financial difficulties.

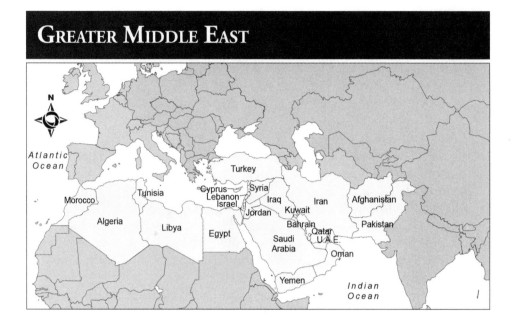

GREATER MIDDLE EAST

With a few notable exceptions, the war went poorly for the Ottomans. Their offensives in Caucasia against the Russians were largely failures, but under the leadership of Liman von Sanders and Ottoman general Mustapha Kemal (the future Kemal Ataturk), the Ottomans turned back a poorly executed British effort to force the Dardanelles with naval power alone, then contained the Allied landing on the Gallipoli Peninsula.

Several Ottoman efforts to seize the Suez Canal failed, although the Ottomans turned back a British effort to secure Baghdad by winning the Battle of Ctesiphon in November 1915. They then laid siege to the British expeditionary force at Kut al-Amara in December and secured its surrender in April 1916. The British built up their strength and reversed the situation, however. Thanks to an arrangement worked out by the British authorities in Cairo, on June 8, 1916, sharif of Mecca Hussein bin Ali began the Arab Revolt (1916–1918), with the British pledge of the creation of a single independent, unified Arab kingdom. The revolt was led by Hussein's son Faisal, working in concert with British Army captain T. E. Lawrence.

At the same time, the British worked to secure Jewish support. On November 2, 1917, British foreign secretary Arthur James Balfour, well aware of the impact of Zionism, the movement to resettle Jews in Palestine owing to religious persecutions (pogroms) in Russia, issued what became known as the Balfour Declaration. The declaration announced British support for the "establishment in Palestine of a national home for the Jewish people."

Finally and most important, there was the Sykes-Picot Agreement. During the war French diplomat François-Georges Picot and British diplomat Sir Mark Sykes negotiated the future disposition of Middle East territory belonging to the Ottoman Empire. Signed on May 16, 1916, it assigned what would be postwar Iraq and

Palestine to Britain, while France was to receive control of what would be Syria and Lebanon.

The punitive Treaty of Sèvres of August 1920 with the Ottoman Empire finalized its partition. Meanwhile, in the Greco-Turkish War (1919–1922), the Greeks attempted to secure Smyrna but were defeated by the Turks. In April 1921 Britain split Palestine into the Emirate of Transjordan, comprising territory east of the Jordan River, and Palestine to the west. Transjordan provided a throne for another Hussein son, Abdullah. Egypt, which had been under British rule since the 1880s, received nominal independence in 1922. Meanwhile, most of the Arabian Peninsula fell under the rule of British ally Ibn Saud, who established the Kingdom of Saudi Arabia in 1932.

In Persia, the British supported a 1921 coup by Reza Khan. Four years later he established the Pahlavi dynasty, with himself as Reza Shah Pahlavi I, and proceeded to lay the foundations of the modern Iranian state. In 1935 he changed the country's name to Iran.

In March 1920 Faisal sought to establish the promised Arab kingdom at Damascus, but his reign lasted only until July, when his forces were defeated by the French. The British then installed Faisal as ruler of the Kingdom of Iraq. The new states, with their arbitrarily drawn borders, were officially recognized as mandates by the new League of Nations.

Early revolts against British and French rule were rather easily crushed. Palestine proved particularly vexing. It had a majority Arab population, but Jews continued to arrive there in significant numbers. Many of them, financed by wealthy West European Jews, were able to purchase land from absentee Arab landholders, creating considerable resentment among many Arabs. The British found themselves in an impossible situation of permitting immigration while trying to win Arab support. Arab anger turned violent in 1936, forcing Britain to dispatch significant troop reinforcements to Palestine.

During World War II, the British openly courted Arab countries. The Suez Canal was of vast importance, and to secure Arab support Britain even turned away Jews attempting to escape the Holocaust and secure refuge in Palestine. Although the British had granted independence to Iraq in 1932, they had retained considerable rights there, including military bases. A coup in 1941 brought a pro-Axis regime to power, and Iraqi forces then attacked British military installations. To prevent Axis aid from reaching Iraq, British and Free French forces overran Vichy French–administered Syria and Lebanon, which were declared independent in 1943 and 1944, respectively. The British crushed the Iraqi revolt and returned a pro-British government to power.

The Maghreb also saw the first major U.S. military offensive of the war. American and British forces invaded Morocco and Algeria in November 1942, then linked up with British forces driving west from Egypt to expel the Axis powers from North Africa in Libya in May 1943.

Also during the war, British and Soviet forces occupied Iran to facilitate Lend-Lease shipments to the Soviet Union through that country. Reza Shah, who sought continued neutrality, was forced to abdicate in favor of his son, Mohammad Reza

Pahlavi. Turkey, which had declared its neutrality, and Saudi Arabia and much of the rest of the Arabian Peninsula were largely unaffected by the war.

After the war, Britain found itself dealing with a nearly impossible situation in Palestine—trying to keep out the surviving Jews—amid great world sympathy for their plight after the deaths of some 6 million Jews in the Holocaust. In February 1947 the British government turned matters over to the new United Nations (UN). That August a UN special commission recommended the creation of two separate independent states in Palestine. Although the Arabs numbered 1.2 million and the Jews numbered just 600,000, the Jews would have received some 56 percent of the land. Understandably, the Arabs were opposed. Desperate to quit Palestine, London announced acceptance of the UN recommendation and declared that its mandate of Palestine would terminate on May 14, 1948.

Immediately following a UN vote approving the partition plan, militant Palestinian Arabs and foreign Arab fighters attacked Jewish communities in Palestine, beginning the Arab-Jewish Communal War (1947–1948). The British completed their pullout as scheduled on May 14, 1948, and that same day David Ben-Gurion, head of the Jewish Agency, declared Israeli independence.

This provoked the Israeli War of Independence (May 15, 1948–March 10, 1949). The Jews defeated the Arab armies and secured an additional 26 percent of the land of Mandate Palestine west of the Jordan River. The war also created some 600,000–700,000 Palestinian Arab refugees in neighboring Arab countries. Israel refused to allow their return, creating a major stumbling block to peace ever since.

In 1960 Britain granted independence to Cyprus, but major tensions continued between the majority Greeks and minority Turks on the island, almost bringing war between the two countries. In 1974 following a Greek coup that pledged union of the island with Greece, Turkish armed forces invaded Cyprus, took significant Greek land, and encouraged Turkish settlement on it. The Turkish government also set up the Turkish Republic of Northern Cyprus.

Meanwhile, the ever-growing importance of Middle Eastern oil to the world economy complicated regional affairs and led to increased U.S. presence in the region. This coincided with mounting Arab nationalism expressed in revolutions throughout the region, with new anti-Western regimes installed in Egypt (1954), Syria (1963), Iraq (1968), and Libya (1969). The Soviet Union took advantage and aligned itself with the new leaders of Egypt, Syria, and Iraq.

Although France granted independence to Morocco and Tunisia in 1956, it was not prepared to do the same in Algeria, which was considered as three French departments: Alger, Oran, and Constantine. Fighting broke out in Algeria in 1954 and brought the collapse of the French Fourth Republic in 1958 and the return to power of Charles de Gaulle, who reluctantly negotiated Algerian independence in 1962.

In 1956 Egyptian president Gamal Abdel Nasser nationalized the Suez Canal. Britain, France, and Israel secretly colluded in an effort to overthrow him. Touching off the Suez Crisis of 1956, Israel forces invaded the Sinai and headed for the canal. Supposedly acting to protect the waterway, French and British forces then invaded

Egypt. Heavy pressure from U.S. president Dwight Eisenhower brought the Suez Crisis to an end, with the invaders withdrawing.

Nasser's support for terrorist attacks against Israel and his major missteps regarding Israel led to a preemptive Israeli strike in the Six-Day War (June 5–10, 1967), a decisive event in the Middle East. Jordan's King Hussein mistakenly took his country into the conflict on the side of Egypt and Syria. The net effect of the war was to make peace between the Arab states and Israel even more difficult, for Israel secured not only Old Jerusalem but also the entire West Bank, the Golan Heights, the Gaza Strip, and the Sinai Peninsula.

During 1975–1990, Lebanon underwent a protracted civil war. From the 1970s also, Israel experienced cross-border raids led by Yasser Arafat's Palestine Liberation Organization (PLO). During 1967–1970 Egypt also mounted the so-called War of Attrition, extensive artillery fire against Israeli defensive positions west of the Suez Canal. Nasser died in 1971, and Anwar Sadat, his successor as Egyptian president, sought to bring Israel to the bargaining table with yet another war. Worked out in conjunction with Syria, the 1973 Yom Kippur War (Ramadan War) caught Israel by surprise, and for the first time the Arab armies fought well, although Israel did win the war. In 1979, however, Sadat concluded a peace treaty with Israel, the first Arab state to do so, which brought Egypt's expulsion from the Arab League. The conclusion of peace brought the Sinai back to Egypt, and in 2005 the Israelis quit Gaza.

In December 1979 in an effort to preserve a communist regime in Afghanistan, Soviet forces invaded that country. The high cost of that war, which saw the United States and Britain supporting the Afghan resistance, ended in a Soviet withdrawal in February 1989 and was a major factor in the collapse of the Soviet Union in 1991.

In 1982, cross-border artillery fire and rocket attacks from the PLO in southern Lebanon led Israel to invade that country. The Israeli forces ultimately forced the PLO to quit Lebanon. Israel then set up a security zone in southern Lebanon, but this did not bring peace.

Shah Reza Pahlavi was a staunch U.S. ally, but a revolution in Iran in January 1979 established a theocratic Islamic republic under conservative Muslim cleric Ayatollah Ruhollah Khomeini. Seeking to take advantage of Iran's disarray in order to secure territory of its longtime rival, Iraqi president Saddam Hussein invaded Iran in September 1980. This caught the Iranians by surprise, but their overly cautious advance cost the Iraqis a chance for early victory, and the fighting settled into attrition warfare resembling that of World War I. The war ended in mutual exhaustion in 1988.

The enormous costs of the Iran-Iraq War were a principal reason for Hussein's decision to send his military into Iraq's neighbor, the small, oil rich nation of Kuwait, in August 1990. U.S. president George H. W. Bush then put together a 34-nation coalition, including a number of Arab states, and rushed forces to Saudi Arabia. With Hussein refusing to quit Kuwait, during January–February 1991 coalition forces drove Iraqi forces from Kuwait (the ground campaign lasted but 100 hours). President Bush refused to invade Iraq and halted the war, some believe prematurely.

He feared that Iraq would break up into Sunni, Shiite, and Kurdish entities and would no longer be able to act as a counterweight to Islamic Iran. This decision left Hussein in power.

The presence of Western forces in Saudi Arabia angered many traditionalist Saudis, among them Osama bin Laden, who formed the Al-Qaeda terrorist organization to do battle with both the West and the Saudi regime.

The collapse of the Soviet Union in 1991 had considerable impact on the Middle East. Large numbers of Soviet Jews were now able to immigrate to Israel, and aid to Russian allies in the Arab world was largely ended. Despite the enhanced role of the United States, peace between most of the Arab states and Israel remained elusive. In 2000, U.S. president Bill Clinton attempted but failed to broker a peace deal between Israel and the Palestinians.

On September 11, 2001, Al-Qaeda, having already attacked U.S. targets abroad, initiated the deadliest terrorist attack in U.S. history, claiming nearly 3,000 lives. When the Taliban government of Afghanistan refused to hand over bin Laden and meet other demands of President George W. Bush, the United States and its allies invaded Afghanistan and, in conjunction with forces of the Northern Alliance, overthrew the Taliban. Much of the Taliban escaped to Pakistan, however. There it found safe haven and proceeded to mount attacks on the new Afghan government and allied troops. The Afghanistan War, begun in 2001, continues.

In 2002, key members of the Bush administration—the so-called Neocons (neo-conservatives)—convinced Bush that Hussein's Iraq either possessed or was attempting to acquire weapons of mass destruction (WMD) and that the United States should invade that country and establish a democratic regime there that would serve as a model for the Middle East. Bush secured congressional approval on evidence now proven incorrect. Glossing over the difficulties involved, the United States, Britain, and a few other allies invaded Iraq in March 2003. Hussein was easily overthrown, but then ethnic and religious violence ensued, pitting the Shiite majority against the minority Kurds as well as the Sunnis (who had long held power and persecuted the Shiites and Kurds). There was also a largely Sunni-led insurgency against both the coalition forces and the Shiite-dominated government. The latter proved inept and corrupt and to a considerable extent allied itself with coreligionists in Iran. The war officially ended with the coalition and U.S. departure in December 2011, but sectarian violence continued apace.

At the same time Israel, under Israeli prime minister Benjamin Netanyahu, moved away from the two-state solution, long promised by Israel and desired by Palestinians and most Western nations. Instead, Netanyahu moved toward a unilateral solution. He pushed for the construction of Jewish settlements and a barrier wall, supposedly to protect Israel from Palestinian suicide bombers but including increasing numbers of Jewish settlements in the West Bank. In 2006 a new conflict erupted between Israel and Hezbollah, the radical Shiite militia organization in southern Lebanon. There were also Israeli invasions of Gaza following rocket attacks from that area.

Beginning in late 2010 in Tunisia, a revolutionary wave promoting democratic reform and popularly known as the Arab Spring brought major protests, uprisings, and even revolutions to several Middle Eastern countries, most notably Tunisia and Egypt. In 2011 the revolutionary wave also brought the Libyan Civil War and the Syrian Civil War. Civil war also erupted in Yemen, with both it and Libya remaining in turmoil. The civil war in Syria was especially bloody. With no end in sight, through mid-2016 it had claimed some 400,000 lives and displaced millions. Continued political instability, corruption, and ethnic violence in Iraq brought the rise of Al-Qaeda and the Islamic fundamentalist Islamic State of Iraq and Syria (ISIS), with the latter securing great swaths of territory in Iraq and Syria. The struggle with ISIS continues as an international coalition does battle with the Islamic extremists. The Greater Middle East seems as volatile as ever.

Spencer C. Tucker

Further Reading

Bacevich, Andrew J. *America's War for the Greater Middle East: A Military History.* New York: Random House, 2016.

Cleveland, William L., and Martin Bunton. *A History of the Modern Middle East.* 5th ed. Boulder, CO: Westview, 2012.

Fromkin, David. *A Peace to End All Peace: The Fall of the Ottoman Empire and the Creation of the Modern Middle East.* New York: Owl, 1989.

Gelvin, James L. *The Modern Middle East: A History.* New York: Oxford University Press, 2005.

Lenczowski, George. *The Middle East in World Affairs.* Ithaca, NY: Cornell University Press, 1952.

Mansfield, Peter. *A History of the Middle East.* 4th ed. London: Penguin, 2013.

Pollack, Kenneth M. *Arabs at War: Military Effectiveness, 1948–1991.* Lincoln: University of Nebraska Press, 2002.

Rabinovich, Abraham. *The Yom Kippur War: An Epic Encounter That Transformed the Middle East.* New York: Schocken Books, 2004.

Yale, William. *The Near East: A Modern History.* Ann Arbor: University of Michigan Press, 1958.

Countries

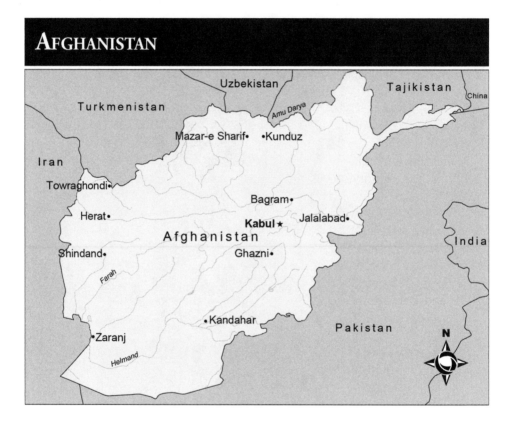

AFGHANISTAN

Uzbekistan

Turkmenistan

Tajikistan

China

Amu Darya

Iran

Mazar-e Sharif• •Kunduz

Towraghondi•

Bagram•

Herat•

Kabul ★ Jalalabad•

Afghanistan

India

Shindand•

Ghazni•

Farah

•Kandahar

Pakistan

•Zaranj

Helmand

N

Afghanistan

Jerry D. Morelock, Daniel E. Spector, and Spencer C. Tucker

The Islamic Republic of Afghanistan is a country of South and Central Asia. Afghanistan is bordered by Pakistan to the south and east; Iran to the west; Turkmenistan, Uzbekistan, and Tajikistan to the north; and China to the northeast. Although landlocked, Afghanistan lies at the gateway of Europe and Asia. The county occupies some 252,000 square miles, making it somewhat smaller than the U.S. state of Texas. Afghanistan's 2016 population was some 33.37 million. Its capital city is Kabul.

Afghanistan is a multiethnic society divided into a wide variety of ethnolinguistic groups, the majority of which are not in one region of the country. Although there are no exact figures, Pashtuns are the most numerous minority. Constituting perhaps 42 percent of the population, they live principally in central and eastern Afghanistan. At some 27 percent, Tajiks are the second most numerous minority. Their largest concentration is in northeastern Afghanistan. Other minorities are Uzbeks, 9 percent; Hazaras, 8 percent; Aimaqs, 4 percent; Turkmens, 3 percent; and Baloichs, 2 percent. Smaller minorities make up the remaining 5 percent. Pashto and Dari are the official languages, with perhaps half of the population speaking Pashto. Fully 99 percent of the population is Muslim, with Sunnis constituting 90 percent and the remainder Shias.

Afghanistan was a cohesive territory as early as 3000 BCE. Its location has made it the object of would-be conquerors, but it has also suffered considerable internal strife from contesting factions and tribal groups. Certainly Afghanistan has seen more than its share of warfare. Among notable conquerors of Afghanistan have been the Persian king Darius I (the Great) around 500 BCE and Alexander the Great of Macedonia in 330 BCE. The Arabs brought Islam in 642 CE. Mahmud of Ghazni conquered both eastern present-day Iran and Afghanistan as well as Pakistan during 997–1030. Genghis Khan and the Mongols took control in 1219, while Timur (Tamerlane) established the Timurid dynasty in 1370. Babur, the founder of India's Mogul Empire, captured Kabul early in the 16th century. Islam was firmly established as Afghanistan's religion in the 19th century. Ahmad Shah Durrani initiated the Durrani dynasty in 1747.

The British and the Russians struggled over control of Afghanistan, with the British seeing it as a buffer to protect their Indian empire. British efforts in this regard ushered in three Anglo-Afghan wars, during 1838–1842, 1878–1880, and

1919. As a consequence of the ability of the Afghans to retain their independence, the country came to be called the "graveyard of empires." In 1838 the British forcibly installed a weak former Afghan emir, precipitating the First Anglo-Afghan War (1838–1842), which ended in an Afghan victory. Nonetheless, this also began a long period of British domination that would not end until the Third Anglo-Afghan War in 1919. The Treaty of Rawalpindi of August 8, 1919, was in effect an armistice that granted Afghanistan's demand of autonomy in its foreign affairs.

Amanullah Khan came to power on February 28, 1919. Declaring himself king in 1926, he sought to capitalize on his early popularity to modernize his country, including constructing schools for both boys and girls, changing the centuries-old dress code for women, instituting efforts to limit the power of the Loya Jirga (the grand assembly), and inaugurating a new constitution to guarantee civil rights for all Afghans. As would be true to the present, the reforms were at odds with traditional Afghan practices and brought an armed rebellion in 1924, which was put down.

Growing opposition to his rule and the introduction of Western ways brought Amanullah's forced abdication on January 14, 1929. He went into exile in British India. An effort to return to power later that year failed, and he died in exile in Europe.

Inayatullah Khan Seraj was briefly king during January 14–17, 1929, but was forced to abdicate. Habibullah Kalakani succeeded him during January 17–October 16, 1929. Muhammad Nadir Shah then ruled until his assassination on November 8, 1933, when he was succeeded by Afghanistan's last king, Mohammed Zahir Shah.

Zahir Shah was able to bring a semblance of stability to the country. Afghanistan was neutral during World War II. In 1947 the British granted independence to the Empire of India. Unable to bridge the hostility between Hindus and Muslims, the British created the predominantly Hindu but secular state of India and the Islamic state of Pakistan. Pakistan enjoys a long porous border with Afghanistan and has frequently sought to influence Afghan affairs.

In September 1953 Afghan Army general Mohammed Daoud Khan, first cousin of the king, became prime minister. Daoud moved Afghanistan toward a close relationship with the Soviet Union. He also introduced reforms, including more rights for women and their access to higher education and the workforce. In 1961 the close Afghan-Soviet ties brought jet aircraft, tanks, and artillery at the heavily discounted price of $25 million. Meanwhile, in January 1965 Afghan communists established the People's Democratic Party of Afghanistan (PDPA), led by Babrak Karmal and Nur Mohammad Taraki.

On July 17, 1973, Daoud seized power from King Zahir Shah in a bloodless coup. Daoud then abolished the monarchy and named himself president. He continued the close Afghan-Soviet ties and in August 1975 secured an arrangement whereby the Soviets agreed to provide economic assistance during a 30-year period.

In early 1978, now alarmed by growing Soviet influence, Daoud reduced the number of Soviet advisers from 1,000 to 200. Too late and ineffectively, he also moved against the Afghan communists. On April 19, 1978, on the occasion of a funeral for a prominent leftist political leader, some 30,000 Afghans gathered to hear speeches by communist leaders Nur Muhammad Taraki, Hafizullah Amin, and Babrak Karmal. Daoud then ordered the arrest of the communist leaders. Taraki was caught, but Karmal escaped to the Soviet Union, and Amin was merely placed under house arrest. Employing his family as couriers, Amin directed planning for a coup d'état against Daoud, who was now unpopular with many Afghans because of his authoritarian rule.

Although on April 26 Daoud placed the Afghan Army on alert, the next day anti-Daoud military units at Kabul International Airport were able to launch the coup attempt. During April 27–28, army units both opposing and loyal to the government battled in and around Kabul. Daoud and most of his family were caught and executed in the presidential palace on April 28, the coup leaders announcing with some understatement that Daoud had "resigned for reasons of health." Soviet involvement in the coup, known as the Saur Revolution, is unclear, but Moscow welcomed the change of government and soon concluded a treaty that renewed assistance to the new government.

On April 30, the country became the Democratic Republic of Afghanistan (DRA). On May 1, Nur Mohammad Taraki assumed the presidency. He was also prime minister and secretary-general of the PDPA. Hafizullah Amin was the new foreign minister and oversaw the rooting out of opponents. The regime also embarked on a modernization program that included women's rights and freedom of religion and also implemented an extensive land reform program. Although most city dwellers welcomed the reforms or were ambivalent about them, their secular nature drew strong opposition in the countryside, with its traditionalist Islamic restrictions regarding women.

On February 14, 1979, U.S. ambassador to Afghanistan Adolph Dubs was taken hostage by Muslim extremists. That same day he was killed in the exchange of gunfire when Afghan security forces and their Soviet advisers stormed the hotel in Kabul where he was being held. The U.S. government protested the Soviet role.

With opposition building against the regime, Islamist leaders soon declared a jihad against "godless communism." By August 1978 this armed revolt included part of the army. On March 15, 1979, the army's 17th Division mutinied at Herat, killed some Soviet citizens, and held that city for about a week until they were crushed by government forces. This Herat Mutiny (Herat Uprising) saw the deaths of between 3,000 and 17,000 people.

On March 27, 1979, Taraki was forced to appoint Amin premier. In these circumstances, in midyear U.S. president Jimmy Carter's administration began Operation CYCLONE, the extension of covert assistance to the conservative Islamic antigovernment mujahideen (freedom fighters, holy warriors) now fighting the Afghan communist government. This program aided and trained the mujahideen through the Pakistani Inter-Services Intelligence (ISI). The mujahideen continued to make steady gains in the rural areas of the country.

On September 14, 1979, Amin ousted President Taraki, who was slain in the coup. This change of power was apparently accomplished without Soviet approval, and friction between the Soviets and Amin increased.

A Muslim rebel commander reviews his men in Kunar province, Afghanistan, on September 4, 1979. The men were fighting the Soviet-supported Marxist government of Afghanistan. (AP Photo/Steve McCurry)

As the mujahideen registered steady gains in the countryside, Moscow grew increasingly concerned. The Soviet leadership was then committed to the so-called Brezhnev Doctrine, elucidated by Soviet leader Leonid Brezhnev, that was employed against the Czech Spring in 1968 and held that the Soviet Union had the right to interfere militarily to prevent the overthrow of a communist government. Moscow was also fearful of the possible impact of an Islamic fundamentalist regime on the large Muslim population of Soviet Central Asia, specifically in the republics bordering Afghanistan. As a consequence, the Soviet leadership moved toward military intervention.

During the last months of 1979, the Brezhnev government dispatched some 4,500 Soviet advisers to assist the DRA, while Soviet aircraft conducted bombing raids against mujahideen positions. Defense Minister Dmitrii Ustinov convinced Brezhnev to undertake a military intervention, arguing that this was the only sure means to preserve the Afghan communist regime. Ustinov also postulated a short and victorious intervention. The deciding factor for Brezhnev was apparently Amin's coup and the death of staunch Soviet ally Taraki in September 1979. Beginning in November, the Soviets increased the size of their garrisons at the two air bases in Kabul and began quietly prepositioning forces on the border, most notably troops of the Fortieth Army of Central Asia.

On December 24, 1979, Soviet troops invaded Afghanistan. Moscow cited as justification the 1978 Treaty of Friendship, Cooperation and Good Neighborliness between the two countries and claimed that the Afghan government had invited in the Soviets. Lieutenant General Viktor S. Paputin commanded the operation. Elements of the 103rd Guards Airborne Division seized strategic installations in Kabul and established an air corridor into the Afghan capital by taking and holding Kabul International Airport. Meanwhile, armored columns of the Soviet's Fortieth Army crossed the border at Kushka in present-day Turkmenistan, with their objective being Kandahar by way of Herat. Other Fortieth Army elements crossed at Termez and proceeded toward Kabul along Highway 1.

Having secured the Kabul airport, on December 25 the Soviets flew in three airborne divisions to Kabul, while the four motorized rifle divisions moved overland from the north. During December 25–28 the 105th Airborne Division occupied Kabul despite considerable resistance from elements of the Afghan Army and Afghanistan's population.

Afghan president Amin and his ministers were cut off in the presidential palace. Amin was killed either in the Soviet assault on December 27 or by execution. Soviet commander Viktor S. Paputin was also killed during the battle. On December 28 the Soviets installed as president Babrak Karmal, former Afghan vice president and then Afghan ambassador to Czechoslovakia.

The more moderate Karmal attempted without great success to win popular support by portraying himself as a devoted Muslim and an Afghan nationalist. Meanwhile, Soviet forces occupied the major Afghan cities and secured the roads.

Unable to meet the Soviets in conventional battle, the mujahideen resorted to guerrilla warfare, ambushing Soviet road-bound convoys and laying siege to several Soviet-occupied towns. During February 21–23, 1980, a popular Afghan uprising occurred in Kabul, but Soviet troops crushed it. Some 500 Afghans were killed, and 1,200 others were imprisoned.

The invasion of Afghanistan had immediate adverse international consequences for the Soviet Union. It effectively ended détente as U.S. president Jimmy Carter reacted strongly to the invasion. He characterized it as a serious threat to world peace, because control of Afghanistan would enable the Soviet Union to dominate the Persian Gulf region and thus interdict at will the flow of Middle East oil.

The so-called Carter Doctrine declared that any effort to dominate the Persian Gulf region would be interpreted as an attack on American interests, to be countered by force if necessary. Carter also moved to limit the transfer of technology and the sale of agricultural products, including grain, to the Soviet Union. He also canceled U.S. participation in the 1980 Moscow Summer Olympic Games and called on America's allies to do the same.

Carter also pushed for the creation of a rapid-deployment force capable of intervening in areas threatened by the Soviets, offered increased military aid to Pakistan, moved to enhance ties with the People's Republic of China, and approved expanded covert assistance to the mujahideen. These steps, except the last, all had but limited impact. Key U.S. allies rejected both economic sanctions and the Olympic boycott, and other states offset the embargo by increasing their own grain sales to the Soviet Union. There was also little interest among the American public for involvement in Afghanistan.

Republican Ronald Reagan, who defeated Carter in the November 1980 presidential election, took a harder stand toward the Soviet Union, which he characterized as an "evil empire." The Reagan administration undertook a massive military buildup to include the development of a missile defense system, the Strategic Defense Initiative. This led Moscow to increase its defense spending, a major factor in the subsequent financial collapse of the Soviet Union.

In the spring of 1980 the Soviets mounted offensive operations. Jet aircraft would bomb rebel positions, followed by armored helicopter gunships firing rockets and machine guns and other helicopters ferrying assault troops. Although the mujahideen inflicted significant casualties on the Soviets, they themselves suffered heavily and were driven into the hills and mountains. The Soviets gradually increased their troop strength to some 105,000 men, but this was insufficient to bring victory. The Soviets never were able to control the mountainous areas where the guerrillas established their bases, nor could they seal the porous frontier with Pakistan, which remained a source of arms and equipment supplied by both Pakistan and the U.S. Central Intelligence Agency (CIA).

Frustrated, the Soviets responded with wanton attacks on villages. Numerous small land mines killed or maimed innocent civilians. The Soviets may also have employed biological and chemical weapons in violation of the Geneva protocols.

The mujahideen, however, remained short of equipment and supplies and were sharply divided by tribal and clan loyalties that prevented them from establishing a unified leadership. In May 1985, however, representatives of seven major mujahideen groups met in Peshawar, Pakistan, to try to establish a united front against the Soviets.

On May 4, 1986, in a bloodless coup engineered by the Soviets, Mohammad Najibullah, former head of the Aghan secret police, replaced Karmal as secretary-general of the PDPA. In November 1987, he was elected president for a seven-year term.

After meeting with new Soviet leader Mikhail Gorbachev, in October 1986 Najibullah offered the mujahideen a unilateral cease-fire agreement and a limited power-sharing arrangement; the mujahideen rejected these, and the war continued. The Soviet leadership found itself committed to waging a war that seemed to offer no acceptable ending.

U.S. aid to the mujahideen ran into the billions of dollars and included food, vehicles, and weapons. The most important CIA-supplied weapon was the shoulder-launched ground-to-air Stinger missile. It and the British-supplied Blowpipe proved to be key in defeating Soviet air-to-ground support and especially the armored helicopter gunships. As casualties mounted, Moscow came under increased domestic criticism, including that by prominent dissidents such as Andrei Sakharov.

By 1986 the Soviet leadership, now headed by the reformist Mikhail Gorbachev, began consideration of how it might extricate itself from Afghanistan. In April 1988, Gorbachev agreed to a United Nations (UN) mediation proposal that provided for the withdrawal of Soviet forces during a 10-month period.

The Soviet withdrawal occurred in two phases: the first from May 15 to August 16, 1988, and the second from November 15, 1988, to February 15, 1989. The withdrawal was generally peaceful. The agreement allowed Soviet military advisers to remain in Afghanistan and provide aid to the more than 300,000-man DRA Army. Moscow also continued to support the DRA with weapons and equipment totaling some $500 million a month.

The Soviet-Afghan War had cost the Soviets some 15,000 dead, 54,000 wounded, and 417 missing. Estimates of Afghan losses are more than 1 million mujahideen combatants and civilians killed and more than 5.5 million displaced, a large number of whom relocated in northwestern Pakistan. Afghanistan was devastated by the fighting. Already one of the world's poorest countries, after the war Afghanistan ranked, according to the UN, 170th of 174 nations in terms of wealth.

The war was a major defeat for the Soviet Union. It cost the Soviets considerable military equipment, seriously damaged that nation's military reputation, and further undermined the legitimacy of the Soviet system. Certainly the war's high financial cost was a major factor in the collapse of the Soviet Union in 1991.

Unfortunately, the United States also lost interest in Afghanistan after the Soviet military withdrawal and extended only scant aid to try to influence events in that war-torn nation. President William Clinton handed this task over to Pakistan and Saudi Arabia. Pakistan was quick to take advantage, developing close relations with warlords and then with the Taliban, a group of radical young Islamists, to secure trade interests and routes. This brought much ecological and agricultural destruction, including the loss of forests and the widespread cultivation of opium.

The Soviet Union continued to support the DRA, and President Mohammad Najibullah, who declared martial law, increased the role of the PDPA and adopted policies favored by the hard-liners. Many observers concluded that Najibullah would soon be driven from power by the mujahideen. Yet the Afghan Army proved more effective than it had ever been under the Soviets. Utilizing large quantities of Soviet-supplied weaponry, including Scud missiles, during March 5–May 16, 1989, the Afghan Army inflicted a surprising defeat on the rebel forces at Jalalabad. Its own losses are unknown, but the mujahideen suffered an estimated 3,000 casualties. Perhaps 12,000–15,000 civilians perished, and another 10,000 fled.

In October 1990, however, the mujahideen opened a major offensive, taking the provincial capitals of Tarin Kowt and Qalat. Although controlling much of the countryside, the mujahideen lacked the heavy weaponry required to secure the cities and were also often at odds with one another. The war appeared to be a stalemate.

Najibullah's government remained in power until 1992. A major reason for its collapse was the refusal in 1992 of new Russian president Boris Yeltsin to sell oil products to Afghanistan because it did not want to support communists. The defection from the government side of General Abdul Rashid Dostam and his Uzbek militia in March 1992 further undermined Najibullah. On April 16 his government fell to the mujahideen, who set up a governing council.

On September 27, 1996, the more Islamic fundamentalist Taliban came to power in Afghanistan. The country became the Islamic Emirate of Afghanistan, with Kandahar as the capital. Afghanistan secured diplomatic recognition from only Pakistan, Saudi Arabia, and the United Arab Emirates. The Taliban enforced sharia law and sharply curtailed women's rights. Its harsh policies included the deliberate destruction of farmlands, tens of thousands of homes, and Afghan archaeological treasures. Hundreds of thousands of Afghans fled, most to Pakistan and Iran. On September 9, 2001, assassins claiming to be journalists killed Ahmed Shah Masood, head of the Northern Alliance and Afghanistan's most effective insurgent leader.

Widely believed to be supported by the Pakistani ISI and military, the Taliban also granted safe haven to Saudi citizen bin Laden and his Islamic fundamentalist Al-Qaeda terrorist organization. On September 11, 2001, Al-Qaeda carried out a devastating attack on the United States. Nearly 3,000 people died in the attacks.

Bin Laden at the time denied responsibility, but the U.S. government quickly established the he was responsible for the attacks. When the Taliban refused to hand over the Al-Qaeda leadership and take other steps demanded by Washington, U.S., British, and some other allied forces invaded Afghanistan under legislation passed by the U.S. Congress on September 14 and signed by President George W. Bush on September 18. The Bush administration did not seek a declaration of war and chose to classify Taliban combatants as "terrorists," which placed them beyond protection offered by the Geneva Convention and due process of law.

Planning was handled by the U.S. Central Command (CENTCOM), headed by U.S. Army general Tommy Franks, who also commanded the invasion itself. The goals were the toppling of the Taliban regime, the capture or death of bin Laden, and the rooting out of terrorist enclaves.

September 11 Attacks

On September 11, 2001, the United States underwent coordinated suicide attacks perpetrated by Al-Qaeda, the Islamic terrorist organization based in Afghanistan and led by Saudi Arabian Osama bin Laden. On that day 19 members of Al-Qaeda, many of whom had undergone pilot training in the United States, used box cutters and pepper spray to hijack four commercial American jetliners and crash them into prearranged targets. Two of the airplanes crashed into the Twin Towers of the World Trade Center in New York City. Another plane hit the Pentagon, the headquarters of the Department of Defense, in northern Virginia. A fourth plane crashed into a field near Shanksville in rural Pennsylvania after some of the passengers, having been informed of the other suicide airplane attacks by cellular phone communications with family members, attempted to storm the cockpit and regain control of the plane. The White House or the U.S. Capitol were the most likely suspected targets of this plane.

Excluding the hijackers, a total of 2,974 people died in the attacks, including 246 from all four planes in which there were no survivors. The attacks crippled not only New York City and its economy but also important sectors of the U.S. economy. Particularly hard hit were the airline and insurance industries, which suffered billions of dollars in losses. The September 11 attacks were the worst terrorist attacks ever committed against the United States, and the resulting death toll surpassed that of the December 7, 1941, Japanese attack on Pearl Harbor.

The George W. Bush administration responded to the attacks by declaring a global war on terror. The next month the United States invaded Afghanistan, toppling the Taliban government that had given sanctuary and support to bin Laden and Al-Qaeda.

Operation ENDURING FREEDOM began on October 7 with U.S. air strikes against Taliban targets. These included Kabul and its airport as well as Kandahar and Jalalabad. The first ground elements were from the CIA's Special Activities Division, followed by U.S. Army Special Forces. Special forces of the United States and the United Kingdom played a key role in aiding the anti-Taliban Northern Alliance forces.

Cruise missiles from ships and bombs from aircraft flying from the United States and British-held Diego Garcia quickly reduced the number of viable military targets. On the ground, the special forces and the CIA were joined by units of the 10th Mountain Division (Light) and Marine Expeditionary Unit 15. In addition to the United Kingdom, Australia and Canada also supplied forces, while other countries granted overflight permission and allowed the use of bases.

U.S. aircraft struck Taliban concentrations and answered appeals from Northern Alliance fighters to attack Taliban frontline positions, while B-52 bombers pummeled Taliban and Al-Qaeda hideouts in the rugged mountains of the Tora Bora area. American close air support proved critical, as some 15,000 members of the Northern Alliance defeated some 45,000 Taliban troops and an estimated 3,000 Al-Qaeda fighters.

The military campaign was also accompanied by large-scale humanitarian assistance, with cargo planes dropping food to starving Afghans in remote locations. Indeed, as many as 6 million people were threatened with starvation. Logistics problems were immense and prompted the seizure of airfields inside Afghanistan early in the campaign.

The Taliban suffered a major defeat with the capture on November 9 of Mazar-i-Sharif, which fell to the Northern Alliance assisted by CIA personnel and special forces. The city, a major transportation hub and home to the Shrine of Hazrat Ali (Blue Mosque), proved to be an important base in subsequent operations against Kabul and Kandahar.

Most Taliban forces fled from Kabul on the night of November 12, although some fighting occurred the next afternoon when coalition forces entered the city. The major cities along the border with Iran also soon fell. Pashtun commanders secured Jalalabad and the rest of northwestern Afghanistan, while in northern Afghanistan Taliban fighters withdrew on Kunduz. It came under siege by November 16. In southeastern Afghanistan the prize was Kandahar. Meanwhile, some 2,000 Taliban and Al-Qaeda members, including bin Laden, were holed up in the cave complexes of Tora Bora some 30 miles southwest of Jalalabad.

Kunduz was taken by November 26. Shortly before its fall, Pakistani aircraft arrived and evacuated key personnel who had been aiding the Taliban in their fight against the Northern Alliance. On November 25 some 600 Taliban prisoners, who had been moved into the Qala-i-Janghi medieval fortress near Mazar-i-Sharif, rose up against their guards and seized half of the fortress, where they secured a cache of small arms and crew-served weapons. Seven days of fighting, including air strikes, ensued. Some 50 Northern Alliance troops were killed, as was 1 American.

Kandahar was the last major Taliban stronghold to fall. It was the home of Taliban head of state Mullah Mohammed Omar Mujahi, better known as Mullah Omar, who ordered his men to fight to the death. Northern Alliance forces soon cut

Kandahar off from resupply, while U.S. marines arrived and set up the first coalition base, known as Camp Rhino, south of the city on November 25. On December 7 Mullah Omar escaped to the north, and Kandahar then fell. The remaining Taliban fled into the mountains or into Pakistan, where they received safe haven.

Victorious to this point, coalition forces suffered a major failure in the mountains of Tora Bora in December, when they endeavored to ferret out members of Al-Qaeda, including bin Laden, in the cave base complexes. U.S. aircraft pounded the area, and some 200 Al-Qaeda members and an unknown number of tribal fighters were killed. While the cave complexes were secured by December 17, the failure to provide the requested number of U.S. troops on the ground resulted in the escape of bin Laden and most members of Al-Qaeda into Pakistan.

Meanwhile, diplomatic efforts were under way to establish a new Afghan government. On December 22, 25 prominent Afghans meeting in Bonn, Germany, established the Afghan Interim Authority (AIA) of 30 members, headed by a chairman, Hamid Karzai. The AIA was to last six months, followed by a two-year Transitional Authority and then national elections. One of the Bonn Agreement provisions called for the establishment of the International Security Assistance Force (ISAF). UN Security Council Resolution 1386, adopted unanimously on December 20, set up the ISAF. Its task was to assist the AIA in maintaining security in Kabul and later all of Afghanistan. The ISAF included forces from 46 nations, although the United States supplied roughly half its manpower.

U.S. forces established their headquarters at the Bagram air base north of Kabul. Another important U.S. base was the Kandahar airport, while outposts were established throughout eastern Afghanistan to enable operations against the remaining Taliban.

In early March 2002, ISAF and Afghan forces launched Operation ANACONDA, aimed at destroying a Taliban buildup in the Shah-i-Kot Valley and Arma Mountain regions. Although Taliban forces sustained heavy casualties, a number regrouped in the tribal regions of northwestern Pakistan and by late 2002 were carrying out hit-and-run guerrilla operations against coalition bases, supply convoys, and nongovernmental agencies in Afghanistan.

Meanwhile, the Bush administration had shifted resources. With the Afghanistan War not yet won, it opened a larger military effort in the form of war with Iraq in March 2003. There can be little doubt that this decision was costly as far as Afghanistan was concerned. Bush's decision to invade Iraq prolonged the Afghanistan War and made it much more expensive in the long run. Meanwhile, on August 11, 2003, the North Atlantic Treaty Organization (NATO) assumed command of the ISAF, which now included non-NATO members.

Although the ISAF and Afghan Army forces responded to the Taliban and Al-Qaeda with military offensives and increased numbers of troops, their operations failed to halt the insurgents, who took advantage of the porous Pakistani-Afghan border to regroup, recruit, train, and resupply in the tribal areas of northwestern Pakistan, controlled by the Pakistani Taliban. Afghan Taliban operations settled into a pattern of avoiding pitched combat with the better-armed and better-supported coalition forces. Organized into units of 50 or more fighters, they would attack isolated ISAF outposts and bases and then break into smaller groups to escape the reaction forces. They also sought to disrupt coalition ground communications through the destruction of bridges and attacked supply convoys and individual vehicles with improvised explosive devices (IEDs). They also employed suicide bombings against government checkpoints and soft targets in the cities. The Taliban also sought to prevent girls from attending school and attacked nongovernmental agencies seeking to improve health care for Afghan citizens.

The year 2006 saw the heaviest fighting to date as coalition forces launched Operation MOUNTAIN THRUST in May and Operation MEDUSA in July. Taliban strength was then estimated at some 10,000 fighters, with 2,000–3,000 dedicated full-time combatants. Perhaps 10 percent of the full-time fighters were foreign volunteers.

Endemic and widespread Afghan government corruption as well as tribalism and the opium trade plagued the coalition military effort. At the same time, the Iraq War took first claim on U.S. military resources, even as commanders in Afghanistan sought more manpower. In 2008 there was a sharp increase in U.S. troop strength, however, from 26,607 in January of that year to 48,250 in June. British troop strength also slightly increased, to 8,030.

On July 13, 2008, the Taliban carried out a spectacular operation, freeing all the prisoners in the Kandahar jail. This raid was a great embarrassment to the Afghan government and the ISAF. It released 1,200 men, 400 of them Taliban members.

Tensions between the United States and the ISAF vis-à-vis Pakistan greatly increased. On September 3, 2008, U.S. commandos, traveling by helicopter, raided across the border into Pakistan and attacked three houses in a known Taliban stronghold. The Pakistani government retaliated by suspending NATO truck resupply into Afghanistan. A spate of incidents involving U.S. and Pakistani forces followed. On September 23, Pakistani forces fired on ISAF helicopters they claimed were in Pakistan's airspace, which the Pentagon angrily denied. U.S. forces did apparently cross into Pakistani territory in an operation against insurgents in Khyber Pakhtunkwa Province, bringing Pakistani government charges that the operation had killed civilians. Despite heightened tensions, the United States increased the use of drone strikes against Taliban targets in Pakistan, resulting in some civilian deaths.

Late that year there were multiple Taliban attacks on supply convoys in Pakistan that included the burning of large numbers of tankers and other cargo trucks and raids on coalition supply dumps. Some 300 trucks and smaller vehicles were destroyed in December alone. Increasing interruption of supplies through Pakistan and the Kyber Pass led the coalition to establish a northern supply network through Russia and Uzbekistan. Azerbaijan also subsequently provided airport facilities and granted use of its airspace. By 2011, 40 percent of supplies were arriving by the northern route as opposed to 30 percent through Pakistan.

Hamid Karzai won the scheduled August 2009 presidential election, defeating challenger Abdullah Abdullah amid widespread charges of voter fraud and intimidation. In November Karzai made a public appeal for direct peace talks with the Taliban. He also made it clear that the U.S. government opposed this.

U.S. president Barack Obama, who took office in January 2009, announced at the end of the year his intent to implement a troop surge in Afghanistan. Despite this, increased use of IEDs by the Taliban led to significantly higher casualties among coalition soldiers, and 2010 saw the largest number of Taliban attacks in the war to date. Some 33,000 additional American troops were sent to Afghanistan and then were withdrawn by September 2012.

Tensions between the United States and Pakistan again increased on September 30, 2010, when two U.S. helicopter gunships attacking members of the Taliban fleeing into Pakistan fired on several Pakistani border posts and killed two Pakistani soldiers. In retaliation the Pakistan government closed the Torkham border crossing point from Pakistan into Afghanistan. The Pakistani Taliban then attacked the backed-up supply convoys, destroying some 100 tanker trucks. Relations with Pakistan were further strained when on May 2, 2011, in Operation NEPTUNE SPEAR, without coordinating with the Pakistani government, U.S. Navy SEALs raided bin Laden's compound in Bilal Town, Abbottabad, Pakistan, and killed him.

During May 7–9, 2011, a major battle occurred at Kandahar when the Taliban tried to capture the city. Although the attack was beaten back, it proved to be a major embarrassment for the Afghan government. Beginning in 2011 also, there were a growing number of so-called insider attacks, with members of the Taliban belonging to, or pretending to belong to, the Afghan Armed Forces and police attacking them and ISAF personnel.

Asserting that sufficient numbers of Afghan soldiers and police were being trained, Obama announced on June 22, 2011, that 10,000 U.S. troops would be withdrawn by the end of the year, with another 22,000 departing by the summer of 2012. Other nations followed suit. During a summit meeting in May 2012, leaders of the NATO member states providing military assistance to Afghanistan agreed that most of the 130,000 ISAF forces would depart by the end of December 2014; meanwhile, all combat missions in the county would be turned over to the Afghan Army and security forces in the summer of 2013, with NATO and coalition partners assuming a training role.

Although the security transfer was completed on schedule in June 2013, the Taliban increased its suicide bombings. As violence against Afghan civilians mounted, Karzai chose to place much blame on NATO and in particular U.S. troops, sharply criticizing the civilian casualties that often accompanied coalition military operations, especially air strikes.

Although Karzai negotiated a new status of forces agreement and then secured its approval by the Loya Jirga, he subsequently refused to sign it, leaving open the possibility that all U.S. and ISAF forces would have to quit Afghanistan at the end of 2014. The two-stage 2014 Afghan national presidential election, however, brought to power Ashraf Ghani, and the security agreement negotiated earlier was signed on September 30, meaning that some U.S. and NATO and other allied forces would remain in a support and training role in Afghanistan.

Meanwhile, violence in Afghanistan was increasing with a large number of Taliban suicide attacks and mounting civilian losses, even in Kabul. On October 26, 2014, however, the United States and Britain officially ended their combat role in Afghanistan, when they handed over their last combat bases to the Afghan Army. U.S. forces would fall to 10,800. Although largely restricted to training and advisory roles, they were authorized to take appropriate measures against direct Taliban threats to U.S. and coalition forces. The NATO-led combat mission in Afghanistan officially ended on December 31, 2014.

Taliban suicide attacks and a major battle for the northern Afghan city of Kunduz made 2015 the bloodiest year of the war for Afghan civilians. The UN tallied 3,545 killed and 7,457 injured, an increase of 4 percent over 2014. Into 2016 the war had claimed more than 91,000 Afghan deaths (civilians, Afghan Army troops, and militants) and 3,517 coalition lives (2,381 of them Americans).

With the Taliban making significant gains and after having courted Pakistan's leadership for more than a year without noticeable result, Ghani changed course on April 10, 2016, and warned that he would lodge a formal complaint with the UN Security Council if Pakistan did not take military action against the Taliban within its borders that was operating against Afghanistan. Also, in June in another sign that the war was not going well, the Obama administration eased engagement rules for U.S. forces remaining in the country. Previously the administration had said that U.S. air strikes could be directed against the Taliban only in the case of direct threats to U.S. troops. Now U.S. air strikes could be employed when commanders saw fit. U.S. forces would also be permitted to accompany Afghan Army forces in combat missions against the Taliban.

Timeline

1838–1842	First Anglo-Afghan War.
1878–1880	Second Anglo-Afghan War.
Feb 28, 1919	Amanullah Khan comes to the Afghan throne as emir.
Aug 8, 1919	The Treaty of Rawalpindi brings to an end the Third Anglo-Afghan War of 1919, with the British granting the Afghans full autonomy in foreign affairs.
1926	Emir Amanullah Khan, who came to the throne in 1919, declares Afghanistan a monarchy, with himself as king.
Jan 14, 1929	Amanullah's attempts to modernize his country with reforms and a new constitution guaranteeing civil rights encounters strong traditionalist Afghan resistance, forcing his abdication.
Nov 8, 1933	Following three short-lived rulers, Mohammed Zahir Shah becomes king and brings a semblance of stability to Afghanistan.
1939–1945	Afghanistan is neutral in World War I.
Sep 7, 1953	General Mohammed Daoud Khan becomes prime minister and seeks Soviet economic and military assistance. He also introduces reforms, including more rights for women.
1956	Soviet leader Nikita Khrushchev agrees to assist Afghanistan, and the two countries become allies.

1961	As a result of its close Soviet ties, Afghanistan acquires significant modern weaponry.
Jan 1, 1965	The communist People's Democratic Party of Afghanistan (PDPA) is established, led by Babrak Karmal and Nur Mohammad Taraki.
Jul 17, 1973	General Daoud Khan overthrows King Zahir Shah in a bloodless military coup. Daoud abolishes the monarchy, names himself president, and continues close ties with the Soviet Union.
Aug 30, 1975	The Soviet Union agrees to provide Afghanistan with economic assistance for a 30-year period.
Jan–Mar 1978	Alarmed over growing Soviet influence, President Daoud orders the number of Soviet advisers sharply reduced.
Apr 19, 1978	Daoud orders the arrest of Afghan communist leaders, but the effort is ineffective, and Hafizullah Amin, who is simply placed under house arrest, plans a coup.
Apr 27–28, 1978	Anti-Daoud military units at Kabul International Airport launch the coup attempt. Fighting erupts in and around Kabul. Daoud and most of his family are caught and executed in the presidential palace on April 28, and the PDPA comes to power.
Apr 30, 1978	Afghanistan becomes the Democratic Republic of Afghanistan (DRA).
May 1, 1978	Nur Mohammad Taraki becomes Afghan president. He also heads the PDPA. The new regime roots out its opponents and embarks on an extensive modernization program that includes women's rights and freedom of religion. The regime also implements land reform. This has considerable opposition in the conservative countryside, with its traditional opposition to secularism and women's rights.
Feb 14, 1979	Taken hostage by Islamic extremists, U.S. ambassador to Afghanistan Adolph Dubs dies in an exchange of gunfire between the Islamists and the Afghan security forces and their Soviet advisers.
Dec 5, 1979	The Afghan government signs a friendship treaty with the Soviet Union.
Mar 15–20, 1979	In the Herat Mutiny (Herat Uprising), soldiers of the Afghan Army's 17th Division mutiny, killing a small number of Soviet citizens before the revolt is crushed. The number of dead in the uprising is variously estimated at between 3,000 and 17,000.
Mar 27, 1979	Taraki is forced to appoint Hafizullah Amin as premier.
Mid-1979	U.S. president Jimmy Carter commences Operation CYCLONE, the Central Intelligence Agency (CIA) program of covert assistance to

the conservative Islamic antigovernment mujahideen (freedom fighters, holy warriors) now fighting the Afghan communist government. The program operates through the Pakistani Inter-Services Intelligence.

Sep 14, 1979   Amin ousts President Taraki, who is slain in the coup. Apparently accomplished without Soviet approval, this change in power brings friction between the Soviets and Amin.

Dec 12, 1979   Soviet leaders, fearing an Iranian-style Islamist revolution and wary of Amin's secret meetings with U.S. diplomats, decide to invade Afghanistan in order to preserve its communist government.

Dec 24, 1979   Soviet armed forces invade Afghanistan. Elements of an airborne division seize strategic installations in Kabul and its airport, establishing an air corridor for additional troops, while armored columns of four divisions cross the border at both Kushka and Termez.

Dec 27, 1979   Amin is killed in Kabul, either in the fighting or by execution. Soviet commander Viktor S. Paputin also dies.

Dec 28, 1979   The Soviets install Babrak Karmal as president. He seeks to rally support as a devoted Muslim and Afghan nationalist.

1980   Resistance to the Soviets intensifies, with various mujahideen groups fighting Soviet forces and the DRA Army. In the first six months of the campaign, the Soviets commit more than 80,000 personnel. The United States, Pakistan, and Saudi Arabia provide arms and financial assistance to the resistance.

1985   More than 5 million Afghans have now been displaced by the war, many seeking refuge in Iran or Pakistan. New Soviet leader Mikhail Gorbachev says that he wants to end the war, but the resulting escalation of troops to pacify the region and bring a quick victory produces the bloodiest year of the war.

May 1985   Representatives of seven major mujahideen groups meet in Peshawar, Pakistan, to establish a united front against the Soviets.

1986   The CIA begins supplying the mujahideen with Stinger antiaircraft missiles, enabling them to shoot down Soviet helicopter gunships.

May 4, 1986   In a bloodless coup engineered by the Soviet Union, Mohammad Najibullah, former head of the Aghan secret police, replaces Karmal as secretary-general of the PDPA.

Oct 1986   After meeting with Soviet leader Gorbachev, Najibullah offers the mujahideen a unilateral cease-fire agreement and limited power-sharing arrangement. They reject these measures, and the war continues.

Nov 1987	Najibullah is elected president of Afghanistan for a seven-year term.
Apr 1988	Gorbachev agrees to a United Nations (UN) mediation proposal worked out in Geneva between the warring parties. Soviet forces will be withdrawn during a 10-month period.
Feb 15, 1989	The Soviet Union announces the departure of its last troops from Afghanistan. Fighting continues, however.
Mar 5–May 16, 1989	The Afghan army wins the Battle of Jalalabad. The mujahideen lose some 3,000 killed.
Apr 16, 1992	Having launched a major offensive, the mujahideen overthrow Najibullah's communist government and then set up a new governing council.
Sep 27, 1996	The Islamic fundamentalist Taliban comes to power and rules Afghanistan as the Islamic Emirate of Afghanistan until December 2001, with Kandahar as the capital. The Taliban enforces sharia law and sharply curtails women's rights. Hundreds of thousands of Afghans flee, most to Pakistan and Iran.
Mar 2001	Despite widespread international protests, the Taliban carries out its threat to destroy ancient Buddhist statues at Bamiyan, claiming that they are an affront to Islam.
Sep 11, 2001	The Taliban had granted safe haven to Saudi Osama bin Laden and his Al-Qaeda Islamic terrorist organization, and on this date Al-Qaeda launches a devastating terrorist attack on the United States, killing nearly 3,000 people. The U.S. government quickly establishes Al-Qaeda's responsibility.
Sep 14, 2001	The U.S. Congress authorizes military operations against the terrorists responsible for the attack. President George W. Bush signs the authorization on September 18.
Oct 7, 2001	With the Taliban refusing to surrender the Al-Qaeda leadership and meet other U.S. demands, the United States, supported by the United Kingdom, launches Operation ENDURING FREEDOM, the invasion of Afghanistan. The invaders are joined by other forces, including the Afghan Northern Alliance.
Nov 9, 2001	The Northern Alliance captures Mazar-i-Sharif, important for subsequent operations against Kabul and Kandahar.
Nov 13, 2001	Coalition forces enter Kabul.
Nov 26, 2001	Coalition forces capture the last Taliban stronghold of Kunduz. The Taliban government is overthrown but reemerges as an insurgency.

Dec 6–17, 2001	With an insufficient number of ground troops committed to the operation, U.S. forces fail to capture bin Laden and many other members of Al-Qaeda, who escape the Tora Bora region into Pakistan.
Dec 7, 2001	Kandahar falls to the coalition forces.
Dec 20, 2001	The UN Security Council authorizes establishment of the International Security Assistance Force (ISAF) for Afghanistan, whose mission involves assisting the Afghan Interim Authority (AIA) in maintaining security in Kabul, later expanded to all Afghanistan. The ISAF includes forces from 46 nations, although the United States supplies roughly half its manpower.
Dec 22, 2001	Twenty-five prominent Afghans meeting in Bonn, Germany, establish the AIA. The AIA is to last six months, followed by a two-year Transitional Authority and then national elections. Hamid Karzai is selected to head the interim government. U.S. forces establish their headquarters at the Bagram air base north of Kabul.
Mar 1–18, 2002	ISAF and Afghan forces launch Operation ANACONDA, aimed at destroying a Taliban buildup in the Shah-i-Kot Valley and Arma Mountain regions.
Late 2002	Having regrouped in the tribal regions of northwestern Pakistan, the Taliban carries out hit-and-run guerrilla operations against coalition bases, supply convoys, and nongovernmental agencies.
Mar 20, 2003	A U.S.-led coalition invades Iraq. The ensuing Iraq War (2003–2011) siphons off much-needed U.S. military resources from Afghanistan.
Aug 11, 2003	The North Atlantic Treaty Organization (NATO) assumes command of the ISAF, which now includes non-NATO members. Meanwhile, Taliban operations settle into a pattern of avoiding pitched combat with better-armed and better-supported coalition forces. The Taliban instead launches small attacks against isolated ISAF outposts and bases and also seeks to interrupt road communication and employ improvised explosive devices. In addition, the Taliban employ suicide bombings against government checkpoints and soft targets in the cities. Meanwhile, endemic and widespread Afghan government corruption and tribalism as well as the opium trade plague the coalition military effort.
2008	Heavy fighting occurs, and there is a sharp increase in U.S. troop strength, from 26,607 in January to 48,250 in June.
Jul 13, 2008	The Taliban frees all 1,200 prisoners held in the Kandahar jail, including 400 Taliban members.

Sep 2008	Tensions between the United States and the ISAF sharply increase when U.S. helicopters and commandos attack known Taliban strongholds in Pakistan. Pakistan responds by halting essential U.S. supply convoys, leading to Taliban attacks on these and the torching of hundreds of trucks. Despite heightened tensions, the United States increases the number of its drone strikes against Taliban targets in Pakistan, resulting in some civilian deaths.
Aug 2009	Karzai wins the presidential election amid widespread charges of voter fraud and intimidation.
Dec 2009	U.S. president Barack Obama announces plans for a temporary U.S. troop surge in Afghanistan. Some 33,000 additional American troops will be sent to Afghanistan to buy time for the training of additional Afghan forces and then will be withdrawn by September 2012.
2010	This year sees the largest number of Taliban attacks to date.
May 2, 2011	In Operation NEPTUNE SPEAR, U.S. Navy SEALs raid bin Laden's compound in Bilal Town, Abbottabad, Pakistan, killing him.
May 7–9, 2011	A major battle occurs for Kandahar. Although the Taliban effort to capture the city is defeated, it is a major embarrassment for the government.
Jun 22, 2011	Asserting that sufficient numbers of Afghan soldiers and police were being trained, Obama announces that 10,000 U.S. troops will be withdrawn by the end of the year, with another 22,000 departing Afghanistan by the summer of 2012. Other nations follow suit.
May 2012	During a NATO summit meeting, leaders of the alliance providing military assistance to Afghanistan agree that most of the 130,000 ISAF forces will depart by the end of December 2014; meanwhile, all combat missions in the county are to be turned over to the Afghan Army and security forces in the summer of 2013, with NATO and coalition partners assuming a training role.
Sep 29, 2014	Having survived a two-stage election process, Ashraf Ghani is sworn in as president of Afghanistan. He promptly signs the security agreement negotiated and approved earlier that Karzai had refused to sign. This ensures that some U.S. and NATO and other allied forces will remain in a support and training role in Afghanistan in 2015 and beyond.
Oct 26, 2014	The United States and Britain officially end their combat role in Afghanistan. U.S. forces will fall to 10,800. Although largely restricted to training and advisory roles, they are authorized to take appropriate measures against direct Taliban threats to U.S. and coalition forces.

Dec 31, 2014   The NATO-led combat mission in Afghanistan officially ends.

2015   The UN concludes that this year is the worst of the war for Afghan civilian casualties, with 3,545 killed and 7,457 injured. This is 4 percent above the 2014 figure.

Spring 2016   A Taliban spring offensive registers significant gains.

Jun 10, 2016   In a sign that the war is going badly for the Afghan government, the Obama administration eases engagement rules on U.S. forces remaining in the country, allowing U.S. air strikes when commanders deem it necessary, with ground troops able to accompany the Afghan Army in combat operations.

Further Reading

Auerswald, David P., and Stephen M. Saideman, eds. *NATO in Afghanistan: Fighting Together, Fighting Alone.* Princeton, NJ: Princeton University Press, 2014.

Barfield, Thomas. *Afghanistan: A Cultural and Political History.* Princeton, NJ: Princeton University Press, 2012.

Braithwaite, Rodric. *Afgantsy: The Russians in Afghanistan, 1979–89.* New York: Oxford University Press, 2011.

Coll, Steve. *Ghost Wars: The Secret History of the CIA, Afghanistan, and Bin Laden, from the Soviet Invasion to September 10, 2001.* New York: Penguin, 2004.

Cordesman, Anthony H. *The Lessons of Afghanistan: War Fighting, Intelligence, and Force Transformation.* Washington, DC: CSIS Press, 2002.

Crile, George. *Charlie Wilson's War: The Extraordinary Story of the Largest Covert Operation in History.* New York: Atlantic Monthly Press, 2003.

Dale, Catherine. *War in Afghanistan: Strategy, Military Operations, and Issues for Congress.* Washington, DC: Congressional Research Service, Library of Congress, 2009.

DeLong, Michael, with Noah Lukeman. *Inside CENTCOM: The Unvarnished Truth about the Wars in Afghanistan and Iraq.* Washington, DC: Regnery, 2004.

Feifer, Gregory. *The Great Gamble: The Soviet War in Afghanistan.* New York: Harper, 2009.

Goodson, Larry P. *Afghanistan's Endless War: State Failure, Regional Politics, and the Rise of the Taliban.* Seattle: University of Washington Press, 2001.

Isby, David C. *Russia's War in Afghanistan.* London: Osprey, 1986.

Lyon, David. *In Afghanistan: Two Hundred Years of British, Russian and American Occupation.* New York: Palgrave Macmillan, 2009.

Rasanayagam, Angelo. *Afghanistan: A Modern History; Monarchy, Despotism or Democracy? The Problems of Governance in the Muslim Tradition.* New York: I. B. Tauris, 2003.

Tanner, Stephen. *Afghanistan: A Military History from Alexander the Great.* Revised ed. Boston: Da Capo, 2009.

Tomsen, Peter. *The Wars of Afghanistan: Messianic Terrorism, Tribal Conflicts, and the Failures of Great Powers.* New York: PublicAffairs, 2013.

Woodward, Bob. *Bush at War.* New York: Simon and Schuster, 2002.

ALGERIA

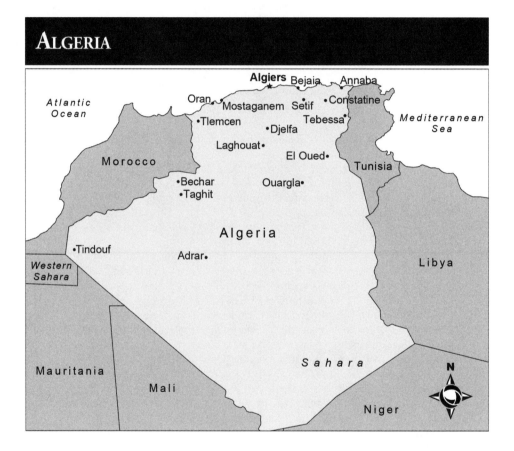

Atlantic
Ocean

Algiers Bejaia   Annaba
Oran•   Setif •Constatine
    •Mostaganem
  •Tlemcen   Tebessa•
        •Djelfa
  Laghouat•
              El Oued•
                    Tunisia

Mediterranean
Sea

Morocco

•Bechar
•Taghit

Algeria

Ouargla•

•Tindouf

Adrar•

Western
Sahara

Libya

Mauritania

Mali

S a h a r a

Niger

N

Algeria

Elun A. Gabriel, Spencer C. Tucker, and William E. Watson

Algeria is located in northeastern North Africa on the southern coast of the Mediterranean Sea. Algeria is bordered to the west by Morocco and Mauritania, to the north by the Mediterranean Sea, to the east by Tunisia and Libya, and to the south by Niger and Mali. Algeria comprises almost 920,000 square miles in area, making it the largest country in Africa, the Arab world, and the Mediterranean Basin. Its population numbered some 40.376 million in 2016. The region was originally peopled by Berbers. While they still make up a sizable national minority, Algeria's population is now predominantly Arab.

Given its strategic location, Algeria has been a part of numerous empires. These include the empires of the ancient Numidians, Phoenicians, Carthaginians, Romans, Vandals, and Byzantines. In more recent history Algeria was conquered and ruled by the Umayyads, Abbasids, Idrisids, Aghlabids, Rustamids, Fatimids, Zirids, Hammadids, Almoravids, and Almohads. Algeria was part of the Ottoman Empire from 1516 until the French government of King Charles X. Hoping to be able to boast an overseas victory in national elections, Charles X sent a sizable invasion force in June 1830 on the excuse of avenging an insult: Dey Hussein, the ruler of Algiers, had struck a French envoy with a fly swatter. The political gambit failed, and Charles X was unseated by a revolution in Paris a month later. Nonetheless, Charles's successors Louis Philippe and Louis Napoleon kept the French forces in place.

Indeed, the French greatly expanded the territorial holdings. The authority of the late dey had been largely limited to only about one-sixth of the territory of present-day Algeria, with the Sahara being outside his control. The French overcame resistance led by Abdelkader El Djezairi in the 1830s, and the process of pacification and territorial expansion was largely complete by the 1870s. The political unit of modern Algeria must therefore be regarded as largely of French creation. French rule also brought modern medicine and an end to tribal warfare. Paradoxically, these would work against French rule, as they helped bring about a rapid expanse in the population from some 1.5 million in 1830 to 11 million in 1960.

From 1848, France administered the entire region of Algeria as an integral part of France. Algeria came to be formed into three departments: Oran, Algiers, and Constantine. Hundreds of thousands of Europeans, chiefly French, settled there, many of them inhabitants of Alsace and Lorraine who did not wish to be part of Germany after these provinces were taken from France following its defeat in the Franco-Prussian War of 1870–1871. Known as colons and later as *pieds-noirs,* the colons settled principally in the cities, where by the early 20th century they constituted the majority of the population in Oran and Algiers. The Europeans constituted the vast majority of the technicians and administrators necessary to a modern state. In a census conducted on the very eve of the beginning of the Algerian War of 1954–1962, Europeans made up 1.2 million of the total Algerian population of some 9.53 million and thus constituted the largest European population in the Arab world.

Europeans controlled key segments of the economy, including the banks, shipping, utilities, and mining. Certainly they benefited from the government's confiscation of communal land, while the amount of land given to agriculture greatly increased with the introduction of modern agricultural methods. The Europeans owned almost half of the land devoted to farming and generally the best land, while the non-European population worked the colons' lands or eked out a meager living on their own far smaller and less productive farms. Although, unlike Indochina, Algeria was considered an integral part of France as three French departments, it was in fact a juridical monster with a complicated political system in place whereby the Europeans exercised complete political control.

World War II had a profound impact on colonial possessions everywhere. During the war many Muslim Algerians had fought with the French Army against the Axis, and some 63,000 were granted French citizenship as a result. At the same time, however, Arab nationalism had come to the fore. On May 8, 1945, on the occasion of a parade in Sétif, Algeria, celebrating the end of the war in Europe, a confrontation between the two communities ended in considerable violence and attacks on Europeans that brought savage French reprisals and the deaths of hundreds of people.

Hopes among moderates in the Arab community that there would be meaningful democratic reform after the end of the war were dashed. The French were not prepared to make the concessions that would have been necessary. The Algerian Statute of September 1947 was largely a sham. It created administrative autonomy for the three departments constituting Algeria and set in place an Algerian Assembly with two colleges. The first college was for the 469,000 non-Muslims eligible to vote and the 63,000 Muslims granted citizenship by dint of army service. The second college was for the 1.301 million eligible to vote of some 8 million Muslims. Each college had 60 seats. While elected separately, the two colleges voted together, so it appeared as if the Muslims could easily control the Algerian Assembly by having only a single vote in the first college. To prevent this from occurring, however, the statute provided that the governor-general or 30 members of the Algerian Assembly could request a two-thirds vote. This ensured continued European control. Adding to this blow to the democratic process was the rigging of the mandatory elections. Final proof that Algeria was not like the rest of France was provided by the fact that although Algeria had representatives in the French Chamber of Deputies, this was not in proportion to population.

The Sétif Uprising

With the end of World War II in Europe, French authorities approved a victory parade on May 8, 1945, in Sétif, a city in the Constantine Department in Algeria. While marchers did carry posters lauding the Allied victory, there were also those calling on Muslims to unite against the French and calling for the release of Algerian nationalist leader Messali Hadj and even death to Frenchmen and Jews. When a French plainclothes policeman shot to death a young marcher carrying an Algerian flag, this touched off a bloody rampage, often referred to as the Sétif Massacre.

Muslims attacked Europeans and their property, and the violence quickly spread. The French response included Foreign Legionnaires and Senegalese troops, tanks, aircraft, and even naval gunfire from a cruiser in the Mediterranean Sea. Settler militias and local vigilantes took prisoners from jails and executed them. An estimated 4,500 Algerians were arrested; 99 people were sentenced to death, and another 64 were given life imprisonment. At least 100 Europeans died. The official French figure of Muslim dead was 1,165, but this was undoubtedly too low, with figures as high as 10,000 cited.

The Sétif Uprising, which was not followed by any meaningful French reform, helped drive a wedge between the two communities in Algeria. French authorities did not understand the implications of this and were caught by surprise when rebellion began in Algeria in November 1954.

At the same time, the two communities of Europeans and Arabs remained separate and distinct, with little mingling between the two. Ethnicity, language, religion, and economic disparity were major barriers that were not overcome. At the same time, Algeria was tied closely to France economically, with most of its products, including wine (which according to their religion Muslims were not to consume) and tobacco, being shipped there.

All pro-Muslim French reform efforts ultimately failed because of political pressure from the sizable colon community and its representatives in Paris. While French political theorists debated between assimilation and autonomy for Algeria's Muslims, the Muslim majority remained largely resentful of the privileged status of the colons. From the first elections of April 1948 tensions steadily increased until the outbreak of the rebellion in 1954.

The first Muslim political organizations had appeared in the 1930s. By the 1950s there were at least four Muslim nationalist parties, including the communists. The most important and radical of the Muslim parties was Messali Hadj's Mouvement pour le Triomphe des Libertés Democratiques (Movement for the Triumph of Democratic Liberties, MTLD). In 1953, 33 of its more radical members who favored violence against the French had broken off from the main party and formed the Comité Révolutionnaire d'Unité et d'Action (Revolutionary Committee of Unity and Action).

The most distinguished of the nationalist leaders was Ferhat Abbas. Originally a proponent of a truly democratic Algeria that would be part of a greater France of 100 million people, by World War II his Union Démocratique du Manifeste Algérien (Democratic Union of the Algerian Manifesto) called for independence but also the maintenance of close ties with France.

Mohamed Ahmed Ben Bella was one of the Muslim veterans returning to Algeria with the end of World War II who were shocked by what they regarded as the French government's heavy-handed actions after Sétif and had then joined the MTLD. Ben Bella went on to form the MTLD's paramilitary branch, the Organization Speciale, and soon fled to Egypt to enlist the support of President Gamal Abdel Nasser. Proindependence Algerian Muslims were certainly emboldened by the Viet Minh's victory over French forces in the Battle of Dienbienphu in Vietnam in May 1954, and when Algerian Muslim leaders met Vietnamese communist leader Ho Chi Minh at the Bandung Conference in April 1955, he assured them that the French could be defeated.

On October 10, 1954, Ben Bella and his compatriots formed the Front de Liberation Nationale (National Liberation Front, FLN). The FLN revolution against France officially began on the night of October 31–November 1, 1954, in a series of small-scale attacks throughout Algeria that caught the French completely by surprise. The FLN organized its manpower into several military districts, or *wilayas*. The goal was complete independence for Algeria and driving out or eliminating the colon population. Wilaya 4, located near Algiers, was especially important, and the FLN was particularly active in Kabylia and the Aures Mountains. The party organization was rigidly hierarchical and tolerated no dissent. In form and style it resembled Soviet bloc communist parties, although it claimed to offer a noncommunist and non-Western alternative ideology, articulated by the Martinique-born Afro-Caribbean psychiatrist, philosopher, revolutionary, and writer Frantz Fanon.

The French government in Paris was determined to prevail and crush what it referred to as "outlaws." The days of colonialism were at an end, but to the French way of thinking there were good reasons to hold onto Algeria. The Algerian entity had been largely created by France, there was the large European French population vehemently opposed to independence, and there were substantial economic interests to be protected. Finally, the professionals of the French Army, which had not tasted victory since World War I, were now transferred to Algeria and would not brook yet another defeat.

In 1956 the bulk of the French Army was transferred to Algeria, and unlike the war in Indochina, this included draftees. As France increased the number of its military forces in Algeria to fight the growing insurgency, French officials sought support from France's North Atlantic Treaty Organization (NATO) partners, arguing that keeping Algeria French would ensure that NATO's southern flank would be safe from communism. Indeed, as a part of France, Algeria was included in the original NATO charter. Washington's position nonetheless was that European colonial empires were obsolete. Furthermore, U.S. officials believed that the United States could positively influence decolonization movements in the developing world. France thus found itself increasingly isolated in diplomatic circles.

The Arab League promoted Pan-Arabism and the image of universal Arab and Muslim support for the FLN. The French grant of independence to both Tunisia and Morocco in March 1956 further bolstered Algeria's Muslims. It also facilitated the shipment of arms and other supplies to the rebels, especially through Tunisia, supplied principally by Egypt at the behest of its leader, Gamal Abdel Nasser. When France, Britain, and Israel invaded Egypt in the Suez Crisis of 1956, both the United States and the Soviet Union condemned the move, and the French, who had been unable to topple Nasser, were forced to contend with an FLN supply base that they could neither attack nor eliminate.

On August 20, 1955, the FLN attacked European civilians in the Philippeville Massacre, and colon reprisals resulted in the deaths of several thousand Muslims. The yearlong Battle of Algiers, a French effort to secure complete control of the Muslim portion of the capital city, began in September 1956 following FLN operative Saadi Yacef's terrorist-style bombing campaign against colon civilians. Meanwhile, other FLN leaders targeted governmental officials for assassination. The FLN movement faced a setback on October 22, however, when Ben Bella was captured. The civilian airliner in which he was a passenger was forced down by French military aircraft.

In December 1956 and January 1957 battle-tested French troops with combat experience in Indochina arrived in Algeria to restore order in Algiers. Among these were General Raoul Salan (commander in chief), paratrooper commander Major General Jacques Massu, and Colonels Yves Goddard and Marcel Bigeard, both of whom were adept at intelligence gathering and infiltration. Massu's men made steady headway, and Goddard himself captured Saadi Yacef in September 1957. The French had won the Battle of Algiers. The 1965 film *The Battle of Algiers,* produced by Gillo

Ahmed Ben Bella after his capture by the French in October 1956. Ben Bella was one of the founders of the FLN (Front de Liberation Nationale, National Liberation Front) that fought the French beginning in 1954. Ben Bella was held by the French until 1962 when Algeria was granted independence. Considered by many Algerians to be the father of their country, he subsequently served as Algeria's first president. (AP Photo)

Pontecorvo and Saadi Yacef (with money provided by the FLN), garnered international support for the FLN, as it depicted the French simply as brutal occupiers. Certainly the French employed torture to force FLN operatives to talk, and others were murdered in the process. The FLN, it needs to be pointed out, also routinely murdered captured French soldiers and colon civilians.

In September 1957 the French military completed the Morice Line, named for French minister of defense André Morice. Designed to prevent the infiltration of men and supplies by the FLN from Tunisia, the line ran for some 200 miles from the Mediterranean Sea in the north into the Sahara in the south. It was centered on an 8-foot tall, 5,000-volt electric fence that ran its entire length. Supporting this was a 50-yard-wide killing zone on each side of the fence rigged with antipersonnel mines. The line was also covered by previously ranged 105mm howitzers. A patrolled track paralleled the fence on its Algerian side. The Morice Line was bolstered by electronic sensors that provided warning of any attempt to pierce the barrier. Searchlights operated at night.

Although manning the line required a large number of French soldiers, this did significantly reduce infiltration by the FLN from Tunisia. By April 1958, the French estimated that they had defeated 80 percent of FLN infiltration attempts. This contributed greatly to the isolation of those FLN units within Algeria that were reliant on support from Tunisia. The French subsequently constructed a less extensive barrier, known as the Pedron Line, along the Algerian border with Morocco.

Despite victory in Algiers and the success of the Morice Line, French forces were not able to quell the Algerian rebellion or gain the confidence of the colons. Some colons were fearful that the French government was about to negotiate with the FLN. In the spring of 1958, colon Ultra groups began to hatch a plan to change the colonial government.

Colon veteran Pierre Lagaillarde now organized hundreds of Ultra commandos and began a revolt on May 13, 1958. Soon, tens of thousands of colons and Muslims arrived outside of the government building in Algiers to protest French government policy. General Massu quickly formed a so-called Committee of Public Safety, and General Salan assumed leadership of the body. Salan then went before the throngs of protesters. Although the plotters would have preferred someone frankly more authoritarian, Salan called for the return to power of General Charles de Gaulle. Although he had been out of power for more than a decade, on May 19 de Gaulle announced his willingness to assume authority.

Massu was prepared to bring back de Gaulle by force if necessary, but military options were not needed. On June 1, 1958, the French National Assembly made de Gaulle premier, technically the last premier of the Fourth Republic. Algeria had thus managed to change the political leadership of the mother country.

De Gaulle visited Algeria five times between June and December 1958. At Oran on June 4, he said about France's mission in Algeria that "she is here forever." A month later he proposed a budget allocation of 15 billion francs for Algerian housing, education, and public works, and that October he suggested an even more sweeping proposal called "The Constantine Plan." The funding for the massive projects was, however, never forthcoming, and true Algerian reform was never realized. It was probably too late in any case for reform to impact the Muslim community of Algeria.

Algeria's new military commander, General Maurice Challe, arrived on December 12, 1958, and then in early 1959 launched a series of attacks on FLN positions in rural Kabylia. Muslim troops loyal to the French guided special mobile French troops called Commandos de Chasse. An aggressive set of sorties deep in Kabylia made much headway, and Challe calculated that by the end of October his men had killed half of the FLN operatives in Kabylia. A second phase of the offensive was to occur in 1960, but by then de Gaulle, who had gradually eliminated options, had decided that Algerian independence was inevitable.

De Gaulle braced his generals for the decision to let go of Algeria in late August 1959 and then addressed the French people on September 19, 1959, declaring his support for Algerian self-determination. Fearing for their future, some Ultras created the Front Nationale Français (National Liberation Front, FNL) and fomented another revolt on January 24, 1960, in the so-called Barricades Week. When policemen tried to restore order, mayhem ensued, and many people were killed or wounded. General Challe and Algerian governor-general Paul Delouvrier fled Algiers on January 28, but the next day de Gaulle, dressed in his old army uniform, turned the tide via a televised address to the nation. On February 1 army units swore loyalty to the government, and the revolt then quickly collapsed. On February 11, increasingly desperate Ultras formed a terrorist group called the Secret Army Organization that targeted colons whom they regarded as traitors.

The Generals' Putsch of April 20–26, 1961, seriously threatened de Gaulle's regime. Challe wanted a revolt limited to Algeria, but Salan and his colleagues (Ground Forces chief of staff General André Zeller and recently retired Inspector General of the Air Force, Edmond Jouhaud) had all prepared for a revolt in France as well. The generals had the support of many frontline officers in addition to almost two divisions of troops. The Foreign Legion arrested Algeria's commander in chief, General Fernand Gambiez, and paratroopers near Rambouillet prepared to march on Paris after obtaining armored support. The coup collapsed, however, as police units managed to convince the paratroopers to depart, and army units again swore loyalty to de Gaulle.

On June 10, 1961, de Gaulle held secret meetings with FLN representatives in Paris and then made a June 14 televised appeal for the FLN's so-called Provisional Government to come to Paris to negotiate an end to the war. Peace talks during June 25–29 failed to lead to resolution, but de Gaulle's mind already was made up. During his visit to Algeria in December he was greeted by large pro-FLN Muslim rallies and Muslim anticolon riots. The United Nations (UN) recognized Algeria's independence on December 20, and on January 8, 1962, the French public voted in favor of Algerian independence.

After the failed coup, a massive exodus of colons commenced. Nearly 1 million returned to their ancestral homelands (half of them went to France, with most others settling in Spain and Italy). Peace talks resumed at Évian-les-Bains, France, and both sides reached a settlement on March 18, 1962. In a national referendum held on April 8, 1962, the accords were approved by almost 91 percent of the electorate. A second vote on the accords, held in Algeria on July 1, saw 5,975,581 votes for independence and just 16,534 against it. De Gaulle pronounced Algeria an independent country on July 3.

The formal handover of power occurred on July 4, 1962, as the FLN's Provisional Committee took control of Algeria. In September Ben Bella, whom many Algerians regard as the father of their country, was elected Algeria's first president. The Algerian War had resulted in some 18,000 French military deaths, 3,000 colon deaths, and about 300,000 Muslim deaths. Some 30,000 colons remained behind in the now-independent Algeria, including the socialist mayor of Algiers, Jacques Chevallier. They were ostensibly granted equal rights in the peace treaty but instead faced the loss of much of their property and official discrimination by the FLN government. The FLN remained in power until 1989, practicing a form of socialism until changes in Soviet foreign policy necessitated changes in Algerian internal affairs.

The FLN government established a decentralized socialist economy and a one-party state. Upon independence, Algerian military forces numbered around 125,000 men including various irregular militias, which were gradually eliminated or integrated into the national force. In October 1963 Colonel Mohand Ou el Hadj led a revolt of Berber tribesmen in the Kabylia region. Government troops soon crushed the revolt, and the surviving rebels took refuge in the mountains.

Ben Bella's inept rule, his attempt to consolidate his power, and popular discontent with the economy's inefficiency sparked a near bloodless military coup by his close associate and war hero, Defense Minister Houari Boumédienne, on June 19, 1965. Boumédienne then established a military-dominated government. He held power as chairman of the Revolutionary Council until December 10, 1976. Ben Bella was under house arrest until 1980, when he was permitted to go into exile abroad.

In 1971, the government endeavored to stimulate economic growth by nationalizing the oil industry and investing the revenues in centrally orchestrated industrial development. Boumédienne's government increasingly took on an authoritarian cast, however. The military expanded rapidly during the 1970s and 1980s, with the army numbering 110,000, the air force 12,000, and the navy 8,000 by 1985.

Algeria's leaders sought to retain their autonomy, joining their country to the Non-Aligned Movement. Boumédienne phased out French military bases. Although Algeria denounced perceived American imperialism and supported Fidel Castro's Cuba, the Viet Cong in South Vietnam during the Vietnam War, Palestinian nationalists, and African anticolonial fighters, it maintained a strong trading relationship with the United States. At the same time, Algeria cultivated economic ties with the Soviet Union, which provided the nation with important military material and training.

Algeria was also involved in the 1973–1991 Western Sahara War, a conflict that pitted the Sahrawi Frente Popular de Liberación de Saguía el Hamra y Río de Oro (Popular Front for the Liberation of Saguia el-Hamra and Río de Oro), better known as Polisario, against first Spain and then Morocco and Mauritania for control of the Spanish colony of Western Sahara (Río de Oro). Sahrawi students in

Moroccan universities formed Polisario in 1971. After trying but failing to win support from various Arab governments, including those of Morocco and Algeria, the students relocated to Spanish-controlled Western Sahara and began an armed uprising against Spain in May 1973. Polisario soon secured support of the vast majority of the population.

With the end of the Francisco Franco regime in Spain the Spanish government began negotiating a handover of power, but in the Madrid Accords of November 14, 1975, Spain reached agreement with Morocco and Mauritania rather than Polisario. Spain agreed to divide the territory between Morocco and Mauritania. Morocco was to secure the northern part of the Spanish Sahara (Saguia el-Hamra), while Mauritania obtained the south (Río de Oro).

In February 1976, Polisario proclaimed the establishment of the Sahrawi Arab Democratic Republic and commenced guerrilla warfare against both Morocco and Mauritania. Algeria provided Polisario with both modern weaponry and other military assistance, along with refugee camps on its territory.

Incapable of a major effort to control the southern Sahara, Mauritania in August 1979 agreed to quit that region entirely and recognize the Sahrawi Arab Democratic Republic. Morocco then immediately claimed for itself the area evacuated by Mauritania. In the mid-1980s Morocco was largely able to keep Polisario at bay by building a large sand berm (the Morocco Wall) to surround the most economically important areas of the Western Sahara. At the same time, Algeria largely withdrew its support for the rebels on the formation in February 1989 of the Arab Maghreb Union, which included both Morocco and Algeria. Finally in September 1991 Polisario and Morocco agreed to a cease-fire, with a referendum to be held the next year. No referendum has been held, however, owing to the issue of who would be eligible to vote. Today Morocco controls two-thirds of the Western Sahara, including virtually the entire Atlantic coast.

During this period, Algeria was too absorbed in its own internal problems to take much interest or participate actively in the Arab-Israeli conflicts, although as an Arab state it did lend strong verbal support to the Palestinians. Algeria did not commit ground troops during the 1973 Yom Kippur War but did supply to Egypt two squadrons of MiG-21 fighters and a squadron of Su-7B fighter-bombers. These aircraft were simply incorporated into Egyptian units. Then in June 1976, Algeria agreed to contribute troops to an Arab League peacekeeping force in Lebanon. Diplomatic relations with the United States warmed after Algeria negotiated the release of American hostages in Iran in 1980 and when Morocco fell out of U.S. favor by allying with Libya in 1984.

In November 1976 a referendum was held on a new Algerian constitution. The referendum established Algeria as a socialist state and confirmed the FLN as the sole legal political party. In addition, the referendum restored the People's National Assembly (which had been suspended since the 1965 coup) and provided for direct election of the president. The government announced approval of the constitutional changes by a 99 percent vote, with a 92.9 percent turnout of eligible voters. When Boumédienne died in December 1978, power passed to Chadli Bendjedid, the army-backed candidate for president. Bendjedid retreated from

Boumédienne's increasingly ineffective economic policies, privatizing much of the economy and encouraging entrepreneurship. Accumulated debt continued to retard economic expansion, however. Growing public anger on the part of labor unions, students, and Islamic fundamentalists against widespread government corruption and Bendjedid's one-party rule resulted in demonstrations and rioting beginning in October 1988, which resulted in more than 500 deaths. The protests forced Bendjedid to decree an end to one-party rule and introduce a new constitution, which was approved by popular vote in February 1989.

The Islamic Salvation Front (Front Islamique du Salut, FIS) proved to be the most successful of the many new political parties established with the end of one-party rule. After large victories by the FIS in local elections in June 1990 and in the first round of voting in Algeria's first multiparty national elections in December 1991, however, the army stepped in. On January 11, 1992, it canceled the second round of voting and forced Benjedid to resign. On January 16 the army leaders put in place a new regime under Mohamed Boudiaf, a former leader of the struggle for independence. The army imposed martial law, arrested tens of thousands of FIS members, and in March 1992 banned all political parties that were based on religion, which of course included the FIS.

Islamist extremists calling themselves the Groupe Islamique Armée (Armed Islamic Group, GIA) now commenced guerrilla warfare and terrorist attacks in what became known as the Algerian Civil War (1992–2002). On June 29, 1992, Boudiaf was assassinated by one of his bodyguards, Lieutenant L. Boumaarafi, which plunged Algeria deeper into chaos.

Fighting raged throughout Algeria in the form of isolated attacks. Although many of the deaths were of the members of the army and militants, a large number of innocent civilians—men, women, and children—also perished, many of them at the hands of the GIA but some apparently by the army and foreign mercenaries and then blamed on various Islamic groups.

Elections resumed in 1995, and on November 16 the voters overwhelmingly rejected Islamic fundamentalist candidates who sought to make Algeria an Islamic republic. The country's high unemployment and inflation served as a major impediment to long-term stability, however. Also, despite the elections allowed by the army-dominated government, there were charges of fraud and rampant corruption, and the violence continued.

On April 16, 1999, Abdelaziz Bouteflika, who was put forward by the military hierarchy, was elected president. The six other candidates for the position had withdrawn the day before to protest organized election fraud. Bouteflika assumed office on April 27. Linguistic rights became a major issue thereafter, and the government recognized Tamazight (Berber) as a national language and permitted it to be taught in schools. Meanwhile, the government sought to take advantage of the substantial increases in the price of oil and natural gas to invest in economic development projects.

The civil war was officially declared at an end on January 11, 2000, when the armed wing of the Islamic Salvation Front agreed to disband following talks with the government. The guerrillas also granted amnesty in return for giving up their weapons. Fighting continued with other guerrilla groups, however, into 2002, by which date all the principal guerrilla organizations had either been destroyed or had surrendered under the government amnesty programs. The violence between January 1992 and June 2002 had brought the deaths of more than 160,000 people. Others had simply disappeared, many of these at the hands of the security forces. By 2005, however, the insurgency greatly diminished in part owing to a concerted effort by the government to promote reconciliation and institute economic reforms.

On August 14, 2005, Bouteflika announced a referendum on a draft charter for "peace and national reconciliation." The government agreed to drop charges against Islamic extremists who surrendered to the authorities and had not participated in massacres, rapes, or bombings. The charter also provided for an amnesty for government security forces. The proposed charter drew sharp protests from families of those who had disappeared, victims of state terrorism and armed groups, human rights organizations, and some opposition parties. They wanted a full accounting of the unrest in Algeria since 1992 and the trial of those responsible for the crimes.

The referendum was held on September 29, 2005. The government claimed that 80 percent of the electorate had gone to the polls and that the charter had been approved by a 97 percent vote. Opposition leaders contested these figures, but foreign governments, including France and the United States, welcomed the results.

Islamist radicals, however, commenced a guerrilla war that has persisted to the present, taking a toll of 150,000 or more lives. Although Algeria's military government managed to gain the upper hand in the struggle after 1998, Islamic groups continue to wage war on the state, which maintains control through brutal repression and tainted elections. The best known of these groups is Al-Qaeda in the Islamic Maghreb (AQIM). It grew out of the militant Islamist movement known as the Armed Islamic Group (GIA), which had violently opposed Algiers's secular leadership in the 1990s. In 1998 several GIA leaders, concerned that tactics such as beheadings were actually counterproductive, formed the Salafist Group for Preaching and Combat (GSPC). The GSPC vowed to continue the rebellion without killing civilians, but the government amnesty program caused it to merge with Al-Qaeda and stage high-profile attacks to enhance recruiting. The merger was announced on September 11, 2006, and the GSPC changed its name to AQIM the following January. The change in name described the AQIM's broadened goal of attacking Western interests in addition to Algerian targets and also benefited Al-Qaeda in enhancing its reach into an area closer to Europe.

On December 11, 2007, AQIM exploded two bombs in Algiers 10 minutes apart. These targeted the regional UN headquarters and the Algerian Supreme Constitutional Court and killed 41 people, including 17 UN personnel. The attack marked a renewal of violence in the ongoing Islamic insurgency.

On August 19, 2008, an AQIM suicide bomber rammed a car filled with explosives into a police training academy about 35 miles east of Algiers. The ensuing blast killed 43 people, most of them civilians waiting to take an entrance exam. On June 17, 2009, AQIM militants employed roadside bombs and small arms to attack a convoy of paramilitary police some 110 miles from Algiers, killing 18 policemen and a civilian.

Protests and demonstrations throughout North Africa and the Middle East (later dubbed the Arab Spring) that began in Tunisia in December 2010 reached neighboring Algeria later that month, on December 28, and widespread demonstrations against the government occurred during January 3–11, 2011, but were ended by police action. On February 22, 2011, the government ended its 19-year-long state of emergency and went on to enact limited reform legislation addressing the election process, political parties, and the representation of women in elected bodies.

On January 16, 2013, in a dramatic terrorist action, some 40 Islamic militants led by Al-Qaeda–linked Mokhtar bel Mokhtar attacked the remote sprawling Amenas natural gas plant in eastern Algeria near the Libyan border, which produced some 10 percent of Algeria's natural gas exports. The raiders seized the workers there, including a significant number of foreigners, with the plan to ransom them in order to secure funds with which to purchase weapons. On January 18 and 19 the Algerian government employed attack helicopters to strike vehicles loaded with the hostages that were departing the facility, which the hostage takers had planned to blow up.

Although the government forces regained control of the facility and freed most of the hostages, the operation came at a high cost. The Algerian government claimed 685 Algerian and 107 foreign hostages freed, but 48 of the hostages were killed in the exchange of fire. The largest death toll among the foreigners was for the Japanese, with 9 slain. The government claimed that 32 of the militants were killed and 5 were captured. A number of the national governments complained regarding what they considered a heavy-handed Algerian action, but the Algerian government appeared bent on making the point that under no circumstances would it negotiate with terrorists.

Terrorism does not appear now to be a major threat to governmental stability in Algeria. Opposition and human rights groups, however, continue to criticize what they characterize as unfair elections, government censorship, and harassment of the political opposition.

Timeline

1516	Algeria becomes part of the Ottoman Empire.
1830s	French forces overcome Arab resistance led by Abdelkader El Djezairi and greatly expand the territory comprising Algeria.
Jun 1830	French forces invade and capture the city of Algiers within a month.
1848	France administers all Algeria as an integral part of France.
1871	As a consequence of the French defeat in the Franco-Prussian War and the loss to Germany of the provinces of Alsace and Lorraine, there is increased French immigration to Algeria of those French citizens not wishing to be under German rule. The

immigrants are known as colons and *pieds-noirs* and come to constitute the vast majority of the technicians and administrators in Algeria. Europeans also come to control the key segments of the economy including banks, shipping, utilities, and mining as well as nearly half of the farming acreage.

May 8, 1945   A confrontation between Arabs and the colons occurs at Sétif during a parade celebrating the end of World War II in Europe. It leads to considerable violence and savage French reprisals, with the deaths of hundreds of people.

Sep 1947   Hopes among moderates in the Arab community that there would be meaningful democratic reform are dashed in the Algerian Statute of this date. It establishes administrative autonomy for the three departments constituting Algeria and sets up the Algerian Assembly with two colleges. The first is for the 469,000 non-Muslim Algerians and the 63,000 Muslims granted citizenship by dint of army service during World War II. The second is for the 1.301 million other Muslims eligible to vote. Each college had 60 seats. While elected separately, the two vote together, but to prevent Muslim control, the statute provides that the governor-general or 30 members of the Algerian Assembly can request a two-thirds vote, thus ensuring continued European control.

Apr 1948   The first elections under the Algerian Statute occur. These are rigged to ensure the election of pliant Muslims, known as yes-men.

May 1954   The Viet Minh defeat the French in the Battle of Dienbienphu in Indochina, dealing a major blow to what remains of European colonialism and leading the French to grant independence to the states of Indochina.

Oct 10, 1954   Mohamed Ahmed Ben Bella and compatriots form the Front de Liberation Nationale (National Liberation Front, FLN).

Oct 31–Nov 1, 1954   The FLN mounts a series of small attacks across Algeria, beginning the Algerian War.

Aug 20, 1955   The FLN attacks colon civilians in what comes to be known as the Philippeville Massacre. Colon reprisals bring the deaths of several thousand Muslims.

Mar 1956   The French grant independence to both Tunisia and Morocco, further bolstering the FLN and enabling the shipment of arms through chiefly Tunisia, supplied by Egyptian president Gamal Abdel Nasser.

Oct 28–Nov 7, 1956   The Suez Crisis. An effort by France, Britain, and Israel to invade Egypt and overthrow Egyptian president Gamal Abdel Nasser fails, owing to strong opposition from the United States as well as the Soviet Union.

Sep 30, 1956–
Sep 24, 1957

The so-called Battle of Algiers begins. FLN operative Saadi Yacef carries out a terrorist-style bombing campaign against European civilians. Other FLN leaders target governmental officials for assassination.

Oct 22, 1956

The French capture FLN leader Ben Bella by forcing down an airliner on which he is a passenger. He is imprisoned for the next six years.

Spring 1958

Fearful that the government in Paris is about to open negotiations with the FLN, colon Ultras begin to plan a change in the colonial government.

May 13, 1958

Colon Pierre Lagaillarde leads a coup in Algiers. French major general Jacques Massu then forms a Committee of Public Safety, and French commander in Algeria General Raoul Salan assumes its leadership and calls for the return to power of General Charles de Gaulle.

Jun 1, 1958

Military options are not necessary, as the French National Assembly votes to make de Gaulle premier. Events in Algeria have changed the political leadership of the mother country.

Jun 4, 1958

During a visit to Oran, de Gaulle pledges, regarding France's mission in Algeria, that "she is here forever."

Oct 3, 1958

During a visit to Constantine, de Gaulle announces a sweeping plan for Algerian economic development, which becomes known as the Constantine Plan. Funding is never forthcoming. In any case, it is probably too late for reform to impact the opinion of the Algerian Muslim community.

Dec 12, 1958

General Maurice Challe assumes command of French forces in Algeria.

Sep 19, 1959

Despite French battlefield successes, especially in rural Kabylia, de Gaulle concludes that Algerian independence is inevitable and addresses the nation to express his support for self-determination.

Jan 24, 1960

Some Algerian colons create the Front Nationale Français and foment another revolt in Algiers. Considerable violence ensues in the so-called Barricades Week.

Jan 28, 1960

General Challe and Algeria's governor-general Paul Delouvrier flee Algiers.

Jan 29, 1960

De Gaulle turns the tide against the putschists in a televised address to the nation while dressed in his old army uniform.

Feb 1, 1960	Army units swear loyalty to the government, and the revolt quickly collapses.
Feb 11, 1960	Extremist colons form a terrorist group called the Secret Army Organization that target colons they regard as traitors. It will also carry out bombings in France and attempt to assassinated de Gaulle.
Apr 20–26, 1961	The Generals' Putsch in Algiers seriously threatens de Gaulle's regime. General Challe wanted a revolt limited to Algeria, but Salan and others prepare for revolt in France as well. The putsch has the support of many frontline officers and almost two divisions of troops. Foreign Legionnaires arrest General Fernand Gambiez, commander of French forces in Algeria and paratroopers near Rambouillet prepared to march on Paris. The coup soon collapses, however, and army units again swear loyalty to de Gaulle. With the failure of this coup, a mass exodus of colons from Algeria commences, ultimately reaching some 1 million.
Jun 10, 1961	De Gaulle meets secretly with FLN representatives in Paris and on June 14 appears on television and appeals for representatives of the FLN's so-called Provisional Government to come to Paris to negotiate an end to the war.
Jun 25–29, 1961	Peace talks fail, but de Gaulle is convinced that independence for Algeria is the only course open.
Dec 20, 1961	The United Nations (UN) recognizes Algerian independence.
Jan 8, 1962	The French public votes in favor of Algerian independence.
Mar 18, 1962	Peace talks having resumed, the two sides conclude the Évian Accords.
Apr 8, 1962	In a national referendum, the French electorate approves the Évian Accords, with almost 91 percent in favor.
Jul 1, 1962	In a second referendum, in Algeria, 5,975,581 vote for independence and just 16,534 vote against.
Jul 3, 1962	De Gaulle pronounces Algeria an independent nation.
Jul 4, 1962	The formal transfer of power occurs in Algeria, with the FLN Provisional Committee assuming control.
Sep 15, 1962	Following a national election, Ben Bella becomes president of Algeria. The FLN establishes a decentralized socialist economy and a one-party state.
Oct 6–12, 1963	Algerian Army colonel Mohand Ou el Hadj leads a revolt of Berber tribesmen in the Kabylia region. Government troops soon crush the revolt, however, and the rebels take refuge in the mountains.

Jun 19, 1965   Ben Bella's attempt to consolidate power and popular discontent regarding the economy result in a bloodless military coup led by Defense Minister Houari Boumédienne. Ben Bella is placed under house arrest until 1980, when he is allowed to go into exile. Boumédienne establishes a military-dominated government and remains in power as chairman of the Revolutionary Council until December 10, 1976.

Dec 13, 1967   Dissident army officers attempt a coup d'état against the Boumédienne government but are promptly crushed by government forces.

1973–1991   The Western Sahara War pits the Sahrawi Frente Popular de Liberación de Saguía el Hamra y Río de Oro (Popular Front for the Liberation of Saguia el-Hamra and Río de Oro), better known as Polisario, against first Spain and then Morocco and Mauritania for control of the Spanish colony of Western Sahara (Río de Oro). Algeria provides both weapons and training camps for Polisario against Morocco, but Algerian support is largely withdrawn on the formation of the Arab Maghreb Union, which includes both Morocco and Algeria, in February 1989. The fighting largely ends with a cease-fire that sees Morocco in control of the vast majority of the Río de Oro, including virtually its entire Atlantic coastline. Although the promised referendum never occurs, an uneasy peace continues.

Jun 10, 1976   Algeria agrees to contribute troops to an Arab League peacekeeping force in Lebanon.

Nov 19, 1976   A national referendum sees (according to the government) a 92.9 percent turnout and a 99 percent favorable vote that restores the People's National Assembly, which had been suspended following the 1965 coup, and provides for the direct election of the president. It also proclaims Algeria as a socialist state and confirms the FLN as the sole legal political party.

Dec 27, 1978   Boumédienne dies while in office.

Feb 9, 1979   The new president is Chadli Bendjedid, the army-backed candidate. Bendjedid privatizes much of the economy and seeks to encourage entrepreneurship.

Oct 1988   Growing public protests from labor unions, students, and Islamic fundamentalists bring the deaths of more than 500 people.

Feb 1989   Considerable public unrest forces the government to end restrictions on political expression in a new constitution approved by popular vote.

1992–2002   In the decade-long civil war, small-scale actions occur throughout much of Algeria. Although many of the deaths occur between the army and militants, a large number of innocent civilians—men, women, and children—also perish, most of them at the hands of Islamist extremists calling themselves the Groupe Islamique Armée (Armed Islamic Group, GIA) but a number apparently by the army and foreign mercenaries and then blamed on various Islamic groups.

Jan 16, 1992   The Islamic Salvation Front (Front Islamique du Salut, FIS) proves to be the most successful of the new political parties, but following its considerable victories in local elections and then the first round of voting for Algeria's first multiparty national elections in December 1991, army leaders step in. They cancel the second round of voting and force Benjedid to resign. On this date, they put in place a new regime under Mohamed Boudiaf.

Mar 1992   The Boudiaf government imposes martial law, arrests tens of thousands of FIS members, and bans all religiously based political parties, which of course includes the FIS. The GIA commence guerrilla warfare and terrorist attacks in what becomes known as the Algerian Civil War (1992–2002).

Jun 29, 1992   Boudiaf is assassinated by one of his bodyguards.

Nov 16, 1995   In a national election, Algerian voters overwhelmingly reject Islamic fundamentalist candidates, who are trying to establish an Islamic republic in the nation and are largely responsible for the civil war. Dissatisfaction with corruption, fraud, and rigged elections, however, prevents stability, and the violence continues.

Apr 3–4, 1997   Fifty-two of the 53 residents of the village of Thalit are massacred by Islamist guerrillas, thought to be affiliated with the GIA.

Apr 16, 1999   Abdelaziz Bouteflika, proposed by the military hierarchy, is elected president. The six other candidates had withdrawn the day before to protest organized election fraud.

Jan 11, 2000   The Algerian government declares the civil war at an end when the armed wing of the Islamic Salvation Front agrees to disband following talks with the government. The guerrillas give up their weapons and are granted amnesty. Other guerrilla groups continue fighting into 2002, by which date all the principal guerrilla organizations had either been destroyed or had surrendered under the government amnesty programs. The Algerian Civil War has claimed more than 160,000 people dead, with others having simply disappeared.

Sep 29, 2005   A referendum occurs on a charter proposed by President Bouteflika. The government will drop charges against Islamic extremists who surrender to the authorities and have not participated in massacres, rapes, or bombings. The charter also provides for amnesty for government security forces. The government claims a 97 percent vote in favor of the referendum with an 80 percent turnout.

Sep 12, 2006   Some Islamist radical groups, principally the Salafist Group for Preaching and Combat (GSPC), continue the rebellion. On this date the GSPC merges with Al-Qaeda and then in January 2007 changes its name to Al-Qaeda in the Islamic Maghreb (AQIM).

Dec 11, 2007   Two bombings occur in Algiers. Only 10 minutes apart, these are against the regional UN headquarters and the Algerian Supreme Constitutional Court. The blasts kill 41 people, including 17 UN personnel. The attack marks a renewal of violence in the ongoing Islamic insurgency.

Aug 19, 2008   An AQIM suicide bomber rams a car filled with explosives into a police training academy near Algiers, killing 43 people.

Jun 17, 2009   AQIM militants employed roadside bombs and small arms to attack a convoy of paramilitary police, killing 18 policemen and a civilian.

Dec 28, 2010   Protests and demonstrations commence in Algeria, part of what will be known as the Arab Spring, a movement that had begun in Tunisia and will spread throughout North Africa and the Middle East.

Jan 3–11, 2011   Antigovernment demonstrations in Algeria are ended by police action.

Feb 22, 2011   The Algerian government ends its 19-year-long state of emergency. The government goes on to enact some reform legislation treating the election process, political parties, and representation of women in elected bodies.

Jan 16–19, 2013   Some 40 Islamic militants led by Al-Qaeda–linked Mokhtar bel Mokhtar attack the sprawling Amenas natural gas plant in far eastern Algeria near the Libyan border and seize the workers there, including a number of foreigners. Reportedly the militants have planned to ransom the hostages to secure funds with which to purchase weapons. On January 18 and 19 the Algerian government employs attack helicopters to strike vehicles, loaded with the hostages, that are departing the facility. The government forces regain control of the facility and free 685 Algerian and 107 foreign hostages, but 48 of the hostages are killed, a number of them foreigners. The government claims that 32 of the militants were slain and 5 were captured.

Further Reading

Horne, Alistair. *A Savage War of Peace: Algeria, 1954–1962*. London: Macmillan, 1977.

Kettle, Michael. *De Gaulle and Algeria, 1940–1960*. London: Quartet, 1993.

Lawless, Richard. *Algeria*. Santa Barbara, CA: ABC-CLIO, 1995.

Ruedy, John. *Modern Algeria: The Origins and Development of a Nation*. Bloomington: Indiana University Press, 1992.

Servan-Schreiber, Jean-Jacques. *Lieutenant in Algeria*. Translated by Ronald Matthews. New York: Knopf, 1957.

Smith, Tony. *The French Stake in Algeria, 1945–1962*. Ithaca, NY: Cornell University Press, 1979.

Stora, Benjamin. *Algeria, 1830–2000: A Short History*. Translated by Jane Marie Todd. Ithaca, NY: Cornell University Press, 2001.

Talbott, John. *The War without a Name: France in Algeria, 1954–1962*. New York: Knopf, 1980.

Watson, William E. *Tricolor and Crescent: France and the Islamic World*. Westport, CT: Praeger, 2003.

BAHRAIN

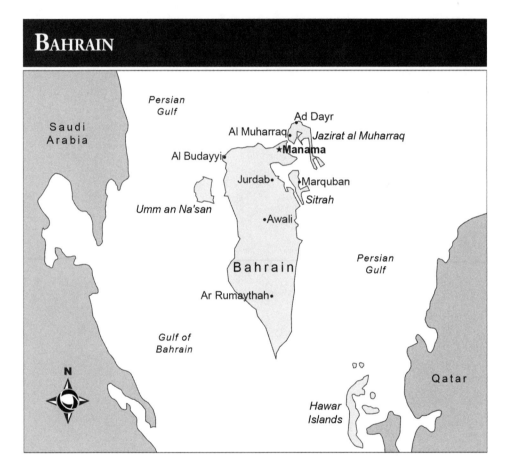

Persian Gulf

Saudi Arabia

Ad Dayr

Al Muharraq

Jazirat al Muharraq

★**Manama**

Al Budayyi•

Jurdab•

•Marquban

Sitrah

Umm an Na'san

•Awali

B a h r a i n

Persian Gulf

Ar Rumaythah•

Gulf of Bahrain

N

Hawar Islands

Qatar

Bahrain

Spencer C. Tucker and Wyndham E. Whynot

Bahrain, officially known as the Kingdom of Bahrain, is an archipelago of more than 30 islands on the western shores of the Persian Gulf. Bahrain continues to create artificial islands for economic and tourism purposes. Only 5 of the islands are permanently inhabited, however. Bordered on the west by the Gulf of Bahrain and by the Persian Gulf on the north, east, and south, Bahrain is about 20 miles from Qatar to the south, while a 16-mile-long causeway westward connects the Bahraini island of Umm al-Nasan to Saudi Arabia. Bahrain's area is only some 295 square miles. The nation's capital is Manama.

Bahrain's 2016 population numbered some 1.397 million. Those of Bahraini descent account for some 45.5 percent of the total. The remainder are 45.5 percent South Asian, 4.7 percent other Arabs, 1.6 percent African, 1 percent European, and 1.2 percent others. Islam is the religion of some 85 percent of the population, with 70 percent of the Muslim population being Shia. The remaining 15 percent practice Bahai, Christianity, and other religions. Arabic, English, and Farsi are the most commonly spoken languages.

Politically, Bahrain consists of a constitutional monarchy, ruled by Emir Khalifa bin Hamad al-Thani, and is a member of the Gulf Cooperation Council, a collective security organization consisting of six countries on the western side of the Persian Gulf. Bahrain also belongs to the Arab League, the United Nations, the Organization of Islamic Conference, the Organization of Arab Petroleum Exporting Countries, and other international organizations.

Although fixing the precise starting date of Bahraini civilization is difficult, Pakistan's Harappa and the Greeks traded their goods for Bahraini pearls in ancient times. Indeed, Bahrain's pearl fisheries were considered the finest in the world into the 19th century. Historically, Bahrain has been known as Dilmun, Tylos, and Awal. Pre-Islamic Bahrain's religions included both paganism and Nestorian Christianity, the latter having a bishopric located on Umm al-Nasan that lasted until at least 835 CE. Bahrain adopted Islam during the lifetime of Prophet Muhammad, and this soon become the dominant religion there. The Ismaili al-Qaramita Islamic sect dominated Bahrain between 900 and 976. Afterward, Shiism eventually became the dominant force in Bahraini Islam.

Throughout Bahrain's history various empires have occupied the country, including those of Babylon, Assyria, Portugal, and Safavid Iran. Portuguese forces captured Bahrain in 1521 and controlled the country until 1602, when Bahrainis overthrew them. Iran's Safavid Empire quickly conquered Bahrain the same year and maintained control until 1717. Iran has used this fact to repeatedly claim Bahraini territory.

In 1783 the al-Khalifa clan, led by Ahmad ibn Mohammed al-Khalifa, invaded and conquered Bahrain. This family line has led the country ever since. The royal family is Sunni Muslim, while as noted the majority of Bahrain's population is Shia Muslim.

In 1820 Bahrain signed a treaty with the British government pledging not to engage in piracy. Britain agreed to provide military protection for Bahrain and official recognition of the al-Khalifa family as the rulers. In exchange, Bahrain agreed not to cede its territory to any country except Britain and not to establish foreign relations with other nations without British consent. Meanwhile, British advisers encouraged the al-Khalifa rulers to adopt a series of social reforms. Iran continued to assert its rights to Bahrain, however. In 1927 Iranian ruler Reza Shah claimed sovereignty over the country in a letter to the League of Nations.

Discovery of oil in 1931 by the Bahrain Petroleum Company, a subsidiary of the Standard Oil Company of California, had immense impact. Production began the next year, and Bahrain soon was an early leading exporter of oil. Meanwhile, relations with Britain became closer, especially after 1935 when London relocated a major naval base there from Iran. Bahrain allied itself with Britain at the onset of World War II, declaring war on Germany on September 10, 1939. During the war Bahrain provided oil to the Allied powers and served as a staging point for the protection of British colonies and oil-production facilities in Asia and Africa.

After India acquired its independence from Britain on August 15, 1947, British interest in the Persian Gulf region diminished markedly, eventually leading to London's decision in 1968 to withdraw from the treaties signed with the Gulf states during the 1800s. Initial attempts to unite Bahrain with other Gulf states failed, and on August 15, 1971, Bahrain declared its full independence.

By 1973 Bahrain's oil reserves were diminishing. Seeking an alternative source of revenue, Bahrain established a robust banking industry seeking to replace that of Lebanon, which had greatly suffered as a consequence of the long Lebanese Civil War (1975–1990). Bahrain soon was recognized as the banking center of the Middle East.

In 1973 Bahrain held its first parliamentary elections. Its members soon quarreled with Emir Isa bin Salman al-Khalifa (r. 1961–1999) regarding implementation of a security law, however. The emir responded by dissolving the assembly in 1975 and putting the law into force by decree. Despite his actions, Bahrain is regarded as quite liberal and tolerant compared to most other Islamic nations in the region.

In 1981 the government of the Islamic Republic of Iran sought to encourage Bahrain's large Shia population to carry out a revolution there. Although some Bahraini Shias attempted a coup d'état that same year, it was unsuccessful. Indeed, Iranian interference in Bahraini affairs encouraged the nation to establish collective security agreements that created the Gulf Cooperation Council on May 25, 1981, and resulted in efforts to improve diplomatic ties with the United States. On January 26, 1982, Bahrain joined Saudi Arabia, Kuwait, Oman, Qatar, and the United Arab Emirates in establishing a joint military command structure and an integrated air defense system. This step was prompted by the perceived threats from Iran, the ongoing Iran-Iraq War (1980–1988), and the Soviet-Afghan War (1979–1989).

Acts against the Bahrainian government included attacks by external and internal sources. One such threat came from the Islamic Front for the Liberation of Bahrain (IFLB), a Shia Islamist militant group that sought to establish a theocratic government in Bahrain. Active from 1981 into the 1990s, the IFLB was based in Iran and trained and financed by Iranian intelligence and the Revolutionary Guards. With the failure of the 1981 coup attempt, the IFLB carried out a number of small terrorist attacks against Bahraini targets, mostly by bombings. The IFLB claimed responsibility for the bombing of the Diplomat Hotel on February 10, 1996, that wounded four people. The perception that the IFLB was closely linked to Iran, however, greatly diminished its support among the wider Bahraini Shia community, and the IFLB disbanded in 2002. Many of its members were amnestied and agreed to work within the political process, becoming active in the Islamic Action Party.

Political dissent within Bahrain grew during the 1980s and 1990s, abetted by the fact that the citizenry lacked the opportunity to actively participate in the governing of their country. Another threat came from the Bahrain Freedom Movement, formed by Bahraini dissidents. It too sought the establishment of an Iranian-styled Islamic republic and toward that end engaged in bombings and other terrorist acts.

The death of Emir Isa ibn Salman al-Khalifa on March 6, 1999, led to significant changes in Bahrain, for his son and new emir Khalifa bin Hamad al-Thani instituted a series of social and political reforms designed to end the unrest associated with the uprising of the 1990s and meet demands for reform. In 2001 Hamad put forward his National Action Charter, among the provisions of which was the resumption of constitutional rule. A referendum on the charter during February 14–15 saw a reported voter turnout of 90 percent and a favorable vote of 98.41 percent. In 2002 King Hamad agreed to parliamentary elections in which women could vote for the first time and run for office, although none won election. Several parties, including the major religious party, the al-Wifaq National Islamic Society, boycotted the election.

Although the United States had sent warships to the Persian Gulf region during the 1800s, Washington had little interest in Bahrain until 1949, when it began leasing British bases there. The United States has maintained at least a minimal force in Bahrain since. Bahrain allowed U.S. forces to use its territory and facilities for launching military operations against Iraq during both the 1991 Persian Gulf War and the 2003–2011 Iraq War. Bahrain was also a major U.S. base for Operation ENDURING FREEDOM in Afghanistan.

Bahrain was actively involved militarily in the Persian Gulf War. It sent a small contingent of 400 troops to serve in the coalition as part of the Joint Forces Command East. Additionally, the Bahraini Air Force, employing F-16 Fighting

Falcon fighters and F-5 Tiger II fighters, engaged in defensive sorties in the region and launched offensives against Iraqi assets.

Bahrain also provided limited military assistance in Operation ENDURING FREE-DOM in Afghanistan with some naval units. Bahrain provided only a support role in Operation IRAQI FREEDOM (the Iraq War), although it did subsequently furnish assistance to the new Iraqi government to help stabilize that country.

The U.S. Naval Forces Central Command is headquartered in Manama, making it the home of the U.S. Navy's Fifth Fleet. Army and air force units operating in Bahrain include the 831st Transport Battalion, located at Mina Sulman, and the Air Mobility Command, which has a detachment at Muharraq Airfield. Additionally, the Isa Air Base serves as a military airfield for various U.S. military aircraft. U.S. military personnel in Bahrain total some 6,000. Flowing from this close U.S.-Bahrain cooperation, in 2004 Bahrain concluded a free trade agreement with the United States.

Discontent in Bahrain with the pace of reforms surfaced in 2011. Inspired by the events in Egypt that toppled Egyptian president Hosni Mubarak on February 11, late on February 15 demonstrators thronged into Pearl Square, the symbolic heart of Manama. They demanded greater political rights, but the upheaval also revealed the religious divide. The crowds demanded that the monarchy give up some powers and end discrimination against Shiites in key positions in the military and the

Demonstrators chanting and waving Bahraini flags near the Pearl Monument in the main square in Manama, Bahrain, on February 15, 2011. Thousands of protesters demanding greater political freedom sought to emulate the events in Egypt of the 2011 Arab Spring. (AP Photo/ Hasan Jamali)

government. Subsequent modest government concessions only served to embolden the demonstrators.

Although the crowds showed restraint and the government had promised to act with moderation, at 3:00 a.m. on February 17 police suddenly charged the demonstrators with tear gas and buckshot. Four people were killed, some 600 were injured, and a reported 60 were missing in the worst violence in the kingdom in decades. The government then sent in tanks and demanded that the people vacate the streets.

This action inflamed the protestors, who vowed that they would not be intimidated. U.S. officials, stunned by the heavy-handed government action, expressed strong support for the U.S. military alliance with Bahrain but urged its government to act with restraint. On February 19 crowds again occupied the strategic center of the capital.

On February 22 in the largest demonstrations to date, tens of thousands marched in Manama, chanting "No Shia, No Sunni. Only Bahraini." Demonstrations continued, and on February 26 Hassan Mushaima, leader of the banned Haq Movement, an opposition party, returned to Bahrain. Long a leader in calling for fundamental reforms, he urged the demonstrators to continue their protests until they had achieved a "successful revolution."

On March 12, U.S. defense secretary Robert Gates met with King Hamad and informed him that "baby steps" to reform were not sufficient to meet the political and economic unrest. In an ensuing press conference Gates told reporters that Iran was looking for ways to exploit the situation and that "time is not our friend."

On March 14, however, Saudi Arabia, acting on a request from Hamad, sent some 150 vehicles and 1,000 troops into Bahrain via the long causeway with the stated goal of protecting government offices and ending the demonstrations. While expressing concern, the Barack Obama administration refused to condemn the Saudi move, which was regarded as a sign on the part of Saudi leaders that concessions by the Bahrainian monarchy could empower Saudi Arabia's own Shia minority and benefit Iran. The government of the United Arab Emirates also supported the Saudi move and issued a statement promising to honor Bahrain's appeal for assistance.

On March 15 Hamad proclaimed a three-month state of emergency, imposed martial law, and ordered the military to restore order. Soldiers and riot police employed tear gas and armored vehicles to drive hundreds of demonstrators from Pearl Square, resulting in the deaths of several demonstrators and police.

On June 4, 2012, Saudi Arabia and Bahrain held talks designed to strengthen their military and political ties in order to meet what they identified as a threat from Iran. Indeed, the Saudis sought common diplomatic and military approaches by all of the Gulf Cooperation Council states. The talks with Bahrain reportedly discussed the possibility of some sort of union of Bahrain and Saudi Arabia. Such a step, however, would be opposed by many Shias in Bahrain. Suggestions of this had resulted in demonstrations by tens of thousands of Shias in Bahrain on May 18.

Bahrain took part with Saudi Arabia and other Arab states in the campaign against the Islamic State of Iraq and Syria (ISIS). On September 23, 2014, cruise missiles and aircraft from the United States and the allied Arab nations struck ISIS targets in Syria. Bahrain also assisted Saudi Arabia in its military intervention in the

Yemen Civil War that had begun on March 19, 2015. On March 26, Saudi Arabia and its Persian Gulf region allies launched air strikes in Yemen in an effort to counter Iran-allied Houthi rebel forces besieging the southern city of Aden, where U.S.-backed Yemeni president Abd-Rabbu Mansour Hadi had taken refuge. The close ties between Bahrain and Saudi Arabia were again demonstrated on January 4, 2016, when rioters stormed the Saudi embassy in Tehran amid a row over the Saudi execution of prominent Shia Muslim cleric Sheikh Nimr al-Nimr and 46 others condemned for alleged terrorist activities. Bahrain promptly followed Saudi Arabia in breaking diplomatic relations with Iran.

Bahrain, a major world banking center and regarded as financially secure, has one of the fastest-growing economies in the Arab world. Its economy is also recognized as the freest in the Arab world. Petroleum accounts for some 60 percent of exports and constitutes 70 percent of government income. Aluminum is the second most exported product. Tourism is an important source of revenue, with most tourists coming from other Arab states.

With little arable land, Bahrain is highly dependent on food imports. The depletion of its oil assets is another concern. However, unemployment remains low, and the country is considered politically stable.

Bahrain has a small but well-equipped military. Known as the Bahrain Defence Force (BDF), it numbers some 13,000 personnel and is commanded by the emir. Most BDF equipment comes from the United States. This includes F-16 Fighting Falcon and F-5 Freedom Fighter aircraft, UH-60 Blackhawk helicopters, M60A3 tanks, and an Oliver Hazard Perry–class former U.S. Navy frigate, RBNS *Sabha*.

In the past five years since the Arab Spring, Bahrain has made a concerted effort to crack down on and silence any form of dissent. This has included the arrest and imprisonment of prodemocracy advocates and opposition leaders, including those who participated in the Arab Spring. These individuals have also been stripped of their citizenship.

Timeline

1521	Portuguese forces capture Bahrain.
1602	Bahrainis overthrows Portuguese forces, but the same year Iran's Safavid Empire conquers Bahrain, and Iran has since used this period of its rule to make repeated claims on Bahraini territory.
1717	Iranian control of Bahrain is ended.
1783	The al-Khalifa clan, led by Ahmad ibn Mohammed al-Khalifa, conquers Bahrain. This family has led the country ever since. The royal family is Sunni Muslim, however, while the majority of Bahrain's population is Shia Muslim.
1820	Bahrain signs a treaty with the British government pledging not to engage in piracy. Britain recognizes the al-Khalifa family as the

rulers and also agrees to provide military protection for Bahrain. Bahrain agrees not to cede its territory to any country except Britain and not to establish foreign relations with other states without British consent.

1927	Iran continues to assert its right to Bahrain, and Iranian ruler Reza Shah claims sovereignty over the country in a letter to the League of Nations.
1931	Oil is discovered in Bahrain by the Bahrain Petroleum Company, a subsidiary of the Standard Oil Company of California.
1932	Production of petroleum in Bahrain commences, and soon the country is a major exporter.
1935	The British relocate a major naval base from Iran to Bahrain.
Sep 10, 1939	Bahrain allies itself with Britain in World War II, declaring war on Germany.
1949	The United States concludes its first basing agreement with Bahrain.
Aug 15, 1971	Bahrain becomes independent.
Sep 21, 1971	Bahrain joins the United Nations.
1973	A first national assembly is elected but soon clashes with Emir Isa bin Salman al-Khalifa (r. 1961–1999) regarding a security law.
1975	Emir Salam dissolves the assembly and puts the security law into force by decree.
May 25, 1981	The Islamic Republic of Iran attempts to foment a coup d'état by the majority Shia population of Bahrain against their Sunni ruler. Its failure and the ongoing Iran-Iraq War (1980–1988) and Soviet-Afghan War (1979–1989) lead to collective security arrangements that create the Gulf Cooperation Council, led by Saudi Arabia and embracing the Gulf states.
Jan 26, 1982	Bahrain joins Saudi Arabia, Kuwait, Oman, Qatar, and the United Arab Emirates in establishing a joint military command structure and integrated air defense system.
1991	Bahrain provides logistical support and contributes its own forces to assist the coalition in driving Iraqi forces from Kuwait in the Persian Gulf War.
Jun 1994	Economic protests against the Bahraini government occur and expand into a call for political reform.
Feb 10, 1996	The Islamic Front for the Liberation of Bahrain (IFLB), a Shia Islamist militant group formed in 1981, based in Iran, and

supported by its Revolutionary Guards, carries out a number of small terrorist attacks against Bahraini targets, mostly bombings. The IFLB claims responsibility for the bombing of the Diplomat Hotel on this date that wounds four people.

Mar 6, 1999   Emir Isa ibn Salman al-Khalifa dies. His son and successor Khalifa bin Hamad al-Thani institutes a series of social and political reforms designed to end unrest.

Feb 22, 2001   A national referendum overwhelmingly approves the emir's National Action Charter.

2003   Bahrain provides logistical support and some naval assistance in the U.S.-led invasion of Afghanistan but provides only logistical support in the U.S.-led invasion of Iraq. The U.S. Naval Forces Central Command is headquartered in Manama, making it the home of the U.S. Navy's Fifth Fleet, and some 6,000 U.S. military personnel are based in the kingdom.

Feb 15, 2011   Discontent in Bahrain with the pace of reforms surfaces, inspired by the events in Egypt that have toppled Egyptian president Hosni Mubarak. Crowds gather in Pearl Square, Manama, demanding greater political rights and an end to discrimination against Shiites in key positions in the military and the government.

Feb 17, 2011   At 3:00 a.m. this day police charge the demonstrators. Four people are killed, some 600 are injured, and a reported 60 are missing in the worst violence in the kingdom in decades.

Feb 22, 2011   In the largest demonstrations to date, tens of thousands march in Manama.

Mar 14, 2011   Saudi Arabia, acting on a request from Hamad, sends some 150 vehicles and 1,000 troops into Bahrain via the long causeway with the stated goal of protecting government offices and ending the demonstrations.

Mar 15, 2011   Hamad proclaims a three-month state of emergency, imposes martial law, and orders the Bahraini military to restore order. Soldiers and riot police employ armored vehicles to drive hundreds of demonstrators from Pearl Square, resulting in the deaths of several demonstrators and police.

Jun 4, 2012   Saudi Arabia and Bahrain hold talks designed to strengthen their military and political ties in order to meet what they identify as a threat from Iran.

Sep 23, 2014   Bahraini Air Force planes take part in joint U.S.-Arab strikes against the Islamic State of Iraq and Syria (ISIS) targets in Syria.

| Mar 26, 2015 | Bahrain assists Saudi Arabia in its military intervention against Iranian-backed Houthi rebels in the Yemen Civil War that began a week earlier. |
| Jan 4, 2016 | Bahrain again acts in solidarity with Saudi Arabia, breaking diplomatic relations with Iran after rioters storm the Saudi embassy in Tehran amid a row over the Saudi execution of prominent Shia Muslim cleric Sheikh Nimr al-Nimr and 46 others condemned for alleged terrorist activities. |

Further Reading

Al-Baharna, Husain. *Legal Status of the Arabian Gulf States: A Study of Their Treaty Relations and Their International Problems.* Manchester, UK: Manchester University Press, 1968.

Congressional Quarterly. *The Middle East.* 10th ed. Washington, DC: CQ Press, 2005.

Faroughy, Abbas. *The Bahrein Islands (750–1951): A Contribution to the Study of Power Politics in the Persian Gulf.* New York: Verry, Fisher, 1951.

Jerry, Sampson. *History of Persian Gulf States, Kuwait, Bahrain, Oman, Qatar, United Arab Emirat: Government, Politics, Economy.* NP: CreateSpace Independent Publishing Platform, 2016.

Matthiesen, Toby. *Sectarian Gulf: Bahrain, Saudi Arabia, and the Arab Spring That Wasn't.* Stanford, CA: Stanford University Press, 2013.

McCoy, Eric Andrew. "Iranians in Bahrain and the United Arab Emirates: Migration, Minorities, and Identities in the Persian Gulf Arab States." Master's thesis, University of Arizona, 2008.

Mojtahed-Zadeh, Pirouz. *Security and Territoriality in the Persian Gulf: A Maritime Political Geography.* London: RoutledgeCurzon, 1999.

Ochsenwald, William, and Sydney Nettleton Fisher. *The Middle East: A History.* 6th ed. New York: McGraw-Hill, 2004.

Palmer, Michael. *Guardians of the Gulf: A History of America's Expanding Role in the Persian Gulf, 1833–1992.* New York: Free Press, 1992.

Pridham, B. R. *The Arab Gulf and the West.* New York: Taylor and Francis, 1985.

Shehabi, Ala'a. *Bahrain's Uprising.* London: Zed Books, 2015.

Spencer, William J. *The Middle East.* 11th ed. Dubuque, IA: McGraw-Hill/Contemporary Learning Series, 2007.

Winkler, David. *Amirs, Admirals & Desert Sailors: Bahrain, the U.S. Navy, and the Arabian Gulf.* Annapolis, MD: Naval Institute Press, 2007.

CYPRUS

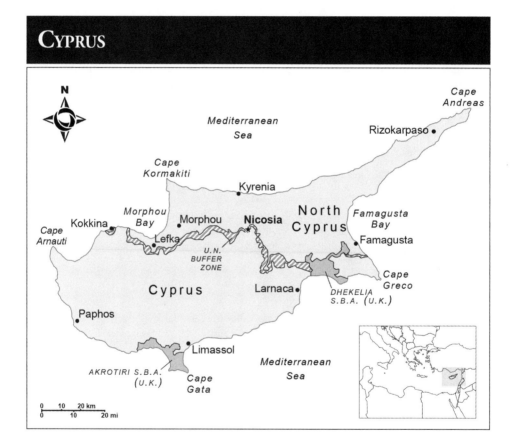

Cyprus

Sedat Cem Karadeli, Lucian N. Leustean, and Spencer C. Tucker

The island of Cyprus, both the third-largest and third most populous Mediterranean island, is situated in the eastern Mediterranean Sea about 40 miles south of Turkey and 60 miles west of Syria. Inhabited by both Greeks and Turks, Cyprus covers a landmass of 3,572 square miles. Its 2016 population was some 1.177 million. Greeks constitute some 77 percent of the total, while Turks are some 18 percent and others make up 5 percent.

Archaeological remains date human activity on Cyprus to around the 10th millennium BCE. A key strategic location in the Middle East, the island was first colonized by Greeks and subsequently conquered by various ancient empires, including those of the Assyrians, Egyptians, and Persians. Alexander the Great of Macedon took Cyprus in 333 BCE. It was subsequently controlled by Ptolemaic Egypt, then the Romans, and for a time Arab caliphates, the French Lusignan dynasty, and the Venetians. Ottoman Turks conquered the island in 1571, and it then became part of the Ottoman Empire. With the passage of time, a large Turkish community developed on Cyprus.

After three centuries of their rule, the Ottomans ceded Cyprus to Britain in 1878 in return for British support against Russia. The British formally annexed the island outright in 1914, and in 1925 it became a crown colony. Until 1960, Cyprus was under British rule. It served as an important strategic base for defense of the Suez Canal in both World War I and World War II. During the Cold War the West used Cyprus to monitor Soviet activities in the Middle East, and Britain launched its 1956 abortive Suez invasion from here.

Greece and Turkey had long been bitter adversaries. Following World War I and the breakup of the Ottoman Empire, the Greeks sought to secure control of Smyrna (modern-day Izmir), the sizable part off western Anatolia that had been home to a large Greek population since ancient times. Although Greece had been late to join the Allied side in World War I and then only under considerable pressure, the Western Allies, particularly the British government of prime minister David Lloyd George, had promised the new Greek government territorial gains at the expense of the Ottoman Empire.

The ensuing Greco-Turkish War (1919–1922) also known as the War of Turkish Independence, began on May 15, 1919, when Greek forces landed in Smyrna. The Greeks soon took control of the western and northwestern parts of Anatolia as well as eastern Thrace. As it turned out, however, the Turkish forces were far better led, organized, and motivated, and they halted the Greek advance in the Battle of the Sakarya (August 23–September 13, 1921). The Turks then took the offensive in August 1922 themselves. For all intents and purposes, the war came to an end with the Turkish liberation of Izmir (September 9, 1922). The conflict officially ended on October 11, 1922.

As a result of the Greek defeat at the hands of the Turks, the Greek government agreed to evacuate all Turkish territory and return to its prewar borders. During the fighting, both sides committed a number of ethnic-based massacres. As a result of the fanning of ethnic animosity during the war, both sides agreed to a major relocation of populations. Some 1.5 million Orthodox Christians, both ethnic Greeks and ethnic Turks, left Turkey, while perhaps 500,000 Turks and Greek Muslims were forced to leave Greece.

The outcome of the war did not affect the status of Cyprus but did add impetus for the Greek demand for enosis, or union of the island with Greece, that developed among the majority Greek population of Cyprus and came to a head following the end of World War II. The sizable minority Turkish population on the island vowed to resist any such step and in this had strong support from the Turkish government. At first Greek agitation was aimed at ending British control. Greek Orthodox archbishop Makarios III became the leader in this effort, condoning terrorism and reprisals against the British.

Greek general Georgios Grivas led the actual terrorist campaign to expel the British. Born in Cyprus, Grivas had fought in the defense of Greece following the 1940 Italian invasion, and during the subsequent German invasion and occupation he established his own guerrilla group (designated "X"). After the end of the Axis occupation in 1944 the group was disbanded, and Grivas rejoined the regular army, seeing duty during the civil war against the communists from 1946 to 1949. Following the Greek army victory over the communists, Grivas had several meetings with Makarios to advance the cause of enosis. In November 1954 Grivas returned to Cyprus and fomented a violent campaign against the British occupation of the island. Taking the name Dighenis, a legendary Byzantine hero, he organized the National Organization of Cypriot Fighters (EOKA) with direct military support from Greece. The EOKA's terrorist campaign commenced on April 1, 1955, and reached its climax in 1956 when British authorities exiled Makarios to the Seychelles Islands in the Indian Ocean. Negotiations in 1955 between Britain, Greece, and Turkey broke down completely, abetted by the Turkish government's demands that Cyprus be partitioned. A total of 504 people died during the EOKA campaign, including 142 Britons and 84 Turks. At the same time, Turks on the island called for partition and toward that end formed the Turkish Resistance Organization (TMT). The British encouraged the TMT in a divide-and-rule effort.

The British government eventually concluded, albeit reluctantly, that Cyprus should become independent, and Prime Minister Harold MacMillan called for negotiations on the matter. On February 11, 1959, Greece and Turkey reached agreement at Zurich on a plan for the independence of Cyprus. On February 19 following a conference at Lancaster House in London, the British government reached final agreement regarding independence in talks with the governments of Greece and Turkey as well as Archbishop Makarios, recalled from exile, for the Greek Cypriot community and Dr. Fazil Küçük, representing the Turkish Cypriots.

Following the Zurich and London agreements, Grivas ordered a cease-fire on March 13. A constitution for Cyprus was drafted and agreed to, and the Republic of Cyprus became independent on August 16, 1960, as a member of the British Commonwealth of Nations. The British retained two military bases on Cyprus but had no executive authority. Greek and Turkish troops on Cyprus were reduced to token forces of only a few hundred men. Britain, Greece, and Turkey all retained limited rights to intervene in Cypriot affairs in order to guarantee the basic rights of both ethnic communities there.

The constitution for the new state contained a power-sharing arrangement. It provided for a Greek Cypriot president elected for a five-year term by the ethnic Greeks, a Turkish Cypriot vice president elected for a similar term by the Turks on the island, and a parliament to reflect the island's 80-20 ethnic split, with each community electing its own representatives. The Council of Ministers consisted of 10 members, 3 of whom had to be Turks. The House of Representatives could not modify the constitution in any respect in regard to its basic articles, and any other modification required a two-thirds majority of both the Greek Cypriot and Turkish Cypriot members. To protect the Turkish minority, the vice president was vested with veto power over any legislation vitally affecting interests of the Turkish population.

Elected the first president of the Republic of Cyprus, Makarios took office on August 16, 1960. On September 20, the island state became a member of the United Nations (UN). Independence only meant the beginning of a new phase of violence on the troubled island, however. In 1962 and 1963, Greek and Turkish leaders held a series of meetings but were unable to resolve their differences in matters of taxation, municipal councils, and local government. In 1963, the Green Line was established in the capital city of Nicosia to separate the two ethnic communities.

In November 1963, Makarios proposed a series of constitutional amendments designed to restrict the rights of the Turkish community. Understandably, Turkish Cypriots opposed these changes, and consequently widespread intercommunal fighting began on December 21, 1963. This ushered in the most violent phase of the Cypriot conflict, with hundreds of casualties on each side. Turkish participation in the central Cypriot government also came to an end. Makarios rejected mediation efforts by Britain and the United States, and on March 4, 1964, the UN Security Council authorized Secretary-General U Thant to establish a peace force and appoint a mediator. Despite the presence of this UN force, Greeks attacked Turkish villages. In response, during August 7–9, 1964, the Turkish Air Force strafed Greek Cypriot positions. With the situation spiraling out of control and Greece and Turkey on the brink of war, the UN was able to secure a cease-fire on August 9.

Although the Turkish parliament voted in 1964 in favor of occupying Cyprus, Turkey was unable to secure support for this from either the UN or the North Atlantic Treaty Organization (NATO). Indeed, U.S. president Lyndon B. Johnson warned Turkish premier Ismet Inönü that his country would resist any Turkish occupation. Turkey did not make good on its threat.

In March 1964 the UN Security Council established the United Nations Peacekeeping Force in Cyprus (UNFICYP) to ward off potential trouble, although fighting continued between the Greeks and Turks. The Turks then formed their own Turkish Cypriot provisional administration. Unhappy over the situation of its countrymen in Cyprus, in August 1966 the Turkish government again threatened military intervention. Following an appeal by U Thant, Makarios relaxed restrictions imposed on the Turkish minority. Another round of intercommunal violence began in November 1967, however, when Makarios attempted to eliminate the veto power vested in the Turkish vice president. War between Greece and Turkey was only narrowly averted by pressure from the United States on both countries.

The Greek Army had seized power in Greece in April 1967. With strong U.S. public opposition to providing military assistance to the Greek junta, the Greek generals authorized Grivas to return to Cyprus in 1971 and resume terrorist activities there. The implication was clear: if the United States refused aid to the junta, there would be no peace on Cyprus, and there would also be new problems for NATO. Washington found itself caught in a dilemma. The junta was a dictatorship, but Greece was of considerable importance to NATO and to the security of the eastern Mediterranean.

Makarios meanwhile shifted from supporting enosis to becoming a Cypriot nationalist. Winning reelection to the presidency in February 1974, he was increasingly reconciled to a Makarios republic. Grivas, who now opposed the Greek junta in Athens and had taken up arms against his former ally, died of heart failure at Limassol, Cyprus, on January 27, 1974. His supporters continued the struggle against Makarios, however.

On July 15, 1974, the Greek Cypriot National Guard seized power. The ruling Greek junta in Athens had fully supported this step to secure enosis and thereby shore up its rapidly diminishing popularity in Greece. The coup ousted Makarios, who fled the island. The new president was proenosis nationalist Nikos Sampson, a former EOKA fighter. Meanwhile, Rauf Denktaş, the Turkish Cypriot leader, called for joint military action by the United Kingdom and Turkey in order to prevent the unification of Cyprus with Greece. Britain could not be persuaded to agree, and Turkey decided to act alone.

On July 20, Turkey carried out its long-standing threat to intervene in the island. Turkey claimed that this action was completely justified under terms of the agreements establishing an independent Cyprus that gave it the right to protect its compatriots there. This justification, however, has been rejected by both the UN and the international community.

The Turkish Air Force bombed Greek positions in Cyprus, and Turkish paratroopers were dropped into the area between Nicosia and Kyrenia, the site of a number of long-established armed Turkish Cypriot enclaves. Turkish troop ships then landed some 6,000 men as well as tanks and other vehicles. The Turkish forces easily defeated the Greek Cypriot National Guard. By July 23, when a ceasefire had been agreed to, there were 30,000 Turkish troops on the island, and Turkish forces had captured Kyrenia, the corridor linking Kyrenia to Nicosia, and the Turkish Cypriot quarter of Nicosia. The Turkish military intervention also brought the collapse of the proenosis Greek Sampson regime.

A Turkish army tank in the Turkish section of Nicosia, Cyprus, on July 24, 1974. The large sign on the roof of a nearby building has a picture of Kemal Ataturk, founder of the modern Turkish republic. The Turkish invasion of Cyprus was sparked by an abortive coup on the island by supporters of a union with Greece. (AP Photo)

The Greek junta in Athens seriously miscalculated both internationally and with the situation in Greece itself when it encouraged the Greeks of Cyprus to seize power there. Junta leaders had believed that this event would rally the mainland Greek population behind their rule. Much to the surprise of the generals, there was little enthusiasm in Greece for war with Turkey. Indeed, widespread discontent regarding the previous seven years of ham-fisted junta rule now came to the fore. The junta leadership—shaken and unsure of itself—disavowed the Greeks in Cyprus, a step that further discredited the generals, who were driven from power on July 24, 1974.

In Cyprus, meanwhile, Glafcos Clerides assumed the presidency of the Republic of Cyprus government in Nicosia, and constitutional order was restored. This removed the pretext for the Turkish invasion, but following negotiations between the sides in Geneva, the Turkish government reinforced its Kyrenia bridgehead and began a second invasion on August 14, quickly seizing Morphou, Karpass, Famagusta, and the Mesaoria. Although international pressure brought a cease-fire, by then the Turks had seized control of some 37 percent of the island and had evicted some 180,000 Greeks from their homes in the northern part of the island. Some 50,000 Turkish Cypriots moved to the areas under the control of the Turkish forces and took over the properties of the displaced Greek Cypriots. The Turkish government subsequently brought in some 20,000 Turks, mainly subsistence farmers from mainland Turkey, to settle and work the underpopulated land. Those who stayed more than five years were granted citizenship in the Turkish Federated State. In the Karpaz region, located on the Turkish side of Cyprus, a Greek-speaking minority remains under UN supervision.

The fighting itself had claimed some 568 Turkish military personnel killed in action; 270 Turkish civilians were killed, and 803 were missing. Greek deaths totaled some 1,378 killed and as many as 1,100 missing. Many others on both sides were wounded. The UNFICYP lost 9 killed and 65 wounded.

The U.S. government voiced its displeasure regarding the Turkish action, which had employed U.S.-supplied military equipment. In mid-1975 Congress imposed a number of sanctions against Turkey, including an arms embargo. This step badly strained Turkish-U.S. relations. The embargo lasted until 1978, when it was lifted by President Jimmy Carter.

Since that time the situation in Cyprus has remained frozen, with the island divided along a line that runs through the center of the city of Nicosia. Ankara retained some 25,000 troops on the island. With the stalemate continuing, on November 15, 1983, Rauf Denktaş, president of the Turkish Cypriot Federal State, unilaterally proclaimed the Turkish portion of the island to be independent as the Turkish Republic of Northern Cyprus. However, it was only recognized as a legitimate independent state by Turkey and members of the Organization of the Islamic Conference. The UN has refused to recognize this political entity. Southern Cyprus is governed by the Republic of Cyprus, which the international community recognizes as having jurisdiction over the entire island and its territorial waters. Negotiations occurred, with the Turkish side prepared to cede some territory taken by Turkish forces in Cyprus in return for recognition of the self-proclaimed Turkish state. But the negotiations soon broke down, with the Greek Cypriots and the government in Athens firmly rejecting partition. An uneasy peace prevails, with the two sides kept apart by some 2,000 UN peacekeeping troops in a buffer zone. Britain retains its military bases in southern Cyprus as sovereign British territory.

On February 19, 1978, terrorists claiming to be members of the Palestine Liberation Organization killed an Egyptian newspaper editor and took 30 people hostage in Cyprus. Egyptian president Anwar Sadat authorized a commando raid to take out those responsible. The Egyptian commandos killed the terrorists but then ran afoul of the Cypriot National Guard, who killed 15 of the Egyptians and captured others. Egypt responded by breaking off diplomatic relations with Cyprus.

In the period since the Turkish invasion, the northern third of Cyprus has become almost exclusively Turkish, while the southern two-thirds is almost exclusively Greek. Thus, the territories are now sometimes referred to as the "Greek part" and the "Turkish part" of Cyprus. Except for occasional demonstrations and infrequent confrontations between border soldiers, few violent conflicts have occurred since 1974. Turkey continued to maintain a significant troop presence in northern Cyprus, although their numbers have been somewhat reduced.

In November 1993 following the election of Cypriot president Glafcos Clerides, Greek Cypriots formed a joint defense pact with Greece. The Turkish Cypriots responded by entering into a joint defense and foreign policy program with Turkey. On January 1, 2004, the Republic of Cyprus was admitted to the European Union.

Having retained its two bases as sovereign British territory, on December 3, 2015, Royal Air Force Tornado aircraft carried out their first air strikes in Syria against the Islamic State of Iraq and Syria (ISIS). Taking off from Akrotiri Air Base, the jets struck an oil field in eastern Syria. The raid occurred only hours after British lawmakers had voted in favor of bombing ISIS strongholds there.

Today the Republic of Cyprus is recognized by the international community as having de jure sovereignty over the island of Cyprus and its surrounding waters except for the British overseas territories of Akrotiri and Dhekelia, which the British administer as sovereign base areas. However, the Republic of Cyprus remains de facto partitioned into two main parts: the area under the effective control of the Republic of Cyprus, comprising some 63 percent of the island's area, and the north, administered by the self-declared Turkish Republic of Northern Cyprus, which covers about 37 percent of the island's area and is recognized by the international community as territory of the Republic of Cyprus occupied by Turkish forces.

Despite these circumstances, Cyprus remains a major tourist destination. It also boasts a high-income economy and a very high Human Development Index. On January 1, 2008, the Republic of Cyprus joined the eurozone.

Timeline

1571   Cyprus becomes part of the Ottoman Empire.

1878   The Ottoman Empire cedes Cyprus to Great Britain. The island serves as an important strategic base during both World War I and World War II.

1919–1922   The Greco-Turkish War.

1925   Cyprus becomes a British crown colony.

Nov 1954   The movement for enosis (the union of Cyprus with Greece) has spread among the majority Greek population. The island's Turkish population, supported by the Turkish government, is determined to prevent this from occurring. Greek Orthodox archbishop Makarios III becomes the leader in the enosis effort, condoning terrorism and reprisals against the British. Cyprus-born Greek general Georgios Grivas returns to the island and organizes the National Organization of Cypriot Fighters (EOKA) with direct military support from Greece.

Apr 1, 1955 The EOKA's terrorist campaign begins. Negotiations among Britain, Greece, and Turkey break down on the Turkish demand for partition of Cyprus. Cypriot Turks form the Turkish Resistance Organization, which the British encourage in an effort to divide and rule.

1956   British authorities exile Makarios to the Seychelles Islands in the Indian Ocean.

Feb 11, 1959   The British government having concluded that Cyprus must become independent, Prime Minister Harold MacMillan calls for negotiations. On this date, Greece and Turkey reach agreement at Zurich on a plan for the independence of Cyprus.

Feb 19, 1959   Following a conference at Lancaster House in London, the British government reaches final agreement with the governments of Greece and Turkey, with Archbishop Makarios, recalled from exile, representing the Greek Cypriot community and Dr. Fazil Küçük representing the Turkish Cypriots on a framework for independence.

Mar 13, 1959   Grivas orders a cease-fire.

Aug 16, 1960   The Republic of Cyprus becomes independent and a member of the British Commonwealth. The British retain as sovereign territory two military bases on Cyprus. Britain, Greece, and Turkey all retain limited rights to intervene in Cypriot affairs in order to guarantee the basic rights of both ethnic communities. The constitution for the new state contains a power-sharing arrangement designed to protect the Turkish minority. On this date also Makarios takes office as the first president of Cyprus.

Sep 20, 1960   The Republic of Cyprus becomes a member of the United Nations (UN).

1962–1963   Tensions in Cyprus increase dramatically following the failure of efforts to resolve differences between the two communities regarding taxation, municipal councils, and local government.

1963   The so-called Green Line is established in the capital of Nicosia to separate Greeks and Turks.

Nov 1963   Makarios proposes a series of constitutional amendments designed to restrict the rights of the Turkish community. Turkish Cypriots oppose this.

Dec 21, 1963   Widespread intercommunal fighting begins in Cyprus, resulting in hundreds of casualties on each side and the end of Turkish participation in the central Cypriot government.

Mar 4, 1964   With Makarios having rejected mediation by Britain and the United States, the UN Security Council authorizes Secretary-General U Thant to establish a peace force (UNFICYP) and appoint a mediator in Cyprus.

Aug 7–9, 1964   With Greeks continuing to attack Turkish villages, Turkey sends aircraft to strafe Greek Cypriot positions.

Aug 9, 1964   With war between Greece and Turkey looming, the UN secures a cease-fire.

Aug 1966	Displeased with the situation of its countrymen in Cyprus, the Turkish government again threatens military intervention. Following an appeal by U Thant, Makarios relaxes restrictions imposed on the Turkish minority.
Nov 1967	A fresh round of intercommunal violence begins in Cyprus when Makarios attempts to eliminate the veto power vested in the Turkish vice president. War between Greece and Turkey is only narrowly averted by U.S. pressure on both countries.
1971	Grivas returns to Cyprus and resumes terrorist activities there but in opposition to Makarios, who has abandoned the plan of union with Greece in favor of a Makarios republic.
Jan 27, 1974	Grivas dies of heart failure at Limassol, Cyprus.
Feb 1974	Makarios wins reelection as president.
Jul 15, 1974	The Greek Cypriot National Guard seizes power in Cyprus, encouraged and supported by the ruling Greek junta in Athens, which sees enosis as a way of shoring up its rapidly diminishing popularity. Makarios flees Cyprus, replaced with proenosis Nikos Sampson. Turkish Cypriot leader Rauf Denktaş calls for joint military action by the United Kingdom and Turkey in order to prevent the unification of Cyprus with Greece. Britain rejects this, and Turkey decides to act alone.
Jul 20, 1974	Turkish forces invade Cyprus and easily defeat the Cypriot National Guard. Ankara cites as justification for its actions the agreements establishing an independent Cyprus that gave it the right to protect its compatriots, although the UN and the international community reject this reasoning.
Jul 23, 1974	A cease-fire is agreed to on Cyprus.
Jul 24, 1974	The Greek junta in Athens, shaken by the Turkish invasion and having itself failed to act, is now totally discredited and driven from power.
Aug 14, 1974	Although Glafcos Clerides has assumed the presidency of the Republic of Cyprus government in Nicosia and constitutional order has been restored, thereby removing the pretext for the Turkish invasion, the Turkish military launches a second invasion, ultimately seizing control of some 37 percent of the island and evicting 180,000 Greeks from their homes in northern Cyprus.
Mid-1975	The U.S. Congress imposes a number of sanctions on Turkey, including an arms embargo.
1978	U.S. president Jimmy Carter lifts the arms embargo against Turkey.

Feb 19, 1978   Members of the Palestine Liberation Organization kill an Egyptian newspaper editor and take 30 people hostage in Cyprus. Egyptian president Anwar Sadat authorizes a commando raid. The Egyptian commandos kill the terrorists, and the Cypriot National Guard kills 15 of the Egyptians and captures others. Egypt then breaks off diplomatic relations.

Nov 15, 1983   With the Cyprus stalemate continuing, Rauf Denktaş, president of the Turkish Cypriot Federal State, unilaterally proclaims the Turkish portion of the island to be independent as the Turkish Republic of Northern Cyprus. It is recognized only by Turkey and members of the Organization of the Islamic Conference. Southern Cyprus is governed by the Republic of Cyprus, which the international community recognizes as having jurisdiction over the entire island and its territorial waters. An uneasy peace prevails, with the two sides kept apart by some 2,000 UN peacekeeping troops in a buffer zone. Britain retains its military bases in southern Cyprus as sovereign British territory.

Nov 1993   Following the election of Glafcos Clerides as president of the Republic of Cyprus, the Greek Cypriots form a joint defense pact with Greece. Turkish Cypriots respond by entering into a joint defense and foreign policy program with Turkey.

Jan 1, 2004   The Republic of Cyprus is admitted to the European Union.

Jan 1, 2008   The Republic of Cyprus joins the eurozone. According to international law, the Republic of Cyprus has de jure sovereignty over the island of Cyprus and its surrounding waters except for the British overseas territories of Akrotiri and Dhekelia, administered as sovereign base areas. However, the Republic of Cyprus is de facto partitioned, with the self-declared Turkish Republic of Northern Cyprus administering the northern part of the island.

Further Reading

Anastasiou, Harry. *Broken Olive Branch: Nationalism, Ethnic Conflict, and the Quest for Peace in Cyprus.* Syracuse, NY: Syracuse University Press, 2008.

Asmussen, Jan. *Cyprus at War: Diplomacy and Conflict during the 1974 Crisis.* New York: I. B. Tauris, 2008.

Brewin, Christopher. *European Union and Cyprus.* Tallahassee, FL: Eothen, 2000.

Durrell, Lawrence. *Bitter Lemons.* New York: Dutton, 1957.

Faustmann, Hubert, and Nicos Peristianis. *Britain and Cyprus: Colonialism and Post-Colonialism, 1878–2006.* Mannheim, Germany: Bibliopolis, 2006.

Hannay, David. *Cyprus: The Search for a Solution.* New York: I. B. Tauris, 2005.

Hitchens, Christopher. *Hostage to History: Cyprus from the Ottomans to Kissinger.* New York: Verso, 1997.

Holland, R. F. *Britain and the Revolt in Cyprus, 1954–1959.* New York: Oxford University Press, 1998.

Joseph, Joseph S. *Cyprus: Ethnic Conflict and International Politics: From Independence to the Threshold of the European Union.* New York: St. Martin's, 1997.

Ker-Lindsay, James. *EU Accession and UN Peacemaking in Cyprus.* New York: Palgrave Macmillan, 2005.

Ker-Lindsay, James, and Hubert Faustmann. *The Government and Politics of Cyprus.* New York: Peter Lang, 2009.

Mallinson, William. *Cyprus: A Modern History.* New York: I. B. Tauris, 2005.

Mirbagheri, Farid. *Cyprus and International Peacemaking.* London: Hurst, 1989.

Nicolet, Claude. *United States Policy towards Cyprus, 1954–1974: Removing the Greek-Turkish Bone of Contention.* Mannheim, Germany: Bibliopolis, 2001.

Richmond, Oliver. *Mediating in Cyprus: The Cypriot Communities and the United Nations.* Portland, OR: Frank Cass, 1998.

Richmond, Oliver, and James Ker-Lindsay, eds. *The Work of the UN in Cyprus: Promoting Peace and Development.* New York: Palgrave Macmillan, 2001.

Richter, Heinz. *A Concise History of Modern Cyprus, 1878–2009.* Mainz: Rutzen, 2010.

Yiorghos, Leventis. *Cyprus: The Struggle for Self-Determination in the 1940s.* New York: Peter Lang, 2002.

EGYPT

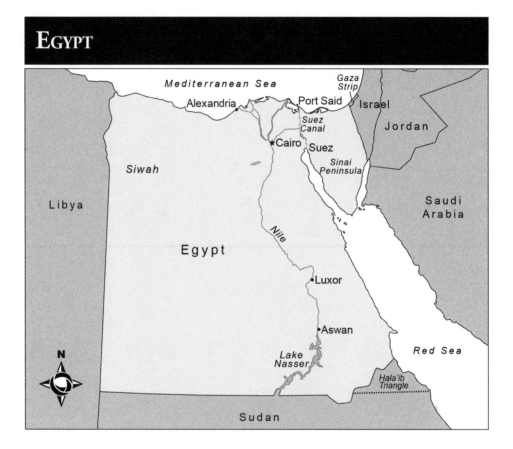

Mediterranean Sea

Gaza Strip

Alexandria

Port Said

Israel

Jordan

Suez Canal

★Cairo

•Suez

Siwah

Sinai Peninsula

Libya

Saudi Arabia

Egypt

Nile

•Luxor

•Aswan

Red Sea

Lake Nasser

Hala'ib Triangle

N

Sudan

Egypt

James B. McNabb, Spencer C. Tucker, Sherifa Zuhur

Egypt is a North African and Middle Eastern nation encompassing 387,048 square miles of territory and thus is the third-largest African nation. Officially the Arab Republic of Egypt, the country is bounded by the Mediterranean Sea to the north, Libya to the west, Sudan to the south, and the Red Sea, the Gulf of Aqaba, and Israel to the east and northeast.

Egypt's 2016 population of some 93.384 million gives the country the largest population in the Arab world and ranks it 15th in the world. Cairo is its capital city. Ethnic Egyptians constitute some 91 percent of the population. Minorities include Abazas, Greeks, Turks, Greeks, Bedouin Arab tribes in the eastern deserts and the Sinai Peninsula, and Nubian communities along the Nile.

President Anwar Sadat made Islam the official state religion. Muslims constitute some 90 percent of the population, the vast majority of them Sunnis. Perhaps 15 million Egyptians follow native Sufi orders, while Shia Muslims could number as many as 3 million, and Salafis (ultraconservatives) are perhaps 5–6 million. Although before the Arab conquest Christians were a majority of the Egyptian population, today they make up only about 10 percent (9 percent are Coptic Christians, and 1 percent are other Christian denominations).

The Egyptian civilization is one of the world's oldest. Egypt is considered a cradle of civilization, and Egyptians call their country the "mother of the world." Egypt's ancient civilization was closely tied to the Nile River, which runs from south to north through the country and empties into the Mediterranean Sea. Ancient Egypt presents some of the world's earliest forms of writing, agriculture, organized religion, and central government. Ancient Egyptian monuments, including the pyramids, are some of the world's greatest archaeological treasures, and tourism is a major source of revenue for the country.

The Achaemenid Persians conquered Egypt in the sixth century BCE. Following a series of native revolts, the Persians again took control of Egypt in the fourth century BCE. Alexander I (Alexander the Great) of Macedon conquered Egypt in 323 BCE. Following his death and rule by the Ptolemies, Egypt was a tributary province of the Roman Empire. Arab armies conquered the country in the seventh century CE. Various Muslim nonindigenous dynasties including the Mamluks then ruled Egypt. In 1517 the Ottoman Turks took control of Egypt.

In 1798 French forces under Napoleon Bonaparte invaded the country. Upon the French departure, Muhammad Ali Pasha, an Ottoman military envoy, held control during May 1805–March 1848. He developed a disciplined army and was the self-proclaimed khedive of Egypt, recognized by the Ottomans in return for his having suppressing rebellions in other Ottoman territories, the Arabian Peninsula, and Syria. Ali's descendants ruled Egypt and modernized Cairo, while Egypt remained nominally an Ottoman province. In 1867, Egypt secured the status of an autonomous vassal (khedivial) state of the Ottoman Empire; this continued until 1914.

In 1869, a French company headed by Ferdinand de Lesseps completed construction of the Suez Canal, which became immediately important to the British as a considerably shorter passage to India. The canal construction led to enormous debt to European banks and caused popular discontent in Egypt because of the onerous taxation required. Khedive Ismail's profligate spending exacerbated the situation, and he was forced to sell Egypt's share in the canal to the British government. Within three years this brought British and French controllers, who in effect became the real power in Egypt. Ismail and his successor Tewfik Pasha governed Egypt as a quasi-independent state under Ottoman suzerainty until the British occupation of 1882.

Egyptian popular dissatisfaction with foreign control brought formation of nationalist groups in 1879, and in February 1881 Ahmet Arabi (Urabi) led a revolt, proclaiming "Egypt for the Egyptians." Arabi becomes minister of war and the key figure in the government. Their position in Egypt threatened, the British and French governments planned a joint military intervention in Egypt, but a change of government in France led to a belated decision in Paris not to participate. London then proceeded alone.

On June 11, 1882, antiforeign riots in Alexandria brought the deaths of 68 Europeans and provided the British with the excuse for action. When Arabi rejected British demands to disarm Alexandria's defenses, British warships shelled the city on July 11 and inflicted considerable damage on the largely antiquated Egyptian shore defenses, while fires, some set by Egyptians, burned much of the city. British marines and seamen sent ashore drove Egyptian troops from the city.

Following the landing of a British expeditionary force, in the Battle of Tel el-Kebir of September 13, British troops under Lieutenant General Garnet Wolseley defeated Arabi's forces in strong defensive positions between Cairo and the Suez Canal. Arabi lost some 2,000 men killed and 500 wounded, while British losses were 58 killed, 379 wounded, and 22 missing.

British cavalry entered Cairo on September 15, almost without opposition. Arabi surrendered, and the revolt quickly collapsed. The British then reinstalled Ismail's son Tewfik as figurehead of a de facto British protectorate. Although British prime minister William Gladstone's government formally notified other powers that the British Army would be withdrawn "as soon as the state of the country, and the organization of the proper means for the maintenance of the Khedive's authority, will admit of it," British troops remained in Egypt. The real ruler of the country for the next 23 years was British consul general and high commissioner Lord Cromer.

When war erupted between the Allied and Central Powers in August 1914, Egypt was still technically an Ottoman tributary, with khedive Abbas Hilmi II subject to the authority of sultan Mehmed V. On October 31, 1914, the Ottoman Empire officially entered the war on the side of the Central Powers, and Abbas Hilmi II declared his support for the Ottoman Muslim caliphate. The British then made the protectorate official, and the title of head of state was changed from khedive to sultan, effectively ending Ottoman control. The British replaced Abbas II with his uncle, Hussein Kamel.

During World War I, Alexandria was the chief support base for the unsuccessful Allied 1915 Gallipoli Campaign. Egypt was threatened by Ottoman forces operating in Sinai, Gaza, and Palestine and from the Libyan desert to the west where the Germans succeeded in persuading the Senussis, the warlike Bedouin tribesmen of Cyrenaica, to rise up against Britain. In the winter of 1915–1916 the Senussis, with German and Ottoman money and arms, invaded Egypt. They then surrounded the garrison at Sollum and forced it to surrender. The British assembled the special Western Desert Force, and operations in early 1916 ended in major defeat for the Senussis and the retaking of Sollum. However, continued raids and incursions from the Libyan desert through the summer of 1916 forced the British to maintain significant forces on the Egyptian western frontier.

In the east, two large Ottoman operations against the Suez Canal were mounted and defeated on February 3, 1915, and August 3, 1916. The British then went over to offensive operations in Palestine. After several rebuffs at Gaza, new British commander Lieutenant General Sir Edmund Allenby prevailed against Gaza in October, and by December 11, 1917, his forces had taken Jerusalem.

Although rising Egyptian nationalism led the British to cede nominal independence to Egypt in 1922 (making Hussein Kamel king), in effect the British retained considerable control over the Egyptian government and also maintained substantial military bases there. During World War II, Egypt was again an important Allied base. Its importance can be seen in that during the 1940 Battle of Britain, Prime Minister Winston Churchill diverted desperately needed military assets there.

Axis and British forces clashed following an Italian invasion of Egypt in 1940, and the ensuing campaigns and battles in Libya and Egypt were some of the most critical of the entire war, especially the First Battle of El Alamein (July 1–27, 1942), in which the British halted the Axis advance on Alexandria and then Cairo and the Suez Canal, and Second Battle of El Alamein (October 23–November 11, 1942), which saw British forces break through the Axis defenses and begin pushing the Germans and Italians back on Tripoli, where the Allies were victorious in May 1943.

The expanded presence of Western troops in Egypt during the war, however, fueled the fires of Egyptian nationalism and especially angered the Muslim Brotherhood, an antisecularist party that sought to dominate the country.

On July 23, 1952, a group of Egyptian Army officers known as the Free Officers overthrew King Farouk and seized power. They called this event a "revolution" because it dislodged from power the former regime and the upper class and also because they claimed legitimacy in the name of common Egyptians in place of the elite. Military and security considerations dominated political life thereafter, and

Egyptian Army officers who led the July 23, 1952, coup d'état that deposed King Farouk. Anwar Sadat, Gamal Abdel Nasser, and Muhammad Najib are seated 5th to 7th from the left. (AP Photo)

the armed forces grew considerably. In fact, since that date all four Egyptian presidents have been military officers.

The Free Officers chose as their leader Muhammad Najib, but he was outmaneuvered by another officer, Gamal Abdel Nasser, who became president of Egypt on June 23, 1956. Nasser preached a populist and anti-imperialist philosophy that called for Arab unity and became known as Nasserism. Starting in 1961, he also promoted certain policies of Arab socialism.

Soon after becoming president, Nasser suppressed Egyptian Marxists, the labor movement, and the Muslim Brotherhood. In 1955 he signed an agreement with Czechoslovakia to purchase Soviet arms. This, his 1955 refusal to sign the pro-Western Baghdad Pact, and his association with the Non-Aligned Movement ran counter to British aims and also concerned policy makers, who did not differentiate local nationalisms from communism, which they hoped to contain in the region.

Angered with Nasser's policies, especially his courting of the Soviet Union, the United States rescinded its pledge to help fund Nasser's ambitious plan to build a high dam on the upper Nile at Aswan. To secure the needed funds, Nasser then nationalized the Suez Canal. This step greatly angered British leaders. The French government was already upset over Nasser's support for insurgent forces in Algeria who were fighting for independence from France, and the Israelis were angered over Nasser's decision to blockade the Gulf of Aqaba (Israel's access to the Indian

Ocean) and Egyptian sponsorship of Palestinian fedayeen raids into the Jewish state. The British, French, and Israeli leaders then secretly colluded to precipitate what became known as the 1956 Suez Crisis.

On July 29, Israeli forces invaded the Sinai. When Egypt refused to allow the British to intervene to "protect" the Suez Canal, Britain and France attacked Egypt and landed troops. The Soviet Union openly supported Egypt, but the key factor was strong financial pressure by U.S. president Dwight D. Eisenhower on Britain. He demanded that the British, French, and Israelis withdraw, which they did. Although Israel benefited from the crisis, Britain and France did not. And far from overthrowing Nasser, the three nations in effect made him a hero in the Arab world. Nasser now expelled many foreigners and minorities from Egypt and seized their property.

Nasser's government turned increasingly to the Soviet bloc, receiving both technical advisers and weaponry. Some 17,000 Soviet advisers eventually arrived in Egypt, and Egyptians were sent to the Soviet Union to receive advanced military training.

In 1958 Syrian officers and politicians prevailed on Nasser to join their two countries in what was known as the United Arab Republic. Seen as a first step toward a larger Pan-Arab state and established on February 1, 1958, it was, however, completely dominated by Egypt. Displeasure in Syria with this brought an army coup in Syria on September 28, 1961. The new Syrian leaders declared Syria's independence. Although the coup leaders expressed their willingness to renegotiate a union under terms that would have placed Syria on a more equal basis with Egypt, Nasser refused. Indeed, he considered military action against Syria, only rejecting this option when he learned that his allies there had all been removed.

In 1961, the Egyptian government also pursued more aggressive Arab socialist policies in the form of land reform, government seizure of private holdings, and further nationalizations. After 1962 the Arab Socialist Union, a single political party, dominated Egypt's bureaucratic and governmental structures. The party became even more important for a time after 1965.

The Egyptian military expanded throughout the Cold War and was equipped primarily by the Soviets. Egypt's chief military challenge was Israel's better-funded and far better-trained armed forces. A struggle developed between more progressive Arab states such as Egypt and Western-aligned monarchies such as Saudi Arabia; some scholars termed this the Arab Cold War. It undoubtedly led Nasser to pursue secondary aims by supporting the Yemeni republicans against the Saudi proxies of the Yemeni royalists in 1962. During the Yemen Civil War (1962–1970), the Egyptian forces there, which grew to some 55,000 men in late 1965, were not highly successful. They were also bogged down there and thus not available to Egypt during the short 1967 Six-Day War with Israel.

By 1967 with Israel's chief supporter, the United States, mired in the Vietnam War, Soviet leaders saw an opportunity to alter the balance of power in the Middle East that would favor their client states of Egypt and Syria. On May 13, the Soviets provided Egypt with false information that Israel was mobilizing troops on the Syrian border. In consequence, on May 16 Nasser declared a state of emergency, and the next day the Egyptian and Syrian governments proclaimed a state of combat readiness. Jordan also mobilized.

Nasser's belligerency caused his popularity to soar in the Arab world with profound impact. On May 16, Nasser demanded that the United Nations Emergency Force (UNEF) in the Sinai depart immediately. Since 1956 it had served as a buffer between the Egyptian and Israeli forces. The UNEF complied on May 19. The day before, Syria and Egypt placed their armed forces on maximum alert while Iraq and Kuwait mobilized.

Nasser then announced Egypt's intention to close the Strait of Tiran to Israeli shipping. The strait was the principal avenue for Israel's trade with Asia and the transit point for 90 percent of its oil imports. Israel's economy would be adversely impacted immediately, and Israel had already let it be known that it would consider such a step a cause for war. Nasser knew that Israel would probably react militarily, but he assumed that the United States would not support this and that Egypt and its allies could count on the Soviet Union. The Kremlin, however, reacted negatively. Having stirred the pot, it now urged restraint. Following a hotline call from U.S. president Lyndon Johnson, Moscow insisted on May 27 that the Egyptians not strike first.

Nasser's announcement regarding the Strait of Tiran was in fact largely a bluff. He assumed that the threat of closing the Strait of Tiran would force Israel to withdraw its supposed increased forces along the Syrian border. On May 22, however, Egyptian minister of defense Field Marshal Abdel Hakim Amer ordered Egyptian forces to close the strait the next day. A countermanding order would have signaled weakness, and Nasser now ordered the Egyptian military to prepare for war.

On May 26, Nasser had announced that if Israel were to strike either Egypt or Syria, this would result in a general war, with the Arab goal being "the destruction of Israel." On May 30 Jordanian king Hussein arrived in Cairo and there concluded a mutual security pact with Egypt.

On paper, the balance of forces heavily favored the Arab states. The Israel Defense Forces (IDF) had 230,000 troops, 1,100 tanks, 200 artillery pieces, 260 combat aircraft, and 22 naval vessels. Egypt and Syria together had 263,000 men, 1,950 tanks, 915 artillery pieces, 521 combat aircraft, and 75 naval vessels. Counting Iraqi and Jordanian forces, the Arab advantage swelled to 409,000 men, 2,437 tanks, 1,487 artillery pieces, 649 combat aircraft, and 90 naval vessels.

Now certain of war and despite strong U.S. opposition, on June 4 Israeli prime minister Levi Eshkol authorized a preemptive strike against Egypt. The Six-Day War began on June 5, 1967, with carefully planned and brilliantly executed Israeli strikes that first destroyed much of the Egyptian Air Force. The Israelis then repeated the process against Syria and Jordan. Israeli ground forces went into action simultaneously, and at the end of only six days Egypt had lost the Sinai and the Gaza Strip, Jordan lost Old Jerusalem and the entire West Bank of the Jordan River, and Syria lost the Golan Heights.

The debacle led Nasser to make the gesture of resigning, but wide-scale popular demonstrations by the Egyptian people blocked this. Marshal Amer was made the scapegoat. Allegedly approached by high-ranking Egyptian officers, he was given a choice to stand trial for treason, which would inevitably have ended with his conviction and execution, or face an honorable death by taking poison. Apparently he chose the latter and received a full military burial.

Recovering politically, Nasser then mounted what became known as the War of Attrition against Israel, consisting largely of artillery fire across the Suez Canal into the Sinai that continued from July 1, 1967, until August 7, 1970. Meanwhile, Nasser pursued his Arabist ideals and supported the Palestinian cause. Growing Palestinian and Syrian pressures on Jordan led to an inter-Arab crisis known as Black September in 1970 when the Jordanian Army expelled the militant Palestinians from that country. Nasser was personally involved in negotiating the aftermath of this crisis just prior to his death on September 28, 1970.

Anwar Sadat, another member of the officer group that had come to power in 1952, succeeded Nasser as president. Under Sadat, Egypt moved toward the West. Sadat expelled communist bloc advisers and purged Nasserists from the governmental elite. Egypt also received more Arab aid, and Sadat gradually opened the economy to foreign investment and joint partnerships.

Sadat opened negotiations with Israel in the hopes of securing the return of the Sinai. Disillusionment with the lack of progress in 1971, however, led him to begin planning a military operation to break the political stalemate. Sadat believed that even a minor Egyptian military success would change the military equilibrium and force a political settlement. Israel's strength was in its air force and armored divisions in maneuver warfare. Egyptian strengths were the ability to build a strong defense line and new Soviet-supplied surface-to-air missiles (SAMs) deployed in batteries along the canal and deep within Egypt. Sadat hoped to paralyze the Israeli Air Force with the SAMs and counter the Israelis' advantage in maneuver warfare by forcing them to attack well-fortified and well-defended Egyptian strongholds.

In an attempt to dilute the Israeli military forces on the Sinai front, Sadat brought in Syria. A coordinated surprise attack by both states would place maximum stress on the IDF. The key to success was secrecy. Were Israel to suspect an imminent attack, it would undoubtedly launch a preventive attack, as in 1967. That part of Sadat's plan, at least, was successful.

A combination of effective Egyptian deceptive measures and Israeli arrogance contributed to Israel's failure to comprehend the threat. One deception consisted of repeated Egyptian drills along the Suez Canal simulating a possible crossing. The Israelis thus interpreted Egyptian preparations for the actual crossings as just another drill. Even the Egyptian soldiers were told as much. Only when the actual crossing was underway were they informed of its true nature.

On the Israeli-Egyptian front, Egypt amassed nearly 800,000 soldiers, 2,200 tanks, 2,300 artillery pieces, 150 SAM batteries, and 550 aircraft. Along the canal, Egypt deployed five infantry divisions with accompanying armored elements, supported by additional infantry and armored independent brigades and backed by three mechanized divisions and two armored divisions. Israel had only a single division supported by 280 tanks. Not until the early morning hours of October 6 did Israeli military intelligence conclude that an Egyptian attack was imminent, but Prime Minister Golda Meir decided against a preemptive strike.

The Yom Kippur War of October 6–26, 1973, also known as the Ramadan War, the October War, and the 1973 Arab-Israeli War, commenced at 2:00 p.m. on October 6 on Yom Kippur, the holiest day for Jews, when Egypt launched a massive air strike against Israeli artillery and command positions. At the same time, Egyptian artillery shelled the Bar Lev Line fortifications. Egyptian commandos crossed the canal followed by engineers, who quickly constructed bridges, allowing the Egyptians to pass across sizable numbers of infantry and armor. By October 8, Egyptian infantry and some 500 tanks had pushed three to five miles east of the canal, defended by the SAM batteries.

The Israelis meanwhile mobilized two armored divisions and on October 8 launched a quick counteroffensive to repel the Egyptians. These encountered the far larger and well-equipped Egyptian force protected by handheld antitank missiles. The Egyptians crushed the Israeli counteroffensive. Israeli ground-support aircraft suffered heavy losses against Egyptian antiaircraft defenses, especially from SAMs. Following this setback, the Israeli General Staff decided to halt offensive actions on the Suez front and give priority to the Syria front.

Sadat now overruled his ground commander, Field Marshal Ahmed Ismail Ali, and, following Syrian pleas for assistance, ordered a resumption of the offensive on October 11. This, however, took Egyptian forces out of their prepared defensive positions and removed them from the effective SAM cover on the other side of the canal. On October 14 the Israelis threw back the Egyptians, inflicting on them heavy losses.

Concurrent with the initial Egyptian assault, Syrian armor and mechanized forces moved in force against the Golan Heights and almost broke through. The Syrian drives were contained, however, and Israeli forces then began their own offensive action and occupied a portion of Syria. Meanwhile, the Israelis crossed the Suez Canal themselves, defeated the Egyptians in the Battle of the Chinese Farm (October 16–18), and cut off Egyptian forces on the east bank. Heavy pressure from the United States, the Soviet Union, and the United Nations (UN) brought a cease-fire agreement on October 25.

Although Egyptian forces had been driven back, they had fought well, and Egyptians regarded the 1973 war as an affirmation of the nation's strength. Sadat knew that his country could not afford another costly war, however. He took the dramatic step of traveling to Tel Aviv in 1977 to address the Israeli parliament and lay the groundwork for a peace agreement with Israel. This was ultimately achieved, with the assistance of U.S. president Jimmy Carter, in the September 17, 1979, Camp David Accords. The settlement returned the Sinai Peninsula to Egyptian control. Egyptian participation in the bilateral agreement with Israel was very unpopular with other Arab governments, however. They promptly cut off aid and tourism to Egypt for a time and expelled Egypt from the Arab League. Because of other political issues, including Sadat's failure to open the political system, the peace agreement also soon became unpopular with many Egyptians.

New Islamic fundamentalist groups began to emerge in Egypt in the 1970s. Sadat had pardoned and released from jail members of the Muslim Brotherhood and allowed Islamist student groups to organize. One of these groups attempted to kill Sadat during a visit to the Military Technical Academy. On October 6, 1981, however, the radical organization Islamic Jihad succeeded in assassinating Sadat in the course of a military review.

Sadat's successor as president, Hosni Mubarak, Egyptian air chief marshal and head of the air force during 1972–1975, continued Egypt's economic opening to the West via privatization and joint ventures, all the while maintaining a large military establishment. The most important challenge to the state internally in the 1980s and 1990s came from Islamist groups that mounted attacks against local officials and tourists. These groups as well as many professionals opposed normalized relations with Israel.

Mubarak joined the international coalition to oppose Iraqi control of Kuwait, and Egyptian troops participated in the liberation of Kuwait during the Persian Gulf War of January–February 1991. As a result of its support, Egypt also received loan waivers from the United States, Western Europe, and several Gulf states in excess of $20 billion.

In the aftermath of the September 11, 2001, terrorist attacks against the United States, the Egyptian government voiced its support for the global war on terror but declined to deploy any troops to the invasion of Afghanistan (Operation ENDURING FREEDOM) or the invasion of Iraq (Operation IRAQI FREEDOM). Indeed, Egypt voiced its displeasure regarding the latter. However, following the overthrow of Iraqi president Saddam Hussein, Egypt publicly supported the Iraqi Governing Council.

Since 2003, U.S.-Egyptian relations have been periodically strained because of disagreements regarding the war in Iraq and the Israeli-Palestinian conflict, U.S. calls for increased Egyptian democratization in Egypt, and suggestions that U.S. aid might be cut off. In December 2006 Egypt's foreign minister called for an end to what he termed "nuclear double standards," which saw economic sanctions imposed against Iran because of its alleged program to acquire nuclear weapons but allowed Israel to develop and deploy nuclear weapons with complete impunity.

Egypt, on U.S. insistence, helped in isolating the radical Palestinian organization Hamas in the Gaza Strip, which after 2007 was under an economic blockade mounted by Israel and Western nations. Egypt closed its borders with Gaza, yet widespread smuggling occurred into Gaza from Egypt through an extensive system of tunnels. Although Egypt took a tougher line with Hamas than that organization expected, Egypt also played a key role in negotiations with Hamas and has hosted various meetings aimed at securing a new truce between it and Israel and ending the economic boycott.

Israeli's all-out attack on the Gaza Strip during December 2008–January 2009 imposed serious strains on Egyptian-Israeli relations. In the spring of 2008 a series of attacks and attempted attacks on tourists in Egypt occurred, and there was mounting discontent in the Egyptian military, both of which were attributed to the Gaza debacle.

As part of the wider Arab Spring movement—a demand for democratic reform that swept much of the Arab world in late 2010 and early 2011—in January 2011 protesters staged massive street demonstrations in Egypt against the repressive Mubarak government. When Egyptian government forces attempted to quash the rebellion, civilians were killed, and Mubarak's grasp on power quickly diminished. This placed the U.S. government in a delicate situation, as it had supported Mubarak for many years. Nevertheless, the Barack Obama administration reluctantly signaled that the Egyptian strongman should step down, which he reluctantly did on February 11, 2011. After that, the Egyptian military took effective control of the country, suspended the constitution and parliament, and promised to hold democratic elections in the near future.

Parliamentary elections occurred during November 28, 2011–January 11, 2012, and in June 2012 Mohamed Morsi was elected president. In August, it was announced that several members of the Muslim Brotherhood would join the government, which caused many Egyptians to question the validity of the new regime. When the Islamist Muslim Brotherhood openly embraced Morsi, most secular and

The Egyptian Revolution of 2011

Prompted by events in Tunisia, on January 25, 2011, Egyptians began massive street protests against the authoritarian rule of President Hosni Mubarak. The rioters were mostly young and were protesting the lack of jobs as well as corruption and rigged elections. Their chief demand was that Mubarak resign. During the next few days the demonstrations grew amid some looting and violence. The police—an object of special hatred for their brutality—tried to confront the demonstrators but were beaten back.

Mubarak went on television on January 28, but while pledging a new government he made no mention of reforms or resignation. With violence increasing, Egyptian Army vehicles took up position in Cairo. Although U.S. president Barack Obama called on Mubarak not to use force, Washington was clearly worried that Egypt might go the way of Iran in 1979, with the Muslim Brotherhood seizing power.

The demonstrators defied government-mandated curfews, and in an important step army leaders announced on January 31 that the troops would not fire on peaceful demonstrations.

On February 1 hundreds of thousands of protestors crowded into Tahrir Square. Mubarak announced that while he would not run for another presidential term in September, he also would not resign. President Obama then called for an immediate orderly transition to a new regime. On the night of February 2 pro- and anti-Mubarak demonstrators clashed, with some killed and many others injured. Meanwhile, the number of demonstrators in Cairo's Tahrir Square continued to swell, with the army keeping the two sides apart.

On the evening of February 10 a large crowd again was in the square, amid reports that Mubarak would announce his resignation. But while he said that he would relinquish some responsibilities, he would not quit. The demonstrators vowed to remain until he left office.

With groups of junior army officers joining the protestors, major new demonstrations were planned for February 11. That evening Vice President Omar Suleiman announced Mubarak's resignation. The military's Supreme Council announced that it would guarantee the transition to democracy that would permit an elected civilian to govern Egypt. Reportedly the Egyptian Revolution claimed 365 dead and thousands injured.

liberal parliament members walked out of the assembly in protest, plunging Egypt into another government crisis. In November 2012, Morsi defended the new constitution and declared his actions to be legal and free from the actions of what he called "reactionaries." This prompted more mass protests. These continued into the summer of 2013, virtually paralyzing Egypt and its economy.

On July 3, 2013, the Egyptian military ousted Morsi from power, and in January 2014 a new constitution was established, receiving more than 98 percent approval (although just 38.6 percent of Egyptians participated in the vote). Egypt's government was then dominated by the military under the aegis of an interim government. In May 2014, nationwide elections resulted in the selection of Abdel Fattah el-Sisi as president. The former head of Egypt's armed forces, he took office on June 8, 2014. El-Sisi's election meant that the Egyptian government would continue to be dominated by the military.

Sisi's government declared the Muslim Brotherhood a terrorist organization and imprisoned scores of Morsi supporters. Then on August 14, Egyptian security forces opened fire on and killed more than 800 pro-Morsi protesters in Rabaa in what is known as the Rabaa Massacre. The U.S. government halted major weapons transfers to Egypt in protest. (At $1.3 billion, Egypt ranked second in U.S. military aid in 2014, behind only Israel at $3.1 billion. The ban on major weapons transfers was lifted by the Obama administration on March 31, 2015.)

Morsi, Egypt's first democratically elected ruler, was brought to trial and found guilty of membership in the now-banned Muslim Brotherhood but acquitted of espionage. He was sentenced to 25 years in prison.

Ongoing violence in Egypt, especially in the Sinai against the government, remains a sizable problem, as does the depressed Egyptian economy, partly owing to a drop in tourism. Terrorism is a constant threat. On October 31, 2015, a Russian Metrojet Airlines Airbus A321 bound for St. Petersburg crashed in the Sinai after takeoff from Sharm el-Sheikh, killing all 224 people on board. A little-known terrorist group, calling itself Ansar Beit al-Maqdis and operating in the Sinai, is believed to have planted a bomb on the aircraft. Then on May 19, 2016, EgyptAir Flight MS804 from Paris to Cairo crashed into the Mediterranean, killing all 66 people on board. The cause of that crash has yet to be determined.

Timeline

600s CE	Arab armies conquer Egypt, and Islam replaces Christianity.
1517	The Ottoman Turks secure control of Egypt.
1798	French forces under Napoleon Bonaparte invade Egypt.
May 1805– Mar 1848	Muhammad Ali Pasha, an Ottoman military commander, secures power in Egypt and establishes the Ali dynasty.
1867	Egypt secures the status of an autonomous vassal state, or khedivate, of the Ottoman Empire, which continues until 1914.

1869	A French company headed by Ferdinand de Lesseps completes construction of the Suez Canal.
1875	Hard-pressed for funds, Khedive Ismail sells Egypt's share in the canal to the British government. Within three years British and French controllers are the real power in Egypt.
1879	Popular dissatisfaction with foreign control brings the formation of nationalist groups in Egypt.
Feb 1881	Ahmet Arabi (Urabi) leads a revolt, proclaiming "Egypt for the Egyptians." Britain sends warships to Alexandria.
Jun 11, 1882	Antiforeign riots in Alexandria result in the deaths of 68 Europeans and provide the British with an excuse for action.
Jul 11, 1882	When Arabi rejects demands to disarm Alexandria's defenses, British warships shell Alexandria, and British forces occupy the city.
Sep 13, 1882	In the Battle of Tel el-Kebir, a British expeditionary force defeats Arabi's forces.
Sep 15, 1882	British cavalry enters Cairo almost without opposition. Arabi surrenders, and the revolt ends. The British then reinstall Ismail's son Tewfik as figurehead of a de facto British protectorate, with British consul general and high commissioner Lord Cromer as the real Egyptian ruler for the next 23 years.
Oct 31, 1914	The Ottoman Empire enters World War I on the side of the Central Powers. With Egypt still technically an Ottoman tributary, anti-British khedive Abbas Hilmi II declares his support for the Ottoman Muslim caliphate.
Dec 19, 1914	The British make their protectorate official and change the title of head of state from khedive to sultan, thus ending Ottoman control. Hussein Kamel replaces Abbas II.
1915–1916	The Germans foment a revolt by the Senussis, the warlike Bedouin tribesmen of Cyrenaica, to rise up against Britain and invade Egypt. The British garrison at Sollum is forced to surrender, but the British retake it and defeat the Senussis in 1916, although their raids continue.
Feb 3, 1915	The British defeat a major Ottoman offensive to take the Suez Canal.
Aug 3, 1916	The British defeat a second Ottoman offensive against the Suez Canal.
Dec 11, 1917	Having gone on the offensive, the British capture Jerusalem.

Feb 28, 1922	Rising Egyptian nationalism forces the British to cede nominal independence to Egypt, although the British still retain considerable control. Hussein Kamel has the title of king.
1939–1945	During World War II, Egypt remains an important British base. The expanded presence of Western troops, however, fuels Egyptian nationalism and especially the Muslim Brotherhood, an antisecularist party seeking to dominate Egypt.
Sep 13, 1940	Italian forces invade Egypt.
Jul 1–27, 1942	In the First Battle of El Alamein, the British halt the Axis advance on Alexandria and then Cairo and the Suez Canal.
Oct 23–Nov 11, 1942	In the Second Battle of El Alamein, British forces break through the Axis defense, driving them west on Tripoli, where the Allies are victorious in May 1943.
Jul 23, 1952	A group of Egyptian Army officers overthrows King Farouk and seizes power. They are initially led by Muhammad Najib.
Sep 1955	An agreement concluded by Nasser with the Soviet Union for a large purchase of arms from Czechoslovakia, coupled with his refusal to sign the pro-Western Baghdad Pact and association with the Non-Aligned Movement, causes alarm and anger in Washington and leads the U.S. government to rescind its pledge to help fund Nasser's ambitious plan to build a high dam on the upper Nile at Aswan.
Jun 23, 1956	Outmaneuvering Najib, Gamal Abdel Nasser becomes the president of Egypt.
Jul 26, 1956	To pay for the Aswan dam, Nasser nationalizes the Suez Canal. The British, French, and Israelis secretly agree to precipitate in what becomes known as the 1956 Suez Crisis.
Jul 29, 1956	Israeli forces invade the Sinai. When Egypt refuses to allow the British to intervene to "protect" the Suez Canal, Britain and France then attack Egypt and land troops. Heavy U.S. pressure forces them to withdraw, greatly enhancing Nasser's prestige in the Arab world.
Feb 1, 1958	The United Arab Republic (UAR) is created by a union of Egypt and Syria, regarded as a first step toward a larger Pan-Arab state.
Sep 28, 1961	With the UAR having been completely dominated by Egypt, discontent in Syria brings an army coup and the end of the UAR.
Sep 27, 1962	Following a coup, the Yemen Civil War begins. It lasts until 1970, with Egypt supporting the Yemeni republicans against the royalists backed by the Saudis. Egyptian numbers steadily increase to

a maximum of 55,000 men in late 1965. Egyptian forces are not highly successful, however, and are bogged down there when the 1967 Six-Day War with Israel occurs.

May 16, 1967   With the Soviets providing Egypt with false information that Israel is mobilizing troops on the Syrian border, Nasser declares a state of emergency, and the next day the Egyptian and Syrian governments proclaim a state of combat readiness. Jordan also mobilizes. His belligerency having caused his popularity to soar in the Arab world, Nasser demands that the United Nations Emergency Force (UNEF) in the Sinai depart immediately. Since 1956 it has been a buffer between Egyptian and Israeli forces.

May 19, 1967   The UNEF complies with Nasser's demand.

May 23, 1967   Egypt closes the Strait of Tiran to Israeli shipping. Nasser announces his intention to do this, but Israel had already let it be known that it would consider such a step a cause for war. Nasser's announcement is in fact largely a bluff. He assumes that the threat will force Israel to withdraw its supposed increased forces along the Syrian border. On May 22, however, Egyptian minister of defense Field Marshal Abdel Hakim Amer orders Egyptian forces to close the strait the next day. A countermanding order would signal weakness, and Nasser now orders the Egyptian military to prepare for war.

May 30, 1967   Jordanian king Hussein arrives in Cairo and there concludes a mutual security pact with Egypt.

Jun 4, 1967   With the military balance heavily favoring the Arab states, Israeli prime minister Levi Eshkol, certain of war and despite strong U.S. opposition, authorizes a preemptive strike against Egypt.

Jun 5–10, 1967   The Six-Day War begins with a preemptive strike against the air forces of Egypt and then Syria and Jordan. The war is an unqualified military success for Israel. By its end, Egypt has lost the Sinai and the Gaza Strip, Jordan has lost Old Jerusalem and the entire West Bank of the Jordan River, and Syria has lost the Golan Heights. The debacle leads Nasser to make the gesture of resigning, but wide-scale popular demonstrations by the Egyptian people block this. Amer is made the scapegoat and is probably forced to commit suicide.

Jul 1, 1967   Nasser mounts the War of Attrition, consisting largely of artillery fire into the Sinai against Israeli forces. It continues until August 7, 1970. He also supports Palestinian raids against Israel.

Jul 21, 1970   With the Soviet Union having provided considerable assistance, the Aswan High Dam officially opens.

Sep 28, 1970	Nasser dies. He is succeeded as president by Anwar Sadat, another member of the officer group that had come to power in 1952. Under Sadat, Egypt moves toward the West. Sadat expels communist bloc advisers and purges Nasserists from the government.
Oct 6–26, 1973	The failure of negotiations with Israel for the return of the Sinai leads Sadat to choose a military option in the Yom Kippur War (Ramadan War) of these dates. Sadat works out an alliance with Syria for a coordinated attack that will force Israel to fight on two fronts simultaneously. He plans to cross forces over the canal, then establish defensive positions and employ handheld antitank missiles and surface-to-air missiles (SAM) to defeat the Israeli counterattacks by armor and aircraft. The Egyptian attack catches the Israelis, who are outnumbered, by surprise. After earlier Egyptian success, however, Sadat overrules his ground commander, Field Marshal Ahmed Ismail Ali, and orders a further advance that takes Egyptian forces away from their SAM umbrella. By the cease-fire of October 26, the Israelis have driven back the Syrians, crossed the Suez Canal, and cut off major Egyptian forces. The Egyptians have fought well, however, and the war reveals that the military balance is evening up.
Nov 20, 1977	Sadat knows that his country cannot afford another costly war, and he takes the dramatic step of traveling to Israel to address the Israeli parliament and lay the groundwork for a peace agreement with Israel.
Sep 17, 1979	In the Camp David Accords, facilitated by U.S. president Jimmy Carter, Egypt and Israel conclude peace. This returns the Sinai Peninsula to Egyptian control. Other Arab governments, however, promptly cut off aid and tourism to Egypt and expel Egypt from the Arab League.
Oct 6, 1981	With many Islamist groups in Egypt unhappy with Sadat, the radical organization Islamic Jihad assassinates him during a military review. Sadat's successor as president is Hosni Mubarak, another military leader. Mubarak will continue Sadat's opening to the West via privatization and joint ventures, all the while maintaining a large military establishment.
Jan–Feb 1991	Egyptian forces take part in the 34-nation coalition of the Persian Gulf War to expel Iraqi forces from Kuwait.
Oct 7, 2001	Although Mubarak expresses support for the United States following the September 11, 2001, terrorist attack on the United States, he refuses to supply troops for the U.S.-led invasion of Afghanistan of this date.

Mar 20, 2003   Mubarak opposes the U.S.-led invasion of Iraq.

2007   On U.S. insistence, Egypt joins Israel in imposing an economic blockade of the radical Palestinian organization Hamas in the Gaza Strip. Egypt plays a key role in negotiations with Hamas and hosts various meetings aimed at securing truce agreements between it and Israel and an end to the economic boycott.

Jan 25–Feb   As a part of the demonstrations in much of the Arab world in
11, 2011   favor of democratic change (the so-called Arab Spring), protesters stage massive street demonstrations in Egypt against the repressive Mubarak government. Government forces attempting to crush the rebellion result in hundreds of civilian deaths and a reluctant call by the administration of U.S. president Barack Obama that Mubarak quit power. Mubarak resigns on February 11. The Egyptian military then takes effective control and suspends the constitution and parliament but promises to hold democratic elections.

Nov 28, 2011–   Parliamentary elections are held in Egypt.
Jan 11, 2012

Jun 30, 2012   Mohamed Morsi is elected president of Egypt. Soon, however, support for Morsi from the Islamist Muslim Brotherhood brings opposition from many secular Egyptians. Members of parliament walk out in protest, and Egypt is again in crisis. Protests against Morsi and his ties with the Muslim Brotherhood continue into the summer of 2013, virtually paralyzing Egypt and its economy.

Jul 3, 2013   The Egyptian military ousts Morsi from power.

Jan 17, 2014   A new constitution is overwhelmingly approved, but the government is dominated by the military under the aegis of an interim government.

Jun 8, 2014   Abdel Fattah el-Sisi takes office as president, the result of nationwide elections in May. He is the former head of Egypt's armed forces, and his election means that the Egyptian military will continue to dominate the government.

Aug 14, 2014   Sisi's government declares the Muslim Brotherhood a terrorist organization and imprisons scores of Morsi supporters. On this date, Egyptian security forces open fire on and kill more than 800 pro-Morsi protesters in Rabaa. The U.S. government halts major weapons transfers to Egypt in protest.

Aug 26, 2014   Following seven weeks of heavy fighting in the 2014 Gaza War between Israeli forces and Hamas, both sides accept an Egyptian-brokered cease-fire.

Nov 29, 2014   An Egyptian court dismisses all charges against former president Hosni Mubarak and his security chief for the deaths of the protesters in the demonstrations prior to Mubarak's resignation and finds him, his sons, and a business associate not guilty of corruption charges.

Feb 16, 2015   The day after the Islamic State of Iraq and Syria (ISIS) releases a gruesome video showing the beheading of 21 Egyptian Coptic Christians who had been working in Libya, Egypt sends aircraft to strike ISIS-affiliated jihadist camps, training areas, and weapons depots in Libya.

Oct 31, 2015   A Russian Metrojet Airlines Airbus A321 flying from Sharm el-Sheikh to St. Petersburg crashes in the Sinai some 24 minutes after takeoff, killing all 224 people on board. Most of the victims are Russians. A little-known terrorist group calling itself Ansar Beit al-Maqdis and operating in the Sinai is believed to have planted a bomb on the aircraft.

May 19, 2016   Egypt suffers another airliner blow when EgyptAir Flight MS804 from Paris to Cairo crashes into the Mediterranean, killing all 66 people on board. Several weeks later the wreckage is discovered, and the damaged flight data and cockpit voice recorders are retrieved. Investigators say that it is too early to rule out any causes for the crash, including terrorism.

Further Reading

Abdel-Malek, Anouar. *Egypt: Military Society.* New York: Random House, 1968.

Aburish, Said. *Nasser: The Last Arab.* New York: St. Martin's and Thomas Dunne Books, 2004.

Beattie, Kirk J. *Egypt during the Sadat Years.* New York: Palgrave, 2000.

Binder, Leonard. *In a Moment of Enthusiasm: Political Power and the Second Stratum in Egypt.* Chicago: University of Chicago Press, 1978.

Cooper, Chester L. *The Lion's Last Roar: Suez, 1956.* New York: Harper and Row, 1978.

Daly, M. W., ed. *The Cambridge History of Egypt,* Vol. 2. Cambridge: Cambridge University Press, 1998.

Ford, Roger. *Eden to Armageddon: World War I in the Middle East.* New York: Pegasus, 2010.

Gordon, Joel. *Nasser's Blessed Movement: Egypt's Free Officers and the July Revolution.* New York: Oxford University Press, 1992.

Hinnebusch, Raymond A., Jr. *Egyptian Politics under Sadat: The Post-Populist Development of an Authoritarian-Modernizing State.* Cambridge: Cambridge University Press, 1985.

Korn, David A. *Stalemate: The War of Attrition and Great Power Diplomacy in the Middle East, 1967–1970.* Boulder, CO: Westview, 1992.

Telhami, Ghada. *Palestine and the Egyptian National Identity.* Westport, CT: Praeger, 1992.

Waterbury, John. *The Egypt of Nasser and Sadat.* Princeton, NJ: Princeton University Press, 1983.

Zuhur, Sherifa. *Egypt: Security, Political and Islamist Challenges.* Carlisle, PA: Strategic Studies Institute, 2007.

IRAN

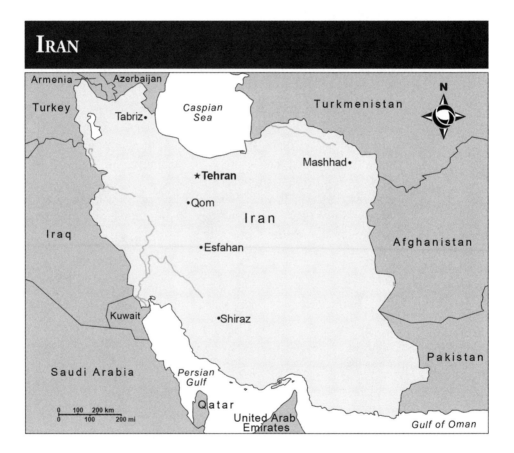

Armenia — Azerbaijan

Turkey

Turkmenistan

N

Tabriz•

Caspian
Sea

Mashhad•

★Tehran

•Qom

Iran

Iraq

Afghanistan

•Esfahan

Kuwait

•Shiraz

Pakistan

Saudi Arabia

Persian
Gulf

0   100   200 km
0   100   200 mi

Qatar

United Arab
Emirates

Gulf of Oman

Iran

Elena Andreeva, Louis A. DiMarco, Adam B. Lowther, Paul G. Pierpaoli Jr., Spencer C. Tucker, and Sherifa Zuhur

The Islamic Republic of Iran is situated in Southwest Asia. "Persia" was, however, the name primarily used by the international community to describe Iran during most of its history. The name "Iran" did not come into wide use until after the mid-1930s. Occupying 636,293 square miles, Iran is slightly larger than the U.S. state of Alaska. Iran is the 2nd-largest nation in the Middle East and the world's 18th largest. Iran is bordered by the Persian Gulf and the Gulf of Oman to the south; Turkey, Azerbaijan, the Caspian Sea, and Armenia to the north; Afghanistan and Pakistan to the east; and Iraq to the west. Iran has long been important because of its strategic location at the geographic nexus of the Middle East, Europe, and Southwest Asia. Iran's population in 2016 was some 80.043 million. Its capital and largest city is Tehran.

Iran's considerable influence in world affairs is due to its location and its considerable reserves of fossil fuels. Iran possesses both the world's fourth-largest oil reserves and the largest natural gas supply. Iran is a member of the United Nations (UN), the Economic Cooperation Organization, the Non-Aligned Movement, the Organization of Islamic Cooperation, and the Organization of Petroleum Exporting Countries. Iran's governmental system is based on the 1979 Iranian Constitution that combines elements of parliamentary democracy with a theocracy governed by Islamic jurists, all headed by a supreme leader.

Iran has numerous ethnic and linguistic groups, but its official language is Persian. Some 90–95 percent of the population adheres to Shia Islam, which is the state religion. Because Sunni Muslims comprise the great majority of Muslims in the Middle East and the world, Shia Iranians have tended to view the actions of Sunni-dominated governments as a direct threat. Sunni Muslims, principally Kurds and Balochs, constitute some 4–8 percent of the population. The remaining 2 percent are non-Muslim religious minorities, including more than a quarter million Christians (most of Armenian background) as well as Jews, Bahais, Mandeans, Yezidis, Yarsanis, and Zoroastrians. Despite the attitude of the current Iranian government toward the State of Israel, Judaism has a long history in Iran dating back to the Persian conquest of the Kingdom of Judah and the so-called Babylonian Captivity of the Jews in the sixth century BCE. As many as 10,000 Jews live in Iran. Although this seems to be a small number, it is the largest Jewish population in the Middle East outside of Israel.

Dating from the Proto-Elamite and Elamite Kingdoms in 3200–2800 BCE, Persia was one of the world's oldest civilizations and came to be one of the most important empires of the ancient world and, for a time, its largest and most powerful. The first Persian Empire appeared in 625 BCE and reached the height of its influence in the Achaemenid Empire established by Cyrus the Great in 550 BCE. At its greatest extent, the empire extended from significant parts of the Balkans in Europe eastward to the Indus Valley of present-day India. Alexander III (the Great) of Macedon conquered Persia in 330 BCE, but his own vast empire was divided following his early death in 323. The Parthian Empire, one of the successor states, lasted only from 247 to 224 BCE. Its successor, the Sassanid Empire, survived until 651. One of the leading world powers, it fought numerous wars with the rival Roman-Byzantine Empire.

Rashidun Arabs conquered Persia by 651 and converted it to Islam. Arabic also replaced Persian as the official language, although Persian remained the language of the common people. During the Safavid dynasty (1501–1736), the Twelver school of Shia Islam became the official religion. Under its great ruler and military leader Nader Shah (1736–1747), Persia was arguably the world's most powerful empire, including all of modern-day Iran, Azerbaijan, Bahrain, and Armenia; most of Georgia, the northern Caucasus, Iraq, Kuwait; and Afghanistan; and parts of Turkey, Syria, Pakistan, Turkmenistan, and Uzbekistan.

Persia's strategic geographical location bordering Russia, India, and the Persian Gulf made it a natural target in the struggle between the Great Powers, primarily Russia and Britain. This was especially true during the weak Qajar dynasty (1795–1925), when Persia was quite unable to resist pressure from outside powers and lost territory in the Caucasus. During the Constitutional Revolution of 1905–1907, Mozzafar-al-Din Shah (r. 1896–1907) was forced to issue a decree in 1906 that created a limited constitutional monarchy. The first Persian parliament, the Majlis, convened in October 1906. Then in 1907 the Anglo-Russian Convention divided Persia into spheres of influence: Russian in the north and center, British in the southeast, and a neutral zone between the two.

Persia declared its neutrality during World War I (1914–1918) but nonetheless became a battleground for German, Ottoman, Russian, and British forces. In March 1915 Russia agreed to British control over the neutral zone, where oil had been discovered in 1908, leading the next year to the establishment of the Anglo-Persian Oil Company.

The Germans and allied Ottomans sought to destroy the British-controlled oil facilities in Khuzestan and secure access to Afghanistan via Persia. The Ottomans also sought to acquire Transcaucasia. Many in Persia favored an Ottoman-German alliance because the Ottomans were Muslims fighting against the much-distrusted Russians and British and also because the Ottoman sultan had proclaimed jihad (holy war) against the Allies. Kaiser Wilhelm II of Germany had also posed as a protector of Islam.

The Ottomans invaded Azerbaijan in the fall of 1914; by May 1916, however, Russian forces had defeated the Ottoman invasion, although the Ottomans were able to arrest the Russian advance and also achieve success in southern Persia against the British. In addition, German agents in southern Persia were able to instigate revolts among the Bakhtiari, Qashqai, and Tangistani tribes. The most famous of those emissaries was Wilhelm Wassmuss, a former consul in Bushire who became known as "the German Lawrence." The British area of influence soon fell under German control, cutting the British off from Tehran and forcing them to divert troops from Mesopotamia to protect the Khuzestan oil fields.

Early in 1916, however, the British formed a new local armed force, the South Persia Rifles, commanded by General Sir Percy Sykes. By the fall of 1916 the South Persia Rifles had recaptured the most important cities from the Germans and linked up with the Russian forces in Isfahan. In late 1917 British forces regained control of the south from the Germans and their tribal allies.

In Tehran in August 1915, Mustawfi al-Mamalik, a nationalist pro-German leader, became prime minister and initiated secret talks with the Germans. The third Majlis was also predominantly pro-German and anti-Russian. The Germans were supported by nationalist members of the Democratic Party, Shia clerics, tribal leaders, and the Swedish-officered Gendarmerie. In November 1915 Russian forces marched from Qazvin toward Tehran. The Majlis was dissolved, but a provisional government was formed first in Qom. It then moved to Hamadan and finally to Kermanshah. The British and Russian ministers persuaded young Ahmad Qajar Shah (r. 1909–1925) and his cabinet to remain in the capital. By March 1917 as a result of Russian and British military successes, the dissident government was forced to withdraw to Ottoman territory. By late 1917, the Russians and the British again controlled most of Persia.

With the Bolshevik Revolution in Russia of November 1917, most Russian military formations in Persia disintegrated, but the British were able to move into that territory in northern Persia. The British also sent expeditions to Transcaucasia, eastern Persia, and Turkistan. Despite the end of the war in November 1918, the British did not withdraw from Persia until 1921.

Persia had suffered greatly from the war. The foreign occupation, the corrupt and ineffective Persian government, tribal rebellions, separatist nationalist movements, and a famine in 1918–1919 all led to a major economic and political crisis. In late 1920 in the midst of growing unrest throughout Persia, some 1,500 men of the so-called Persian Soviet Socialist Republic, reinforced by elements of the Russian Bolshevik Red Army, prepared to march from Rasht on Tehran. Ahmad Shah Qajar was both weak and inept. The British, who now had a major economic stake in Iran, were greatly concerned.

On January 14, 1921, British general Edmund Ironside, then commanding the Allied force in Persia, chose Reza Khan, commander of the Tabriz Battalion, to lead the major Persian military formation, the 3,000- to 4,000-man Cossack Brigade, as a brigadier general and the first Persian so selected. The next month with British support, Reza Khan marched on Tehran, and on February 21 he seized control in a largely bloodless coup d'état.

Although military actions extended well into 1922, Reza Khan was able to pacify the entire country. On October 28, 1923, he became prime minister, serving until November 1, 1925. On December 15, 1923, he established the Pahlavi dynasty, with himself as Reza Shah Pahlavi I.

Reza Shah laid the foundations of the modern Iranian state. He instituted agricultural, economic, and educational reforms and began the modernization of the country's transportation system. He also built up the military. These and other reforms threatened the status of the Shia clerics in Iran, who began to oppose the shah and policies that were seen as impinging on their areas of authority. Desiring to stress the country's pre-Islamic traditions and to include Iranians who were not from Fars (the central province), Reza Shah in 1935 changed the country's name from Persia to Iran.

Germany had a significant economic influence and presence in Iran prior to the outbreak of World War II (1939–1945), for in the 1930s Reza Shah had turned to it for economic assistance. His admiration of Germany, which had no tradition of imperial intervention in Iran or in the Middle East, was well known, as was his distrust of Britain and the Soviet Union.

Reza Shah declared Iran neutral in the war. However, after the Germans attacked the Soviet Union in June 1941, Iranian involvement became inevitable. The Soviet Union was now allied with Britain, and as German forces drove farther eastward and threatened the Caucasus, the strategic significance of Iran grew. The Allies sought to protect the British-controlled oil fields in Khuzestan and to use Iran and, in particular, its newly built Trans-Iranian Railroad to transport military supplies to the Soviet Union. The British and Soviet representatives in Iran demanded that the government expel German nationals and allow the Allies to utilize the railroad to transport war materials. When Reza Shah refused on the grounds of Iranian neutrality, the Allies invaded and occupied the country.

On August 25, 1941, Soviet forces entered Iran from the northwest, while the British entered from Iraq. The Allies suppressed Iranian military and naval resistance in just three days. Reza Shah was forced to abdicate on September 16, 1941. Sent into exile, he died in South Africa in 1944. He was succeeded as shah by his 22-year-old son, Mohammad Reza.

The Soviet and British zones of occupation closely mirrored the spheres of influence into which Iran had been divided by the Anglo-Russia Convention of 1907. The Soviets occupied the north, the British took control in the south, and Tehran and other central areas were placed under joint Anglo-Soviet protection. In January 1942 Iran, the Soviet Union, and Great Britain signed the Tripartite Treaty of Alliance. The Great Powers promised to respect Iranian territorial integrity, sovereignty, and political independence; safeguard the Iranian economy from the effects of the war; and withdraw from Iranian territory within six months of the end of hostilities.

By the spring of 1942, Iran had severed diplomatic relations with Germany, Italy, and Japan and expelled their nationals, and on September 9, 1943, Iran declared war on Germany. Two months later, U.S. president Franklin D. Roosevelt, British prime minister Winston L. S. Churchill, and Soviet leader Joseph Stalin met in Tehran in one of the most important conferences of the war. The three Allied leaders promised during the meeting to provide economic assistance to Iran and address its problems after the war.

During the war, much of the central government strength built up by Reza Shah was lost. The war years saw political instability, social disintegration, the rise of separatist movements, and economic hardship brought on by inflation and a poor harvest in 1942 with widespread famine. The Soviet Union and Britain also revived their long-standing rivalry for influence in Iran. The Soviets closed their occupation zone to free entry and supported left-wing trade unions and the Communist Party (banned in 1937, it was revived in 1941 under the new name Tudeh [Masses]). The Soviets also supported separatist leftist movements in Iranian Kurdistan and Azerbaijan. Indeed, Soviet activities led to the establishment of an autonomous state of Azerbaijan in December 1945. Meanwhile, the British in the south supported conservative elements, including the tribes, Muslim clerics, and the proponents of monarchy. The British sponsored the right-wing, pro-Western, anticommunist National Will Party.

The U.S. government was aware of the strategic importance of Iran, and after the United States entered the war in December 1941, American troops arrived in Iran. The Persian Gulf Command, which eventually numbered 30,000 men, helped orchestrate the movement through Iran of Lend-Lease supplies to the Soviet Union. American financial and military advisers also arrived at the request of the Iranian government. One U.S. mission worked on reorganizing Iran's finances, while another took charge of the reorganization of the Iranian Gendarmerie (rural police).

In the first half of 1944, two American oil companies and then the Soviet government attempted to secure oil concessions from the Iranian government in order to undermine the monopoly of the Anglo-Iranian Oil Company (AIOC), which during the war had artificially deflated the price of oil in order to minimize the cost of the war to the British economy. The Majlis (parliament), however, passed a bill, authored mainly by Mohammad Mosaddegh, leader of the National Front Party, that prohibited oil-concession agreements with any foreign company until after the end of the war. Certainly, the popularity of the shah suffered because of his ties to the West.

Mosaddegh became prime minister on April 28, 1951, and soon became the shah's most prominent critic. Mosaddegh secured the nationalization by the Majlis of the AIOC on May 1. Washington chose to regard this as a clear example of Mosaddegh's communist tendencies. Britain responded by imposing an embargo on Iranian oil and blocking the export of products from the formerly British properties. Because Britain was Iran's primary oil consumer, this had great impact on the Iranian economy. On July 16, 1952, Mosaddegh insisted on the right of the prime minister to name the minister of war and the chief of staff of the army, something that had been vested in the shah. The shah's refusal precipitated a political crisis.

Aware of his great popularity with the Iranian people, Mosaddegh promptly resigned. This led to widespread protests and demands that he be returned to power. Unnerved, on July 21 the shah reappointed Mosaddegh, who then took steps to consolidate his power. These included the implementation of land reforms and other measures, which to many in Britain and the United States seemed socialist. Although Mosaddegh had not had any direct contact with the Soviets, the events in Iran were nevertheless of great concern to U.S. policy makers who, based on Soviet efforts to annex northern Iran at the end of World War II, feared a communist takeover.

Washington refused Mosaddegh's repeated requests for financial aid because he refused to reverse the AIOC nationalization. By the summer of 1953, Mosaddegh's intransigence and his legalization of the leftist Tudeh Party led the United States to

Mohammad Mosaddegh

While the British were correct in viewing Mohammad Mosaddegh as a threat to their position in Iran, U.S. policy makers were wrong to presume that he was a communist. Rather, Mosaddegh was an Iranian nationalist and reformer who sought to improve the dire domestic conditions faced by so many Iranians and to establish a more independent foreign policy.

In December 1953, Mosaddegh was sentenced to three years' solitary confinement in a military prison. He was then kept under house arrest at his Ahmadabad residence until his death in March 1967. To this day Mosaddegh is regarded as one of the most popular figures in Iranian history.

join Britain and the temporarily exiled shah in a covert plot in August to overthrow him. Known as Operation TPAJAX (the "TP" referring to the Tudeh Party), the coup was successful on August 19, and the shah returned to power from Rome on August 22. The overthrow of Mosaddegh would be a rallying point in anti-U.S. protests during the 1979 Iranian Revolution.

The decade that followed saw the creation in 1957 of the Sazeman-e Ettelaat va Amniyat-e Keshvar (National Information and Security Organization, SAVAK), the shah's dreaded secret police. It also brought a number of failed or overly ambitious economic reforms. Iranian economic policy gave preference to large state projects rather than a true free market economy, and the largely state-run economy failed to perform as promised. This and pressure by the United States finally led the shah to propose the White Revolution. This ambitious undertaking included land reform, privatization of government-owned firms, electoral reform, women's suffrage, the nationalization of forests, rural literacy programs, and profit sharing for industrial workers. The White Revolution proved far less than revolutionary, however. It was also accompanied by a brutal crackdown on Iranian dissidents and fundamentalist clerics, which did nothing to endear the shah to his own people.

By the early 1960s Ayatollah Ruhollah Khomeini, a conservative Muslim cleric, was the shah's most prominent opponent. Khomeini attacked the regime for its secular focus and the shah for his elaborate and regal Western lifestyle. A staunch foe of Israel, Khomeini was also critical of Iran's close relationships with the United States, which was the chief supporter of Israel, and with Israel, which was helping to train SAVAK. Thus, when SAVAK arrested, tortured, and killed activists opposed to the regime, the United States and Israel were blamed along with the shah. Khomeini's considerable popularity prevented the shah from eliminating him but not from exiling him. Forced to leave Iran in 1964, Khomeini continued to denounce the shah, Zionism, and the United States.

When the White Revolution failed to achieve the desired results, leftist groups such as the Mujahideen-e Khalq and Fidiyann-e Islami Khalq joined the National Front Party and religious conservatives in opposing the regime. During the 1970s, opposition to the regime saw overt acts of defiance such as the wearing of the *hijab* by Iranian women; attendance at mosques, the imams of which openly criticized the shah; performance of religious plays on holidays; and demonstrations to memorialize slain protesters.

When an article critical of Khomeini ran in a Tehran newspaper in January 1978, the city's streets filled with Khomeini supporters and regime opponents. The shah's failure to quell the riots that followed emboldened his opponents, and each demonstration led to another riot and a new set of martyrs and then memorial demonstrations.

Following massive general strikes in the autumn of 1978, the shah lost control. Announcing that he was going abroad for a short holiday, he left Iran on January 16, 1979, never to return (he died of cancer in Cairo, Egypt, where he was granted asylum, on July 27, 1980). Meanwhile, a transitional government composed of the various opposition groups took power in Iran.

Khomeini made a triumphant return to Iran from exile on February 1, 1979, and immediately set about resurrecting the country's Islamic heritage. It was clear that he was no liberal, but Iranian secular and leftist politicians gave him their full support on the false assumption that he was merely a figurehead who would eventually cede power to the secular groups.

Within two weeks of Khomeini's return, the military announced its intention to remain neutral, thereby avoiding prosecution by local Islamic Revolutionary Committees, or Komitehs, composed of armed militant Shiites organized around local mosques who functioned as vigilantes enforcing Islamic values and laws. Meanwhile, senior officials of the former regime were arrested, tried by a revolutionary court, and executed.

In March 1979, a 97 percent vote in a national referendum ratified Khomeini's decision to establish an Islamic republic. He went on to create a separate

Ayatollah Ruhollah Khomeini thronged by supporters after having delivered a speech at the Tehran airport on February 1, 1979, the day of his return from 14 years of exile. (AP Photo)

paramilitary force, the Revolutionary Guard Corps, which served as a secret police. On April 1, 1979, the Islamic Republic of Iran came into being.

During the summer of 1979, Khomeini loyalists crafted a new constitution and government that was nominally democratic with an elected parliament, elected municipal councils, and an elected president but also had a Council of Guardians composed of 12 clerics and jurists. The Council of Guardians held real power, as it approved candidates seeking elected office and also approved or vetoed legislation passed by the parliament. The council was tasked with assuring that legislation and politics remained strictly Islamic. The constitution also confirmed Khomeini and his successors as the supreme leaders of the government, with the right to appoint the heads of the armed forces, the head of the Revolutionary Guard Corps, and half of the members of the Council of Guardians. The Communist Party, liberal organizations, and even moderate groups that had initially supported the revolution and now opposed Khomeini's theocratic state were marginalized and excluded from the new government, and some of their members were executed for allegedly being anti-Islamic.

Relative moderates such as Mehdi Bazargan and Abolhasan Bani-Sadr, the first prime minister and president, respectively, after the shah's departure, were soon forced from power by Khomeini, the supreme *faqih* (expert in Islamic law) and de facto national leader.

Angered by U.S. president Jimmy Carter's decision to allow the shah to undergo cancer treatments in the United States, on November 4, 1979, Iranian students stormed the U.S. embassy in Tehran and seized 53 American diplomatic personnel as hostages. Khomeini had supported the students and their demands that the United States turn over the shah for trial in exchange for releasing the hostages. The ensuing diplomatic crisis, which lasted for 444 days (November 4, 1979–January 20, 1981), paralyzed the Carter administration; brought an aborted U.S. military rescue mission, Operation EAGLE CLAW on April 24, 1980, that nonetheless claimed through accident the lives of eight Americans and the injuring of five others; and may well have cost Carter reelection as president.

The incoming administration of President Ronald Reagan (1981–1989) viewed the new Iranian regime as a threat to American interests in the Middle East and to its closest ally, Israel. This led the United States to support Iraq in the Iran-Iraq War of 1980–1988.

The war was in many ways a continuation of the ancient Persian-Arab rivalry fueled by 20th-century border disputes and competition for hegemony in the Persian Gulf and the Middle East. The long-standing rivalry between these two nations was abetted by a collision between the Pan-Islamism and revolutionary Shia Islamism of Iran and the Pan-Arab nationalism of Iraq.

The border between the two states had been contested for some time, and in 1969 Iran had abrogated its treaty with Iraq on the navigation of the Shatt al-Arab waterway, Iraq's only outlet to the Persian Gulf. Iran had seized islands in the Persian Gulf in 1971, and there had been border clashes between the two states in middecade. Minorities issues also intruded. Both states, especially Iraq, have large Kurdish populations in their northern regions, while an Arab minority inhabits the oil-rich Iranian province of Khuzestan, and a majority Shia Muslim population in Iraq is concentrated in the south of that country.

Given circumstances, it was natural that the leaders of both states would seek to exploit any perceived weakness in the other. Thus, Iraqi president Saddam Hussein sought to take advantage of the upheaval following the fall of the shah and the establishment of Khomeini's Islamic fundamentalist regime. This had brought an end to U.S. military assistance to Iran, which meant a shortage of spare parts. Hussein saw an opportunity to punish Iran for its support of Kurdish and Shia opposition to Sunni Muslim domination in Iraq. More important, it was a chance for Iraq to secure both banks of the Shatt al-Arab as well as Khuzestan, acquire the islands of Abu Musa and the Greater and Lesser Tombs on behalf of the United Arab Emirates, and overthrow the militant Islamic regime in Iran.

On the eve of the war Iraq enjoyed an advantage in ground forces, while Iran had the edge in the air. Iraq had a regular army of some 300,000 men, 1,000 artillery pieces, 2,700 tanks, 332 fighter aircraft, and 40 helicopters. Iran had a regular army of 200,000 men, somewhat more than 1,000 artillery pieces, 1,740 tanks, 445 fighter aircraft, and 500 helicopters.

The Iraqi invasion on September 22, 1980, came as a complete surprise. Hussein justified it as a response to an alleged assassination attempt sponsored by Iran on Iraqi foreign minister Tariq Aziz. Striking on a 300-mile front, Iraqi troops were initially successful against the disorganized Iranian defenders. The Iraqis drove into southwestern Iran and secured the far side of the Shatt al-Arab. In November they captured Khorramshahr in Khuzestan Province and in places penetrated as much as 30 miles into Iran. But the Iraqis threw away the opportunity for a quick and decisive victory by their overly cautious advance. Another factor was certainly the rapid Iranian mobilization of resources, especially the largely untrained but fanatical Pasdaran (Revolutionary Guard Corps) militia.

Recovering from the initial shock of the invasion, the Iranians soon established strong defensive positions. Their navy also carried out an effective blockade of Iraq. Although on the first day of the war Iraqi aircraft destroyed much of the Iranian Air Force infrastructure, most of the Iranian aircraft survived, and Iraq lacked the long-range bombers to achieve strategic effectiveness against such a large country. Indeed, Iranian pilots flying U.S.-manufactured aircraft soon secured air superiority over the Iraqi Soviet-built aircraft, enabling the Iranians to carry out ground-support missions with both airplanes and helicopters.

Far from breaking Iranian morale as Hussein hoped, the Iraqi invasion rallied public opinion behind the Islamic regime. Ideologically committed Iranians flocked to join the army and Pasdaran. By March 1981 the war had settled into a protracted stalemate, with much of the ground combat resembling the trench warfare of World War I. During March 22–30, however, the Iranians launched a highly successful counteroffensive, driving the Iraqis back as much as 24 miles in places. The Iranians resumed their offensive during April 30–May 20, again pushing the Iraqis back, and on May 24 recaptured the city of Khorramshahr, securing there large quantities of Soviet-manufactured weapons. Flush with victory, the Iranians proclaimed as their war aim the overthrow of Hussein.

With the war now going badly, Hussein proposed a truce and the withdrawal of all Iraqi troops from Iranian soil. He also declared a unilateral cease-fire. Sensing victory, Iran rejected the proposal and reiterated its demand for Hussein's ouster.

With the Iranian rebuff, Hussein withdrew his forces back into well-prepared static defenses within Iraq, reasoning that Iraqis would rally to his regime in defense of their homeland. For political reasons, Hussein announced that purpose of the withdrawal was so Iraqi forces might assist Lebanon, which had been invaded by Israeli forces in June 1982.

Iranian leaders also rejected a Saudi Arabian–brokered deal that would have secured it $70 billion in war reparations by the Arab states to Iran and complete Iraqi withdrawal from Iranian territory in return for peace. Iranian leaders continued to insist on Hussein's removal and also insisted that some 100,000 Shiites expelled from Iraq before the war be permitted to return home and that the reparations figure be $150 billion. There is some suggestion that Iran did not expect these terms to be accepted and hoped to be able to continue the war with an invasion of Iraq. Indeed, Khomeini announced his intention to see the establishment of an Islamic republic in Iraq, presumably with the Iraqi Shiite majority in charge.

The Iranians sought to utilize their numerical advantage in a new offensive, although Hussein had managed to substantially increase the number of Iraqis under arms. Launched on July 20, 1982, the offensive was directed against Shiite-dominated southern Iraq, with the goal of capturing Basra, Iraq's second-largest city. Iranian human-wave assaults, prompted by a shortage of ammunition, encountered well-prepared Iraqi static defenses, supported by artillery. The Iraqis also employed poison gas. Hussein had managed, however, to substantially increase the number of Iraqis under arms.

Although the Iranians registered modest gains, these were at heavy human cost. Particularly hard-hit were the untrained and poorly armed units of boy-soldiers who volunteered to march into Iraqi minefields to clear them with their bodies for the trained Iranian soldiers to follow. On July 21, Iranian aircraft struck Baghdad. Iraq retaliated in August with attacks on the Iranian oil-shipping facilities at Khargh Island and also sank several ships.

During September–November the Iranians launched new offensives in the northern part of the front, securing some territory inside Iraq before Iraqi counterattacks drove the Iranians back into their own territory. In the southern part of the front in November, the Iranians advanced to within artillery range of the vital Baghdad-Basra highway.

Between February and August 1983, Iran launched five major offensives against Iraq. Before the first of these, however, beginning in early February the Iraqi Air Force carried out large-scale air attacks against Iranian coastal oil-production facilities, producing the largest oil spill in the history of the Persian Gulf region. In their first ground offensive of February, the Iranians hoped to take advantage of their greater troop strength to isolate Basra by cutting the Baghdad-Basra road at Kut al-Amara. Their drive was halted and then thrown back, with the Iraqis claiming to have destroyed upwards of 1,000 Iranian tanks. The later Iranian 1983 offensives included a drive into northern Iraq. These, however, registered scant gains, and both sides suffered heavy casualties.

Determined to prevent the spread of Islamic fundamentalism regimes in the Middle East, the Ronald Reagan administration in the United States made a firm commitment to support Iraq. Washington supplied Baghdad with intelligence information in the form of satellite photography and also provided economic aid and weapons.

Believing that more aggressive tactics were necessary to induce Iran to talk peace, Hussein announced that unless Iran agreed to halt offensive action against Iraq by February 7, 1984, he would order major attacks against 11 Iranian cities. Iran's answer was a ground attack in the northern part of the front, and Hussein then ordered the air and missile attacks against the cities to proceed. Iran then retaliated in what became known as the War of the Cities. There were five such air campaigns during the course of the war.

In February 1984 the Iranians launched the first in a series of ground offensives, in the central part of the front. It saw a quarter million men engaged on each side, with the Iranians attempting to take Kut al-Amara to cut the vital Baghdad-Basra road there. The Iranians came within 15 miles of the city but were then halted.

The Iranians enjoyed more success in a February–March drive against Basra, which almost broke through. The Iranians did capture part of the Majnun (Majnoon) Islands with their undeveloped oil fields, then held them against an Iraqi counterattack supported by poison gas. The Iranians occupied the islands until near the end of the war.

With his forces having benefited from substantial arms purchases financed by the oil-rich Gulf states, in January 1985 Hussein launched the first Iraqi ground offensive since 1980. It failed to register significant gains, and the Iranians responded with an offensive of their own in March. Now possessing better-trained troops, the Iranians eschewed the costly human-wave tactics of the past, and their more effective tactics brought the capture of a portion of the Baghdad-Basra road. Hussein responded to this emergency with chemical weapons and renewed air and missile strikes against 20 Iranian cities, including Tehran.

On February 17, 1986, in a surprise offensive employing commandos, Iranian forces captured the strategically important Iraqi port of al-Faw, southeast of Basra at the southeast end of the al-Faw Peninsula on the Shatt al-Arab waterway. In January 1987 Iran launched Operation KARBALA-5, a renewed effort to capture the city of Basra in southern Iraq. When it ground to a halt in mid-February, the Iranians launched Operation NASR-4 in northern Iraq, which threatened the Iraqi city of Kirkuk (May–June).

On March 7, 1987, the United States initiated Operation EARNEST WILL to protect oil tankers and shipping lanes in the Persian Gulf. The so-called Tanker War had begun in August 1982 with the Iraqi air attack on Kharg Island and nearby oil installations. Iran then retaliated with attacks, including the use of mines, against tankers carrying Iraqi oil from Kuwait as well as those of the Gulf states supporting Iraq. On November 1, 1986, Kuwait petitioned the international community to protect its tankers, whereupon the United States announced that it would provide protection for any U.S.-flagged tankers, with other tankers free to accompany them. These steps protected neutral tankers proceeding to or from Iraqi ports and ensured that Iraq would have the economic means to continue the war.

On the night of May 17, 1987, an Iraqi Mirage F-1 fighter on antiship patrol fired two Exocet antiship missiles at a radar contact, apparently not knowing that it was the U.S. Navy frigate *Stark*. Although only one of the missiles detonated, both struck home and badly crippled the frigate, killing 37 crewmen and injuring another 50. The crew managed to save the ship, which made port under its own power.

During February 1988, the Iraqis launched a renewed wave of attacks against Iranian population centers, and the Iranians reciprocated. The attacks included not only aircraft but also surface-to-surface missiles, principally the Soviet-built Scud type. Iraq fired many more missiles than did Iran (some 520 as opposed to 177). Also during February and extending into September, the Iraqi Army carried out a massacre of Kurds in northern Iraq. Known as the al-Anfal (Spoils of War) Campaign, it claimed as many as 300,000 civilian lives and destroyed some 4,000 villages.

On April 14, 1988, meanwhile, the U.S. Navy frigate *Samuel B. Roberts*, taking part in Operation EARNEST WILL, struck an Iranian mine in the Persian Gulf. No one was killed, but the ship nearly sank. On April 18, the U.S. Navy responded with Operation PRAYING MANTIS, its largest battle involving surface warships since World War II and the first surface-to-surface missile engagement in the navy's history. U.S. forces damaged two Iranian offshore oil platforms, sank one Iranian frigate and a gunboat, damaged another frigate, and sank three Iranian speedboats. The U.S. lost one helicopter.

By the spring of 1988, Iraqi forces were sufficiently regrouped to enable them to launch major operations. By contrast, Iran was now desperately short of spare parts, especially for its largely U.S.-built aircraft. The Iranians had also lost a large number of aircraft in combat. As a result, by late 1987 Iran was less able to mount an effective defense against the resupplied Iraqi Air Force, let alone carry out aerial counterattacks against a ground attack.

The Iraqis mounted four separate offensives. In the process they were able to recapture the strategically important al-Faw Peninsula lost in 1986, drive the Iranians away from Basra, and also make progress in the northern part of the front. The Iraqi victories came at little cost to themselves, while the Iranians suffered heavy personnel and equipment losses. These setbacks were the chief factor behind Khomeini's decision to agree to a cease-fire in 1988.

On July 3, 1988, the crew of the U.S. Navy cruiser *Vincennes*, patrolling in the Persian Gulf and believing that they were under attack by an Iranian jet fighter, shot down Iran Air Flight 655, a civilian airliner carrying 290 passengers and crew. There were no survivors. The U.S. government subsequently agreed to pay $131.8 million in compensation for the incident. It expressed regret only for the loss of innocent life and did not apologize to the Iranian government. This incident may have helped to convince Khomeini of the dangers of the United States actively entering the war, thus making him more amenable to ending it.

War weariness and pressure from other governments induced both sides to accept a cease-fire agreement on August 20, 1988, bringing the eight-year war to a close. Iran announced a death toll of nearly 300,000 of its citizens, but some analysts place this figure as high as 1 million or more.

The war ended with none of the outstanding issues resolved, as the UN-arranged cease-fire merely ended the fighting, leaving these two isolated states to pursue an arms race with each other and with the other states in the region. Negotiations between Iraq and Iran remained deadlocked for two years after the cease-fire. In 1990 Iraq, concerned with securing its forcible annexation of Kuwait, reestablished diplomatic relations with Iran and agreed to withdraw its troops from occupied Iranian territory, divide sovereignty over the Shatt al-Arab, and exchange prisoners of war. The war, while very costly to Iran, did serve to consolidate popular support behind the Islamic Revolution.

Khomeini died on June 3, 1989. His Islamic Religious Party continued to dominate the government bureaucracy and the policy-making apparatus. It also eliminated many political or religious rivals. Iranian president Akbar Hashemi Rafsanjani, who assumed office that August, pursued a pragmatic probusiness policy in an effort to rebuild the national economy without effecting any dramatic break in revolutionary ideology. In August 1997, moderate reformist Mohammad Khatami succeeded Rafsanjani as president. Khatami attempted, without success, to introduce democratic reforms.

According to the U.S. government, Iran in the 1980s was the single most important state sponsor of terrorism. Certainly Iran strongly supported the Palestinian struggle against Israel and criticized the United States for its blind support of the Jewish state. Iran also supported both Hamas in Gaza and Hezbollah in Lebanon. Hezbollah was founded by Shia clerics trained in Iraq, and Iran has provided it financial support, military training, and arms, greatly aiding Hezbollah in its efforts to confront Israel and gain political control in Lebanon.

The leaders of Iran have routinely stated that Israel must be destroyed. With Israel possessing nuclear weapon and having the most powerful military in the Middle East, any direct Iranian strike against the Jewish state would be suicidal, however. For their part, Israeli leaders have regularly argued that Israel might need to mount a preemptive strike against Iran's nuclear facilities in order to prevent it from acquiring nuclear weapons.

During the 1990s, U.S. president Bill Clinton attempted without success to pursue détente with Iran and sought to restore economic relations with that country. More recently, however, the United States accused Iran of being a key supporter of the insurgency in Iraq following the Anglo-American invasion of that nation in 2003.

In 2007 Washington grudgingly agreed to talks with Iranian officials, the first of their kind since the 1979 Iranian Revolution, this in an attempt to discuss key issues, including Iranian pilgrim traffic into Iraq and the alleged Iranian aid to anti-American elements in that country. A chief concern not only for Israel but also for its strongest ally, the United States, remains the threat of Iran acquiring nuclear weapons and the long-range missile technology needed to deliver them against Israel and Europe.

The 2005 presidential election brought conservative populist candidate Mahmoud Ahmadinejad to power. Reelected twice, he served from August 2005 to

August 2013. Ahmadinejad took a hard-line stance toward Israel and the United States and was an outspoken Holocaust denier. During the George W. Bush administration (2001–2009), Secretary of State Condoleezza Rice announced that the U.S. government would try to spur regime change in Iran through "soft approaches" and dedicated $74 million to that project. This, together with threats against Iran regarding its nuclear development program, tended to galvanize Iranian sentiment against external interference.

When Barack Obama became president of the United States in January 2009, he signaled a willingness to engage Iran diplomatically. At the same time, his government came under intense pressure from Israel and conservatives in the United States to force the Iranians' hands vis-à-vis their suspected nuclear weapons program. Between 2009 and 2013, the Obama administration worked diligently with the international community, including China and Russia, to impose tougher sanctions on Iran, which it was hoped would result in a softening of Iran's position regarding its nuclear program. The sanctions indeed hurt the Iranian economy and made Ahmadinejad, Iran's hard-line and controversial president, increasingly unpopular among many Iranians.

In June 2013, Hassan Rouhani was elected as Ahmadinejad's successor. Rouhani, who is considerably more moderate than his predecessor, vowed to improve relations with the West and signaled his determination to enter into serious multilateral talks in order to resolve the issue of his nation's nuclear program. On September 13, 2013, Rouhani spoke directly with Obama via telephone, making it the highest-level exchange between Iranian and American leaders since the 1979 Iranian Revolution. Meanwhile, nuclear talks continued, and by year's end a preliminary framework for an eventual agreement had been reached.

Finally, after 2 additional years of grueling negotiations between Iran and leading Western powers, including Russia, a historic accord was achieved on July 14, 2015. The agreement, which was widely criticized in Israel and among Republican politicians in the United States, placed stringent controls on Iran's nuclear activities, which were designed to keep the country at least 1 year away from producing a nuclear bomb. It did so by cutting the number of Iranian centrifuges by two-thirds and by placing strict caps on uranium enrichment and uranium stockpiles for at least 15 years. The agreement also subjected Iran's nuclear facilities to regular inspections and verification by UN weapons inspectors. Iran, in turn, saw significant frozen funds freed and economic sanctions lifted after compliance with the deal was verified.

The development of long-range missiles by Iran that would be capable of striking Israel and even Europe continues to be a concern. In April 2016, Iran announced that the Russian government had begun shipping to Iran SD-300 surface-to-air missiles. This came in spite of strong objections from the United States, Israel, and Saudi Arabia. The $800 million contract, signed in 2007, had been frozen by Russia in 2010 because of the international sanctions but was unfrozen by Russian president Vladimir Putin in 2015 even before sanctions were lifted. Israel and the United States fear that the missiles could be used to protect Iranian nuclear sites from air strikes. Reportedly the S-300 has a speed of five times that of sound and a range of some 150 miles and can shoot down any medium-range missile in the world today.

Iran would seem to be at a crossroads. As the West had hoped, Iranian moderates backing President Rouhani made substantial gains in the spring 2016 parliamentary elections but failed to achieve a majority. The apparent yearning of younger well-educated Iranians for a more open, tolerant, and democratic society, with closer ties with the West, has not weakened the hold of the clerics on the instruments of state power. Iran also continues to be, along with Russia, the chief support of the regime of President Bashar al-Assad in Syria and also supplies weapons and financial assistance to Hezbollah in Syria and actively supports the Shiite Houthi rebels in Yemen. Iran is also very much involved in seeking to influence policies of the Shiite-dominated Iraqi government. Indeed, the Sunni-Shiite confrontation between Iran and Saudi Arabia has, if anything, intensified in the last few years. An attack by Iranians on the Saudi embassy in Tehran that followed the execution by Saudi Arabia of a prominent Shiite cleric accused by the Saudi government of treason in January 2016 led Saudi Arabia to break diplomatic ties with Iran.

Timeline

651	By this date Rashidun Arabs conquer Persia and convert it to Islam.
1501–1736	The Safavid dynasty rules Persia, during which the Twelver school of Shia Islam becomes the official religion.
1736–1747	The reign of Persian emperor Nader Shah, during which Persia is arguably the world's most powerful empire.
1800s	Persia comes under increasing pressure from both imperial Russia and Great Britain and suffers the loss of significant territory in the Caucasus.
1905–1907	The Constitutional Revolution of 1905–1907, during which Mozzafar-al-Din Shah (r. 1896–1907) is forced to create a limited constitutional monarchy.
Oct 1906	The first Persian parliament, the Majlis, convenes.
1907	With Persia weak under young Ahmad Qajar Shah (1909–1925), an Anglo-Russian convention divides the country into spheres of influence: Russian controls the north and center, while British controls the southeast, and there is a neutral zone between the two.
1908	Oil is discovered in Persia.
1909	The Anglo-Persian Oil Company, later the Anglo-Iranian Oil Company (AIOC), is established.

1914–1918	Although officially neutral during World War I, Persia becomes a battleground for the Ottomans, Germans, Russians, and British. There is considerable pro-German sentiment in the Majlis, and German agents instigate some tribal revolts, but by late 1917 the British regain control of southern Persia.
Nov 1917	With the Bolshevik Revolution in Russia, Russian forces are withdrawn, and the British secure control of most of Persia. They now have a considerable economic stake in the country.
Jan 14, 1921	With a force of the self-proclaimed Persian Soviet Socialist Republic, reinforced by elements of the Russian Bolshevik Red Army, preparing to march on Tehran, British general Edmund Ironside, commanding Allied troops in Persia, selects Reza Khan to command the Cossack Brigade, the major Persian military formation.
Feb 21, 1921	With British support and having led his men to Tehran, Reza Khan stages a relatively bloodless coup d'état and by the next year has pacified all of Persia.
Oct 28, 1923	Reza Khan becomes prime minister of Iran, serving in this post until November 1, 1925.
Dec 15, 1923	Reza Khan establishes the Pahlavi dynasty, with himself as Reza Shah Pahlavi I, and proceeds to lay the foundations of the modern Iranian state.
Jun 1935	Reza Shah changes the country's name from Persia to Iran.
Jun 22, 1939	With the beginning of World War II, Reza Shah proclaims Iranian neutrality, but after the Germans invade the Soviet Union on this date, the involvement of Iran is inevitable. The Allies seek to protect the British-controlled oil fields in Khuzestan and utilize the newly built Trans-Iranian Railroad to transport military supplies to the Soviet Union, but Reza Shah rejects this on the grounds of Iranian neutrality.
Aug 25, 1941	Soviet forces invade Iran from the northwest, and the British do the same from Iraq. Iranian military resistance is quickly crushed, and Iran is again divided into spheres of influence along the lines of the Anglo-Russian Convention of 1907.
Sep 16, 1941	Reza Shah is forced to abdicate and is sent into exile. His 22-year-old son, Mohammad Reza, becomes shah.
1942	A poor harvest brings widespread famine.
Jan 29, 1942	Iran, the Soviet Union, and Great Britain sign the Tripartite Treaty of Alliance by which the British and Soviets promise to respect Iranian territorial integrity, sovereignty, and political independence;

safeguard the Iranian economy from the effects of the war; and withdraw from Iranian territory within six months of the end of hostilities. Iran then severs relations with the Axis powers and expels their nationals.

Sep 9, 1943	Iran declares war on Germany.
Nov 28–Dec 1, 1943	U.S. president Franklin D. Roosevelt, British prime minister Winston L. S. Churchill, and Soviet leader Joseph Stalin meet in Tehran in one of the most important conferences of the war. The three leaders pledge economic assistance to Iran and promise to address its problems after the war. Despite this, the Soviet Union and Britain revive their long-standing rivalry for influence in Iran. The Soviets close their zone of occupation to free entry and support leftist trade unions and the Communist Party, along with separatist leftist movements in Iranian Kurdistan and Azerbaijan. In southern Iran, meanwhile, the British favor conservative elements supporting the monarchy.
Apr 28, 1951	Reformer and nationalist politician Mohammad Mosaddegh becomes prime minister and soon clashes with the shah.
May 1, 1951	Mosaddegh secures nationalization of the AIOC by the Majlis. Britain then embargoes Iranian oil and blocks the export of products from the former British properties, causing considerable financial hardship in Iran.
Jul 16, 1952	Mosaddegh insists on the right of the prime minister to name the minister of war and the chief of staff of the army. When the shah refuses, Mosaddegh resigns, creating a political crisis.
Jul 21, 1852	The shah gives way and reappoints Mosaddegh, who then consolidates his power, introducing land reform and other reform measures.
Aug 19, 1953	Seeing Mosaddegh as a communist, the United States joins Britain and the temporarily exiled shah in Operation TPAJAX (the "TP" standing for "Tudeh Party"), a successful coup this date that overthrows Mosaddegh and restores the temporarily exiled shah to power on August 22.
1957	Assisted by the Israeli government, the shah establishes the Sazeman-e Ettelaat va Amniyat-e Keshvar (National Information and Security Organization, SAVAK), a secret police force.
1963	A national referendum overwhelmingly approves the shah's so-called White Revolution, an ambitious economic reform program that is urged by the U.S. government but largely proves to be a failure.

Nov 4, 1964   Ayatollah Ruhollah Khomeini, a conservative Muslim cleric and the shah's most prominent opponent, is sent into exile. He will be abroad for the next 14 years, first in Najif, Iraq, and then in a Paris suburb.

Jan 7, 1978   With the failure of the White Revolution, opposition to the shah's rule grows. On this date an article critical of Khomeini appears in a Tehran newspaper and brings out Khomeini supporters and regime opponents. Rioting ensues, but the shah shrinks from force. His failure to quell the riots emboldens his opponents, and a pattern emerges of demonstrations, martyrs, and memorial demonstrations. SAVAK minimizes the real threat to the regime, and the shah rejects force until it is too late, losing control of the situation following a massive general strike in the autumn.

Jan 16, 1979   The shah announces that he is going abroad on a short holiday and flees from Tehran. He never returns and dies in Cairo of cancer on July 27, 1980.

Feb 1, 1979   Khomeini returns from exile and sets about erecting an Islamic state. The moderate secular politicians heading the transition government give him full support in the mistaken belief that he is a mere figurehead who will cede power. Iranian military leaders meanwhile announce that the military will remain neutral, avoiding possible prosecution by local Islamic Revolutionary Committees that are enforcing Islamic values and laws and rounding up former senior officials for trial and execution.

Mar 30–31,   A 97 percent vote in a national referendum approves Khomeini's
1979   decision to establish an Islamic republic. Khomeini creates a separate paramilitary force, the Revolutionary Guard Corps, which serves as a secret police.

Apr 1, 1979   Establishment of the Islamic Republic of Iran. A new constitution confirms Khomeini and his successors as supreme leaders of the government, with the right to appoint the heads of the armed forces, the head of the Revolutionary Guard Corps, and much of the government. Khomeini soon forces from power relative moderates such as Mehdi Bazargan and Abolhasan Bani-Sadr, the first prime minister and president, respectively.

Nov 4, 1979   Angered by U.S. president Jimmy Carter's decision to allow the former shah to undergo cancer treatments in the United States, Iranian students storm the U.S. embassy in Tehran and seize 53 American diplomatic personnel as hostages. Khomeini supports the students and their demands that the United States turn over the shah for trial in exchange for releasing the hostages.

Apr 24, 1980   Under the press of public opinion to do something to secure the return of the U.S. hostages held by Iran, President Carter authorizes Operation EAGLE CLAW. The mission is aborted but nonetheless claims the lives of eight U.S. servicemen and wounds four others. This failure and the fact that the hostages are not released may well have cost Carter reelection.

Sep 22, 1980   Iraqi forces invade Iran, beginning the long and costly Iran-Iraq War (1980–1988). A long-standing rivalry between these two nations is abetted by the collision between the Pan-Islamism and revolutionary Shia Islamism of Iran and the Pan-Arab nationalism of Iraq. Iraqi president Saddam Hussein seeks to take advantage of the upheaval following the fall of the shah and the establishment of Khomeini's Islamic fundamentalist regime.

The Iraqi attack comes as a complete surprise. Iraqi forces are initially successful, penetrating up to 30 miles into Iran, but they throw away the chance for a quick, decisive victory by their overly cautious advance. Another factor is certainly the rapid Iranian mobilization of resources, especially the largely untrained but fanatical Pasdaran (Revolutionary Guard Corps) militia.

Far from breaking Iranian morale as Hussein hoped, the Iraqi invasion rallies public opinion behind the Islamic regime.

Jan 20, 1981   Iran releases the American hostages, and also on this date Ronald Reagan is inaugurated as president.

Mar 22–30 1981   The war having settled into stalemate with ground combat resembling that of World War I, the Iranians launch a highly successful counteroffensive.

Apr 30–May 20, 1981   The Iranians renew their offensive.

May 24, 1981   The Iranians recapture the city of Khorramshahr, lost early in the war, securing there large quantities of weapons. Flush with victory, the Iranians proclaim as their war aim the overthrow of Hussein. They reject Hussein's call for a truce and pledge to withdraw Iraqi troops from Iranian soil. Indeed, Khomeini announces his intention to see the establishment of an Iraqi Islamic republic, presumably with the Iraqi Shiite majority in charge.

Jul 20, 1982   The Iranians launch a new offensive in southern Iraq with the goal of capturing Basra, Iraq's second-largest city. The Iraqis blunt the attack with artillery and poison gas.

Jul 21, 1982   Iranian aircraft attack Baghdad.

Aug 1982	Iraqi aircraft attack Iranian oil-shipping facilities at Khargh Island and sink several ships.
Sep–Nov 1982	The Iranians launch new offensives in the northern part of the front, securing some territory inside Iraq, but then are driven back. In November the Iranians advance to within artillery range of the vital Baghdad-Basra highway.
Early Feb 1983	The Iraqis carry out large-scale air attacks against Iranian coastal oil-production facilities, producing the largest oil spill in the history of the Persian Gulf region.
Feb–Aug 1983	Iran launches five major offensives against Iraq. Iran's effort to isolate Basra by cutting the Baghdad-Basra road at Kut al-Amara fails at high cost, however. The later Iranian offensives include a drive into northern Iraq. These secure scant gains at high cost to both sides.
Feb–Mar 1984	An Iranian effort to take Kut al-Amara and cut the vital Baghdad-Basra road there fails. A March drive against Basra almost succeeds, and the Iranians capture part of the Majnun (Majnoon) Islands with undeveloped oil fields and holds them until near the end of the war.
Feb 7, 1984	With Hussein having announced that unless Iran halts all offensive action by this date he would order major attacks against 11 Iranian cities, Iran answers with an offensive, and Hussein orders the air and missile attacks against the cities to proceed. Iran retaliates in what becomes known as the War of the Cities. There are five such air campaigns in the course of the war.
Jan 1985	Hussein launches the first Iraqi ground offensive since 1980. It fails to achieve significant gains.
Mar 1985	The Iranians launch a new offensive, capturing a portion of the Baghdad-Basra road. Hussein responds to this emergency with chemical weapons and renewed air and missile strikes against 20 Iranian cities, including Tehran.
Feb 17, 1986	In a surprise offensive, Iranian forces capture the strategically important Iraqi port of al-Faw, on the Shatt al-Arab waterway.
Jan 1987	Iran launches another effort to capture Basra, but this comes to a halt in February.
Mar 7, 1987	The United States, now siding with Iraq in the war, initiates Operation EARNEST WILL to protect oil tankers and shipping lanes in the Persian Gulf. The so-called Tanker War had begun in March 1984 with the Iraqi air attack on Kharg Island and nearby oil installations. Iran then retaliated with attacks, including the use of

mines, against tankers carrying Iraqi oil from Kuwait and those of the Gulf states supporting Iraq. The U.S. move helps ensure that Iraq will have the economic means to continue the war.

May–Jun 1987   The Iranians launch a drive in northern Iraq, attempting to take Kirkuk.

May 17, 1987   An Iraqi Mirage F-1 fighter on antiship patrol fires two Exocet antiship missiles at a radar contact, apparently not knowing it was the U.S. Navy frigate *Stark*. Although only one of the missiles detonates, both strike home and badly cripple the frigate, killing 37 crewmen and injuring another 50. The crew manages to save their ship, which makes port under its own power.

Feb 1988   The Iraqis launch new attacks against Iranian population centers, and the Iranians reciprocate. The attacks include aircraft and surface-to-surface missiles.

Spring 1988   Reequipped and regrouped Iraqi forces launch four separate offensives. Iran is now short of spare parts, especially for its U.S.-built aircraft, and is thus less able to counter the Iraqi drives. The Iraqis recapture the strategically important al-Faw Peninsula and drive the Iranians away from Basra and also make progress in the northern part of the front. These setbacks are the chief factor behind Khomeini's decision to agree to a cease-fire in 1988.

Apr 14, 1988   The U.S. Navy frigate *Samuel B. Roberts,* assigned to Operation EARNEST WILL, strikes an Iranian mine in the Persian Gulf. No one is killed, but the ship nearly sinks.

Apr 18, 1988   The U.S. Navy responds with Operation PRAYING MANTIS, its largest battle involving surface warships since World War II and the first surface-to-surface missile engagement in the navy's history. U.S. forces damage two Iranian offshore oil platforms, sink an Iranian frigate and a gunboat, damage another frigate, and sink three Iranian speedboats. The U.S. loses one helicopter.

Jul 3, 1988   In the Persian Gulf, the crew of the U.S. Navy cruiser *Vincennes,* believing that they are under attack by an Iranian jet fighter, shoot down Iran Air Flight 655, a civilian airliner carrying 290 passengers and crew. There are no survivors. The U.S. government subsequently pays $131.8 million in compensation. The incident may, however, have helped convince Khomeini of the possibility of the United States actively entering the war and thus helped make him more amenable to ending it.

Aug 20, 1988   A cease-fire agreement brokered by the United Nations (UN) brings the war to an end but resolves none of the outstanding issues. Iran puts the number of dead on its side in the war at nearly

300,000, but some place this figure as at high as 1 million or more.

The cease-fire merely ends the fighting. Negotiations between Iraq and Iran remain deadlocked until 1990, when Hussein, concerned with securing the annexation of Kuwait, reestablishes diplomatic relations with Iran and agrees to withdraw its troops from occupied Iranian territory, divide sovereignty over the Shatt al-Arab, and exchange prisoners of war. The war, while very costly to Iran, does consolidate popular support behind the Islamic Revolution.

Jun 3, 1989   Khomeini dies. His Islamic Religious Party continues to dominate the government bureaucracy and policy-making apparatus, however.

Aug 3, 1989   Akbar Hashemi Rafsanjani becomes president of Iran and pursues a pragmatic probusiness policy in an effort to rebuild the national economy, but there is no dramatic break in revolutionary ideology. Iran continues to support Islamic groups pitted against unfriendly regimes, earning it the characterization by the U.S. government of the single most important state sponsor of terrorism. This includes Hamas in Gaza and Hezbollah in Lebanon. Succeeding decades add aid to President Bashar al-Assad in the Syrian Civil War (2011–) and the Houthi rebels in Yemen (2015–). Israel and the United States remain constant targets of bellicose statements, and Iran seeks to supplant U.S. influence with the majority Shia government in Iraq.

Aug 3, 1997   Moderate reformist Mohammad Khatami succeeds Rafsanjani as president. Khatami fails in his effort to introduce democratic reforms.

Aug 3, 2005   Conservative populist candidate Mahmoud Ahmadinejad becomes president and takes a hard-line position regarding Israel. Elected twice, he will be president until August 3, 2013.

2007   Washington agrees to talks with Iranian officials, the first of their kind since the 1979 Iranian Revolution, in an attempt to discuss key issues, including Iranian intervention in Iraq, but a chief concern is the perceived effort by Iran to acquire nuclear weapons and missile technology, a threat most felt by Israel.

Jan 2009   Barack Obama becomes U.S. president and signals a willingness to engage Iran diplomatically. The Obama administration works tirelessly to impose tougher international sanctions on Iran, which it hopes will bring Iran to the bargaining table regarding its nuclear program. The sanctions imposed indeed hurt the Iranian economy and cause Ahmadinejad to become increasingly unpopular with many Iranians.

| Aug 3, 2013 | Hassan Rouhani takes office as Iranian president. Much more moderate than his predecessor, he vows to improve relations with the West and signals his determination to enter into serious multilateral talks in order to resolve the issue of his nation's nuclear program. |

Aug 3, 2013   Hassan Rouhani takes office as Iranian president. Much more moderate than his predecessor, he vows to improve relations with the West and signals his determination to enter into serious multilateral talks in order to resolve the issue of his nation's nuclear program.

Sep 13, 2013   Rouhani speaks directly with Obama via telephone, making it the highest-level exchange between Iranian and American leaders since the 1979 Iranian Revolution. Meanwhile, nuclear talks continue, and by year's end a preliminary framework for an eventual agreement is reached.

Jul 14, 2015   Following lengthy grueling negotiations between Iran and leading Western powers, including Russia, a historic accord is signed. Although widely criticized in Israel and among Republican politicians in the United States, it places stringent controls on Iran's nuclear activities, designed to keep Iran at least one year away from producing a nuclear bomb. The agreement also subjects Iran's nuclear facilities to regular inspections and verification by UN weapons inspectors. Iran, in turn, sees considerable frozen funds freed and economic sanctions lifted after compliance with the deal is verified.

Apr 2016   Over the strong objections of Israel, Saudi Arabia, and the United States, the Russian government ships to Iran SD-300 surface-to-air missiles. A contract, signed in 2007, had been frozen by Russia in 2010 because of the international sanctions but was unfrozen by President Vladimir Putin in 2015 even before sanctions were lifted. Israel and the United States fear that the missiles may be used to protect Iranian nuclear sites from air strikes. Reportedly, the S-300 can shoot down any medium-range missile currently in service. Meanwhile, Iran continues to test longer-range missiles.

Further Reading

Abrahamian, Ervand. *A History of Modern Iran.* Cambridge: Cambridge University Press, 2008.

Ahmad, Ishtiag. *Anglo-Iranian Relations, 1905–1919.* New York: Asia Publishing House, 1974.

Ansari, Ali. *A History of Modern Iran since 1921: The Pahlavis and After.* Boston: Longman, 2003.

Cordesman, Anthony H., and Abraham R. Wagner. *The Lessons of Modern War: The Iran-Iraq War,* Vol. 2. Boulder, CO: Westview, 1990.

Draper, Theodore. *A Very Thin Line: The Iran-Contra Affairs.* New York: Hill and Wang, 1991.

Jordan, Hamilton. *Crisis: The Last Year of the Carter Presidency.* New York: Putnam, 1982.

Karsh, Ifraim. *The Iran-Iraq War, 1980–1988.* Oxford, UK: Osprey, 2002.

Katouzian, Homa. *The Persians: Ancient, Medieval, and Modern Iran.* New Haven, CT: Yale University Press, 2010.

Lenczowski, George. *Russia and the West in Iran, 1918–1948: A Study in Big-Power Rivalry.* Ithaca, NY: Cornell University Press, 1949.

Majd, Mohammad Gholi. *Persia in World War I and Its Conquest by Great Britain.* Lanham, MD: University Press of America, 2003.

Marr, Phebe. *The Modern History of Iraq.* 2nd ed. Boulder, CO: Westview, 2004.

Olson, William J. *Anglo-Iranian Relations during World War I.* London: Cass, 1984.

Palmer, Michael A. *Guardians of the Gulf: A History of America's Expanding Role in the Persian Gulf, 1833–1992.* New York: Free Press, 1992.

Rajaee, Farhang. *The Iran-Iraq War: The Politics of Aggression.* Gainesville: University Press of Florida, 1993.

Ramazani, Rouhollah K. *The Foreign Policy of Iran: A Developing Nation in World Affairs, 1500–1941.* Charlottesville: University Press of Virginia, 1966.

Ramazani, Rouhollah K. *Iran's Foreign Policy, 1941–1973: A Study of Foreign Policy in Modernizing Nations.* Charlottesville: University Press of Virginia, 1975.

Ryan, Paul. *The Iranian Rescue Mission.* Annapolis, MD: Naval Institute Press, 1985.

Saikal, Amin. *The Rise and Fall of the Shah.* Princeton, NJ: Princeton University Press, 1980.

Wilber, Donald N. *Iran: Past and Present.* Princeton, NJ: Princeton University Press, 1955.

Willet, Edward C. *The Iran-Iraq War.* New York: Rosen Publishing Group, 2004.

Wise, Harold L. *Inside the Danger Zone: The U.S. Military in the Persian Gulf, 1987–1988.* Annapolis, MD: Naval Institute Press, 2007.

Wright, Robin. *In the Name of God: The Khomeini Decade.* New York: Simon and Schuster, 1989.

IRAQ

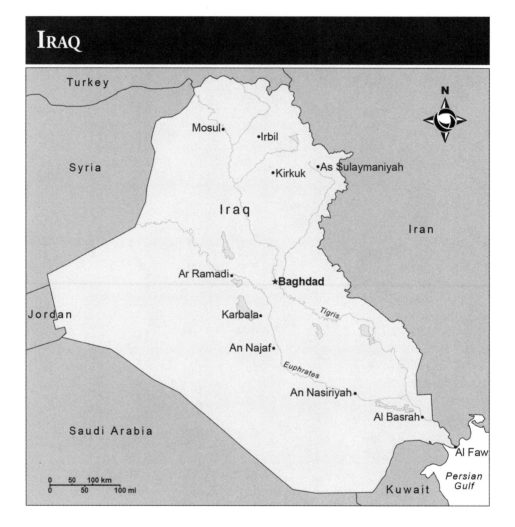

Turkey

Syria

Mosul•

•Irbil

•Kirkuk

•As Sulaymaniyah

Iraq

Iran

Ar Ramadi•

★**Baghdad**

Jordan

Karbala•

Tigris

An Najaf•

Euphrates

An Nasiriyah•

Al Basrah•

Saudi Arabia

Al Faw

Persian
Gulf

Kuwait

| 0 | 50 | 100 km |
| 0 | 50 | 100 mi |

Iraq

*Louis A. DiMarco, Jack Vahram Kalpakian,
Adam B. Lowther, Gregory Wayne Morgan,
Paul G. Pierpaoli Jr., and Spencer C. Tucker*

The Republic of Iraq encompasses 169,234 square miles. Slightly smaller in size than the U.S. state of California, Iraq is the third-largest state in the Middle East behind only Saudi Arabia and Iran. Iraq is bordered by Saudi Arabia on the west and south, Kuwait and the Persian Gulf (for 36 miles) to the south, Iran to the east, and Syria and Turkey to the north. Because of its size, oil wealth, and strategic location, Iraq has played a key regional role.

Iraq's 2016 population was some 37.548 million. Baghdad is the capital and largest city. Arabs constitute 75–80 percent of the population, while 15 percent are Kurds. Assyrians, Turkmen, and much smaller minorities such as Mandeans, Armenians, Circassians, Iranians, Shabakis, Yazidis, and Kawliyas constitute 5–10 percent. Around 95 percent of the population is Muslim. Although Sunnis dominated the Iraqi power structure in the second half of the 20th century, Shiites, concentrated in southern Iraq, constitute as much as 65 percent of Iraqi Muslims. Christianity, Yarsanism, Yezidism, and Mandeanism are also present.

Known as the "Cradle of Civilization," Iraq occupies Mesopotamia, the historic fertile "land between the rivers," referring to the Tigris and Euphrates Rivers, that saw the world's oldest civilization, the Sumerian, about 4,000 BCE. Sumeria introduced the first writing system and thus recorded history. The Babylonian and Assyrian Empires that followed projected their power as far as the Caucasus, Persia, Egypt, and Arabia. In the sixth century BCE, Cyrus the Great of Persia defeated the Neo-Babylonian Empire. In the fourth century BCE, it was Alexander the Great's turn. The Parthians conquered the region in the second century BCE. The Romans then took control. The Sassanid Persians absorbed the region in 224 CE, and for the next four centuries today's Iraq was a Persian province.

The Arabs conquered Mesopotamia during 633–644 and established Islam as the predominant religion. The move of the Abbasid Empire's capital in 750 from Damascus to Baghdad gave Iraq renewed prominence. By the ninth century, Baghdad was an economic and cultural center for the entire Muslim world.

Iraq fell under Black Sheep Turkmen rule in the 14th and 15th centuries, but in 1466 the White Sheep Turkmen defeated their rivals and assumed control. In 1533 Iraq came under rule by the Ottoman Turks, although there were periods of Persian hegemony, and in 1747 Iraq was ruled by the Mamluks. In 1831, however, the Ottomans overthrew the Mamluks and assumed direct rule.

During World War I the Ottoman Empire declared for the Central Powers. The Allied victory in the war saw Britain as master of the former Ottoman provinces of Mosul, Baghdad, and Basra, which form modern-day Iraq, and on April 28, 1920, the San Remo Agreement awarded Iraq to Britain as a League of Nations mandate.

British ally Faisal bin Hussein bin Ali al-Hashimi of the Hashemite dynasty had led the Arab Revolt against the Ottomans in World War I and been proclaimed king of Syria by the Syrian National Congress in Damascus in March 1920. Syria had been assigned to the French, however, and a French army drove him out in July. The British then promised Faisal Iraq as a new kingdom. During May–October 1920, however, the British were obliged to put down a revolt in Iraq against their rule, which they accomplished largely through Royal Air Force bombers.

On August 23, 1921, the British formally installed Faisal as king of Iraq. The Anglo-Iraqi Treaty of October 10, 1922, granted Iraq independence but left Britain in control of foreign and military affairs. Faisal was king until his death, probably through poisoning, on September 8, 1933.

Iraq's strategic importance was greatly enhanced by the discovery of oil in 1925. Although the British formally granted Iraq its independence on October 3, 1932, they retained considerable influence. The treaty protected British oil interests and granted Britain military bases. Faisal attempted to build a unified nation, but Iraq, like so much else of the Middle East, was an arbitrary creation and was badly fractured between Sunnis and Shias; among Arabs, Kurds, and Turkman; and between urban and rural attitudes.

In December 1938, pro-British general Nuri al-Said became prime minister. Instability increased when King Ghazi I died in an accident on April 4, 1939. With the new king Faisal II being only four years old, his uncle Abdul Illah became regent. Nuri put down an attempted army coup in March 1939 and another in February 1940. Nuri wanted to declare war on Germany but encountered opposition from Iraqi nationalists, who insisted on concessions from Britain first. In consequence, Nuri declared Iraq's neutrality, severing relations with Germany but not those with Italy.

Axis successes in the Mediterranean beginning in the fall of 1940 encouraged Iraqi nationalists, who saw circumstances favorable to ending remaining British control. In March 1940 Rashid Ali Rashid Ali al-Gaylani replaced Nuri and came under the influence of four nationalist pro-Axis generals who called themselves the "Golden Square." In May 1941, however, the regent forced Gaylani to resign because of the latter's pro-Axis connections. Taha al-Hashimi became prime minister.

Axis military successes and hints of aid emboldened the Golden Square, who staged a coup on April 2 and restored Gaylani to power. He immediately formed a cabinet with men of Axis inclinations. The regent and Nuri both fled.

Iraq was now a major oil producer (2.5 million metric tons in 1940), and were it to side with the Axis, its location on the Persian Gulf would also have enabled Germany to threaten the British lifeline to India. Encouraged by hints of Axis aid, on May 2, 1941, Iraqi troops opened artillery fire on the British air base at Habbaniya. The Royal Air Force immediately went into action, and Britain also dispatched some 5,800 troops, including the 1,500-man Arab Legion from

Transjordan. It was clear that without immediate Axis assistance the British would triumph.

The German government brought pressure to bear on Vichy France, which allowed Axis aid to transit through Syria to Mosul, albeit it in insufficient quantities to affect the outcome. British forces broke the siege at Habbaniya, occupied Falluja, and surrounded Baghdad by the end of May. Gaylani and some supporters then fled to Iran. In deference to Nuri and Regent Abdul Illah, the British did not enter Baghdad, a decision that allowed the remnants of the Golden Square to attack Baghdad's Jewish community and kill some 150 Jews.

Again prime minister, Nuri set up a pro-British administration, and Iraq became an important supply center for Allied assistance to the Soviet Union. Iraq declared war on the Axis on January 16, 1943.

Israel's declaration of independence on May 14, 1948, brought declarations of war from the Arab states. Iraq provided some 18,000 troops to the Arab side in the Israeli War of Independence (1948–1949). Arab military failure in the war brought persecution of Iraqi Jews, whose loyalty was suspect, a process repeated during subsequent Arab-Israeli wars.

In 1955 Iraq joined the pro-Western Baghdad Pact, allying itself with Turkey, Iran, and Pakistan in a mutual defense agreement sponsored by the United States, which, however, was not a member. The pact was a direct affront to the long-simmering nationalist sentiments within the Iraqi Army. Indeed, the pact became the catalyst that ignited revolution in 1958, the first in a string of coups and countercoups plaguing Iraq until the Baathists finally consolidated power in 1968.

On July 14, 1958, members of the secret nationalist organization known as the Free Officers Movement, led by Colonel Abd al-Karim Qasim, seized control of Baghdad and executed both Faisal II and Nuri. The revolutionaries then abolished the monarchy, proclaimed Iraq a republic, and sought closer ties to the Soviet Union. Qasim became prime minister, but his policies ultimately brought internal conflict. In the Ramadan Revolution of February 9, 1963, a coalition of anticommunist military officers and secular Arab nationalists and Baathists in Baghdad overthrew Qasim, who was slain.

Colonel Abdul Salam Arif became president, with Hasan al-Bakr as prime minister. But members of the National Council of the Revolutionary Command who had taken the reins of power soon turned against one another. The military and the Baath Party were fundamentally at odds regarding policy. President Arif died in a helicopter crash on April 13, 1966, perhaps the result of sabotage by Baathist elements in the military. His more pliable brother, Abdul Rahman Arif, took over and was president until 1968.

Iraq's failure to support fellow Arab states in the Six-Day War (June 5–10, 1967) led to widespread rioting in Baghdad. Then on July 17, 1968, members of the Baath Party seized key locations in Baghdad. Ahmed Hasan al-Bakr became president, prime minister, and secretary-general of the Revolutionary Command Council. His cousin Saddam Hussein worked to eliminate opponents of the new regime. Hussein proved to be an adroit though ruthless operator, and his patronage system broke down the historic bonds in Iraqi society.

The new Baathist regime did institute numerous needed reforms. These included agricultural investment, land reform, the renegotiation of oil contracts, and hospital and school construction. All were designed to bring all of the country into the regime's broader network of patronage. With corruption widespread, most economic reforms were unsuccessful. From 1973 onward Iraq was largely dependent on oil revenues. Iraq played only a minor role in the Yom Kippur War (Ramadan War) of October 1973, with an armored division assisting the Syrians on the Golan Heights front. On July 16, 1979, al-Bakr left office, ostensibly for reasons of health. Hussein was now president, ruler of Iraq in name and fact.

Early in 1979 Iran underwent a revolution that led to an Islamic Republic under Khomeini. The long-standing rivalry between Iran and Iraq for regional hegemony was abetted by border disputes and a collision between the Pan-Islamism of Iran and the Pan-Arab nationalism of Iraq. In many ways, however, the ensuing clash was a continuation of the ancient Persian-Arab rivalry, fueled by 20th-century border disputes and competition for hegemony in the Persian Gulf region and the Middle East.

The border had been contested for some time, and in 1969 Iran had abrogated its treaty with Iraq on the navigation of the Shatt al-Arab waterway, Iraq's only outlet to the Persian Gulf. Iran had seized Persian Gulf islands in 1971, and there were border clashes between the two states in middecade. Minorities' issues also intruded. Both states, especially Iraq, have large Kurdish populations in their northern regions, while an Arab minority inhabits the oil-rich Iranian province of Khuzestan, and the Shia Muslim majority population of Iraq is concentrated in the south of that country.

Hussein sought to take advantage of the upheaval following the establishment of Khomeini's Islamic fundamentalist regime, which had ended U.S. military assistance to Iran, meaning a shortage of spare parts. In deciding to go to war with Iran, Hussein sought to secure both banks of the Shatt al-Arab and Khuzestan Province, acquire islands on behalf of the United Arab Emirates, and overthrow Iran's Islamic regime. On the eve of war Iraq enjoyed an advantage in ground forces, while Iran had the edge in the air.

The Iraqi invasion on September 22, 1980, caught Iran by surprise. Hussein justified it as a response to an alleged assassination attempt sponsored by Iran on Iraqi foreign minister Tariq Aziz. Striking on a broad front, the Iraqis enjoyed initial success. They secured the far side of the Shatt al-Arab and in November captured Khorramshahr in Khuzestan. But Hussein threw away the chance for a quick, decisive victory by an overly cautious advance, while Iran rapidly mobilized its resources.

The Iranians soon established a strong defense, while their navy also carried out an effective blockade of Iraq. Far from breaking Iranian morale, the invasion rallied public opinion behind the Islamic regime, and by March 1981 the war had become a protracted stalemate greatly resembling the trench warfare of World War I.

An Iranian offensive in March 1981 drove the Iraqis back, and on May 24 they recaptured Khorramshahr. Hussein then proposed a truce and an Iraqi withdrawal from Iranian territory. He also declared a unilateral cease-fire. Sensing victory, Iran rejected the proposal and demanded Hussein's ouster.

Iraqi president Saddam Hussein speaking at a news conference in Baghdad on November 11, 1980, during the Iran-Iraq War. (AP Photo/Zuheir Saade)

Hussein then withdrew his forces into well-prepared static defenses within Iraq. Iranian leaders meanwhile rejected as insufficient a Saudi Arabian–brokered deal that would have given Iran $70 billion in reparations by the Arab states and a complete Iraqi withdrawal from Iranian territory. Khomeini apparently now hoped to establish an Islamic republic in Iraq, presumably with its Shiite majority in charge.

In July 1982 the Iranians launched a new offensive, this time against Shiite-dominated southern Iraq with the goal of capturing Basra, Iraq's second-largest city. Iraqi resistance included the use of poison gas, and Iran secured only modest gains at heavy human cost. Each side also employed aircraft and missiles against the other's cities, with five separate such campaigns during the war. Iraq attacked Iranian oil-shipping facilities and later production facilities, which produced the largest oil spill in the history of the Persian Gulf region.

New Iranian offensives that autumn in the northern part of the front secured some territory inside Iraq before being driven out. In the southern part of the front, Iranian forces secured gains in a drive on the vital Baghdad-Basra highway. Between February and August 1983 Iran launched five major offensives, first against Basra and then in the north, but had only slight gains for heavy casualties. Determined to prevent the spread of Islamic fundamentalism regimes in the Middle East, U.S. president Ronald Reagan supported Iraq, providing it with satellite photography as well as economic aid and weapons.

In February 1984, the Iranians launched the first in a series of ground offensives in the central part of the front to take Kut al-Amara and there cut the vital

Baghdad-Basra highway. The Iranians came within 15 miles of the city before being halted. An Iranian drive against Basra also almost broke through.

With his forces having benefited from substantial arms purchases financed by the Gulf states, in January 1985 Hussein launched his first ground offensive since 1980 but scored only scant gains. The Iranians responded with an offensive of their own in March, capturing a portion of the Baghdad-Basra road. Hussein responded to this emergency with chemical weapons and renewed air and missile strikes against Iranian cities, including Tehran.

On February 17, 1986, Iranian forces captured the strategically important Iraqi port of al-Faw, southeast of Basra on the Shatt al-Arab waterway. During January–February 1987, Iran again tried but failed to take Basra. During May–June the Iranians tried to capture Kirkuk in northern Iraq.

On March 7, 1987, the United States initiated Operation EARNEST WILL, an effort to protect oil tankers and shipping lanes in the Persian Gulf. Iran had responded to the March 1984 Iraqi air attack on Kharg Island and nearby oil installations by employing sea mines against tankers carrying Iraqi oil from Kuwait as well as those of the Gulf states supporting Iraq. Responding to a Kuwaiti appeal, Washington agreed to provide protection for any U.S.-flagged tankers and other tankers accompanying these to and from Iraqi ports. This action ensured that Iraq would have the economic means to continue the war.

On the night of May 17, 1987, an Iraqi Mirage F-1 fighter on antiship patrol fired two Exocet antiship missiles at a radar contact, its pilot apparently not knowing that his target was the U.S. Navy frigate *Stark*. Although only one detonated, both missiles struck home and badly crippled the frigate, killing 37 crewmen and injuring another 50. The crew managed to save the ship, however.

Air and missile attacks by both sides against the cities of the other continued. Also during February 1988 and extending into September, the Iraqi Army carried out a massacre of its own Kurdish population in northern Iraq. Known as the al-Anfal (Spoils of War) Campaign, it claimed as many as 300,000 Kurdish lives and the destruction of some 4,000 villages.

On April 14, 1988, meanwhile, the U.S. Navy frigate *Samuel B. Roberts,* taking part in Operation EARNEST WILL, was badly damaged by an Iranian mine in the Persian Gulf. No one was killed, but the ship nearly sank. On April 18, the U.S. Navy responded with Operation PRAYING MANTIS, its largest battle involving surface warships since World War II and the first surface-to-surface missile engagement in the navy's history. U.S. forces damaged two Iranian offshore oil platforms, sank an Iranian frigate and a gunboat, damaged another frigate, and sank three Iranian speedboats. The U.S. lost one helicopter.

In the spring of 1988, with Iran now desperately short of spare parts, especially for its largely U.S.-built aircraft, Iraq launched four major offensives, recapturing the strategically important al-Faw Peninsula lost in 1986, driving the Iranians away from Basra, and making progress in the northern part of the front. These Iraqi victories came at little cost to themselves, while the Iranians suffered heavy personnel and equipment losses. These setbacks were the chief factor behind Khomeini's decision to agree to a cease-fire in 1988.

On July 3, 1988, the crew of the U.S. Navy cruiser *Vincennes,* patrolling in the Persian Gulf and believing that they were under attack by an Iranian jet fighter, shot down Iran Air Flight 655, a civilian airliner carrying 290 passengers and crew. There were no survivors. The U.S. government subsequently agreed to pay $131.8 million in compensation. This incident may have helped to convince Khomeini of the dangers of the United States actively entering the war, thus making him more amenable to ending it.

Both sides accepted a cease-fire agreement, arranged by the United Nations (UN), on August 20 1988. There are no reliable casualty totals, but each side probably suffered at least 300,000 dead. Negotiations between Iraq and Iran remained deadlocked for two years after the cease-fire, but in 1990, concerned with securing its forcible annexation of Kuwait, Iraq reestablished diplomatic relations with Iran and agreed to withdraw its troops from occupied Iranian territory, divide sovereignty over the Shatt al-Arab, and exchange prisoners of war.

With Iraq having sustained war costs of some $561 billion, Hussein turned to Saudi Arabia and Kuwait for financial relief, only to meet rebuff. During Ottoman rule, Kuwait had been part of Basra Province; it had only become an independent emirate during the British mandate, and this provided Hussein with the claim that Kuwait was an Iraqi province. Hussein also accused the Kuwaitis of overdrilling that had forced down the price of oil, much to the detriment of the Iraqi economy. He also asserted that Kuwait was illegally slant-drilling into Iraqi oil fields along their common border.

Meeting between April Glaspie and Saddam Hussein, July 25, 1990

April Glaspie, U.S. ambassador to Iraq, met with Iraqi president Saddam Hussein on July 25, 1990, eight days before the Iraqi invasion of Kuwait. Two transcripts exist of this meeting. Based particularly on the Iraqi version, some have alleged that Glaspie encouraged Hussein to invade Kuwait by giving him the impression that the United States was disinterested in Iraq's feud with Kuwait, including its military buildup along the Kuwaiti border. According to the Iraqi transcript, Glaspie told Hussein that the United States had "no opinion on the Arab-Arab conflicts, like your border disagreement with Kuwait." According to the U.S. cable, however, this was taken out of context, and Glaspie made clear that the United States could "never excuse settlements of dispute by other than peaceful means."

Although Glaspie clearly did not take a position regarding Iraq's dispute with Kuwait, this was not the same thing as inviting or endorsing an Iraqi invasion. Also, it should be remembered that few in the Arab world, especially Egyptian President Hosni Mubarak, who was mediating the dispute between Iraq and Kuwait, expected an invasion. Hussein was believed to merely be bluffing in an effort to intimidate Kuwait into forgiving Iraq's large debts to Kuwait.

On August 2, 1990, Iraqi troops invaded their small neighbor of Kuwait and quickly occupied it. Hussein then proclaimed its annexation. Much of the international community condemned the action and demanded an Iraqi withdrawal. UN Security Council Resolution 661 imposed wide-ranging sanctions on Iraq. These included a trade embargo that excluded only medical supplies, food, and other essential items. The UN also authorized a naval blockade of Iraq.

The U.S. government was deeply concerned about the occupation of Kuwait and a possible Iraqi military incursion into Saudi Arabia or at least pressure on that country and the threat to world oil supplies. It also worried about Iraqi programs to produce chemical, biological, and nuclear weapons, the so-called weapons of mass destruction (WMD). U.S. officials also feared that the balance of power in the region would be upset and would imperil Israel.

On paper, Iraq appeared formidable. Its army numbered more than 950,000 men, and it had some 5,500 main battle tanks, 6,000 armored personnel carriers (APCs), and about 3,500 artillery pieces. Saddam ultimately deployed 43 divisions to Kuwait, positioning most of them along the border with Saudi Arabia.

In Operation DESERT SHIELD, designed to protect Saudi Arabia and prepare for the liberation of Kuwait, U.S. president George H. W. Bush put together an impressive coalition that included Syria, Egypt, and Saudi Arabia as well as Britain, France, and many other states. Altogether 34 nations participated, and coalition assets grew to 665,000 troops and substantial air and naval assets.

Saddam remained intransigent but also quiescent, allowing the coalition buildup to proceed unimpeded. When the deadline to withdraw from Kuwait passed without Iraqi action, coalition commander U.S. Army general H. Norman Schwarzkopf unleashed Operation DESERT STORM on January 17, 1991. It began with a massive air offensive against targets in Kuwait and throughout Iraq, including Baghdad. Although Iraq possessed nearly 800 combat aircraft and an integrated air defense system controlling 3,000 antiaircraft missiles, coalition aircraft soon had destroyed the bulk of the Iraqi Air Force. Complete air superiority ensured success on the ground.

Night after night B-52s dropped massive bomb loads in classic attrition warfare; many Iraqi defenders were simply buried alive. Schwarzkopf also mounted an elaborate deception to convince the Iraqis that the coalition was planning an amphibious assault against Kuwait, thereby pinning down there a number of Iraqi divisions. In reality, Schwarzkopf planned a return to large-scale maneuver warfare.

The coalition campaign involved three thrusts. On the far left, 200 miles from the coast, highly mobile U.S. and French forces were to swing wide and cut off the Iraqis on the Euphrates River, preventing resupply or retreat. The center assault of VII Corps would occur some 100 miles inland and consisted of the heavily armored mailed fist of U.S. and British divisions. Its mission was to thrust deep and destroy the elite Iraqi Republican Guard divisions. The third and final thrust would be on the coast. Consisting of the U.S. 1st Marine Expeditionary force, one U.S. armored division, and allied Arab units, it would drive on Kuwait City.

On February 24 Allied forces executed simultaneous drives, while the 101st Airborne Division established a position 50 miles behind the border. As they moved up the coast toward Kuwait City, the U.S. marines were hit in the flank by Iraqi armor. In the largest tank battle in their history, the marines, supported by coalition airpower, easily defeated the Iraqis in a surrealist day-into-night atmosphere caused by the smoke of burning oil wells set afire by the retreating Iraqis.

As the marines, preceded by a light Arab force, prepared to enter Kuwait City, the Iraqis fled north with whatever they could loot. Thousands of civilian vehicles and personnel were caught in the open on the highway from Kuwait City and were there pummeled by air and artillery on what became known as the "Highway of Death."

On February 27 the Allies came up against an Iraqi rear guard of 300 tanks and APCs covering the withdrawal north toward Basra of four Republican Guard divisions. In perhaps the most lopsided tank battle in history, in the Battle of Medina Ridge units of the U.S. 1st Armored Division easily defeated the Iraqis at scant cost to themselves. The afternoon of February 27 also saw VII Corps engaged in intense combat. An armored brigade of the Medina Republican Guard Division was in defensive positions hoping to delay the coalition. The advancing 2nd Brigade of the U.S. 1st Armored Division spotted the Iraqis and took them under fire. The ensuing Battle of Norfolk was the largest single engagement of the war. In only 45 minutes, 69 Iraqi tanks and 38 APCs were destroyed. As VII Corps closed to the sea, XVIII Corps to its left, with a much larger distance to travel, raced to reach the fleeing Republican Guard divisions before they could escape to Baghdad.

In only 100 hours of ground combat coalition forces had liberated Kuwait, but on February 28 Bush stopped the war. He feared both the wisdom and cost of an assault on Baghdad with the possibility that Iraq might break up into a Kurdish north, a Sunni Muslim center, and a Shiite Muslim south. Bush wanted to see Iraq intact to counter a resurgent Iran.

The war was among the most lopsided in history. Iraq lost 3,700 tanks, more than 1,000 other armored vehicles, and 3,000 artillery pieces. The coalition lost 4 tanks, 9 other combat vehicles, and 1 artillery piece. The coalition sustained 500 casualties (150 dead), many from accidents and friendly fire. Iraq sustained perhaps 60,000 deaths and some 80,000 taken prisoner. Perhaps an equal number simply deserted.

It did not take long for Saddam Hussein to reestablish his authority. Bush had called for the Iraqi people to force Hussein to resign. Shiite Muslims in southern Iraq and Kurds in northern Iraq, both of which had been persecuted by Hussein, rebelled against the government. The refusal of the coalition to support the insurgents, however, allowed Hussein to suppress the uprisings with brutal force. The cease-fire agreement ending the war negotiated by Schwarzkopf permitted the Iraqi government to continue to fly helicopters, and these were employed with devastating effectiveness. Both the Kurds and the Shiites underwent persecution during the rest of Hussein's presidency. Hussein also defied UN inspection teams by refusing to account for all of his biological and chemical weapons, the so-called WMD.

To protect the Kurds and the Shias, the United States, Britain, and France belatedly established two no-fly zones (NFZs) in Iraq. The NFZ in northern Iraq, Operation NORTHERN WATCH, was established on April 10, 1991, and ran from the 36th parallel northward. Not until August 2, 1992, however, did the Bush administration establish an NFZ in the south to the 32nd parallel. In 1996 it was expanded to the 33rd parallel. The northern NFZ was initially part of Operation PROVIDE COMFORT, the relief operation aiding the Kurds. The southern NFZ was maintained by Operation SOUTHERN WATCH. After the French withdrew in 1998, U.S. and British aircraft continued to enforce the NFZs until the Iraq War that began in March 2003.

Continuing UN sanctions devastated the already-reeling Iraqi economy. The sanctions had called for 30 percent of Iraqi oil exports to be set aside for war reparations, but the Iraqi economy had grown to depend on its oil exports at the expense of other industries, especially agriculture. With the diminishment in oil revenues, many Iraqis experienced malnourishment and grinding poverty, while hyperinflation nearly wiped out the middle class. Food rationing did little to improve the situation. Power shortages caused widespread problems, and many manufacturing facilities had to be shut down.

In 1991, the Iraqi government had rejected UN proposals to trade its oil for food and other humanitarian supplies. On May 20, 1996, however, a memorandum of understanding was reached between the Iraqi government and the UN by which Iraq could sell oil to purchase food and other humanitarian supplies. This program suffered from deliberate illegal diversion of funds and did little to alleviate the plight of average Iraqis. By 2000, as many as 16 million Iraqis depended on some form of government assistance merely to survive.

The United States, Britain, and France (until 1998) continued to limit Hussein's power through punitive military operations. These aircraft and missile strikes damaged infrastructure and put even more of a strain on the Iraqi economy. Operation VIGILANT WARRIOR of October 8, 1994, was a U.S. response to the deployment of Iraqi troops toward the Kuwaiti border. After some 170 U.S. aircraft and 6,500 military personnel were deployed to southern Iraq, Hussein recalled his troops. Operation DESERT STRIKE of September 3, 1996, was in response to the movement of 40,000 Iraqi troops into northern Iraq, which threatened the Kurds. More than two years later on December 16, 1998, the United States and Great Britain began Operation DESERT FOX, a four-day bombing campaign, after Iraq's refusal to comply with UN Security Council resolutions that called for the dismantling of certain weapons and the Iraqi government's interference with UN weapons inspectors charged with ensuring Iraqi compliance with UN resolutions. DESERT FOX targeted research and developmental facilities in order to destroy any hidden WMD and the Iraqi government's ability to produce them. Then on February 16, 2001, U.S. and British aircraft launched missiles to damage Iraq's command and control facilities.

All the bombing to force Iraqi compliance with UN mandates did little to weaken Hussein's hold on power. The secular Baath government embarked on a so-called faith campaign, depicting the struggle as a jihad (holy war). Meanwhile, Hussein insisted on absolute loyalty.

Following the Al-Qaeda terrorist attacks on the United States on September 11, 2001, that killed nearly 3,000 people, the George W. Bush administration took a more assertive stance with Iraq. Bush and his closest advisers saw Iraq as a threat. Many Bush advisers mistakenly insisted that Iraq possessed WMD or was attempting to acquire such, and they claimed that an invasion of Iraq would easily remove Hussein, secure the alleged WMD, and serve as a warning to other rogue states. Beyond that, they saw a democratic Iraq as a force for change in the entire region. Some even held that Iraqi oil would pay for the invasion.

As invasion plans proceeded, Bush hoped to secure UN approval. On September 12, 2002, he addressed the UN Security Council and made his case for an invasion. Much of the international community was skeptical and did not believe that Iraq posed a threat or had links to such terrorist organizations as Al-Qaeda, which the Bush administration also alleged. On October 10 and 11, however, the U.S. Congress passed the Authorization for Use of Military Force against Iraq Resolution of 2002 (Iraq War Resolution), which Bush signed into law on October 16. On November 8, 2002, the UN Security Council passed Resolution 1441, which offered Iraq a final chance to comply with its disarmament agreements. This required that Iraq destroy all WMD and means to deliver them and also provide complete documentation of such.

On February 5, 2003, U.S. secretary of state Colin Powell addressed the UN General Assembly and presented evidence, some of which was later proven to be false, that Iraqi officials were impeding the work of the weapons inspectors, continuing to develop WMD, and directly supporting Al-Qaeda. The United States and Great Britain, among others, then proposed a UN resolution calling for the use of force against Iraq. Other countries, including U.S. allies Canada, France, and Germany, urged continued diplomacy. Bush then decided to pursue an invasion without UN authorization.

On March 20, 2003, a U.S. and British-led coalition invaded Iraq. The operation was mounted solely from Kuwait. It was also hastily reworked, for after lengthy negotiations Turkey refused to allow the 4th Infantry Division to stage from that country. Nonetheless, coalition forces advanced north quickly and on April 3–12

Saddam Hussein and Weapons of Mass Destruction

The belief that Iraqi president Saddam Hussein was actively seeking to acquire biological, chemical, and even nuclear weapons—collectively known as weapons of mass destruction (WMD)—was one of the major reasons stated by U.S. president George W. Bush's administration as justification for the invasion of Iraq in March 2003.

No such weapons were ever found. Before his execution in December 2006, Hussein informed U.S. Federal Bureau of Investigation interrogators that he had misled the world to give the impression that Iraq had WMD in order to make Iraq appear stronger in the face of its enemy, Iran.

fought the Battle of Baghdad. After the fall of the capital and the official end to the Iraqi government, Hussein went into hiding. Coalition forces entered Kirkuk on April 10 and Hussein's hometown of Tikrit on April 15.

On May 1, 2003, Bush declared that major combat operations in Iraq had ended and that the postinvasion reconstruction phase had begun. However, the war was far from over; indeed, the postinvasion period would prove very difficult for coalition forces. With insufficient numbers of coalition forces to keep order, Iraq soon fell into chaos with the looting of palaces, museums, and even arms depots.

On April 20, 2003, the United States had established the Coalition Provisional Authority (CPA), and on May 11 Bush selected diplomat Lewis Paul Bremer III as its head. Bremer made two most unfortunate decisions. On June 3, he ordered the de-Baathification of Iraq. Some 30,000 Baath Party officials were removed from their positions and banned from future employment in the public sector. The next day, Bremer dissolved Iraq's 500,000-member army. This order left Iraq without a military or police force to stop the continuing chaos. These moves also produced a large number of opponents to the coalition presence. Violence against the occupation forces steadily increased. Individuals, largely Sunnis, employed ambush tactics, improvised explosive devices, and suicide bombings against coalition forces, who now faced a long battle with Iraqi insurgents in their attempt to bring peace to Iraq. This led to a number of costly battles, including two for the city of Falluja (April 4–May 1 and November 7–December 23, 2004).

Sectarian strife also increased, and by mid-2004 Iraq appeared perched on the edge of full-blown civil war. Sunni extremists, rightly fearful of dominance by the Shiite majority, employed car bombs and suicide bombings against Shiites, while Shiite members of the new Iraqi Army used extralegal means against Sunni civilians. Shiite death squads killed many Iraqi civilians and sought to cleanse neighborhoods of Sunni residents.

With the ongoing violence, on June 28, 2004, governing authority was transferred to the Iraqi Interim Government, led by Prime Minister Iyad Allawi. The generally pro-Western Allawi launched a campaign to weaken the rebel forces of Shiite cleric Muqtada al-Sadr. On September 1 Allawi pulled out of peace negotiations with Sadr, and fighting ensued in what became known as the Battle of Sadr City. Sadr eventually agreed to a cease-fire and took part in the legislative elections on January 30, 2005.

In the elections, the Iraqi people chose representatives for the 275-member National Assembly. Some 8.4 million people cast their ballots. Two Shiite parties won a majority of the seats, with 85 women among those elected. Many Sunnis boycotted the elections, however. The assembly was immediately charged with writing a constitution and approved the Iraqi Transitional Government on April 28, 2005, which went into operation on May 3. The constitution was approved on October 15, 2005, and described Iraq as a democratic, federal, representative republic.

On December 15, 2005, a second general election was held to elect a permanent Iraqi Council of Representatives. Following approval by the National Assembly, a permanent Iraqi government was established on May 16, 2006. Turnout for this election was high, at 79.4 percent, and the level of violence was lower than during the previous election. The United Iraqi Alliance, a coalition of Arab Shiite parties, won the most votes, at 41.2 percent. Nouri al-Maliki, a member of the Islamic Dawa Party, a conservative Shiite group, became prime minister. Maliki negotiated a peace treaty with Sadr's rebel forces in August 2007.

U.S. forces had captured Saddam Hussein on December 13, 2003, in Dawr, a small town north of Baghdad. He was eventually tried by an Iraqi Special Tribunal for crimes committed against the inhabitants of the town of Dujail, which had been the site of an unsuccessful assassination attempt against Hussein in 1982. Hussein was charged with the murder of 148 people and with having ordered the torture of women and children and illegally arresting 399 others. Found guilty on November 5, 2006, he was sentenced to death by hanging and was executed on December 30.

In January 2007 President Bush presented a new U.S. military strategy, the stated goal of which was to reduce the sectarian violence and secure both Baghdad and Al Anbar Province. In what became known as a troop surge, five additional U.S. Army brigades totaling some 20,000 troops were deployed to Iraq between January and May 2007. Other troops had their tours extended. The success of the surge has been debated. Certainly another key factor in the reduction of violence was the decision of many Sunnis to work with the coalition forces.

On December 4, 2008, the U.S. and Iraqi governments concluded a status of forces agreement, which stipulated that U.S. troops would depart from all Iraqi cities by June 30, 2009, and leave Iraq entirely by December 31, 2011. U.S. forces were no longer allowed to hold Iraqi citizens without charges for more than 24 hours. Also, U.S. contractors were to lose immunity from prosecution in Iraqi courts. It was widely assumed that a new status of forces agreement plan would be negotiated after expiration of the 2008 version, but new U.S. president Barack Obama had run on a pledge of ending the Iraq War, and he announced soon after taking office in January 2009 that U.S. combat operations would cease in 2010. About 200 marines were to remain to help train the Iraqi Army and provide security for U.S. diplomatic personnel.

When it came time to renegotiate a new agreement, however, there was no consensus. U.S. military leaders wanted as many as 24,000 troops. But the Obama administration rejected this in favor of perhaps 10,000 troops in strategic locations after the exit. A figure of 3,500 was also bandied about, but even that low figure ran up against opposition from within the Iraqi parliament and Washington's insistence that any troops be immune to Iraqi—although not American—criminal prosecution. Thus no agreement was ever reached, for which U.S. Republican Party leaders chose to blame Obama. The last U.S. troops left Iraq on December 18, 2011, two weeks ahead of the schedule provided by a status of forces agreement.

Iraq meanwhile continued to experience major problems. Although the economy had improved somewhat, corruption was endemic, and unemployment remained astronomically high (60–70 percent in 2008). At the same time, the Iraqi foreign debt rose. Since the withdrawal of coalition troops, the Iraqi economy has failed to make any major gains, and in many sectors it has steadily deteriorated.

Much of this was due to a growing insurgency and ongoing sectarian violence, combined with the ineffective and graft-ridden Maliki government. Although unemployment had dropped to 30 percent by the end of 2013, most Iraqis were employed in the public sector (60 percent), and per capita gross domestic product was only about $4,000 per year.

In the last few years, Iraq has witnessed an alarming reemergence of the antigovernment insurgency. This has included sectarian violence and the rise to prominence of Islamic extremist groups, including most notably Al-Qaeda in Iraq and the Islamic State of Iraq and Syria (ISIS). By early 2014, ISIS had seized control of virtually all of Iraq's vast Anbar Province. Maliki's government was unable to stem the rising tide of deadly violence. Indeed, Maliki's policies saw the Shiites run roughshod over the Sunnis and Kurds, setting the stage for a renewal of deadly violence in the form of sectarian car bombings and suicide bombings. May 2013 was the deadliest month in Iraq since the height of the Iraqi insurgency in 2006–2007.

In May 2014, the U.S. government announced an arms deal with Iraq that promised at least $1 billion in new aircraft, armored vehicles, and surveillance technology. Meanwhile, the Iraqis also engaged in a major arms deal with the Russians, who agreed to sell them aircraft and bunker-busting rockets, among other items.

By midsummer 2014 the Iraqi situation appeared dire, with ISIS having secured both Falluja (December 30, 2013–January 4, 2014) and Mosul (June 4–10) and having advanced to within 90 miles of Baghdad. Until then, the Iraqi Army had performed abysmally in its fight against ISIS; indeed, many soldiers simply deserted or fled in the face of ISIS military operations. In August, Maliki was now under great domestic and international pressure to step down. Even those in his own party believed that he must go. In the meantime, the United States began dispatching growing but relatively small numbers of military advisers to Iraq even as U.S. and allied aircraft began bombing raids against ISIS targets in northern and western Iraq.

Maliki finally agreed to relinquish his office on September 8, 2014. He was succeeded by Haider al-Abadi, also of the Dawa Party. The Shiite Abadi vowed to reinvigorate Iraq's army and work closely with the new international coalition formed to stop and eventually eradicate ISIS. He also pledged more governmental transparency and efforts to bridge the gaping chasm between the majority Shiite and minority Sunni and Kurdish populations.

Throughout 2015 Iraqi forces battled ISIS, achieving modest success in winning back some territory claimed by the extremist group. Worrisome to Washington, Iran had also begun providing direct military support to the Iraqi government. The collapse of oil prices during the second half of 2015 has had a chilling effect on Iraq's economy, still highly dependent on oil exports. Indeed, by early 2016 the Abadi government announced that the greatly reduced oil revenues were beginning to affect its ability to continue the fight against ISIS.

Violence continued, with bombings a frequent occurrence. A January 2016 UN report stated that between January 2014 and November 2015, nearly 19,000 Iraqi civilians had died owing to violence in Iraq, while at least 40,000 others had been injured. An additional 3 million Iraqis had been displaced from their homes. In May 2016 the government began a long-anticipated offensive to retake Falluja, the essential prelude to moving against the ISIS stronghold of Mosul. On June 26 General Abdul Wahab al-Saadi, commander of Iraq operations against Falluja, announced that the final ISIS strongpoint in the city, the neighborhood of al-Jolan, had been taken. The government claimed that more than 1,800 ISIS militants had been killed during the battle to retake Falluja and the villages surrounding it. Meanwhile, large numbers of Sunni civilians who had fled the fighting were in dire straits, living in hastily prepared refugee camps without even the basic amenities, such as toilets. The Sunnis are, of course, the very group the Shia-dominated government is trying to win over.

Timeline

1831	The Ottoman Turks overthrow the Mamluks and assume direct rule over the territory of present-day Iraq.
1914–1918	The Ottoman Empire joins the Central Powers in World War I and is defeated. Britain is then master of the former Ottoman provinces of Mosul, Baghdad, and Basra, which form modern-day Iraq.
Apr 28, 1920	The San Remo Agreement awards Iraq to Britain as a League of Nations mandate.
May–Oct 1920	The British put down a revolt in Iraq, largely by Royal Air Force bombers.
Aug 23, 1921	Having secured formal control of Iraq as a League of Nations mandate, the British install their ally, Faisal bin Hussein bin Ali al-Hashimi of the Hashemite dynasty, as king of Iraq.
Oct 10, 1922	The Anglo-Iraqi Treaty of October 10, 1922, grants Iraq independence but leaves Britain in control of its foreign and military affairs.
1925	Oil is discovered, greatly increasing Iraq's strategic importance.
Oct 3, 1932	The British formally grant Iraq its independence, but the treaty protects British oil interests and grants Britain military bases.
Sep 8, 1933	Faisal dies in Basel, Switzerland, probably as a result of being poisoned. Ghazi I succeeds him.
Dec 25, 1938	Pro-British general Nuri al-Said becomes prime minister.
Mar 1939	Nuri puts down an attempted army coup.
Apr 4, 1939	King Ghazi I dies in an accident. With new king Faisal II only four years old, his uncle Abdul Illah acts as regent.

Sep 1939	World War II begins. Nuri wants to declare war on the Axis, but the opposition forces him to declare Iraqi neutrality instead.
Feb 1940	Nuri puts down another attempted army coup.
Mar 31, 1940	Rashid Ali Rashid Ali al-Gaylani replaces Nuri as prime minister and comes under the influence of four nationalist, pro-Axis generals, the so-called Golden Square.
Apr 2, 1941	Continued Axis military success and hints of Axis aid lead the Golden Square to mount a corp d'état and restore Gaylani to power. He forms a cabinet of Axis sympathizers. The regent and Nuri flee.
May 2, 1941	Iraqi troops open artillery fire on the Royal Air Force base at Habbaniya. The Royal Air Force immediately goes into action, and Britain dispatches troops. Although some German military aid reaches the rebels, it is insufficient, and superior British firepower breaks the siege at Habbaniya. The British occupy Falluja on May 20 and surround Baghdad by the end of the month.
May 29, 1941	Regent Abdul Illah forces Gaylani to resign because of the latter's pro-Axis connections. Taha al-Hashimi then becomes prime minister.
Oct 10, 1941	Nuri again becomes prime minister with a pro-British administration.
Jan 16, 1943	Iraq declares war on the Axis.
1948–1949	Iraq provides some 18,000 troops to the Arab side in the Israeli War of Independence.
1955	Iraq joins the pro-Western Baghdad Pact, which angers many Iraqi nationalists.
Jul 14, 1958	The Free Officers Movement, a secret nationalist organization led by Colonel Abd al-Karim Qasim, seizes power and executes both Faisal II and Nuri. The revolutionaries abolish the monarchy, proclaim Iraq a republic, and seek closer ties to the Soviet Union.
Feb 9, 1963	Qasim is overthrown and killed by a coalition of anticommunist military officers and secular Arab nationalists and Baathists. Colonel Abdul Salam Arif then becomes president, with Hasan al-Bakr as prime minister.
Apr 13, 1966	Arif dies in a helicopter crash, and his brother, Abdul Rahman Arif, becomes president.
Jun 5–12, 1967	Iraq's failure to support fellow Arab states in the Six-Day War brings widespread rioting in Baghdad.

Jul 17, 1968	The Baath Party seizes power. Ahmed Hasan al-Bakr becomes president. His cousin, Saddam Hussein, eliminates the opposition.
Oct 6–26, 1973	Iraq plays only a minor role in the Yom Kippur War (Ramadan War), sending an armored division to assist the Syrians on the Golan Heights front.
Jul 16, 1979	Hussein becomes president in form as well as in fact, with al-Bakr departing ostensibly for health reasons.
Sep 22, 1980	Seeking to capitalize on unrest in Iran following the Islamic revolution there to secure Iranian territory, Hussein sends Iraqi forces into Iran, beginning the long Iran-Iraq War. The overly cautious Iraqi advance negates the chance of an early Iraqi victory, and by the spring of 1981 the war has settled into a protracted stalemate greatly resembling World War I trench warfare, with the each side mounting costly offensives that result in little gain. There are also a half dozen air campaigns by the two sides, and Iran institutes a highly successful naval blockade of Iraq.
Feb 17, 1986	Iranian forces capture the strategically important Iraqi port of al-Faw, at the southeast end of the al-Faw Peninsula on the Shatt al-Arab waterway.
Mar 7, 1987	The United States initiates Operation EARNEST WILL, protecting oil tankers and shipping lanes in the Persian Gulf against Iranian attack. This ensures that Iraq will have the economic means to continue the war.
May 17, 1987	An Iraqi jet fighter fires two missiles at an unknown radar contact that turns out to be the U.S. Navy frigate *Stark*. The attack kills 37 crewmen and injures another 50, although the ship is saved.
Feb 2–Sep 6, 1988	In the al-Anfal (Spoils of War) Campaign, the Iraqi military carries out a massacre of Kurds in northern Iraq, killing as many as 300,000 civilians and destroying some 4,000 villages.
Apr 18, 1988	Retaliating for the mining of the frigate *Samuel B. Roberts* by Iran on April 14, the U.S. Navy responds with Operation PRAYING MANTIS, sinking and damaging a number of Iranian vessels and also damaging two oil platforms, for the loss of one helicopter.
Jul 3, 1988	The crew of the U.S. Navy cruiser *Vincennes* in the Persian Gulf, believing that they are under attack by an Iranian jet fighter, shoots down Iran Air Flight 655, a civilian airliner carrying 290 passengers and crew. There are no survivors. The U.S. government subsequently agrees to pay compensation.
Aug 20, 1988	War weariness and pressure from other governments induces both sides to accept a cease-fire agreement arranged by the United

Nations (UN). Negotiations continue, and only in 1990 does Iraq reestablish diplomatic relations with Iran and agree to withdraw its troops from occupied Iranian territory, divide sovereignty over the Shatt al-Arab, and exchange prisoners of war.

Aug 2, 1990   Hussein sends the Iraqi Army into Kuwait. Claiming that it was part of Basra Province under the Ottomans and desiring its oil to help pay for the Iran-Iraq War, he declares the annexation of Kuwait.

Aug 6, 1990   UN Security Council Resolution 661 imposes wide-ranging sanctions on Iraq, including a trade embargo to be enforced by a naval blockade. Meanwhile, the United States rushes forces to Saudi Arabia in Operation DESERT SHIELD as President George H. W. Bush puts together a coalition of 34 nations that includes Syria, Egypt, and Saudi Arabia.

Jan 17, 1991   With Hussein intransigent, coalition forces commanded by U.S. Army general H. Norman Schwarzkopf commence the Persian Gulf War (Operation DESERT STORM) to expel Iraq from Kuwait. It begins on this date with an extensive bombing campaign in Kuwait and Iraq itself.

Feb 24, 1991   The Persian Gulf War ground war commences.

Feb 27, 1991   U.S. forces defeat the Iraqis in the Battle of Medina Ridge and the Battle of Norfolk. U.S. marines, having secured Kuwait International Airport, stop at the outskirts of Kuwait City and allow coalition Arab forces to take and occupy it, effectively ending combat operations in the Kuwaiti theater of the war.

Feb 28, 1991   President Bush ends the war. He fears the cost of an assault on Baghdad and also fears that Iraq might then break up into Kurdish, Sunni, and Muslim entities. Bush favors a strong Iraq to counter a resurgent Iran. He had called for the Iraqi people to force Hussein to step aside, but although there are uprisings by Shias in the south and Kurds in the north, Hussein survives politically and indeed crushes the revolts with great ferocity.

Apr 10, 1991   To protect the Kurds, the United States, Britain, and France establish a no-fly zone (NFZ) for Iraqi aircraft in northern Iraq. Enforced by U.S., British, and (until 1998) French aircraft, this operation, named NORTHERN WATCH, runs from the 36th parallel northwards and is part of Operation PROVIDE COMFORT to alleviate Kurdish suffering.

Aug 2, 1992   The Bush administration establishes an NFZ in the south to the 32nd parallel. This operation, SOUTHERN WATCH, is expanded in 1996 to the 33rd parallel to protect the Shias. The two NFZs continue until the U.S.-led invasion of Iraq in March 2003.

Oct 8–Dec 15, 1994	U.S. forces carry out Operation VIGILANT WARRIOR in response to the deployment of Iraqi troops toward the Kuwaiti border. The United States deploys some 170 aircraft and 6,500 military personnel, whereupon Hussein recalls his troops.
May 20, 1996	A memorandum of understanding between the UN and the Iraqi government permits the Iraqi government to sell oil to purchase food and other humanitarian supplies, but this is marked by corruption and does little to improve the desperate situation faced by many Iraqis.
Dec 16–19, 1998	The United States and Great Britain carry out Operation DESERT FOX, a bombing campaign in response to the Iraqi government's refusal to comply with UN Security Council resolutions that called for the dismantling of certain weapons and an end to the government's interference with UN weapons inspectors.
Feb 16, 2001	The United States and Great Britain launch a bombing campaign to damage Iraq's air defense network.
Sep 11, 2001	Operatives of the Al-Qaeda terrorist network attack the United States. Seizing control of four airliners, they crash two into the World Trade Center towers in New York City and another into the Pentagon. The fourth plane crashes in Pennsylvania as passengers attempt to overtake the hijackers. Nearly 3,000 people are killed in the attacks. The events of 9/11 lead the George W. Bush administration to take a more assertive stance with Iraq, which many of his advisers believe has links to Al-Qaeda.
Sep 12, 2002	Bush addresses the UN Security Council and makes his case for an invasion of Iraq. Much of the international community is skeptical of his claims and opposes such a course.
Oct 16, 2002	Bush signs the Authorization for Use of Military Force Against Iraq Resolution of 2002 (Iraq War Resolution) passed by Congress.
Nov 8, 2002	The UN Security Council passes Resolution 1441, which offers Iraq a final chance to comply with its disarmament agreements.
Feb 5, 2003	U.S. secretary of state Colin Powell addresses the UN General Assembly and presents evidence, some of which is later proven false, that Iraqi officials are impeding the work of the weapons inspectors, continuing to develop weapons of mass destruction, and directly supporting Al-Qaeda.
Mar 20, 2003	A U.S.- and British-led coalition invades Iraq from Kuwait with the objectives of disarming Iraq, ousting Hussein, and freeing the Iraqi people.

Apr 3–12, 2003	Advancing quickly, coalition forces capture Baghdad and topple the Iraqi government, forcing Hussein into hiding.
Apr 20, 2003	The United States establishes the Coalition Provisional Authority (CPA) to govern Iraq.
May 1, 2003	Bush declares major combat operations in Iraq over and announces that the postinvasion reconstruction phase has begun. With the absence of government authority and social order, the country soon experiences widespread civil disorder and massive looting, which the limited number of coalition troops are unable to prevent.
May 11, 2003	Bush appoints diplomat Lewis Paul Bremer III to head the CPA.
Jun 3, 2003	Bremer orders the de-Baathification of Iraq, removing some 30,000 members of the Baath Party from the public sector. The next day he dissolves Iraq's 500,000-member army. This order leaves Iraq without a military or police force to stop the widespread looting. These two mistaken decisions ensure a huge number of disgruntled, unemployed dissidents who view the CPA with great enmity, and violence against the occupation forces steadily increases. Sectarian strife also is on the upswing, with Sunni extremists attacking and killing many Shiite civilians.
Dec 13, 2003	U.S. forces capture Hussein in a small town north of Baghdad.
Jun 28, 2004	Governing authority is transferred to the Iraqi Interim Government, led by Prime Minister Iyad Allawi.
Jan 30, 2005	Iraqi legislative elections occur, and the Shiite majority dominates. The new National Assembly has 275 members, of whom 85 are women, and is charged with writing a constitution
Apr 25, 2005	The National Assembly approves the Iraqi Transitional Government, which comes into being on May 3.
Oct 15, 2005	The Iraqi Constitution is approved and describes Iraq as a democratic, federal, representative republic.
Dec 15, 2005	A second general election is held to elect an Iraqi Council of Representatives.
May 16, 2006	A permanent Iraqi government is formed. Nouri al-Maliki, a member of the Islamic Dawa Party, a conservative Shiite group, becomes prime minister.
Dec 30, 2006	Saddam Hussein, having been brought to trial and found guilty of crimes against his own people, is executed by hanging.
Jan–May 2007	The Bush administration deploys some 20,000 additional personnel to Iraq in what is described as a troop surge, with the goal of

decreasing the rampant sectarian violence gripping the country. The troop surge and deals struck between the U.S. military and Sunni minority leaders help bring a reduction in violence.

Dec 4, 2008   The U.S. and Iraqi governments conclude a status of forces agreement. It stipulates that U.S. troops will depart from all Iraqi cities by June 30, 2009, and leave Iraq entirely by December 31, 2011.

Dec 18, 2011   U.S. president Barack Obama, who has pledged to remove U.S. troops from Iraq before 2012, makes good on his promise as the last U.S. troops quit Iraq on this date. The insurgency and sectarian violence remain, as does rampant corruption. The coming years also see the rise of the Islamic extremist groups Al-Qaeda in Iraq and the Islamic State of Iraq and Syria (ISIS).

Spring 2014   ISIS seizes control of virtually all of Iraq's Anbar Province. Maliki proves unable to stem the rising tide of deadly sectarian violence; indeed, his exclusionary tactics toward the Sunni minority largely set the stage for a renewed insurgency.

May 2014   The U.S. government announces an arms deal with Iraq that promises at least $1 billion in new aircraft, armored vehicles, and surveillance technology. Meanwhile, the Iraqis also engage in a major arms deal with the Russians, who agree to sell them aircraft and bunker-busting rockets, among other items.

Summer 2014   The situation in Iraq appears dire, with ISIS having advanced within 90 miles of Baghdad. The Iraqi Army performs abysmally in the fight against ISIS. In this situation, the United States sends small deployments of military advisers to Iraq even as U.S. and allied aircraft began bombing raids against ISIS targets in northern and western Iraq.

Sep 8, 2014   Under considerable pressure, Maliki relinquishes his post as prime minister and is succeeded by Haider al-Abadi, also a Shiite. He vows to reinvigorate Iraq's army, work closely with the new international coalition battling ISIS, provide more governmental transparency, institute anticorruption efforts, and bridge the divide between Iraq's Sunni and Shiite populations.

2015   Iraqi forces battle ISIS, achieving only modest success. They are aided in part by direct military support from Iran as well as U.S. air strikes.

May 23, 2016   Iraqi forces commence operations to retake the city of Falluja from ISIS. In Sunni-dominated Anbar Province, Falluja was the scene of two major battles during the Iraq War and has been under ISIS control since January 2014.

Jun 26, 2016   The Iraqi government announces that its forces have retaken the final ISIS strongpoint in Falluja and that the city has been liberated.

Further Reading

Abdullah, Thabit. *A Short History of Iraq.* London: Pearson, 2003.

Allawi, Ali A. *The Occupation of Iraq: Winning the War, Losing the Peace.* New Haven, CT: Yale University Press, 2007.

Butt, Gerald. *The Lion in the Sand: The British in the Middle East.* London: Bloomsbury, 1995.

Dodge, Toby. *Inventing Iraq: The Failure of Nation-Building and a History Denied.* New York: Columbia University Press, 2003.

Hamdi, Walid M. *Rashid al-Gailani and the Nationalist Movement in Iraq, 1939–1941: A Political and Military Study of the British Campaign in Iraq and the National Revolution of May 1941.* London: Darf, 1987.

Hopwood, Derek, Habib Ishow, and Thomas Koszinowski, eds. *Iraq: Power and Society.* Reading, UK: Ithaca Press, 1993.

Inati, Shams Constantine. *Iraq: Its History, People, and Politics.* Amherst, MA: Humanity Books, 2003.

Karsh, Efraim. *Islamic Imperialism.* New Haven, CT: Yale University Press, 2006.

Makiya, Kanan. *Republic of Fear: The Politics of Modern Iraq.* Berkeley: University of California Press, 1998.

Marr, Phebe. *The Modern History of Iraq.* 2nd ed. Boulder, CO: Westview, 2003.

Murray, Williamson, and Robert H. Scales Jr. *The Iraq War: A Military History.* Cambridge, MA: Harvard University Press, 2003.

Oren, Michael B. *Six Days of War: June 1967 and the Making of the Modern Middle East.* Novato, CA: Presidio, 2003.

Pelletiere, Stephen. *The Iran-Iraq War: Chaos in a Vacuum.* New York: Praeger, 1992.

Polk, William R. *Understanding Iraq: The Whole Sweep of Iraqi History, from Genghis Khan's Mongols to the Ottoman Turks to the British Mandate to the American Occupation.* New York: Harper Perennial, 2006.

Tripp, Charles. *A History of Iraq.* Cambridge: Cambridge University Press, 2007.

ISRAEL

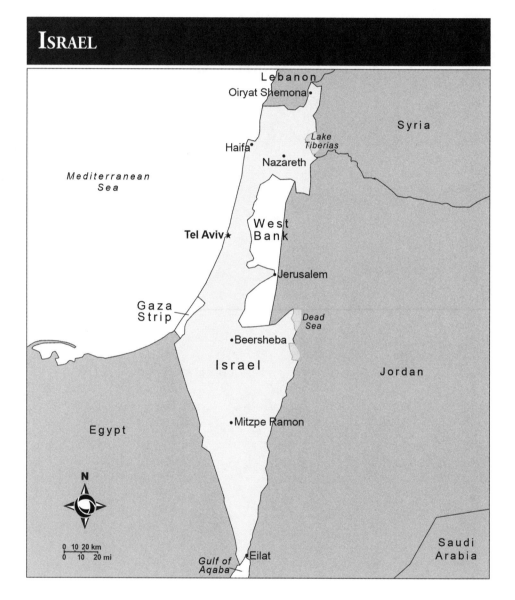

Lebanon

Oiryat Shemona•

Syria

Haifa•

Lake Tiberias

Nazareth•

Mediterranean Sea

Tel Aviv★

West Bank

•Jerusalem

Gaza Strip

Dead Sea

•Beersheba

Israel

Jordan

•Mitzpe Ramon

Egypt

N

0 10 20 km
0 10 20 mi

Saudi Arabia

Gulf of Aqaba

•Eilat

Israel

Stefan M. Brooks, Paul G. Pierpaoli Jr., Daniel E. Spector, and Spencer C. Tucker

The State of Israel, the only Jewish nation in the world, has an area of some 8,019 square miles and is thus slightly larger than the U.S. state of Massachusetts. Israel's population in 2016 was some 8.515 million, and its capital is Tel Aviv. Israel is bordered to the west by the eastern Mediterranean, to the north by Lebanon, to the east by Jordan and Syria, and to the southwest by Egypt. Israel's government is a parliamentary democracy, and the country boasts an advanced Western-style economy. Israel also possesses atomic weapons.

According to the Jewish bible, the Torah (or the Christian Old Testament), Jews trace their origins to some 4,000 years ago to the prophet Abraham and his son Isaac. A series of Jewish kingdoms and states intermittently ruled Palestine for more than a millennium thereafter. For many centuries Jews were the majority population of Palestine or, as the Jews called it, Israel (meaning "land of God"), but they were forced to endure diaspora, or dispersion from their homeland. The first of these exiles came under Tiglath-Pileser III of Assyria in 733 BCE and was completed by Sargon II with the destruction of the Kingdom of Israel in 722. In 586 BCE King Nebuchadnezzar II of Babylon conquered the Kingdom of Judah and, according to the Bible, destroyed the Temple and exiled part of the Jewish population to Babylon. This exile ended after 70 years on the declaration of King Cyrus I of Persia, with the Jews allowed to return home and construct the Second Temple. Alexander the Great of Macedon conquered the region in 334 BCE. After his death it was part of the Ptolemaic Empire and then the Seleucid Empire.

In 63 BCE Roman armies invaded and established a protectorate, with a vassal Judean kingdom under Herod the Great. In 6 CE the kingdom was organized as the Roman province of Judea. Following a revolt by the Jews in 66, the Romans laid siege to and destroyed the Second Temple and most of Jerusalem. This event marked the beginning of the Roman Exile (Edom Exile), with many Jews killed or sold into slavery.

Another Jewish revolt, this time under Bar Kokhba during 132–135, brought another defeat. Emperor Hadrian changed the name of Jerusalem to Aelia Capitolina. He turned it into a pagan city and prevented Jews from living there. Much of the population then became Greco-Roman. After a period of Byzantine rule, in 634–641 the Arabs, having adopted Islam, conquered the region. It remained under Muslim control for the next 1,300 years.

Securing Jerusalem was a primary goal of the Christian Crusades (1096–1291). In 1099 the crusaders laid siege to and captured the city, after which they massacred some 60,000 people, including 6,000 Jews seeking refuge in a synagogue. In 1260 control passed to the Mamluk sultans of Egypt, but in 1516, with their victory over the Mamluk Sultanate, the Ottoman Turks took charge.

In the 19th century, nationalism became a primary force in European affairs. The large Jewish population of the Russian Empire was then undergoing periodic savage persecutions (pogroms), but anti-Semitism was also rife in many countries including France, as in the Dreyfus Affair. Jews came to the conclusion that the only way they could secure protection was to establish their own state. The result at the end of the 19th century was Zionism, whereby Jews sought a national homeland. Under Austrian Jew Theodor Herzl, the first World Zionist Congress (WZC) met in Basel, Switzerland, in 1897. Subsequent WZCs affirmed that the Jewish national homeland had to be Palestine.

In 1914 the Ottoman Empire entered World War I on the side of the Central Powers. During the conflict French diplomat François-Georges Picot and British diplomat Sir Mark Sykes negotiated an agreement regarding the disposition of the Middle East territory belonging to the Ottoman Empire. Signed on May 16, 1916, it assigned what would be postwar Iraq, Transjordan, and Palestine to Britain, while France was to receive control of what would be Syria and Lebanon. At the same time, however, British authorities in Egypt negotiated with the Arabs and promised the establishment of an Arab kingdom if they would rise up against the Ottomans. This occurred in the Arab Revolt (1916–1918). In another major demarche, in order to secure Jewish support for the Allied war effort, British foreign secretary Arthur James Balfour on November 2, 1917, issued what became known as the Balfour Declaration. It announced British support for the "establishment in Palestine of a national home for the Jewish people."

Following the Allied victory in World War I, at the San Remo Conference in Italy in April 1920 Britain and France secured approval of the other major Allied powers for the establishment of the former Ottoman Middle East as League of Nations mandates along the lines of the Sykes-Picot Agreement. In April 1921, however, Britain split Palestine into the Emirate of Transjordan, comprising territory east of the Jordan River, and Palestine to the west.

Already a growing number of Jews had arrived in Palestine and settled there. Many of them, financed by wealthy West European Jews, had purchased land from the Arabs. These numbers increased after the war, which the Palestinian Arabs came to view with growing alarm, seeing themselves becoming marginalized in their own land. In response to continuing Jewish immigration, sporadic Arab attacks occurred against Jews as well as British officials in Palestine. The escalating violence was the result of the impossible British policy of permitting Jewish immigration while at the same time attempting to safeguard Arab rights. Continued immigration brought more Jewish land purchases and in turn more violence.

In 1920 Arabs began sporadically attacking Jewish settlements, and in response Jews formed the Haganah, a clandestine defense organization. Heightened violence by 1929 led the British to halt all Jewish settlement in Palestine, but Jewish outcries caused the British to reverse this policy. Militant Jewish groups also began to take action against what they saw as restrictive British immigration policies. A three-way struggle thus ensued between the British and militant Arabs and Jews. In 1936, a full-fledged Arab revolt began. Lasting until 1939, it forced the British to dispatch to Palestine 20,000 additional troops and resulted in the deaths of some 5,000 Arabs and many more injured. It also brought a temporary alliance between the British and the Jews.

In 1937 the British government considered partitioning Palestine into separate Arab and Jewish states but then a year later rejected this as not feasible. In 1939 London announced that Palestine would become an independent state within 10 years. The British also sharply curtailed Jewish immigration and restricted the sale of Arab land to Jews. This policy of attempting to favor the Arabs continued during World War II, when the British even diverted warships to intercept and turn back ships carrying Jews attempting to escape the Holocaust, the Nazi scheme to exterminate all the Jews within their grasp.

Realization of the full extent of the Holocaust, which had brought the deaths of more than 6 million Jews, dramatically changed attitudes throughout most of the world in favor of Jewish settlement in Palestine and even the creation of a Jewish state there. Probably most Jews now believed that the only way to prevent a new Holocaust was the creation of a Jewish nation state. Armed Zionist terrorist organizations, such as Lohamei Herut Yisrael (Lehi) and Irgun, were increasingly at war with the British Palestine administration, which was refusing to allow the resettlement in Israel from Europe of more than 250,000 Jewish Holocaust survivors. For their part, the Arabs failed to understand why they should be made victims for something not of their doing in the Holocaust.

On February 14, 1947, exasperated by its inability to solve the Palestinian problem, the British government turned matters over to the new United Nations (UN). That August the United Nations Special Commission on Palestine (UNSCOP) recommended that the British mandate be terminated and that Palestine be granted its independence on the basis of separate Arab and Jewish states. Although the Arabs numbered 1.2 million and the Jews just 600,000, the Jews would have had some 56 percent of the land. Jews supported the plan; understandably, the Arabs did not. Now desperate to quit Palestine, the British government announced acceptance of the UNSCOP recommendation and declared in September 1947 that its mandate of Palestine would terminate on May 14, 1948.

On November 29, 1947, the UN General Assembly officially approved the partition of Palestine. The Council of the Arab League announced that it was prepared to prevent the creation of a Jewish state by force if necessary, and immediately following the UN vote, militant Palestinian Arabs and foreign Arab fighters attacked Jewish communities in Palestine, beginning the Arab-Jewish Communal War (November 30, 1947–May 14, 1948). The United States, with the world's largest Jewish population, became the chief champion and most reliable ally of a Jewish state, a position that cost it dearly in its relations with the Arab world and greatly impacted subsequent geopolitics in the Middle East and throughout the world.

The British completed their pullout on May 14, 1948, and that same day David Ben-Gurion, the executive chairman and defense minister of the Jewish Agency, immediately declared the independence of the Jewish State of Israel. Leader of the Mapai (Worker's Party), Ben-Gurion became the new state's first prime minister.

At first, the interests of the United States and those of the Soviet Union regarding the Jewish state converged. U.S. recognition of Israel came only shortly before that of the Soviet Union. Moscow found common ground with Jewish suffering at the hands of the Nazis in World War II and also identified with the socialism espoused by the early Jewish settlers in Palestine and their anti-British stance. The Cold War, the reemergence of official anti-Semitism in the Soviet Union, and Moscow's desire to court the Arab states soon changed that, however.

Immediately following Ben-Gurion's declaration of independence, Egypt, Lebanon, Jordan, Syria, and Iraq invaded Palestine, beginning the Israeli War of Independence (May 15, 1948–March 10, 1949). In the war, the Jews successfully defended their new state and defeated the Arab armies. A series of armistices with neighboring states ended the fighting, with Israel left in control of an additional 26 percent of the land of Mandate Palestine west of the Jordan River. Jordan, however, controlled large portions of Judea and Samaria, later known as the West Bank.

The establishment of Israel and the subsequent war created some 600,000–700,000 Palestinian Arab refugees. Why these refugees fled their homes is much disputed, but clearly a great many were forced to flee by the Israelis. In any case, Israel refused to allow their return after the war. The matter of the right of return has been a major stumbling block to any peace settlement ever since.

Meanwhile, the Israelis set up the machinery of state. Mapai and its successor parties would govern Israel for the next 30 years. These were social democratic parties with strong roots in Zionism. As such, they were hawkish on defense but inclined toward moderate socialism in the socioeconomic sphere. The provisional government governed until February 14, 1949, following democratic elections on January 25, 1949, that established a unicameral parliament—later known as the Knesset—of 120 members. The executive (cabinet) was selected by the Knesset and was subject to it. Israel also adopted a system of proportional representation in which Knesset seats were based on the percentage of votes received. Even parties receiving relatively few votes had representation. Such parties included those representing the Arab population, those espousing various degrees of Jewish orthodoxy, the communists, and Revisionist Zionist groups.

On May 11, 1949, meanwhile, Israel was admitted to the UN. The Mapai Party remained the dominant political party after the second Knesset elections on July 30, 1951, which saw the formation of a coalition government with the religious parties.

Legislation of July 1950 established the Law of Return, granting any Jew the right to settle in Israel. In 1951 alone 687,000 Jews arrived, some 300,000 of these from Arab states. Ben-Gurion remained prime minister until 1953. He returned to that position in October 1955 and remained in office until 1963.

Israel's early years were dominated by the great challenge of absorbing and integrating into society hundreds of thousands of Jewish immigrants, including those from Eastern and Central Europe (Ashkenazi Jews), West European Jews (Sephardim

Jews), and Middle Eastern or Oriental Jews (Arabs who practice the Jewish religion). The differences in terms of cultural background and socioeconomic status among the various groups of Jews initially proved to be a challenge for the Israeli government.

In addition to money raised from Jewish communities overseas, especially in the United States, and the U.S. government, financial assistance came from an unlikely source. Chancellor Konrad Adenauer of the Federal Republic of Germany (West Germany) secured passage of legislation to provide billions of dollars in assistance to Israel during a 12-year period with payments to individual victims of the Holocaust. Israel's formative years also witnessed the creation of a mixed socialist-capitalist economy. Included in the expansion and maturation of the economy were agricultural incentives for the cultivation of additional land.

The 1949 cease-fires that ended the 1948–1949 war were not followed by peace agreements. The Arab states not only refused to recognize the existence of Israel but also refused to concede defeat in the war. They soon had imposed an economic and political boycott on Israel. Also, throughout most of the 1950s Israel suffered from repeated attacks and raids from the neighboring Arab states as well as from Palestinian Arab paramilitary and terrorist groups. Aggressive Israeli retaliation failed to stop the attacks and raids. Tension increased with the 1952 coup and revolution in Egypt led by Gamal Abdel Nasser. Indeed, Nasser proved to be an outspoken opponent of Israel and the West and a champion of Arab nationalism and unity. He supported cross-border raids into Israeli territory by so-called fedayeen (guerrilla fighters) from the Gaza Strip and formed alliances with other Arab states. He also cultivated close ties with the Soviet Union.

In 1956 Nasser nationalized the Suez Canal, which provided the pretext for the French, British, and Israeli governments to secretly plan war against Egypt. The British sought to retake control of the canal, while the French wanted to end Nasser's support of the Algerian independence movement. Israel saw the Suez Crisis as an opportunity to cooperate with Britain and France to check Nasser's power and influence, if not overthrow him.

On October 29, 1956, Israeli forces invaded the Sinai and headed for the Suez Canal. This provided the excuse for the British and the French to intervene. The U.S. government applied considerable pressure, and all three states soon agreed to withdraw. Israel, however, secured the right to free navigation through the Suez Canal and on the waterways through the Strait of Tiran and the Gulf of Aqaba. On November 7, the UN deployed a United Nations Emergency Force (UNEF) as a buffer between Egypt and Israel.

During 1957–1967, Israel was primarily preoccupied with domestic politics, including continued agricultural and industrial development. Its border with Egypt generally remained calm, although incidents with Syria in particular increased, especially over water rights as Israel diverted water from the Jordan River for irrigation purposes. This led Syria and Lebanon to divert water upstream from the Jordan. In response to this so-called water war, Israel destroyed Lebanese and Syrian projects designed to reduce water flow downstream.

Ben-Gurion resigned as prime minister in 1963 and two years later defected from the Mapai Party to create a new political organization, the Rafi Party (Israeli

Labor List). Upon Ben-Gurion's resignation, Levi Eshkol of Mapai was prime minister until his death in 1969, when Foreign Minister Golda Meir replaced him as Israel's fourth prime minister.

On May 23, 1960, in Buenos Aires, Argentina, Israeli agents captured fugitive Nazi official Adolf Eichmann, who had charge of the deportation of Jews to the death camps during World War II. Spiriting him out of Argentina, Eichmann was brought to Israel, where he was placed on trial for crimes against humanity and the Jewish people. Convicted, he was hanged on May 31, 1962, the only time the death penalty was imposed according to Israeli law. In 1965 after much internal debate and controversy, Israel established formal diplomatic relations with West Germany.

On February 22, 1966, a coup brought a military government to power in Syria. It was committed to the Palestinian cause and the liberation of Palestine, and incidents along Israel's border with Syria increased significantly. Throughout the spring of 1967, Israel faced increasing attacks from Syria and from the Palestine Liberation Organization (PLO), a quasi-terrorist organization created in 1964 to represent the Palestinians Arabs and coordinate efforts with Arabs states to liberate Palestine. The PLO also mounted raids from Jordan.

On May 13, 1967, the Soviet Union provided Egypt with false information that Israel was mobilizing troops on the Syrian border, and on May 16 Nasser declared a state of emergency. Egypt, Syria, and Jordan then all mobilized their forces.

Buoyed by strong support in the Arab world for his belligerent stance, Nasser on May 16 demanded that the UNEF quit the Sinai immediately. The UNEF complied on May 19. Syrian and Egyptian forces were now on maximum alert.

Nasser then announced Egypt's intention to close the Strait of Tiran to Israeli shipping. This was the principal route for Israeli trade with Asia and the transit point for 90 percent of its oil imports. Israel had already let it be known that it would consider such a step a cause for war.

Nasser's announcement regarding the Strait of Tiran was largely a bluff, for he assumed that the threat of closing the strait would force Israel to withdraw its supposed increased forces along the Syrian border. On May 22, however, Egyptian minister of defense Field Marshal Abdel Hakim Amer ordered Egyptian forces to close the strait the next day. A countermanding order would have signaled weakness, and Nasser now ordered the Egyptian military to prepare for war. On May 30 Jordanian king Hussein arrived in Cairo and there concluded a mutual security pact with Egypt.

On paper, the balance of forces heavily favored the Arab states. The Israel Defense Forces (IDF) had 230,000 troops, 1,100 tanks, 200 artillery pieces, 260 combat aircraft, and 22 naval vessels. Egypt and Syria together had 263,000 men, 1,950 tanks, 915 artillery pieces, 521 combat aircraft, and 75 naval vessels. Counting Iraqi and Jordanian forces, the Arab advantage swelled to 409,000 men, 2,437 tanks, 1,487 artillery pieces, 649 combat aircraft, and 90 naval vessels.

Now certain of war and unwilling to allow the Arab forces time to fully mobilize their much larger resources, on June 4, despite strong U.S. opposition, Israeli prime minister Levi Eshkol authorized a preemptive strike against Egypt.

The Arab-Israeli war of 1967, known to history as the Six-Day War, began on the morning of June 5 and for all practical purposes was over by noon. The Israeli

Air Force (IAF) offensive of that day remains one of the most stunning successes in modern warfare. Destruction of the Egyptian Air Force was essential if the Israeli Army was to enjoy success, yet Israel was outnumbered by Egypt and Syria two to one in combat aircraft. It would also be difficult for the Israeli Army to defend against Egyptian and Syrian air attacks coming from two different directions, and Israel was too small in area for early warning systems to provide sufficient time for Israeli fighters to scramble.

The IAF achieved a brilliant success not only against the Egyptians but also against Syria and Jordan. And following an Iraqi air strike on Israel, the IAF also attacked Iraqi air bases in the Mosul area. The IAF could now turn to close air support of Israeli mechanized ground forces, which had begun operations in the Sinai simultaneous with the initial air attacks.

The Egyptians, it should be noted, were handicapped by the fact that 50,000 of their best troops were tied down in the civil war in Yemen. Gaza surrendered on June 6. As the Israelis drove forward in the Sinai, Egyptian Army commander Field Marshal Amer ordered a general withdrawal. Meanwhile, Israeli air and amphibious forces secured Sharm el-Sheikh.

On June 8 Israeli units reached the Suez Canal, and by the end of the day the Sinai east of the Suez Canal was firmly under Israeli control. A cease-fire went into effect on June 10. Egypt had lost 80 percent of its military equipment and had

The Israeli Air Strikes of June 5, 1967

At the start of the Six-Day War, the Israeli Air Force (IAF) was outnumbered by Egypt and Syria two to one in combat aircraft. The Israeli air attack plan relied on accurate, timely, and precise intelligence. The initial aircraft took off from airfields all around Israel and flew west, under radio silence and at low altitude to avoid radar out over the Mediterranean, and then turned south to strike Egyptian airfields simultaneously. This also coincided with the return of Egyptian aircraft to base from morning patrols, when most pilots were having breakfast.

Israeli air and ground crews were highly trained and able to reduce turnaround time between missions to a minimum. They could thus fly up to four sorties a day, twice the number for their opponents. The operation was extremely risky, however, in that it committed almost all Israeli strike aircraft, leaving only a dozen fighters behind to defend Israel itself.

The IAF achieved complete tactical surprise. The first attack wave struck 10 Egyptian airfields. Only 4 Egyptian aircraft, all trainers, were in the air at the time, and all were shot down. Subsequent waves arrived at 10-minute intervals. Only eight Egyptian MiGs managed to take off during the strikes, and all were shot down. In all, the IAF attacked 17 major Egyptian airfields with some 500 sorties in just under three hours, wiping out half of Egyptian Air Force strength of 431 combat aircraft. In all, during the war the Arab side lost 390 aircraft of their prewar strength of 969 aircraft. Total IAF losses were 32 aircraft shot down of 354 at the beginning of the war, only 2 of these to aerial combat.

some 11,500 troops killed, 20,000 wounded, and 5,500 taken prisoner. The IDF sustained 338 killed. On June 9, meanwhile, Nasser had offered his resignation, but large supportive Egyptian public demonstrations caused him to remain.

Israeli leaders had urged King Hussein of Jordan to stay out of the war, informing him at the onset of fighting that their dispute was with Egypt. Hussein wanted to avoid participation but came under heavy public pressure to act, in one of the most fateful decisions of the modern Middle East. He was also deceived by false early Cairo broadcasts claiming major Egyptian military successes. Hussein hoped to satisfy his allies with minimum military action short of all-out war. Jordanian 155mm guns went into action against Tel Aviv, and Jordanian aircraft attempted to strafe a small Israeli airfield. These steps, however, led Israel to declare war on Jordan.

The Israelis quickly surrounded the Old City of Jerusalem. Although Jordanian forces there put up a stiff fight, the Israelis were able to prevent them from relieving. The Israelis also captured Latrun, opening the road between Tel Aviv and Jerusalem to Jewish traffic for the first time since 1947. On June 7 the Israelis stormed the Old City, forcing a Jordanian withdrawal. That same day the Israelis captured Bethlehem, Hebron, and Etzion. Despite Jordanian counterattacks, the Israelis also advanced on and seized Nablus. Jordanian forces then withdrew across the Jordan River, and both Israel and Jordan agreed to a cease-fire.

The Syrian front at first saw only artillery duels, with the Syrians not wishing to initiate offensive action. On June 9, with resources released from other fronts, the Israelis began major offensive action and broke through Syrian defenses in the northern Golan, resisting calls from the United States not to occupy the Golan Heights. Instead the Israelis advanced on and captured Quneitra. Only when the Golan Heights was firmly in their hands did they agree to a cease-fire of June 10.

There also was some fighting at sea. On June 8 the *Liberty,* a U.S. electronic intelligence-gathering ship, was in international waters some 13 miles off El Arish when it came under attack by Israeli air and naval units. Thirty-four Americans died in the attack, and another 172 were wounded, many seriously. Although the ship was badly damaged, its crew managed to keep it afloat and make Malta, escorted by ships of the U.S. Sixth Fleet. The Israeli government later apologized for the attack and paid nearly $13 million in compensation. Official inquiries concluded that it was a matter of mistaken identity.

In the Six-Day War, Israel suffered some 800 dead, 2,440 wounded, and 16 missing or taken prisoner. Arab losses, chiefly Egyptian, were some 14,300 dead, 23,800 wounded, and 10,500 missing or taken prisoner. Israel lost 100 tanks and 40 aircraft, while the Arabs lost 950 tanks and 368 aircraft.

The Six-Day War vastly increased the amount of territory controlled by Israel. Israel gained from Egypt all of the Sinai east of the Suez Canal, including the Gaza Strip; from Jordan, it secured the entire east bank of the Jordan River and the Old City of Jerusalem; and from Syria, it added the Golan Heights.

These Israeli territorial acquisitions would make securing a Middle East peace settlement much more difficult. Although Israel returned the Sinai to Egypt in 1978 and withdrew from the Gaza Strip in 2005, it has showed a marked reluctance to yield the Golan Heights, the West Bank, and Old Jerusalem. Politically

Israeli Sherman M4 tanks moving toward the Sinai during Israel's invasion of the Sinai Peninsula in the Six-Day War, June 6, 1967. (Universal History Archive/UIG via Getty Images)

conservative Israelis and Ultra-Orthodox Jews consider the West Bank part of the ancient Jewish state never to be given up.

Humiliated by their defeat, the Arab states refused to negotiate with, recognize, or make peace with Israel. This was spelled out in the Khartoum Arab Summit Communiqué of September 1, 1967. The war united much of Israeli society and muted, if not silenced, most political disputes for several years. On January 21, 1968, the Mapai Party merged with two other socialist political parties to form the Labor Party.

In 1967, the so-called War of Attrition began with Egyptian forces shelling Israeli targets in the Sinai along the Suez Canal and with Israel responding with retaliatory raids and air strikes. Israel also constructed the Bar Lev Line, an elaborate series of defensive fortifications to shield Israeli forces from Egyptian artillery fire. Nasser sought Soviet military aid and support, including surface-to-air missiles (SAMs). By 1969, the euphoria from Israel's decisive 1967 victory had turned into disillusionment with rising Israeli casualties and the fact that peace was still elusive.

Israel also experienced increasing incidents along its border with Jordan in PLO raids. These triggered retaliatory Israeli attacks that ultimately provoked a civil war between the PLO and the Jordanian government in 1970, which culminated in the so-called Black September that saw heavy fighting between the Jordanian Army and the PLO, which was expelled from Jordan to Lebanon. During Black September, Syria sought to intervene on the side of the PLO but was deterred from doing so by Israel.

On August 7, 1970, with American support, UN-brokered peace talks between Egypt and Israel brought a cease-fire and a temporary end to the War of Attrition. But no settlement was reached regarding Israel's 1967 occupation of Arab territories.

Egyptian president Gamal Abdel Nasser died in September 1970. His successor, Anwar Sadat, was determined to change the status quo regarding Israel. Sadat sought a peace process that would lead to Israeli withdrawal from the Sinai but without a formal general peace agreement. Toward that end, he resumed negotiations that Nasser had ended in 1955.

The failure of his diplomatic efforts in 1971, however, led Sadat to begin planning a military operation to break the political stalemate. Sadat believed that even a minor Egyptian military success would change the military equilibrium and force a political settlement. Israel's strength was in its air force and armored divisions in maneuver warfare. Egyptian strengths were the ability to build a strong defense line and new Soviet-supplied SAMs deployed in batteries along the canal and deep within Egypt. Sadat hoped to paralyze the IAF with the SAMs and counter the Israelis' advantage in maneuver warfare by forcing them to attack well-fortified and well-defended Egyptian strongholds.

In an attempt to dilute the Israeli military forces on the Sinai front and place maximum stress on his opponent, Sadat brought in Syria for a coordinated surprise attack. The key to success was secrecy. Were Israel to suspect that an attack was imminent, it would undoubtedly launch a preventive attack, as in 1967. That part of Sadat's plan, at least, was successful. A combination of effective Egyptian deceptive measures and Israeli arrogance contributed to Israel's failure to comprehend the threat.

On the Israeli-Egyptian front, Egypt amassed nearly 800,000 soldiers, 2,200 tanks, 2,300 artillery pieces, 150 SAM batteries, and 550 aircraft. Along the canal, Egypt deployed five infantry divisions with accompanying armored elements, supported by additional infantry and armored independent brigades. This force was backed by three mechanized divisions and two armored divisions. Israel had only a single division supported by 280 tanks.

Not until the early morning hours of October 6 did Israeli military intelligence conclude that an Egyptian attack was imminent. Brigadier General Eliahu Zeira, Israeli director of intelligence, warned Lieutenant General David Elazar, IDF chief of staff, but Prime Minister Golda Meir decided against a preemptive strike.

The Yom Kippur War of October 6–26, 1973, also known as the Ramadan War, the October War, and the 1973 Arab-Israeli War, commenced at 2:00 p.m. on October 6, on Yom Kippur, the holiest day for Jews, when Egypt launched a massive air strike against Israeli artillery and command positions. At the same time, Egyptian artillery shelled the Bar Lev Line fortifications. Egyptian commandos crossed the canal followed by engineers, who quickly constructed bridges, allowing the Egyptians to pass across sizable numbers of infantry and armor. By October 8, Egyptian infantry and some 500 tanks had pushed three to five miles east of the canal, which was defended by the SAM batteries.

The Israelis meanwhile mobilized two armored divisions and on October 8 launched a quick counteroffensive to repel the Egyptians. These encountered the far larger and more well-equipped Egyptian force protected by handheld antitank missiles. The Egyptians crushed the Israeli counteroffensive. Israeli ground-support aircraft also suffered heavy losses against Egyptian antiaircraft defenses, especially from SAMs. Following this setback, the Israeli General Staff decided to halt offensive actions on the Suez front and give priority to the Syria front.

Sadat now overruled his ground commander, Field Marshal Ahmed Ismail Ali, and, following Syrian pleas for assistance, ordered a resumption of the offensive on October 11. This, however, took Egyptian forces out of their prepared defensive positions and removed them from the effective SAM cover on the other side of the canal. On October 14 the Israelis threw back the Egyptians and inflicted heavy losses.

On October 15–16 the Israelis located a gap, unknown to the Egyptian high command, between the two Egyptian divisions. One Israeli division drove through that gap, and part of it crossed the canal. An Israeli paratroop brigade then established a bridgehead on the west bank. The Israeli high command now sought to establish a SAM-free zone over which Israeli aircraft could maneuver and to cut off Egyptian troops east of the canal.

With the Egyptians threatening the Israelis west of the canal, heavy fighting occurred in the so-called Battle of the Chinese Farm during October 16–18. The Egyptians suffered heavy losses, and a second Israeli armored division crossed the canal and drove westward, rolling up Egyptian base camps and capturing antiaircraft positions and SAM sites. An Israeli effort to capture Ismailia failed, however. The Egyptians also turned back an Israeli effort to take Suez during October 23–24, and a cease-fire went into effect on October 25.

On the Syrian front, President Hafez al-Assad sought to regain the Golan Heights, captured by Israel in 1967, thereby gaining security for its northern settlements from sporadic Syrian bombardment. Unlike Sadat, Assad had no intention of using the war as leverage for a settlement with Israel.

On October 6, simultaneous with the Egyptian air strikes to the south, Syria launched a massive air strike accompanied by heavy artillery fire against Israeli positions on the Golan Heights. Syrian ground forces then advanced. They counted some 60,000 men in two armored divisions (600 tanks) and two infantry divisions (another 300 tanks). The Syrians also had some 140 artillery batteries. Opposing them, the Israelis had some 12,000 troops, 177 tanks, and 11 artillery batteries.

With the exception of one important outpost, Israeli forces were not taken by surprise. Israeli tanks were in hull-down positions behind earthen barricades, with infantry in their fighting positions. The one exception was Mount Herman. Syrian helicopters carried commandos to the back of the fortified Israeli observation post on Mount Hermon, which provided an excellent view of the Golan Heights and the Damascus Plateau. The two-platoon Israeli garrison was taken completely by surprise, and all were slain, including those who surrendered.

The main Syrian attack by the four divisions occurred against two Israeli brigades, but Israeli mobilization was rapid, with reservists soon in place. Within a day the Israelis halted the northern Syrian thrusts. The two southern Syrian thrusts, however, nearly entered the Jordan River Valley. Had they been able to push beyond the escarpment, the Syrians could have cut Israel in two.

The IAF went into action, and although many of the Israeli jets fell prey to Syrian SAMs and mobile antiaircraft guns, a great many Syrian tanks were knocked out. Israeli close air support, the rapid arrival of reserves, and unimaginative Syrian attacks prevented the Syrians from retaking the southern Golan.

During October 8–9 the Israelis counterattacked in the south, and on October 10 they mounted a major counteroffensive north of the Quneitra-Damascus road, pushing the Syrians back to and beyond the prewar Israeli-Syrian border.

Beginning on October 9 also, Israel launched an air campaign deep within Syria, striking the Ministry of Defense in Damascus as well as seaports, industrial sites, and fuel-storage areas. Profoundly impacting the Syrian economy, these attacks continued until October 21.

On October 12 the Israelis began to withdraw some units south to fight on the Sinai front. Nonetheless, by October 14 they had opened up a salient inside Syria some 10 miles deep, 30 miles wide, and only 25 miles from Damascus. The Israelis held it during October 15–19, despite fierce Syrian and Iraqi counterattacks, with Iraq having now entered the war. On October 15 the Israelis repulsed an Iraqi armored division, and on October 19 they halted another counterattack against the salient, this one spearheaded by Jordanian units. The Israelis maintained these positions until the cease-fire of October 24. On October 22 following two failed assaults on October 8 and 21, Israeli helicopter-borne forces retook Mount Hermon.

In the fighting for the Golan Heights, Israel lost nearly 800 dead and 250 tanks put out of action, along with a number of ground-support aircraft shot down. Certainly a key factor was the ability of the Israelis to quickly return disabled tanks to battle. Syrian losses were perhaps 8,000 men killed, 1,150 tanks destroyed, and 118 aircraft lost.

There was also fighting at sea, with the Egyptians imposing a naval blockade of Israel's Mediterranean coast while also halting seaborne traffic to Eilat. On the first night of the war, Israeli missile boats attacked the chief Syrian Mediterranean port of Latakia (Ladhaqiyya). Syrian missile boats engaged them, and in the first naval battle in history between missile-firing ships, the Israelis defeated the incoming Syrian fire-and-forget Styx missiles while using their own radar-guided Gabriel ship-to-ship missiles to destroy three Syrian missile boats and a minesweeper. The Syrian Navy then remained in port for the rest of the war. The Battle of Latakia brought new prestige for the Israeli Navy, previously regarded as only a poor relation of its highly regarded army and air force.

Among other naval engagements, on October 8–9 off the Egyptian port of Damietta, Egyptian missile boats sortied to engage an Israeli missile boat task force, which sank four of them for no losses of its own. In an action the next night off Port Said in Egypt, another Egyptian missile boat was sunk. The remaining Egyptian missile boats then withdrew to Damietta and Alexandria.

Both the United States, supporting Israel, and the Soviet Union, supporting the Arab states, were caught off guard by the war, although the Soviets probably learned of the Egyptian and Syrian plans several days in advance of the actual attacks. Both the Soviets and the Americans sent supplies to their sides during the war. Between October 14 and 21 the United States airlifted some 20,000 tons of supplies to the Israelis, as opposed to some 15,000 tons by the Soviet Union to the Arab states.

A Soviet announcement on October 24 that it was placing seven airborne divisions on alert brought a U.S. announcement the next day that its armed forces were on precautionary alert. Any possibility of a Soviet-U.S. armed clash ended with a UN Security Council resolution, with both the Soviet and U.S. representatives voting in the affirmative, that established a 7,000-man force to enforce the cease-fires in the Sinai Peninsula and the Golan Heights. The cease-fires went into effect on October 25.

Casualty figures for the Yom Kippur (Ramadan) War vary. Israel suffered 2,521–2,800 killed in action, 7,250–8,800 wounded, and 293 taken prisoner. Some 400 Israeli tanks were destroyed; another 600 were disabled but returned to service. The IAF lost 102 airplanes and 2 helicopters. There were no navy losses.

Arab losses were some 5,000–15,000 Egyptians and 3,000–3,500 Syrians killed; the number of wounded is unknown. Iraq lost 278 killed and 898 wounded, while Jordan suffered 23 killed and 77 wounded. A total of 8,372 Egyptians, 392 Syrians, 13 Iraqis, and 6 Moroccans were taken prisoner. The Arab states lost 2,250–2,300 tanks, 400 of which were taken by the Israelis in good working order and added to their inventory. Arab aircraft losses were 450–512. Nineteen Arab naval vessels, including 10 missile boats, were sunk.

Although the outcome secured Israel's borders, the war shocked the Israeli people. An investigatory agency, the Agranat Commission, led to the removal of several high-ranking officers. The commission did not assess civilian leadership responsibility. The Yom Kippur War shook Israel's confidence and morale. In the December 1973 Knesset elections the Labor Party lost seats, and the newly formed right-wing Likud Party gained strength. Political fallout from the war led Prime Minister Golda Meir to resign on April 10, 1974. Minister of Defense Moshe Dayan followed her in June. Meir was succeeded by Yitzhak Rabin, also of the Labor Party.

Although the Arab states lost the war, Egyptian president Anwar Sadat achieved his aim of erasing the trauma of their rapid defeat in the Six-Day War of 1967. The Yom Kippur War also allowed him to negotiate as an equal with Israel. On January 18, 1974, Israel and Egypt signed a disengagement agreement by which Israel agreed to pull back its forces from west of the Suez Canal and from the length of the front to create security zones. Another agreement, known as Sinai II, of September 4, 1975, saw Israel withdraw another 12–24 miles, with UN observer forces taking over that area. Still, Israel held more than two-thirds of Sinai.

During this period, Arab states along with the PLO proved much more effective in publicizing the plight of the Palestinians. Increasing acts of terrorism by the PLO also focused world attention on the Arab-Israeli conflict and the Palestinian cause. On October 14, 1974, the UN General Assembly authorized the PLO to participate in a series of debates. Included was PLO chairman Yasser Arafat, considered a terrorist in Israel and the West. He addressed the body, and on November 10, 1975, in Resolution 3379 the General Assembly declared Zionism as racist. (Resolution 3379 was revoked in 1991 by General Assembly Resolution 4686.) Israeli prime minister Rabin refused to negotiate with the PLO because it refused to recognize Israel and proclaimed as its goal the destruction of the Jewish state.

With little loss of life, on July 4, 1976, in a daring raid, Israeli commandos rescued 94 Israeli passengers and 12 crew members of an Air France plane taken by Palestinian hijackers to Entebbe, Uganda, under the protection of Ugandan dictator Idi Amin. The hijackers threatened to kill the passengers unless 40 Palestinian terrorists in Israeli and West European prisons were released. The successful operation proved to be a major morale boost for Israel and its military.

In May 1977 Likud ended Labor's 29-year political reign, and Menachem Begin became prime minister. Now seeking to jump-start the peace process, Egyptian president Sadat shocked the world by announcing on November 9, 1977, his willingness to go to Jerusalem for a face-to-face meeting with the Israelis to negotiate peace. Accepting an invitation by Begin, Sadat arrived in Israel on November 19, the first Arab head of state to do so, effectively recognizing Israel's right to exist. Sadat both met with Begin and addressed the Knesset. Although every other Arab state refused to negotiate with Israel, after two years of negotiations mediated by U.S. president Jimmy Carter, Egypt and Israel made peace on March 26, 1979. In these Camp David Accords, Israel withdrew from the Sinai in exchange for Egypt recognizing Israel. Discussions about the status of the Palestinians took place but never achieved common ground. Sadat's assassination on October 6, 1981, effectively ended the process. Meanwhile, most Arab leaders condemned the peace treaty, and Egypt was suspended from the Arab League.

On July 7, 1981, the IAF bombed the Osiraq nuclear reactor in Iraq, thwarting possible Iraqi efforts to acquire nuclear weapons. Then on June 6, 1982, Israeli forces invaded Lebanon, which had been experiencing a civil war since 1975, ostensibly to defend its northern border from increasing terrorist attacks from Lebanon but also to expel both the PLO and Syrian forces from Lebanon, which it did by laying siege to Beirut and forcing the PLO to relocate to Tunisia. The 1982 Lebanon War came at terrible human cost and material destruction in Lebanon, and Israel failed to achieve its broad policy objectives of creating a stable pro-Israeli government in Lebanon. In 1983, Begin resigned and was replaced by fellow Likud member Yitzhak Shamir. Israel withdrew from most of Lebanon in June 1985 but maintained a buffer zone there in southern Lebanon until May 24, 2000, when it surrendered that territory as well.

A major Palestinian uprising, the First Intifada, erupted in 1987 in the Israeli-occupied territories of the West Bank and the Gaza Strip and demanded significant Israeli military resources. The images of armed Israeli soldiers battling Palestinian youths, mostly throwing stones, led to considerable international criticism of Israel. In 1991 following Iraq's August 1990 invasion of Kuwait, Iraq targeted Israel with Scud missiles in an ultimately unsuccessful attempt to provoke Israel into attacking Iraq and cause the Arab states to withdraw from the multinational U.S.-led coalition force.

The collapse of the Soviet Union in December 1991 and the end of the Cold War brought into Israel hundreds of thousands of Jews from the Soviet Union. This also left many Arab states, previously allied with Moscow, isolated and gave the United States much more influence and leverage in the region. Accordingly, peace

Israel's Goals during the 1982 Invasion of Lebanon

Operation PEACE FOR GALILEE, the June 6, 1982, Israeli invasion of southern Lebanon, was in response to numerous attacks by the Palestine Liberation Organization (PLO) in southern Lebanon across the border against northern Israel. Understandably, the Israeli cabinet was loath to place its forces in an urban combat situation that would undoubtedly bring heavy civilian casualties and opposition from the United States and Western Europe. Israeli prime minister Menachem Begin and Defense Minister Ariel Sharon, both of whom had a deep commitment to Eretz Israel, the ancestral homeland of the Jews that embraces territory beyond Israel's borders into Lebanon and across the Jordan River, merely informed the cabinet that the goal was merely to break up PLO bases in southern Lebanon and push back PLO and Syrian forces in Lebanon some 25 miles, beyond rocket range of Galilee. Once the operation began, however, Sharon quickly expanded it to incorporate Beirut, which is well beyond the stated 25-mile mark. Although it was then too late, many in the cabinet believed that they had been deliberately misled.

talks were held in 1991 and 1992 among Israel, Syria, Lebanon, Jordan, and the Palestinians. Those talks paved the way for the 1993 Oslo Accords between Israel and the PLO, stipulating the beginning of Palestinian self-rule in the West Bank and the Gaza Strip and peace between Israel and Jordan on October 26, 1994.

Initial Israeli support for the Oslo Accords waned following a series of terrorist attacks by Hamas—a Palestinian terrorist group founded in 1987 at the beginning of the First Intifada—which opposed peace with Israel. On November 4, 1995, a right-wing Jewish nationalist assassinated Prime Minister Rabin for his peace efforts with the Palestinians and willingness to cede occupied territory in the West Bank. Many observers believe that Rabin's death effectively ended Israeli willingness to make meaningful territorial concessions for peace.

Continued Hamas terrorism led to the election as prime minister of hard-liner Benjamin Netanyahu of Likud. Netanyahu refused to pursue the "land for peace" dialogue with the Palestinians, and the peace process stalled. In 1999 Labor's Ehud Barak defeated Netanyahu, and in 2000 talks between Barak and Yasser Arafat, mediated by U.S. president Bill Clinton, came very close but failed to produce agreement on a Palestinian state owing to Arafat's intransigence.

Collapse of the peace talks and a provocative visit on September 28, 2000, by Likud's Ariel Sharon to the contested religious site known to Jews as the Temple Mount and to Muslims as the Dome of the Rock sparked the Second or Al-Aqsa Intifada, which lasted until February 8, 2005. Sharon was elected prime minister in March 2001 and was reelected in 2003.

Under Sharon, the Israeli government began constructing a series of solid wall barriers to separate Israel proper from most of the West Bank. The stated purpose of the barrier was the prevention of terrorist attacks. The barrier itself, known in Hebrew as the Separation Wall and to the Arabs as the Apartheid Wall, runs only partly along the 1949 Jordanian-Israeli armistice line (the Green Line) and partly through the West Bank, diverging eastward from the armistice line by up to 12 miles in order to include on the western (Israeli) side concentrations of highly populated Jewish settlements, such as East Jerusalem. The barrier has been widely condemned as a violation of international law and a major impediment to the establishment of a viable independent Palestinian state.

In the face of Second Intifada and stalled peace talks with the Palestinians, in September 2005 Israel withdrew from the Gaza Strip, although it controlled its borders, coast, and airspace. Hamas soon came to dominate Gaza. After Sharon suffered a massive stroke on January 4, 2006, Ehud Olmert became acting prime minister. Olmert was formally elected to the post following the victory of his Kadima Party in the legislative elections of April 14, 2006.

On January 25, 2006, elections were held for the second Palestinian Legislative Council, the legislature of the Palestinian National Authority. To the surprise of many, these were won by the more militant Hamas, which campaigned on a platform of change and reform, winning 74 of the 132 seats, while the ruling Fatah won only 45 seats. The Hamas victory was regarded as a major setback for the peace process.

On June 25, 2006, after a Hamas raid killed two Israeli soldiers and captured another, Israel launched Operation SUMMER RAINS, a series of attacks into the Gaza Strip and arrests of Hamas leaders in the West Bank. The next month, the Olmert government became involved in a monthlong conflict in Lebanon following an attack by Hezbollah on Israel that killed three Israeli soldiers and captured two. Hezbollah is an Iranian- and Syrian-backed Shia Islamic extremist group and a major political entity in Lebanon. To the surprise of many, Hezbollah, which was well armed and had established strong defensive positions in southern Lebanon, fought very well indeed. This July 12–August 14, 2006, Lebanon War (also called the 2006 Israel-Hezbollah War and known in Lebanon as the July War and in Israel as the Second Lebanon War) devastated much of southern Lebanon. Israel failed to achieve its broad policy objectives, and Hezbollah appeared strengthened.

Meanwhile, Israeli voters remained keenly interested in such issues as the role of the Orthodox minority, the rights of Israeli Arabs, the fate of Israeli settlements in the West Bank, and the ups and downs of the economy. The two nearest and most direct threats to Israel remained Hamas and Hezbollah, although the Israeli government expressed great concern regarding threats by Iran and what it asserted was Iran's desire to acquire nuclear weapons. Iranian president Mahmoud Ahmadinejad, a Holocaust denier, repeatedly called for the destruction of Israel.

After midnight on September 6, 2007, the IAF carried out Operation ORCHARD, a surprise raid on a suspected nuclear development facility in the Deir ez-Zor region of Syria. Yet in early 2008, Syrian president Bashar al-Assad revealed that Israel and Syria had been engaged in secret peace discussions, with Turkey as a mediator.

In December 2008, the shaky Hamas-Israeli cease-fire ended when Hamas fighters began launching rockets on Israel from Hamas-controlled Gaza. Israel responded with heavy air strikes, and on January 3, 2009, the government sent troops into Gaza. This First Gaza War (Israeli Operation CAST LEAD) of December 27, 2008–January 18, 2009, wrought considerable physical destruction in Gaza and killed perhaps 1,300 Palestinians, while Israel lost 13 dead (10 of them military personnel). Tensions remained high thereafter.

In February 2009 after Olmert declared his intention to resign the premiership, parliamentary elections occurred but resulted in an unclear mandate. Israeli president Shimon Peres then asked Netanyahu to form a coalition government, which by necessity would include members from the Likud, Kadima, and other parties. During his second premiership, Netanyahu showed very little inclination to try to resolve the Israeli-Palestinian conflict through meaningful negotiation, all the while increasing the number of Jewish housing settlements on the West Bank. Netanyahu repeatedly warned of the dangers of Iran's suspected nuclear weapons ambitions, and his hard-line approach resulted in badly strained relations with the Barack Obama administration in Washington. Netanyahu's political coalition won a majority of seats in the 2013 elections, which saw him continue as prime minister. While he continued his policies toward economic liberalization, renewed peace talks with the Palestinians that commenced in the summer of 2013 yielded no tangible results.

After the kidnapping of 3 Israeli teenagers in the West Bank on June 12, 2014, the IDF initiated Operation BROTHER'S KEEPER to find the teens. Israeli authorities arrested some 350 Palestinians, including nearly all Hamas leaders in the West Bank. Five Palestinians were also killed. The bodies of the 3 teenagers were subsequently discovered, and Netanyahu blamed Hamas. Palestinian president Mahmoud Abbas maintained that there was no evidence that Hamas was behind the kidnappings, and others were also skeptical. In response, however, Hamas in Gaza began launching rockets that targeted Israeli cities. Netanyahu responded with overwhelming force.

During July 8–August 26, 2014, Israeli forces again invaded Gaza, in Operation PROTECTIVE EDGE. In the 2014 Gaza conflict, Israel lost 66 soldiers and 6 civilians killed, while Palestinian dead were about 2,300. Many more were wounded on each side, and physical damage in Gaza was immense.

Angered by the April 2014 agreement between the Fatah-dominated Palestinian National Authority and Hamas to hold national elections in late 2014 and form a compromise unity government, Netanyahu increased Jewish housing construction in Arab areas. This brought sharp condemnation internationally, including from the European Community and the Obama administration.

On December 2, 2014, Netanyahu fired his cabinet and called for new elections to be held in March 2015, in advance of the date mandated by law. This occurred amid rising criticism of Israel from the United States and Western Europe, with many believing that Netanyahu had rejected the two-state solution in favor of outright Israeli annexation of the West Bank. In a stunning development, on December 23, 2014, Foreign Minister Avigdor Lieberman denounced Netanyahu's Palestinian policy, accusing him of not doing anything to advance the peace process.

On March 3, 2015, in an unprecedented interjection in U.S. politics, Netanyahu was invited by the majority Republican Party members in the U.S. Congress to address a joint session to voice his adamant opposition to a pending diplomatic agreement with Iran regarding that country's nuclear weapons program. The speech greatly angered the Obama administration and brought U.S.-Israeli relations to a historic low. On March 16, the day before Israeli national elections, in order to attract right-wing votes, Netanyahu announced his opposition to a two-state solution. His coalition narrowly won, whereupon he publicly reversed his position on a two-state solution.

On August 22, only weeks after the nuclear deal with Iran was concluded, U.S. and Israeli media outlets revealed that in 2009 and 2010 Israeli leaders, including Netanyahu, had drawn up plans to attack Iran but shelved the scheme when it encountered stiff resistance from some Israeli cabinet members. In October 2015 Netanyahu created an international stir when he stated that Haj Amin al-Husseini, Jerusalem's grand mufti during World War II, had helped convince Nazi leaders to implement the Holocaust. This claim, which has long been debunked by scholars, created even more antipathy between Muslims and Israelis.

By March 2016, Netanyahu's coalition government showed considerable signs of strain as a number of Ultra-Orthodox members threatened to revolt over the government's plans to create non-Orthodox prayer space at the Western Wall. On May 20 Israeli defense minister Moshe Yaalon resigned, claiming that the nation was being taken over by "extremist and dangerous elements" after Netanyahu moved to replace him with longtime Netanyahu rival and far-right politician Avigdor Lieberman to strengthen the governing coalition. As the Defense Ministry also runs civil affairs in the occupied West Bank, this did not bode well for the Palestinians there. A former chief of Israel's armed forces, Yaalon had shored up relations with the Pentagon that provided a counterweight to Netanyahu's policy feuds with President Obama regarding peace talks with the Palestinians and Iran's nuclear program. By contrast, Lieberman is inexperienced militarily and is known for his past hawkish talk against Palestinians, Israel's Arab minority, and Egypt, an important Israeli regional security partner.

Meanwhile, ongoing construction of new Israeli settlements in the West Bank, undertaken in defiance of public opinion, makes a two-state solution far more difficult. In mid-2016, peace between Israel, the Palestinians, and Israeli's Arab neighbors remained as elusive as ever.

Timeline

1516	The Ottoman Turks establish control over the region encompassing present-day Palestine.
1897	Desiring to escape persecution in many parts of Europe and live together in peace, the first World Zionist Congress (WZC) meets in Basel, Switzerland. Subsequent WZCs confirm Palestine as the location for the Jewish national homeland.
May 16, 1916	With the Ottoman Empire having sided with the Central Powers in World War I (1914–1918), the French and British enter into discussions regarding the possible disposition of Ottoman territory in the

Middle East. On this date, French diplomat François-Georges Picot and British diplomat Sir Mark Sykes sign an agreement assigning what will be postwar Iraq, Transjordan, and Palestine to Britain, while France will receive control of what will be Syria and Lebanon.

Nov 2, 1917   The British government issues the Balfour Declaration, named for British foreign secretary Arthur James Balfour. An effort to secure Jewish support for the Allied war effort, it announces British support for the "establishment in Palestine of a national home for the Jewish people."

1920   Steadily increasing Jewish immigration to Palestine and Jewish purchases of Arab lands bring sporadic Arab attacks against the Jewish settlements. In response, Jews form the Haganah, a clandestine defense organization.

Apr 1920   At the San Remo Conference in Italy, Britain and France secure the approval of the other Allied powers for their division of the former Ottoman Empire's Middle Eastern territory as League of Nations mandates along the lines of the Sykes-Picot Agreement.

Apr 1921   Britain splits Palestine into the Emirate of Transjordan, the territory east of the Jordan River, and Palestine to the west.

1929   Heightened violence leads the British to halt all Jewish settlement in Palestine, but Jewish outcries cause the British to reverse this policy. Soon there is a three-way struggle between the British and militant Arabs and Jews.

1936–1939   Resentment brings an Arab revolt, forcing the British to dispatch to Palestine 20,000 additional troops and resulting in the deaths of some 5,000 Arabs and many more injured.

1937   The British government considers partitioning Palestine into Arab and Jewish states but a year later rejects this as not feasible.

1939   The British government announces that Palestine will become an independent state within 10 years. The British also sharply curtail Jewish immigration and restrict the sale of Arab land to Jews. This policy of attempting to favor the Arabs continues during World War II, when the British even intercept and turn back ships carrying Jews attempting to escape the Holocaust in Europe.

1945   Realization of the full extent of the Holocaust, which has caused the deaths of more than 6 million Jews, dramatically changes attitudes throughout most of the world in favor of Jewish settlement in Palestine and even the creation of a Jewish state there. Armed Zionist terrorist organizations, such as Lohamei Herut Yisrael (Lehi) and Irgun, are increasingly at war with British authorities in Palestine, who are refusing to allow the resettlement in Israel of more than 250,000 Jewish Holocaust survivors.

Feb 14, 1947   The British government turns matters over to the new United Nations (UN).

Aug 1947   The UN Special Commission on Palestine (UNSCOP) recommends that the British mandate be terminated and that Palestine be granted its independence, with separate Arab and Jewish states. Although the Arabs have two-thirds of the population, the Jews would receive a majority of the land. Understandably, the Arabs reject this.

Sep 1947   Desperate to quit Palestine, the British government announces acceptance of the UNSCOP recommendation and declares that its mandate of Palestine will end on May 14, 1948.

Nov 29, 1947   The UN General Assembly officially approves the partition of Palestine.

Nov 30, 1947–   The Arab-Jewish Communal War. The Arab League announces
May 14, 1948   that it is prepared to prevent the creation of a Jewish state by force, and militant Palestinian Arabs and foreign Arab fighters attack Jewish communities in Palestine.

May 14, 1948   With the British having completed their pullout on this date, David Ben-Gurion, executive chairman and defense minister of the Jewish Agency, declares the independent Jewish State of Israel. He is the Jewish state's first prime minister.

May 15, 1948   The Arab armies of Egypt, Lebanon, Jordan, Syria, and Iraq invade Palestine, beginning the Israeli War of Independence. A series of armistices with neighboring states bring the war to a close on March 10, 1949, with Israel controlling an additional 26 percent of the land of Mandate Palestine west of the Jordan River. Some 600,000–700,000 Palestinian Arabs flee their homes into the neighboring Arab states, but Israel refuses their efforts to return.

Feb 14, 1949   Elections on January 25, 1949, lead to an Israeli unicameral parliament, later known as the Knesset, of 120 members.

May 11, 1949   Israel is admitted to the UN.

1950   The Arab states impose an economic and political boycott on Israel. Also throughout most of the 1950s, Israel suffers from repeated attacks and raids from the neighboring Arab states as well as from Palestinian Arab paramilitary and terrorist groups.

Jul 5, 1950   Israel's Law of Return stipulates that any Jew has the right to settle in Israel. In 1951 alone 687,000 Jews arrive, some 300,000 of these from Arab states.

Oct 29, 1956   Israeli forces invade the Sinai. With Egyptian president Gamal Abdel Nasser having nationalized the Suez Canal, British, French, and Israeli leaders develop a secret plan to topple him from power and restore the status quo ante. Israel is to invade Egyptian territory in the Sinai, and Britain and France will use this as an excuse to themselves invade and take control of the canal. It does not work out as planned. After some fighting, heavy pressure by the Dwight Eisenhower administration forces the three states to withdraw their forces. Israel, however, secures the right of navigation through the Suez Canal and on the waterways through the Strait of Tiran and the Gulf of Aqaba.

Nov 7, 1956   The UN authorizes the United Nations Emergency Force between Egypt and Israel.

May 23, 1960   Israeli agents capture fugitive Nazi official Adolf Eichmann in Argentina and bring him to Israel, where he is placed on trial. Convicted, he is hanged on May 31, 1962.

May 23, 1967   Egypt closes the Strait of Tiran and blockades the Gulf of Aqaba, thereby cutting off access to the Israeli port of Eliat.

Jun 5, 1967   Fearing an imminent Arab attack and invasion, Israel launches a preemptive and massive air attack, beginning the Six-Day War and crippling the air forces of Egypt, Syria, Jordan, and Iraq. Having achieved air supremacy, Israel then easily defeats the Arab armies, securing the Sinai and the Gaza Strip from Egypt, the West Bank and East Jerusalem from Jordan, and the Golan Heights from Syria. This doubles the size of the Jewish state and provides buffer zones in the new territories. In the wake of its military victory in the Six-Day War, Israel announces that it will not withdraw from the captured territories until the Arab states recognize its right to exist. Humiliated by their utter defeat, however, the Arab states refuse to make peace with Israel.

Jun 8, 1967   During the Six-Day War, units of the Israeli Air Force (IAF) and the Israeli Navy attack the *Liberty,* a U.S. electronic intelligence-gathering ship in international waters some 13 miles off El Arish on the Sinai Peninsula. Thirty-four Americans die in the attack, and another 172 are wounded, many seriously. The crew manages to keep the *Liberty* afloat and make Malta. The Israeli government later apologizes for the attack and pays compensation. Official inquiries conclude that the attack was a matter of mistaken identity.

Jul 1, 1967   The War of Attrition begins. Egypt shells Israeli targets in the Sinai along the Suez Canal, and Israel launches retaliatory raids and air strikes. Israel constructs the Bar Lev Line to shield its forces from Egyptian artillery fire. At the same time, Israel experiences increasing incidents along its border with Jordan as the Palestine Liberation Organization (PLO) launches raids, triggering retaliatory Israeli attacks.

Sep 1967   A near civil war in Jordan between the PLO and the government culminates in so-called Black September. Heavy fighting between the Jordanian Army and the PLO brings the expulsion of the latter from Jordan to Lebanon.

Aug 7, 1970   Beginning in 1970 and with American support, UN-sponsored peace talks between Egypt and Israel result in a cease-fire and a temporary end to the War of Attrition.

Oct 6–26, 1973   The Yom Kippur War. Egyptian president Anwar Sadat, frustrated at the lack of progress toward peace, arranges with Syria a combined surprise attack on Israel on the Jewish holy day of Yom Kippur. (The war is also known as the Ramadan War for the Muslim holy month of Ramadan.) Egyptian forces cross the Suez Canal, and heavy Syrian armor units smash into the Golan Heights. Although both attacking powers enjoy initial success, Israel rallies, repulses both offensives, and retains control of the Sinai and the Golan Heights. Both sides suffer heavy personnel and materiel losses. Clearly the military balance between Israel and its Arab foes has shifted, and the notion of Israeli invincibility is ended.

Apr 10, 1974   Widely blamed for having been caught by surprise, Israeli prime minister Golda Meir resigns, and Defense Minister Moshe Dayan follows her in June. Meir is succeeded by Yitzhak Rabin, also of the Labor Party.

Nov 10, 1975   With much of world opinion turning against Israel for its failure to withdraw from the occupied territories, on this date the UN General Assembly declares Zionism to be racist.

Jul 4, 1976   With little loss of life, Israeli commandos rescue Israeli airline passengers kidnapped by Palestinian hijackers and taken to Entebbe, Uganda. The hijackers had threatened to kill the passengers unless Palestinian terrorists in Israeli and West European prisons were released.

Jun 27, 1977   With the Likud Party winning the May 1977 elections, ending Labor's 29-year political reign, Menachem Begin becomes prime minister.

Nov 19, 1977   Egyptian president Sadat shocks the world by traveling to Israel, the first Arab head of state to do so. Sadat meets with Begin and also addresses the Knesset.

Mar 26, 1979	After two years of negotiations, aided by U.S. president Jimmy Carter, Egypt and Israel make peace in the Camp David Accords with the Egypt-Israel Peace Treaty, concluded in Maryland in the United States. Israel withdraws from the Sinai in exchange for Egypt recognition of Israel. In consequence, Egypt is expelled from the Arab League.
Jul 7, 1981	The IAF bombs and destroys the Osiraq nuclear reactor in Iraq, thwarting possible Iraqi efforts to acquire nuclear weapons.
Oct 6, 1981	Sadat is assassinated in Egypt by army officers opposed to peace with Israel.
Jun 6, 1982	Following increasing shelling and cross-border attacks by the PLO from Lebanon, Israeli forces invade that country, push back the PLO, and lay siege to Beirut. After considerable destruction in the city, Israel forces an agreement whereby the PLO quits Lebanon. Israel, however, fails to achieve its broad policy objectives of creating a stable pro-Israeli government in Lebanon.
Jun 1985	Israel withdraws from most of Lebanon except for a buffer zone in southern Lebanon.
Dec 8, 1987	A major Palestinian uprising, the First Intifada, erupts in the Israel-occupied territories of the West Bank and the Gaza Strip.
Jan 1991	Iraq fires 39 Scud missiles on Israel during the Persian Gulf War in an attempt to provoke Israel into attacking Iraq and causing the Arab states to withdraw from the multinational U.S.-led coalition force battling Iraq. Under intense U.S. pressure, Israel does not retaliate.
Sep 13, 1993	The First Intifada ends.
Dec 13, 1993	Peace talks between Israel and the Arab states pave the way for the signing of the Oslo Accords, between Israeli prime minister Yitzhak Rabin and PLO chairman Yasser Arafat, stipulating the beginning of Palestinian self-rule in the West Bank and the Gaza Strip.
Oct 26, 1994	Israel and Jordan sign a peace treaty.
Nov 4, 1995	A right-wing Jewish nationalist assassinates Prime Minister Rabin for his peace efforts with the Palestinians and willingness to cede occupied territory in the West Bank. Many observers believe that Rabin's death effectively ends Israeli willingness to make meaningful territorial concession to secure peace.
Jun 18, 1996	A series of attacks by Hamas, a Palestinian terrorist group formed in 1987 at the beginning of the First Intifada that opposes peace

with Israel, leads to the election as prime minister of hard-liner Benjamin Netanyahu of Likud. Netanyahu refuses to pursue the "land for peace" dialogue with the Palestinians, and the peace process stalls.

Jul 5, 1999   Ehud Barak of the Labor Party becomes prime minister.

May 24, 2000   Barak withdraws Israeli forces from southern Lebanon.

Jul 11–25,   Talks between Barak and Yasser Arafat at Camp David, Maryland,
2000   mediated by U.S. president Bill Clinton, fail on Arafat's intransigence regarding a Palestinian state.

Sep 28, 2000   A provocative visit by Likud's Ariel Sharon to the contested religious site known to Jews as the Temple Mount and to Muslims as the Dome of the Rock sparks the Second or Al-Aqsa Intifada.

Mar 7, 2001   Sharon becomes prime minister.

Jun 23, 2002   The Sharon cabinet approves the construction of solid wall barriers to separate Israel proper from most of the West Bank.

Feb 8, 2005   The Second or Al-Aqsa Intifada ends.

Sep 12, 2005   The Israeli evacuation of Gaza, carried out by the Sharon government, is completed. Hamas soon dominates Gaza.

Jan 3, 2006   Sharon suffers a massive stroke, and Ehud Olmert became acting prime minister. He is formally elected to the post following the victory of his Kadima Party in the legislative elections of April 14, 2006.

Jan 25, 2006   Elections for the Palestinian Legislative Council, the legislature of the Palestinian National Authority, end in a victory for Hamas. It secures 74 of the 132 seats; the ruling Fatah wins only 45. This is regarded as a major setback for the peace process.

Jun 25, 2006   Following a raid by Hamas that kills two Israeli soldiers and captures another, Israel launches attacks into the Gaza Strip and arrests Hamas leaders in the West Bank.

Jul 12–Aug   Following a raid by the Shiite Islamic extremist Hezbollah
14, 2006   organization in Lebanon into northern Israel that kills three Israeli soldiers and captures two, Israeli forces invade southern Lebanon. Hezbollah, well armed and having established strong defensive positions, fights well in this 2006 Lebanon War. Much of southern Lebanon is devastated, and Hezbollah is strengthened.

Sep 6, 2007   The IAF launches Operation ORCHARD, a surprise raid on a suspected nuclear development facility in Syria.

Dec 27, 2008–
Jan 18, 2009

The shaky Hamas-Israeli cease-fire ends in December 2008 when Hamas begins launching rockets on Israeli from Gaza. Israel responds with air strikes and on January 3, 2009, sends ground forces into Gaza. This First Gaza War (Israeli Operation CAST LEAD) brings considerable physical destruction in Gaza and kills some 1,300 Palestinians. Israel loses 13 killed (10 of them military personnel).

Mar 31, 2009

Benjamin Netanyahu becomes prime minister. During this, his second premiership, Netanyahu has shown very little inclination to engage in meaningful negotiations, all the while increasing the number of Jewish settlements on the West Bank. Many observers believe that Netanyahu is bent on outright Israeli annexation of the entire West Bank.

Jun 12, 2014

Three Israeli teenagers are kidnapped in the West Bank, causing Israel to launch Operation BROTHER'S KEEPER. Some 350 Palestinians are arrested, including nearly all Hamas leaders in the West Bank. Five Palestinians are killed. The bodies of the 3 teenagers are subsequently discovered, and Hamas then begins launching rockets from Gaza, targeting Israeli cities.

Jul 8–Aug 26,
2014

Netanyahu responds with overwhelming force, and Israeli forces again invade Gaza in Operation PROTECTIVE EDGE. Israel loses 66 soldiers and 6 civilians killed, while Palestinian dead are about 2,300. Many more are wounded, and physical damage in Gaza is immense.

Mar 3, 2015

Netanyahu's acceptance of an invitation from the Republican Party–controlled U.S. Congress to address a joint session of Congress to voice his (and the Republicans') opposition to a pending diplomatic agreement with Iran regarding that country's nuclear weapons program greatly angers President Barack Obama and brings U.S.-Israeli relations to a historic low.

Mar 16, 2015

The day before Israeli national elections in order to attract right-wing votes, Netanyahu announces his opposition to a two-state solution. His coalition narrowly wins, whereupon he reverses his position on a two-state solution.

May 20, 2016

Israeli defense minister Moshe Yaalon resigns, claiming that the nation was being taken over by "extremist and dangerous elements" after Netanyahu moves to replace him with longtime Netanyahu rival and far-right politician Avigdor Lieberman in an effort to strengthen his governing coalition. As the Defense Ministry also runs civil affairs in the occupied West Bank, this does not bode well for the Palestinians there. Lieberman is inexperienced militarily and is known for his past hawkish rhetoric regarding Palestinians.

Further Reading

Bickerton, Ian J. *A Concise History of the Arab-Israeli Conflict.* Upper Saddle River, NJ: Prentice Hall, 2005.

Bowen, Jeremy. *Six Days: How the 1967 War Shaped the Middle East.* London: Simon and Schuster, 2003.

Bregman, Ahron. *Israel's Wars: A History since 1947.* London: Routledge, 2002.

Bright, John. *A History of Israel,* 4th ed. Louisville, KY: Westminster John Knox Press, 2000.

Dunstan, Simon. *The Yom Kippur War, 1973.* Oxford, UK: Osprey, 2007.

Ephron, Dan. *Killing a King: The Assassination of Yitzhak Rabin and the Remaking of Israel.* New York: Norton, 2015.

Flapan, Simha. *The Birth of Israel: Myths and Realities.* New York: Pantheon Books, 1987.

Fromkin, David. *A Peace to End All Peace: The Fall of the Ottoman Empire and the Creation of the Modern Middle East.* New York: Owl, 1989.

Gilbert, Martin. *Israel: A History.* New York: RosettaBooks, 2014.

Hammel, Eric. *Six Days in June: How Israel Won the 1967 Arab-Israeli War.* New York: Simon and Schuster, 1992.

Herzog, Chaim. *The Arab-Israeli Wars: War and Peace in the Middle East.* New York: Random House, 1982.

Krämer, Gudrun. *A History of Palestine: From the Ottoman Conquest to the Founding of the State of Israel.* Princeton, NJ: Princeton University Press, 2011.

Morris, Benny. *1948: The First Arab-Israeli War.* New Haven, CT: Yale University Press, 2008.

Oren, Michael B. *Six Days of War: June 1967 and the Making of the Modern Middle East.* New York: Presidio, 2003.

Pappe, Ilan. *A History of Modern Palestine: One Land, Two Peoples.* Cambridge: Cambridge University Press, 2004.

Quandt, William B. *Peace Process: American Diplomacy and the Arab-Israeli Conflict Since 1967.* Washington, DC: Brookings Institution and University of California Press, 1993.

Rabinovich, Abraham. *The Yom Kippur War: An Epic Encounter That Transformed the Middle East.* New York: Schocken Books, 2004.

Reich, Bernard. *A Brief History of Israel.* New York: Checkmark Books, 2005.

Rosenberg, Joel C. *Israel at War.* Carol Stream, IL: Tyndale House Publishers, 2012.

Ross, Dennis. *Doomed to Succeed: The U.S.-Israel Relationship from Truman to Obama.* New York: Farrar, Straus and Giroux, 2015.

Sachar, Abram L. *The Redemption of the Unwanted: From the Liberation of the Death Camps to the Founding of Israel.* New York: St. Martin's, 1983.

Sachar, Howard M. *A History of Israel: From the Rise of Zionism to Our Time.* New York: Knopf, 1976.

Shapira, Anita. *Israel, A History.* Lebanon, NH: Brandeis University Press of New England University Press, 2012.

Shepherd, Naomi. *Ploughing Sand: British Rule in Palestine, 1917–1948.* New Brunswick, NJ: Rutgers University Press, 1999.

JORDAN

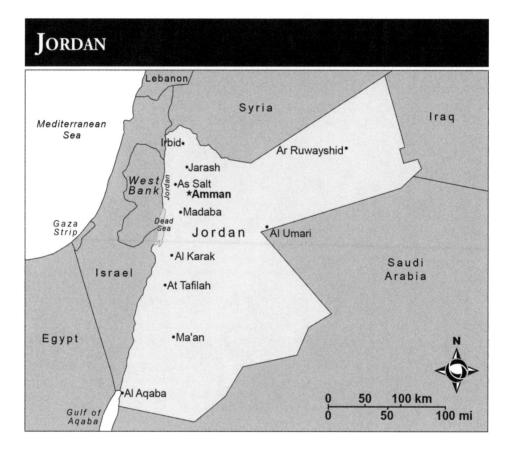

Mediterranean
Sea

Lebanon

Syria

Iraq

Irbid•

Ar Ruwayshid•

•Jarash

West
Bank

•As Salt

★Amman

Gaza
Strip

•Madaba

Dead
Sea

Jordan

•Al Umari

•Al Karak

Israel

Saudi
Arabia

•At Tafilah

Egypt

•Ma'an

•Al Aqaba

Gulf of
Aqaba

N

0   50   100 km
0   50   100 mi

Jordan

Paul G. Pierpaoli Jr. and Spencer C. Tucker

The Arab state of Jordan occupies 35,637 square miles (making it about the size of the U.S. state of Indiana) on the east bank of the Jordan River. Officially known as the Hashemite Kingdom of Jordan, it is bordered by Israel and the West Bank to the west, Syria and the Golan Heights to the north, Iraq to the east, and Saudi Arabia to the east and south. Its 2016 population was some 7.748 million. Jordan's capital city is Amman.

Arabs constitute some 98 percent of Jordan's population, while Circassians and Armenians each number about 1 percent. Islam is the dominant religion. Muslims make up about 92 percent of the country's population, with 93 percent of these adhering to Sunni Islam. Christians constitute some 6 percent, but this percentage is down sharply from some 30 percent in 1950, owing to substantial Muslim immigration into Jordan and high Muslim birth rates. Traditionally Christians hold two cabinet positions in the government and are reserved 9 seats out of the 130 in parliament. Other, smaller religious minorities include Druzes and Baha'is.

Jordan is a constitutional monarchy, but the king wields considerable power. Among many international organizations to which it belongs, Jordan is a founding member of both the Arab League and the Organization of Islamic Cooperation.

Jordan saw human habitation early in prehistory. Later a succession of tribal kingdoms appeared and were in near constant warfare with the Hebrew Kingdom of Israel and the Kingdom of Judah west of the Jordan River. The region then became part of the Akkadian Empire, followed by the Egyptian, Hittite, Assyrian, Neo-Babylonian, and Achaemenid Empires. Macedonian king Alexander III (the Great) conquered the Achaemenid Empire in 332 BCE. Following his death in 323, Jordan was fought over between the Ptolemies in Egypt and the Seleucids in Syria. The Romans arrived in 63 BCE. When in 324 CE the Roman Empire split into the Western and Eastern (Byzantine) Empires, Jordan became part of the latter, and Christianity was the state religion. For some of this time the Sassanian Empire controlled parts of the region, however.

In 636 the Arabs defeated the Byzantines in the decisive Battle of Yarmouk and secured control of the Levant. Rule by the Rashidun, Ummayad, and Abbasid Caliphates followed. Twelfth-century Fatimid rule was interrupted by the Christian Crusades, but Saladin defeated the crusaders and founded the Ayyubid dynasty (1189–1260). Mamluk rule followed, but in 1516 the Ottomans defeated the Mamluks, and the Levant became part of the Ottoman Empire.

Ottoman control over Transjordan and much else of the region came to an end during World War I (1914–1918). In 1915 the British opened secret negotiations with Hussein bin Ali, sharif and emir of Mecca, promising the creation of an independent Arab state in the Hejaz and the Levant in return for military assistance against the Ottomans. Beginning in 1916, Jordanians took part in what became known as the Arab Revolt in alliance with the British. The war ended with most of the territory of the Hejaz and the Levant, including land east of the Jordan River, liberated from Ottoman control.

At the same time that the British had been promising the Arabs an independent state, they had also been secretly negotiating with the French, and the ensuing Sykes-Picot Agreement of 1916 divided much of the Levant into British and French spheres of influence. The Balfour Declaration of November 2, 1917, was another blow to the Arabs, for in it the British government promised its support for a Jewish homeland in Palestine. Arab nationalists certainly regarded this as a betrayal of their wartime agreement with the British.

With the end of the war the region was divided, and the borders of five new states were arbitrarily drawn for Iraq, Syria, Lebanon, Transjordan, and Palestine. The French secured mandates for Syria and Lebanon; the British mandates were Palestine, Iraq, and Transjordan. On October 22, 1920, after taking over Transjordan, the United Kingdom formed what was known as the Mobile Force, a military unit of 150 men commanded by British Army captain (later major general) Frederick Gerard Peake, known as Peake Pasha. It was to defend the territory from tribal warfare or invasion and protect the important Jerusalem-to-Amman road. Soon the Mobile Force had grown to some 1,000 men. On October 22, 1922, it merged with the Reserve Mobile Force, with Peake now an employee of the Emirate of Transjordan. This new force, paid for by the British and with British officers, was officially named Al Jeish al Arabi (the Arab Army) but was better known as the Arab Legion.

The territory known as Transjordan was from April 1, 1921, ruled by Emir Abdullah ibn Hussein, the second of three sons of Hussein, sharif of Mecca. On July 24, 1922, the League of Nations recognized Transjordan as a state under the British mandate for Palestine.

In 1930 Captain (later lieutenant general) John Bagot Glubb became second-in-command of the Arab Legion. A close personal friend and trusted adviser of Abdullah, he was widely known to Jordanians as Glubb Pasha. Glubb took command of the Arab Legion on Peake's retirement in 1939 and made it into the best-trained military force in the Arab world. Certainly the Arab Legion rendered effective service during World War II in the British-led Iraq and Syria campaigns of 1941.

World War II marked the effective end of the colonial era, and on May 25, 1946, Transjordan received its independence, now officially known as the Hashemite Kingdom of Jordan. Abdullah I ruled as king. The ground force of the Arab Legion, which now numbered some 8,000 men, became the Jordanian Arab Army.

Britain was unable to resolve the matter of Palestinian governance, and a three-way war developed there between Arab nationalists, Jews, and the British Army.

With the Arab rejection of a partition agreement, the British simply terminated their Palestine mandate, and on May 14, 1948, the Jews in Palestine proclaimed the independence of the State of Israel. As with most other Arab leaders, Abdullah flatly rejected this, and a day later the Arab Legion joined the armies of other nations in an invasion that became the Israeli War of Independence (May 15, 1948–March 10, 1949). Officially, the Arab forces were under the auspices of the Arab League, which had been formed in 1945. Abdullah held nominal command of the Arab armies, but cooperation among these forces was almost nonexistent and a chief cause of their ensuing military failure.

At the beginning of the war in the central part of the front, Arab forces from Transjordan and Iraq advanced on Jerusalem with the aim of driving the Jews from the city. The Arab Legion, which was certainly the best Arab fighting force in the war, secured the eastern and southern portions of the new part of the city and occupied most of Old Jerusalem.

The Israeli-Transjordan armistice at the end of the war on April 3, 1949, saw Transjordan retain control of the West Bank of the Jordan River and East Jerusalem. To reflect this territorial change, on December 1, 1948, Abdullah officially changed his country's name to the Hashemite Kingdom of Jordan. During the war, a great many Palestinian Arabs were displaced by the fighting and fled into Transjordanian territory. Jordan, unlike other Arab states, allowed Palestinians to take Jordanian citizenship.

On July 20, 1951, a Palestinian assassinated Abdullah while he was in the Al-Aqsa Mosque in Jerusalem, purportedly because of the belief that Abdullah was secretly negotiating with Israel. He was succeeded by his son Talal; as Talal was mentally ill, his son Prince Hussein became the effective ruler as King Hussein I on August 11, 1962, at age 17. He would rule Jordan for the next 47 years.

A series of anti-Western demonstrations in Jordan, combined with the October 1956 Suez Crisis, compelled Hussein to sever military ties with Britain. He also dismissed Glubb Pasha in order to show political independence from the United Kingdom and to Arabize the Jordanian officer corps.

The Assassination of King Abdullah I

On July 16, 1921, Riad Bey al-Solh, a former prime minister of Lebanon, was assassinated in Amman on rumors of peace talks between Lebanon and Jordan regarding Israel. On July 20, King Abdullah I was in Jerusalem to give a eulogy at the funeral. While attending prayers at the Al-Aqsa Mosque with his grandson, Prince Hussein, Abdullah was confronted by a Palestinian gunman who fired three fatal bullets into his head and chest. Prince Hussein was at Abdullah's side and was also hit. A medal pinned to Hussein's chest at his grandfather's insistence deflected the bullet and saved the prince's life. It was said that once Hussein became king, the assassination of Abdullah influenced him not to enter peace talks with Israel in the aftermath of the Six-Day War in order to avoid a similar fate.

In February 1958, Hussein formed the Arab Federation with Iraq. The king viewed this as a needed countermeasure to the newly established United Arab Republic (UAR), formed between Egypt and Syria and dominated by Egypt's Pan-Arab president Gamal Abdel Nasser. The Arab Federation fell apart by the autumn, however, after the Iraqi king was overthrown and slain in a coup. Later that same year, leaders of the UAR called for the overthrow of the Lebanese and Jordanian governments. Hussein then requested aid from the British, who sent troops to Jordan to quell antigovernment protests. The Americans simultaneously sent forces to Lebanon to bolster its besieged Christian-led government.

Jordan's relations with the UAR remained tense. Indeed, in 1963 when a rival Jordanian government-in-exile was set up in Damascus, Hussein declared a state of emergency. The crisis subsided when the Americans and British publicly endorsed Hussein's rule. For good measure, Washington placed on alert the U.S. Navy's Sixth Fleet in the Mediterranean.

After the mid-1960s and more than a decade of crises and regional conflicts, Hussein turned his attention to domestic issues. Determined to improve the welfare of his people, he launched major programs to increase literacy, enhance educational opportunities, bolster public health initiatives, and lower infant mortality. Hussein achieved considerable success. By the late 1980s literacy rates approached 100 percent, and infant deaths were down dramatically. Jordan's economy also began to expand as the nation engaged in more international trade, while relations with Egypt improved. Hussein also began to build a modern and reliable transportation system and moved to modernize the country's infrastructure. Notably, he accomplished this without resorting to overly repressive tactics. Indeed, throughout the period Jordanians enjoyed a level of freedom virtually unrivaled in the Middle East.

By the spring of 1967, however, the Middle East was on the brink of a new war. Considerable low-key fighting had been occurring in the form of Palestinian raids against Israel mounted from Syria and Jordan. Israel met this undeclared war on its territory by retaliatory strikes against guerrilla camps and villages in the Golan Heights of Syria and in Jordan. The year 1965 saw an Arab attempt to divert the flow of the Jordan River, and this brought Israel Defense Forces (IDF) attacks against the diversion sites in Syria. This in turn led to a mutual defense pact between Egypt and Syria against Israel on November 4, 1966. On November 13, 1966, the IDF also mounted a large-scale attack on the Es Samu Palestinian refugee camp in Jordan, said to be a terrorist base. Jordan dispatched troops and aircraft and in the ensuing clash with the IDF suffered 16 killed, 51 wounded, a number of vehicles destroyed, and one plane shot down. The Israelis lost 1 soldier killed and 10 wounded. Three civilians died, and 96 were wounded.

After Egypt blockaded Israeli shipping in the Gulf of Aqaba on May 22, 1967, Egyptian minister of defense Field Marshal Abdel Hakim Amer ordered Egyptian forces to close the straits the next day. A countermanding order by Nasser would have signaled weakness, and he now issued orders to the Egyptian military to prepare for war.

With both sides mobilizing, on May 30 King Hussein, normally a moderating force, arrived in Cairo and concluded with Egypt a mutual security pact. The

Six-Day War (June 5–10, 1967) began with a preemptive Israeli air strike on Egypt. As Israel was locked in combat with both Egypt and Syria, Israeli leaders employed diplomatic channels to urge Hussein to stay out of the war. Hussein wanted to avoid participation but came under heavy pressure to act, and he was deceived by early Cairo broadcasts claiming major Egyptian military successes. Hussein hoped to satisfy his allies with minimum military action short of all-out war. Jordanian 155mm Long Tom artillery went into action against Tel Aviv, and Jordanian aircraft attempted to strafe a small Israeli airfield near Kfar Sirkin. These steps, however, led Israel to declare war on Jordan.

Hussein's decision had great consequences for the Middle East, as the IDF captured all of Jerusalem and the entire West Bank. Also, as many as 300,000 Palestinians fled to Jordan from the West Bank, swelling the Palestinian refugee population there to almost 1 million. This massive influx severely taxed Jordanian infrastructure, schools, health care, and other resources and engendered considerable resentment among some Jordanians.

The large number of Palestinians in Jordan by 1968 also brought greatly increased influence for Palestinian militants—especially militants such as the fedayeen. These groups were well armed (receiving significant assistance from Syria and Egypt) and posed a serious threat to Hussein's rule. By 1970, it appeared as if the Palestinian resistance fighters were in the process of creating a Palestinian state within a state, much as they would do in Lebanon.

Members of a guerrilla unit of the Palestine Liberation Front receiving instructions before moving out from their position in Jordan on November 4, 1968. The unit was to cross the Jordan River into Israel at night and establish an ambush position. (AP Photo)

By early 1970 Palestinian guerrilla groups and the Palestine Liberation Organization (PLO) were skirmishing with Jordanian troops. Open warfare erupted in June. On June 9, Hussein escaped death when would-be assassins opened fire on his motorcade. In particularly bloody fighting during September 1970, the Jordanian Army triumphed, and thousands of Palestinians, including the leadership of the PLO, fled Jordan for Syria and Lebanon. From the Palestinian perspective, the fighting and forced expulsion of the PLO leadership was a great betrayal. Indeed, they referred to the events of September 1970 as Black September.

The early 1970s saw continued unrest. In 1972 King Hussein tried to create a new Arab federation, which would have included the West Bank. Israel as well as most of the Arab states flatly rejected the idea. Hussein played only a minor rule during the 1973 Yom Kippur War (Ramadan War), ordering a limited troop deployment of one brigade to fight in Syria. In 1974, however, Hussein finally agreed to recognize the Arab League's position that the PLO was the sole representative of the Palestinian people.

Hussein strengthened relations with neighboring Syria beginning in the late 1970s and vigorously opposed the 1979 Egypt-Israel Peace Treaty. He supported Iraq in the long Iran-Iraq War (1980–1988).

The 1980s were difficult years economically for Jordan, as job creation failed to keep pace with population growth, resulting in high unemployment. Inflation became a major problem, foreign investment fell off, and exports declined. In 1989, riots occurred in southern Jordan because of the lack of jobs and a government-mandated increase in the cost of basic commodities, including electricity and water. This situation led Hussein to seek U.S. financial aid in the late 1980s when the nation's foreign debt burden grew substantially.

King Hussein miscalculated when he chose to back Iraqi president Saddam Hussein in his August 1990 seizure of Kuwait, for U.S. and much European aid to Jordan was sharply curtailed. Saudi Arabia and (later) Kuwait also withheld financial assistance, and the economy went from bad to worse. When some 700,000 Jordanians returned to Jordan because they were now unwelcome in Saudi Arabia and in Kuwait following its liberation in the 1991 Persian Gulf War, the economic situation became truly dire. Jordan's tourism declined precipitously, oil prices were high, and exports suffered. By 1995 the government put unemployment at 14 percent, but other sources claimed that it was perhaps twice that figure. Not until 2001 did the economy begin to regain its footing. Hussein's decision to back Iraq also put Jordanian-U.S. relations in a holding pattern, and relations with other major Western powers were little better.

By 1993–1994, however, Jordanian-U.S. relations were on an upswing. Jordan became an active partner in the Arab-Israeli peace process, and Hussein supported United Nations–imposed sanctions on Iraq. On July 25, 1994, King Hussein signed a historic nonbelligerent agreement with the Israelis in the Washington Declaration. This was followed by the October 26, 1994, signing of the Israel-Jordan Peace Treaty.

King Hussein died of cancer on February 7, 1999. He had named his eldest son as crown prince and successor, who now ruled as King Abdullah II. Abdullah has tried to continue Jordan's role as the force of moderation in the Middle East. He has attempted to keep dialogue open between the Israelis and the Palestinians and continues to counsel both sides that discussions and agreements are preferable to conflict and war.

Although Abdullah publicly criticized the Anglo-American war in Iraq that began in March 2003, he quietly provided assistance to the United States and Britain during the invasion and its aftermath and partnered with the coalition forces in an attempt to bring a semblance of order to that war-torn country.

Jordan itself has been surprisingly free of terrorist activity. A notable exception was the November 2005 terrorist bombing of three hotels in Amman by Al-Qaeda in Iraq, an organization led by a native Jordanian. The blasts killed 57 people and wounded at least 100 others.

On February 1, 2011, in an effort to preempt the opposition and avoid the events that had swept Tunisia and then Egypt and became known as the Arab Spring, Abdullah ordered his entire cabinet to resign, brought back a reformist prime minister, and pledged to embark on democratic reform. He also met with the leaders of the Muslim Brotherhood for the first time in nearly a decade.

Jordan firmly supported efforts to combat the Islamist State of Iraq and Syria (ISIS) when it seized large stretches of Syria and Iraq following the start of the Syrian Civil War in 2011. By 2013 Jordan was serving as a conduit for the shipment of small arms to rebel groups fighting both ISIS and the Syrian government of president Bashar al-Assad. In June 2013 Jordan was host to EAGER LION, a military exercise involving some 15,000 military personnel from 18 different nations that saw the United States deploy to Jordan both F-16 fighter aircraft and Patriot missiles. In mid-June the Pentagon announced that the aircraft and the Patriot missiles would remain in Jordan after the end of the exercise on June 23.

On September 23, 2014, Jordanian aircraft joined other Arab nations and the United States in attacking ISIS targets in Syria. On December 24, however, one of the anti-ISIS coalition aircraft, a Jordanian F-16, was downed in Syria's eastern Raqqa Province in territory controlled by ISIS, and its pilot, Lieutenant Muath al-Kaseasbeh, was captured. On February 3, 2015, ISIS released a video showing his murder. Placed in a cage, al-Kaseasbeh was doused with inflammable fluid and then set on fire and burned to death. As recently as a few days before ISIS had been negotiating for an exchange involving female suicide bomber Sajida al-Rishawi, whose explosive vest had failed to detonate during the 2005 Amman hotel bombing and who was on death row in Jordan. King Abdullah, then in Washington for talks with U.S. president Barack Obama, immediately returned home and addressed the nation amid widespread anti-ISIS demonstrations. The Jordanian government promptly executed al-Rishawi and Ziad al-Karbouly, another terrorist, and launched a series of bombing raids against ISIS targets. ISIS leaders apparently hoped that the video would put pressure on Jordan to leave the coalition, as air attacks on fellow Sunni Muslims in ISIS by the U.S.-led coalition had not been popular in Jordan, but the deed served to unite Jordanian public opinion against ISIS.

In March 26, 2015, Jordanian aircraft joined Saudi Arabia and its Persian Gulf region allies in launching air strikes in Yemen in an effort to counter Iran-allied Houthi rebel forces besieging the city of Aden. Then in December, Jordan and a coalition of 34 predominately Muslim nations, formed under Saudi leadership, pledged to fight terrorism.

In 2016 the Jordanian political situation appeared stable, despite the addition of some 1.4 million Syrian refugees from the long-running Syrian Civil War, added to the 2 million Palestinians. Jordan also welcomed thousands of Christians fleeing ISIS. All of this placed a considerable strain on Jordanian resources and infrastructure. Tourism has been a major boon to the economy and helped to offset Jordan's lack of natural resources.

Timeline

1516–1918	The Levant, of which Jordan is a part, is part of the Ottoman Empire.
Nov 2, 1914	The Ottoman Empire sides with Germany and Austria-Hungary in World War I (1914–1918).
1915	British authorities in Cairo open negotiations with Sharif Hussein of Mecca, promising the Arabs military assistance and an independent state if they will fight on the Entente side against the Ottoman Empire.
1916	The Arab Revolt against the Ottomans commences.
May 16, 1916	The French and the British negotiate secretly and then sign the Sykes-Picot Agreement, which divides much of the Levant into British and French spheres of influence.
Nov 2, 1917	In the Balfour Declaration, the British government pledges its support for a Jewish homeland in Palestine. Arab nationalists see this as a betrayal of their wartime agreement with the British.
1919	With the end of World War I, five new states that will be League of Nations mandates are created in the Levant: Iraq, Syria, Transjordan, Palestine, and Lebanon.
Apr 1, 1921	Emir Abdullah ibn Hussein becomes the ruler of Transjordan.
Jul 24, 1922	The League of Nations officially recognizes Transjordan as a state under the British mandate for Palestine.
Oct 22, 1922	The British create what will become the Arab Legion, a military force for Transjordan with Arab soldiers and British officers. It will come to be recognized as the best-trained fighting force in the Arab world.
May 25, 1946	Transjordan becomes independent as the Hashemite Kingdom of Jordan, ruled by King Abdullah I.
May 14, 1948	Unable to work out a partition agreement between Arabs and Jews, Britain simply ends its mandate in Palestine, and the Jews there declare the independence of the State of Israel.

May 15, 1948	The Arab Legion joins other Arab armies in an invasion of Israel in what becomes the Israeli War of Independence (May 15, 1948–March 10, 1949). Abdullah is commander in chief of the Arab armies, although cooperation is minimal and a major cause of the Arab failure in the war.
May 15–Jun 1, 1948	The Arab Legion drives on Jerusalem and secures a good bit of the city.
Apr 3, 1949	The Israeli-Transjordanian armistice allows the Arab Legion to remain in control of the West Bank and East Jerusalem. Abdullah then changes the name of his country to Jordan to differentiate the new territories west of the Jordan River from the broader Transjordan.
Jul 20, 1951	A Palestinian assassinates Abdullah in Jerusalem. Abdullah is succeeded by his son Talal.
Aug 11, 1952	With Talal mentally ill, his son Prince Hussein becomes the effective ruler as King Hussein I and will rule Jordan for the next 47 years.
1956	The Suez Crisis, in which Britain joins France and Israel in trying to topple Egyptian president Gamal Abdel Nasser and wrest back control of the Suez Canal, brings demonstrations in Jordan and compels Hussein to sever military ties with Britain.
Feb 14, 1958	Hussein forms with Iraq the Arab Federation. It is intended as a counter to the newly established United Arab Republic (UAR) between Egypt and Syria which is dominated by Egyptian president Nasser. The federation ends that autumn, after the Iraqi king is killed in a coup d'état. Later that same year, leaders of the UAR call for the overthrow of the governments in Lebanon and Jordan. Hussein then calls on Britain for assistance, and it sends troops to Jordan to quell antigovernment protests.
1963	Jordan's relations with the UAR remain tense, and when a rival Jordanian government-in-exile is set up in Damascus, Hussein declares a state of emergency. Strong support for Hussein from Britain and the United States ends the emergency, enabling Hussein to deal with pressing domestic concerns.
Nov 4, 1966	Egypt and Syria conclude a mutual defense pact against Israel.
Nov 13, 1966	With Palestinian militants launching raids against Israel from Jordan and Syria, Israel retaliates with strikes of its own against Palestinian bases and villages in the two countries. On this date, the Israel Defense Forces (IDF) mounts a large-scale attack on Es Samu in Jordan, a Palestinian refugee camp said to be a terrorist base. This leads to a large clash with Jordanian forces dispatched there.

May 22, 1967	Egypt blockades Israeli shipping in the Gulf of Aqaba and the next day closes the straits. Nasser then orders the Egyptian military to prepare for war.
May 30, 1967	King Hussein arrives in Cairo and concludes a mutual security pact with Egypt.
Jun 5–10, 1967	The Six-Day War. Israel mounts a preemptive strike on Egypt and then Syria, beginning the war. Hussein wants to avoid participation but comes under heavy pressure to act. He hopes to satisfy his allies with only a minimal response, but this leads Israel to declare war on Jordan. In the ensuing fighting the IDF takes all of Jerusalem and the territory of the West Bank of the Jordan River. As many as 300,000 Palestinians flee to Jordan, swelling the Palestinian refugee population there to almost 1 million.
Jun 1970	The great influx of Palestinian refugees into Jordan sharply increases the influence of the radical groups bent on attacking Israel. Armed by Egypt and Syria, these groups threaten to become a state within a state. They and the Palestine Liberation Organization (PLO) embark on open warfare with the Jordanian Army.
Jun 9, 1970	King Hussein escapes an assassination attempt by gunmen firing on his motorcade.
Sep 16–29, 1970	In what the Palestinians come to know as Black September, heavy fighting occurs between Palestinian militants and the Jordanian armed forces. In the end a number of Palestinians, including the leadership of the PLO, flee Jordan for Syria and Lebanon.
1972	King Hussein tries to create a new Arab federation, which would have included the West Bank. Israel and most of the Arab states reject this.
Oct 6–26, 1973	Hussein played only a minor rule during the 1973 Yom Kippur War (Ramadan War) of these dates, ordering a limited troop deployment (one brigade) to fight in Syria.
1974	Hussein finally agrees to recognize the Arab League's position that the PLO is the sole representative of the Palestinian people.
1980–1988	The Iran-Iraq War.
Jan 1982	Jordanian volunteers assist Iraq in its war with Iran.
1989	Riots occur in southern Jordan over the lack of jobs and a government-mandated increase in the cost of basic commodities.
Aug 1990	King Hussein miscalculates when he backs Iraqi president Saddam Hussein in the Iraqi seizure of Kuwait. This decision brings a

sharp curtailment in U.S. and other aid to Jordan. The economy nosedives sharply, especially with the return of some 700,000 Jordanians expelled from Saudi Arabia and also from Kuwait, following its liberation in the 1991 Persian Gulf War.

Jul 25, 1994   Hussein signs a historic nonbelligerent agreement with the Israeli government,

Oct 26, 1994   The Israel-Jordan Peace Treaty is signed.

Feb 7, 1999   King Hussein dies of cancer. He is succeeded by his son Abdullah, who rules as Abdullah II.

Mar 2003   Although publicly criticizing the Anglo-American invasion of Iraq, Abdullah quietly provides assistance to coalition forces during the war and its aftermath.

Nov 8, 2005   The terrorist Al-Qaeda in Iraq organization, led by a native Jordanian, detonates three bombs in hotels in Amman, killing 57 people and wounding at least 100 others.

Feb 1, 2011   Seeking to preempt the opposition and avoid the events that have swept Tunisia and now Egypt in the so-called Arab Spring, King Abdullah orders his entire cabinet to resign, brings back a reformist prime minister, and pledges democratic reform.

Dec 2012   With the beginning of the Syrian Civil War in 2011 and the rise of the Islamic State of Iraq and Syria (ISIS), Jordan acts as a conduit for small arms supplied by Saudi Arabia to the rebels fighting ISIS and the Syrian regime of President Bashar al-Assad.

Sep 23, 2014   Jordanian aircraft participate with those from other Arab nations and the United States in attacks on ISIS targets in Syria. Its $300 million total in aid this year makes Jordan the fourth-largest recipient of U.S. military aid in 2014.

Feb 3, 2015   Jordanians and many others are shocked by a video released this date showing the murder by ISIS of Jordanian Air Force lieutenant Muath al-Kaseasbeh, who had been taken prisoner on December 24, 2014, when his F-16 fighter crashed in ISIS-controlled territory. King Abdullah, in Washington for previously scheduled talks with U.S. president Barack Obama, immediately returns to Jordan and addresses the nation. Amid widespread demonstrations in Jordan hailing the pilot as a hero, the Jordanian government executes two condemned terrorists and launches a series of bombing raids against ISIS targets.

Mar 26, 2015   Jordan joins Saudi Arabia and Persian Gulf region allies in air strikes in Yemen in an effort to counter Iran-allied Houthi rebel forces besieging the southern city of Aden.

Dec 15, 2015   Jordan joins a coalition of 34 predominately Muslim nations formed under the leadership of Saudi Arabia to fight terrorism.

Further Reading

Abdullah ibn al-Husayn, King. *King Abdallah of Jordan: My Memoirs Completed (al-Takmilah)*. Translated by Harold W. Glidden. Washington, DC: American Council of Learned Societies, 1954.

Cordesman, Anthony H. *The Military Balance in the Middle East*. Westport, CT: Praeger, 2004.

El Edross, Syed Ali. *The Hashemite Arab Army, 1908–1979*. Amman, Jordan: Central Publishing House, 1986.

Lunt, James D. *Hussein of Jordan: Searching for a Just and Lasting Peace*. New York: William Morrow, 1989.

Mutawi, Samir A. *Jordan in the 1967 War*. Cambridge: Cambridge University Press, 2002.

Nevo, Joseph, and Illan Pappe, eds. *Jordan in the Middle East: The Making of a Pivotal State*. London: Frank Cass, 1994.

Salibi, Kamal S. *The History of Modern Jordan*. New York: William Morrow, 1993.

Satloff, Robert B. *From Abdullah to Hussein: Jordan in Transition*. New York: Oxford University Press, 1993.

Wilson, Mary C. *King Abdullah, Britain and the Making of Jordan*. Cambridge and New York: Cambridge University Press, 1988.

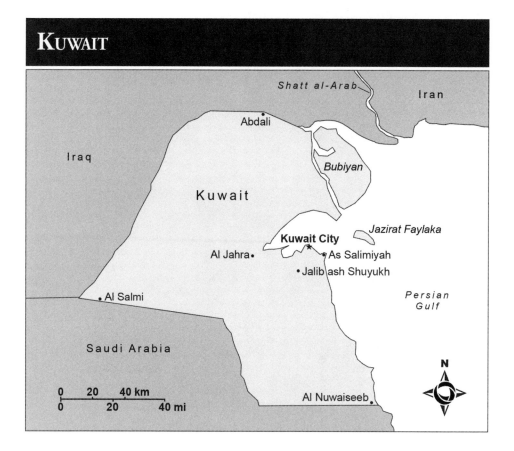

Kuwait

Stefan M. Brooks, Benedict Edward DeDominicis, Gregory Wayne Morgan, Daniel E. Spector, and Spencer C. Tucker

The State of Kuwait is strategically located at the northern end of the Persian Gulf. It is bordered by Saudi Arabia to the south, Iraq to the west and north, and the Persian Gulf to the east. Kuwait occupies some 6,880 square miles, including the Kuwaiti share of the neutral zone defined by agreement with Saudi Arabia in 1922 and partitioned by mutual agreement in 1966. Kuwait is thus about the size of the U.S. state of Hawaii. Kuwait's 2016 population was some 4.026 million. More than half of this number are noncitizen workers attracted by job opportunities in the oil-rich Persian Gulf nation.

Kuwait had been part of Ottoman-ruled Basra Province since the 17th century. The Utub tribes that settled in the area early in the 18th century called their central town Kuwait (founded in 1613 and originally primarily a fishing village), the Arabic diminutive for *kut,* meaning "a fortress built near water." During 1775–1779 the Persians laid siege to Basra, at which time a number of Iraqi merchants took refuge in Kuwait and helped expand Kuwait's trade as well as its boat-building industry. Indeed, in the 18th century Kuwait was the center of the regional boat-building trade. In 1756 the al-Sabah family established an autonomous sheikhdom in Kuwait and focused on developing the local pearl beds and taking advantage of location to promote regional trade. Thereafter the Ottoman Empire exercised only nominal rule. In 1792 the British East India Company arrived in Kuwait and secured lucrative trading routes. In the late 19th century, the British government grew concerned when Kuwait was touted as the possible terminus of the German-backed Berlin-to-Baghdad railroad project. Kuwait had now eclipsed Basra as an important regional training center. The British were also greatly concerned about possible German domination, as the Persian Gulf controlled access to the Suez Canal, which had become Britain's imperial lifeline to India.

In 1898 the Ottoman government in Istanbul (Constantinople) sought to exert more control over Kuwait. To forestall this and being anxious to prevent German influence in the Persian Gulf region, the British concluded an agreement with Kuwait on January 23, 1899, whereby Kuwait became a British protectorate. In return for a financial subsidy, Kuwaiti sheikh Mubarak al-Sabah granted Britain control of Kuwait's foreign affairs and defense and promised not to grant economic concessions or conclude a military alliance with any other power.

In 1904 Kuwait's territory was formally drawn as a 40-mile radius around its center at Kuwait City. In 1913 the Anglo-Ottoman Convention defined Kuwait as an "autonomous caza" of the Ottoman Empire. Kuwaiti sheikhs were regarded as Ottoman provincial subgovernors. In the convention Britain recognized Ottoman interests in Kuwait in return for a pledge that Istanbul would not interfere in Kuwaiti internal affairs.

The Ottoman Empire sided with the Central Powers in World War I, but during the war the British maintained a troop presence in Kuwait. Following the war the British had to deal with Wahhabi attacks into Kuwait, which they repulsed in 1919 and 1927–1928. As a consequence of the Allied victory in World War I, Britain also secured a League of Nations mandate over Iraq. The 1922 Treaty of Ugair set the Kuwaiti southern border with Saudi Arabia and established the Saudi-Kuwaiti neutral zone, an area of some 2,000 square miles. In the Treaty of Lausanne of 1923, Turkey renounced all claims to the former Ottoman possessions in the Arabian Peninsula.

In December 1934 Kuwait granted an oil concession to a consortium of the American Gulf Oil Company and the British Anglo-Persian Oil Company. A significant oil find occurred in February 1938, and soon thereafter Kuwait had become one of the world's major oil producers.

In October 1960 the rulers of Kuwait and Saudi Arabia met and decided that the neutral zone between their two countries should be divided. An agreement to that effect was signed on July 7, 1965, and formally took effect in December 1969.

On June 19, 1961, Britain granted Kuwait full independence, and six days later Iraqi leader Abd al-Karim Qasim claimed that Kuwait was part of Iraq because parts of Kuwait had been in the province of Basra during the period of Ottoman rule. Qasim also threatened an invasion. The British sent troops to Kuwait, and the crisis passed. As a consequence, however, Kuwait firmly aligned itself with the West—the United States in particular. The 1979 Iranian Revolution served to further strengthen this alliance, with Kuwait—which has a majority Sunni Muslim population—worried about its minority Shiite Muslims. No precise figures are available, but Sunnis are believed to account for 60–70 percent of Kuwait's population, with the Shiites at 30–40 percent.

Kuwait strongly supported Iraq during the 1980–1988 Iran-Iraq War. Assistance included nearly $35 billion in grants, loans, and other aid to the Iraqi government. With the end of the war, Iraq was essentially bankrupt. Having amassed a debt of some $70 billion, it was desperate for cash. Because his country was a major oil producer and oil was the principal Iraq export, Iraqi leader Saddam Hussein counted on oil revenues to rebuild the Iraqi economy and ensure the stability of his regime.

Casting his war with Iran largely as an effort to protect the Arab states on the Persian Gulf, especially Kuwait, from Iranian Shiite Islamic fundamentalism, Hussein chose to regard these states as ungrateful for Iraq's wartime sacrifices. Hussein now pressed for forgiveness of the debt, but Kuwait refused.

Finally, there was the long-standing Iraqi government claim of Kuwait as a province dating back to the arbitrary administrative boundaries during the period of the Ottoman Empire. This was a matter of securing not only Kuwaiti oil but also that nation's long coastline. Iraq's sole access to the Persian Gulf was the Shatt al-Arab waterway, sovereignty over which was a point of contention with its enemy, Iran. Securing Kuwait would give Iraq easy access to the Persian Gulf.

The war with Iran had left Iraq with one of the world's largest military establishments, and Hussein was determined to use this to advantage. For some time Washington had been concerned over Iraq's expanding nuclear industry and a chemical and biological capability that Hussein had employed in the war against Iran as well as against some of his own people, the Kurds. Then in mid-July 1990, American intelligence satellites detected Iraqi forces massing near the Kuwaiti border.

In February 1990 at a summit meeting of the Arab Cooperation Council in Amman, Jordan, Saddam Hussein asked King Hussein of Jordan and President Hosni Mubarak of Egypt to inform the Gulf states of Iraq's insistence that its debts be forgiven and that it needed an immediate infusion of some $30 billion. Saddam Hussein reportedly said that if he were not given the money, he "would know how to get it." This not-so-veiled threat was accompanied by Iraqi military maneuvers near the Kuwaiti border.

In late May 1990 at an Arab League summit in Baghdad, Saddam Hussein claimed that Iraq was being subjected to "economic warfare" and that it would not long tolerate such treatment. He now demanded $27 billion from Kuwait. The Kuwaitis replied that they did not have such a large sum to give or lend. A month later at a meeting of the Organization of Petroleum Exporting Countries (OPEC) meeting, Kuwait offered $500 million to Iraq over three years, which Hussein characterized as paltry and insulting.

On July 16, 1990, Iraq publicly accused Kuwait both of violating the OPEC oil-production quotas through excessive production and thus driving down the price of oil and of employing slant drilling to steal Iraqi oil from the Rumaila oil field shared by both countries. That same day, Iraqi foreign minister Tariq Aziz informed an Arab summit meeting in Tunisia that "we are sure some Arab states are involved in a conspiracy against us" and vowed not to "kneel."

On July 17 in a speech to the Iraqi people, Hussein repeated his claim that Kuwait and the United Arab Emirates (UAE) were violating OPEC oil-production quotas and threatened unspecified military action if it continued. Iraq also demanded $2.4 billion from Kuwait for oil allegedly "stolen" in drilling from the Rumaila oil field. The next day, Kuwait canceled all military leaves and placed its small military on alert. It also called for an emergency session of the Gulf Cooperation Council, a defense group of Gulf states, and the Arab League. Kuwait leaders concluded that Hussein's demands were tantamount to extortion and would only invite more blackmail later. They also refused to believe that Hussein would invade another Arab state.

On July 21 the U.S. Central Intelligence Agency reported that Iraq had moved some 30,000 troops and hundreds of tanks to the Kuwaiti border. U.S. policy in this crisis was unclear. Fearful of radical Islam in Iran, both the Soviet Union and the United States had assisted Iraq in its war with Iran. Indeed, Washington had provided valuable satellite intelligence. Washington assumed that Hussein was weary of war and would in any case need a protracted period of peace to rebuild. At the same time, U.S. ambassador to Iraq April Glaspie had followed the George H. W. Bush administration's policy of delivering mixed messages, which Hussein chose to interpret as allowing him operational freedom in the Persian Gulf region. Hussein probably believed that his moves against Kuwait would not be challenged by the United States. For its part, the U.S. State Department did not believe that Hussein would actually mount a full-scale invasion. If military action occurred, Washington expected only a limited offensive to force the Kuwaitis to accede to Iraqi demands of bringing the cost of oil in line. Clearly Washington underestimated Hussein's ambitions. The intelligence was there, but the administration failed to act on a Pentagon call for a show of force to deter possible Iraqi aggression. Indeed, the Bush administration did not draw a firm line in the sand until Hussein had already crossed it.

Kuwaiti leaders also concluded that Iraq's provocative action was a bluff to increase the price of oil and blackmail Kuwait into acceding to Hussein's demands. On July 22, Tariq Aziz repeated his criticism of Kuwait and the UAE after Hussein met in Baghdad with Egyptian president Hosni Mubarak, acting as a mediator between Iraq and Kuwait. Mubarak subsequently claimed to have received assurances from Hussein that Iraq would not attack Kuwait, but Iraqi officials asserted that Hussein had said that nothing would happen to Kuwait so long as negotiations continued.

On July 26 Kuwait agreed to lower its oil-production quotas, which would have the effect of increasing the worldwide price of oil, but Hussein had already begun moving additional troops and armor to the Kuwaiti border. Under Saudi Arabian auspices, Kuwaiti and Iraqi representatives met in Jeddah on July 31 in an effort to resolve their differences. The Iraqis claimed that Kuwait was unwilling to negotiate in good faith. The Kuwaitis said that the Iraqis were not interested in negotiations but rather sought to dictate a solution. Iraqi demands now included Kuwait ceding disputed territory along the border, increasing Iraq's oil-pumping rights, and providing a $10 billion cash payment to Iraq. On August 1 the meeting adjourned early because one of the Iraqi diplomats was taken ill, but both sides agreed to resume talks in Baghdad in a few days.

At 2:00 a.m. local time on August 2, 1990, Iraq invaded Kuwait. Iraq then reportedly possessed the world's fourth-largest standing army, numbering some 450,000 men. The invading force numbered perhaps 100,000 men and as many as 700 tanks. Iraqi Republican Guard commander Lieutenant General Ayad Futahih al-Rawi had command. Surprisingly, given Hussein's saber rattling in the weeks before the invasion, the small Kuwaiti armed forces were not on alert.

The invasion force consisted of four Republican Guard divisions: the 1st Hammurabi Armored, the 2nd al-Medinah al-Munawera Armored, the 3rd Tawalkalna ala-Allah Mechanized Infantry, and the 6th Nebuchadnezzar Motorized Infantry Division. There were also Iraqi Army special forces units equivalent to a full division. The Hammurabi and Tawakalna divisions easily overcame the sole Kuwaiti brigade deployed along the common border, then headed south to Jahrad at the head of the Gulf of Kuwait before turning east to Kuwait. Kuwaiti armored cars had no chance of stopping the massed Iraqi T-72 tanks.

Meanwhile, elite Iraqi troops were airlifted by helicopter into Kuwait City, preventing any Kuwaiti withdrawal back into it, while some six squadrons of Iraqi aircraft struck targets in Kuwait City and also attacked the two principal Kuwaiti Air Force bases in an effort to secure air superiority. At the same time, Iraqi seaborne commandos sealed off the Kuwaiti coast.

Caught by surprise, the Kuwaiti armed forces did what they could. Kuwaiti Dassault Mirage F1 and Douglas A-4 Skyhawks tangled with Iraqi Mirage F1s, Sukhoi Su-22s and Su-25s, and Mikoyan Gurevich MiG-23s over Kuwait City, while an approximate battalion of Chieftain tanks of the 35th Armored Brigade fought delaying actions near Al Jahra, west of the capital. To the south, the 15th Armored Brigade evacuated to Saudi Arabia. Two missile boats of the small Kuwaiti Navy also escaped. Refueled and rearmed at Saudi air bases, Kuwaiti Air Force aircraft flew missions against the Iraqis and delivered ammunition to isolated Kuwaiti ground units until the morning of August 4, when the last remaining Chieftain tanks of the 35th Armored Brigade withdrew into Saudi Arabia as well.

The Medina Armored Division screened the Iraqi invasion force against the remote possibility of any intervention by the Gulf Cooperation Council's Peninsula Shield Brigade, situated in northern Saudi Arabia. Four Iraqi infantry divisions then moved in behind the mobile forces to occupy the country and conduct mopping-up operations, while the Iraqi heavy divisions took up defensive positions along the border with Saudi Arabia to the south. Kuwait was completely occupied in only 48 hours.

The Iraqis failed in their effort to seize the emir of Kuwait, Sheikh Jabir al-Ahmad al-Jabir al-Sabah. He managed to escape, although Iraqi commandos killed his brother, Sheikh Fahd, who was in the palace.

Losses on the two sides are hard to pin down. Kuwait subsequently claimed that its air force and Hawk antiaircraft batteries had downed 37 Iraqi helicopters and 2 jet aircraft and that numerous Iraqi armored vehicles were also destroyed. The Kuwaitis subsequently reported that they had lost 19 aircraft but that 80 percent of its aircraft were able to reach refuge in Saudi Arabia. Iraq captured a half dozen Kuwaiti aircraft intact on the ground as well as other military equipment. Personnel losses are not known, although thousands of Kuwaitis escaped to Saudi Arabia before that border was sealed on August 11. The Iraqis then built up their forces along the Saudi-Kuwaiti border.

Following the Iraqi incursion into Kuwait, Iraqi president Saddam Hussein moved quickly to consolidate his hold on Kuwait. He appointed his first cousin, Ali Hassan Abd al-Majid al-Tikriti, as the governor of Kuwait. With the full support of Hussein, al-Tikriti instituted a brutal and repressive regime. It included the plundering of Kuwaiti resources and infrastructure and the killing of many Kuwaiti citizens. Iraq's military looted and pillaged Kuwait's consumer economy almost at will, sending back to Iraq large quantities of automobiles and luxury goods. Kuwait soon was a virtual ghost town of looted and burned shops and stores; in many cases, these establishments were stripped of light fixtures and furniture. The

Kuwaiti National Museum was not spared. Its collection of priceless Islamic arti-
facts was looted, and almost every room in the museum was gutted by fire.

The Iraqi occupiers did not spare the Kuwaiti people. Crimes against the citizenry included murder, rape, and torture. Nor were these limited to Kuwaitis, for
expatriates and foreign nationals suffered equally. In the aftermath of the six-month
occupation, the Kuwaiti government reported that 5,733 people had been systematically tortured by Iraqi troops. Iraqi documents captured after the liberation of
Kuwait revealed orders from Baghdad for the summary execution of home owners
whose buildings bore anti-Iraqi or pro-Kuwaiti slogans. Orders also directed troops
to kill on sight any civilian caught on the streets after curfew or anyone suspected
of being involved in any resistance activity. Iraqi forces were also accused of engag-
ing in extrajudicial killings of government officials and members of the Kuwaiti
military.

Following the liberation of Kuwait, numerous Iraqi torture facilities were discovered. Reports from the few who managed to escape Kuwait following the invasion recounted public executions and bodies left hanging from lampposts or
dumped by the side of the street. According to both the United Nations (UN) and
Kuwait, some 600 Kuwaiti nationals were abducted and were taken to Iraq and
disappeared. Iraqi officials also used Westerners captured in Kuwait as hostages, or
human shields, until they were released as an alleged act of goodwill on the part of
Iraq in December 1990. It is worth pointing out, however, that some allegations by
the exiled Kuwaiti government of human rights abuses were subsequently proven
false. Despite this, the wanton brutality of Iraq's occupation of Kuwait cannot be
denied.

Washington's reaction to the invasion was surprisingly swift. President Bush was
deeply concerned over the impact of the invasion on the supply of oil and oil
prices as well as on Saudi Arabia, which possessed the world's largest oil reserves
and shared a common border with Kuwait. Bush and others of his generation
styled Hussein's aggression as a challenge akin to that of Adolf Hitler and made
much of a supposed and quite inaccurate contrast between dictatorship (Iraq) and
democracy (Kuwait). On August 8 Bush ordered the deployment of forward forces
to Saudi Arabia in what became Operation DESERT SHIELD. The troops were to bolster the Saudis and demonstrate resolve in the midst of diplomatic maneuvering.
Hussein proved intransigent, and war loomed between Iraq and a growing U.S.-led
coalition of nations. Hussein then began building up Iraqi forces along the Kuwait-
Saudi border.

Bush led the effort to forge an international coalition, first to defend Saudi
Arabia against possible Iraqi attack and then to force Iraq to quit Kuwait. U.S.
Army general H. Norman Schwarzkopf Jr., commander of the U.S. Central
Command, oversaw military operations. As the a buildup of international coalition
forces went forward, the UN Security Council imposed a January 15, 1991, deadline for Iraq's unconditional withdrawal. Ultimately 34 nations were involved in
the coalition efforts.

With Iraqi's refusal to leave Kuwait and the expiration of an ultimatum,
Operation DESERT STORM began on January 17, 1991, in a bombing campaign

against targets in Kuwait and Iraq. Coalition forces enjoyed complete air superiority and greatly degraded Iraqi ground force units. Hussein remained defiant, however.

The impending assault to liberate Kuwait, as part of Operation DESERT SABRE, the ground component of DESERT STORM, included tying down elite Iraqi Republican Guard divisions by a left-wing flanking maneuver into southern Iraq by the U.S. Army XVIII Airborne and VII Corps. The U.S. Navy and 5th Marine Expeditionary Brigade, feinting an amphibious landing on the Kuwaiti coast, also tied down as many as 10 of 43 Iraqi divisions there.

At 4:00 a.m. local time on February 24 after preliminary infiltration operations, the U.S. 1st and 2nd Marine Divisions in Marine Central Command, followed by Joint (Arab) Forces Command–North on their left and Joint (Arab) Forces Command–East on the Persian Gulf coast, initiated the ground assault with pinning attack operations against Iraqi fortifications in Kuwait. Meanwhile, XVIII and VII Corps, along with French and British divisions, sought to neutralize reinforcements of the Iraqi Republican Guard, the elite units of the Iraqi armed forces. Of the 14 coalition divisions, 6 (Joint Arab Forces and U.S. Marine Corps) were initially devoted to a northerly attack into Kuwait from Saudi Arabia, directly confronting only 5 Iraqi divisions.

After breaching extensive minefields and taking al-Jaber airfield with 1 dead and 12 wounded from Iraqi rocket fire, both U.S. Marine Corps divisions repulsed repeated Iraqi counterattacks launched on February 25 from the burning Burgan oil field, part of some 700 Kuwaiti oil wells that would be set afire by Iraqi troops. This gratuitous destruction not only crippled Kuwait's oil production for many months but also created an environmental disaster.

The marines destroyed or captured nearly 200 Iraqi tanks. Meanwhile, the Joint Arab Forces, both Saudi and Qatari, advanced up the coast on February 24 after heavy shelling by U.S. warships, quickly passing through gaps in the first line of defenses (with 2 Saudis dead and 4 wounded in an air-ground friendly-fire incident) to reach the second line, which they overran on February 25. This operation resulted in 6 coalition troops killed and 21 wounded. Iraqi resistance then largely collapsed, and the Joint Arab troops reached Kuwait City by the evening of February 26. Marine forces approaching on the left from al-Jaber continued to advance and destroyed more than 100 additional Iraqi tanks. Employing a combination of U.S. naval gunfire and marine ground units, the coalition eliminated the remnants of the Iraqi armored brigade based at Kuwait International Airport.

Joint Arab Forces–North consisted of Saudi, Kuwaiti, and Egyptian forces, with Syrian troops in reserve. Beginning their northerly advance into western Kuwait on February 24, they encountered only light resistance and took large numbers of Iraqi prisoners before turning east to reach Kuwait City by 5:00 p.m. on February 26.

On February 26 Hussein ordered his surviving forces to evacuate Kuwait, emptying fortifications around Kuwait City that may have been more difficult for coalition forces to take. Iraqi units fleeing west and north from Kuwait along the highways linking it with Basra in southern Iraq had been under continuous air attack from U.S. Navy and U.S. Air Force aircraft since the previous night. The planes dropped aerial mines to prevent their advance or retreat on the roads out of Kuwait. The U.S. Army's 1st Tiger Brigade of the 2nd Armored Division attacked, cleared, and occupied the 25-foot-high Mutla Ridge outside of the Jahrah suburb of Kuwait next to the juncture of two multilane highways, destroying numerous Iraqi antiaircraft emplacements and adding its firepower to the assault below on what became known as the "Highway of Death."

The chaotic flight of Iraqi military and commandeered civilian vehicles, as well as Kuwaiti hostages, prisoners, and refugees including Palestinian militiamen, were trapped on the main highway to the north of Jahrah to Basra as well as on the coastal road spur to Basra by the continuous and unhindered U.S. and British attacks and the ensuing turmoil. Many of those who abandoned their vehicles and fled into the desert were also killed. Estimates of the casualties among the total of 1,500–2,000 vehicles destroyed along these two conflated stretches of the Highway of Death remain in dispute, ranging between a low of 200 to as many as 10,000. Officers of the Tiger Brigade, the first American unit to arrive at the Highway of Death, stated that the unit found only about 200 Iraqi corpses among the thousands of destroyed vehicles. The unit also reported the capture of some 2,000 Iraqis who had taken refuge in the desert. Other observers reported that hundreds of bodies, including those of women and children, continued to be buried several days later. Most of the vehicles destroyed on the main northern highway route were commandeered civilian vehicles seized by regular Iraqi Army personnel. Predominantly military vehicles belonging to Republican Guard units were destroyed on the coastal route, with the U.S. Army 3rd Armored Division joining the assault.

On February 27 Saudi-commanded units passed through Marine Central Command sector, along with Joint Arab Forces Command–North columns, to liberate Kuwait City itself. After making contact with Egyptian Army units, U.S. Army Tiger

Kuwaiti soldiers, armed with AK-47 assault rifles and rocket propelled grenade launchers, wave their weapons and cheer from atop an armored vehicle in Kuwait City on February 27, 1991. Kuwaitis took to the streets to celebrate their liberation during the Persian Gulf War. (AP Photo/J. Scott Applewhite)

Brigade troops cleared the major military airfield, the Kuwaiti Royal Summer palace, and bunker complexes.

A cease-fire went into effect at 8:00 a.m. on February 28. Iraq accepted unconditionally all UN Security Council resolutions regarding Iraq's occupation of Kuwait, thereby renouncing for good the annexation of Kuwait. The ground war had lasted 100 hours.

Although Kuwait had been heavily damaged during the Iraqi occupation and subsequent war, the nation's immense oil wealth and small size allowed it to rebuild quickly and efficiently. Thereafter, Kuwait remained a firm ally of the United States, and, with Saudi Arabia and Turkey opposed to the plan, Kuwait was the major staging area for the U.S.-led effort to oust Saddam Hussein from power in March 2003. In return the United States has been restrained in any criticism of Kuwaiti internal affairs. In May 2005, however, Kuwait's parliament did grant full political rights to women. The United States maintains a significant military and naval presence in the region that helps protect the al-Sabah ruling family of Kuwait.

Kuwait has not been a major player in the Arab-Israeli conflict. As Kuwait did not obtain independence from Britain until 1961, it did not participate in the 1948 and 1956 wars in and around Israel. After independence Kuwait aligned itself with the Arab side in the Arab-Israeli conflict, sending only small numbers of troops to fight in the 1967 and 1973 wars. These were token forces, and Kuwait focused on internal development of its oil resources. The large proportion of Palestinians in the Kuwaiti workforce has not led to an active support of the Palestinian cause but may indeed have led to a suspicion of Palestinians as a possible source of problems, as had occurred in Jordan and Lebanon in the 1970s and 1980s. Palestine Liberation Organization support for Iraq in the 1990 conflict with Iraq did not enhance Kuwaiti support for anti-Israeli activities. Kuwait did not provide any substantial support for Hezbollah in its 2006 conflict with Israel. The fact that Hezbollah is a Shia group while the ruling family in Kuwait is Sunni likely played a role in this, along with the fact that Kuwait has a substantial Shia minority and remains wary of Shia-dominated Iran.

Kuwaiti emir Jaber died in January 2006. Saad al-Sabah succeeded as emir but was removed nine days later by the Kuwaiti parliament owing to his poor health. Sabah al-Sabah then became emir and continues in that position today.

The Kuwaiti economy is based largely on petroleum, which accounts for some 94 percent of export revenue and perhaps half of the national income. Kuwait has led the Arab world in efforts at economic diversification. Nonpetroleum enterprises include shipping, water desalination, and financial services. Kuwait has some of the Arab world's largest banks, and the Kuwait Stock Exchange is its second largest. The Kuwaiti dinar is the highest valued currency in the world, and Kuwait is the world's fourth-richest nation in terms of per capita income.

When the Arab Spring commenced in 2011, Kuwait experienced street protests calling for reforms. To head off trouble, the parliament was dissolved in December 2011, and the prime minister resigned. New parliamentary elections were held in 2013. Distrust of the government remains amid ample evidence of graft and corruption. Nevertheless, Kuwait's ruling family has managed to stay somewhat aloof from the political instability. During the 2008–2009 Hamas-Israeli conflict, some Kuwaiti legislators publicly protested Israeli tactics, but the Kuwaiti government did not take any significant punitive measures against Israel. There were more anti-Israeli protests during the Hamas-Israeli conflict of 2014, which prompted the Kuwaiti government to call for an end to the Israeli blockade of the Gaza Strip.

On June 26, 2015, a suicide bombing occurred at a Shia Muslim mosque in Kuwait. The blast killed 27 people and injured another 227. The Islamic State of Iraq and Syria claimed responsibility. Twenty-nine people were arrested and subsequently tried for the bombing. Fifteen were found guilty, and 7 were sentenced to death (5 in absentia). It remains the largest terror attack in Kuwait's history.

Timeline

1600s	The territory of present-day Kuwait becomes part of the Ottoman Empire's Basra Province.
1613	The town of Kuwait is founded.
1700s	Utub tribes settle the area, calling their principal town Kuwait, the Arabic diminutive for *kut,* meaning "a fortress built near water."
1756	The al-Sabah family establish an autonomous sheikdom in Kuwait.
Jan 23, 1899	Kuwait is now an important regional trading center, and the Ottoman government in Istanbul is seeking to restore its control. Worried about growing German influence in Istanbul and the threat this might pose in the Persian Gulf region, which controls access to the Suez Canal, the British government concludes an agreement with Kuwait on this date whereby Kuwait becomes a British protectorate. In return for a financial subsidy, Kuwaiti sheikh Mubarak al-Sabah grants Britain control of Kuwait's foreign affairs and defense and pledges not to grant economic concessions or conclude a military alliance with any other power.
1904	Kuwait's territory is formally drawn as a 40-mile radius around Kuwait City.
Jul 29, 1913	An Anglo-Ottoman convention defines Kuwait as an "autonomous caza" of the Ottoman Empire. Kuwaiti sheikhs are regarded as Ottoman provincial subgovernors. Britain recognizes Ottoman interests in Kuwait in return for a pledge that Istanbul will not interfere in Kuwaiti internal affairs.
Nov 2, 1914	With Ottoman warships (former German warships under command of a German admiral) shelling Russian ports in the Black Sea, Russia declares war on the Ottoman Empire. The British maintain a troop presence in Kuwait during the war.

1919	British forces in Kuwait repulse Wahhabi attacks.
1922	The Treaty of Ugair sets the Kuwaiti southern border with Saudi Arabia and establishes the Saudi-Kuwaiti neutral zone, an area of some 2,000 square miles.
Jul 24, 1923	In the Treaty of Lausanne, Turkey renounces all claims to the former Ottoman possessions in the Arabian Peninsula.
1927–1928	British forces in Kuwait repulse Wahhabi attacks.
Dec 1934	Kuwait grants an oil concession to a consortium of the American Gulf Oil Company and the British Anglo-Persian Oil Company.
Feb 1938	Significant oil is discovered in Kuwait. Soon Kuwait is one of the world's major oil producers.
Oct 1960	The rulers of Kuwait and Saudi Arabia meet and decide that the neutral zone between their two countries should be divided.
Jun 19, 1961	Britain grants Kuwait full independence, and six days later Iraqi leader Abd al-Karim Qasim claims that Kuwait was part of Iraq, as parts of Kuwait had been in the province of Basra during the period of Ottoman rule. Qasim also threatens an invasion. The British send troops to Kuwait, and the crisis passes. As a consequence, however, Kuwait firmly aligns itself with the West—the United States in particular. The 1979 Iranian Revolution serves to further strengthen this alliance, with Kuwait—which has a majority Sunni Muslim population—worried about its minority Shiite Muslims.
Jul 7, 1965	An agreement dividing the aforementioned neutral zone is signed and formally takes effect in December 1969.
1980–1988	Kuwait strongly supports Iraq during the Iran-Iraq War, including some $35 billion in grants, loans, and other assistance.
1988	Iraqi president Saddam Hussein puts heavy pressure on Kuwait to forgive the loans to Iraq. He also claims that Kuwait is an Iraqi province.
Aug 2, 1990	Hussein sends Iraqi forces into Kuwait, securing it in several days and proclaiming it to be Iraq's 19th province.
Aug 7, 1990–Jan 17, 1991	Fearful of Iraqi pressure on Saudi Arabia, the United States sends forces to Saudi Arabia in Operation DESERT SHIELD.
Jan 17–Feb 28, 1991	Following the failure of Iraq to withdraw its forces from Kuwait and with United Nations authorization, an international coalition of 34 nations, led by the United States and including Arab nations, drives Iraqi forces from Kuwait in Operation DESERT STORM

	(the Persian Gulf War). Iraq is then compelled to recognize Kuwaiti independence.
2003	Kuwait serves as the major staging area for the U.S.-led invasion of Iraq.
Jan 29, 2006	Sabah al-Sabah becomes emir of Kuwait.
Jun 26, 2015	A terrorist bombing at a Shia mosque in Kuwait kills 27 people and injures another 227. The Islamic State of Iraq and Syria claims responsibility.

Further Reading

Abu-Hakima, Ahmad Mustafa. *The Modern History of Kuwait, 1750–1965.* London: Luzac, 1983.

Al Yahya, Mohammad Abdul Rahman. *Kuwait: Fall and Rebirth.* London: Kegan Paul International, 1993.

Assiri, Abdul-Reda. *Kuwait's Foreign Policy: City-State in World Politics.* Boulder, CO: Westview, 1990.

Casey, Michael S., Frank W. Thackeray, and John E. Findling. *The History of Kuwait.* Westport, CT: Greenwood, 2007.

Cordesman, Anthony J. *Kuwait: Recovery and Security after the Gulf War.* Boulder, CO: Westview, 1997.

Crystal, Jill. *Kuwait: The Transformation of an Oil State.* Boulder, CO: Westview, 1992.

Daniels, John. *Kuwait Journey.* Luton, UK: White Crescent, 1971.

Gordon, Michael R., and Bernard E. Trainor. *The Generals' War: The Inside Story of the Conflict in the Gulf.* New York: Little, Brown, 1995.

Jassan, Hamdi A. *The Iraqi Invasion of Kuwait: Religion, Identity, and Otherness in the Analysis of War and Conflict.* Sterling, VA: Pluto, 1999.

Polk, William R. *Understanding Iraq: The Whole Sweep of Iraqi History, from Genghis Khan's Mongols to the Ottoman Turks to the British Mandate to the American Occupation.* New York: HarperCollins, 2005.

Ray, Kurt. *A Historical Atlas of Kuwait.* New York: Rosen, 2003.

Scales, Robert H. *Certain Victory: The U.S. Army in the Gulf War.* Washington, DC: Brassey's, 1994.

Tripp, Charles. *A History of Iraq.* New York: Cambridge University Press, 2002.

Tucker, Spencer C. *Persian Gulf War Encyclopedia: A Political, Social, and Military History.* Santa Barbara, CA: ABC-CLIO, 2014.

United States Army. *Area Handbook Series: Persian Gulf States.* Washington, DC: U.S. Government Printing Office, 1984.

LEBANON

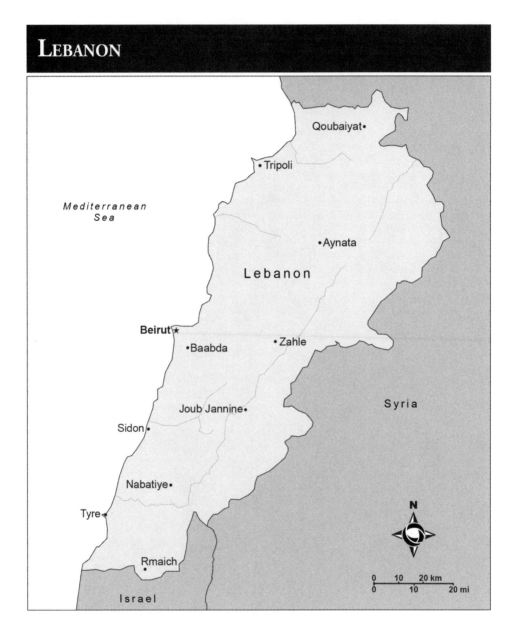

Qoubaiyat

• Tripoli

Mediterranean Sea

• Aynata

L e b a n o n

Beirut ★

• Baabda

• Zahle

S y r i a

Joub Jannine•

Sidon •

Nabatiye •

Tyre •

Rmaich •

I s r a e l

N

0   10   20 km
0   10   20 mi

Lebanon

*Brent M. Geary, Daniel E. Spector,
and Spencer C. Tucker*

Lebanon (officially the Lebanese Republic) is located on the eastern end of the Mediterranean Sea and is bordered by Israel to the south and Syria to the east and north. Lebanon covers 4,015 square miles, and its 2016 population was some 5.988 million. Because the relative size of the religious groups is a sensitive issue, there has been no national census since 1932. Muslims number perhaps 54 percent (Shias, 27 percent; Sunnis, 27 percent). Druzes constitute 5.6 percent; the Druze sect emerged during the 11th century from a branch of Shia Islam. Christians are some 40.5 percent of the Lebanese population. There are also small numbers of Jews, Baha'is, Buddhists, Hindus, and Mormons.

Lebanon's strategic location led to frequent invasions in ancient times, resulting in a chaotic history and great religious and cultural diversity. Its location fostered a maritime culture under the Canaanites and Phoenicians during circa 1550–539 BCE. In 64 BCE, Rome established control. Lebanon became a Christian center under the Maronites, who survived the Arab conquest. The Druzes also established themselves there. During the Christian Crusades (1096–1291) the Maronites reestablished ties with the Roman Catholic Church.

Lebanon passed under the rule of the Ottoman Empire in 1516. The Ottoman Empire joined World War I on the side of the Central Powers. The defeat of the latter in 1918 saw the areas of modern-day Lebanon and Syria controlled by France as a League of Nations mandate from October 29, 1923. Britain meanwhile secured mandates over Iraq and Palestine.

During World War II a pro-Axis coup occurred in Iraq, and the Germans applied pressure on the Vichy French government to permit the transport of arms there through Syria. Deeply concerned about the possible loss of Iraqi oil and the threat to British communications with India, British and Free French forces invaded Syria and Lebanon in June–July 1941. Free French high commissioner to the Levant General Georges Catroux announced on November 26 that Lebanon would become independent under the authority of the Free French government. Elections were held in 1943, and on November 8 the new Lebanese government unilaterally abolished the mandate. The French responded by imprisoning the members of the government. Following strong international pressure, Free French authorities released those arrested on November 22, 1943, celebrated by Lebanese as their independence day. Foreign troops withdrew from Lebanon entirely on December 31, 1946.

Lebanon became a charter member of the United Nations (UN) in 1945, the same year it joined the Arab League. Although independence and international status were welcomed by the Lebanese, sectarian tensions have continually threatened internal peace. This along with 60 years as a participant in the Arab-Israeli conflicts has left Lebanon with only a few years absent of internal and external conflict since 1945.

The Lebanese government operated under an unusual political arrangement of confessionalism in which power was shared among the different religious communities. Lebanon's unwritten National Pact of 1943 was based on the 1932 census and awarded the Maronite Christians a privileged place in the government. Generally a Maronite is the president, the prime minister is a Sunni, the speaker of parliament is a Shiite, and the deputy speaker of parliament and deputy prime minister is Greek Orthodox.

As demographic developments led to a Muslim majority by the 1960s, Maronite predominance came under increasing pressure from various Muslim groups. The fact that the Muslims were not a monolithic force further complicated matters. The Shias, along with the Druzes and a small number of Alawites, outnumbered the Sunnis, and these groups often had contentious relations. On top of this, the Cold War and the ongoing Arab-Israeli conflict presented Lebanon with major challenges.

As a member of the Arab League, Lebanon was a reluctant participant in the Arab military effort to defeat Israel on the latter's declaration of independence in May 1948. Lebanese forces and Lebanese volunteers in the Arab Liberation Army fought alongside those from Syria in the northern front of the Israeli War of Independence (1948–1949), but the fighting ended with Israel in control of the Jordan River, the lakes of Galilee and Huleh, and a panhandle of territory jutting north and bordering on both Lebanon and Syria. Lebanon's only success of the war was the June 5–6, 1948, capture of Al-Malkiyya. Lebanon was directly impacted by the war, with the flight there of some 100,000 Palestinians from Israeli occupied areas. Israel then refused to permit their return. Lebanon was not a major player in the subsequent Arab-Israeli wars and thus avoided military losses and potential occupation.

This did not mean that Lebanon remained at peace, however, for sectarian troubles and the evolving Cold War between the United States and the Soviet Union brought their own challenges. Both sides in the Cold War sought to support regimes that they believed would aid them in the worldwide conflict.

In January 1957, President Dwight Eisenhower requested a congressional resolution authorizing use of force in the Middle East to prevent the spread of communism. Known as the Eisenhower Doctrine, it was in response to waning British influence in the region following the 1956 Suez Crisis. Having lost faith in British capabilities, Eisenhower declared his intention to take the lead in keeping the region from Soviet control.

Events in the region during 1957 and 1958 were seen by the United States as a warning of the rise of both communism and radical Arab nationalism. In 1957 King Hussein of Jordan established diplomatic relations with the Soviet Union. In February 1958 the most radical regimes in the region, Egypt and Syria (both supported by the Soviet Union) merged to form the United Arab Republic (UAR).

Then in July 1958, the pro-Western Iraqi monarchy was overthrown by a radical military junta.

Faced with these developments, along with relentless propaganda by Arab nationalists against his more pro-Western regime and internal threats to his rule, including an insurrection demanding that Lebanon join the UAR, Lebanese president Camille Chamoun requested direct American intervention to defend his government. Eisenhower invoked his new doctrine and ordered 5,000 U.S. marines to Lebanon. They arrived in Beirut on July 15. Meanwhile, the British sent forces into Jordan.

The main issue at stake in Lebanon became Chamoun's effort to change the constitution to allow him to continue to rule the nation after his term of office expired. Eisenhower instructed his personal representative and experienced international troubleshooter Robert Murphy to pressure Chamoun to yield power to circumvent civil war. Chamoun eventually conceded, and former general Fuad Chehab, a popular figure in Lebanon, replaced him, allowing American forces to be withdrawn.

For the next decade and a half, the Muslim and Christian populations seemed to be working well together. Indeed, during the 1960s Lebanon was often referred to as the "Switzerland of the Middle East," a nation where diverse communities thrived in mutual tolerance. Lebanon enjoyed considerable prosperity owing to tourism, agricultural production, commerce, and extensive banking.

The apparent harmony did not last long, however. Gradually, the Muslim population became the clear majority, and Lebanon could not avoid becoming involved in the Arab-Israeli conflict. A number of the Palestinian refugees in Lebanon began carrying out hit-and-run actions across the border in Israel. Lebanese Christians opposed this, fearing that Israeli reprisals would threaten Lebanese independence.

The Six-Day War in 1967 and the 1973 Yom Kippur War (Ramadan War), coupled with the expulsion of radical Palestinians from Jordan in 1970 and 1971, saw more Palestinians relocate to Lebanon, greatly increasing their influence there. The refugees lived in wretched camps that served as breeding grounds for anti-Israeli terrorists. While the Lebanese military tried to maintain order and restrain the Palestinian guerrillas from using Lebanon for attacks against Israel, this was largely unsuccessful. In 1975, clashes between Lebanese Christians and Muslims expanded into full-scale civil war (April 13, 1975–October 13, 1990), pitting Christian groups against the forces of the Palestine Liberation Organization (PLO) and Druze and Muslim militias. In the fighting between March 1975 and November 1976 alone, some 40,000 died and 100,000 more were wounded.

In June 1976 Lebanese president Elias Sarkis requested Syrian Army intervention to help restore peace, and that October the Arab League agreed to establish a predominantly Syrian Arab deterrent force to restore calm.

Attacks by the PLO across the border into northern Israel meanwhile led Israeli prime minister Menachem Begin to send troops into southern Lebanon in March 1978 in Operation LITANI. The operation brought the deaths of 1,100–2,000 Lebanese and Palestinians and 20 Israelis. It also resulted in the internal displacement of 100,000 to 250,000 people in Lebanon. PLO forces retreated north of the Litani River. U.S. pressure forced an Israeli withdrawal and brought creation of the United Nations Interim Force in Lebanon (UNIFIL), charged with providing security in southern Lebanon.

With UNIFIL incapable of fulfilling its mandate, major PLO cross-border strikes resumed in April 1982. While Israel conducted both air strikes and commando raids across the border, it was unable to prevent increasing numbers of PLO personnel from locating there. PLO rocket and mortar attacks regularly forced thousands of Israeli civilians to flee homes and fields in northern Galilee to seek protection in bomb shelters.

The attempted assassination and serious wounding in London on June 3, 1982, of Israeli ambassador to Britain Shlomo Argov led Begin to order the bombing of Palestinian targets in western Beirut and southern Lebanon during June 4–5, 1982. The PLO responded by attacking Galilee with rockets and mortars, triggering the Israeli decision to invade Lebanon.

On June 6, Israeli defense minister Ariel Sharon, acting under instructions from Begin, ordered a massive Israeli military invasion in Operation PEACE FOR GALILEE (the Lebanon War). Ultimately the Israel Defense Forces (IDF) committed some 76,000 troops, 800 tanks, 1,500 armored personnel carriers (APCs), and 364 aircraft. Syria committed perhaps 22,000 men, 352 tanks, 300 APCs, and 96 aircraft, while the PLO had perhaps 15,000 men, 300 tanks, and 150 APCs.

The Israelis sought to destroy the PLO in southern Lebanon, evict the Syrian Army from Lebanon and bring about the removal of its missiles from the Beqaa Valley, and influence Lebanese politics. Israel sought an alliance with the Maronite Christians, specifically Bashir Jumayyil (Gemayel), leader of the Phalange (al-Kata'ib) and head

An overturned Israeli tank along the Damour highway in Lebanon on June 17, 1982. The tank had been hit by a Palestine Liberation Organization rocket during the 1982 Israeli invasion. (AP Photo/Merliac)

of the unified command of the Lebanese Forces. While the Phalange was mainly a political association, the unified command of the Lebanese Forces was an umbrella organization of Christian militias. Jumayyil opposed growing Muslim power in Lebanon and the Syrian presence, and he sought close ties with the West and Israel.

Within a few days, IDF forces had reached the outskirts of Beirut. Tyre and Sidon, two cities within the 25-mile limit, were both heavily damaged in the Israeli advance. Rather than stand their ground and be overwhelmed by the better-equipped Israelis, the PLO withdrew back on western Beirut.

Fighting also occurred between the Israelis and Syrian forces in the Beqaa Valley. Unable to meet Israel on equal footing and being bereft of allies, Syria rejected an all-out military effort. Most of the battle was in the air. The Israeli Air Force neutralized Syrian surface-to-air missiles in the Beqaa Valley and downed dozens of Syrian jets, perhaps as many as 80. The Israelis also employed helicopter gunships to attack and destroy Syrian tanks and APCs. The Israelis trapped the Syrian forces in the Beqaa Valley and were on the verge of severing the Beirut-Damascus highway on June 11 when Moscow and Washington brokered a cease-fire.

Fighting between the IDF and the PLO continued, however, with the IDF closing a ring around Beirut by June 13. Israeli hopes that the Maronite Christian militias would ferret out the PLO trapped in the city proved illusory. The IDF was not prepared to undertake street-by-street fighting that would entail heavy casualties for its own forces and so for some seven weeks carried out land, sea, and air attacks against Beirut, cutting off its electricity and access to food and water. International observers accused the Israelis of indiscriminate shelling of the city that destroyed some 500 buildings in the first week alone.

Although Sharon secured Begin's support for a large-scale operation to conquer western Beirut, on July 16 the full Israeli cabinet rejected this. On August 10, with American envoy Philip Habib having submitted a draft agreement to Israel, Sharon ordered saturation bombing of Beirut, during which at least 300 people died. U.S. president Ronald Reagan formally lodged a protest with the Israeli government, and on August 12 the Israeli cabinet stripped Sharon of most of his powers.

On August 21 following U.S. mediation, 350 French paratroopers arrived in Beirut, followed by 800 U.S. marines and Italian Bersaglieri, plus additional international peacekeepers, for a total multinational force (MNF) of 2,130 men. It supervised the removal of the PLO, first by ship and then overland, to Tunisia, Yemen, Jordan, and Syria. By the end of the operation on September 1, some 8,500 PLO troops had departed for Tunis and 2,500 to other Arab countries.

Following the evacuation of the PLO, the ongoing civil war escalated among various Christian, Muslim, and Druze factions vying for control of Lebanon. Furthermore, Israeli and Syrian forces in Lebanon continued to clash, threatening an all-out war between the two nations. The MNF returned after the assassination on September 14 of Jumayyil, then Lebanese president-elect, and massacres by Lebanese Christian militias in several refugee camps.

As time passed, MNF forces were embroiled in the fighting and came to be viewed as supporters of the Lebanese government. On October 24, 1983, a suicide bomber, believed to be a Shiite, drove a van filled with explosives through a barrier and into the marine barracks at the Beirut airport, killing 241. At the French head-quarters, another bomb killed 58 soldiers. Public pressure in the United States and the collapse of the Lebanese Army in February 1984 forced Reagan to withdraw the marines, and the other MNF nations soon followed.

The Lebanese Civil War raged on, and Israel and Syria continued to maintain significant forces in Lebanon. The Lebanese government was not able to assert its authority over large parts of the country, and Israel kept forces in the south to pre-vent raids and rocket attacks against its territory. Syrian strongman president Hafez al-Assad dispatched additional forces and attempted to control Lebanese policies as well as provide arms and training to militias sympathetic to Syria. Nevertheless, this did bring some stability to Lebanon and some semblance of economic recovery. The relative calm was, however, periodically interrupted by conflict between Israeli forces and Shiite militias, predominantly Hezbollah, which was armed by Syria.

A political impasse continued as the Lebanese parliament deadlocked regarding the election of a successor to Jumayyil as president. In May 1888 the Arab League established a committee to try to resolve the situation, and on September 16, 1989, it secured acceptance of its peace plan. A cease-fire went into effect, and ports and airports were reopened. The Lebanese parliament agreed to the National Reconciliation Accord, also known as the Taif Agreement (it was negotiated at Taif, Saudi Arabia). This specified a timetable for the withdrawal of Syrian forces and established a for-mula to end the confessionalist political arrangement, although there was no timeta-ble for implementation. The agreement increased the Chamber of Deputies to 128 members, with seats to be shared equally between Christians and Muslims rather than elected by universal suffrage, which would have provided a Muslim majority (excluding the expatriate community, a majority of which is Christian). The cabinet was also to be equally divided between Christians and Muslims.

The agreement was ratified on November 5, 1989. That same day the parlia-ment elected René Mouawad as president. Mouawad was assassinated only 17 days later in a car bombing in Beirut as his motorcade returned from Lebanese Independence Day ceremonies. Elias Hrawi succeeded him.

The Lebanese Civil War formally ended on October 13, 1990. Its toll was 150,000 dead and 200,000 injured as well as the displacement of nearly 1 million civilians. The physical destruction was immense, with major damage to the Lebanese infrastructure.

In May 2000 Israel had withdrawn its forces from southern Lebanon, hoping that this would lead to a stable border. Instead the border became more dangerous, as Hezbollah soon controlled much of southern Lebanon, fortifying positions there with Syrian assistance.

On February 14, 2005, former prime minister Rafik Hariri was assassinated by a car bomb. Many Lebanese blamed Syria, while the Syrian government claimed that Israeli intelligence services were responsible. Other prominent Lebanese were also killed, but Hariri's assassination triggered the Cedar Revolution, a series of demonstrations demanding withdrawal of Syrian troops and an international in-vestigation into the assassination. International pressure did bring a Syrian with-drawal, completed by April 26, 2005. Although a UN investigation into Hariri's death concluded that the assassination was most likely carried out by the Syrian intelligence services, no individuals have ever been brought to justice.

On July 12, 2006, Hezbollah launched rockets into Israel and carried out a cross-border raid, killing three Israeli soldiers and capturing two others. The Israeli reaction was massive and was not anticipated by Hezbollah leader Hassan Nasrallah, who later admitted that the raid would not have been launched if he had known the likely Israeli response.

Israel commenced air attacks and a massive ground invasion of southern Lebanon in what is known as the 2006 Lebanese War: a month of heavy fighting in southern Lebanon until a tenuous UN cease-fire was negotiated on August 14. Hezbollah had about 1,000 fighters well dug into prepared positions in southern Lebanon, backed by other militias and a civilian population that largely supported them, facing up to 30,000 members of the IDF.

Hezbollah claimed 74 dead during the monthlong fighting, while Israel reported 440 confirmed Hezbollah deaths. Militias supporting Hezbollah suffered 31 dead, while the Lebanese Army sustained 41 dead and about 100 wounded. Israel reported 119 dead, 400 injured, and 2 captured. UN observer forces in the area suffered 7 dead and 12 wounded. The worst toll was among Lebanese civilians, with perhaps 1,200 dead and 3,600 more injured. As many as 250,000 Lebanese were displaced by the fighting. Israel suffered 44 civilian deaths and more than 1,300 injured. Lebanon also suffered extensive damage to its infrastructure from Israeli artillery fire and air strikes.

The robust defense put up by Hezbollah came as a surprise. Hezbollah was able to fire 4,000 rockets into Israeli territory, including not only short-range Katyushas but also middle-range missiles capable of hitting Haifa and other points believed to be safe from the usual Hezbollah rockets. In southern Lebanon, Hezbollah was able to resist Israeli armored attacks, destroying 20 main battle tanks in two engagements. A missile attack against an Israeli warship was also a surprise.

The cease-fire called for a halt in the fighting, an end to the Israeli blockade, the deployment of UN forces to southern Lebanon to maintain peace, and a Lebanese Army takeover of areas previously dominated by Hezbollah.

During May 20–September 7, 2007, fighting occurred between the Lebanese Armed Forces and Fatah al-Islam, an Islamist militant organization. The fighting, centered in Nahr al-Bared, a Palestinian refugee camp near Tripoli, was the most severe internal warfare since the 1975–1990 Lebanese Civil War. Minor clashes also occurred in the Ain al-Hilweh refugee camp in southern Lebanon, and there were several bombings in and around Beirut. At least 169 soldiers, 287 insurgents, and 47 civilians died.

During 2006–2008 there were a series of protests against pro-Western prime minister Fouad Siniora demanding the creation of a national unity government in which mostly Shia opposition groups would have veto power. When Émile Lahoud's presidential term ended in October 2007, the opposition refused to vote for a successor unless a power-sharing deal was reached, leaving Lebanon without a president.

On May 9, 2008, Hezbollah and Amal forces seized control of western Beirut, leading to more fighting in which at least 62 people died. The Doha Agreement of

May 21, 2008, ended the fighting, and Michel Suleiman became president, heading a national unity government. This was, however, a victory for the opposition, which secured the veto. In early January 2011, the national unity government collapsed owing to the belief that the Special Tribunal for Lebanon was expected to indict members of Hezbollah for the assassination of Hariri. The parliament elected Najib Mikati as prime minister. He was the candidate of the Hezbollah-led March 8 Alliance.

In 2011, the Arab Spring brought civil war in Syria. This conflict threatened to expand to Lebanon, causing more incidents of sectarian violence and armed clashes between Sunnis and Alawites in Tripoli. By March 2016 there were some 1.069 million Syrian refugees in Lebanon, representing one-fifth of that nation's population and threatening to undermine Lebanon's already fragile political system. Also on March 2, 2016, Saudi Arabia, apparently bent on punishing Lebanon for Hezbollah forces having taken part in the fighting in support of the Assad regime in the Syrian Civil War, slashed billions in aid for Lebanon, urged Sunnis not to visit Lebanon as tourists, and identified Hezbollah, Lebanon's most powerful political and armed organization, as a terrorist group.

Timeline

1516	Lebanon passes under rule of the Ottoman Empire.
Oct 29, 1923	With the collapse of the Ottoman Empire following its defeat in World War I, France secures a League of Nations mandate over Lebanon, formally established on this date.
Jun–Jul 1941	The threat posed by a pro-Axis coup in Iraq and the shipment of German arms there through Syria lead Britain to invade Syria and Lebanon.
Nov 26, 1941	Free French high commissioner to the Levant General Georges Catroux announces that Lebanon will become independent under the authority of the Free French government.
Nov 8, 1943	Following elections, the new Lebanese government unilaterally abolishes the mandate.
Nov 22, 1943	French authorities respond by imprisoning the members of the government, but following international pressure, on this date the French release those arrested. This date is celebrated by Lebanese as their independence day.
Dec 31, 1946	All foreign troops are withdrawn from Lebanon by this date.
Jun 5–6, 1948	Lebanese Army forces capture Al-Malkiyya, their only success of the Israeli War of Independence. Some 100,000 Palestinians flee into Lebanon as a result of the war, not to return.
Jul 15, 1958	With internal threats, including an insurrection demanding that Lebanon join the United Arab Republic, Lebanese president

Camille Chamoun requests American intervention, and U.S. president Dwight D. Eisenhower dispatches 5,000 U.S. marines to Lebanon. They arrive in Beirut on this date.

Apr 13, 1975   The Lebanese Civil War begins, pitting Christian and Muslim militias against one another.

Jun 1976   Lebanese president Elias Sarkis requests Syrian Army intervention to help restore peace.

Oct 1976   The Arab League agrees to establish a predominantly Syrian Arab deterrent force to restore calm in Lebanon.

Mar 14–21,   Attacks by the Palestine Liberation Organization (PLO) from
1978   Lebanon into northern Israel lead Israeli prime minister Menachem Begin to send troops into southern Lebanon in Operation LITANI. U.S. pressure forces their withdrawal, and the United Nations (UN) creates the United Nations Interim Force in Lebanon (UNIFIL), charged with providing security in southern Lebanon.

Apr 1982   With UNIFIL incapable of fulfilling its mandate, major PLO cross-border strikes resume. While Israel conducts both air strikes and commando raids across the border, it cannot prevent a growing number of PLO personnel from locating there. Rocket and mortar attacks regularly force thousands of Israelis to seek protection in bomb shelters.

Jun 4–5, 1982   The serious wounding of Israeli ambassador to Britain Shlomo Argov on June 3, 1982, leads Begin to order the bombing of Palestinian targets in western Beirut and southern Lebanon.

Jun 6, 1982   PLO attacks on Galilee with rockets and mortars trigger the Israeli decision to invade Lebanon, Operation PEACE FOR GALILEE. Committing some 76,000 troops, the Israelis seek to destroy the PLO in southern Lebanon, evict the Syrian Army from Lebanon, and influence Lebanese politics. Although Begin and Defense Minister Ariel Sharon inform the cabinet that their goal is merely to break up PLO bases in southern Lebanon and push back PLO and Syrian forces some 25 miles, beyond rocket range of Galilee, Sharon expands the mission to incorporate operations against the PLO headed by Yasser Arafat in western Beirut.

Jun 11, 1982   With Israel having destroyed substantial Syrian forces in the Beqaa Valley and downed dozens of Syrian aircraft, a cease-fire takes hold.

Jun 14–Aug 21,   The Siege of Beirut. Israeli forces, having closed around the city
1982   and shut off essential services, seek to drive the PLO out. Maronite Christian forces are unable to drive out the PLO, and Israel mounts major artillery and air strikes on western Beirut, inflicting

considerable damage and casualties. U.S. mediation brings a multinational force (MNF) of 2,130 men, including French and Italian troops and U.S. marines. They oversee the departure of some 11,000 PLO members, principally to Tunis.

Despite departure of the PLO, the ongoing civil War continues among various Christian, Muslim, and Druze factions. Israeli and Syrian forces in Lebanon also clash, threatening all-out war between the two nations.

Sep 1982	The MNF returns after the assassination on September 14 of the president-elect Bashir Jumayyil (Gemayel), head of a Christian militia coalition, and massacres by Lebanese Christian militias in several Palestine refugee camps.
Oct 24, 1983	A suicide bomber, believed to be from a Shiite Muslim terrorist group, drives an explosive-filled van through a barrier and into the marine barracks at the Beirut airport, killing 241. At the French headquarters, another bomb kills 58 soldiers. Public pressure in the United States and the collapse of the Lebanese Army in February 1984 force President Ronald Reagan to withdraw the marines, and the other MNF nations follow suit. The Lebanese Civil War rages on.
Nov 5, 1989	The Taif Agreement (the National Reconciliation Accord) worked out in Taif, Saudi Arabia, is ratified by the Lebanese parliament, which also elects René Mouawad president. The Taif Agreement includes a timetable for the withdrawal of Syrian forces from Lebanon and establishes a formula that would end the confessionalist Lebanese political arrangement, although there is no timetable for its implementation.
Nov 22, 1989	Mouawad is assassinated in a car bombing in Beirut.
Oct 13, 1990	The Lebanese Civil War comes to an end. It has claimed some 150,000 killed and 200,000 injured, displaced nearly 1 million civilians, and brought immense physical destruction.
May 24, 2000	Israel withdraws its forces from southern Lebanon. South Lebanon now becomes more dangerous for the Israelis as the area comes under the control of the radical Shiite Hezbollah organization.
Feb 14, 2005	Former Lebanese prime minister Rafik Hariri is assassinated by a car bomb. Many blame the Syrian government, triggering the so-called Cedar Revolution, a series of demonstrations demanding the withdrawal of Syrian troops and an international investigation into the assassination.
Apr 26, 2005	International pressure forces a Syrian withdrawal from Lebanon, completed by this date. Despite the departure of the Syrians, Lebanon continues to experience internal conflict.

Jul 12, 2006	Hezbollah launches rockets into Israel and carries out a cross-border raid, killing three Israeli soldiers and capturing two others. Israel responds with air attacks and a massive ground invasion of southern Lebanon in what is known as the 2006 Lebanese War.
Aug 14, 2006	A UN-brokered cease-fire goes into effect, ending the 2006 Lebanese War. The cease-fire calls for an end to the Israeli blockade, deployment of UN forces to southern Lebanon to maintain peace, and a Lebanese Army takeover of areas previously dominated by Hezbollah.
May 20–Sep 7, 2007	The most serious fighting in Lebanon since the 1975–1990 civil war occurs between the Lebanese Armed Forces and Fatah al-Islam, an Islamist militant organization in Nahr al-Bared, a Palestinian refugee camp near Tripoli.
May 9, 2008	Hezbollah and Amal forces seize control of western Beirut, leading to more fighting, which is ended by the Doha Agreement of May 21, 2008. Michel Suleiman becomes president, heading a national unity government.
Jan 2011	The national unity government collapses.
Mar 15, 2011	The Syrian Civil War begins. Threatening to expand into Lebanon, it leads to more sectarian violence and armed clashes between Sunnis and Alawites in Tripoli. By March 2016 there are some 1.069 million Syrian refugees in Lebanon.

Further Reading

Friedman, Thomas. *From Beirut to Jerusalem.* New York: Anchor Books, 1995.

Gendzier, Irene. *Notes from the Minefield: United States Intervention in Lebanon and the Middle East, 1945–1958.* New York: Columbia University Press, 1997.

Harris, William. *Lebanon: A History, 600–2011.* New York: Oxford University Press, 2014.

Herzog, Chaim. *Arab-Israeli Wars: War and Peace in the Middle East from the War of Independence through Lebanon.* New York: Vintage, 1984.

Hurewitz, J. C. *Middle East Politics: The Military Dimension.* New York: Praeger, 1969.

Kaufman, Burton I. *The Arab Middle East and the United States: Inter-Arab Rivalry and Superpower Diplomacy.* New York: Twayne, 1996.

Levitt, Matthew. *Hezbollah.* Washington, DC: Georgetown University Press, 2016.

Mackey, Sandra. *Lebanon: A House Divided.* New York: Norton, 2006.

Rabil, Robert G. *Embattled Neighbors: Syria, Israel and Lebanon.* Boulder, CO: Lynne Rienner, 2003.

Traboulsi, Fawwaz. *A History of Modern Lebanon.* 2nd ed. London: Pluto, 2012.

U.S. Army. *Area Handbook Series: Lebanon.* Washington, DC: U.S. Government Printing Office, 1989.

Warner, Geoffrey. *Iraq and Syria, 1941.* London: Davis-Poynter, 1974.

Wright, Robin. *Sacred Rage: The Wrath of Militant Islam.* New York: Simon and Schuster, 2001.

Zweig, Ronald W. *Britain and Palestine during the Second World War.* Suffolk, UK: Boydell and Brewer, 1986.

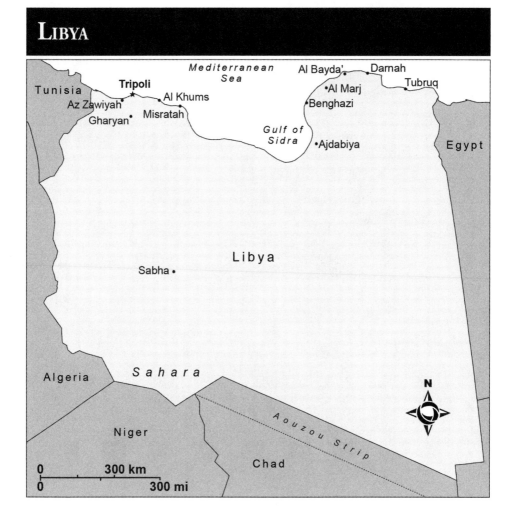

LIBYA

Tunisia

Mediterranean Sea

Al Bayda' Darnah
Tripoli Al Marj Tubruq
Az Zawiyah Al Khums Benghazi
Gharyan Misratah
Gulf of Sidra

Egypt

Ajdabiya

Libya

Sabha

Algeria Sahara

Niger Aouzou Strip

Chad

N

| 0 | 300 km |
| 0 | 300 mi |

Libya

Robert S. Kiely, Larissa Mihalisko, Paul G. Pierpaoli Jr., Spencer C. Tucker, and Bruce Vandervort

Libya is a predominantly Muslim nation located in North Africa. Comprising 679,359 square miles, it is Africa's 4th-largest country and the world's 16th largest. Libya is bordered by the Mediterranean Sea to the north, Egypt to the east, the Sudan to the southeast, Niger and Chad to the south, Algeria to the west, and Tunisia to the northwest. The three traditional parts of the country are Tripolitania in the west, centered on Tripoli; Cyrenaica in the east, centered on Benghazi; and much of the Sahara Desert known as the Fezzan in the southwest. Libya boasts an important natural resource in the world's 10th-largest proven oil reserves.

Libya's population in 2016 was some 6.33 million. Its capital and largest city is Tripoli. The other large urban center is Benghazi. About 97 percent of Libyans are Muslims, and most belong to the Sunni branch of Islam. Christians constitute fewer than 1 percent of the population.

Libya has been inhabited by Berbers since the late Bronze Age. The Phoenicians established trading posts in western Libya, and Greek colonists established toeholds in eastern Libya. Libya was ruled by Persians, Egyptians, and Greeks before becoming part of the Roman Empire and was also an early center of Christianity. The Vandals then controlled Libya, but Arab armies invaded and colonized it in the 7th century. In the 16th century, the Spanish Empire and the Knights of St. John occupied Tripoli, while Ottoman rule commenced in 1551. The United States and Libya, then known as Tripoli, clashed in the Barbary Wars of 1801–1805 and 1815.

In the late 19th century with the Ottoman Empire in obvious decline, Italian leaders began to plan the acquisition of Libya. The French already had conquered Algeria; they also controlled Tunis and were on the brink of securing Morocco. If Italy did not act, any hope of a colony across the Mediterranean would be lost. Italian leaders hoped to bolster Italy's status as a major power and secure territory in which to settle its surplus population.

The pretext employed by the Italian government to justify the invasion of Libya was alleged Ottoman bias against Italian businesses in Libya and the presumed inability of Ottoman authorities to guarantee the security of expatriates. An Italian ultimatum presented to the Sublime Porte on September 28, 1911, gave the Ottoman government 24 hours to agree to Italian military occupation. Although the response was conciliatory, the Italian government declared it unsatisfactory and ordered its navy into action. The army was mobilized, but it took time to assemble and outfit the 45,000 soldiers assigned to the invasion force.

The Italian Navy subjected Tripoli to a short shore bombardment, and Italian sailors and troops then occupied the city and set up a defensive ring around it within naval gunfire range. Meanwhile, the small Ottoman garrisons, totaling fewer than 5,000 men, withdrew into the Libyan interior to join with Arab and Berber militia and tribal levies to resist the invaders.

The Italians had expected that the Arab and Berber populations of Libya, who viewed the Turks as corrupt and repressive, would greet the Italians as liberators. This proved false, for the shared faith of Islam outweighed all other considerations. The Ottoman military commitment also proved stronger than expected.

On October 23, 1911, Ottoman forces aided by civilians killed some 500 Italian soldiers in a surprise attack on a weakly defended sector of the Tripoli defenses. This Massacre of Sciara Sciat brought severe Italian reprisals, including summary executions and the opening of concentration camps.

From October 1911 well into 1912, Italian forces were largely confined to their coastal beachheads despite reinforcements and a considerable advantage in weaponry, including aircraft and dirigibles used to bomb enemy positions. (This was in fact the first time that aircraft were used in a combat role rather than simply for reconnaissance.) The Italians also pioneered the use of armored cars and developed a system of battlefield wireless communication.

Ottoman Army regulars, denied reinforcements by a tight Italian naval blockade, were consistently outnumbered in the field and seldom able to take the offensive. The Senussis played an important role. This powerful Sufi brotherhood served as the spiritual and, to some extent, political leaders of the Bedouin to the interior, particularly in Cyrenaica. They joined the Ottoman side, with the result that Italians troops were unable to penetrate into the interior of that province for the duration of the conflict.

The fighting between Italy and the Ottoman Empire was brought to an end only when the Italians expanded the war to the eastern Mediterranean, something they earlier had promised they would not do, as there were fears that such action might encourage the Balkan states such as Serbia and Bulgaria to try to end what remained of Ottoman control in Southeastern Europe. A naval raid on the Dardanelles was followed by Italian occupation of Rhodes in May 1912 and other islands in the Dodecanese chain in the Aegean. This plus looming conflict in the Balkans brought the Turks to the negotiating table.

On October 18, 1912, a settlement was reached at Lausanne, Switzerland, that gave Italy sovereignty over Libya. Fighting in Libya did not end with the Treaty of Lausanne, however. An Arab and Berber insurrection festered until 1932, when Benito Mussolini's army employed scorched-earth tactics to finally stamp it out. Indeed, in 1916 with Italy then engaged in World War I (1914–1918), more than 40,000 of its soldiers were still battling guerrillas there. The indigenous struggle against the Italians in Libya gained support, largely moral, from Muslims around the world and has been called the first Pan-Islamic resistance movement against Western colonialism. It is credited with providing modern-day Libya with the necessary credentials to declare itself an independent nation-state.

Libya saw significant fighting in the North African campaigns of World War II between the Allied and Axis forces until it was ultimately secured by the British and the Americans in 1943. Ultimately, in 1949 the United Nations (UN) passed a resolution calling for a united, independent Libya. Dutch diplomat Adrian Pelt acted as the UN commissioner to oversee the establishment of the new nation. Negotiations with the varied regions in Libya proved difficult. Those in and around Tripoli supported a large degree of national unity, while the more established government of Cyrenaica preferred a federal system and insisted on choosing the monarch. The process resulted in a constitutional monarchy, an elected bicameral parliament, and a federal system of government. Emir Idris of Cyrenaica became the hereditary king of Libya, and Libya was declared independent on December 24, 1951.

The new Kingdom of Libya had strong links to the West. Both Britain and the United States maintained military bases on its soil and in return supported the state financially. Libya maintained a strong Arab identity, however, joining the Arab League in 1953. Libya was strongly influenced by the growth of Arab nationalist movements in response to the 1948 creation of the State of Israel. The emergence of Gamal Abdel Nasser's Pan-Arabic nationalist regime in Egypt in 1954 encouraged similar political thought within Libya, and the 1956 Suez Crisis only increased this trend. In 1959, Libya's first oil fields were discovered at Amal and Zelten. This economic windfall gave Libya both wealth and increased geopolitical significance. By 1968 oil exports had reached $1 billion.

Arab nationalism and Middle Eastern conflict continued to affect Libya and its pro-Western policies in the 1960s. In 1964, Nasser charged that American and British bases in Libya might be used to support Israel in a conflict, and he pressured the Libyan government to close them. The 1967 Six-Day War proved to be a turning point for Libyan politics, for on June 5, 1967, the day hostilities began, anti-Jewish and anti-Western riots broke out in Tripoli. When Nasser falsely blamed the Arab defeat on American and British assistance to Israel, Libyan oil workers refused to load American, British, and German tankers. Prime Minister Hussein Maziq was forced to resign, and the king appointed a new cabinet.

In the months after the war, the Libyan government was under continued pressure from Arab nationalists internally and externally. It pledged financial aid to Egypt and Jordan and called for, but did not press, the closing of all foreign bases in Libya. Then on September 1, 1969, a group of junior army officers seized power while King Idris was out of the country. The Revolution Command Council, headed by Colonel Muammar Gaddafi, took control with little opposition.

Gaddafi, an adherent of Nasser's version of Arab nationalism, stressed Arab unity, opposition to Western imperialism, and socialist economic policies. Unlike Nasser, however, Gaddafi maintained that this agenda could be reconciled with a strong emphasis on Islamic law. Gaddafi rejected the Western presence in the Middle East and considered Israel an imperialist outpost. He also completed the removal of foreign bases in Libya. After Nasser's death, Gaddafi actively sought leadership in the Muslim world, promoting his "Third International Theory," a middle way between the communism of the Soviet Union and the capitalism of the

Colonel Muammar Gaddafi, shown here in 1970. Gaddafi held power in Libya from 1969 until the Libyan Revolution (Libyan Civil War) of 2011, when he was overthrown and killed. (AP Photo)

West. Although Gaddafi succeeded in convincing more than 30 African countries to reject relations with Israel, he never gained the confidence of other Muslim nations.

To implement his unconventional governing system within Libya, Gaddafi relied heavily on Revolutionary Committees, which reported directly to him. The committees were also used as vehicles for internal surveillance, and by the 1980s anywhere from 10 percent to 20 percent of all Libyans performed some type of surveillance work for these committees. Only in North Korea and Iraq under Saddam Hussein were there more citizens working as covert informants. In 1973 the Gaddafi regime outlawed political dissent, so the committees were vitally important to his government. With so many informants, it is not surprising that a large number of Libyans were at one time or another detained, arrested, or imprisoned.

Oddly perhaps, Gaddafi's regime generally refrained from perpetrating violent repression at home, and the dictator publicly condemned torture. Those accused of torture could receive lengthy prison sentences. Gaddafi was far more willing to engineer violent acts outside Libya, however. Always an enemy of Zionism, he supported Yasser Arafat's Fatah faction of the Palestine Liberation Organization and sponsored terrorist attacks against Israel and related Western targets. As the 1970s progressed, Gaddafi voiced his support for revolutionary movements around the world, and Libya played host to a number of insurgent groups. Gaddafi also sought to build up the Libyan military and pursued significant arms purchases from France and the Soviet Union after 1970. However, his suspicion of the atheist dimension of communism kept Libya out of the Soviet orbit in the strict sense. Nevertheless, his anti-Western activities assured him of Soviet support.

Internally, Gaddafi sought to remake Libyan society, insisting that a mixture of socialism and Islam would ensure social justice. He created a welfare state buttressed by oil revenues and reformed the legal system to include elements of sharia (Islamic law). Gaddafi's *Green Book* (1976) laid out his political philosophy. In it he rejected representative government in favor of direct democracy. In 1977, he set up Basic People's Congresses across the nation but still retained real power himself. Finally, Gaddafi transformed Libya's oil industry by taking production away from international oil companies, setting a pattern that would be imitated by other oil-rich states.

Despite Gaddafi's radical politics, Libya and the United States avoided direct confrontation for much of the 1970s because of their economic relationship. This changed when Libya vehemently opposed Egyptian-Israeli peace negotiations. Gaddafi viewed any Arab rapprochement with Israel as a betrayal. In 1977, the Jimmy Carter administration listed Libya, Cuba, and North Korea as states that supported international terrorism.

U.S.-Libyan relations continued to sour. On December 2, 1979, rioters targeted the U.S. embassy in Tripoli in imitation of the attack on the American embassy in Tehran earlier that year. As a result, in May 1980 the United States withdrew its diplomatic personnel from Libya.

With the election of President Ronald Reagan in 1980, relations between the United States and Libya chilled further. On May 6, 1981, Reagan officially labeled Libya as a state supporter of terrorism and expelled Libyan diplomats from the United States. The administration also pursued a freedom of navigation policy and challenged Libya's 1973 claims of sovereignty over the Gulf of Sidra in the Mediterranean. On July 19, 1981, the *Nimitz* carrier battle group was patrolling near the Gulf of Sidra when two of the carrier's fighters were approached and attacked by two Libyan fighters. The American aircraft evaded the attack and shot down both Libyan planes.

Tensions increased further, and in March 1982 the United States banned the import of Libyan oil. The sanctions had only limited effect, as European nations did not adopt U.S. policies. Meanwhile, Gaddafi continued to support revolutionary and terrorist activity. On April 5, 1986, an explosion in a Berlin discotheque frequented by U.S. military personnel killed 3 (2 U.S. soldiers and a Turkish woman) and wounded 230 others, including 63 U.S. servicemen.

Telex messages from the Libyan government to its East Berlin embassy congratulating the bombers on carrying out their assignment led the Reagan administration to order a military strike against Libya. Dubbed Operation EL DORADO CANYON, the strike occurred early on April 15 and involved U.S. Air Force aircraft flying from Britain and U.S. Navy aircraft flying off two carriers. The planes struck a half dozen targets around Tripoli and Benghazi, sank two missile boats, and destroyed a number of Libyan aircraft. At least 15 Libyans died in the air strikes, including Gaddafi's adopted 15-month-old daughter (Gaddafi, forewarned by a phone call from Malta prime minister Karmenu Mifsud Bonnici that unauthorized aircraft were flying over Malta heading for Libya, escaped just in time with most other members of his family, although 2 of his sons were among more than 100 people injured.). One U.S. Air Force F-111 was lost and its two aircrew killed when it was shot down over the Gulf of Sidra.

The Reagan administration maintained that its raid had resulted in significant disruptions to Libyan-supported terrorism, and such activity did decline for a

The Destruction of Pan Am Flight 103

On December 21, 1988, Pan Am Flight 103, a Boeing 747-100 aircraft, departed London's Heathrow Airport for New York City. It exploded at 31,000 feet over Lockerbie in Scotland, killing all 243 passengers and 16 crew members on board as well as 11 people on the ground. Investigation revealed that a bomb destroyed the plane. Although originally thought to have been planned by the Iranian government, evidence surfaced linking the terrorist attack to Libya.

Two Libyans were subsequently charged, and on January 31, 2001, Abdelbaset Ali al-Megrahi, a Libyan intelligence officer and head of security for Libyan Arab Airlines, was found guilty of murder by a panel of three Scottish judges and sentenced to 27 years in prison. The coaccused, Lamin Khalifah Fhimah, was found not guilty and was acquitted. On May 29, 2002, the Libyan government accepted responsibility for the bombings and agreed to pay $2.7 billion to compensate the families of the 270 victims.

Suffering from terminal colon cancer and reputedly having only three months to live, al-Megrahi was released from prison in August 2009 by a Scottish court on "compassionate grounds." He received a hero's welcome on his return to Libya and died there in May 2012.

number of years. On December 21, 1988, however, Pan Am Flight 103, a Boeing 747-100 aircraft flying from London to New York City, blew up over Lockerbie, Scotland, killing all 243 passengers and 16 crew members on board and 11 people on the ground. Subsequent investigations proved that a bomb had downed the plane and pointed to 2 Libyan men as primary suspects. When Gaddafi refused to extradite the men for trial, the UN imposed sanctions on Libya in 1992.

American confrontations with Libya continued, and a second incident over the Gulf of Sidra resulted in the destruction of two Libyan fighter aircraft on January 4, 1989. Gaddafi, however, remained steadfast in his support of revolutionary movements and terrorist actions against Israel and the West. The United States continued to view Libya as a sponsor of international terrorism.

On June 29, 1996, a massive riot at Libya's Abu Salim maximum security prison, which housed many political dissidents and enemies of the state, caused the deaths of 1,270 inmates. The prisoners were protesting the dreadful living conditions at the facility. The Gaddafi regime dispatched government troops to quash the revolt, which they did using automatic weapons. To this day, the precise events of that event remain unclear.

In the late 1990s Gaddafi began to take a more conciliatory tone with the West. In 1999 he turned over the men responsible for the Pan Am bombing and in 2003 acknowledged Libyan responsibility for the bombing and agreed to pay restitution to the victims' families. Gaddafi also denounced radical Islamic terror groups such as Al-Qaeda. Then in February 2004 Libya declared that it would give up its weapons of mass destruction program and comply with the Nuclear Non-Proliferation

Treaty, beginning a thaw in relations with the United States. The George W. Bush administration resumed diplomatic relations with Libya that June and lifted all remaining economic sanctions in September 2004.

Despite these developments, Gaddafi's regime remained dictatorial. Gaddafi's hold on power was loosened by the so-called Arab Spring, however. Demonstrations in neighboring Tunisia in December 2010 touched off calls for reform and democratization throughout much of the Middle East, including Libya, where the result was civil war (also known as the Libyan Revolution and the Libyan Insurgency).

By 2011 Gaddafi had ruled Libya for 42 years and was the focal point of considerable popular unrest, which was strongest in the eastern region of Libya but also manifest in parts of the western and southern provinces. Opponents protested decades of authoritarianism, corruption, and repression that had produced economic and political dysfunction. Libyans tired of the Gaddafi regime now sought to ride the Arab Spring to oust the long-ruling dictator.

The situation in Libya had been tense since the ousting in January 2012 of Tunisian president Ben Ali, and Libyans abroad who made up the preponderance of organized opposition to the Gaddafi regime began mobilizing prior to the beginning of peaceful demonstrations in Benghazi on February 15, 2011, usually given as the date for the start of the civil war, protesting the arrest of a human rights lawyer. Two days later the demonstrations escalated, and Libyan security forces opened fire on the crowds. Some 150 people were killed before protesters overwhelmed the security forces, who withdrew from Benghazi on February 18. Violence also erupted in al-Bayda, Derna, and Tobruk, and Libyan rebels advanced across the country in makeshift vehicle caravans with incredible speed. Gaddafi meanwhile made clear that he would not yield political power and preferred a civil war.

The opposition in Libya was far more organized than in some other Arab Spring nations. This proved critical in establishing a transitional political movement as well as garnering international support. On February 27, 2011, the opposition leaders formed the Interim Transitional National Council (TNC). It was originally made up of 31 members representing regions of the country as well as the many clans. Local councils from throughout the country selected representatives and charged them with removing Gaddafi and installing democratic rule. The first TNC chairman was Mustafa Mohammad Abdul Jalil, while Mahmoud Jibril chaired the TNC's Executive Board. The TNC also set up a military committee, led by Omar al-Hariri, although Abdul Fatah Younis Al-Obeidi had actual charge of ground operations.

In the first few days of revolt, Libyan minister of the interior Abdul Fatah Younis Al-Obeidi defected, bolstering rebel support. On February 20, protests reached the Gaddafi stronghold of Tripoli. By late February, Gaddafi's regime had lost control of Cyrenaica, Misrata, Zawiyah, and the Berber areas. Fighting in eastern Libya was intense in February and March, with rebels not only securing Benghazi but also advancing to Brega, site of a major oil and gas refinery. Gaddafi loyalists counterattacked and drove the rebels out of Brega and back to the town of Ajdabiya, a strategic access point to Benghazi. On March 15, Gaddafi mounted a drive on Ajdabiya that ousted the rebels and carried on toward Benghazi.

Meanwhile, the Battle of Misrata raged from February 18 until May 15, as Gaddafi's forces laid siege to this city that had been taken by rebels and that in their possession threatened his hold on Tripoli. The rebels quickly organized the Misrata Street and Military Councils. Although not as well financed as the TNC, the Military Council led by General Ramadan Zarmuh was able to stave off a loyalist onslaught that ultimately reached more than 10,000 men and saw widespread shelling of the city. Misrata was saved thanks to a sealift of rebel manpower, weapons, and supplies from Benghazi.

During the fighting in Cyrenaica, fears abounded that Gaddafi would wreak havoc on Benghazi, resulting in the deaths of countless innocent civilians in what was Libya's second-largest city. This led Libyan opposition leaders to call for international intervention. On March 17 the UN Security Council adopted Resolution 1973 calling for a no-fly zone over Libya and granting permission for member states to take all necessary measures to protect civilians there. The resolution did not authorize foreign ground troops, however.

Acting under the authority of the UN resolution, beginning on March 19 French warplanes halted Gaddafi's advance on Benghazi and drove his forces back to Ajdabiya. In U.S.-named Operation ODYSSEY DAWN, U.S. and British ships and submarines joined the French planes by attacking Libyan targets with 110 Tomahawk cruise missiles. The coalition forces enforced a no-fly zone and destroyed loyalist aircraft, armor and artillery, air defenses, and command-and-control centers.

The North Atlantic Treaty Organization (NATO) reached agreement on intervention and air strikes. Operation UNIFIED PROTECTOR, which began on March 23 and ran until October 31, enforced the arms embargo and had command of all NATO operations in Libya. NATO aircraft kept the loyalists from massing the forces needed to take Misrata and Benghazi.

Even with international intervention, the conflict dragged on for many more months. The battle for Misrata continued, with Gaddafi seeking to exploit tribal antagonisms to his advantage. He also sought to use his naval forces against the port, with the result that NATO carried out an attack on the Libyan Navy on May 20.

The three-month battle for Misrata ended in an insurgent victory on May 15. The battle had claimed more than 1,500 rebel and civilian dead. Meanwhile, Gaddafi's forces employed tanks and artillery against rebel towns in the Nafusa Mountains. This went on for some four months, with rebel forces there in dire straits until several key victories reopened supply lines and NATO air strikes deflected the loyalists.

Another major battle erupted in late February in the city of Zawiyah, only 30 miles west of Tripoli. More important than its proximity to the capital were its oil refinery and port facilities. Rebel forces under the command of Colonel Hussein Darbouk were unable to hold the city against Gaddafi's onslaught, and Zawiyah remained under loyalist control until August. When the rebels retook Zawiyah, this prompted a drive from the Nafusa Mountains into Tripoli on August 20.

The campaign to secure control of Tripoli involved rebel elements from the Nafusa Mountains and Misrata as well as from Tripoli itself. Fighting was block by block, with the last government stronghold falling on August 28. Gaddafi, who had vowed to fight to the end in Tripoli, had already departed for his hometown of Sirte, which was the objective of a rebel attack in mid-October. Gaddafi was captured while attempting to escape from Sirte on October 20 and executed on the spot. Also killed were his son Mutassim Gaddafi and Libyan Army chief General Abu Bakr Younis.

On October 23 the TNC declared victory and set elections for 18 months in the future. The NATO mission ended on October 31. The death toll in the civil war is estimated at some 32,000.

Vast challenges remained. These included rebuilding the Libyan economy and the military, constructing institutions capable of governing a country unused to such, and maintaining political unity in a nation sharply divided along tribal and ethnic lines. Large quantities of Libyan government weapons, including antiaircraft missiles, also had passed into private hands during and after the war, and with no internationally sanctioned peacekeeping force on the ground, the situation soon deteriorated as fighting for power commenced between the various Libyan tribes and political factions. This chronic instability permitted Islamic extremist groups such as Al-Qaeda and the Islamic State of Iraq and Syria (ISIS) to assert themselves within Libya. Indeed, some of these groups have already perpetrated attacks on foreign interests in Libya, most notably on September 11–12, 2012, when radicals with ties to Al-Qaeda attacked the U.S. consulate at Benghazi, killing 4 Americans including ambassador J. Christopher Stevens and wounding 10 others.

In July 2014 in the worst fighting since the civil war, extended combat occurred on the outskirts of Tripoli as militia groups battled for control of the airport. In August, catching Washington by surprise, Egypt and the United Arab Emirates secretly teamed up to launch air strikes against the Islamist-allied militias battling for control of Tripoli. On September 4, a UN report concluded that four months of fighting for Tripoli and Benghazi had displaced some 250,000 people, with 150,000 of these, including migrant workers, departing Libya altogether.

On February 15, 2015, ISIS-affiliated jihadists in Libya released a gruesome video showing the beheading of 21 Egyptian Coptic Christians who had been working in Libya. The next day Egyptian aircraft bombed reported ISIS camps, training areas, and weapons depots in Libya. The United States also augmented aerial surveillance and air strikes in Libya. On November 13, 2015, one such strike killed Abu Nabil, also known as Wissam Najm Abd Zayd al-Zubaydi, the senior ISIS leader in Libya. In February 2016, Washington officials estimated that ISIS then had increased its strength there to some 6,500.

In 2016 Libya was split into at least a half dozen fiefdoms. Two principal political entities claimed to be the legitimate government of Libya. The first, the Council of Deputies, was located in Tobruk. It controlled eastern and southern Libya and enjoyed international recognition. The second, the General National Congress, established in 2014 and located in Tripoli, claimed to be the legal continuation of the General National Congress elected in 2012 and then dissolved following elections in June 2014, only to be reconvened by a minority of its membership. The rest of

Libya meanwhile remained outside the control of either government and was under Islamist extremists and tribal militias.

UN-sponsored peace talks between the Tobruk- and Tripoli-based governments led to a December 17, 2015, agreement under which a 9-member Presidency Council and a 17-member interim Government of National Accord were to be established, with new national elections to occur within two years. The leaders of the new government, called the Government of National Accord (GNA), arrived in Tripoli on April 5, 2016. Whether this will last and avert even more devastating conflict than in 2011 is open to considerable question. Also in April, U.S. president Barack Obama declared that not preparing for a post-Gaddafi regime in Libya was probably the "worst mistake" of his presidency.

On June 11, 2016, following a two-week offensive, forces backing the GNA retook much of the Mediterranean port city of Sirte from ISIS. The government forces also secured complete control of the al-Sarawa area east of Sirte. The GNA's air force carried out six air raids against the militants and their weaponry in Buhari, about two miles south of Sirte. This advance paralleled those against ISIS in Iraq and Syria. Still, Kiubya remained ISIS's most important base of operations outside of Iraq and Syria, with an estimated 4,000–6,000 militants in Libya. The United State has, however, stepped up military assistance to counter ISIS there.

Timeline

1551	The territory of modern-day Libya passes under rule of the Ottoman Empire.
1801–1805, 1815	The United States and Libya, then known as Tripoli, clash in the so-called Barbary Wars.
Sep 28, 1911	The Italian government presents an ultimatum to the Ottoman Sublime Porte demanding an Italian military occupation of Libya.
Sep 29, 1911	Italy declares war on the Ottoman Empire, beginning the Tripolitan War of 1911–1912.
Oct 9, 1911	Following a brief Italian naval bombardment, Italian forces occupy Tripoli.
Oct 20, 1911	Italian forces capture Benghazi.
Oct 23, 1911	Some 500 Italian soldiers are killed in a surprise Ottoman attack at Tripoli. Known as the Massacre of Sciara Sciat, it brings severe Italian reprisals, including summary executions and concentration camps.
May 1912	Italian forces occupy Rhodes and other islands in the Dodecanese chain in the Aegean Sea. This and looming conflict in the Balkans brings the Turks to the negotiating table.

Oct 18, 1912   A peace treaty is signed at Lausanne, Switzerland, in which the Ottoman Empire grants Italy sovereignty over Libya. An Arab and Berber insurrection festers until 1932, however.

1943   Libya is secured by the British and Americans following significant fighting there during the North African campaigns of World War II.

Nov 21, 1949   The United Nations (UN) passes a resolution calling for a united, independent Libya.

Dec 24, 1951   Libya is declared a fully independent state, with Emir Idris of Cyrenaica as hereditary king.

1959   Oil is discovered at Amal and Zelten.

Jun 5, 1967   On this first day of the Six-Day War, anti-Jewish and anti-Western riots occur in Tripoli.

Sep 1, 1969   With King Idris out of the country, a group of junior army officers calling themselves the Revolution Command Council and headed by Colonel Muammar Gaddafi seize power in Libya. Gaddafi is soon dictator.

Dec 2, 1979   With U.S.-Libyan relations in a tailspin, rioters target the U.S. embassy in Tripoli.

May 1980   The United States terminates diplomatic relations with Libya.

May 6, 1981   The Ronald Reagan administration officially labels Libya a state supporter of terrorism and expels Libyan diplomats from the United States.

Jul 19, 1981   The U.S. Navy challenges the Libyan claim of sovereignty over the Gulf of Sidra. On this date the *Nimitz* carrier battle group is patrolling near the Gulf of Sidra when two of its fighters are approached and attacked by two Libyan fighters. The American aircraft shoot down both Libyan aircraft.

Mar 1982   The United States bans the import of Libyan oil.

Apr 5, 1986   A bomb in a Berlin discotheque frequented by U.S. military personnel kills 3 people (2 U.S. soldiers and a Turkish woman) and wounds some 230 others. Evidence links the deed to the Libyan government.

Apr 15, 1986   In Operation EL DORADO CANYON, a retaliatory U.S. raid, U.S. aircraft strike a half dozen targets in Libya, sink 2 Libyan missile boats, and destroy 17–19 Libyan aircraft. One U.S. aircraft is lost, and its two aircrew are killed.

Dec 21, 1988   Pan Am Flight 103, a Boeing 747-100 aircraft flying from London to New York City, blows up over Lockerbie, Scotland, killing 270 people in the plane and on the ground. Investigations prove that a bomb had downed the plane and point to 2 Libyan men as primary suspects. When the Gaddafi regime refuses to extradite the 2 for arrest and trial, the UN imposes sanctions on Libya in 1992.

Jan 4, 1989   A second Gulf of Sidra incident results in U.S. Navy aircraft downing two Libyan fighters.

Jun 29, 1996   A riot at Libya's Abu Salim maximum security prison, housing many political dissidents and enemies of the state, brings the deaths of 1,270 inmates.

1999   Gaddafi turns over to Scottish authorities the two Libyans accused of downing Pan Am Flight 103.

Aug 16, 2003   Libya accepts responsibility for the Pan Am bombing and agrees to pay compensation to the victims' families.

Feb 2004   Libya declares that it is renouncing its weapons of mass destruction program and will comply with the Nuclear Non-Proliferation Treaty.

Jun 2004   The George W. Bush administration resumes U.S. diplomatic relations with Libya and lifts all remaining economic sanctions against the country in September 2004.

Dec 2010   Beginning in Tunisia, demonstrations demanding reform and democratization and known as the Arab Spring occur in much of the Arab world.

Feb 15, 2011   Prompted by events in Tunisia, peaceful demonstration against the Gaddafi regime begin in Benghazi. This is usually given as the start of the Libyan Civil War.

Feb 16–20, 2011   The demonstrations in Benghazi escalate, and Libyan security forces open fire on the crowds. During the next several days some 150 people are killed. Protesters overwhelm the security forces, which withdraw from Benghazi on February 18. Violence also erupts in al-Bayda, Derna, Tobruk, and, by February 20, Tripoli. Gaddafi makes clear that he will not yield political power.

Feb 18–May 15, 2011   The Battle of Misrata occurs, with government forces laying siege to this rebel stronghold that threatens Gaddafi's hold on Tripoli. Despite heavy fighting, the rebels manage to hold out and win the battle.

Feb 24–Mar 12, 2011   The First Battle of Zawiyah. Located only 30 miles west of Tripoli, Zawiyah is the site of a major oil refinery and port facilities. Rebel forces are unable to hold the city against a loyalist onslaught, however, and Zawiyah passes under loyalist control until August.

Feb 27, 2011   Opposition leaders form a new government, the Interim Transitional National Council (TNC), representing regions of the country and the many clans.

Mar 2011   Gaddafi mounts a drive on Benghazi. Fighting in eastern Libya is intense, with rebel forces securing Benghazi and advancing to Brega, the site of a major oil and gas refinery. Gaddafi loyalists counterattack and drive the rebels out of Brega and back to Ajdabiya, a strategic access point to Benghazi. On March 15, Gaddafi's forces begin a drive on Ajdabiya that ousts the rebels and carries on toward Benghazi.

Mar 17, 2011   To avoid an anticipated bloodbath in Benghazi, opposition leaders call for international intervention, and on this date the UN Security Council calls for a no-fly zone over Libya and the granting of permission for member states to take all necessary measures to protect civilians there. The resolution does not authorize foreign ground troops, however.

Mar 19, 2011   Acting under the authority of the UN resolution, French warplanes disrupt Gaddafi's advance on Benghazi. In the U.S.-named Operation ODYSSEY DAWN (March 19–31), French aircraft and U.S. and British ships and submarines strike Libyan targets with munitions that include 110 Tomahawk cruise missiles, enforcing a no-fly zone and destroying loyalist armor and artillery, air defenses, and command-and-control centers.

Mar 23, 2011   With the North Atlantic Treaty Organization (NATO) having reached agreement on intervention, NATO commences Operation UNIFIED PROTECTOR. Running until October 31, it enforces the arms embargo and carries out NATO operations in Libya.

Aug 13–20, 2011   In the Second Battle of Zawiyah, rebel forces retake this important port city only 30 miles from Tripoli, then commence a drive from it and the Nafusa Mountains into Tripoli.

Aug 20–28, 2011   In the Battle of Tripoli, rebel forces secure control of the Libyan capital.

Oct 20, 2011   Attempting to escape from Sirte, Gaddafi is captured and immediately executed along with his son Mutassim Gaddafi and army chief General Abu Bakr Younis.

Oct 23, 2011   The TNC declares victory.

Oct 31, 2011   The NATO mission comes to an end.

Sep 11–12, 2012	Radicals with ties to Al-Qaeda attack the U.S. consulate at Benghazi, killing 4 Americans, including ambassador J. Christopher Stevens, and wounding 10 others.
Jun 25, 2014	Legislative elections are held for the Council of Deputies.
Jul 2014	In the worst fighting since the civil war, extended combat occurs on the outskirts of Tripoli as militia groups battle for control of the airport.
Aug 2014	Catching Washington by surprise, aircraft of Egypt and the United Arab Emirates secretly team up to launch air strikes against the Islamist-allied militias battling for control of Tripoli.
Feb 15, 2015	Jihadists affiliated with the Islamic State of Iraq and Syria (ISIS) in Libya release a video showing the beheading of 21 Egyptian Coptic Christians who had been working in Libya. The next day Egyptian aircraft bomb reported ISIS camps, training areas, and weapons depots in Libya.
Dec 17, 2015	UN-sponsored peace talks between the two leading and rival political factions, each claiming to be the legitimate government of Libya—the Council of Deputies, which is located in Tobruk, controls most of eastern and southern part of the country, and enjoys the support of the international community, and the General National Congress in Tripoli, which controls most of western Libya, result in an agreement for the establishment of a provisional government and new national elections to occur within two years.
Apr 5, 2016	The leaders of the new government, called the Government of National Accord, arrive in Tripoli.

Further Reading

Askew, W. C. *Europe and Italy's Acquisition of Libya, 1911–1912*. Durham, NC: Duke University Press, 1942.

Bosworth, R. J. B. *Italy, the Least of the Great Powers: Italian Foreign Policy before the First World War*. Cambridge: Cambridge University Press, 1979.

Cooley, John. *Libyan Sands: The Complete Account of Qaddafi's Revolution*. New York: Holt, Rinehart and Winston, 1982.

Lobban, Richard A., Jr. and Christopher H. Dalton. *Libya: History and Revolution*. Santa Barbara, CA: ABC-CLIO, 2014.

Pargeter, Alison. *Libya: The Rise and Fall of Qaddafi*. New Haven, CT: Yale University Press, 2012.

Simons, Geoff. *Libya and the West: From Independence to Lockerbie*. London: I. B. Tauris, 2004.

St. John, Ronald B. *Libya: From Colony to Revolution*. Oxford, UK: Oneworld, 2012.

Vandervort, B. *To the Fourth Shore: Italy's War for Libya, 1911–1912*. Rome: Stato Maggiore dell'Esercito, Ufficio Storico, 2012.

Vandewalle, Dirk J. *A History of Modern Libya*. Cambridge: Cambridge University Press, 2012.

Wright, John. *Libya: A Modern History*. Baltimore: Johns Hopkins University Press, 1981.

MOROCCO

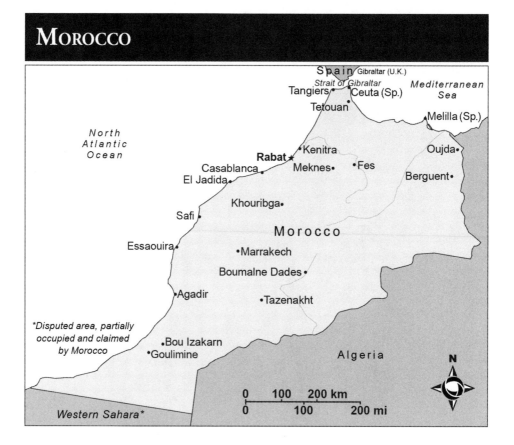

Spain
Gibraltar (U.K.)
Strait of Gibraltar
Tangiers•   •Ceuta (Sp.)   Mediterranean
Tetouan   Sea

North
Atlantic
Ocean   •Melilla (Sp.)

                  •Kenitra
          Rabat ★   •Oujda
Casablanca•   Meknes•   •Fes
El Jadida•   Berguent•

       Khouribga•

Safi•   M o r o c c o

Essaouira•
              •Marrakech
          Boumalne Dades•

   •Agadir   •Tazenakht

*Disputed area, partially
occupied and claimed   •Bou Izakarn   Algeria
   by Morocco   •Goulimine

                          N
        0   100   200 km
        0   100   200 mi

Western Sahara*

Morocco

William T. Dean III, Mark M. Sanders, and Spencer C. Tucker

Located in Northwest Africa, the Kingdom of Morocco borders on the Mediterranean Sea to the north, the Atlantic Ocean to the west, Western Sahara to the south, and Algeria to the east. Morocco has an area of 172,410 square miles, making it slightly larger than the U.S. state of California. Morocco occupied and then annexed most of the Western Sahara and claims that region as its Southern Provinces, although this action has not been recognized by the international community.

Rabat is the capital of Morocco. The population of the country in 2016 was some 34.817 million. Arabs and Berbers constitute some 99 percent of the population, with Islam being the predominant religion. Sunni Islam is both the official and majority religion. Shia Islam, Judaism, Christianity, and Baha'i are minority faiths. Moroccan culture is a blend of Berber, Arab, sub-Saharan African, and European influences.

The Kingdom of Morocco is a constitutional monarchy with an elected parliament. The king holds considerable power, especially regarding the formation of foreign policy, the military, and religious matters. He can also issue decrees (*dahirs*) that have the force of law and has the power to dissolve the parliament after consultation with the prime minister and president of the constitutional court. The parliament consists of two houses: the Assembly of Representatives and the Assembly of Councillors. Morocco is a member of the Arab League and boasts the sixth-largest economy in Africa.

Morocco has a long history. The region has been inhabited since Paleolithic times. The Phoenicians established trading colonies and coastal settlements here in the sixth century BCE, and Morocco became part of the Carthaginian Empire. The earliest known independent Moroccan state was the Berber kingdom of Mauretania, which lasted from the third century BCE until it became a Roman province in 44 BCE. Morocco was under Roman rule until 432 CE, when it was conquered first by the Vandals and then by the Visigoths. From the sixth century the Byzantine Empire controlled the northern part of Morocco, with the interior remaining under Berber control. In 670 Uqba ibn Nafi, an Umayyad Muslim general, began the conquest of Morocco. The Umayyads then converted most of the population to Islam. Independent Muslim states emerged in Morocco as early as 710. That same year the governor of North Africa, Musa ibn Nusair, sent Muslim forces across the Strait of Gibraltar to Spain in a raiding expedition, ultimately leading to Islamic control of Spain.

In 1549 the region fell to successive Arab dynasties, but in 1666 Morocco was reunited under the Alaouite dynasty, the ruling family of the country ever since. Morocco was the first country to recognize the United States as an independent nation, in 1777, and the Moroccan-American Treaty of Friendship, signed in 1786, is the oldest U.S. nonbroken friendship treaty.

From the early 16th century the so-called Barbary states of Morocco, Algiers, Tunis, and Tripoli were centers of corsair activity, sending out warships to seize the merchant shipping and hold for ransom the crews of trading nations that failed to pay them tribute. The new United States fought a series of naval wars against these states during 1801–1805 and 1815, but these Barbary Wars did not involve Morocco.

In the 19th century there was considerable interest by the major European powers in colonizing overseas territories, especially Africa. Morocco, coveted by both France and Spain, was no exception. France wanted Africa in order to secure the western flank of Algeria. The French had seized Algiers in 1830 and then expanded their holdings, creating modern-day Algeria. Morocco was also important for its strategic location, controlling access to the Mediterranean from the Atlantic through the Strait of Gibraltar, and for its frontage on the eastern Atlantic. Spain was, of course, the closest European nation to Morocco. A dispute involving Spain's small coastal enclave of Ceuta led to the Spanish-Moroccan War of 1859–1860. (Ceded by Morocco to Spain in 1668, Ceuta is today a 7.1-square-mile autonomous Spanish city separated from the Iberian Peninsula only by the Strait of Gibraltar and located along the boundary between the Mediterranean Sea and the Atlantic Ocean.) The Spanish victory in the war brought the enlargement of Ceuta and the cession of another Spanish enclave, that of Melilla (today another autonomous Spanish city of 4.7-square miles). Morocco was also forced to pay reparations. Then in 1884, Spain created a protectorate in the coastal areas of Morocco.

Internal turmoil in Morocco invited further European penetration, for both France and Spain were interested in controlling Morocco, more for strategic reasons and national prestige than economic concerns. This, however, brought two international crises (1905–1906 and 1911) that almost produced war between France and Germany, which would have meant world war and had implications for World War I that began in 1914.

In April 1904 the French and British governments concluded a series of agreements that resolved points of tension between their two nations in what became known as the Entente Cordiale. One of the agreements called for French recognition of British interests in Egypt in return for British recognition of France's paramount position in Morocco. That October the French and Spanish governments also concluded an agreement, providing for a sharing of power in Morocco between them. With British and Spanish support for its anticipated takeover secure, in December 1904 the French government sent St. René Taillandier to the Moroccan capital of Fez to demand of Moroccan sultan Abdelaziz (r. 1894–1906) a series of reforms in the police, the state bank, and communications that would have given France a virtual protectorate.

At this point the German government, with no vital national interests at stake and virtually no investment in Morocco, decided to challenge the French move as part of Kaiser Wilhelm II's determination to assert German power on the world stage. In January 1905 Chancellor Bernard von Bülow wired Abdelaziz his government's support in resisting French demands. Bülow also underscored Berlin's opposition to a French takeover by setting up a brief visit to Tangier by Wilhelm II on March 31, 1905.

The next day, April 1, Berlin announced that the kaiser's visit underscored Germany's commitment to Morocco's continued independence. This was in fact typical of the ill-considered, blustering, and erratic nature of German diplomacy in the decade before 1914 but also had profound implications, for Berlin also informed Madrid that it must abandon its agreement with France and told French premier Maurice Rouvier that unless the architect of this French foreign policy gambit, Foreign Minister Théophile Delcassé, resigned, there could be "no possibility of an improvement in Franco-German relations."

Rouvier considered war, but the army had been torn apart by the Dreyfus Affair, and France's principal ally Russia was in the midst of war with Japan (1904–1905). Rouvier then tried negotiation, offering Germany territorial compensation elsewhere in Africa. But having posed as the champion of African independence, however dishonestly, Bülow could not now abandon the sultan. Finally an international conference was proposed. Bülow accepted, believing that he could count on Triple Alliance allies Austria-Hungary and Italy, the United States, and the small nations of Europe to support his proposal of an "open door" in Morocco. Spain would then switch sides, and Britain would provide France only moral support.

If the German plan was to destroy or weaken the Entente Cordiale between France and Great Britain, this failed. British public opinion stood firmly with France. Indeed, British foreign secretary Sir Edward Grey informed the German ambassador that if Germany actually attacked France, Great Britain could hardly remain aloof. Thus, this first Moroccan crisis served to consolidate the Franco-British entente and increase tensions between France and Germany.

With Delcassé opposing concession, Rouvier was forced to reorganize his cabinet, dropping him as foreign minister. The international conference on Morocco opened in Algeciras, Spain, in January 1906, and for the next three months the conferees haggled over the terms of an agreement. Able French diplomat Paul Révoil played a key role, courting the representatives of the smaller powers present and securing the support of the U.S. representative. Aided by maladroit German bullying, Révoil was able to shift the balance toward France and secure complete victory. Even nominal German ally Italy sided with France. Germany had the support only of Austria-Hungary.

The crisis ended with Germany's world position weaker than before. German claims to uphold the independence of an Islamic state were shown to be mere rhetoric. France and Britain were closer together; indeed, military staff talks between the two countries were authorized in January 1906.

Under the terms of the Algeciras Agreement, France and Spain shared police duties in Morocco's port cities. French banks controlled the Moroccan state bank. With Moroccans frustrated, attacks on foreigners increased, as in Tangier in 1906. France then moved to secure order through full control of Morocco.

In the spring of 1911 French troops occupied Fez to protect Europeans there from antiforeign agitation. Germany now demanded compensation for what was a violation of the Algeciras Agreement. Berlin backed this up by sending to the Moroccan port of Agadir the German gunboat *Panther*. This so-called Spring of the *Panther* again served to bring together Britain and France. This triggered the Second Moroccan Crisis. London gave wholehearted diplomatic support to France. Indeed, on July 21 Minister of the Exchequer David Lloyd George delivered a speech in which he used threatening language against Germany. Had Paris refused meaningful concessions there might have been war, but neither government wanted this in 1911, and eventually a settlement was achieved whereby Germany agreed to a French protectorate over Morocco and received two strips of the French Congo connecting German Cameroon with the Congo and Ubangi Rivers.

In accordance with the Treaty of Fez of March 30, 1912, Moroccan sultan Mulay Hafid was forced to accept a protectorate. Spain continued to operate its coastal protectorate, but Spain also now assumed the role of the protecting power of the northern and southern Saharan zones of Morocco. France secured control of the bulk of the country. Although the Moroccan sultan theoretically was sovereign, he reigned but did not rule. The French resident general held real power.

Tens of thousands of Europeans now settled in Morocco. Much of the best agricultural land passed into their hands, and they were also involved in mining, banking, and shipping. These individuals pressed France to increase its control over Morocco as being necessary to end the nearly continuous warfare between the various tribes of Morocco. French general Louis Hubert Lyautey, who had cut his teeth in the colonial administration first in Madagascar and then in Algeria, was appointed resident general in Morocco in 1912 and served in that position until 1925. An admirer of Moroccan culture and an adroit colonial administrator, Lyautey had long pressed the French government to take control of Morocco, but he also believed that if France was to be successful in colonial affairs it would have to respect the existing civilizations and cultures and work with the native elites of the lands it sought to manage.

Morocco was little affected by World War I. Moroccan soldiers known as Goumiers, who served in auxiliary units attached to the French Army of Africa, did not see service outside Morocco during the war, but they did enable Lyautey to withdraw a substantial portion of the regular French military forces from Morocco for service on the Western Front.

Lyautey continued to press French pacification of the Moroccan interior, extending French control into the Atlas Mountains region. Concurrent with military operations, Lyautey pushed the construction of roads, railroads, and bridges and was instrumental in the creation of a modern educational system. Slavery was abolished in Morocco in 1925.

Lyautey also had to deal with continued armed opposition to European control of Morocco, notably from Berber tribesmen in the interior Rif Mountains region who in 1893 had threatened the Spanish enclave of Melilla and forced Spain to send substantial reinforcements to North Africa. Indeed, during World War I both the French and Spanish governments were obliged to carry out counterinsurgency operations there.

A new leader against foreign rule in Morocco arose after World War I in 1920 in the person of Muhammad ibn Abd el-Krim al-Khattabi. In 1921 Abd el-Krim, joined by his brother, who became his chief adviser and commander of the rebel army, raised the standard of resistance against foreign control of Morocco. This marked the beginning of the Rif War (1921–1926), although some date the conflict from 1920.

In late July 1921 Spanish general Fernandes Silvestre, determined to destroy the rebels, moved into the Rif Mountains with some 20,000 men. Silverstre failed to carry out adequate reconnaissance or even take sufficient security precautions, and at Annual (Anual) on July 21, Rif forces fell on the Spaniards, killing as many as 12,000 and taking several thousand others prisoner. The rebels also seized important quantities of arms and equipment there as well as from Spanish regional outposts.

Some of the Rif forces now advanced on Melilla, the principal Spanish base in the eastern Rif region, held by 14,000 Spanish troops. Fearful that an attempt to take Melilla might lead to a widened war in consequence of the many citizens of other European states living there, Abd el-Krim ordered his troops not to attack. Later he characterized this decision as his biggest mistake of the war.

Meanwhile, news of the Spanish military disaster of Annual shook Spain to its core and led directly to the establishment of a virtual military dictatorship in Spain under General Miguel Primo de Rivera in 1923.

In 1923 Abd el-Krim proclaimed the Republic of the Rif, with himself as president. He endeavored to create a centralized Berber government that would respect traditional values but override tribal rivalries. Fighting continued, and by the end of 1924 Spanish authority was reduced to the coastal enclaves of Melilla and Tetuán. At its peak insurgent strength numbered some 80,000–90,000 men, although the Rifs had only some 20,000 rifles available at any one time, and many of the modern weapons in their hands were poorly maintained.

Aircraft played a key role in this war. During the fighting the Spanish Army of Africa employed up to 150 planes, including British-built Airco DH-4s bombers, to drop conventional ordnance and also considerable quantities of German-developed mustard gas on Rifian villages. Targets included *souks* (markets), livestock, and Abd el-Krim's headquarters. The Spaniards also used their aircraft to resupply encircled posts. Rifian antiaircraft fire did bring down a number of low-flying Spanish planes, however.

On April 12, 1925, an overconfident Abd el-Krim opened a major offensive against the French part of Morocco in what many historians hold was a major miscalculation. Lyautey had only limited resources, and Abd el-Krim's forces were initially able to overrun 45 of 66 French posts in the Ouergha River Valley. Lyautey used French air assets to good effect. The Goumiers of the French Army of Africa also provided important service and subsequently became a form of gendarmerie, keeping order in rural districts of Morocco.

In July, Lyautey was able to halt the Berber advance short of Fez. Faced with the Rif threat, that same month the French and Spanish governments agreed to close cooperation against Abd el-Krim. The French contributed 150,000 men under Marshal Henri Philippe Pétain, while the Spanish assembled 50,000 under General José Sanjurjo.

Pétain abandoned Lyautey's population-centric methods in favor of a highly kinetic industrial approach to the war that employed infantry along with cavalry but also tanks, artillery, and attack aircraft. By late summer, Rifian forces were under attack by the French and Spanish from the north and south.

In September 1925, coalition forces carried out an amphibious landing at Alhucemas Bay near Abd el-Krim's headquarters. Within a month, 90,000 French and Spanish troops were ashore in what was the most significant operation of its kind in any irregular war during the interwar period.

The period November 1925–April 1926 saw both sides in winter quarters, with only limited French and Spanish air operations occurring. Facing overwhelming force and technological superiority in the form of modern aircraft and artillery, and with his own weapons stocks dwindling and forces melting away, Abd el-Krim surrendered to the French on May 26, 1926. This brought the Rif War to a close, although the French continued to fight various insurgent tribes in the Atlas Mountains until the early 1930s.

Indigenous Moroccans also played an important role in the Spanish Civil War of 1936–1939 on the Nationalist (fascist) side. These Fuerzas Regulares Indígenas (Indigenous Regular Forces), known simply as the Regulares (Regulars), were volunteer infantry and cavalry units serving in the Spanish Army of Africa that included the Spanish Foreign Legion. The Regulares were officered by Spaniards. The Spanish Army of Africa grew from about 30,000 men at the onset of the civil war to some 60,000 at its end. The Regulares were the most decorated units of the Nationalist forces and were accorded a prominent place in the victory parade in Madrid at war's end.

On the defeat of France by the Germans in June 1940 during World War II, the Vichy France government in unoccupied France retained control of French territory overseas, including Morocco, Algeria, and Tunisia. In November 1942, however, U.S. and British forces invaded French North Africa and occupied Morocco. Morocco contributed significant manpower against Axis forces in North Africa and in Europe.

World War II signaled the end of the colonial era, and despite deep ties to France and French culture, the Moroccan people increasingly embraced nationalism. In January 1943 U.S. president Franklin D. Roosevelt traveled to Casablanca, where he met with Winston Churchill to plan military strategy. At that time Roosevelt also met with Moroccan Sultan Mohammed V (r. 1927–1953, 1955–1957) and proclaimed American support for Morocco's eventual independence.

With growing nationalist sentiment in Morocco, the French government exiled the sultan and his family, first to Corsica and then to Madagascar during 1953–1955. In the wake of the Indochina War and with the outbreak of rebellion in Algeria in 1954, France granted independence to both Morocco and Tunisia in

King Mohammed V's Protection of Jews

After the German defeat of France, the Vichy French government controlled Morocco. In 1941 under German pressure, the Vichy government attempted to enact laws that would discriminate against Moroccan Jews, including restricting the number of Jewish doctors and lawyers and removing Jewish students from French schools.

Moroccan king Mohammed V stated that these laws were inconsistent with Moroccan law and called for Jews to be treated equally with Muslims. Defying Vichy, Mohammed invited all the Moroccan rabbis to his 1941 throne celebrations. Owing to his strong stance, Vichy administrators were unable to implement their discriminatory laws in Morocco.

After the creation of Israel, Mohammed warned Moroccans against persecution of Jews, reminding his people that Jews had always been protected there.

1956, although Spain continued to control the Western Sahara region until the mid-1970s and still retains the small enclaves of Ceuta and Melilla along the Mediterranean coast.

Returning from exile a national hero in November 1955, the sultan took the title King Mohammed V in 1957 following Moroccan independence on March 2, 1956. The king was both the nation's head of government and its spiritual leader, as a direct descendent of Prophet Muhammad. In this period, Morocco maintained close ties with the United States.

Upon Mohammed V's unexpected death on February 26, 1961, his son, Crown Prince Moulay Hassan, became king as Hassan II and ruled for the next four decades until his death in July 1999. Hassan, while lacking the charisma and unifying ability of his father, nonetheless proved to be an effective leader. He was

Mohammed V, King of Morocco, in 1957, a year after Morocco gained its independence from France. The king was both head of government and, as a direct descendant of the Prophet Muhammad, Morocco's spiritual leader. (AP Photo)

able to balance relations with the West, whose economic and political aid helped modernize his country, and the Middle East, whose Islamic heritage was his basis for power.

Although the Moroccan government was ostensibly a constitutional monarchy, in reality Hassan controlled nearly all sectors of government, including the military. Strongly opposed to communism, he oppressed the leftist Union Socialiste des Forces Populaires (Socialist Union of Popular Forces) for much of the 1960s. Notwithstanding its opposition to communism, Morocco enjoyed cordial relationships with communist countries such as the Soviet Union and the People's Republic of China.

In 1970 a new constitution providing for a unicameral legislature came into being, but this failed to placate political and military opponents of Hassan's centralized authority. Army elements led by General Muhammad Oufkir staged two unsuccessful attempts at a coup d'état, including an effort to assassinate the king. The first occurred on July 10, 1971, and the second occurred on August 16, 1972. To strengthen his position, Hassan embarked on an effort to secure the Western Sahara.

This conflict, known as the Western Sahara War, pitted the Sahrawi Frente Popular de Liberación de Saguía el Hamra y Río de Oro (Popular Front for the Liberation of Saguia el-Hamra and Río de Oro, better known as Polisario) against first Spain and then Morocco and Mauritania for control of the Spanish colony of Western Sahara (Río de Oro). Spain had acquired the Western Sahara in the 1880s and then in 1958 had joined the district of Saguia el-Hamra (in the north) with Río de Oro (in the south) to form the province of Spanish Sahara.

Sahrawi students in Moroccan universities formed the Polisario in 1971. After trying but failing to win support from various Arab governments, including those of Morocco and Algeria, the students relocated to Spanish-controlled Western Sahara and there commenced an armed uprising against Spain in May 1973. Polisario soon gained the support of the vast majority of the population. A number of the Spanish auxiliary troops, the Tropas Nomidas, deserted to them, bringing with them their weapons and military training.

With the end of the Francisco Franco regime in Spain in 1975, the new Spanish government began negotiations for a transfer of power in the Western Sahara. On November 6, 1975, acting on the behest of King Hassan II, some 350,000 unarmed Moroccans in the so-called Green March, as a symbol of Islam, advanced several miles into Western Sahara territory, escorted by nearly 20,000 Moroccan troops, and met very little response from Polisario. In the Madrid Accords of November 14, 1975, the Spanish government reached agreement with Morocco and Mauritania rather than Polisario, dividing the territory between the two. Morocco was to receive the northern part of the Spanish Sahara (Saguia el-Hamra), while Mauritania obtained the south (Río de Oro).

Polisario meanwhile proclaimed the establishment of the Sahrawi Arab Democratic Republic on February 27, 1976, and then commenced guerrilla warfare against both Morocco and Mauritania. Polisario never had more than 10,000 fighters, while Morocco alone ultimately committed as many as 120,000 men to control the north. Algeria provided both modern weaponry and other military assistance to

Polisario, the ranks of which swelled as a consequence of large numbers of refugees from the fighting who relocated to camps in Algeria. Polisario was soon mounting highly effective hit-and-run attacks against both Moroccan and Mauritanian forces in the Western Sahara.

The weak Mauritanian government headed by Ould Daddah was never able to make a major effort to control the southern Sahara, committing there only about 3,000 men. When Polisario guerrillas attacked Mauritania's iron mines, its chief source of income, the Daddah government was overthrown in 1978 by the Mauritanian Army. It then entered into negotiations with Polisario and reached agreement on August 5, 1979, to quit the southern Sahara altogether and recognize the Sahrawi Arab Democratic Republic. Morocco, however, responded by immediately claiming for itself the area of Western Sahara evacuated by the Mauritanians.

In this struggle the United States supported Morocco, the result of the long-standing alliance between the two countries. As part of this arrangement, U.S. forces enjoyed access to bases in the country, although they relinquished control of their last air base in Africa, at Kenitra, to Morocco in October 1978.

In the mid-1980s Morocco largely managed to keep the Polisario guerrillas at bay by building a large sand berm (the Morocco Wall) to surround the most economically important areas of the Western Sahara, which was manned by roughly as many troops as there were Sahrwais. At the same time, Algerian support for the rebels was largely withdrawn on the formation in February 1989 of the Arab Maghreb Union, which includes both Morocco and Algeria. The result was a stalemate. Although Morocco controlled more than two-thirds of the Western Sahara, including virtually the entire Atlantic coastline, maintaining the wall and its troops in the Western Sahara proved to be a heavy economic burden for Morocco.

On September 6, 1991, both sides agreed to a cease-fire and a referendum to be held in 1992. The cease-fire was monitored by the United Nations Mission for the Referendum in Western Sahara (MINURSO). The referendum did not occur, however. It was stalled largely over the issue of who would be eligible to vote. An uneasy peace continued, with Polisario threatening on numerous occasions to resume the war.

On March 18, 2016, Morocco ordered the United Nations (UN) to pull 84 members from the MINURSO staff of 496 after accusing UN secretary-general Ban Ki-moon of no longer being neutral in a conflict over the disputed territory following his visit to Sahrawi refugee camps in southern Algeria when he used the word "occupation" to describe Morocco's annexation of the region. Rabat's position was that it was prepared to grant only semiautonomy. The controversy was Morocco's worst dispute with the UN since 1991, when the UN brokered the cease-fire. Ban had wanted to restart stalled negotiations between the two sides.

The early 1980s saw increasing domestic difficulties, including the cost of war in Western Sahara, a sluggish economy, rising inflation, and a severe drought. A sharp rise in the price of necessities brought a general strike and then a bread riot on June 6, 1981, in the city of Casablanca that claimed as many as 1,000 lives. A $1.2 billion loan from the International Monetary Fund, changes in the tax structure, improvements in agriculture, and increased revenue from trade and tourism ameliorated many of these problems in the second half of the decade.

Hassan pursued a conciliatory foreign policy. In the 1980s he worked to secure Arab recognition of Israel and an end to the Arab-Israeli conflict. In July 1986 he held talks on Palestinian issues with Israeli prime minister Shimon Peres. Hassan also sought to improve relationships among other Arab states as a result of the Cold War. In 1984 he organized the Islamic Congress of Casablanca and created the Arabic-African Union with Libya. During the 1990–1991 crisis following Iraq's annexation of Kuwait that resulted in the Persian Gulf War, Morocco aligned itself squarely with the United States and sent troops to help defend Saudi Arabia.

During Hassan's reign, literacy, women's equality, and economic well-being all increased substantially. The social and economic disparity between urban and rural populations decreased through improved education, health care, and communications. But rising Islamic fundamentalism posed difficult challenges for Morocco in the late 1980s and early 1990s. These problems continue to the present under Hassan's son and successor Mohammed VI, who became king on July 23, 1999, on the death of his father. Challenges include the status of the Western Sahara, reducing constraints on private activity and foreign trade, and achieving sustainable economic growth.

Moroccan internal security is generally effective, and acts of political violence have been rare with the notable exception of the May 16, 2003, Casablanca bombings, when 14 young terrorists struck various locations. Forty-five people died, including 12 of the 14 bombers, and more than 100 people were wounded. Salafia Jihadia, an offshoot of the Moroccan Islamic Combatant Group and believed to have Al-Qaeda links, was blamed for the attack, which was probably ordered by Abu Musab al-Zarqawi.

In March 2015, Morocco joined other Arab states led by Saudi Arabia in sending aircraft to support a military effort in Yemen intended to counter Iran-allied Houthi rebel forces besieging the southern city of Aden.

Timeline

1549	Morocco is taken over by a succession of Arab dynasties.
1666	Morocco is reunited under the Alaouite dynasty, the ruling family of the country ever since.
1777	Morocco is the first country to recognize the United States as an independent nation.
1786	The Moroccan-American Treaty of Friendship remains the oldest U.S. nonbroken friendship treaty.
1859–1860	The Spanish-Moroccan War, caused by a dispute over Spain's small coastal enclave of Ceuta, results in a Spanish victory. Under the terms of the peace settlement, Ceuta is enlarged, and Spain secures Melilla, another enclave in Morocco (today both are autonomous Spanish cities), as well as an indemnity.

1884   Spain creates a protectorate in the coastal areas of Morocco.

Apr 1904   In one of a series of agreements between their two governments, the French recognize British interests in Egypt in return for British recognition of French paramount interest in Morocco. The agreements reached create what is known as the Entente Cordiale.

Oct 1904   France and Spain reach agreement on a power-sharing arrangement in Morocco.

1905–1906   The First Moroccan Crisis. In December 1904 the French government sends St. René Taillandier to Fez to demand of Moroccan sultan Abdelaziz (r. 1894–1906) a series of reforms in the police, the state bank, and communications. These will give France a virtual protectorate.

            German leaders decide, with no vital national interests at stake and virtually no investment in Morocco, to challenge the French move as part of Kaiser Wilhelm II's determination to assert German power on the world stage. In January 1905 Chancellor Bernard von Bülow informs Abdelaziz of his government's support in resisting French demands.

Mar 31, 1905   Wilhelm II makes a brief visit to Tangier, supposedly underscoring Germany's support for Morocco's continued independence. Germany puts heavy pressure on France, the government of which eschews war and holds out territorial compensation for Germany elsewhere in Africa, but Bülow insists on an international conference to resolve the matter, believing that Germany will secure support from a majority of the nations represented.

Jan 16–Apr 7, 1906   The international conference on Morocco ends in a French victory. France and Spain are to share police duties in Morocco's port cities. French banks control the Moroccan state bank. Moroccan frustration results in attacks on foreigners, as in Tangier, and the French government moves to secure order through full control of Morocco.

Spring 1911   French troops occupy Fez to protect Europeans there from anti-foreign agitation. Germany then demands compensation for what is a violation of the Algeciras Agreement and sends the German gunboat *Panther* to Agadir. In the ensuing Second Moroccan Crisis Britain formally supports France. Had Paris refused meaningful concessions there might have been war, but neither government wants this in 1911, and a settlement is reached whereby France secures German agreement for a French protectorate over Morocco in return for two strips of the French Congo connecting German Cameroon with the Congo and Ubangi Rivers.

Mar 30, 1912   In the Treaty of Fez, Moroccan sultan Mulay Hafid is forced to accept the French protectorate over his country. France secures control of most of Morocco, while Spain continues its coastal protectorate and now receives control of the northern and southern Saharan zones of Morocco. The sultan still reigns but no longer rules. Real power is vested in French resident general Louis Hubert Lyautey, who holds the post until 1925.

Lyautey presses French pacification of the Moroccan interior, extending French control into the Atlas Mountains. Concurrent with military operations, he also pushes the construction of roads, railroads, and bridges and is instrumental in the creation of a modern educational system.

1914–1918   Moroccan soldiers known as Goumiers, who serve in auxiliary units attached to the French Army of Africa, while not seeing service outside Morocco during World War I, do enable Lyautey to withdraw a substantial portion of the regular French military forces in Morocco for service on the Western Front.

1921–1926   Muhammad ibn Abd el-Krim al-Khattabi begins a revolt against foreign control of Morocco. This becomes known as the Rif War.

Jul 21, 1921   Spanish general Fernandes Silvestre moves into the Rif Mountain region with some 20,000 men but fails to take sufficient security precautions, and at Annual (Anual) on this date, Rif forces defeat the Spaniards, killing as many as 12,000 and taking several thousand others prisoner. The rebels also secure important quantities of arms and equipment.

1923   Abd el-Krim proclaims the Republic of the Rif, with himself as president.

1924   By the end of this year Spanish authority is reduced to the coastal enclaves of Melilla and Tetuán. The Spaniards use aircraft to drop mustard gas on Rifian villages.

Apr 12, 1925   Abd el-Krim opens a major offensive against the French part of Morocco in what many consider to be his greatest mistake. He takes advantage of Lyautey's limited resources to overrun 45 of 66 French posts in the Ouergha River Valley. Lyautey employs French air assets to good effect, however, and in July is able to halt the Berber advance short of Fez. The Goumiers provide valuable service.

The Spanish and French governments also agree to cooperate and furnish additional military manpower. Rifian forces find themselves under attack by the French and Spanish from the north and south.

Sep 1925	Coalition forces carry out an amphibious landing at Alhucemas Bay near Abd el-Krim's headquarters. Involving some 90,000 French and Spanish troops, it is the most significant operation of its kind in any irregular war during the interwar period.
May 26, 1926	Abd el-Krim, facing overwhelming force and modern aircraft and artillery and with his own weapons stocks dwindling and his forces melting away, surrenders to the French, bringing the Rif War to a close.
1936–1939	During the Spanish Civil War, indigenous Moroccan forces play an important role fighting on the Nationalist (fascist) side. These Fuerzas Regulares Indígenas (Indigenous Regular Forces), known simply as the Regulares (Regulars) of the Spanish Army of Africa, are led by Spanish officers and are the most decorated units of the Nationalist forces.
Nov 8–10, 1942	In Operation TORCH, U.S. and British forces invade French North Africa and occupy Morocco. Morocco then contributes substantial forces to fight in the defeat of Axis forces in North Africa and Europe.
Jan 14–24, 1943	U.S. president Franklin D. Roosevelt travels to Casablanca to meet with British prime minister Winston Churchill and plan military strategy. Roosevelt also meets with Moroccan sultan Mohammed V and proclaims American support for Morocco's eventual independence.
1953	With growing nationalist sentiment in Morocco, the French government exiles Mohammed V and his family, first to Corsica and then to Madagascar.
Nov 1955	Mohammed V returns from exile.
Mar 2, 1956	France grants independence to both Morocco and Tunisia. Spain continues to control the Western Sahara region until the mid-1970s and still retains the small Mediterranean coastal enclaves of Ceuta and Melilla.
Feb 26, 1961	Mohammed V dies unexpectedly and is succeeded by his son, Crown Prince Moulay Hassan, as King Hassan II.
Jul 24, 1970	A referendum results in overwhelming approval of a new constitution that establishes a unicameral legislature.
Jul 10, 1971	Dissident army elements led by General Muhammad Oufkir attempt to assassinate Hassan II and seize power.
Aug 16, 1972	A second attempt by dissident army officers to assassinate the king and seize power also fails.

1975–1991	The Western Sahara War. In an effort to enhance his position in Morocco, King Hassan II endeavors to secure the Western Sahara. The conflict pits the Sahrawi Frente Popular de Liberación de Saguía el Hamra y Río de Oro (Popular Front for the Liberation of Saguia el-Hamra and Río de Oro, better known as Polisario) against first Spain and then Morocco and Mauritania for control of the Spanish colony of Western Sahara (Río de Oro). Spain had acquired the Western Sahara in the 1880s and then in 1958 had joined the district of Saguia el-Hamra (in the north) with Río de Oro (in the south) to form the province of Spanish Sahara.
	Sahrawi students in Moroccan universities had formed Polisario in 1971 and commenced warfare against Spanish forces in the Western Sahara in May 1973. Polisario soon gained the support of the vast majority of the indigenous population. With the end of the Francisco Franco regime in Spain in 1975, the new Spanish government commences negotiations for a transfer of power in the Western Sahara.
Nov 6, 1975	The Green March. Acting on the behest of King Hassan II, some 350,000 unarmed Moroccans in the so-called Green March, as a symbol of Islam, advance several miles into Western Sahara territory, escorted by nearly 20,000 Moroccan troops, and meet very little response from Polisario.
Nov 14, 1975	In the Madrid Accords, the Spanish government reaches agreement with Morocco and Mauritania rather than Polisario, dividing the Spanish Sahara between them. Morocco receives the northern part of the Spanish Sahara (Saguia el-Hamra), while Mauritania obtains the south (Río de Oro).
Feb 27, 1976	Polisario proclaims establishment of the Sahrawi Arab Democratic Republic and then commences guerrilla warfare against both Morocco and Mauritania. Algeria provides weapons and other military assistance to Polisario and establishes refugee camps on its territory.
Oct 1978	The United States quits its last military base in Morocco, at Kenitra.
Aug 5, 1979	Polisario's attacks on Mauritania's iron mines cause the weak Mauritanian government to quit the southern Sahara altogether and recognize the Sahrawi Arab Democratic Republic. Morocco, however, immediately claims for itself the area evacuated by the Mauritanians.
Mid-1980s	Morocco builds a large sand berm (the Morocco Wall) to surround the most economically important areas of the Western

Sahara. At the same time, Algerian support for the rebels is largely withdrawn on the formation in February 1989 of the Arab Maghreb Union, which includes both Morocco and Algeria. The result is a stalemate, although Morocco controls more than two-thirds of the Western Sahara, including virtually the entire Atlantic coastline.

Jun 6, 1981   A hike in the price of necessities lead to a strike and then a bread riot in the city of Casablanca, in which as many as 1,000 people are killed.

Jul 1986   Seeking to secure Arab recognition of Israel and an end to the Arab-Israeli conflict, King Hassan II holds talks with Israeli prime minister Shimon Peres.

1990–1991   Hassan II aligns Morocco firmly on the side of the U.S.-led coalition against Iraq, following the latter's annexation of Kuwait in August 1990. Morocco sends troops to help defend Saudi Arabia.

Sep 6, 1991   Both sides agree to a cease-fire, with a referendum to be held in 1992. The cease-fire is monitored by the United Nations Mission for the Referendum in Western Sahara (MINURSO). The referendum does not occur, stalled largely over the issue of who is eligible to vote. An uneasy peace continues, with Polisario threatening on numerous occasions to resume the war.

Jul 23, 1999   Mohammed VI becomes king of Morocco on the death of his father, Hassan II.

May 16, 2003   On this night fourteen suicide bombers of Salafia Jihadia, an offshoot of the Moroccan Islamic Combatant Group believed to be linked to Al-Qaeda, attack a number of targets in Casablanca. Forty-five people die, including 12 of the bombers. More than 100 people are wounded.

Mar 2015   Morocco joins the Arab coalition led by Saudi Arabia in sending aircraft to support a military effort in Yemen intended to counter Iran-allied Houthi rebel forces besieging the southern city of Aden.

Mar 18, 2016   Morocco orders the United Nations (UN) to pull 84 members from the MINURSO staff of 496 after accusing UN secretary-general Ban Ki-moon of no longer being neutral. Ban had used the word "occupation" to describe Morocco's annexation of the region when he visiting Sahrawi refugee camps in southern Algeria and has been attempting without success to restart stalled negotiations between the two sides.

Further Reading

Alvarez, Jose E. *The Betrothed of Death: The Spanish Foreign Legion during the Rif Rebellion, 1920–1927*. Westport, CT: Greenwood, 2001.

Balfour, Sebastian. *Deadly Embrace: Morocco and the Road to the Spanish Civil War*. Oxford: Oxford University Press, 2002.

Barbour, Nevill. *Morocco*. New York: Walker, 1965.

Entelis, John P. *Culture and Counterculture in Moroccan Politics*. Boulder, CO: Westview, 1989.

Findlay, Anne Margaret, and Allan M Findlay. *Morocco*. Santa Barbara, CA: ABC-CLIO, 1995.

Nelson, Harold D., ed. *Morocco: A Country Study*. Washington, DC: American University, 1985.

Pennell, C. R. *Morocco since 1830: A History*. New York: New York University Press, 2000.

Woolman, David S. *Rebels in the Rif: Abdel Krim and the Rif Rebellion*. Stanford, CA: Stanford University Press, 1968.

OMAN

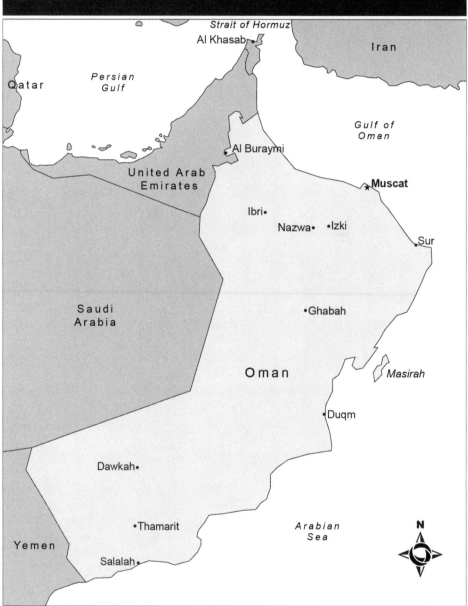

Strait of Hormuz

Al Khasab

Iran

Qatar

Persian
Gulf

Gulf of
Oman

Al Buraymi

United Arab
Emirates

Muscat

Ibri

Nazwa   Izki

Sur

Saudi
Arabia

Ghabah

Oman

Masirah

Duqm

Dawkah

Thamarit

Arabian
Sea

N

Yemen

Salalah

Oman

Paul G. Pierpaoli Jr. and Spencer C. Tucker

The Sultanate of Oman is an Arab nation located along the southeastern coast of the Arabian Peninsula and strategically situated at the mouth of the Persian Gulf.

Oman is 119,498 square miles in area and is bordered by Yemen to the southwest, Saudi Arabia to the west, the United Arab Emirates (UAE) to the northwest, the Arabian Sea to the southeast, and the Gulf of Oman to the northeast. Oman also shares marine borders with Iran and Pakistan. The two Omani territorial exclaves of Madha and Musandam are surrounded by the UAE on their land sides, with the Strait of Hormuz and the Gulf of Oman forming Musandam's coastal boundaries.

Oman had a 2016 population of some 4.654 million. Its capital and largest city is Muscat. Islam is practiced by some 95 percent of the population and is the state religion. There are no governmental statistics on religious affiliation, but nearly half the Muslims, including the sultan, are of the Ibadi School of Islam, which resulted from one of the first schisms in Islam and is close to mainstream Islam. Another 20 percent are Sunni Muslims. The remainder are Shias, who generally live in coastal communities. Virtually all the non-Muslims in Oman are foreign workers. In religion they include Jains, Buddhists, Zoroastrians, Sikhs, Baha'is, Hindus, and Christians.

Oman enjoys a relatively high standard of living primarily as a consequence of its petroleum revenues, ranking 25th globally. Oil was discovered in 1964, and production began in 1967. In sharp contrast to most of its neighboring states, which rely heavily on oil exports, much of Oman's economy is based on trade and tourism.

Oman is an absolute hereditary monarchy based on male primogeniture. Sultan Qaboos bin Said al-Said is the longest-serving ruler of any country in the Middle East, having ascended the Omni throne in 1970. Although the sultan has enacted some political reforms, he retains much control over the government and has sole control over the armed forces. There are no political parties, and there is no official opposition to the sitting government. Sharia law is the source of all legislation.

Arabs came to dominate Oman and introduced Islam in the late 600s. In 1507 the Portuguese attacked and sacked the port of Muscat and captured much of the Omani coast. They were not driven out until 1650. From the late 17th century, however, the Omani Sultanate was a powerful empire with considerable influence in the Persian Gulf and Indian Ocean regions. Indeed, Muscat was the principal trading port of the Persian Gulf region. The height of Omani influence came in the 19th century, when it included parts of the Indian subcontinent and reached as far south as Zanzibar (now part of Tanzania) and Mombasa. The Persians invaded Oman in 1737 but were driven out in 1749. Ahmad bin Said al-Busaidi became sultan on June 10, 1749, beginning the Al Said dynasty that continues to rule Oman to the present.

In 1913 the interior of Oman came under the control of Ibadite imams, restricting the power of the sultan to the coastal areas. Under a British-brokered agreement in 1920, the sultan recognized the autonomy of the interior. On February 10, 1932, Said bin Taimur became sultan. He took a feudal and isolationist approach. In 1954, however, fighting resumed between the imamate forces who sought an independent state and those of the sultan.

In July 1957 Imam Ghalib bin Ali, who had conspired against the sultan in 1955 and been exiled, received the support of Egypt and Saudi Arabia and led a new revolt. After major fighting near Nizwa on July 15, 1957, the sultan requested British military assistance. This aid, consisting mostly of air support, enabled the sultan's forces to crush the revolt in mid-August. An effort by Arab states in the United Nations to censure the British for their intervention failed to win approval, and by 1959 the sultan's forces had regained control of the interior.

During 1962–1976 the government had to contend with a rebellion in the southern dependency of Dhofar in which leftist forces were pitted against government troops. Said bin Taimur had attempted to outlaw most aspects of 20th-century life

Jebeli tribesmen, known as Firqa, patrol Dhofar province in Oman on behalf of the government on February 2, 1975. Most of them were rebels themselves before they defected from the Popular Front for the Liberation of Oman. (AP Photo/Holger Jensen)

and had subjected Dhofar to greater restrictions and economic exploitation than in the rest of Oman. The rebellion was led by tribal leader Mussalim bin Nafl, who formed the Dhofar Liberation Front (DLF). Saudi Arabia, which had already attempted to gain control of the Buraimi Oasis, provided arms and equipment to the insurgents. Ghalib bin Ali, the exiled imam of Oman, also supported the revolt.

Fighting commenced in December 1962, with hit-and-run raids against the British air base at Salalah. This intensified in 1964 with hit-and-run attacks against government installations and oil industry facilities. Following a failed assassination attempt in April 1966, Sultan Said bin Taimur retired to his palace and was never again seen in public. His forces, however, launched major search-and-destroy missions in Dhofar, in which villages were attacked and laid waste and wells were destroyed.

Egypt and leftist movements in Yemen and Aden furnished aid to the rebels. With the establishment of the People's Democratic Republic of Yemen in 1967, the rebels secured a steady stream of arms, but this also led to a split, with some of the rebels breaking off to form the Popular Front for the Liberation of the Occupied Arabian Gulf (PFLOAG) with the aim of establishing a Marxist-Leninist state. The PFLOAG received the support of South Yemen and the People's Republic of China.

By 1969, the DLF and the PFLOAG controlled large stretches of Dhofar. The sultan's forces were outnumbered, with only some 1,000 men in the rebel province. The British were then forced to deploy small military detachments to protect the airfield at Salalah. Meanwhile, another guerrilla organization appeared in northern Oman in the National Democratic Front for the Liberation of Oman and the Arabian Gulf (NDFLOAG).

With it now clear that the insurgency could not be ended without new leadership, on July 23, 1970, Said bin Taimur was deposed in a coup led by his son, Qaboos bin Said, who then commenced a liberalization and modernization program, pledging to use Oman's wealth to benefit its people. Assisted by the British Special Air Service, he launched a comprehensive counterinsurgency program that included a hearts-and-minds component and amnesty for the rebels. At the same time, government forces assisted by the British endeavored to cut off rebel resupply. Aircraft proved to be a major assist, as did training personnel and military assistance provided by the shah of Iran. Indeed, on February 2, 1975, Oman signed a defense pact with Iran whereby that country pledged to support Oman in the event of an attack. The Kingdom of Jordan also sent aid. Government forces now made steady gains, and the rebellion was declared at an end in January 1976, although isolated incidents continued into 1983.

Under Sultan Qaboos, Oman's foreign and economic policies have generally favored the West. On June 4, 1980, the United States concluded an agreement with Oman whereby it secured rights to certain air and naval bases in return for military and economic assistance. Oman also regularly participated in regional multinational military exercises involving the United States, Egypt, and other nations.

On June 6, 1982, Oman joined Saudi Arabia, Bahrain, Kuwait, Qatar, and the United Arab Emirates (UAE) in establishing a joint military command structure and integrated air defense system. This was prompted by the perceived threats of the Islamic Republic of Iran, the ongoing Iran-Iraq War (1980–1988), and the Soviet-Afghan War (1979–1989).

In the years leading up to the Persian Gulf War of 1991, Sultan Qaboos steadily increased the size and effectiveness of Oman's armed forces especially in the Iran-Iraq War, during which al-Said deployed an infantry battalion to serve in the Peninsula Shield force, a military arm of the Gulf Cooperation Council meant to deter aggression from either Iraq or Iran. Meanwhile, Britain's Royal Air Force continued to use an air base on Masirah Island off Oman's southern coast.

After Iraq invaded and occupied Kuwait in August 1990, Oman became a strong supporter of the international military coalition that drove Iraqi forces from Kuwait. Coalition forces used several of Oman's air bases as key staging areas for the conflict. The country also contributed 6,300 ground troops, who were deployed to Saudi Arabia. On the second day of the ground war in February 1991, Omani troops, along with the Saudi 10th Mechanized Brigade, entered Kuwait, helping to effect its liberation by February 28.

In 1999 Oman and the UAE signed a border agreement delineating most of their disputed common frontier. In October 2001, large-scale British-Omani military exercises in the Omani desert coincided with the launch of strikes against the Taliban in Afghanistan prompted by the terror attacks on the United States on September 11.

Suntan Qaboos meanwhile continued his liberalization program. In 1997 he decreed that women could vote and stand for election to the Majlis al-Shura (Consultative Council). Two women were duly elected. In November 2002 he extended voting rights to all citizens over the age of 21, the voters having previously been chosen from among tribal leaders, intellectuals, and businessmen. The first elections under universal suffrage occurred in October 2003.

In January 2005, nearly 100 suspected Islamists were arrested in Oman. Thirty-one were subsequently convicted of trying to overthrow the government, but they were pardoned in June. In late February 2011 as part of the so-called Arab Spring, protests erupted, with demonstrators demanding jobs and political reform. One demonstrator was shot dead by the police. Sultan Qaboos sought to tamp down the protests with a pledge of more jobs and improved benefits. On March 5 he also replaced three of his top government officials, and late that year he granted the newly elected Majlis al-Shura greater powers. There was a limit to criticism allowed, however, for in September 2012 trials occurred of activists who had criticized the government online. Six were given jail terms of 12–18 months, but the next March Qaboos pardoned a number of those convicted.

Oman's military consists of an army, a navy, and an air force. Its military establishment is well equipped with modern hardware and weapons systems purchased chiefly from Great Britain, the United States, and France. Sultan Qaboos has long worried about potential incursions from rival Arab nations and remains particularly concerned about Iran's foreign and military policies. As such, the nation spends a huge portion of its gross domestic product (GDP) on defense expenditures, which are currently estimated at about $2.1 billion a year, or 11.5 percent of

GDP. Active military personnel number some 44,000. The ground forces are equipped with some 117 main battle tanks and 37 light tanks. The air force has approximately three dozen combat aircraft.

Although Oman's armed forces did not actively participate in the subsequent Afghan War and Iraq War, Oman cooperated with coalition forces by permitting overflights of its airspace and allowing coalition forces to utilize some of its bases as staging areas.

Timeline

Late 600s	Arabs come to dominate Oman and introduce Islam.
1507	The Portuguese sack the port of Muscat and secure much of the Omani coast.
1650	The Portuguese are driven out.
1737	The Persians invade Oman in 1737 but are driven out in 1749.
Jun 10, 1749	Ahmad bin Said al-Busaidi becomes sultan, beginning the Al Said dynasty that rules Oman to the present.
1800s	The Omani Sultanate is a powerful empire with considerable influence in the Persian Gulf region and Indian Ocean area.
1913	Ibadite imams secure control of the Oman interior, restricting the power of the sultan to the coastal areas.
1920	The British broker an agreement whereby the sultan recognizes the interior as autonomous.
Feb 10, 1932	Said bin Taimur becomes sultan. He takes an archaic, feudalistic approach, eschewing the 20th century.
1954	Fighting resumes between the imamate forces seeking an independent state and those of the sultan.
Jul 1957	Imam Ghalib bin Ali, who had conspired against the sultan in 1955 and been exiled, receives the support of Egypt and Saudi Arabia and leads a new revolt.
Jul 15, 1957	Major fighting occurs near Nizwa, whereupon the sultan asks for British military assistance.
Mid-Aug 1857	British aid, mainly air support, enables the sultan's forces to crush the revolt. By 1959 the sultan's forces have regained control of the interior.
Dec 1962–Jan 1976	The Dhofar Rebellion sees leftist forces pitted against the government. Mussalim bin Nafl leads the rebellion, forming the Dhofar Liberation Front (DLF). Saudi Arabia, which had already

	attempted to gain control of the Buraimi Oasis, provides arms and equipment. Ghalib bin Ali, the exiled imam of Oman, also supports the revolt.
1964	Oil is discovered, although production does not commence until 1967.
1967	Egypt, Aden, and Yemen all now furnishing aid to the rebels. However, a split develops in the rebel ranks when some of them form the Popular Front for the Liberation of the Occupied Arabian Gulf (PFLOAG) with the aim of establishing a Marxist-Leninist state. It receives the support of South Yemen and the People's Republic of China.
Apr 1967	An attempt to assassinate Sultan Said bin Taimur fails, but he goes into seclusion.
1969	The DLF and the PFLOAG now control large swaths of Dhofar, and another threat appears in the creation in northern Oman in the National Democratic Front for the Liberation of Oman and the Arabian Gulf.
Jul 23, 1970	With it clear that only new leadership can save the situation, Qaboos bin Said deposes his father, Said bin Taimur, and announces a liberalization and modernization program for Oman. Assisted by the British Special Air Service, he launches a comprehensive counterinsurgency program that includes a hearts-and-minds component and amnesty for the rebels. Britain, Iran, and Jordan all provide assistance.
Feb 2, 1975	Oman signs a defense pact with Iran whereby that country pledges to support Oman in the event of an attack.
Jan 1976	The Dhofar Rebellion is declared at an end, although isolated incidents continue into 1983.
Jun 4, 1980	The United States concludes an agreement with Oman, securing air and naval bases in return for military and economic assistance.
Jun 6, 1982	Oman joins Saudi Arabia, Bahrain, Kuwait, Qatar, and the United Arab Emirates in establishing a joint military command structure and integrated air defense system.
Jan–Feb 1991	Oman is a strong supporter of the international military coalition driving Iraqi forces from Kuwait. Coalition forces use several of Oman's air bases as key staging areas for the conflict, and Oman contributes 6,300 ground troops who participate in the liberation of Kuwait City.

| 1997 | Sultan Qaboos decrees that women may vote and stand for election to the Majlis al-Shura (Consultative Council). Two women are duly elected. |

Oct 2001   Military strikes are launched from Oman following the September 11, 2001, terror attacks on the United States.

Nov 2002   Sultan Qaboos extends voting rights to all citizens over the age of 21.

Mar 2003   Although Oman does not take part in the U.S.-led invasion of Iraq, it does permit overflights of its airspace and allows coalition forces to utilize some of its bases as staging areas.

Jan 2005   Nearly 100 suspected Islamists are arrested and 31 are subsequently convicted of trying to overthrow the government but are pardoned in June.

Late Feb 2011   As part of the so-called Arab Spring, several weeks of protests erupt in Oman, with the demonstrators demanding jobs and political reform. One demonstrator was shot dead by the police. Sultan Qaboos pledges changes, replaces several of his top officials, and grants the newly elected Majlis al-Shura greater powers.

Further Reading

Jones, Jeremy, and Nicholas Ridout. *A History of Modern Oman.* Cambridge: Cambridge University Press, 2015.

Kechichian, Joseph A. *Oman and the World: The Emergence of an Independent Foreign Policy.* Santa Monica, CA: RAND, 1995.

Owtram, Francis. *A Modern History of Oman: Formation of the State since 1920.* London: I. B. Tauris, 2004.

Valeri, Marc. *Oman: Politics and Society in the Qaboos State.* Oxford: Oxford University Press, 2015.

PAKISTAN

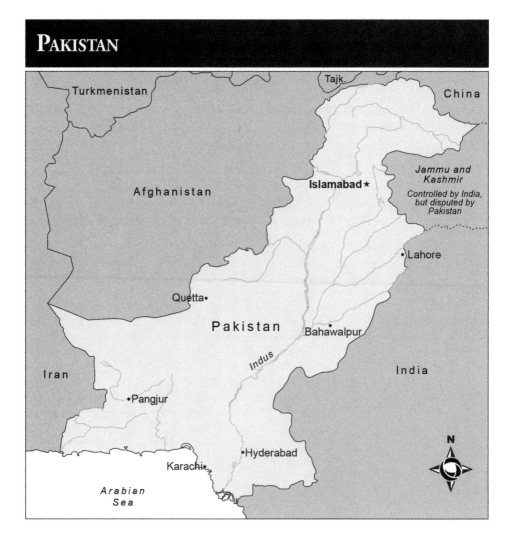

Pakistan

Arne Kislenko and Spencer C. Tucker

The Islamic Republic of Pakistan occupies a strategic position in South Asia. Pakistan is bordered by Afghanistan to the west and Iran to the southwest, the People's Republic of China and India to the east, and the Arabian Sea and Gulf of Oman (on which it has a 650-mile coastline) to the south. It is separated from Tajikistan only by Afghanistan's narrow Wakhan Corridor in the north. Pakistan also shares a maritime border with Oman.

With a 2016 population of some 192.827 million people, Pakistan is the world's sixth most populous nation and is second only to Indonesia as the nation with a Muslim majority. Pakistan also has a large diaspora, including Great Britain and the United States. The city of Islamabad, built in the 1960s, is the Pakistani capital. A major regional power, Pakistan has the world's 41st ranked economy in terms of gross domestic product and, with half a million men, the world's seventh-largest standing armed forces. It is also one of only nine nations and the only Muslim state possessing nuclear weapons.

Pakistani history since its independence in 1947 has been marked by political instability accompanied by periods of military rule. There have also been major wars with India in 1947, 1965, and 1971 as well as an undeclared war in 1999 and a series of smaller border clashes. Pakistan is a member of the United Nations (UN), the Commonwealth of Nations, and the Organization of Islamic Cooperation.

Some 97 percent of Pakistan's population is Muslim. The majority are Sunnis, but the 5–20 percent of the population who adhere to Shia Islam are second in number only to those of Iran. The Ahmadis are a much smaller minority sect but are officially classified by Pakistan as non-Muslim. During the past two decades sectarian violence between Sunni and Shia Muslims has sharply increased, with targeted killings not an uncommon occurrence.

The territory of present-day Pakistan formed part of a number of ancient empires. Situated along the famous Silk Road linking China and the West, Pakistan was a strategic crossroads. Aryans, Persians, Macedonians, Greeks, Afghans, Arabs, Mongols, and Turkic groups all fought over its territory. Empires and dynasties included the Indian Mauryan and Persian Achaemenid Empires, the empire created by King of Macedon Alexander III (Alexander the Great), the Arab Umayyad Caliphate, the Delhi Sultanate, the Mongol Empire, the Mogul Empire, the Durrani

Empire, and the Sikh Empire. During 1526–1857 most of the subcontinent was under the sway of the Mogul Empire, the rulers of which were Muslim.

In the late 15th century the Portuguese established coastal trading posts, but it was the British who came to exercise control over the subcontinent. Adroit leadership and enterprise coupled with superior weaponry enabled the British East India Company, a private corporation, to defeat the rival Portugese, French, and native princely rulers and establish control over the entire subcontinent. The 1857 Sepoy Revolt (known in India as the First Indian War of Independence), however, prompted the British Crown to assume responsibility for the administration of the subcontinent. In 1858 it established the British Raj (Hindi for "rule" or "reign"). Trade with India was immensely important to Britain, with India often referred to as the "jewel in the British Crown." On May 1, 1876, at the height of British rule, Queen Victoria took the title "Empress of India." The British governed India through a mixed system of direct control and indirect rule, with a small but talented pool of British administrators, working largely through the native princely rulers, playing one against the other and dominating the affairs of the entire subcontinent.

The days of British rule were numbered, however. Western education, increased contact between Indians and the rest of the world through trade and war, and modern nationalism all worked to undermine the British position. Resistance to British rule gradually took root in the 1870s among the Western-educated Indian elite. The Indian National Congress (INC), Britain's principal vehicle, was established on December 28, 1885, by British civil servants to enable the Westernized Indian elite to engage in gentlemanly discourse with their British rulers.

As with other colonial areas of the world, India experienced a wave of nationalism as a result of World War I. This was in part based on the sizable Indian contribution to the Allied victory. In addition to manufactured goods, India provided some 1.4 million men to the war effort, rendering excellent service principally against Ottoman Empire forces in the Middle East but also in Africa. At the same time the concept of self-rule was gaining wide currency in the developing world, thanks to such declarations as the call for the "self-determination of peoples" by U.S. president Woodrow Wilson in his Fourteen Points of 1918. As with the Chinese, however, Indians were to be disappointed to learn at the Paris Peace Conference of 1919 that "self-determination" applied only to Europe.

In India Mohandas Karamchand Gandhi led an increasing successful campaign of noncooperation based on civil disobedience and passive resistance to British rule. Following a series of meetings, especially the Round Table Conferences of 1930–1932, to discuss constitutional changes for India, the British Parliament passed the lengthy Government of India Act in August 1935. The act authorized the creation of a central government for India that would incorporate both the British provinces and the princely states, independent legislative assemblies in all the provinces of British India, and mechanisms to protect the Muslims and other minorities. The future constitution of independent India would be based on this act and would not be repealed until 1998.

The population of the subcontinent was not only enormous but was also exceptionally diverse and sharply divided by religion, ethnicity, and social caste. The independence movement spearheaded by the INC, and unofficially led by Gandhi, was a multifaith, multiethnic front. Gandhi, a Hindu, espoused nonviolence and also insisted on India's territorial integrity but could not entirely bridge the gaps between the different groups. Founded on December 30, 1906, the All-India Muslim League (AIML) advocated the separation of British India into Muslim and Hindu states, and support for the creation of an Islamic state grew during the 1930s. On March 24, 1940, AIML leaders approved the Lahore Declaration that called for the division of British India, with the majority Muslim areas of the northwest and northeast becoming independent states. Thereafter AIML's adroit and forceful leader, Muhammad Ali Jinnah, pushed the British for separate recognition.

During World War II, with Great Britain stretched to the limit and in desperate need of Indian support as the Japanese threatened to invade India, in March 1942 British prime minister Winston Churchill dispatched to India Sir Stafford Cripps, leader of the House of Commons. Cripps brought a pledge of what amounted to Indian independence through dominion status following the defeat of Japan. But the plan also contained a clause to the effect that no part of the Indian Empire would be forced to join the postwar dominion, and this could clearly be interpreted as supporting the creation of an independent Muslim state.

Gandhi strongly opposed the British proposal owing to the possibility of separate Hindu and Muslim states. Indeed, in August 1942, despite the war and the Japanese threat, he called on the British to simply quit India immediately. This brought his arrest, along with that of most of the INC leadership. Gandhi's decision played directly into the hands of Jinnah, whose Muslim League strongly supported the Allied war effort and thereby greatly advanced the possibility of the creation of a separate Muslim state after the war.

Indian Army forces played an important role in World War II. When the Japanese captured Singapore in February 1942, however, 60,000 Indian troops became prisoners of war. Radical Indian nationalist politician Subhas Chandra Bose and the Japanese convinced some 25,000 of them to join the Azad Hind Fanj (Indian National Army, INA) and fight to end British rule in India. The Japanese viewed this force as an effective tool against British power, whereas its members saw themselves as an army of national liberation. Ultimately some 7,000 INA troops were attached to Japanese units and fought in the Imphal Offensive into India. The remainder were employed as auxiliaries. Most of the poorly trained and inadequately equipped INA forces were taken prisoner or deserted. In all 2,644,323 men served in the Indian Army during the war, of whom approximately 2 million were combatants. Indian forces fought in Syria, North Africa, East Africa, the Middle East, Malaya, Greece, Sicily, and Italy.

The Labour Party won the July 1945 British elections and, much to the chagrin of Churchill, pledged the creation of a single independent Indian state by June 1948. To placate Muslim concerns, the new independent India was to be a federated state with a weak central government. In February 1947 Admiral of the Fleet Louis Francis Albert Victor Nicholas Mountbatten, 1st Earl Mountbatten of Burma, was appointed the last British viceroy to carry out the transition.

Unfortunately for the British plan, Mountbatten could not get the Indian politicians to agree on a constitutional framework. Failing this and despite the strong opposition of Gandhi and other Hindu leaders, Mountbatten concluded that partition was the only viable option, with both states to remain members of the British Commonwealth of Nations. The British government passed the Indian Independence Act on July 18, 1947.

Independence officially came for both states on August 15, 1947. Three former Indian provinces (the North-West Frontier Province, West Punjab, and Sind) joined with the Baluchistan States Union, an array of princely states, tribal areas, and the Federal Capital Territory around the city of Karachi to form chiefly Urdu-speaking West Pakistan. Pakistan also included the province of East Bengal, now known as East Pakistan, but it was separated from West Pakistan by nearly 1,000 miles of India and had a predominantly Bengali-speaking Muslim population.

The first capital of Pakistan was the port city of Karachi, which remains its largest urban center. Liaquat Ali Khan became the first prime minister, while Jinnah was both governor-general and president-speaker of the state parliament. Jinnah died on September 11, 1948. Bengali leader Sir Khawaja Nazimuddin succeeded him as the governor-general of Pakistan.

Mountbatten would be much criticized for the haste of the British departure, for the partition of India ignited massive riots, rampant violence, and the migration of some 15 million people in what was probably the largest single movement of people in history. The population of 1947 prepartition India was some 390 million people. After partition, there were perhaps 330 million people in India and

Muhammad Ali Jinnah

Muhammad Ali Jinnah was the most influential figure in the creation of Pakistan. Born in Karachi in 1876, he was educated in India before training as a lawyer in England. In 1909, Jinnah was elected to represent Muslims of Bombay in India's Supreme Legislative Council. Unlike Mohandas Gandhi's approach of boycott and passive resistance to bring an end to British rule in India, Jinnah advocated cooperation and a gradual transfer of power.

In December 1920, Jinnah resigned from the Indian National Congress in protest of Gandhi's call for noncooperation. For several decades Jinnah labored to unite colonial India's Hindu and Muslim populations in a working democratic union, but he finally became convinced that there was no alternative to the creation of a separate Muslim political entity. While Gandhi opposed this, Jinnah's strong support of the British in World War II was certainly key in winning British support for partition.

After Pakistani independence in 1947 Jinnah served as the nation's first governor-general, setting the course for the future of his country. Unfortunately, he died of tuberculosis in September 1948 after less than a year in office. Most scholars consider Jinnah to have been Pakistan's greatest leader.

60 million in Pakistan (30 million in West Pakistan, now Pakistan, and 30 million in East Pakistan, now Bangladesh). Pakistan was also at considerable disadvantage geographically, for its two halves were separated by India.

Violence was particularly pronounced in the Punjab region, where arbitrary boundary lines caused chaos, separating farms from markets and factories from the raw materials they needed in order to operate. Estimates put the total death toll from the violence accompanying partition at between a quarter million and 1 million people.

The planned allocation of assets (to be at a ratio of four to one in favor of India) also created major problems, with Pakistan accusing India of blocking the transfer of resources to which Pakistan was due. The partition agreement also called for India to receive two-thirds and Pakistan one-third of the military assets, but India received the vast bulk of the armor and aircraft assets, while Pakistan secured most of the larger naval vessels. The military officers of both states were all British trained, although few had experience at higher command. Technically, British field marshal Sir Claude Auchinleck commanded both armies.

A pressing issue was the future disposition of several disputed territories. The latter included Junagadh, Hyderabad, and Jammu and Kashmir. Junagagh and Hyderabad were predominantly Hindu states with Muslim leaders. They were quickly absorbed by India. The dispute over Jammu and Kashmir was not so easily resolved, however. There a Sikh, Maharajah Hari Singh, had ruled since 1925. As Kashmir was 77 percent Muslim, it was assumed that he would join the kingdom to Pakistan. However, he wanted Kashmir to remain independent and neutral, and while he was hesitating joining Pakistan, Pathan Muslims of Poonch in southeastern Kashmir rebelled against their Hindu landowners.

On October 22, 1947, Pakistan sent Muslim tribal militias into Kashmir claiming that they were needed to suppress the rebellion. These tribal militias and irregular Pakistani forces moved against the Kashmiri capital of Srinagar. They reached Uri, but Singh then appealed to India for assistance. Indian prime minister Jawaharlal Nehru made this contingent on Singh signing an instrument of accession to join India, which he did on October 26. India then quickly airlifted troops to Kashmir, marking the formal beginning of the India-Pakistan War of 1947.

At first the Indians were successful, securing the Kashmiri capital of Srinagar in the Battle of Shalateng on November 7, 1947, but with Indian forces overextended, the Pakistanis triumphed at Jhangar on December 24. By the beginning of 1948 and with the war stalemated, Nehru requested UN mediation.

As the UN-brokered talks slowly progressed, India made military progress against both the Pakistani irregulars and increasing numbers of Pakistani regular forces who crossed into Kashmir to take part in the fighting. In 1948 the Indian Army was victorious at Naoshera on February 6, Gurais on May 22–27, and Zojila on October 19. Following protracted negotiations, the fighting largely ended in December 1948, with the Line of Control dividing Kashmir into territories administered by Pakistan (northern and western Kashmir) and India (southern, central, and northeastern Kashmir). India retained the most fertile and populous regions of Kashmir, but about 30 percent of Kashmir—some 5,000 square miles—remained in Pakistani hands when the cease-fire took hold on January 1, 1949. Each side had sustained about 1,500 casualties.

The UN resolution of January 5, 1949, called for a plebiscite to determine the future status of Kashmir, but India refused to permit this vote, so tensions between India and Pakistan remained high. Indeed, Kashmir continues to be the principal cause of animosity between India and Pakistan to the present.

Since the partition of India, the United States had cultivated Pakistan as an ally, drawing it into multilateral pacts such as the Southeast Asian Treaty Organization in September 1954 and the Central Treaty Organization, or Baghdad Pact, in February 1955. The United States also supplied substantial military aid to Pakistan. Washington, however, also sought better relations with nonaligned India, which courted both the United States and the Soviet Union for material assistance. The Indians attracted more Western support following the Sino-Indian War (1962), which saw the Chinese invade and occupy their disputed border region. With no resolution to the conflict over Jammu and Kashmir by 1965, the United States feared renewed hostilities between what were ostensibly its two allies. U.S.-Pakistani ties were undermined by what Pakistani leaders saw as American duplicity in providing aid to their enemy, India, especially given India's victory in the 1947 war. As a consequence, Pakistan pursued ties with China, America's major rival in the region.

Internal politics within Pakistan also significantly shaped its international relations. Between 1947 and 1958, the country had a succession of largely unstable civilian governments. On October 7, 1958, with the Muslim League, Pakistan's dominant political party, unable to establish a consensus and govern effectively, Pakistani president Iskander Mirza abrogated the constitution and declared martial law, only to be deposed himself on October 27 in a bloodless military coup d'état carried out by General Muhammad Ayub Khan, commander of the Pakistani Army, who took the presidency himself.

In April 1965 Pakistan and India again collided in the Second Kashmir War, when president Ayub Khan sought to test Indian resolve. Indian leader Jawaharlal Nehru had died, and his successor as prime minister of India, Lal Bahadur Shastri, appeared vulnerable. Ayub had also just signed a friendship pact with the People's Republic of China. Ayub commenced military operations in the Rann of Kutch, where the frontier was poorly defined. Within several weeks the fighting had escalated into full-scale hostilities in which the Pakistanis appeared to have had the upper hand until monsoon rains suspended the fighting. Shastri then agreed to a mediated settlement.

Emboldened by this and convinced that the Indian Army was weak, Pakistani foreign minister Zulfirkar Ali Bhutto urged renewal of the fighting. In August, border clashes occurred in both Kashmir and the Punjab as both sides violated the Kashmir cease-fire line. Then on August 24, Indian forces launched a major raid across it.

In retaliation for the Indian raid, on September 1, 1965, Ayub launched Operation GRAND SLAM, a major military offensive to cut the road linking India to Kashmir and isolate two Indian Army corps in the Ravi-Sutley corridor. Both sides

Three Pakistani soldiers stand next to an armed Willys jeep on September 7, 1965. The jeep was abandoned by Indian soldiers who had penetrated into the Lahore region during the Second Indo-Pakistani War, which was fought over Kashmir. (Keystone-France/Gamma-Keystone via Getty Images)

also carried out air attacks against the other not only in the Punjab but also in Indian raids on Karachi and Pakistani attacks on New Delhi. On September 6, however, India sent some 900,000 men across the border into Pakistan. Superior numbers soon told. In one of the largest tank battles in history, the Indians defeated the Pakistanis at Chawinda (September 14–19) during their Sialkot Campaign and reached Lahore, claiming to have destroyed 300 Pakistani tanks in the process. There was no fighting at sea during the war.

On September 20, the UN Security Council passed Resolution 211 calling for an end to the fighting and negotiations to settle the issue of Kashmir. Both the United States and the United Kingdom supported the UN decision by cutting off arms supplies to both belligerents. This affected both sides, but Pakistan, with a weaker military, felt the ban more than India. The UN resolution, the halting of arms sales, and China's threat to initiate military operations against India all had their effects. Both sides accepted a cease-fire on September 27.

India then occupied a good deal of Pakistani territory, but under terms of the cease-fire both sides agreed to withdraw to the prewar boundaries.

Finally on January 10, 1966, both sides agreed to a peace settlement at Tashkent in the Soviet Union that also included Britain and the United States. It formally reestablished the cease-fire line as it had been in 1949, restored diplomatic and economic relations between the two countries, and provided for an orderly transfer of prisoners of war. The two sides also agreed to work toward the establishment of good relations, and India again pledged to hold a plebiscite in Kashmir. Unfortunately, Indian prime minister Shastri died shortly thereafter, and his successor, Indira Gandhi, failed to implement the Kashmir plebiscite, with the result that tensions continued.

Along with Pakistan's defeat in the 1965 war, rampant corruption and heavy-handed rule undermined Ayub Khan's popularity. Increasing violence led Ayub Khan to resign in March 1969. He was replaced by another general, Aga Muhammad Yahya Khan, who served as Pakistani president from March 26, 1969, to December 20, 1971. When some questioned his ascension to power, Yahya Khan declared martial law and cracked down on all dissenters, including leaders in East Pakistan who pushed for separation.

Meanwhile, unrest was growing in East Pakistan. Although more populous than West Pakistan, East Pakistan received proportionally less of the national wealth, and Bengalis found themselves marginalized in the government and the military. Compounding matters, one of the worst cyclones in history hit East Pakistan on November 12, 1970, killing as many as 500,000 people. Ayub Khan was much criticized for his handling of the situation, for the government response to the disaster was both slow and insufficient, adding to Bengali alienation.

The Awami League political party, which sought autonomy for East Pakistan, triumphed in the December 1970 national elections. Led by Sheikh Mujibur Rahman (known simply as Mujib and regarded as the father of present-day Bangladesh), it won 167 of 169 East Pakistan seats in the National Assembly (along with 288 of the 300 seats in East Pakistan's provincial assembly). Although it won none of West Pakistan's 138 seats, the Awami League now held a majority in the 313-seat National Assembly and was thus in position to establish a government without having to form a coalition. West Pakistan's leaders found this unacceptable; they feared that such a step would lead to the breakup of Pakistan. Yahya Khan refused to ask Mujib to form a government. On March 7, 1971, Mujib announced a civil disobedience movement to press for convening the National Assembly.

The Pakistani government's response was a declaration of martial law and Operation SEARCHLIGHT on March 25, 1971. Mujib was arrested and flown to West Pakistan, where he was jailed on a charge of treason. Protests in East Pakistan were violently suppressed by the military, especially after Bengali officers within its ranks declared independence on behalf of Mujib on March 26, 1971. The number of dead is in dispute, with estimates ranging widely from 30,000 to 3 million. Perhaps 10 million refugees fled East Pakistan into India.

With Indians demanding that their armed forces intervene, Prime Minister Indira Gandhi appealed unsuccessfully to world leaders to end the repression in East Pakistan. During June–November 1971, India and Pakistan exchanged artillery fire and conducted small raids across the border against each other. Meanwhile, on August 9, 1971, India concluded a treaty of friendship with the Soviet Union.

Alarmed by West Pakistani actions in East Pakistan, the United States terminated arms shipments to Pakistan on November 8.

Meanwhile, East Pakistani refugees calling themselves the Mukti Bahini and supported by India engaged the West Pakistani forces. This goaded Pakistan into taking the first hostile action against India, a Pakistani Air Force strike into eastern India on November 22, followed by major air attacks from West Pakistan against the principal Indian air bases on December 3. The Pakistanis hoped to achieve the same surprise garnered by the Israeli Air Force against Egypt in the 1967 Six-Day War, but the Indians, well aware that they were goading the Pakistanis into armed conflict, were well prepared, and the Pakistani air strikes were largely unsuccessful.

The Pakistani air attacks on December 3 marked the official beginning of the 1971 war, which lasted until December 16. India was concerned that China, with which it had fought a border war in 1962, might seek to take advantage of the situation to invade northern India. Nonetheless, Indian forces were ready and had at least three times the strength of the 90,000 West Pakistani forces in East Pakistan. Moving swiftly and well supported by air force and naval units, the Indians launched an invasion from the north and west. During December 14–16 the Indian Army captured the East Pakistan capital of Dhaka (Dacca).

On the western front, on December 4 Pakistani forces invaded Jammu and Kashmir and registered gains of up to 10 miles into Indian territory until they were halted. During December 5–6 the Soviet Union supported its Indian ally by vetoing UN Security Council resolutions calling for a cease-fire and forcing Pakistani foreign minister Zulfikar Ali Bhutto to work through the dilatory UN General Assembly. On December 6, India officially recognized the independence of East Pakistan as Bangladesh. On December 15, with the fighting there all but over, the UN General Assembly demanded a cease-fire in East Pakistan. Indian troops also recaptured some of the territory in Kashmir and the Punjab lost to the Pakistanis earlier and invaded West Pakistan in both Hyderabad and the Punjab.

Meanwhile, the Indian Navy neutralized Pakistani naval units on the first day of the war. The Indian Eastern Fleet completely controlled the Bay of Bengal, blockading East Pakistan. Indian antisubmarine warfare units sank the Pakistani submarine *Ghazi*, which tried to ambush the Indian aircraft carrier *Vikrant*. In the largest surface action in the Indian Ocean since 1945, the Indian Western Fleet sank the Pakistani destroyer *Khaibar* and a minesweeper off Karachi. Indian surface units then shelled and rocketed the naval base at Karachi. Pakistan's only naval success in the war came when the submarine *Hangor* torpedoed and sank the Indian frigate *Khukri*.

On December 16 in Dhaka, Pakistani commander Lieutenant General Amir Abdullah Khan Niazi officially surrendered to Indian commander General Sam Hormusji Framji Jamshedji Manekshaw, effectively ending the war. On December 17 both sides accepted a cease-fire agreement. The war saw the highest number of casualties of any of the three major Indian-Pakistani conflicts. Indian losses were some 2,400 killed, 6,200 wounded, and 2,100 taken prisoner. India also admitted that it had lost 73 tanks and 45 aircraft. Pakistan, however, lost more than 4,000 dead and 10,000 wounded, along with 93,000 prisoners (the latter figure included some of the wounded). Pakistan thus had lost a third of its army, half of its navy, and a quarter of its air force.

The United States found itself widely condemned, even by some of its allies such as Britain and France, for its support of Pakistan. Because of Moscow's support of India and of Bengali independence, the conflict had become a Cold War issue. U.S. president Richard M. Nixon had acted against the wishes of Congress and funneled aid to the Pakistanis via Iran, hoping in part to curry favor with China, another supporter of Pakistan with which he was beginning to move toward détente.

Thoroughly discredited, Yahya Khan resigned on December 20, 1971, and was replaced by Zulfikar Ali Bhutto. The last Indian troops were withdrawn from Bangladesh in March 1972, and on March 19 India and Bangladesh concluded a treaty of friendship. On July 2, India and Pakistan formally concluded an agreement at Simla, India. President Bhutto signed for Pakistan, and Prime Minister Gandhi signed for India. Both sides agreed to a a general troop withdrawal and restoration of the prewar western border but postponed action on settlement of the dispute over Kashmir and the return of Pakistani prisoners of war. India did not agree to the release of the prisoners of war until August 1973, with the last of them returning to Pakistan in April 1974.

The one positive consequence for India and Pakistan of the 1971 war was the Simla Agreement. In it, both nations pledged to resolve all future disputes through diplomatic means. Although this brought an almost major war between India and Pakistan, it did not mean a complete halt to fighting. Border incidents continued to occur regularly thereafter, threatening wider wars. In 1984, war nearly broke out over India's belief that Pakistan was involved in the Sikh insurgency of that year. This crisis was headed off by diplomacy. Fighting initiated by a local Indian commander also occurred in 1987 but was contained.

On taking power in 1971, Bhutto promptly placed Yahya Khan and senior Pakistani generals under arrest. Bhutto also restored civilian rule and shifted the country's foreign policy away from dependence on the United States. He sought to build up the Pakistani military, a decision that included development of nuclear weapons beginning in 1973. Bhutto also presided over the suppression of an independence movement in Baluchistan in 1973 and constitutional changes that made Pakistan an Islamic republic later that same year. However, personal and political rivalries led to his overthrow in a military coup (Operation FAIR PLAY), led by General Mohammed Zia al-Haq on July 5, 1977. Found guilty of the murder of political rivals in what many still see as a political move by the military, Bhutto was executed in April 1979.

General Zia presided over considerable change within Pakistan, most notably the increasing Islamization of the country with the 1978 intermingling of sharia (Islamic law) with civil and secular law. Zia also facilitated an important reconciliation with the Americans predicated on the Soviet invasion of Afghanistan in December 1979. Almost immediately, Zia backed factions within the mujahideen (jihadists or holy warriors), a loose federation of Afghan tribes opposed to the Soviet occupation. With the United States having lost Iran as an ally following the

Islamic revolution there earlier in the year and fearing Soviet expansion in the Middle East, U.S. president Jimmy Carter offered Zia $400 million in aid to help fight in Afghanistan, which the general famously denounced as "peanuts."

It was not until President Ronald W. Reagan took office in January 1981 that the Americans and Pakistanis worked together, largely through their intelligence services, to supply and train the mujahideen. Thus, Pakistan once again became a major ally of the United States, in return receiving substantial military aid of $1.36 billion between 1985 and 1991 alone. Worried about the Pakistani military buildup, in 1985 the U.S. Congress passed the Pressler Amendment, requiring the president to certify that Pakistan did not possess nuclear weapons before aid was approved. Zia's hard-line regime gradually became a liability for Washington, especially after the Soviets began withdrawing from Afghanistan in 1987.

Elements within the Pakistani military and particularly the Inter-Service Intelligence (ISI) service were opposed to the Islamization of the country, as were moderate, secular Pakistani politicians. Zia was also hated by the Soviets, while chieftains in Pakistan's tribal areas resented his suppression of their autonomy. In August 1988 Zia died in a plane crash, widely seen as an assassination carried out by at least one of these disaffected groups.

A caretaker government took control briefly before Benazir Bhutto—the daughter of Zulfikar Ali Bhutto—was elected in December 1988 as the first female prime minister of an Islamic country. Almost immediately her government battled charges of corruption, ultimately resulting in its collapse in August 1990. She was replaced by Nawaz Sharif in November 1990. He served until July 1993, when elections returned Bhutto as prime minister until November 1996. During Bhutto's second term, Pakistan was once again active in Afghanistan, supporting the Taliban, a Sunni Muslim fundamentalist group formed from segments of the mujahideen. The Taliban came to power in Afghanistan in September 1996, shortly before Bhutto's government was again dismissed amid accusations of corruption. Sharif returned to power, but he had a difficult time managing the Pakistani military. In May 1998 Pakistan had successfully exploded six nuclear weapons. These tests, despite the threat of sanctions by the United States and other Western powers, were in response to nuclear tests conducted by India less than a month before (India's first successful nuclear test occurred in May 1974).

In 1999 another armed conflict occurred between Pakistan and India. Known as the Kargil War but more limited than the three previous armed conflicts, it took place during May–July 1999 in the Kargil district of Kashmir when Pakistani forces, along with Kashmiri insurgents, infiltrated across the Line of Control (the de facto border between India and Pakistan in Kashmir) into the Indian-occupied Kargil district. India responded with a major military offensive to drive out the invaders. With the real danger of another full-scale war in the Indian subcontinent, the United States, then supporting Pakistan, pressured that country to withdraw, and by the end of July organized hostilities in the Kargil district had ended. The Kargil War has been the only instance of direct conventional warfare between two states possessing nuclear weapons. Pakistan maintains that it would only employ nuclear weapons first if its armed forces were not able to halt an invasion or if a nuclear strike was initiated against Pakistan. India, according to stated policy, would not be the first to employ their use.

Following Pakistan's defeat in the 1999 fighting with India, Prime Minister Sharif tried to court-martial senior military officers, but on October 12, 1999, they turned the tables when army chief of staff General Pervez Musharraf seized power in a coup d'état. Musharraf's regime, which came to be widely viewed as oppressive and corrupt, was largely condemned in the West. Musharraf also continued to support the fundamentalist Taliban regime in Afghanistan, while some members of the Pakistani intelligence services were believed to have ties with international terrorist organizations, including Al-Qaeda.

Following the September 11, 2001, terrorist attacks on the United States, carried out by Al-Qaeda in Afghanistan, Musharraf decided not to risk incurring the wrath of the Americans and a possible alliance between the United States and India. He then declared himself an ally of the United States in its October 2001 invasion of Afghanistan to destroy Al-Qaeda bases (Operation ENDURING FREEDOM).

Musharraf also denounced militants in Kashmir whom he had previously supported and condemned all forms of Islamic extremism. This provoked public anger within Pakistan, especially in the tribal areas where members of Al-Qaeda and the Taliban had received refuge. Having survived several attempts on his life, Musharraf also faced challenges from within his own government, especially by prodemocracy elements and those who supported a return of Benazir Bhutto. As the U.S.-led global war on terror progressed, many in Washington called into question Musharraf's commitment to fighting Islamic radicals. Remnants of the Taliban and Al-Qaeda operated with renewed vigor along the long, desolate, and porous border between Pakistan and Afghanistan but also within the Punjab region.

Pressure from Washington on the Pakistani government to move against the Federally Administered Tribal Areas of northern Waziristan helped cause Musharraf to finally send troops into the region. On March 16, 2004, he ordered some 80,000 troops to the area. Known as the War in North-West Pakistan and the War in Waziristan, it continues to the present. This had the goal of removing Al-Qaeda and Taliban forces that had long enjoyed safe haven there supported by elements of the Pakistani intelligence service. The government billed this as Pakistan's contribution to the global war on terror. At the same time, the United States mounted drone aircraft attacks in the tribal areas. Pakistani forces, however, sustained heavy casualties throughout 2004 and into early 2005, when the government switched to negotiations.

Despite doubts, the U.S. government continued to court Pakistan as an ally, for to have turned its back on Musharraf might have opened the way for a radical anti-American government to take hold in Karachi. Since 2001 the United States has continued to rely on Pakistan as its most important regional ally.

As it turned out, Musharraf sowed the seeds of his own downfall. In the autumn of 2007 he precipitated a full-blown political crisis when he sacked most of the Pakistani Supreme Court, suspended the constitution, ordered the mass arrests of dissidents and regime opponents, and declared a state of emergency on November 3, 2007. His actions provoked mass protests, sporadic violence, and much criticism from the international community, including the United States. Musharraf lifted the state of emergency on December 15, but Benazir Bhutto had returned to Pakistan, and both she and Nawaz Sharif, who had been disallowed from returning to the country, were outspoken critics of Musharraf. The crisis grew worse when Bhutto was assassinated in Ralapindi on December 27. Her supporters alleged involvement of either the government or Musharraf. After that Musharraf's hold on power grew ever more tenuous, and he finally resigned in August 2008.

Musharraf was succeeded by Benazir Bhutto's widower, Asif Ali Zardari, who assumed the presidency in September. Zardari's government cooperated with the United States, although it protested U.S. drone strikes from Afghanistan into northwestern Pakistan against the Taliban and Al-Qaeda. The government faced great challenges at home, not the least of which was Islamic radicalism. Ongoing tensions with India remained high and raised the specter of nuclear war in the subcontinent, especially with the November 26–29, 2008, terrorist attacks in Mumbai, when 10 Pakistani members of the militant Islamic Lashar-e Taiba organization carried out 12 coordinated attacks in that Indian city, resulting in the deaths of 164 people and the wounding of at least 308. Ajmal Kasab, the sole attacker taken alive, confessed to Indian interrogators that the attacks had the support of the ISI.

Zardari's government also set off alarm bells in Washington when it concluded a truce with the Taliban in northwestern Pakistan that allowed the imposition of sharia, law based on the Qur'an, in effect conceding rule of the Swat Valley to the Taliban. However, when Taliban forces broke the truce by moving into the Buner district of the Khyber Pakhtunkhwa Province of Pakistan only some 60 miles north of the capital of Islamabad, Zardari responded with force.

Under heavy pressure from the U.S. government and from moderate elements within Pakistan itself, he declared the truce with the Taliban to be at an end and in late April 2009 sent the army into Buner but also into the Swat Valley. After two weeks of heavy fighting the government claimed that it had killed some 1,000 Taliban and Al-Qaeda extremists, but the fighting displaced some 2 million people in the greatest refugee crisis in recent years. The United States promised additional financial and military aid to Pakistan. Zardari also pledged cooperation with Afghan president Hamid Karzai in fighting the Taliban and Al-Qaeda in Afghanistan.

U.S. president Barack Obama authorized a May 2, 2011, raid by U.S. Army Special Forces that killed Al-Qaeda leader Osama bin Laden in Abbottabad, Pakistan. This action, however, won the United States no friends in Pakistan, for it was carried out without the knowledge or support of Pakistani authorities. There were also questions about how bin Laden could have hidden in plain sight in Pakistan for so long without assistance from the ISI.

The Pakistani general election of 2013 resulted in the return to power of Nawaz Sharif as prime minister in July for the third time after a lapse of 14 years, although claims of electoral fraud and corruption have clouded his tenure.

The Obama administration substantially increased U.S. drone strikes in Pakistan's tribal areas as well as in border areas with Afghanistan. A number of these resulted in the deaths of innocent civilians, which increased tensions between Washington and Islamabad. Meanwhile, by early 2014 Al-Qaeda was on the upswing in Pakistan, along with sectarian-based violence.

In June 2014 the Pakistani Army undertook a major offensive aimed at clearing out the militants in its restive regions along the Afghan border. The offensive displaced tens of thousands of people, and in response to army inroads, Islamic militants mounted terror attacks throughout Pakistan, the most spectacular and horrific of which occurred on December 16, 2014, when 7 Taliban suicide bombers attacked an army-run school in the city of Peshawar and systematically executed 145 people, 132 of them children, with many others wounded. All of the attackers also perished. Two other costly attacks mounted by Islamic extremists against innocent civilians occurred in January and March 2016.

Tensions regarding Kashmir also remain high. Military skirmishes continue to be a common occurrence, with Pakistan accused by numerous sources of having been behind a number of terrorist attacks in Indian-occupied portions of Jammu and Kashmir, including in 2013 and 2014.

Pakistan certainly continues to meddle in Afghanistan. After courting the Pakistani government for more than a year in hopes of winning its support for action but with no result, in late April 2016 Afghan president Ashraf Ghani changed course and warned Islamabad that he would lodge a formal complaint with the UN Security Council if Pakistan did not take military action against Taliban forces operating from Pakistan against Afghanistan in what has been increasingly bloody fighting. The killing of Afghan Taliban leader Mullah Akhtar Muhammad Mansour in a U.S. drone strike in May 2016 was another strong message to Pakistan, for the attack took place in Baluchistan, a Pakistani province, and the United States had not informed the Pakistani government in advance.

Because of its proximity to Afghanistan and its familiarity and ties with major militant groups in South and Central Asia, Pakistan remains critical to regional order. Nonetheless, with ongoing internal instability, widespread poverty, illiteracy, corruption, terrorism, and ever-present tensions with India, Pakistan's future remains clouded at best.

Timeline

1857	The Sepoy Rebellion (known in India as the First War of Indian Independence) occurs against British East India Company rule.
1858	The British government assumes direct rule of the subcontinent, beginning the British Raj (Hindi for "rule" or "reign").
May 1, 1876	Queen Victoria takes the title "Empress of India."
Dec 28, 1885	Founding of the Indian National Congress (INC).
Dec 30, 1906	Founding of the All-India Muslim League (AIML).
1914–1918	During World War I, the Indian Army plays a major role principally in the Middle East.

1930–1932	The Round Table Conferences discuss constitutional reform in India.
Aug 1935	The British Parliament passes the Government of India Act, conceding a degree of autonomy.
1939–1945	World War II. Indian Army units again play a sizable role.
Mar 24, 1940	AIML leaders approve the Lahore Declaration calling for the division of British India with the majority Muslim areas to become independent states.
Mar 1942	In the Cripps Mission to India, the British government offers Indian independence after the war, but the INC rejects the conditions, which imply the possibility of partition based on religion.
Aug 1942	Indian nationalist leader Mohandas Karamchand Gandhi calls on the British to quit India. He and most of the INC leadership are arrested.
Jul 1945	The anticolonial Labour Party wins the British national elections and pledges to grant independence to a single Indian state by June 1948.
Feb 12, 1947	Viscount Louis Mountbatten becomes viceroy of India. He serves in this position until August 5, 1947, when he becomes governor-general of India until June 21, 1948.
Jul 18, 1947	The British Parliament passes the Indian Independence Act.
Aug 15, 1947	The British grant independence to the Union of India and the Dominion of Pakistan. Muhammad Ali Jinnah becomes Pakistani governor-general and president-speaker of Parliament.
Oct 22, 1947	Fighting commences between India and Pakistan in the 1947 India-Pakistan War.
Oct 26, 1947	Maharajah Hari Singh signs the Instrument of Accession, assigning his kingdom of Kashmir, which has a majority Muslim population, to India. This action formally begins the India-Pakistan War.
Nov 7, 1947	Indian forces win the Battle of Shalateng.
Dec 24, 1947	The Pakistanis win the Battle of Jhangar.
Jan 30, 1948	Mahatma Gandhi is assassinated in Delhi.
Feb 6, 1948	Indian forces prevail in the Battle of Naoshera.
May 22–27, 1948	Indian forces win the Battle of Gurais.

Sep 11, 1948   Jinnah dies and is succeeded by Sir Khawaja Nazimuddin as governor-general of Pakistan.

Oct 19, 1948   Indian forces win the Battle of Zojila.

Jan 1, 1949   The 1947 war comes to an end.

Jan 5, 1949   A United Nations resolution calls for a plebiscite to determine the future status of Kashmir, but India refuses to permit this.

Sep 1954   Pakistan is a founding member of the Southeast Asia Treaty Organization, formed by its ally, the United States.

Feb 24, 1955   Pakistan become a founding member of the Central Treaty Organization on the urging of the United States, which, however, is not a member.

Oct 7, 1958   Following a succession of unstable civilian governments, President Iskander Mirza abrogates the constitution of Pakistan and declares martial law.

Oct 27, 1958   General Muhammad Ayub Khan, commander of the Pakistani Army, seizes power and assumes the office of president.

Apr 1965   The 1965 Indo-Pakistani War begins.

Aug 24, 1965   Indian forces launch a major raid across the cease-fire line in Kashmir.

Sep 1, 1965   Pakistan launches Operation GRAND SLAM.

Sep 14–19, 1965   The Indians defeat the Pakistanis in a major tank battle at Chawinda.

Sep 27, 1965   A cease-fire brings the 1965 fighting to a close.

Jan 10, 1966   Indian and Pakistani representatives meeting at Tashkent in the Soviet Union conclude a peace agreement.

Mar 28, 1969   Ayub Khan resigns the presidency and is succeeded by another general, Yahya Khan.

Nov 12–13, 1970   A great cyclone hits East Pakistan, killing as many as 500,000 people.

Dec 1970   The Awami League political party, which is led by Sheikh Mujibur Rahman (known as Mujib) and seeks autonomy for East Pakistan, wins an absolute majority in the national elections. Fearing that this will bring the breakup of Pakistan, Yahya Khan refuses to allow Mujib to form a government. Widespread demonstrations occur in East Pakistan.

Mar 7, 1971   Mujib announces a civil disobedience movement to force the convening of the National Assembly.

Mar 25, 1971	Yahya Khan declares martial law and sends in the army in Operation SEARCHLIGHT. Mujib is arrested and flown to West Pakistan, where he is jailed on a charge of treason.
Mar 26, 1971	Bengali Army officers declare independence on behalf of Mujib. A major Pakistani military repression follows in East Pakistan, resulting in a substantial number of deaths. Perhaps 10 million refugees flee East Pakistan into India.
Jun–Nov, 1971	India and Pakistan exchange intermittent artillery fire and carry out small cross-border raids against each other.
Aug 9, 1971	India concludes a treaty of friendship with the Soviet Union.
Nov 8, 1971	Alarmed at events, the United States terminates arms to Pakistan.
Nov 22, 1971	Pakistani aircraft raid eastern India.
Dec 3, 1971	The third major Indo-Pakistani war begins with a major Pakistani air assault against Indian airfields.
Dec 4, 1971	Pakistani forces invade Jammu and Kashmir.
Dec 6, 1971	India recognizes the independence of East Pakistan as Bangladesh.
Dec 14–16, 1971	Indian forces capture Dhaka (Dacca).
Dec 16, 1971	Pakistani forces surrender, and the next day a cease-fire agreement enters into force.
Dec 16, 1971	The 1971 Indo-Pakistani war officially ends.
Dec 20, 1971	President Ayub Khan resigns. Zulfikar Ali Bhutto replaces him as president.
Jul 2, 1972	In the Simla Agreement, India and Pakistan renounce the use of force against each other.
Jul 5, 1977	Bhutto is overthrown in a military coup (Operation FAIR PLAY) led by General Mohammed Zia al-Haq, who takes power. Bhutto is later tried and executed in what most observers see as an effort by Zia to get rid of a political rival.
Dec 1979	Soviet forces invade Afghanistan. Zia immediately supports the Afghan resistance and effects reconciliation with the United States to train, equip, and supply the Afghan mujahideen resistance. Pakistan is thus once again a major U.S. ally and the beneficiary of substantial aid.
Aug 17, 1988	President Zia dies in a plane crash, widely seen as an assassination carried out by one of many groups opposed to his rule.

Dec 2, 1988	Benazir Bhutto, the daughter of Zulfikar Ali Bhutto, becomes prime minister. She is the first female head of state of an Islamic country.
Sep 1996	Supported by Pakistan, the Sunni Muslim fundamentalist Taliban comes to power in Afghanistan.
May 1998	Pakistan successfully carries out nuclear tests. These are in response to India having already developed nuclear weapons.
May–Jul 1999	The Kargil War occurs, with fighting in the Kargil district of Kashmir between Indian and Pakistani forces.
Oct 12, 1999	With Prime Minister Sharif endeavoring to dismiss senior military officers, army chief of staff General Pervez Musharraf stages a coup d'état. Musharraf continues to support the fundamentalist Taliban regime in Afghanistan, and some members of the Pakistani Inter-Service Intelligence (ISI) are widely thought to have ties with Al-Qaeda, the Islamic terrorist organization.
Sep 11, 2001	Following the Al-Qaeda terrorist attacks on the United States of this date, Musharraf declares his country an ally of the West in the U.S.-defined global war on terror.
Mar 16, 2004	With Washington questioning his commitment to fighting Islamic radicals, Musharraf sends some 80,000 troops into the Federally Administered Tribal Areas of northern Waziristan, with the goal of removing Al-Qaeda and Taliban forces that have long enjoyed safe haven there supported by elements of the ISI. This begins the War in North-West Pakistan (also known as the War in Waziristan), which continues to the present. The United States also mounts drone attacks in the tribal areas.
Nov 3, 2007	Musharraf precipitates a full-blown political crisis when he sacks most of the Pakistani Supreme Court, suspends the constitution, orders the mass arrests of dissidents and regime opponents, and declares a state of emergency on this date.
Dec 15, 2007	Widespread criticism of Musharraf's actions from within Pakistan and abroad lead him to lift the state of emergency.
Dec 27, 2007	Having returned to Pakistan a strong critic of Musharraf, Bhutto is assassinated in Ralapindi. Her supporters allege involvement of the government or Musharraf.
Aug 18, 2008	Under increasing pressure, Musharraf resigns and is succeeded by Bhutto's widower, Asif Ali Zardari, who becomes president in September. Islamic radicalism continues.
Nov 26–29, 2008	Ten Pakistani members of the militant Islamic Lashar-e Taiba organization mount 12 coordinated attacks in Mumbai, India,

causing the deaths of 164 people and the wounding of at least 308 others. The sole attacker taken alive confesses that the attacks were supported by the ISI.

Apr 2009   Zardari declares an end to a truce with the Taliban and sends forces into Buner and the Swat Valley. The ensuing heavy fighting displaces some 2 million people in the greatest refugee crisis in recent years.

May 2, 2011   U.S. Army Special Forces kill Al-Qaeda leader Osama bin Laden in his compound in Abbottabad, Pakistan. This action is carried out without the knowledge or support of Pakistani authorities, as many believe that bin Laden had been protected by the ISI.

Jul 6, 2013   Following national elections, Sharif returns to power as prime minister for the third time after a lapse of 14 years.

Jun 2014   The Pakistani Army undertakes a major offensive to clear militants from the restive regions along the Afghan border.

Dec 16, 2014   Islamic militants retaliate with terrorist attacks throughout Pakistan. The most spectacular and horrific of these sees 7 Taliban suicide bombers attacking an army-run school in Peshawar, systematically executing 145 people, 132 of them children, with many others wounded.

Jan 20, 2016   Four gunmen kill 21 students at Bacha Khan University in Charsadda in northwestern Pakistan.

Mar 26, 2016   An Islamic terrorist bomb in Lahore kills at least 72 people and injures more than 300 in a park where Christian families are celebrating the Easter holiday. Many women and children are among the victims. Jamat-ul-Ahrar, a splinter group of the Pakistani Taliban, claims responsibility and says that the attack deliberately targeted Christians.

Further Reading

Afzal, M. Rafique. *Pakistan: History and Politics, 1947–1971.* New York: Oxford University Press, 2001.

Ayub, Muhammad. *An Army, Its Role and Rule: A History of the Pakistan Army from Independence to Kargil, 1947–1999.* Pittsburgh: RoseDog Books, 2005.

Bose, Sumantra. *Kashmir: Roots of Conflict, Paths to Peace.* Cambridge, MA: Harvard University Press, 2003.

Cheema, Pervaiz Iqbal. *The Armed Forces of Pakistan.* New York: New York University Press, 2002.

Choudhury, G. W. *The Last Days of United Pakistan.* Bloomington: University of Indiana Press, 1974.

Cohen, Stephen P. *The Pakistan Army.* Karachi: Oxford University Press, 1998.

Dixit, J. N. *India-Pakistan in War and Peace.* London: Routledge, 2002.

Dodwell, H. H. *Cambridge History of India,* Vol. 6, *1858–1969.* New Delhi: S. Chand, 1972.

Farwell, Byron. *Armies of the Raj: From the Mutiny to Independence, 1858–1947*. New York: Norton, 1989.

Ganguly, Sumit. *The Origins of War in South Asia: The Indo-Pakistani Wars since 1947*. Boulder, CO: Westview, 1994.

Haggani, Husain. *Magnificent Delusions: Pakistan, the United States, and an Epic History of Misunderstanding*. New York: PublicAffairs, 2013.

Haqqani, Husain. *Pakistan: Between Mosque and Military*. Washington, DC: Carnegie Endowment for International Peace, 2005.

Hiro, Dilip. *The Longest August: The Unflinching Rivalry between India and Pakistan*. New York: Nation Books, 2015.

Hussain, Rizwan. *Pakistan and the Emergence of Islamic Militancy in Afghanistan*. Aldershot, UK: Ashgate, 2005.

Jones, Owen Bennett. *Pakistan: Eye of the Storm*. New Haven, CT: Yale University Press, 2002.

Khan, Yasmin. *The Great Partition: The Making of India and Pakistan*. New Haven, CT: Yale University Press, 2008.

Kiessling, Hein. *Faith, Unity, Discipline: The Inter-Service-Intelligence (ISI) of Pakistan*. New York: Hurst, 2016.

Kux, Dennis. *The United States and Pakistan, 1947–2000: Disenchanted Allies*. Washington, DC: Woodrow Wilson Center Press, 2001.

Lieven, Anatol. *Pakistan: A Hard Country*. New York: PublicAffairs, 2012.

Menezes, S. L. *Fidelity and Honour: The Indian Army from the 17th to the 21st Century*. New Delhi: Viking, 1993.

Rashid, Ahmed. *Pakistan on the Brink: The Future of America, Pakistan, and Afghanistan*. New York: PublicAffairs, 2012.

Sathasivam, Kanishkan. *Uneasy Neighbors: India, Pakistan, and U.S. Foreign Policy*. Aldershot, UK: Ashgate, 2005.

Talbot, Ian. *Pakistan: A New History*. Rev ed. New York: Oxford University Press, 2015.

Weaver, Mary Anne. *Pakistan: In the Shadow of Jihad and Afghanistan*. New York: Farrar, Straus and Giroux, 2003.

Wirsing, Robert. *India, Pakistan, and the Kashmir Dispute: On Regional Conflict and Its Resolution*. New York: St. Martin's, 1994.

Ziring, Lawrence. *Pakistan: At the Crosscurrents of History*. Oxford: Oxford University Press, 2003.

QATAR

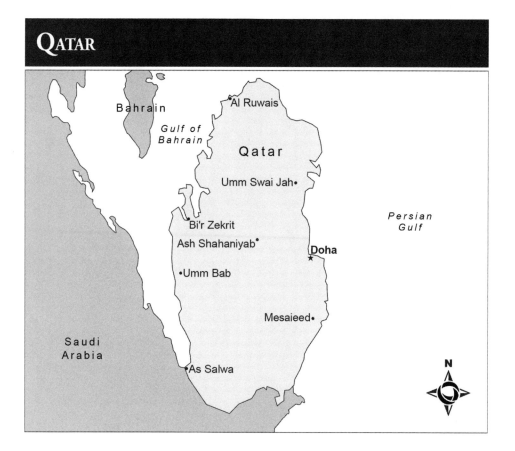

Bahrain

Gulf of
Bahrain

•Al Ruwais

Qatar

Umm Swai Jah•

•
Bi'r Zekrit

Ash Shahaniyab•

Persian
Gulf

Doha
★

•Umm Bab

Mesaieed•

Saudi
Arabia

•As Salwa

N

Qatar

Stefan M. Brooks and Spencer C. Tucker

Qatar, officially the State of Qatar, is located in Southwest Asia. It comprises the Qatar Peninsula on the northeastern coast of the Arabian Peninsula and, at 4,416 square miles, is a bit smaller than the U.S. state of Connecticut. Qatar's sole land border is to the south with Saudi Arabia. The remainder of Qatar is surrounded by the Persian Gulf. A strait separates Qatar from the nearby island of Bahrain, and Qatar also shares sea borders with the United Arab Emirates (UAE) and Iran.

Qatar's population in 2016 was some 2.291 million. Nearly 80 percent of the people live in the capital city of Doha and its suburbs. Qatar is a hereditary constitutional monarchy headed by an emir. Some 67.7 percent of Qataris are Muslim, and Islam is the state religion, with the vast majority of Muslims belonging to the Salafi sect of Sunni Islam. Another 13.8 percent are Christians (almost all of these foreigners), while 13.8 percent are Hindu and 3.1 percent are Buddhist. Other religions and religiously unaffiliated people make up the remaining 1.6 percent. Qatar is regarded as the most conservative of the states, after Saudi Arabia, of Gulf Cooperation Council members.

Qatar enjoys considerable per capita wealth and a modern infrastructure. Indeed, Qatar has the world's highest per capita income as a result of possessing the world's third-largest natural gas and oil reserves. Qatar has used this wealth to become a major power in the Arab world and also enjoys great influence beyond the region through its highly regarded Al Jazeera Media Network.

Qatar has been inhabited for some 50,000 years. In 224 CE it became part of the Sasanian Empire. Islam was introduced in 621. Qatar was known for its trade in pearls and a purple dye and as a horse- and camel-breeding center. Ruled by Bahrain during 1783–1868, in 1871 Qatar became part of the Ottoman Empire. The country shook off Ottoman rule in the Arab Revolt in 1916 during World War I (1914–1918). Qatar became a British protectorate on November 3, 1916, when Sheikh Abdullah bin Jassim al-Thani signed a treaty in which he pledged not to enter into relations with any other power without the prior consent of the British government. The British pledged in return to protect Qatar from seaborne attack. Another treaty between Qatar and Britain on May 5, 1935, provided Qatar further protection against internal and external threats.

Although Qatar's vast oil holdings were discovered in 1939, exploitation was delayed by World War II. Following the independence of India and Pakistan in 1947,

British interest in the Persian Gulf region declined considerably. At the same time, the considerable wealth from oil production led the people of Qatar to support independence. Thus, on January 24, 1968, British prime minister Harold Wilson announced his government's decision to let the treaties with the emirates lapse in three years. This was reaffirmed in March 1971 by Prime Minister Edward Heath. Qatar then joined other states of the eastern Persian Gulf region in a federation. Regional disputes, however, led Qatar to resign and declare its independence from this coalition of small states that would become the UAE, and on September 3, 1971, Qatar became an independent sovereign state. On February 22, 1972, Sheikh Khalifa bin Hamad al-Thani deposed his cousin Sheikh Ahmed bin Ali al-Thani as ruler of Qatar.

On January 26, 1982, Qatar joined with Saudi Arabia, Bahrain, Kuwait, Oman, and the UAE in establishing a joint military command structure and integrated air defense system. This move was prompted by the perceived threats posed by the Islamic Republic of Iran, the ongoing Iran-Iraq War (1980–1988), and the Soviet-Afghan War (1979–1989).

The United States established diplomatic relations with Qatar in March 1973. Since then, relations between the two governments have been mainly cordial. Qatar has only a small military establishment numbering only some 11,000 troops, 34 tanks, and about a dozen aircraft. Its most extensive role in combat operations came during January 29–31, 1991, in the first battle of the 1991 Persian Gulf War, when a Qatari tank battalion and Saudi troops, backed by American artillery and air support, repulsed an Iraqi cross-border assault on the Saudi city of Khafji. During that war U.S., French, and Canadian aircraft staged from Qatar. The era since the end of the Persian Gulf War has been marked by greater political, economic, and military cooperation with the West and the United States in particular, as the 1990 Iraqi invasion of Kuwait and the resulting threat to other small Gulf states forced Qatar to significantly alter its defense and foreign policy priorities.

On June 27, 1995, Crown Prince Hamad bin Khalifa al-Thani carried out a bloodless coup, overthrowing the repressive regime of his father, Emir Sheikh Khalifa bin Hamad al-Thani. The crown prince vowed to liberalize Qatar, and during the next several years he allowed women far more freedom, including the right to vote in municipal elections; ended censorship; introduced Qatar's first constitution; and established Al Jazeera. He also permitted the construction of U.S. military facilities.

Strains with Saudi Arabia and Bahrain and aspirations for a more assertive and influential position in foreign affairs explain Qatar's recent foreign policy, which has become more Western oriented. On June 23, 1992, Qatar and the United States signed a bilateral defense cooperation agreement that provided the United States access to Qatari bases, the prepositioning of U.S. military equipment in the nation, and future joint military exercises. Qatar also allowed construction of an extensive American military air base—Al Udeid—in the country, which served as the command center for the Anglo-American invasion of Iraq in March 2003. Presumably for this reason, Iraq launched Scud missiles at Qatar upon the commencement of the conflict. Al Udeid boasts the longest runway (15,000 feet) in the Persian Gulf region and currently houses some 5,000 U.S. troops. It is equipped to accommodate as many as 10,000 troops and 40 aircraft in a 76,000-square-foot

Sheikh Hamad bin Khalifa al-Thani, the Emir of Qatar, talks with King Hussein of Jordan in Doha on August 2, 1995. Two months before, the emir had overthrown his father's repressive regime in a bloodless coup. (AP Photo)

hangar. Qatar also allowed the construction of the As-Sayliyah Army Base, the largest prepositioning facility for U.S. equipment in the world.

Shortly after the terror attacks against the United States on September 11, 2001, Qatar granted the Americans permission to deploy warplanes to Al Udeid, and these flew missions in Afghanistan during Operation ENDURING FREEDOM in the fall of 2001 to overthrow the Taliban government, which had given sanctuary to Osama bin Laden and his Al-Qaeda terrorist organization.

In the months leading up to Operation IRAQI FREEDOM (the Iraq War) in 2003, the United States moved significant troops, weapons, and equipment, along with its Air Operations Command Center, from Prince Sultan Air Base in Saudi Arabia to Qatar, the consequence of Saudi Arabia's opposition to the invasion. Indeed, during the Iraq War, Saudi Arabia forbade the United States from using its territory to launch attacks against Iraq.

In March 2005, a suicide bombing carried out by an Egyptian with suspected ties to Al-Qaeda in the Arabian Peninsula killed a British teacher, shocking the country, which had not previously experienced such acts of terrorism. Qatar firmly aligned itself with the United States and the North Atlantic Treaty Organization in the latter's intervention in the 2011 Libyan Civil War. Along with the United States, Qatar has also been the chief supplier of arms and financial support for the rebels battling the regime of Syrian president Bashar al-Assad in the ongoing Syrian Civil War (2011–)

and has hosted several meetings of representatives of states supporting the rebels. On September 23, 2014, Qatari Air Force planes took part in a U.S. and Arab coalition attack on Islamic State of Iraq and Syria (ISIS) rebels in Syria. Qatar has also served as a base for U.S. aircraft taking part in the fight against ISIS. These included B-1 and B-52 strategic bombers, the latter from April 2016. Qatar has also been active in trying to broker a peace agreement with the Taliban in Afghanistan.

On June 25, 2013, Sheikh Tamim bin Hamad al-Thani became the Emir of Qatar upon his father ceding power. Sheikh Tamim stated his intention to improve the welfare of Qatari citizens by improving both advanced health care and education. He has also supported major improvements in the country's infrastructure in preparation for the hosting of the 2022 World Cup, the first Arab country to do so.

During 2013–2014 Qatar earned the enmity of some of its Persian Gulf neighbors, especially Saudi Arabia, Bahrain, and the UAE, because of its support of the Muslim Brotherhood, a group that is both feared and despised in those nations. On March 26, 2015, Qatar sent aircraft to participate in the Saudi Arabian–led military intervention in Yemen against Iranian-backed Houthi rebels. Qatar's relations with the West have remained solid.

Timeline

224	Qatar becomes part of the Sasanian Empire.
621	Islam is introduced into Qatar.
1783–1868	Bahrain controls Qatar.
1871–1916	Qatar is part of the Ottoman Empire.
Nov 3, 1916	Qatar becomes a British protectorate when Sheikh Abdullah bin Jassim al-Thani signs a treaty with the British.
May 5, 1935	A second treaty between Qatar and Britain provides additional British guarantees to protect Qatar from attack.
1939	Oil is discovered in Qatar.
Jan 24, 1968	British prime minister Harold Wilson announces his government's decision to let the treaties with the Persian Gulf states lapse in three years.
Sep 3, 1971	Qatar becomes an independent sovereign state.
Feb 22, 1972	Sheikh Khalifa bin Hamad al-Thani deposes his cousin Sheikh Ahmed bin Ali al-Thani as ruler of Qatar.
Mar 1973	The United States opens an embassy in Doha.
Jan 26, 1982	Qatar joins Saudi Arabia, Bahrain, Kuwait, Oman, and the United Arab Emirates in establishing a joint military command structure and integrated air defense system.

Jan 29–31, 1991	Qatari forces take part in the Battle of Khafji against Iraqi forces in the first engagement of the Persian Gulf War.
Jun 27, 1995	In a bloodless coup, Crown Prince Hamad bin Khalifa al-Thani overthrows the repressive regime of his father, Emir Sheikh Khalifa bin Hamad al-Thani, and then introduces a number of reforms.
Jun 23, 1992	Qatar and the United States signed a bilateral defense cooperation agreement that provides U.S. access to Qatari bases, the prepositioning of U.S. military equipment in Qatar, and future joint military exercises. Qatar also allows the construction of major U.S. bases.
Sep 2001	After the terror attacks against the United States on September 11, 2001, Qatar grants the Americans permission to deploy warplanes to Al Udeid Air Base and then fly missions in Afghanistan during Operation ENDURING FREEDOM to overthrow the Taliban government there.
Mar 2003	With Saudi Arabia opposed, Qatar serves as the command center for the Anglo-American invasion of Iraq.
Mar–Oct 2011	Qatar firmly aligns itself with the United States and the North Atlantic Treaty Organization in the latter's intervention in the Libyan Civil War. Along with the United States, Qatar is also the chief supplier of arms and financial support for rebels in the ongoing Syrian Civil War (2011–).
Jun 25, 2013	Sheikh Tamim bin Hamad al-Thani becomes the emir of Qatar after his father abdicates.
Sep 23, 2014	Qatari Air Force planes participate in the U.S.-Arab coalition attack on Islamic State of Iraq and Syria rebels in Syria.
Mar 26, 2015	Qatar sends aircraft to participate in the Saudi Arabian–led military intervention in Yemen against the Iranian-backed Houthi rebels.

Further Reading

Blanchard, Christopher. *Qatar: Background and U.S. Relations*. Washington, DC: Congressional Research Service, Library of Congress, 2005.

Cleveland, William F. *A History of the Modern Middle East*. Boulder, CO: Westview, 2004.

Fromherz, Allen J. *Qatar: A Modern History*. Washington, DC: Georgetown University Press, 2012.

Kamrava, Mehran. *Qatar: Small State, Big Politics*. Ithaca, NY: Cornell University Press, 2015.

Potter, Lawrence, and Gary Sick. *Security in the Persian Gulf: Origins, Obstacles, and the Search for Consensus*. New York: Palgrave Macmillan, 2002.

Roberts, David. *Qatar: Securing the Global Ambitions of a City-State*. London: Hurst, 2016.

Ulrichsen, Kristian Coates. *Qatar and the Arab Spring*. Oxford: Oxford University Press, 2014.

SAUDI ARABIA

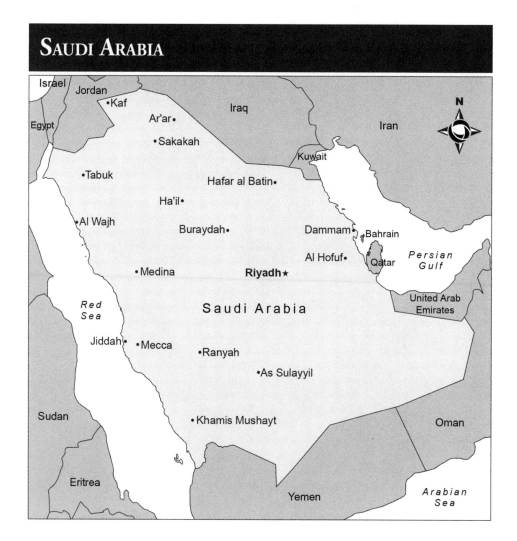

Israel
Jordan
•Kaf
Iraq
Iran
N
Egypt
Ar'ar•
•Sakakah
Kuwait
•Tabuk
Hafar al Batin•
Ha'il•
Al Wajh
Buraydah•
Dammam•
Bahrain
Al Hofuf•
Qatar
Persian Gulf
•Medina
Riyadh★
Red Sea
Saudi Arabia
United Arab Emirates
Jiddah•
•Mecca
•Ranyah
•As Sulayyil
Sudan
•Khamis Mushayt
Oman
Eritrea
Yemen
Arabian Sea

Saudi Arabia

Robert S. Kiely, Spencer C. Tucker,
and Sherifa Zuhur

The Kingdom of Saudi Arabia is located in West Asia. Constituting nearly the entire Arabian Peninsula, Saudi Arabia occupies some 830,000 square miles and is thus nearly three times the area of the U.S. state of Texas. Saudi Arabia is second in size in the Arab world only to Algeria. The kingdom borders on Jordan, Iraq, and Kuwait to the north; the Persian Gulf, Qatar, and the United Arab Emirates to the east; Oman and Yemen to the south; and the Red Sea to the west. Saudi Arabia's capital and largest city is Riyadh.

Arabs predominate in the kingdom, and Saudi Arabia is an absolute monarchy. The ruling House of Saud has historical ties to the Wahhabi sect of Islam, which is a branch of Sunni Islam and the official state religion. Adherents prefer the term "Salafism" rather than "Wahhabism," but what is described as the true faith by adherents is seen by many in the West as intolerant or at best ultraconservative. Regardless, Saudi Arabian law and society are based on a strict interpretation of Islamic law. Virtually all Saudi citizens are Muslims, and the vast majority (75–90 percent) are Sunni Muslims, with the remainder being Shiites. Saudi Arabia is home to the two holiest places in the Muslim world, Al-Masjid al-Haram in Mecca and Al-Masjid an-Nabawi in Medina.

Some 1.5 million Christians live in Saudi Arabia. Almost all of them are foreign workers, but they are not permitted to practice their faith openly. Saudi Arabia also forbids religious conversion from Islam and punishes it by death. There are perhaps 390,000 Hindus, again foreign workers, in the kingdom.

Saudi Arabia had a total population in 2016 of some 32.158 million. A high percentage of these are foreign workers. The figure varies widely according to source, with the Saudi Arabian government putting it at about one-third of the total. One source estimates the leading foreign populations and country of origin as follows: Pakistan, 1.5 million; India, 1.3 million; Egypt, 900,000; Yemen, 800,000; Bangladesh, 500,000; the Philippines, 500,000; Jordan and Palestine, 260,000; Indonesia, 250,000; Sri Lanka, 350,000; Sudan, 250,000, Syria, 100,000; and Turkey, 100,000. Perhaps 100,000 Westerners also reside in Saudi Arabia, most of them in compounds or gated communities.

What would become the Kingdom of Saudi Arabia was early peopled by nomadic tribes surviving in a hostile desert environment. Two population centers developed in Mecca and Medina. The Islamic prophet Muhammad (ca. 571–632) was born in Mecca, and in the early 600s he led a military effort that ended with his securing control of both Mecca and Medina and uniting the tribes into a single Islamic religious state.

Muhammad's followers aggressively expanded the territory under Islamic control until it reached as far west as the Iberian Peninsula and as far east as present-day Pakistan. With other areas far richer in terms of resources and wealth, Arabia was soon eclipsed as the center of Islamic power. From the 10th century the sharif of Mecca, who ruled the Hejaz, was the leading figure, but most of the territory that would become modern Saudi Arabia remained under tribal rule. The sharif was hardly independent, as most of the time he owed allegiance to one of the Islamic empires in Baghdad or Cairo and then in Istanbul. In the 16th century the Ottoman Empire came to control the coastal areas on the Red Sea and the Persian Gulf (the Hejaz, Asir, and Al-Ahsa) and claimed suzerainty over the Arabian interior. Actual Ottoman control varied during the course of the next four centuries, however.

In 1744 in central Arabia, Muhammad bin Saud, founder of the dynasty that continues to rule Saudi Arabia, formed an alliance with Muhammad ibn Abd al-Wahhab, who founded the Wahhabi movement (Wahhabism), a strict puritanical form of Sunni Islam. The alliance was formalized in the marriage of Muhammad bin Abdul-Wahhab's daughter to Abdul Aziz bin Muhammad bin Saud, son and successor of Ibn Saud, who ruled from 1765 to 1803. The descendants of these two families have remained closely linked ever since.

This alliance gave Saud control of the area around Riyadh. He then rapidly expanded his control until he ruled most of what today constitutes Saudi Arabia. Ottoman viceroy of Egypt Muhammad Ali Pasha invaded and destroyed this state in 1818. By 1824, however, Saud had established a new state in Nejd. For the remainder of the 19th century the Al Saud family dueled with another ruling family, the Al Rashid, to see which would control the Arabian interior. By 1891, the Al Rashid family won out, and the Al Saud family was forced into exile in Kuwait.

In 1902, Abdulaziz ibn Abdul Rahman ibn Faisal ibn Turki ibn Abdullah ibn Muhammad al-Saud (known in the Arab world as Abdulaziz and in the West as Ibn Saud), then age 27, recaptured control of Riyadh. The role played by Ibn Saud in the history of Saudi Arabia cannot be overstated. Securing the assistance of the Ikhwan, a tribal army inspired by Wahhabism, by 1913 Ibn Saud had conquered Arabia'a easternmost province of Al-Ahsa from the Ottomans.

The British were eager to protect their imperial lifeline to India, and during World War I (1914–1918) when the Ottoman Empire was fighting against them on the side of the Central Powers, on December 26, 1915, the British signed the Treaty of Darin with Ibn Saud, securing the latter's benevolent neutrality. With Ibn Saud holding aloof from direct involvement in the war, British authorities in Cairo that same year had entered into negotiations with Hussein bin Ali, sharif of Mecca and a rival of Ibn Saud, to lead a Pan-Arab revolt against the Ottoman Empire with the pledge of the creation of a united Arab state at the end of the conflict.

Although the Arab Revolt of 1916–1918 greatly aided the British forces in their defeat of the Ottoman forces in the Middle East and helped bring finis to the

Ottoman Empire, it did not lead to the creation of a single independent Arab state. Indeed, the British and French had secretly agreed to divide control of the region among themselves. The result was the creation of new states as League of Nations mandates, formed from territory of the former Ottoman Empire. The British had de facto control of Palestine, Transjordan, and Iraq, while the French controlled Syria and Lebanon.

Ibn Saud had avoided involvement in the Arab Revolt, choosing instead to continue his struggle with the Al Rashids. After World War I, he received support for that effort from the British, including munitions. He launched his campaign in 1920, leading to their defeat by 1922. On November 3, 1921, Ibn Saud had taken the title "Sultan of Nejd." His victory doubled the size of Saudi territory.

Assisted by the Ikhwan, on August 24, 1924, Ibn Saud invaded the Hejaz and drove on Mecca. Sharif Hussein abdicated on October 3, succeeded by his son Ali. Mecca surrendered to Ibn Saud on October 14. On December 8, 1925, Ali, who had withdrawn to Jidda, also abdicated, and Ibn Saud's forces took Jidda on December 23. Now in effective control of the entire area, on January 8, 1926, Ibn Saud declared himself king of the Hejaz. A year later, he added the title "King of Nejd," although both kingdoms were administered separately.

Following the conquest of the Hejaz, the Ikhwan leadership wanted to expand Wahhabism northward, and they began raids into the British protectorates of Transjordan, Iraq, and Kuwait. This greatly concerned Ibn Saud, who was anxious not to antagonize the British. Another point of contention between him and the Ikhwan was Ibn Saud's domestic program, which the Ikhwan said smacked of modernism. They also objected to an influx of non-Muslims into the kingdom. Fighting began in 1927 between the Ikhwan and forces loyal to Ibn Saud, and a two-year civil war ensued. The decisive engagement in the so-called Ikhwan Revolt was the Battle of Sabilla (March 29–31, 1929). Ibn Saud's forces were victorious, and the Ikhwan leaders were massacred. On September 23, 1932, Ibn Saud merged his two kingdoms of the Hejaz and Nejd to form the Kingdom of Saudi Arabia.

The ruling House of Saud has dominated Saudi Arabia for its entire modern history. Ibn Saud ruled the kingdom until his death on November 9, 1953, and all succeeding kings have been his sons, of which he had more than 50. The present ruler, Salman, is said to be Ibn Saud's 25th son.

Despite its vast size, however, Saudi Arabia was one of the world's poorest countries, apparently bereft of natural resources and dependent economically to a considerable extent on religious pilgrimages to its holy sites. That changed in 1938 with the discovery of significant oil deposits by the American-owned California-Arabian Standard Oil Co., which paid royalties for the right to extract and ship Saudi oil. The importance of oil during World War II enhanced the U.S.-Saudi relationship, and in 1944 the Arab-American Oil Corporation (ARAMCO) was formed.

President Franklin Roosevelt helped cement the growing relationship between the United States and Saudi Arabia when he met with Ibn Saud aboard the U.S. Navy cruiser *Quincy* in Egypt's Great Bitter Lake on February 14, 1945, the first time that the Saudi king had left his country. The Saudi monarchy has maintained close economic and strategic ties to the United States ever since, although that relationship has not always been a smooth one.

Because of the growing strategic importance of the Middle East and its oil reserves to geopolitics, during the Cold War (1945–1991) both the United States and the Soviet Union sought increased influence in the region. The Soviets endorsed the rise of secular, socialist Arab nationalist regimes in Egypt, Iraq, and Syria, and Soviet military assistance was crucial to these nations in their ongoing struggle with the State of Israel after its establishment in 1948. The United States tightened its ties to the royal regimes in Iran and Saudi Arabia.

In September 1962 civil war broke out in the Kingdom of Yemen (North Yemen) and came to involve Saudi Arabia. On the death of Imam Ahmed on September 19, Crown Prince Seif al-Islam Mohammed al-Badr assumed the throne of the Kingdom of Yemen. However, a republican revolt began on September 27 in the capital city of Sana'a (Sanaa, Sana) when rebels headed by Colonel Abdullah al-Sallal proclaimed the establishment of the "Free Yemen Republic" and easily seized key locations in Sana'a and moved against Al-Bashaer Palace, capturing it the next day. Meanwhile, an insurgency was ongoing in South Yemen, which remained under British rule until 1967.

Al-Badr escaped into far northern Yemen, where he received the support of royalist tribes and also the Saudi monarchy. President Gamal Abdel Nasser of Egypt meanwhile decided to back al-Sallal, even sending Egyptian forces. Indeed, by late 1965 there were some 55,000 Egyptian troops in North Yemen. Saudi Arabian leaders were greatly angered by Nasser's move, seeing this as a direct challenge to their influence. By the mid-1960s, the royalists also secured the help of Iraq, Jordan, Pakistan, Iran, and Britain as well as covert assistance from Israel, while the Soviet Union and several other communist bloc nations supported the republican side. The conflict thus became politicized along Cold War lines, with the United States, the United Kingdom, and other Western powers siding with the royalists. Attempts by the United Nations (UN) to bring about an end to the fighting were unsuccessful.

The Egyptian forces initially performed poorly, and in January 1964 the royalists laid siege to Sana'a. When the Egyptians staged air strikes on Najran and Jizan, staging areas within Saudi Arabia for the royalist forces, this almost led to war between the two countries. U.S. president John F. Kennedy supplied air defense systems to Saudi Arabia and also dispatched U.S. aircraft to Dhahran Airbase, demonstrating the American commitment to defend Saudi Arabia.

The war becomes a stalemated guerrilla conflict and a huge drain on the Egyptian treasury and military. Indeed, the presence in Yemen of so many trained troops and so much equipment certainly impacted the June 1967 Six-Day War. Egypt's ignominious defeat in that conflict forced Nasser to begin withdrawing his troops from Yemen. That same year the British withdrew from South Yemen. By 1969, both sides in the struggle agreed that the first step to ending the war was the withdrawal of all foreign troops from Yemeni territory. On April 14, 1970, Saudi Arabia recognized the republican government of Yemen in return for the inclusion of royalists in several key government posts.

The Israeli issue greatly complicated U.S.-Saudi relations. The Saudis strongly objected to the 1948 formation of Israel and opposed the displacement of Palestinian Arabs. Although the Saudis played only a minor military role in the Israeli War of Independence (1948–1949), they contributed significant funds to Palestinian causes. Indeed, Saudi Arabia became a primary source of economic aid for the Palestine Liberation Organization (PLO). While PLO support for Iraqi president Saddam Hussein during the Persian Gulf War of 1991 effectively curtailed Saudi financial support, the Saudis continued to insist on a comprehensive peace settlement that would include the right of return for Palestinian refugees.

Despite its opposition to Israel, the Saudi government maintained only perfunctory relations with Arab nationalist regimes in Syria, Egypt, Iraq, and Jordan, Israel's principal enemies. Thus, Saudi Arabia did not participate in the Arab-Israeli wars of 1956, 1967, and 1973. As American support for Israel increased after the 1967 war, however, the Saudis sought to influence American policy, and the Arab-Israeli confrontation laid the foundation for the 1973 oil embargo.

Saudi oil was largely controlled by American oil companies until the early 1970s, when the House of Saud negotiated the gradual takeover of ARAMCO by Saudi interests. This transfer of control had begun by 1973. When Egypt and Syria attacked Israel in October 1973, prompting the Yom Kippur War, Saudi Arabia's King Faisal obtained U.S. president Richard Nixon's assurances of American nonintervention. The Israelis suffered severe reversals in the opening stages of the conflict, however, prompting Nixon to send U.S. military assistance to Israel beginning on October 19. The next day, working through the Organization of Petroleum Exporting Countries (OPEC), the Saudi government implemented an oil embargo directed at the United States. This severely impacted the U.S. economy, with prices at the pump rising 40 percent during the five months of the crisis. Even after the embargo ended, oil prices remained high for the rest of the decade.

During his reign as king of Saudi Arabia from 1964 to 1975, Faisal ibn Abd al-Aziz al-Saud raised his country from near feudal status to a modern society that still strongly adhered to Islamic teachings. (Library of Congress)

Saudi Arabia emerged from the crisis as the clear leader of OPEC and with renewed respect in the Arab world. Massive increases in oil revenues (from $5 billion in 1972 to $119 billion in 1981) helped transform Saudi Arabia into an affluent, urbanized society with generous government subsidies and programs for its citizens and no taxation. The U.S.-Saudi relationship eventually recovered and remained close; indeed, Saudi Arabia often used its influence in OPEC to keep oil prices artificially low during from the mid-1980s to late 1990s.

Such policies, however, had a downside. When oil prices dipped dramatically during 1981–1985, the Saudi economy plunged into recession, presenting the government with significant domestic unrest. A similar scenario was played out in the late 1990s. This time the Saudis acted aggressively, hiking oil prices in 2000 and 2001 to right their foundering economy. An effort begun by the Saudis in November 2014 to keep production high and thereby sharply lower prices, with one aim being to drive the U.S. oil companies into bankruptcy, has thus far not been successful.

Despite the considerable power the Saudis wielded in international relations beginning in the 1970s and the tremendous increase in wealth as a result of oil revenues, the House of Saud maintained strict control over Saudi society, culture, and law. Opposition emerged to King Faisal, however, particularly from conservatives. On March 25, 1975, Faisal was assassinated by his nephew, the stated reason being revenge for the death of his brother who had been killed by Saudi Defense Force members during a demonstration in 1965. Faisal was succeeded by his half brother, Khalid bin Abdulaziz al-Saud.

On November 20, 1979, Juhayman al-Otaybi, a member of an influential Najd family, led hundreds of followers, many of them theology students at the Islamic University in Medina, to seize control of the Grand Mosque in Mecca. Al-Otaybi declared his brother-in-law Mohammed Abdullah al-Qahtani to be the Mahdi, or redeemer, whom Muslims believe will arrive on Earth several years before Judgment Day. This event triggered a full-scale political crisis. Fighting lasted until December 4, when the mosque was finally secured. The military suffered 127 dead and 451 injured, while the insurgents lost 117 killed and suffered an unknown number of wounded. On January 9, 1980, 63 of the rebels were publicly beheaded in the squares of eight different Saudi cities.

The Saudis continued to oppose Israel's treatment of the Palestinians and its continued presence in the occupied territories. Saudi relations with Egypt also declined precipitously after the 1978 signing of the Camp David Accords between Israel and Egypt. The Saudis objected to any individual peace deals with Israel that did not settle the entire Arab-Israeli conflict and address the plight of the Palestinian Arabs and the refugees of the 1948–1949 war.

On August 7, 1981, Crown Prince Fahd presented an eight-point proposal to resolve the Arab-Israeli conflict and give the Palestinians an independent state. Loosely based on UN Resolutions 242 and 338, the plan called for recognition of Israel but with Israel to withdraw from territories captured in 1967, including East Jerusalem (but not the whole city). Israel was also to dismantle its settlements, recognize the PLO as the representative of the Palestinian people, and agree to the establishment of an independent Palestinian state with Jerusalem as its capital. There were also to be secure guarantees of peace. Fahd's plan was not popular at home with the Saudi intelligentsia, middle class, and clergy, who were strongly critical of any proposal that recognized Israel. At the Twelfth Arab Summit Conference, held in Fez, Morocco, on September 9, 1982, however, the Arab League adopted a version of the Fahd plan, which became known as the Fez Initiative. It received a mixed reception in Arab capitals because it implicitly recognized Israel but found support among European countries, anxious to secure their oil supplies. At the time the United States was more interested in what became known as the Reagan Plan that kept Jordan in place as the sovereign in the West Bank. On April 26, 2002, during a trip to the United States, Saudi crown prince Abdullah presented an eight-point Mideast peace proposal to U.S. president George W. Bush. Similar to Fahd's 1981 proposal, it was rejected by the Israeli government.

Saudi Arabia strongly backed Iraq during the Iran-Iraq War (1980–1988), providing some $20 billion to help fund the Iraqi war effort. Thus, the Saudis were greatly angered when Iraqi president Saddam Hussein decided to invade and annex Kuwait beginning on August 2, 1990, especially as the Saudis had been trying to broker a deal between the two states. U.S. president George H. W. Bush immediately rushed forces to Saudi Arabia (Operation DESERT SHIELD) and took the lead in the formation of an international coalition to force Iraq to withdraw.

The Saudis took the highly unusual step of allowing foreign troops into their territory, from which the coalition invasion of Kuwait would be mounted. This decision, which led to the presence in the kingdom of some half million foreign troops—most of them Americans—was billed as a protective measure to keep Iraq from continuing its offensive into Saudi Arabia itself. It did, however, cause a negative reaction among influential ultraconservatives in Saudi Arabia, who claimed that the foreigners were defiling Islamic traditions and law and that this was thus a motivation behind the formation of the Al-Qaeda Islamic terrorist organization, headed by Saudi citizen Osama bin Laden.

Saudi Arabia was confirmed as a significant regional military force during the ensuing 1991 Persian Gulf War. Two Arab task forces were organized under the command of Saudi prince Khalid ibn Sultan al-Saud, with the Saudi ground commitment totaling nearly 50,000 men. The Saudis deployed some 270 tanks and 930 other armored fighting vehicles as well as artillery and more than 250 aircraft that flew 6,852 sorties. Saudi forces took part in the Battle of Khafji (January 29–February 1, 1991) and in the four-day ground war that began on February 24 and helped drive the Iraqis from Kuwait.

U.S.-Saudi relations suffered following the September 11, 2001, terrorist attacks on the United States, which involved 15 Saudi Arabian nationals or citizen. The Saudis, however, strongly disapproved of Operation IRAQI FREEDOM, the U.S.- and British-led invasion of Iraq that began in March 2003, and they refused to allow use of their territory as a base of operations for the invasion. The Saudis disapproved because of the likelihood of Iraqi fratricide following regime change and the advantage that a destabilized Iraq would create for Iran. However, many Saudis were also concerned that if the coalition forces pulled out too soon, Iraq would degenerate into full-scale civil war. Also, the U.S. engagement in Iraq provided a

The Battle of Khafji

Saudi Arabian and Qatari forces participated in the Battle of Khafji (January 29–31, 1991) during Persian Gulf War. Iraqi president Saddam Hussein had predicted the "mother of all battles," with coalition ground forces halted along the now heavily fortified Saudi-Kuwaiti border. With punishing coalition air strikes steadily degrading his ground strength, however, Hussein sought to initiate that ground war by ordering his commanders to attack across the border into Saudi Arabia. Only III Corps commander Lieutenant General Salah Abdul Mahmud complied, sending his forces against the lightly defended border towns of Khafji and Wafrah, the civilian inhabitants of which had been evacuated at the start of the war.

The Battle of Khafji, the first major ground confrontation of the war, initially was an Iraqi success but ended with the Iraqis being driven back by Saudi and Qatari troops, supported by U.S. troops, artillery, and airpower. The allies suffered 43 dead, 52 wounded, and 2 captured, while the Iraqis suffered some 60–100 killed and 400 taken prisoner. At least 50 Iraqi tanks were destroyed in Khafji itself, while heavy coalition air strikes to the north of Khafji may have inflicted more than 2,000 Iraqi casualties and destroyed 300 vehicles, constituting the majority of three Iraqi mechanized/armored divisions.

rationale for Saudis who opposed their government's alliance with America. Indeed, some joined the insurgents in Iraq. At the same time, an effort to close down U.S. military operations in the kingdom had been in progress for some time, and by August 2003 all remaining U.S. troops had been withdrawn.

During 2003–2005 a series of attacks by a hitherto unknown group calling itself Al-Qaeda fi Jazirat al-Arabiyya (Al-Qaeda in the Arabian Peninsula, AQAP) attacked and killed a number of Westerners. These included the bombing in May and November 2003 of housing compounds for foreign workers and an attack on the American consulate in Jeddah. Attacks and attempted sabotage by this group continued despite numerous arrests and the deaths of most of the AQAP leadership, a strong counterterrorism effort carried out by Saudi authorities, and a thorough reeducation program designed by the Saudi Ministry of the Interior. The Saudis also cooperated with numerous American requirements such as exerting control over Islamic charitable groups, addressing extremism in parts of the Islamic educational system, cutting off funding to the *mutawa'in* (morals police), and providing information to the international counterintelligence effort.

In January 2011 as revolution swept Egypt and sparked what became known as the Arab Spring, protests occurred in Jeddah. The demonstrations were quickly crushed, and a number of people were arrested. The following month, the Saudi government announced a major multibillion-dollar initiative designed to ameliorate living conditions for its poorer citizens. In March, the government rolled out a plan that would provide some 500,000 new housing units and create at least 60,000 new jobs. The plan was estimated to cost $93 billion. In a bid to further mollify Saudis, King Abdullah declared that women would be able to vote beginning in 2015 and would be eligible for positions on the Shura Council. This was seen as a major political reform measure in a profoundly conservative nation that had all but excluded women from public life.

On March 14, 2011, following massive prodemocracy demonstrations in neighboring Bahrain, Saudi Arabia acted on a request from that government and sent some 150 vehicles and 1,000 troops eastward into Bahrain via the long 12-mile causeway that connects the two states. The stated goal here was to protect Bahrain's government offices and end the demonstrations. While expressing concern, the U.S. government refused to condemn the Saudi move, which was regarded as a signal by Saudi leaders that concessions by the Bahrainian monarchy could empower Saudi Arabia's own Shia minority and benefit Iran.

The Sunni-Shia religious confrontation has come to impact much of Saudi foreign policy. Saudi Arabia has assumed the former Iraqi role of opposing the spread of Iranian influence in Lebanon, Syria, and Yemen. Thus, the Saudis have strongly supported opposition forces battling the Iranian-backed Syrian government of President Bashar al-Assad in the Syrian Civil War (2011–present), first with funds and then by early 2013 with small arms shipped through Jordan. Saudi demands that Assad resign brought the severing of diplomatic ties between the two states.

The Saudis have also viewed the rise of the Islamic State of Iraq and Syria (ISIS) with great concern. On September 23, 2014, Saudi aircraft joined those of the United States and some other Arab states in striking ISIS targets in Syria. In September 2014, Saudi Arabia reportedly encouraged air attacks against radical Islamists in Libya carried out by the United Arab Emirates, Qatar, and Egypt. Then in December 2015, the Saudi government announced the formation of a coalition of 34 predominately Muslim nations to fight terrorism, specifically referencing such activity in Syria, Iraq, the Sinai, Yemen, Libya, Mali, Nigeria, Pakistan, and Afghanistan. The new coalition's joint operations center is based in Riyadh.

Saudi Arabia also intervened more forcefully in the Yemen Civil War that had begun on March 19, 2015. With clear evidence that Iran had been arming the Shiite Muslims there, on March 26 Saudi Arabia and its Persian Gulf region allies launched air strikes in an effort to counter the Iran-allied Houthi rebel forces besieging the southern city of Aden. The Saudi military intervention in Yemen, primarily through airpower with attendant civilian casualties, continues.

On January 4, 2016, after rioters stormed the Saudi embassy in Tehran amid a row over the Saudi execution of prominent Shia Muslim cleric Sheikh Nimr al-Nimr and 46 others condemned for alleged terrorist activities, Saudi Arabia terminated diplomatic relations with Iran.

King Abdullah bin Abdulaziz al-Saud died at age 90 on January 22, 2015. He was succeeded by his 79-year-old brother, Salman bin Abdulaziz, whose brother Prince Muqrin, a decade younger, is the new crown prince. Salman has been both defense minister and deputy prime minister.

Saudi Arabia's crackdown on dissent and history of human rights abuses remains the subject of harsh criticism from Western nongovernmental organizations such as Amnesty International and Human Rights Watch. In April 2016, however, in a significant step Saudi Arabia stripped its religious forces of their powers to arrest, urging them to act "kindly and gently" in enforcing Islamic rules. Then in May, King Salman reshuffled the government and replaced a number of key cabinet ministers. With the price of oil at low levels and the regional order that Saudi Arabia had long supported now apparently in tatters, with civil war raging in Syria and Yemen, and with an intensified challenge from regional rival Iran, the king is seeking to reduce the kingdom's dependence on oil as a source of revenue while also improving the quality of life for the kingdom's citizens. The cabinet changes have included the reshuffling of the duties of the oil ministry and the replacement of its long-standing minister, Ali al-Naimi.

Timeline

ca. 571	Islamic prophet Muhammad is born in Mecca in Arabia. In the early 600s he secures control of both Mecca and Medina and creates a single Islamic religious state. Although his successors and their Arab armies aggressively expand the frontiers of Islam, Arabia's paucity of resources bring its eclipse as a center of Islamic power.
1500s	The Ottoman Empire secures control of the coastal areas on the Red Sea and the Persian Gulf (the Hejaz, Asir, and Al-Ahsa) and claims suzerainty over the Arabian interior.
1744	In central Arabia, Muhammad bin Saud, founder of the dynasty that continues to rule Saudi Arabia, forms an alliance with Muhammad ibn Abd al-Wahhab, founder of the Wahhabi movement (Wahhabism), a strict puritanical form of Sunni Islam.
1765–1803	Rule of Abdul-Aziz bin Muhammad bin Saud, son and successor of Muhammad bin Saud, who expands Al Saud control and comes to rule most of what today constitutes Saudi Arabia.
1818	Ottoman viceroy of Egypt Muhammad Ali Pasha invades and destroys the Al Saud "state."
1824	The Al Sauds establish a new state in Nejd. For the remainder of the century the Al Sauds duel with another ruling family, the Al Rashids, to see which will control the Arabian interior.
1891	The Al Rashids defeat the Al Sauds and force them into exile in Kuwait.
1902	Abdulaziz ibn Abdul Rahman ibn Faisal ibn Turki ibn Abdullah ibn Muhammad al-Saud (known in the Arab world as Abdulaziz and in the West as Ibn Saud) recaptures control of Riyadh.
1913	Assisted by the Ikhwan, a tribal army inspired by Wahhabism, Ibn Saud conquers from the Ottoman Empire Arabia's easternmost province of Al-Ahsa.

Oct 2, 1914	The Ottoman Empire enters World War I (1914–1918).
Dec 26, 1915	The British government signs the Treaty of Darin with Ibn Saud, securing his benevolent neutrality.
1920–1922	Having avoided participation in the Arab Revolt of 1916–1918 against the Ottoman Empire, Ibn Saud continues his struggle with the Al Rashids. Assisted by the British, he launches his campaign in 1920 and defeats the Al Rashids in 1922.
Nov 3, 1921	Ibn Saud takes the title of sultan of Nejd.
Aug 24, 1924	Assisted by the Ikhwan, Ibn Saud invades the Hejaz.
Oct 3, 1924	Hussein, sharif of Mecca, abdicates.
Oct 14, 1924	Ibn Saud takes the surrender of Mecca.
Dec 23, 1924	Ibn Saud's forces capture Jidda.
Jan 8, 1926	Ibn Saud declares himself king of the Hejaz. A year later, he adds the title "King of Nejd," although both kingdoms are administered separately.
1927–1929	The Ikhwan Revolt occurs when the leaders of the Ikhwan turn against Ibn Saud.
Mar 29–31, 1929	Ibn Saud's forces defeat the Ikhwan in the decisive Battle of Sabilla, massacring the Ikhwan leaders.
Sep 23, 1932	Ibn Saud merges the two kingdoms of the Hejaz and Nejd to form the Kingdom of Saudi Arabia.
1938	Significant deposits of oil are discovered in Saudi Arabia by the American-owned California-Arabian Standard Oil Co.
1944	The Arab-American Oil Corporation (ARAMCO) is formed.
Feb 14, 1945	U.S. president Franklin Roosevelt meets with Ibn Saud aboard the U.S. Navy cruiser *Quincy* in Egypt's Great Bitter Lake. The Saudi monarchy has maintained close economic and strategic ties with the United States ever since.
Nov 9, 1953	King Ibn Saud dies. He is succeeded by his son, Saud bin Abdulaziz al-Saud. All kings of Saudi Arabia to the present have been Ibn Saud's sons, of whom he had more than 50.
Sep 27, 1962	Civil war breaks out in the neighboring Kingdom of Yemen (North Yemen), and the Saudis actively support the monarchists against the republican faction backed by Saudi Arabia. Saudi Arabia comes close to war with Egypt before the civil war is brought to an end in 1970.
Nov 2, 1964	King Saud dies. He is succeeded by Faisal bin Abdulaziz al-Saud.

Oct 20, 1973	Despite a pledge to the Saudis that the United States would remain neutral, on October 19, 1973, President Richard Nixon extends military aid to the Israelis, who are hard-pressed by the surprise Egyptian-Syrian attack of the Yom Kippur War. The next day, with the Saudi government having already commenced the takeover of ARAMCO, King Faisal works through the Organization of Petroleum Exporting Countries (OPEC) to implement an oil embargo directed at the United States. This five-month-long action has a severe negative impact on the American economy. Saudi Arabia emerges from the crisis as the clear leader of OPEC and with renewed respect in the Arab world.
Mar 25, 1975	King Faisal is assassinated by his nephew and is succeeded as king by his half brother, Khalid bin Abdulaziz al-Saud.
Nov 20–Dec 4, 1979	Juhayman al-Otaybi leads some 300–600 followers to seize control of the Grand Mosque in Mecca. Al-Otaybi declares his brother-in-law, Mohammed Abdullah al-Qahtani, to be the Mahdi, or redeemer, whom Muslims believe will arrive on Earth several years before Judgment Day. Saudi security forces and the military do not recover control of the mosque until December 4. The military suffers 127 dead and 451 injured, while the insurgents lose 117 killed and an unknown number wounded. During 1980–1988 Saudi Arabia provides strong support to Iraq during the Iran-Iraq War, giving it some $20 billion.
Jan 9, 1980	Sixty-three rebels are publicly beheaded in the squares of eight different Saudi cities.
Aug 7, 1981	Saudi crown prince Fahd proposes an eight-point peace plan to resolve the Arab-Israeli conflict and give the Palestinians an independent state. The plan receives a mixed reception in Arab capitals because it implicitly recognizes Israel but finds support in the West. Israel is to withdraw from 1967-captured territories, including East Jerusalem (but not the whole city), dismantle the Jewish settlements, recognize the Palestine Liberation Organization (PLO) as the Palestinian representative, establish an independent Palestinian state with Jerusalem as its capital, and secure guarantees of peace. Fahd's plan is not popular at home with much of the population because of its recognition of Israel.
Jun 13, 1982	King Khalid bin Abdulaziz al-Saud dies and is succeeded by King Fahd bin Abdulaziz al-Saud.
Sep 9, 1982	At the Twelfth Arab Summit Conference in Fez, Morocco, the League of Arab States adopts a version of the Fahd plan, which becomes known as the Fez Initiative.

Aug 2, 1990	Iraqi forces invade Kuwait and within a few days annex it. This poses a direct threat to Saudi Arabia. U.S. president George H. W. Bush rushes forces to Saudi Arabia (Operation DESERT SHIELD) and takes the lead in the formation of an international coalition to force Iraq to withdraw. The Saudis take the highly unusual step of allowing a half million foreign troops into their territory. Billed as a protective measure to keep Iraq from continuing its offensive into Saudi Arabia itself, it produces a negative reaction among influential ultraconservatives in Saudi Arabia who claim that the foreigners are defiling Islamic traditions and law and proves to be a motivation for the formation of the Al-Qaeda Islamic terrorist organization headed by Saudi citizen Osama bin Laden. Saudi Arabia will also underwrite much of the cost of the coalition military effort to drive the Iraqis from Kuwait.
Jan 17–Feb 28, 1991	Saudi Arabia contributes considerable military assets of its own during the Persian Gulf War of these dates. Saudi prince Khalid ibn Sultan al-Saud commands two Arab task forces, and Saudi ground forces total nearly 50,000 men. The Saudis also deploy some 270 tanks, 930 other armored fighting vehicles, artillery, and more than 250 aircraft.
Jan 29–Feb 1, 1991	Saudi forces take part in the Battle of Khafji (January 29–February 1, 1991) and then help drive the Iraqis from Kuwait on the commencement of the coalition ground campaign from February 24.
Jan 1, 1993	Publication of the Saudi Basic Law for governance of the kingdom.
Sep 11, 2001	Fifteen of the 19 members of the Al-Qaeda Islamic terrorist organization who carry out the attacks in the United States this day, which kill nearly 3,000 people, are Saudi Arabian nationals or citizens. U.S.-Saudi relations suffer as a result, even though the Saudi government decries the terrorist actions.
Apr 26, 2002	During a trip to the United States, Saudi crown prince Abdullah presents an eight-point Mideast peace proposal to U.S. president George W. Bush. Very similar to Crown Prince Fahd's 1981 proposal, it is rejected by the Israeli government.
Mar 2003	The Saudis strongly oppose Operation IRAQI FREEDOM, the U.S.- and British-led invasion of Iraq, and refuse to allow use of their territory as a base of operations for the invasion. This provides justification for an ongoing effort to close down U.S. military operations, and in August 2003 all remaining U.S. troops are withdrawn.
May 2003–2005	Al-Qaeda in the Arabian Peninsula (Al-Qaeda fi Jazirat al-Arabiyya, AQAP), an Islamic extremist group led by Yusuf Salah

Fahd al-Uyayri (Ayiri) that seeks to overthrow the Saudi monarchy, mounts a series of attacks aimed at foreigners residing in the kingdom. On May 12, 2003, AQAP carries out three simultaneous suicide vehicle bombings at the al-Hamra, Vinnell, and Jedewahl housing compounds used by foreigners (mainly Westerners) in Riyadh, killing 35 people, including 9 of the terrorists, and wounding 200 others. On November 8, AQAP attacks the al-Muhayya housing complex in Riyadh, killing 18 people and wounding scores of others.

The group continues to launch attacks on Saudi and foreign targets, including a Riyadh government building on April 21, 2004, and an oil company office in Yanbu on May 1, which results in the killing of 5 Western workers. AQAP also kills a number of foreigners in single attacks, the most widely publicized of which is the June 12, 2004, kidnapping of Paul M. Johnson Jr., an American employee of U.S. defense contractor Lockheed Martin. When Saudi authorities reject AQAP's demand for the release of all detainees held by Saudi authorities, which is denied, on June 18 AQAP beheads Johnson, filming the deed and then releasing the video on websites. Meanwhile, on May 29 the group succeeds again in carrying out attacks on three targets in the city of al-Khobar, taking hostages in oil business offices and housing complexes. Saudi police and soldiers storm the buildings the next day, but 22 of the hostages are killed. Shortly after this attack, the U.S. Department of State issues a statement that urges U.S. citizens to leave the kingdom. The year is capped off with a spectacular attack on December 6 on the U.S. consulate in Jeddah in which 5 consulate employees, 4 Saudi national guardsmen, and 3 AQAP members are killed.

Saudi security forces arrest hundreds of people and engage in shootouts with the AQAP members, killing a number of them including most of the leaders.

Aug 1, 2005   King Fahd bin Abdulaziz al-Saud dies and is succeeded by Abdullah bin Abdulaziz al-Saud. A cautious reformer, he introduces somewhat broader freedoms in this very conservative kingdom and also invests considerable sums from the nation's vast oil wealth in large-scale education and infrastructure projects.

Jan 2011   As revolution sweeps through much of the Middle East (the so-called Arab Spring), protests occur in Jeddah but are quickly crushed, with as many as 50 people arrested.

Feb 2011   In an attempt to circumvent the unrest taking part in other Arab nations, the Saudi government announces a major multibillion-dollar initiative designed to ameliorate living conditions for poorer

Saudis and the next month rolls out a plan to provide some 500,000 new housing units and create at least 60,000 new jobs. King Abdullah also announces that beginning in 2015 women will be able to vote and will be eligible for positions on the Shura Council.

Mar 14, 2011   Acting on a request from the Bahraini government, Saudi Arabia sends some 150 vehicles and 1,000 troops into Bahrain via the 12-mile causeway that connects the two states. The stated goal is to protect government offices and end the massive demonstrations there. The Saudis are clearly worried that concessions by the Bahrainian monarchy could empower Saudi Arabia's own Shia minority and benefit Iran. Indeed, the Sunni-Shia confrontation drives much of Saudi policy.

Jan 2013   Reports surface that Saudi Arabia is shipping arms through Jordan to the opposition forces in the Syrian Civil War (2011–present), first with funds and then by early 2013 with small arms shipped through Jordan. Saudi demands that Assad must resign bring the severing of diplomatic ties between the two states.

Sep 23, 2014   Saudi aircraft join those of the United States and some other Arab states in striking Islamic State of Iraq and Syria (ISIS) targets in Syria.

Jan 22, 2015   King Abdullah bin Abdulaziz al-Saud dies at age 90 and is succeeded by his brother, 79-year-old King Salman bin Abdulaziz al-Saud, who had been both defense minister and deputy prime minister.

Mar 26, 2015   Saudi Arabia intervenes in the Yemen Civil War that began on March 19. With clear evidence that Iran has been arming the Houthi Shiite insurgents, Saudi Arabia and its Persian Gulf region allies begin air strikes in an effort to counter Houthi rebel forces besieging the southern city of Aden. The Saudi military intervention in Yemen, primarily through airpower, continues.

Dec 15, 2015   The Saudi government announces the formation of a coalition of 34 predominately Muslim nations to fight terrorism. In making the announcement, Saudi deputy crown prince and defense minister Mohammed bin Salman specifically references terrorism in Syria, Iraq, the Sinai, Yemen, Libya, Mali, Nigeria, Pakistan, and Afghanistan. The new coalition's joint operations center will be based in Riyadh.

Jan 4, 2016   After rioters stormed the Saudi embassy in Tehran amid a row over the Saudi execution of prominent Shia Muslim cleric Sheikh Nimr al-Nimr and 46 others condemned for alleged terrorist activities, Saudi Arabia terminates diplomatic relations with Iran.

Further Reading

Aarts, Paul, and Carolien Roelants. *Saudi Arabia: A Kingdom in Peril*. New York: Hurst, 2015.

Cooper, Andrew Scott. *The Oil Kings: How the U.S., Iran, and Saudi Arabia Changed the Balance of Power in the Middle East*. New York: Simon and Schuster, 2011.

Darlow, Michael, and Barabara Bray. *Ibn Saud: The Desert Warrior Who Created the Kingdom of Saudi Arabia*. New York: Skyhorse Publishing, 2009.

Hourani, Albert. A *History of the Arab Peoples*. Cambridge, MA: Harvard University Press, 1991.

House, Karen Elliott. *On Saudi Arabia: Its People, Past, Religion, Fault Lines-and Future*. New York: Vintage, 2012.

Lacey, Robert. *Inside the Kingdom: Kings, Clerics, Modernists, Terrorists, and the Struggle for Saudi Arabia*. New York: Penguin, 2009.

Lacey, Robert. *The Kingdom*. New York: Harcourt Brace Jovanovich, 1982.

Lewis, Bernard. *The Middle East*. New York: Scribner, 1997.

Wynbrandt, James. *A Brief History of Saudi Arabia*. New York: Checkmark, 2004.

Zuhur, Sherifa. *Saudi Arabia: Islamic Threat, Political Reform and the Global War on Terror*. Carlisle Barracks, PA: Strategic Studies, 2005.

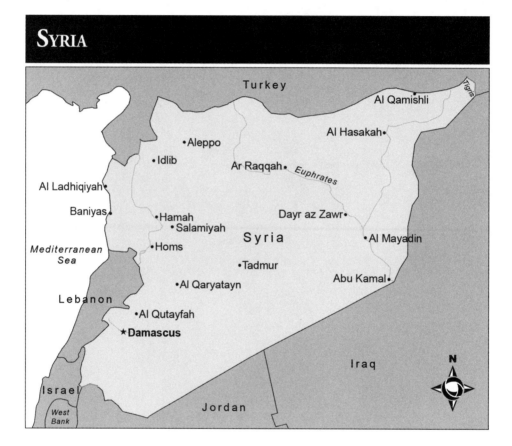

SYRIA

Turkey

Tigris

Al Qamishli

Al Hasakah

Aleppo

Idlib

Ar Raqqah

Euphrates

Al Ladhiqiyah

Baniyas

Hamah

Salamiyah

Syria

Dayr az Zawr

Mediterranean
Sea

Homs

Al Mayadin

Tadmur

Al Qaryatayn

Abu Kamal

Lebanon

Al Qutayfah

Damascus

Iraq

N

Israel

West
Bank

Jordan

Syria

*Larissa Mihalisko, Paul G. Pierpaoli Jr.,
and Spencer C. Tucker*

The Syrian Arab Republic borders on Jordan and Israel to the south, Lebanon and the Mediterranean Sea to the west, Turkey to the north, and Iraq to the east. Occupying 71,479 square miles, Syria is thus slightly larger than the U.S. state of North Dakota. Syria's 2016 population was some 18.564 million. Its capital of Damascus is one of the world's oldest cities. Syrian Arabs and some 600,000 Palestinian Arabs constitute some 74 percent of the population. Kurds, most of whom live in northeastern Syria, are about 10 percent of the population, or some 1.6 million people. Smaller Syrian ethnic groups include Turkmen, Circassians, Greeks, and Armenians (most of whom arrived there during Worlds War I). Syria was once home to a large number of Jews, but most emigrated either to Europe or Latin America and then to the new State of Israel. Today only a few Jews remain. Sunni Muslims number about 74 percent of the population, while some 13 percent are Shias (Alawites, Twelvers, and Ismailis). Christians make up 10 percent, with the majority bring orthodox. Some 3 percent are Druzes. Despite their minority status, Alawites dominate the Syrian power structure. President Bashar al-Assad is an Alawite, as are other leading figures in the government and military.

Syria is home to one of the world's oldest civilizations, preceded perhaps only by those of Mesopotamia. The Kingdom of Ebla was founded in northern Syria around 3500 BCE. A succession of empires and kingdoms followed: Akkadian, Old Babylonian, Old Assyrian, Yamhad, Hittite, and Egyptian. From the 12th century BCE, Canaanites known as Phoenicians dominated the eastern Mediterranean coast. They established colonies through the Mediterranean, including Carthage. Syria was then part of the Neo-Assyrian Empire, followed by the Neo-Babylonian Empire. The Achaemenid Persian Empire held sway until conquered by King Alexander III (the Great) of Macedon. After his death, it became part of the Seleucid Empire. The Greeks introduced the name "Syria" for the region, basing it on "Assyria."

Syria briefly came under Armenian control but was conquered by the Roman Empire in 64 BCE. The division of the Roman Empire in 295 CE saw Syria become part of the Eastern Roman (Byzantine) Empire. The Arabs conquered Syria by 640, and the Umayyad dynasty made Damascus it capital (the Abbasid dynasty moved the capital to Baghdad in 750). Arabic became the dominant language. Syria passed under Muslim Egyptian control in 887. During the Crusades of 1096–1291 a number of Christian city-states were established on the eastern Mediterranean, the most important of these being Antioch. After rule by the Seljuk Turks, Syria was conquered in the late 12th century by the Kurdish warlord Saladin, founder of the Ayyubid dynasty in Egypt. The Mongols invaded in 1260 but were defeated by Mamluks from Egypt. In 1400, Muslim conqueror Timur (Tamerlane) invaded, sacked Aleppo, and took Damascus.

In 1516 Ottoman Empire forces invaded the Mamluk Sultanate of Egypt, conquered Syria, and incorporated it into their empire. Ottoman rule lasted until the end of World War I. The Ottoman leaders had chosen to join the war on the side of the Central Powers, and defeat brought an end to the empire, which shrank to Anatolia and a small bit of Europe. During the war the Armenians had rebelled, seeking independence. This forced the Ottoman government to divert troops there from major campaigns elsewhere, and in an effort to stabilize the situation, the government forcibly relocated the Armenians to Deir ex-Zor in the Syrian Desert. Inadequate water, food, clothing, and medical supplies brought the deaths of as many as 1.2 million Armenians in the forced march, which has been called the Armenian Massacre and, controversially, the Armenian Genocide.

During the war, in 1916 French diplomat François Georges-Picot and Briton Mark Sykes reached a secret agreement on behalf of their governments to divide much of the Ottoman Empire into spheres of influence. With their borders arbitrarily drawn by Britain and France, four new states were created in Syria and Lebanon (to be controlled by the French) and Iraq and Palestine (to pass under British control).

On March 8, 1920, Faisal bin Hussein of the Hashemites as Faisal I established a short-lived independent Kingdom of Syria. He had led the Arab Revolt against the Ottomans during World War I and been promised establishment of an Arab kingdom by the British. His reign lasted only until July 24, when the French Army of the Levant defeated his forces in the Battle of Maysalun. French troops then occupied Syria. Syria and Lebanon were officially recognized as French mandates by the League of Nations in 1923.

In 1925 a prominent Arab Druze, Sultan al-Atrash, led a revolt that spread to include all of Syria and parts of Lebanon. Al-Atrash's forces won several battles against the French, with the most notable being at al-Kafr (July 21, 1925) and al-Mazraa (August 2–3, 1925). France dispatched troops from Morocco and Senegal, but the revolt simmered on until the spring of 1927. Although captured and sentenced to death, al-Atrash escaped to Transjordan and was eventually pardoned. He returned to Syria in 1937.

In 1934 the French government proposed independence for Syria under an arrangement beneficial to France. Strong opposition to this was organized in Syria by nationalist leader Hashim al-Atassi. In September 1936 in Paris, Syria and France negotiated a new treaty. It called for immediate recognition of Syrian independence as a sovereign republic but with full emancipation to occur during a 25-year period. The previously autonomous Druze and Alawite regions were to be incorporated into Syria, but not so with Lebanon, with which the French signed a similar treaty in November. The treaty with Syria pledged curtailment of French intervention in Syrian domestic affairs as well as a reduction in the number of French troops and military bases. For its part, Syria pledged to support France in times of war, including the use of its airspace, and allowed France to retain two military bases. There were also political, economic, and cultural provisions. Atassi was elected president of Syria in November.

The treaty was stillborn, because faced with the threat to French security posed by Germany under Adolf Hitler, the French Legislature refused to ratify it. In 1940 during World War II Germany defeated France, and Syria passed under the control of the Vichy French government.

A pro-Axis coup against the British in Iraq in April 1941 led to fighting between British forces and the Iraqi military and caused Berlin to demand from the Vichy government the right to ship arms and supplies through Damascus to Iraq. The Vichy government acquiesced, and French high commissioner to Syria Henri Dentz granted German and Italian aircraft landing rights in Syria for Axis aircraft on their way to Iraq.

The British government responded with an invasion of Syria and Lebanon in June 1941 by British, Australian, and Free French forces as well as the Transjordan Arab Legion. By mid-July the Allies fully controlled both Syria and Lebanon. Syria was then turned over to the Free French authorities. Although they recognized Syrian independence, the French continued to occupy the country and declared martial law, imposed strict press censorship, and arrested political subversives.

In July 1943 under pressure from its allies, the Free French government-in-exile announced new Syrian elections. A nationalist government came to power that August, electing Syrian nationalist Shukri al-Quwatli as president. France granted Syria independence on January 1, 1944, but the country remained under Allied occupation for the rest of the war. On February 26, 1945, Syria declared war on the Axis powers and became a member of the United Nations (UN) the next month.

In early May 1945 anti-French demonstrations erupted throughout Syria, whereupon French forces bombarded Damascus, killing some 400 people before the British intervened. A UN resolution in February 1946 called on France to evacuate the country, and by mid-April all French and British forces had departed Syrian soil. Evacuation Day, April 17, is celebrated as a Syrian national holiday.

Syria was a cofounder of the Arab League on March 22, 1945. The league advocated Pan-Arab nationalism but without the consolidation of states and the resultant problems that would have ensued. The Arab League was also aimed at blocking the creation of a Jewish state in Palestine, which the Syrian government strongly opposed.

Syria played a relatively small role in the failed Israeli War of Independence (1948–1949) that arose from the creation of the State of Israel in May 1948. At the beginning of the fighting Syria had only some 4,500 troops to commit, almost all of whom were dispatched to the Syrian-Palestinian border. These were repelled with heavy casualties early in the fighting. Quwatli was widely blamed for the setback and reacted by firing his defense minister and chief of staff. As time progressed, Syrian troops enjoyed some modest success but then remained rather quiescent for the remainder of the war.

The Israeli victory and disagreements regarding a possible Syrian union with Iraq torpedoed Quwatli's government. He was overthrown in a bloodless military coup on March 29, 1949, by former chief of staff Husni al-Za'im. Quwatli was briefly imprisoned and then was allowed to go into exile in Egypt. This first Syrian military coup shattered that country's democratic rule and set off military revolts. Two more coups quickly followed.

On August 14, 1949, Za'im was himself overthrown in a coup headed by Colonel Sami al-Hinnawi that included Lieutenant Colonel Adib al-Shishakli. After the coup, Hinnawi ordered Za'im and Prime Minister Muhsin al-Barazi executed. Hinnawi was the titular head of the military junta ruling Syria, but Shishakli was its strongman and on December 19, 1949, mounted the third coup of that year. Shishakli governed with a heavy hand until 1954.

Growing discontent eventually led to another coup on February 24, 1954, in which Shishakli was overthrown. The plotters included members of the Syrian Communist Party, Druze officers, and members of the Baath Party. Shishakli resigned rather than risk civil war and fled abroad.

The period 1954–1958 in Syria was marked by party politics and weak national governments. Late in 1954 elections were held to install a civilian government. In the end, a coalition of the People's Party, the National Party, and the Baath Party emerged, with National Party chief Sabri al-Asali as its head. The coalition was a shaky one. In succeeding years the Baathists, who combined Arab nationalism with socialist economic policies, became the most powerful political force in Syria.

In October 1955 Syria signed a defense pact with Gamal Abdel Nasser's Egypt, and Syria followed Egypt's lead in cultivating relations with the Soviet bloc, including arms purchases. On February 1, 1958, Syria and Egypt joined to form the United Arab Republic (UAR) as a step toward realizing Nasser's dream of one large Pan-Arab state. Many Syrians had assumed that this would be a federation of equals, but Egypt completely dominated, imposing Nasser's centralized socialistic political and economical system on a weaker Syria. A strong backlash from Syrian business interests and the military resulted in yet another coup on September 28, 1961, and the end of the UAR.

The new coup saw the establishment of the Syrian Arab Republic. Elections on December 1, 1961, for a new National Assembly resulted in the selection of Nazzim al-Qudsi as president. Another army coup occurred on March 28, 1962; although Qudsi was retained as president, there were other personnel changes. On September 13, 1962, Khalid al-Azm became prime minister. He quickly dissolved the parliament and announced that he would govern by decree until new elections in one year.

Yet another military coup on March 8, 1963, brought a new government, largely controlled by the Baath Party. It nationalized most industrial and large commercial concerns and engaged in land reforms, redistributing land to the peasants. One significant development was the decline in political influence of the Syrian Sunni Muslim majority and dominance of the Alawite minority.

A schism in the Baath Party resulted in more instability, and on February 26, 1966, the radical wing of the party staged yet another coup and removed the military government of Salah al-Din al-Bitar. There was some fighting, and the coup claimed perhaps 400 lives. The victorious faction was principally Alawite Muslim. The two key figures in the coup were Salah Jadid and Hafez al-Assad. The new regime tightened Syria's ties with both the Soviets and Egyptians.

Syria fought Israel again in the June 1967 Six-Day War, with disastrous consequences. This time, Syria's defeat included the loss of the Golan Heights to the Israelis. The outcome of the war eviscerated the ruling government, and when Syrian forces had to pull back after attempting to aid the Palestinians in Jordan during Black September (1970), the scene was set for yet another change of government. On November 13, 1970, General Assad, now Syrian minister of defense, seized power in a bloodless coup. Assad referred to this as the "Corrective Revolution," which essentially ousted from power civilian Baathists in favor of the military Baathists. An ardent Baath nationalist himself, Assad sought to strengthen ties to other Arab states, de-emphasize Syrian reliance on the Soviet Union, and defeat Israel.

In early 1971 Assad was elected president and immediately began to consolidate his power. He would rule the country until his death in 2000. He modernized and greatly enlarged the Syrian Army (it went from about 50,000 men in 1968 to 500,000 men in 1986). To fortify his own power, he saw to it to that only trusted figures were in command positions, and he also greatly increased the security apparatus, composed primarily of Alawites. He engaged in modest economic reforms, with the state playing a central role in economic planning and implementation. Assad's tactics could be brutal, and there was little room for dissent or democracy.

Syria joined with Egypt in the 1973 October Yom Kippur (Ramadan) War with Israel. At the beginning of the fighting, Syria launched a massive ground attack that included 1,500 tanks (900 in the initial attack and 600 in reserve) and 144 batteries of artillery in an attempt to retake the Golan Heights. After some initial success and although Syrian forces this time fought quite well, the Israelis rallied and drove the attackers back beyond their original positions. Syria did regain control over a small portion of the Golan Heights as a result of negotiations after the war.

In the late 1970s and 1980s, Sunni Muslim fundamentalists began challenging the Baath Party's secular outlook. From 1976 to 1982, urban areas all across Syria became hotbeds of political unrest. Assad brutally crushed a February 1982 uprising by the Muslim Brotherhood in Hama. Large parts of the old city were destroyed. Estimates of the dead, including 1,000 soldiers, range from 10,000 to 40,000, with 20,000 being a likely figure.

Assad also sent his army into Lebanon in June 1976, ostensibly as a peacekeeping force during the civil war there that had broken out the year before. The troops stayed on, however, with Assad siding with the Muslims who were fighting Christian militias. By the mid-1980s, Syrian forces had become the preponderant political and military force in Lebanon. Although the Lebanese Civil War was declared to have ended in 1990, Syrian troops were not withdrawn from Lebanon until April 2005. As a result of the long Syrian presence in Lebanon, nearly 1 million Syrians moved into Lebanon to seek work. In 1994 the Lebanese government granted citizenship to 250,000 Syrians, a move that for obvious reasons was controversial among the Lebanese people.

On June 6, 1982, substantial Israeli forces began an invasion of southern Lebanon to attack Palestine Liberation Organization (PLO) forces that had been striking northern Israel from Lebanon. There was also heavy fighting between the Israelis and Syrian forces in and over the Begaa Valley, in which Israel downed a substantial number of Syrian aircraft before a cease-fire took hold between Israel and Syria on June 11.

At the same time, the 1980s saw the Assad regime taking harder-line Arab positions and moving closer to the Soviets, accompanied by massive arms purchases. Assad's get-tough approach in regional politics included the funding and encouragement of terrorism, both in the Middle East and internationally. He openly supported the radical Kurdish Workers' Party in its insurgency against the Turkish government. When some 10,000 Turkish troops massed on the Syrian border, however, on October 21, 1998, Assad agreed to halt all Syrian aid to the rebels.

Assad, always a pragmatist, sought to ameliorate relations with the West as the Soviet Union imploded in 1990. When Iraq invaded Kuwait in August 1990, Assad was the first Arab leader to denounce the attack. Syria provided 20,000 troops to the international coalition that defeated Iraqi forces in the 1991 Persian Gulf War. Assad's frontline position in the war reflected both his desire to strengthen relations with the West and his strong dislike of Iraqi dictator Saddam Hussein. Although Hussein was a Baathist at least in name, Assad saw himself as the predominant leader in the region.

In 1991, Assad's government entered into peace negotiations with Israel in an effort to regain the Golan Heights, although the process broke down with no firm agreement in January 2000. After 30 years in power, Assad died unexpectedly on June 10, 2000. His oldest son, Basil al-Assad, was the presumed heir apparent but had died in an automobile accident in 1994, and the mantle passed to his younger brother, Bashar al-Assad, who had studied medicine and then trained in ophthalmology, including at the Western Eye Hospital in London. After his brother's death, Bashar al-Assad enrolled in the military academy at Homs and became a colonel in the Syrian Army in 1999.

In 2000, Assad was elected secretary-general of the Baath Party and stood as a presidential candidate. The People's Assembly amended the Syrian Constitution to lower the minimum presidential age to 35, and Assad was elected president for a 7-year term. A general referendum soon ratified the decision.

A reform movement emerged during the first year of Assad's rule, dubbed the Damascus Spring. Some Syrians hoped that their young president—who had announced governmental reforms, an end to corruption, and economic liberalization—would open Syria to a greater degree. Indeed, reformers hoped to end the State of Emergency Law, which allowed for the abuse of legal and human rights. Assad released some political prisoners from the notorious Mezze Prison, and certain intellectual forums were permitted. However, by mid-2001 Assad reined in the reformists, some of whom were imprisoned and accused of being Western agents.

Under Assad, Syria opened somewhat in terms of allowing more media coverage, although censorship remained a contentious issue. Cellular phones became prevalent, and Syria finally allowed access to the Internet, whereas under Hafiz

Assad, even facsimile machines were prohibited. Economic reform and modernization received top priority. Job creation, the lessening of Syria's dependence on oil revenue, the encouragement of private capital investments, and the mitigation of poverty were goals in the economic sphere. The government created foreign investment zones, and private universities were legally permitted, along with private banks. Employment centers were established after 2000, and Bashar Assad announced his support of an association with the European Union. However, these changes were too few and too gradual to instill much confidence in Syrian modernization. Assad's pledges of democratic reform failed to materialize.

After the September 11, 2001, terrorist attacks against the United States, Syria pledged its cooperation in the so-called war on terror. But with the beginning of the U.S.-led Iraq War in 2003, which Assad refused to support, U.S.-Syrian relations sharply deteriorated. Syria's continued support of militant Palestinian groups and terrorist organizations such as Hezbollah in Lebanon seriously strained relations with the United States and much of the West. To make matters worse, Syria's long and porous border with Iraq to the east served as a conduit for Syrian weaponry and terrorist fighters involved in the ensuing insurgency in Iraq. U.S. president George W. Bush's administration repeatedly warned Damascus not to aid the Iraqi insurgents, but the warnings were little heeded.

Although Syrian troops were finally out of Lebanon by 2005, evidence suggests that the Syrians continued to involve themselves in the internal politics of that nation. Indeed, most observers agree that Syrian operatives were responsible for the assassination of former Lebanese prime minister Rafik Hariri in February 2005. By late 2006 there were fears that Syria, working in tandem with Iran, was attempting to undermine the shaky government in Lebanon in a bid to exert de facto control over that country.

The so-called Arab Spring, a reform movement that began in Tunisia in December 2010 and impacted much of the Arab world, triggered the Syrian Civil War. It began on March 15, 2001. Protesters in Damascus demanded democratic reforms, action against corruption, and the release of political prisoners. The security forces retaliated by opening fire on the demonstrators, but the protests quickly spread. The city of Daraa became an opposition center, and Assad sent in the army. In the ensuing Siege of Daraa (April 25–May 5, 2011), some 6,000 army troops supported by tanks and helicopters moved against the city. By the time it was secured, as many as 244 civilians had been killed, along with 81 soldiers. Some 1,000 people were arrested. Nonetheless, the demonstrations increased, becoming full-scale civil war. By the end of 2012, this civil strife had claimed an estimated 60,000 lives and showed no sign of abating.

In the wake of the uprisings Assad attempted to address some concerns raised by protesters, such as formally ending the five decades of emergency law in the country and dissolving the security courts that had angered locals with unfair and corrupt adjudication. He also issued a decree legalizing political parties and indicated that he was even open to changing the constitution. However, such measures were offset by the harsh actions of the government security forces, especially in Daraa and Damascus.

A member of the Free Syrian Army stands guard during an anti-Syrian government protest in Idlib, Syria, on February 6, 2012. The effort to overthrow the regime of Syrian president Bashar al-Assad began in March 2011. (AP Photo)

The demonstrations brought to the fore long-standing resentments held by the majority Sunnis as well as by minority Christians, Druzes, and others against rule by the minority Alawites. Much of the fighting was along sectarian lines, with the Sunni areas experiencing the brunt of the government attacks. Thus, the Syrian people were not only fighting for fundamental governmental reform but were also revisiting historic rivalries. It was thus no surprise that cities such as Hama, Daraa, and Deir al-Zor, where there had been past sectarian violence, should see heavy fighting.

Establishing a united political and military front against Assad's forces proved challenging for the opposition. The UN, the Arab League, and the international community long argued that intervening in the conflict without an established political and military opposition leadership in place would be disastrous. By August 2011 the Free Syrian Army had been established. It was a conglomeration of the country's opposition forces and was made up of defected members of Assad's military. The next month, the Syrian National Council and National Coordinating bodies were set up in Turkey. Despite these bodies, opposition unity remained tenuous at best.

The Assad regime enjoyed the support of Iran (with Iranian weaponry passing to the Syrian government through Iraqi airspace). The regime also received support from Russia, which was a major trading partner and maintained a Mediterranean naval base in the Syrian city of Tartus. The Syrian opposition looked to neighboring countries for assistance. Some Salafists and other jihadists joined the insurgency. Fighters who had fought the Americans and security forces in Iraq transitioned to

Syria and pushed an Islamist agenda. The most notorious of these organizations was the Islamic State of Iraq and Syria (ISIS), which soon held sway over a substantial portion of central Syria and northern Iraq.

Concerns abounded that the uprising in Syria would disrupt the delicate Sunni-Shia balance in neighboring countries. Lebanon was particularly vulnerable, and fighting triggered by the Syrian crisis occurred along sectarian lines in Tripoli and other cities. Syrian Christians, fearing repression under a new Syrian regime, sought support from their coreligionists in Lebanon and Iraq. Turkey has played a critical role in the conflict by providing sanctuary to tens of thousands of Syrian refugees and also hosted the opposition leadership until September 2012, when the latter moved back into Syria. Turkish president Recep Tayyip Erdoğan demanded Assad's departure.

Attempts by the UN, the Arab League, and the Gulf Cooperation Council to bring an end to the violence proved futile, as was Assad's prompting of parliamentary elections on May 7, 2012, which saw opposition forces rejecting the elections altogether.

Assad's forces shelled neighborhoods and cities and increasingly relied on airpower in an effort to defeat the opposition forces (which Assad referred to as terrorists), a weapon of choice being barrel bombs with high attendant civilian casualties. The cities of Homs and Bab Amr each endured more than a month of shelling, driving civilians out of the cities and forcing a temporary rebel withdrawal in March 2012. Opposition forces, albeit somewhat disorganized, mounted regular attacks against government targets such as the Damascus intelligence headquarters and military buildings. Suicide attacks increased during 2012, as did the use of roadside bombs.

During 2012, attacks by security forces against civilians and opposition forces increased dramatically. In the town of Darayya, an August battle between rebels and security forces brought the massacre of more than 300 people. Increasing government firepower against the Syrian civilian population brought major defections, including in July 2012 close Assad supporter Brigadier General Manaf Tlas as well as several Syrian ambassadors and legislators.

In July, the Syrian rebels began to retake some of the towns they had been driven from earlier, capturing a military base near Aleppo. Their downing of military aircraft indicated improving weaponry and tactics. By November 2012, the military balance appeared to be tipping toward the opposition as its fighters edged closer to Assad's stronghold of Damascus. Concerns in December 2012 that Assad would employ chemical weapons in a last-ditch effort against the opposition brought warnings by the United States and West European countries that such a step would have serious consequences. Indeed, in the United States the Barack Obama administration called this a red line and said that crossing it would have dire consequences, with the clear implication of U.S. military intervention. In midmonth Syria for the first time employed Scud missiles against rebel concentrations. The United States then dispatched to Turkey Patriot missile batteries and 400 troops to man them in a largely symbolic gesture designed to help protect the long Turkish border with Syria against possible missile or aircraft attack.

By July 2013, the UN estimated that the fighting had claimed some 93,000 dead. The war, which had seemed to be going in favor of the rebels, turned in favor of government forces when on June 5 Assad's forces captured the key city of al-Qusayr near the Lebanese border. The city was of great importance as a supply route for rebels fighting Syrian government forces in Homs but also for the Syrian government, as it is situated between Damascus and the Alawite stronghold on the Syrian coast. The Battle for al-Qusayr (May 19–June 5, 2013) saw the participation of fighters from the radical Lebanese Shiite organization Hezbollah, which was strongly supported by Iran. The participation of Hezbollah angered many Sunnis and raised the prospect of a widened Middle East sectarian war to include at least Lebanon. Indeed, on June 15 Egypt broke diplomatic ties with Syria and called for the overthrow of Assad.

Also on June 15, the American government, following similar announcements by France and Britain, concluded that the Syrian government had indeed employed chemical weapons against its own people. Much to the disappointment of many, the Obama administration did not undertake military action, despite a plea on September 2 by the Arab League for military action against Syria for the use of chemical weapons. Washington did agree to provide limited arms to the Free Syrian Army, but this did not include the heavy weapons the rebels most required, such as antiaircraft missiles; nor did it include the establishment of a no-fly zone. Under immense pressure, Assad's regime did at last agree to turn over its chemical weapons stockpiles in order that they might be destroyed.

Representatives of 11 states, including the United States, met in Qatar and pledged increased aid to the rebels. Clearly the rebels—armed basically with small arms—were outgunned by Syrian government forces, with their tanks, artillery, and especially aircraft.

With Iran and Russia firmly supporting Assad—indeed, Russian president Vladimir Putin announced that Russia intended to proceed with the sale to the Syrian government of advanced antiaircraft missiles—peace appeared as elusive as ever. Saudi Arabia and some other Sunni Muslim states provided limited arms to the rebels, while the U.S. government gave only nonlethal military assistance.

In September 2014 a U.S.-led coalition began waging an air war against ISIS targets in Syria, but the situation in that nation continued to deteriorate. Iran was already active militarily in Syria, ostensibly to defeat ISIS but also to prop up Assad. In the summer of 2015 at the invitation of Assad, Russia began to construct new bases in the country, and in late September Russia began its own intervention, employing withering air strikes supposedly against ISIS but, according to most observers, largely against the anti-Assad rebels, something Moscow vehemently denied.

In late 2015, the Obama administration sent a small contingent of special operations troops to Syria in recognition that an air war alone might not be sufficient to destroy ISIS. Turkey's downing in November 2015 of a Russian warplane, which it claimed had violated its airspace, was a stark reminder of how the conflict might result in a direct confrontation between Russia and the West.

In July 2013 the Syrian government was said to have control of approximately 30–40 percent of Syrian territory and 60 percent of the population, but by August

2015 the territory fully controlled by the Syrian Army had shrunk to only about 16 percent of the country, although this still contained the majority of the population. From October 2015, however, the Syrian government, backed up by direct Russian military involvement, made significant advances against both ISIS and the other rebels, most notably in retaking Palmyra from ISIS in March 2016.

It is difficult to determine with any accuracy the casualty total from the war because Assad would not permit access to the international media, but in April 2016 the UN estimated the death toll at some 400,000 people. Multinational human rights organizations have accused the Syrian government of massive human rights violations, including the direct targeting of civilians. The civil war has also created about 4 million refugees and at least 7.5 million internally displaced persons.

Although UN-sponsored peace talks commenced at Geneva on February 1, 2016, there was little letup in the fighting, and the talks collapsed in April. On June 7 in his first major address since the breakdown of the talks, Assad struck a defiant note, vowing to retake "every inch" of Syria.

Timeline

1516	Ottoman forces invade the Mamluk Sultanate of Egypt, conquer Syria, and incorporate it into their empire.
1915	The Armenian Massacre claims the deaths of some 1.2 Armenians in a forced removal to Syria.
1916	French diplomat François Georges-Picot and Briton Mark Sykes reach a secret agreement on behalf of their governments to carve out of the Ottoman Empire four new states in Syria and Lebanon (to be controlled by the French) and Iraq and Palestine (to pass under British control).
Mar 8–Jul 24, 1920	The Kingdom of Syria is established under Faisal I of the Hashemites. The French Army of the Levant defeats his forces in the Battle of Maysalun on July 24, then occupy all of Syria.
Oct 29, 1923	The League of Nations places Syria under a French mandate.
1925	Sultan al-Atrash, a Druze, leads a revolt against the French that spreads to all of Syria and parts of Lebanon. Al-Atrash's forces win several battles against the French, but French reinforcements crush the revolt.
1934	The French government proposes independence for Syria under an arrangement beneficial to France. Strong opposition to this in Syria is organized by nationalist leader Hashim al-Atassi.
Sep 1936	Syria and France negotiate a new treaty. It calls for immediate recognition of Syrian independence as a sovereign republic but with full emancipation to occur during a 25-year period. Faced

with the threat to French security posed by Germany, the French legislature refuses to ratify it, however.

Jun 22, 1940   Germany defeats France in World War II, and Syria passes under the control of the new Vichy French government.

Jun–Jul 1941   A pro-Axis coup in Iraq and the shipment of arms there by Germany through Vichy-controlled Syria bring a British and Free French invasion and the takeover of Syria and Lebanon.

Jul 1943   Under pressure from its allies, the Free French government-in-exile announces new Syrian elections, and a nationalist government comes to power that August, with Syrian nationalist Shukri al-Quwatli as president.

Jan 1, 1944   France grants Syria independence on January 1, 1944, but the country remains under Allied occupation for the rest of the war.

Feb 26, 1945   Syria declares war on the Axis powers and becomes a member of the United Nations (UN) the next month.

Mar 22, 1945   Syria is a cofounder of the Arab League.

May 1945   Anti-French demonstrations throughout Syria bring the French bombardment of Damascus, killing some 400 people before the British intervene.

Feb 1946   A UN resolution calls on France to evacuate Syria.

Apr 17, 1946   Evacuation Day, with all French troops having left Syria, is celebrated as a Syrian national holiday.

Mar 29, 1949   Following Syria's poor showing in the Israeli War of Independence of 1948–1949 and disagreements regarding a possible Syrian union with Iraq, former Syrian Army chief of staff Husni al-Za'im seizes power in a bloodless coup d'état.

Aug 14, 1949   Za'im is himself overthrown in a coup headed by Colonel Sami al-Hinnawi that includes Lieutenant Colonel Adib al-Shishakli.

Dec 19, 1949   Shishakli takes power in the third coup of 1949.

Feb 24, 1954   Shishakli is overthrown in a coup. Late this year elections install a civilian government, but it is weak and marked by fractious party politics. In the succeeding years the Baathists, who combine Arab nationalism with socialist economic policies, becomes the most powerful political force in Syria.

Oct 20, 1955   Syria signs a defense pact with Egypt and joins Egypt's lead in cultivating relations with the Soviet bloc, to include arms purchases.

Feb 1, 1958   Syria and Egypt form the United Arab Republic (UAR).

Sep 28, 1961   With Egypt completely dominating the UAR, Syrian opposition brings another coup, the end of the UAR, and the establishment of the Syrian Arab Republic.

Dec 1, 1961   Syrian elections for a new National Assembly result in the selection of Nazzim al-Qudsi as president.

Mar 28, 1962   Another army coup leaves Qudsi as president but brings other personnel changes.

Sep 13, 1962   Khalid al-Azm becomes prime minister. He quickly dissolves the parliament and announces that he will govern by decree until new elections in one year.

Mar 8, 1963   A military coup brings yet another new government, largely controlled by the Baath Party.

Feb 26, 1966   The radical wing of the Baath Party mounts yet another coup, removing the government of Salah al-Din al-Bitar. This coup claims some 400 lives. The victorious faction is principally Alawite. The two key figures in the coup are Salah Jadid and Hafez al-Assad.

Jun 5–10, 1967 Syria again fights Israel in the Six-Day War, with disastrous consequences. This time, Syria's defeat includes the loss of the Golan Heights.

Nov 13, 1970   Assad, now minister of defense, seizes power in a bloodless coup. He will rule Syria with an iron first until his death in 2000.

Oct 6–26, 1973 Syria joins Egypt in a surprise attack on Israel in the Yom Kippur (Ramadan) War. Syria's massive armor offensive at the beginning of the fighting carries into the Golan Heights, but the Israelis rally and throw the attackers back beyond their original positions.

Jun 1976   Assad sends his army into Lebanon, ostensibly as a peacekeeping force, during the Lebanese Civil War of 1975–1990. The troops stay on, however, with Assad siding with the Muslims who are fighting Christian militias. By the mid-1980s, Syrian forces are the preponderant political and military force in Lebanon and are not withdrawn from there until April 2005.

Feb 2–28, 1982 Assad brutally crushes an uprising by the Muslim Brotherhood in Hama, killing as many as 40,000 people and destroying much of the old city.

Jun 6–11, 1982 Israeli forces invade southern Lebanon to attack Palestine Liberation Organization forces that have been striking northern Israel from Lebanon. There is also heavy fighting between the

Israelis and the Syrians in the Begaa Valley that sees Israel downing a substantial number of Syrian aircraft before a cease-fire takes hold.

Oct 21, 1998   With Assad openly supporting the radical Kurdish Workers' Party (PKK) in its insurgency against the Turkish government and with Turkish troops massing on the Syrian border, Assad agrees to halt all Syrian aid to the PKK.

Aug 1990   A staunch opponent of Iraqi president Saddam Hussein, Assad condemns the latter's decision to invade and absorb Kuwait. He provides 20,000 troops to the international coalition that defeats Iraqi forces in the 1991 Persian Gulf War.

Jun 10, 2000   Assad dies unexpectedly and is succeeded by his son Bashar al-Assad, who is duly elected president. After some modest reforms, mostly in the economic sphere, he reversers course.

2003–2011   During the Iraq War, Syria's long and porous border with Iraq is a conduit for Syrian weaponry and terrorist fighters involved in the ensuing insurgency in Iraq.

Apr 2005   Syrian troops are withdrawn from Lebanon.

Mar 15, 2011   Beginning of the Syrian Civil War, prompted by the so-called Arab Spring of widespread demonstrations for change throughout much of the Arab world. Demonstrators in Damascus demand democratic reforms, action against corruption, and the release of political prisoners. The security forces open fire on the protesters, but the demonstrations spread.

Apr 25–May 5, 2011   The siege of Daraa. Following antigovernment protests, some 6,000 army troops supported by tanks and helicopters lay siege to Daraa. By the time it is secured as many as 244 civilians have been killed, along with 81 soldiers, and 1,000 people are arrested.

Aug 2011   The Free Syrian Army, a conglomeration of the country's opposition forces and made up of defected members of Assad's military, is established.

Sep 2011   The Syrian National Council and National Coordinating bodies are established in Turkey, but opposition unity proves elusive.

Dec 2012   Syria for the first time employs Scud missiles against rebel concentrations. The United States dispatches to Turkey Patriot missile batteries in a largely symbolic gesture designed to help protect the long Turkish border with Syria against possible missile or aircraft attack. Meanwhile the Syrian fighting seesaws back and forth, with growing casualties.

Feb 11, 2013	Syrian rebel forces capture the nation's largest dam, al-Furat. Lake Assad, backed up by the dam, is one of the largest artificial lakes in the region and the greatest freshwater reserve in Syria.
May 17, 2013	Russia furnishes the Syrian government advanced antiship cruise missiles. This is probably intended to send a message to the West in that the weapons would force any Western or allied naval activity farther from the coast, rendering far more difficult any effort to supply Syrian opposition forces from the sea.
May 19–Jun 5, 2013	The Battle of al-Qusayr. Assad's forces capture the key city of Qusayr near the Lebanese border. The region is of great importance as a supply route for rebels fighting Syrian government forces in Homs but also for the Syrian government, as it is situated between Damascus and the Alawite stronghold on the Syrian coast. The battle sees the participation of fighters from the radical Lebanese Shiite organization Hezbollah, which is strongly supported by Iran. The participation of Hezbollah angers many Sunnis and raises the prospect of a widened Middle East sectarian war that would include at least Lebanon.
Jun 1, 2013	The European Union lifts its embargo on arms to the Syrian opposition.
Jun 15, 2013	The Egyptian government breaks diplomatic ties with Syria and calls for the overthrow of Assad.
	The U.S. government concludes, with the governments of Britain and France, that Syria has employed chemical weapons against its own people. Much to the disappointment of many, the Barack Obama administration fails to undertake a major military intervention as threatened. The United States will now arm the Free Syrian Army, but this does not include the heavy weapons most required, including antiaircraft missiles; nor will it include the establishment of a no-fly zone. Under heavy pressure, however, Assad does agree to turn over Syria's chemical weapons stockpiles in order that they might be destroyed.
Jun 23, 2013	Representatives of 11 states, including the United States, meet in Qatar and pledge increased aid to the rebels. Russian president Vladimir Putin, however, announces that Russia intends to go ahead with the sale to the Syrian government of advanced antiaircraft missiles.
Aug 25, 2014	The United States begins drone surveillance flights over Syria.
Sep 23, 2014	Cruise missiles and aircraft from the United States and allied Arab nations are launched at Muslim extremist Islamic State of Iraq and Syria (ISIS) targets in Syria in the first U.S. military offensive in

the war-torn country. ISIS now controls great swaths of territory in Iraq and Syria. The air campaign is ongoing, with the United States bearing its brunt.

Sep 9, 2015   Russia begins its own active military intervention in the civil war, beginning air strikes supposedly against ISIS but, according to most observers, largely against anti-Assad rebels.

Nov 21, 2015   Turkey downs a Russian warplane that it claims violated its airspace, leading to an angry Russian response and serving as a reminder of how the conflict could bring a direct confrontation between Russia and the West.

Feb 1, 2016   UN-sponsored peace talks to end the Syrian Civil War begin in Geneva, but prospects are not encouraging, and the effort breaks down in April.

Mar 27, 2016   Syrian government forces, backed up by direct Russian military involvement, make significant territorial gains in the fighting, culminating on this date in the retaking of Palmyra from ISIS.

Apr 2016   A UN estimate holds that 400,000 people have died in the civil war, which has also created some 4 million refugees and at least 7.5 million internally displaced persons.

Jun 7, 2016   In his first major address since the breakdown of the Geneva peace talks, Assad strikes a defiant note, vowing to retake "every inch" of Syria.

Further Reading

Ajami, Fouad. *The Syrian Rebellion.* Stanford, CA: Hoover Institution, Stanford University, 2012.

Darraj, Susan Muaddi. *Bashar al-Assad.* New York: Chelsea House, 2005.

George, Alan. *Syria: Neither Bread nor Freedom.* London: Zed Books, 2003.

Glass, Charles. *Syria Burning: A Short History of a Catastrophe.* New York: Verso, 2016.

Herzog, Chaim. *The Arab-Israeli Wars: War and Peace in the Middle East from the War of Independence to Lebanon.* Westminster, MD: Random House, 1984.

Lesch, David W. *The New Lion of Damascus: Bashar Al-Assad and Modern Syria.* New Haven, CT: Yale University Press, 2005.

Lesch, David W. *Syria: The Fall of the House of Assad.* New Haven, CT: Yale University Press, 2012.

Leverett, Flynt. *Inheriting Syria: Bashar's Trial by Fire.* Washington, DC: Brookings Institution Press, 2005.

Lustick, Ian. *From War to War: Israel vs. the Arabs, 1948–1967.* New York: Garland, 1994.

Maoz, Moshe, and Avner Yaniv, eds. *Syria under Assad: Domestic Constraints and Regional Risks.* London: Croom Helm, 1987.

McHugo, John. *Syria: A Recent History.* London: Saqi, 2015.

Pipes, Daniel. *Greater Syria: The History of an Ambition.* New York: Oxford University Press, 1990.

Pollack, Kenneth M. *Arabs at War: Military Effectiveness, 1948–1991.* Lincoln: University of Nebraska Press, 2002.

Rabil, Robert G. *Embattled Neighbors: Syria, Israel, and Lebanon.* Boulder, CO: Lynne Rienner, 2003.

Roberts, David. *The Ba'th and the Creation of Modern Syria.* New York: St. Martin's, 1987.

Rubin, Barry, and Thomas A. Keaney, eds. *Armed Forces in the Middle East: Politics and Strategy.* Portland, OR: Frank Cass, 2002.

Seale, Patrick. *Assad of Syria: The Struggle for the Middle East.* Berkeley: University of California Press, 1988.

Solomon, Brian. *Chemical and Biological Warfare.* New York: H. W. Wilson, 1999.

Starr, Stephen. *Revolt in Syria: Eye-witness to the Uprising.* New York: Columbia University Press, 2012.

Torr, James D. *Weapons of Mass Destruction: Opposing Viewpoints.* San Diego: Greenhaven, 2005.

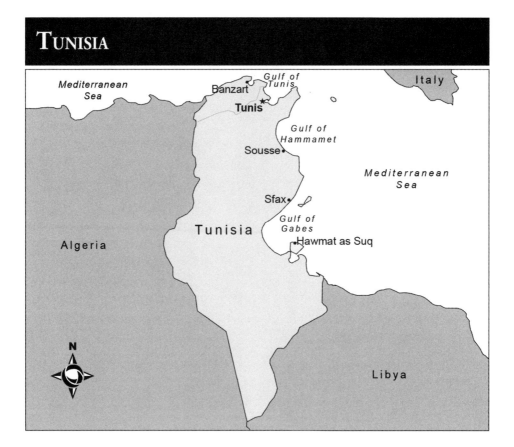

TUNISIA

Mediterranean
Sea

Gulf of
Tunis

Banzart

Tunis

Gulf of
Hammamet

Sousse

Mediterranean
Sea

Sfax

Gulf of
Gabes

Tunisia

Hawmat as Suq

Algeria

Italy

Libya

N

Tunisia

Mark M. Sanders and Spencer C. Tucker

The Republic of Tunisia is located in central North Africa. The northernmost country of the African continent, Tunisia lies on the southern shore of the Mediterranean and comprises 63,170 square miles. Algeria is to its west, Libya is to its southeast, and the Mediterranean Sea is to its north. Tunisia's population in 2016 was some 11.375 million. Tunis is the capital city.

Tunisia is the sole democracy in the Arab world and has extraordinarily close ties with Europe, especially France and Italy, and also with the United States. Tunisia has an association agreement with the European Union and enjoys the status of a major non–North Atlantic Treaty Organization (NATO) ally. The country is a member of numerous international organizations, including the Arab Maghreb Union, the Arab League, the African Union, and the United Nations (UN).

Tunisia was initially inhabited by Berber tribes. Phoenician immigration began in the 12th century BCE and led to the founding of Carthage near present-day Tunis; it became the capital of the Carthaginian Empire that fought three major wars with Rome (264–241, 218–201, and 149–146 BCE). The second of these almost brought Carthaginian victory, but Rome ultimately triumphed and, with its victory in the Third Punic War, utterly destroyed Carthage (leading to the term "Carthaginian Peace"). The Romans ruled Tunisia during from 146 BCE to 435 CE and introduced Christianity. The Vandals held sway during 435–534, followed by the Byzantine Empire in 534–698. Arab armies had established themselves in Tunisia by 670 and completed its conquest by 698. A series of Arab caliphates followed, with some periods of Berber rule. During 1574–1705, Tunisia was part of the Ottoman Empire. The Husainid dynasty took control in 1705. The first of these rulers was al-Husayn I ibn Ali; his father was a Greek from Crete, and his mother was a Tunisian. The Hussinids beys (kings) ruled until 1956.

Bankruptcy resulting from the nonpayment of high-interest loans advanced by European banks to the bey, in order to finance public works projects but also his own lavish spending, provided the excuse for European intervention and control. In 1869 Tunisia declared bankruptcy, and this brought an international commission with British, Italian, and French representation that took control of the Tunisian economy.

Given their close geographic proximity and the large number of their countrymen already living there, the Italians expected to dominate. The British were also interested, but the French had taken control of neighboring Algeria in 1830, and Tunisia seemed the logical next step. In the end the British government supported the French in exchange for French support for a British protectorate over Cyprus.

Tribal raiding from Tunisia into Algeria in the spring of 1881 provided the excuse for the French takeover. France responded by sending a force of some 36,000 men into Tunisia. With its rapid advance on Tunis, the bey was compelled to come to terms. On May 12, 1881, Sadik Bey signed the Treaty of Bardo establishing a French protectorate. The bey remained as figurehead ruler, but the French held actual power. Some resistance occurred, but French rule was firmly established within several years.

Tunisian society and culture were greatly affected by the long period of French colonial rule. Vichy France controlled Tunisia after France was defeated by the Germans during World War II in June 1940, but U.S. and British forces invaded North Africa in November 1942 and, advancing eastward, linked up with British forces driving west from Egypt. On May 13, 1943, the Allies won the major Battle of Tunis, effectively clearing Axis forces from North Africa.

World War II marked the effective end of the colonial era. A strong nationalist movement in Tunisia had emerged, headed by the Neo-Destour (New Constitution) Party. On March 20, 1956, following two years of difficult negotiations, France granted independence to Tunisia. Morocco had secured its independence the same month. The French were, however, determined to hold on to Algeria, which it had conquered in 1830; Algeria had a large European population and was officially regarded as an integral part of France as three French departments. Fighting had broken out in Algeria between the National Liberation Front (FLN) and the French in late 1954 in a war that lasted until 1962.

In Tunisia, meanwhile, on July 25, 1957, the Constituent Assembly ousted the bey, Muhammad VIII al-Amin, who was sympathetic to France and had long been unpopular. The assembly established the Tunisian republic and elected Habib Bourguiba as president.

Bourguiba, who would rule until 1987, was decidedly pro-Western in his outlook and foreign policy. He also maintained cordial communications with Israel, although this was not made public until years later. Bourguiba made known his opinion that Arab states should accept the existence of Israel and pertinent UN resolutions as a condition for solving the Palestinian problem. The Bourguiba administration was also tolerant of its Jewish citizens, distinguishing between them and the often unpopular policies of the State of Israel.

Bourguiba's efforts to transform Tunisia into a modern democratic state had the backing of the majority of young Westernized Tunisian intellectuals. His main political support came from the well-organized Neo-Destour Party, which he had founded in 1934 and constituted the country's chief political force. Bourguiba was not without political rivals, however. Early in his presidency, he was strongly challenged by Salah ben Youssef, who favored Egypt and Pan-Arabism and championed the continuation of Tunisia's ancient Islamic traditions.

Meanwhile, the Algerian War (1954–1962) continued, and considerable military aid flowed from Egypt through Tunisia to the FLN rebels. The French responded by

President Habib Bourguiba, seen lifting a sword while on horseback, is welcomed during a trip to Tataouine in southern Tunisia on June 20, 1956. Tunisia had only recently secured independence from France. (AP Photo/Agipan)

building an extensive defensive line along the Tunisian border. Completed in 1957, it included a 286-mile-long electrified fence. Clashes between the French and Tunisians occurred during May 26–June 7, 1957, and on February 8, 1958, the French staged an air attack on the Tunisian border town of Sakiet-Sidi-Youssef. The Tunisian government responded by placing all French military establishments in Tunisia under a virtual state of siege. It also lodged a formal complaint with the UN. The U.S. and British governments were anxious to secure a continuation of Tunisia's pro-Western policies, which were now under considerable Arab pressure, and the crisis was resolved by Anglo-American mediation, but not before the forced resignation of French premier Félix Gaillard on May 14. All French troops would be evacuated from all bases in Tunisia except for Bizerte, where a force of approximately 12,000 troops would remain, although Tunisian sovereignty over the base was recognized.

The continued French presence at the major air, land, and naval base at Bizerte led to another crisis. On July 17, 1961, Tunisian militiamen fired on French helicopters and attempted to lay siege to the base, while Tunisian Navy ships sought to block the harbor. The French responded with overwhelming force during July 19–21, carrying out some 150 air sorties that killed hundreds of Tunisians before a UN-brokered cease-fire took hold on July 23. France gave up the base in October 1963, when it passed under Tunisian control and was closed.

Despite this, Tunisia almost always aligned itself squarely with the West. Certainly it has long been considered a strong American ally. During the June 1967 Six-Day War, for example, Bourguiba refused to sever relations with the United States over its support of Israel, despite considerable pressure to do so from other Arab states. Tunisia also faced hostility from Egyptian leader Gamal Abdel Nasser, with whom Bourguiba often found himself at odds, even going so far as to briefly sever diplomatic relations in October 1966.

In spite of Bourguiba's support of Western-style democracy, his regime nevertheless exerted strong, centralized authority. The government closely controlled the economy and, as fears of Islamic fundamentalism increased, especially after the late 1970s, increasingly relied on censorship, illegal detentions, and other decidedly undemocratic schemes.

As Tunisia increasingly lost influence among its Arab neighbors, the government's stance on Israel hardened and often resulted in contradictory and paradoxical policies. Thus, Tunisia supported the October 1973 Egyptian-Syrian attack on Israel, sparking the Yom Kippur War (Ramadan War), and sent close to 1,000 combatants to fight, despite its having historically urged diplomatic solutions to Arab-Israeli conflicts. Although Tunisia distanced itself from the Middle East's continued problems throughout the rest of the decade, from 1979 to 1989 Tunis served as the headquarters of the Arab League when the organization suspended Egypt's membership and abandoned Cairo following President Anwar Sadat's peace agreement with Israel.

In 1982, Bourguiba reluctantly allowed the Palestine Liberation Organization (PLO) to move the majority of its operations from Beirut to Tunis following the Israeli invasion of Lebanon. When a PLO attack killed 3 Israelis on a yacht off Cyprus, on October 1, 1985, Israel sent eight fighter aircraft nearly 1,300 miles to Tunisia to bomb the PLO headquarters in the Tunis suburbs. The attack killed 67 people and injured many more. The U.S. government at first defended the action as a "legitimate response" to terrorism, but with this stand adversely affecting U.S.-Tunisian relations, Washington then reversed itself and condemned the strike. Then on April 16, 1988, Israeli commandos killed the PLO's second-in-command, Khalil al-Wazir (Abu Jihad), and 3 other individuals at al-Wazir's residence in Tunis. Following the PLO's acceptance of Israel's right to exist in December 1988, the organization left Tunis and returned to the Middle East, much to the relief of the Tunisian government.

Bourguiba had been president since Tunisia's independence in 1956, but his heavy-handed rule and frail health combined to bring about his ouster in a bloodless coup on November 7, 1987, by career army officer and premier Zine el-Abidine Ben Ali, who became acting president and then president. Ben Ali held power until January 2011. Under his tenure, Tunisia maintained a moderate nonaligned stance in its foreign relations. Domestically, it sought to diffuse rising pressures for a more open political system while at the same time dealing with increased Islamic radical fundamentalist activities and growing anti-Western sentiments.

During the 1991 Persian Gulf War, Tunisia declined to support the international coalition arrayed against the Iraqi forces that had seized Kuwait. Ben Ali's government viewed the conflict not as one of liberation but rather as one for the control of Middle

Eastern oil. This stance ran counter to many of its Arab neighbors, who did join the coalition.

In April 1996, Tunisia followed the lead of Morocco and opened a liaison office in Tel Aviv to strengthen cultural ties with Israel, especially with respect to Jewish tourism. While the rise of Israel's conservative Likud Party strained emerging Tunisian-Israeli relations during the next several years, on February 6, 2000, Tunisia's secretary of state met with the Israeli foreign minister in Tel Aviv, marking the first ever visit of such high-ranking officials.

The 21st century saw a cooling of relations between Israel and Tunisia. At the 2002 Arab Summit in Beirut, President Ben Ali supported the peace plan that called for an independent Palestinian state with Jerusalem as its capital and the return of all occupied territories. In 2004, Ben Ali won a fourth five-year term. Meanwhile, he strengthened his ties to the United States and the West, voicing support for the post-2001 war on terror and likening it to his own battle to fight Islamic radicalism at home. While Tunisia did not participate in the U.S.-led invasions of Afghanistan in 2001 and of Iraq in 2003, the Ben Ali regime cooperated with the George W. Bush administration's efforts to stymie international terrorism.

Beginning on December 18, 2010, demonstrations began in Tunisia. They were sparked by the self-immolation and eventual death the day before of 26-year-old university graduate Mohammed Bouazizi, who was selling fruit in Sidi Bouzid in central Tunisia. The demonstrations soon reached Tunis, with the participants employing social media to communicate. The demonstrators were protesting corruption, lack of jobs, and restrictions on civil liberties, and dozens of people died at the hands of the security police. On January 14, 2011, Ben Ali fled Tunisia for Saudi Arabia.

During the next several days Tunisia was in chaos, with widespread looting and gunfire, and there were two leadership changes within 24 hours. The first was longtime Ben Ali ally and prime minister Mohamed Ghannouchi, who left open the option of Ben Ali's return, and the second was speaker of parliament Fouad Mebazaa who, sworn in as interim president, asked Prime Minister Mohamed Ghannouchi to form a national unity government and organize new elections. The events in Tunisia opened the possibility of democracy and were regarded as a warning to other autocratic Arab regimes. Indeed, they began what has been called the Arab Spring as the demand for democratic reform and an end to corruption soon spread to Egypt, Libya, and other countries of the Arab world.

On October 23, 2011, Tunisians went to the polls and selected representatives to the Constituent Assembly. The formerly banned Ennahda Islamic party won the election by capturing 41 percent of the vote. On December 12, 2011, former dissident and veteran human rights activist Moncef Marzouki was elected president. In March 2012, Ennahda declared that it would not support making sharia the main source of legislation in the new constitution, thus continuing the secular nature of the Tunisian state, a stance slammed by hard-line Islamists but welcomed by the secular parties. On February 6, 2013, Chokri Belaid, the leader of the leftist opposition and a prominent critic of Ennahda, was assassinated.

On December 21, 2014, Mohamed Beji Caid Essebsi won the runoff in Tunisia's first free and democratic election with 55.7 percent of the vote. The victory was regarded as a major setback for the Islamists, as Essebsi's anti-Islamist Nidaa Tounes party had also won a plurality in parliament the month before.

That Tunisia was not immune from terrorism was revealed on March 18, 2015, when gunmen associated with the Islamic State of Iraq and Syria (ISIS) armed with assault rifles opened fire on tourists at they left buses in front of the National Bardo Museum in central Tunis near the parliament building, where the deputies were, ironically, debating antiterrorist legislation. The gunmen killed 23 and wounded 44, most of them foreigners. Two of the gunmen also died, but several others escaped. Clearly, the terrorists sought to inflict an economic blow by crippling Tunisia's important tourist industry.

On May 21, 2015, Essebsi met with U.S. president Barack Obama in Washington. In a move intended to bolster the fledgling Tunisian democratic regime, Obama accorded Tunisia the status of a major non-NATO ally. Only a month later, however, on June 26 ISIS again struck when Tunisian student Seifeddine Rezgui, age 23, systematically shot foreign tourists on the beach near the Hotel Riu Imperial Marhaba in coastal Sousse, then entered the hotel lobby and detonated several grenades before being shot dead by the police on a city street. Thirty-eight tourists were killed, 15 of them Britons, and another 39 were wounded. On December 15, 2015, Tunisia was among 34 Arab nations in a coalition formed by Saudi Arabia to fight terrorism.

On January 11, 2016, Fannahda, Tunisia's principal Islamist party, reemerged as the dominant force in the national parliament following resignations from Essebsi's secular Nidaa Tounes Party, largely in protest of his son's position as head of the party. The individuals who resigned said that this was not a protest regarding policy but rather Hafedh Caid Essebsi's takeover of the party leadership and what they regarded as an effort to create a dynastic transfer of power. Tunisian politics had become more complicated.

The collapse of order in Libya also threatened to engulf Tunisia. On March 7, 2016, radical Islamist militiamen crossed the border into Tunisia and attacked an army barracks at Ben Gardane. The ensuing fighting claimed 65 people dead: 46 jihadists, 12 members of the Tunisian security forces, and 7 civilians. Tunisian premier Habib Essid blamed ISIS.

Although Tunisia has been widely praised for its democratic practices since the Arab Spring, it has also had five different governments in this same time period, and it is a major concern that some 5,500 Tunisians have joined ISIS, more than from any other nation. That moderate Rachid Ghannouchi, a renowned Islamic thinker, was reelected in May 2016 as leader of the Ennahda Party was seen as a most encouraging sign, for Ghannouchi has steadily worked to move Ennahda away from its Islamic roots to be more in line with the country's democratic revolution.

Timeline

698	After initial settlement by Berber tribes and having been the center of the Carthaginian Empire, then held by the Romans, Vandals, and Byzantines, the Arabs establish their control and introduce

Islam. A series of Arab dynasties follow, with occasional Berber interludes.

1574–1705	Tunisia is part of the Ottoman Empire.
1705	The Husainid dynasty assumes control of Tunisia under al-Husayn I ibn Ali. This family will rule as beys (kings) of Tunisia until 1956.
1869	The government of Tunisia declares bankruptcy, following profligate spending financed by high-interest European bank loans. This ushers in European economic control by the British, French, and Italians.
Spring 1881	Following Tunisian tribal raiding into Algeria, the French send a large military force to Tunis and seize control there.
May 12, 1881	Sadik Bey signs the Bardo Treaty that establishes a French protectorate. The bey remains as figurehead ruler, but the French hold actual power. There is some resistance, but within several years the French have full control.
May 13, 1943	The Allied victory in the major Battle of Tunis completes the British and French clearance of Axis forces from North Africa in World War II.
1954–1962	The Algerian War occurs between National Liberation Front rebels seeking independence and the French Army.
Mar 20, 1956	France grants independence to Tunisia.
May 26–Jun 7, 1957	Clashes occur between the French and Tunisians along the Algerian-Tunisian border.
Jul 25, 1957	The Tunisian Constituent Assembly ousts the pro-French unpopular bey Muhammad VIII al-Amin, establishes the Tunisian republic, and elects Habib Bourguiba the first president.
Feb 8, 1958	French forces in Algeria mount an air attack on the Tunisian border town of Sakiet-Sidi-Youssef. The Tunisian government then places all French military establishments in Tunisia under a virtual state of siege. Anglo-American mediation resolves the crisis. The French agree to abandon all their bases in Tunisia except the major air, land, and naval facility at Bizerte.
Jul 17–23, 1961	Fighting erupts when Tunisian forces attempt to drive the French from Bizerte. The French respond with major air strikes, killing several hundred Tunisians before a United Nations–brokered cease-fire takes hold. France agrees to give up the base in October 1963, when it passes under Tunisian control and is closed.
Oct 1973	Tunisia sends some 1,000 troops to fight against Israel in the Yom Kippur War (Ramadan War).

1979–1989	Tunis serves as the headquarters of the Arab League.
1982	Bourguiba reluctantly allowed the Palestine Liberation Organization (PLO) to move the majority of its operations from Beirut to Tunis following the Israeli invasion of Lebanon.
Oct 1, 1985	Following a PLO attack that kills 3 Israelis on a yacht off Cyprus, Israel sends eight aircraft nearly 1,300 miles to bomb the PLO headquarters in the Tunis suburbs. The attack kills 67 people and injures many more.
Nov 7, 1987	Bourguiba, who has been president since 1956, is ousted by career army officer and premier Zine el-Abidine Ben Ali in a coup. Ben Ali becomes first acting president and then president and holds power until January 2011.
Apr 16, 1988	Israeli commandos kill the PLO's second-in-command, Khalil al-Wazir (Abu Jihad), and three other individuals in Tunis. Following the PLO's acceptance of Israel's right to exist in December 1988, the organization leaves Tunis.
Apr 1996	Tunisia follows the lead of Morocco and opens a liaison office in Tel Aviv to strengthen cultural ties with Israel.
Feb 6, 2000	Tunisia's secretary of state meets with the Israeli foreign minister in Tel Aviv, marking the first ever visit of such high-ranking officials.
Dec 18, 2010	Demonstrations began in Tunisia, sparked by the self-immolation and eventual death the day before of a 26-year-old university graduate. The demonstrators are protesting corruption, lack of jobs, and restrictions on civil liberties. Dozens of people are killed by the security police.
Jan 14, 2011	With the protests continuing, President Ben Ali flees the country for Saudi Arabia.
Oct 23, 2011	The first postrevolution election occurs, with Tunisians selecting members of a Constituent Assembly. The formerly banned Ennahda Islamic party wins the greatest number by capturing 41 percent of the total vote.
Dec 12, 2011	Moncef Marzouki is elected president of Tunisia.
Mar 2012	Much to the relief of secularists, Ennahda declares that it will not support sharia as the main source of legislation in the new constitution.
Feb 6, 2013	Chokri Belaid, leader of the leftist opposition and prominent critic of Ennahda, is assassinated.

Dec 21, 2014   Mohamed Beji Caid Essebsi is elected president. This is regarded as a major setback for the Islamists, as his anti-Islamist Nidaa Tounes Party had also won a plurality in parliament the month before.

Mar 18, 2015   Islamic State of Iraq and Syria (ISIS) terrorists armed with assault rifles kill 23 people and wound another 44 outside the Bardo National Museum in Tunis in an effort to cripple the economy by striking at the tourist trade. Two of the gunmen also die, but several others escape.

May 21, 2015   U.S. president Barack Obama, meeting with President Essebsi in Washington, designates Tunisia a major non-NATO ally.

Jun 26, 2015   Tunisian student Seifeddine Rezgui, age 23, a member of ISIS, systematically shoots foreign tourists on the beach near the Hotel Riu Imperial Marhaba in coastal Sousse, then enters the hotel lobby and detonates several grenades before being shot dead by the police. Thirty-eight tourists are killed, 15 of them Britons, and another 39 are wounded.

Dec 15, 2015   Tunisia is among 34 Arab nations in a coalition formed by Saudi Arabia to fight terrorism.

Mar 7, 2016   Terrorists from strife-torn Libya cross the border and attack an army barracks at Ben Gardane. The ensuing fighting claims 65 dead: 46 jihadists, 12 members of the Tunisian security forces, and 7 civilians. ISIS is blamed. Some 5,500 Tunisians have joined ISIS, more than from any other nation.

Further Reading

Beinin, Josel. *Workers and Thieves: Labor Movements and Popular Uprisings in Tunisia and Egypt.* Stanford, CA: Stanford University Press, 2015.

Fraihat, Ibrahim. *Unfinished Revolutions: Yemen, Libya, and Tunisia after the Arab Spring.* New Haven, CT: Yale University Press, 2016.

Geyer, Georgie Anne. *Tunisia: The Story of a Country That Works.* London: Stacey International, 2002.

Perkins, Kenneth. *A History of Modern Tunisia.* New York: Cambridge University Press, 2014.

Willis, Michael. *Politics and Power in the Maghreb: Algeria, Tunisia and Morocco from Independence to the Arab Spring.* Oxford: Oxford University Press, 2014.

TURKEY

Bulgaria

Black Sea

Georgia

•Kirklareli

•Sinop

Istanbul

•Artvin

Greece

Armenia

•Amasya

Ankara★

Erzincan•

•Balikesir

Turkey

Tunceli•

Iran

•Bingol

•Izmir

•Nevsehir

Tigris

Aegean
Sea

Hakkari•

•Aydin

•Isparta

Kahramanmaras•

Euphrates

Iraq

Mediterranean
Sea

Syria

N

Cyprus

Lebanon

Azb

Azb

Turkey

Timothy L. Francis, Laura J. Hilton,
Sedat Cem Karadeli, Keith A. Leitich,
Paul G. Pierpaoli Jr., and Spencer C. Tucker

The Republic of Turkey is a Eurasian nation covering 300,948 square miles. Bordering eight countries, Turkey is strategically located in both Europe and Asia Minor and includes the important Turkish Straits (the Dardanelles, the Sea of Marmara, and the Bosporus) connecting the Black Sea with the Mediterranean and separating Thrace from Anatolia. Eastern Thrace is the small geographical area of European Turkey. It is bordered by Greece to the west and Bulgaria to the northwest. The Aegean Sea is to the east, and the Mediterranean is to the south. Most of Turkey lies in Asia Minor, in Anatolia. In Asia Minor, Turkey shares common borders with Georgia to the northwest; Armenia, Iran, and the Azerbaijani enclave of Nakhchivan to the east; and Syria and Iraq to the south. The Black Sea is to the north.

Turkey is a democratic, secular, unitary, constitutional republic. A president, elected by popular vote, is head of state. There is also a prime minister, elected by parliament. In 2016 Turkey had a population of some 79.622 million. Its capital city is Ankara. Ethnic Turks constitute some 70–75 percent of the population, while Kurds make up perhaps 18 percent. Muslims are said to make up between 96.4 and 99.8 percent of the population. Three-quarters of these are Sunni Muslims. There are perhaps 200,000 Christians and 26,000 Jews.

An important regional power, Turkey has a strong military. Its 411,000 active-duty personnel and 186,000 personnel in the active reserve give Turkey the second-largest military establishment of the North Atlantic Treaty Organization (NATO). One source ranks Turkey's military as the world's eighth strongest. Turkey, which is a member of the United Nations (UN), NATO, the Council of Europe, and the G-20, became an associate member of the European Economic Commission in 1963, joined the European Union Customs Union in 1995, and started full membership negotiations with the European Union (EU) in 2005.

Turkey was home to many ancient civilizations, including those of the Greeks, Thracians, Armenians, and Assyrians. It then formed the eastern reaches of the Persian Empire, which was conquered by King Alexander III (the Great) of Macedon in 334 BCE and Hellenized. Although Turkey was subsequently part of the Roman Empire, Greek language and culture predominated.

In 324 CE, Emperor Constantine I designated Byzantium on the Bosporus as the new capital of the Roman Empire. In 395 the empire was permanently divided, and Byzantium, popularly known as Constantinople, became the capital of the Eastern

Roman Empire, later designated the Byzantine Empire. Between the 3rd and 7th centuries the Byzantine Empire engaged in frequent warfare with the Sassanid Empire to the east, with the result that both were weakened to the extent that they fell prey to Muslim conquest. The Seljuk Turks became a threat in the 11th century and defeated the Byzantines in the important Battle of Manziker in 1071.

Osman I established the Ottoman Empire in 1299. Constantinople (now Istanbul) fell in 1453, and the empire subsequently included a considerable swath of the Mediterranean Basin, including much of Southeastern Europe, Western Asia, North Africa, and the Middle East. The empire reached the peak of its power and influence from the 15th to 17th centuries, especially under Sultan Suleiman the Magnificent (r. 1526–1566). After the failure of a second Ottoman siege of Vienna in 1683 and the end of the Great Turkish War in 1699, the Ottoman Empire underwent steady decline and came to be known as "the Sick Man of Europe."

Russian efforts to secure control of the Bosporus and gain access to the Mediterranean brought the Crimean War of 1853–1856. Britain and France supported the Ottomans. Most of the fighting occurred in the Crimean Peninsula, with the major military operation being the siege of the Russian Black Sea port and the naval base of Sevastopol (October 17, 1854–September 9, 1855). The allies, joined by the Kingdom of Sardinia (Sardinia-Piedmont), at last secured Sevastopol and victory in the war.

Nonetheless, Russia persisted. It formed a coalition with the Ottoman principalities of Romania, Bulgaria, Serbia, and Montenegro and then in the Russo-Turkish War of 1877–1878 secured Kars and Batumi in the Caucasus and annexed the Budjak region. Romania, Serbia, and Montenegro were all formally recognized as independent, and Bulgaria was recognized as a principality. The subsequent Congress of Berlin also allowed Austria-Hungary to occupy Bosnia and Herzegovina and allowed Great Britain to secure Cyprus, ceded by the Ottomans in return for British protection against Russia.

Ottoman weakness brought increasing demands from within the empire for reform. Turkish nationalism was also on the rise. In 1908 the Committee of Union and Progress (CUP), part of the Young Turk movement, convinced Sultan Abdul Hamid II (r. 1876–1909) to restore the parliament. Following an attempted counterrevolution later that year the CUP deposed the sultan and then on April 27, 1909 replaced him with his younger brother, Mehmed V.

Italy also sought to take advantage to secure Tripoli (present-day Libya). Italy declared war on September 29, 1911. Although Italian forces quickly occupied the city of Tripoli and outnumbered the scattered Ottoman garrisons, Italian forces were largely confined to coastal beachheads well into 1912. The war was brought to an end only when the Italians expanded the conflict to the eastern Mediterranean. In the Treaty of Lausanne of October 18, 1912, Italy secured sovereignty over Libya.

As many observers had predicted, Italy's success encouraged the Balkan states to try to take the remaining Ottoman territory in Europe. Montenegro declared war on October 8, 1912, followed by Bulgaria, Serbia, and Greece. During the next eight months, the larger and better-armed military establishments of the Balkan powers overcame the numerically inferior and strategically disadvantaged Ottoman armies. During October 28–November 3, the Bulgarians won a major victory over the Ottomans at Lulé Burgas. They then advanced to the last Ottoman defenses before Istanbul, although the Russians then warned the Bulgarians not to attempt to occupy the city. On November 16–18 the Serbs defeated the badly outnumbered Ottomans in the Battle of Monastir (Bitola), giving the Serbs control of southwestern Macedonia.

An acute international crisis ensued on November 24 when the Austro-Hungarian government announced its opposition to Serbian access to the Adriatic and insisted on the creation of an independent Albania. Italy supported the Austrians, while Russia backed Serbia. With both Austria and Russia mobilizing and with Austria allied to Germany and Russia allied to France, a general European war threatened. The crisis receded when Russia—clearly unready for war—withdrew its support from Serbia. On December 3 the Ottomans concluded an armistice with Bulgaria and Serbia, and a peace conference opened in London, only to collapse when the Ottomans refused to surrender Adrianople, the Aegean Islands, and Crete.

On January 23, a day after the major powers convinced the Ottoman government to yield Adrianople, a coup d'état occurred in Istanbul. The empire's steady stream of military defeats greatly discredited Mehmed V, and the CUP Young Turks seized power. A triumvirate now dominated Ottoman affairs: Ismail Enver Pasha as minister of war, Mehmed Talât Pasha as minister of the interior, and Ahmed Djemal Pasha as naval minister.

A photograph of the battlefield during the Siege of Adrianople (November 3, 1912–March 26, 1913) during the Balkan Wars. Adrianople, now known as Edirne, is in northeastern Turkey. (Library of Congress)

On February 3 the war resumed. The Bulgarians secured Adrianople on March 26. On April 16 the Ottomans concluded an armistice with Bulgaria, and the other warring Balkan powers soon followed suit. Tensions remained high over Albania, however, with both Montenegro and Serbia opposing its independence and occupying territory assigned to it and only yielding it under threat of war with Austria-Hungary. Talks in London resumed, and the Balkan states accepted the settlement developed by the Great Powers. In the Treaty of London of May 30 the Ottoman Empire ceded to the Balkan states the vast majority of its territory in Europe.

The victorious Balkan states now fell to quarreling among themselves regarding the spoils. Bulgaria had been the big winner territorially, but there were sharp differences between it and Serbia and Greece over Macedonia. Greece and Serbia resolved their own differences, and on June 1, 1913, they concluded a treaty of alliance against Bulgaria. With Greece and Serbia now planning war, on June 29 Bulgarian commander General Michael Savov opted for a preemptive strike without informing his government. Although the Bulgarian government subsequently disavowed Savov's action, the Serbs and Greeks, joined by Romania and even Ottoman forces, attacked Bulgaria in the Second Balkan War. By July 30, Bulgaria had been defeated. Under the terms of the Treaty of Bucharest of August 10, Bulgaria was left with only a small portion of Macedonia. On September 29 in a treaty between the Ottoman Empire and Bulgaria, the Ottomans recovered Adrianople in Europe and territory up to the Maritza River.

The Balkans were now largely a tinderbox. The rival European big power alliance systems of the Dual Alliance of Germany and Austria-Hungary and the Triple Entente of Russia, France, and Great Britain courted the Ottoman Empire, for in 1914 it still controlled all Anatolia, Mesopotamia, Syria, and Palestine. Germany won the struggle for influence, and in December 1913 a military mission led by Lieutenant General Otto Liman von Sanders arrived in Istanbul to help reorganize the Ottoman Army.

Following the assassination of Archduke Franz Ferdinand in Sarajevo on June 28, 1914, the Austrian government actively sought war with Serbia, seeing the opportunity to end the threat to its own existence posed by Slavic nationalism. On July 28 Austrian forces invaded Serbia, beginning the Third Balkan War, which a few days later became World War I when Russia mobilized and Germany declared war on it. On August 2, Ottoman leaders signed a secret alliance with Germany promising joint action if Russia intervened militarily in the conflict between Austria-Hungary and Serbia. The next day the Ottoman Empire mobilized its military.

The Entente rejected Enver Pasha's offer of neutrality in return for a large loan and modification of the financial concessions enjoyed by the European powers in the Ottoman Empire. The British government had sequestered two Ottoman dreadnoughts under construction in British yards. As the ships had been paid for by public subscription, this action rallied Ottoman public opinion against the Entente. Enver also accepted a gift of the German battle cruiser *Goeben* and light cruiser *Breslau*, both of which had eluded French and British warships in the Mediterranean and escaped into the straits and then to Istanbul.

On September 8 the Ottoman Empire abolished the financial capitulations. And on October 28 the *Goeben* and *Breslau* (given Turkish names but still under German command) attacked Russian ports and shipping in the Black Sea. Russia declared war on November 4, followed by Britain and France the next day. On November 14 Mehmed V proclaimed jihad (holy war) against the Entente.

The Ottoman Empire's entry into World War I had immense consequences. Closure of the Dardanelles isolated Russia from its allies and severely weakened its ability to wage war. Great Britain was also forced to shift major resources to protect the Suez Canal. Soon Ottoman forces were fighting in Caucasia, Egypt, and Mesopotamia as well as in Europe at the Dardanelles.

At home the CUP leadership instituted numerous administrative and bureaucratic reforms and also worked to improve infrastructure. The government also challenged the power of the influential Islamic clerics by bringing Islam more under its own control. Prior to the war, the government had subordinated the Islamic courts to its secular system. During the war, the government secularized the religious courts and schools. The government also carried out major reforms in the emancipation of women, equalizing their legal rights in marriage and inheritance and enhancing educational and employment opportunities for girls and women.

The Ottoman leadership believed that the war would be short and thus failed to institute planning to secure sufficient food and civilian supplies for an extended conflict. By 1915, there was a grain shortage in Istanbul and many other cities. Famine became widespread because of the lack of agricultural laborers (many had been conscripted into the military), a prolonged drought, and the monopolization of railroads by the military. War refugees fleeing to the cities brought instability and a further drain on resources. Inflation skyrocketed, reaching perhaps 400 percent in the first year of the war alone.

While the potentially most dangerous front for the Ottomans was Thrace, where the frontier was less than 180 miles from the national capital, the major Ottoman military effort came in Caucasia. Enver hoped to catch the Russians off guard, regain territory lost to the Russians earlier, and stimulate revolts among Muslims in southern Russia.

The Ottoman Army was, however, unready for war. Ignoring this, the weather, mountainous terrain, and supply problems, Enver launched his Third Army from Armenia on December 17, 1914. Following some initial success, the Ottomans were badly mauled by the Russians in the Battle of Sariklamish (December 22, 1914–January 17, 1915). Rebuilt in the spring of 1915, the Third Army was almost destroyed in the Russian Erzurum Offensive early in 1916. Later in the same year, the Second Army was nearly destroyed in an offensive farther south in the Caucasus. After that, the war in the east ground to a halt. In 1918, after the November 1917 Bolshevik Revolution brought a Russian military withdrawal from Caucasia, the Third Army went over to the offensive and penetrated deep into Armenia and Azerbaijan.

In the European portions of the empire, the First and Fifth Armies under Liman von Sanders turned back and inflicted heavy losses on the Entente's Gallipoli landing of April 1915. But when the Allies broke out from Salonika in 1918, there was nothing left to prevent them from entering Istanbul.

The British easily rebuffed Ottoman efforts to seize the Suez Canal from Palestine in 1915 and 1916. Afterward, the Sinai-Palestinian front evolved into a state of protracted, indecisive warfare, aggravated by the rising Arab Revolt. During 1916–1917 the British built up their resources, and in 1918 the German-Ottoman army group finally collapsed under repeated attacks, and British forces seized Jerusalem and Damascus.

In Mesopotamia, an Anglo-Indian thrust toward Baghdad ended in a Turkish triumph on April 29, 1916, when an entire division surrendered to the Ottoman Sixth Army at Kut. Thereafter this theater remained more or less quiet until the British renewed their advance in 1918. Several Turkish invasions of Persia proved to be insignificant.

The war badly weakened the empire's internal stability. Two groups in particular rebelled against rule from Istanbul: the Armenian Christians in eastern Anatolia and the Arabs in the Hejaz. The Armenians, who sought independence, forced the Ottomans to divert troops there from major campaigns elsewhere. In an effort to stabilize the situation, the government forcibly relocated the Armenian population to the Syrian Desert, an area remote from potential collusion with the Russians. Inadequate water, food, clothing, and medical supplies brought the deaths of as many as 1.5 million Armenians in the forced desert march and other government operations both during and after World War I. This episode in Turkish history has been called the Armenian Massacre and, controversially, the Armenian Genocide.

The other major source of revolt was the Arab community of the Hejaz. Its push for independence began in June 1916 under the leadership of Sharif Hussein ibn

The Armenian Genocide

The Armenian Genocide, as it is generally referred to in the West (it is also known as the Armenian Massacre and the Armenian Holocaust), refers to the Ottoman government's systematic extermination of much of its minority Armenian populations within the territory of the present-day Republic of Turkey during World War I. Rising Armenian nationalism, the service of many Armenians in the Russian Army, and fears of Armenian collusion with the Russians in the fighting in Caucasia led to the massacre. It began on April 24, 1915, with the Ottoman government's arrest of some 250 Armenian leaders in Istanbul (Constantinople) and their deportation to Ankara, where most were murdered or died in confinement. Ottoman Army commanders then oversaw the murder of able-bodied Armenian men, while chiefly Armenian women, children, the elderly, and the infirm were forced into death marches into the Syrian Desert. Other Christian groups, including Greeks, were also targeted. The total death toll may have been as high as 1.5 million of the 2 million Armenians in the empire in 1914.

The Turkish government continues to deny the genocide as an impossibility, but a growing number of governments and prominent individuals have asserted it as such.

Ali. His third son, Prince Faisal, and British lieutenant colonel T. E. Lawrence played key roles in this, supporting the British military campaign in Palestine and Syria in 1917 and 1918. The Arab insurgents forced the Ottomans to divert troops and attention from the main British advances.

An armistice ending Ottoman participation in the war was signed on October 30, 1918, aboard the British battleship *Agamemnon* off the island of Mudros. Allied troops then occupied much of the empire. According to recent estimates, in the war the Ottomans suffered some 770,000 dead and 760,000 wounded, each about 27 percent of the manpower mobilized; some 145,000 were taken prisoner.

The government at Istanbul meanwhile disintegrated, and its leaders fled. The Ottoman Empire unofficially ended on November 15 when Sultan Mehmed VI, who had succeeded to the throne only in October on the death of Mehmed V, established a new government under the control of Greek and British troops. The British, French, and Italians then established a tripartite administration of Istanbul, garrisoned the Alexandretta-Smyrna-Constantinople Railway, and encouraged the creation of independent Georgian and Armenian armies. A buildup of British, Italian, French, and Greek forces also occurred.

Turkish nationalist resistance to these moves developed first in eastern Anatolia, particularly under General Mustafa Kemal in Samsun and General Kazim Karabekir in Erzurum. The nationalists turned to the Bolsheviks of Russia for military aid, concluding an agreement the following spring. Contact with the Bolsheviks also provided a bargaining chip with the anticommunist British.

On May 15, 1919, a large Greek force occupied Smyrna (Izmir). The Turkish War of Independence (1919–1923) can be said to have begun on May 19 with clashes between Greek and Turkish nationalist forces. The Greco-Turkish War is known to the Turks as the Western Front. Fighting in the east was largely between the Turks and Armenians. During September 4–11, an assembly of Turkish nationalist representatives from all the Anatolia provinces met in the city of Sivas in east-central Turkey.

On March 16, 1920, British troops seized government buildings in Istanbul and set up a pro-Allied cabinet, preparatory to forcing the Ottoman government to sign the punitive Treaty of Sèvres (August 10, 1920). In it, Ottoman control would be largely restricted to Anatolia, with the economy controlled by the Entente. The treaty made the Kingdom of Hejaz independent, gave Smyrna and many Aegean islands to Greece, ceded the Dodecanese Islands to Italy, internationalized the Turkish Straits, and granted Armenia independence. In addition, Syria, Palestine, and Mesopotamia were established as independent states under French and British mandates. The latter two powers also signed the San Remo oil agreement, delimiting their oil interests in Persia, Mesopotamia, and the Caucasus. These demands were presented to the sultan and the pro-Allied cabinet on June 10, 1920. Twelve days later, about 60,000 Greek troops advanced from Smyrna.

The Turkish forces were unprepared for the Greek military advance, and the Greek columns soon seized major cities in western Anatolia and Adrianople in Thrace. In the east an Armenian attack collapsed near Erzurum, and a Turkish counterattack forced the Armenians to sue for peace. The ensuing peace treaty reduced

Armenia to the province of Erivan. On March 16, 1921, the Turkish nationalists signed a treaty with Soviet Russia delimiting the border in the east and securing additional military assistance.

On March 23, 1921, the Greeks opened a new offensive toward Ankara. It soon stalled, but the Greeks regrouped and advanced again in July. The Turks withdrew across the Sakarya River and stood on the defensive. During August 23–September 16, they fought a successful series of meeting engagements known as the Battle of the Sakarya across a 120-mile front. At this point the French (as with the Italians earlier in the summer) agreed to withdraw from Anatolia in return for economic concessions.

During the winter, the British attempted to negotiate an end to the war through a partial revision of the Treaty of Sèvres. The nationalists in Ankara refused, and the Turks took the offensive on August 18, 1922. Superior Turkish cavalry forced the Greeks back; the retreat then turned into a rout, and the Greeks fled to the coast.

In response to the Turkish advance toward Istanbul, a British force landed to protect the straits. Armistice negotiations began shortly thereafter. The Greeks agreed to an armistice on October 11, 1922. The opposing sides opened negotiations in November and signed the Treaty of Lausanne on July 24, 1923. Although the Turks agreed to relinquish all prewar non-Turkish territory in the Middle East and lost almost all the offshore islands in the Aegean and the Mediterranean, the Greeks departed Anatolia, the Turks avoided any reparations, and no legal restrictions remained on their government.

The war had seen widespread atrocities committed by Greeks against Turks and by Turks against Greeks and Armenians, and an ensuing population exchange treaty concluded by the two governments saw Greek orthodox citizens of Turkey and Turkish and Greek Muslim citizens residing in Greece subjected to a forced exchange. Some 1.5 million Orthodox Christians from Turkey and 500,000 Turks and Greek Muslims from Greece were uprooted from their homelands.

The last British troops evacuated Istanbul on October 2, and the Republic of Turkey was formally established under the presidency of Kemal on October 29, 1923. Determined to see his country a modern, secular nation, Kemal (known as Ataturk and regarded as the father of modern-day Turkey) immediately embarked on an ambitious reform program. Expanding education was a major priority, with primary education made free and compulsory. Women were accorded equal civil and political rights, and taxation was reformed. Ataturk also pushed a policy of Turkification and sharply limited the influence of Islam. The new Turkey, although much more homogeneous than before, was also far smaller, and its foreign policy centered on preserving the status quo.

Ataturk died in 1938, and Premier Ismet Inönü, his closest associate, took over the leadership of the nation and its one political party, the People's Party. Inönü was reelected president in 1943.

During World War II, Turkey resisted pressure from both sides to join the war. With the consequences of World War I still fresh, Turkish leaders were understandably reluctant to embark on a new conflict, especially as their military was obsolete. Turkey did keep its large army mobilized throughout the conflict, however, worried by the ambitions not only of Germany and the Soviet Union but also those of Italy. Once the Germans controlled the Balkans, Ankara signed the Treaty of Territorial Integrity and Friendship with Berlin on June 18, 1941. The treaty extended economic concessions to Germany. İnönü strongly resisted pressure by the Germans to enter the war on the Axis side, however.

When the tide of war turned against the Axis, Turkey resumed its general pro-West position, although it also resisted pressure from the United States and Britain to enter the war on their side. Although Turkey declared war on Germany on February 23, 1945, this was to ensure membership in the UN.

Following the war, the Soviet Union applied tremendous pressure on Turkey to secure the two northeastern Turkish provinces of Kars and Ardahan, both of which had long been in contention between the two countries. Moscow also demanded a share of control over defense of the Turkish Straits. This Soviet pressure on Turkey and the simultaneous communist threat to Greece led to the 1947 U.S. Truman Doctrine and to Turkish membership in NATO in 1952. During the Cold War, Turkey was firmly in the Western camp and sent troops to fight on the UN side in the Korean War (1950–1953).

The Turkish single-party period ended in 1945. During the next decades Turkey experienced a tumultuous transition to multiparty democracy marked by a fragmented party system and unstable governments. With increasing domestic strife, the Turkish military, which regarded itself as the principal defender of the ideals of Ataturk and a secular state, mounted coup d'états in 1960, 1971, and 1980. To their credit, however, each time the army leaders restored the democratic process.

In foreign affairs, ongoing tensions between Turkey and Greece regarding Cyprus almost brought war between the two NATO states. Following a decade of violence in Cyprus and a coup on July 15, 1974, by the Greek EOKA B paramilitary organization that sought enosis (union with Greece), five days later Turkish forces invaded the island. The Turks took additional territory in northern Cyprus, encouraged Turks to migrate there, and set up the Turkish Republic of Northern Cyprus. The standoff regarding Cyprus continues, with the Turkish-installed republic recognized only by Turkey itself.

Turkey was a member of the international coalition that expelled Iraqi forces from Kuwait in the 1991 Persian Gulf War. Although Turkey provided no ground troops, it dispatched two frigates to the Persian Gulf and was heavily involved in basing coalition forces, including air assets. Ankara also allowed overflights of its airspace when the air war began in January. Rigid enforcement of the international economic blockade against Iraq cost Turkey an estimated $3 billion in revenues, chiefly from shutting down an oil pipeline through the country.

Generally speaking, aside from strong opposition to the creation of a Kurdish state, Turkey maintained a policy of alleged noninvolvement in Middle Eastern affairs for fear of being dragged into one of the region's internecine conflicts, especially the Arab-Israeli conflict. Turkey generally enjoyed cordial diplomatic relations with both Israel and its Arab neighbors. Turkey's involvement in the 1955 Baghdad Pact, pushed by the United States and scorned by Muslim states except for Iraq and Iran, did alienate it from much of the Middle East, especially Egypt. In the early 1960s, Turkey sought a more evenhanded Middle East policy that meant less cooperation with the United States and greater rapprochement with the Arab states.

An entente developed between Turkey and Israel in the 1990s. Both were Western-oriented states with close ties to the United States, and both sought closer ties with Europe. Leaders in both countries worried about the threats to this posed by terrorism, Islamic radicalism, and perceived hostile regimes in Syria and Iran. Cooperation included trade and tourism but also military cooperation, with Israeli upgrades of Turkish military equipment and the sharing of intelligence. Inhibiting this cooperation was strong public sympathy in Turkey toward the Palestinians.

Turkish-Israeli relations plummeted on May 31, 2010, when Israeli commandos mounted a raid in international waters of the Mediterranean against a flotilla of six ships, carrying humanitarian assistance to Gaza, that had originated in Turkey. Violence flared, and the Israeli commandos killed 10 people in one of the ships. Condemnation of Israel was especially strong in Turkey, which recalled its ambassador from Israel. The 2014 Israel-Gaza War also saw Turkish president Recep Tayyip Erdoğan strongly condemn Israel's policies, characterizing them as more "barbaric" than those of Adolf Hitler.

Following the terrorist attacks on the United States of September 11, 2001, Ankara immediately offered its full support. It extended airspace and refueling rights as the U.S.-led coalition began operations against Afghanistan's Taliban regime in October 2001, and the next year Turkey dispatched troops to join the International Security Assistance Force–Afghanistan. The deployment numbered some 1,700 personnel in 2009, but the troops were not engaged in combat operations, and Erdoğan, then Turkish prime minister, resisted pressure from Washington to offer more combat troops in large part because Turkish public opinion was ambivalent about the mission in Afghanistan. Erdoğan initially opposed any NATO military intervention in the 2011 Libyan Civil War, and when Turkey did go along with the operation, its military remained largely on the sidelines. Erdoğan also angered Washington when he engaged the Russians in a series of bilateral commercial and energy agreements to include a major pipeline deal in December 2014. He was also largely silent regarding the Russian seizure of Crimea and intervention in eastern Ukraine.

In recent years, three political parties have vied for power in Turkey. The largest by far is the Justice and Development Party (AKP), followed in order of magnitude by the Republican People's Party and the far-right Nationalist Movement Party (MHP). Erdoğan's AKP won a surprise landslide victory in the November 2002 legislative elections, and the charismatic Erdoğan became prime minister in 2003. He held that post until 2014, when he was elected president. Concerns have been raised about the AKP's Islamic-based ideology, but Erdoğan initially focused on economic reform and securing Turkey's entrance into the EU.

Erdoğan did move against the Turkish military, long regarded as the guardian of the secular state, and dramatically purged its leadership. In July 2011, the nation's top four military commanders abruptly resigned to protest the detention of hundreds of military officers on charges of conspiring against the government in 2009. In September 2012, a Turkish court convicted 330 military officers, including the top former commanders of the army, navy, and air force, of the plot and sentenced them to as much as 20 years in prison. In August 2013, there were additional sentences. Former chief of staff of the army General Ilker Basbug received a life sentence; 3 former members of the Turkish parliament also received prison terms, as did 20 journalists. This purge brought international condemnation regarding judicial fairness and was seen by many as a move to stifle dissent.

Erdoğan also secured constitutional changes in 2010 that served to strengthen his authority. While the Turkish economy has registered solid gains, Erdoğan's Islamic stance and his authoritarianism remain concerns for many secular Turks as well as Western governments.

Erdoğan has also taken a hard line regarding the Kurds. The Kurds live in the mountainous region known as Kurdistan, encompassing southeastern Turkey, eastern Syria, northern Iraq, and western Iran. Kurdistan includes the oil fields in Iraq around Kirkuk and is rich in other natural resources. Most Kurds are Sunni Muslims.

Turkey is home to 15 million Kurds, representing nearly half of the world's Kurdish population of 30 million, the world's largest ethnic group without a state. (Some 7 million Kurds live in Iran, 6 million live in Iraq, and 2 million live in Syria.) Statehood appeared on the verge of realization following World War I. Indeed, the 1920 Treaty of Sèvres promised the Kurds autonomy leading to statehood after a plebiscite, but the Treaty of Lausanne of 1923 recognized Turkish sovereignty over northern Kurdistan, while the remainder of Kurdish territory fell in Iran and the new states of Iraq and Syria.

Kurdish rebellions occurred in the 1960s and 1970s in Iraq, while Kurds revolted in Iran during the Iranian Revolution of 1979. In 1988, Iraqi president Saddam Hussein ordered military force against the Iraqi Kurds. Conventional attacks and chemical warfare destroyed some 2,000 villages and killed upwards of 180,000 Kurds. The Iraqi Army crushed other Kurdish revolts following the Persian Gulf War in 1991 and also in 1995.

Turkey's Kurds have long claimed discrimination and attempts by the government to eradicate their culture. On November 27, 1978, Abdullah Öcalan established the Partiya Karkerên Kurdistan (Kurdistan Workers' Party, PKK), initially composed largely of students. In addition to stressing Kurdish nationalism, the PKK initially espoused a Marxist ideology.

Almost immediately the PKK was locked in combat with right-wing parties in Turkey and with those Kurdish leaders it accused of collaboration with the government. Beginning in 1984 the PKK commenced an insurgency in southern Turkey, home to most Turkish Kurds. This took the form of attacks and bombings against government institutions and military installations. In the mid-1990s the PKK initiated suicide bombings, the majority of which were carried out by women.

In March 1995 the Turkish Army responded with Operation STEEL CURTAIN, sending 35,000 troops into the Kurdish zone of northern Iraq in an effort to trap several thousand guerrillas and halt PKK cross-border raids. In the late 1990s, Turkey increased pressure on the PKK when an undeclared war between Turkey and Syria ended open Syrian support for the PKK.

In February 1999 Turkish commandos, assisted by U.S. intelligence, seized Öcalan in Kenya. Brought before a Turkish court, he was condemned to death, but this was commuted to life imprisonment as part of negotiations for Turkish membership in the EU. That same month the Turkish Army again invaded northern Iraq to wipe out PKK bases there.

Meanwhile, the Turkish government sought to allay international criticism of its actions by somewhat relaxing legislation directed against the Kurds, including bans on broadcasting and publishing in the Kurdish language. At the same time, the PKK found itself blacklisted in a number of states. Both the United States and the EU characterized the PKK as a terrorist organization.

No reliable casualty figures exist, but the Turkish Army has set the numbers of killed through 1984 at 6,482 Turkish military personnel, 32,000 PKK troops, and 5,560 civilians. The army also claims 14,000 PKK troops taken prisoner. The PKK claims that the Turkish armed forces destroyed some 8,000 Kurdish communities and displaced 3 million to 4 million people.

Kurdish hopes for at least autonomy received a boost from the 2003–2011 Iraq War, when Kurds in northern Iraq all but established their own state, a development long opposed by Ankara, which long feared that if Iraq were to break into separate states, this would mean an independent Kurdish nation that would lay claim to Turkish territory. This was a major factor in Ankara's decision to refuse support for the U.S.-led invasion, despite strong financial incentives offered by Washington. This decision by Ankara denied a secure northern base of operations for the U.S. Army's 4th Infantry Division and forced a recasting of the coalition's military plans, severely straining relations between the United States and Turkey. The war also saw Ankara accusing Washington of failing to wipe out PKK bases in northern Iraq.

In February 2008, Turkish military forces launched an incursion into northern Iraq again against the PKK. This brief eight-day incursion was preceded by Turkish air strikes against PKK targets beginning in December 2007. Perhaps 550 PPK fighters died in the fighting. Both the Iraqi and U.S. governments voiced their displeasure at the Turkish action.

Talks between the Turkish government and the PKK between 2009 and 2011 in Oslo failed, and in January 2013 the Erdoğan government entered into peace talks with Öcalan, who signaled an immense shift in PKK policy by calling for a cease-fire. A shaky cease-fire ensued in April, and despite isolated attacks thereafter, there was cautious optimism about resolving the conflict. The government demanded disarmament and withdrawal of PKK forces, while the Kurds sought more language and cultural rights within Turkey as well as a degree of autonomy.

On October 13, 2014, however, the Kurds were angered when Turkish aircraft, rather than coming to the relief of Kurds under attack by the Islamic extremist Islamic State of Iraq and Syria (ISIS) at Kobanî just across the Turkish border with Syria, attacked PKK positions in southeastern Turkey even though the PKK was aligned with the Kurds fighting ISIS in Syria. Then on July 20, 2015, an ISIS suicide bombing killed more than 30 Kurdish activists in the southern Turkish town of Suruc. The PKK blamed the government for not preventing the attack and declared the cease-fire at an end, although Öcalan had not issued such a statement. On

July 22, a PKK-linked car bombing killed 2 Turkish soldiers. In retaliation, Turkey launched air strikes against PKK camps in northern Iraq and ISIS militants in Syria and also rounded up alleged supporters from both groups. On July 28, Erdoğan announced an end to the peace process. This occurred just as the liberal Kurdish-based People's Democratic Party (HDP) was becoming a rising force in Turkey's politics.

On February 17, 2016, a bomb-laden vehicle exploded near the Turkish parliament building in Ankara, targeting military vehicles stopped in traffic. The blast killed 28 people and injured 61 others. The next day Turkish prime minister Ahmet Davutoglu identified the assailant as having links to the People's Protection Units, the military wing of the Kurdish Democratic Union Party, a PKK offshoot. The Turkish military retaliated with air strikes in northern Iraq targeting the PKK.

Another blast occurred in Ankara in a busy square on March 13, 2016, killing 37 people and wounding 125. Turkish aircraft then mounted air strikes on what were described as PKK bases in northern Iraq, although subsequently the Kurdish Freedom Falcons, another PKK offshoot, claimed responsibility. Despite all this, Turkey imported oil from the Kurdish region of northern Iraq.

Erdoğan now found himself engaged on three separate fronts not only against the militant Kurds and ISIS but also the Syrian regime president of Bashar al-Assad. Washington and Ankara often seemed at odds on policy decisions regarding Syria, however. Thus, Erdoğan extended aid to antigovernment rebels in the Syrian Civil War that began in 2011 without coordinating with Washington, which failed to support his calls for the imposition of a no-fly zone over portions of Syria. In 2012 Turkey joined Saudi Arabia and Qatar in establishing a center in Adana in southeastern Turkey to assist the rebel Free Syrian Army in its fight with Syrian government forces. In 2013, 2014, and 2015, Turkey shot down Syrian military aircraft that it claimed had violated its airspace.

In the early fall of 2014, Washington sought permission to use Turkey's Incirlik Air Base as a staging area for its aircraft attacking ISIS targets in Iraq and Syria. Erdoğan said that he would accede to the request only after Assad had been removed from power, a stance that angered Washington and may have cost Turkey a seat on the UN Security Council. On October 12, 2014, however, Erdoğan relented and permitted U.S. and other coalition forces some basing rights. On February 19, 2015, Turkey and the United States signed an agreement to train and arm Syrian rebels at a base in Kirsehir, Turkey.

Although the Turkish government had long been reluctant to attack ISIS, on August 24, 2015, a day after ISIS militants fired on a Turkish border outpost, Turkish aircraft attacked ISIS targets in Syria. Ankara also announced that it would allow U.S.-led coalition forces to base manned and unmanned aircraft at its air bases for operations against ISIS and that Turkey's military would take part in the operations. This meant far shorter distances for U.S. aircraft to travel in order to strike ISIS targets. On August 28, the Turkish Air Force carried out its first air strikes as part of the coalition against ISIS.

On the morning of October 10 two powerful bombs exploded near the main train station in Ankara, targeting a peace rally. In this deadliest terrorist attack in modern Turkish history, 103 people were killed and some 400 others were injured.

The explosions occurred during a gathering of some 14,000 people for a peace march at noon. The demonstrators included members of the Kurdish-based HDP, with the demonstrators calling for an end to the renewed conflict between the government and the PKK.

Critics charged that this attack impacted the national elections, held only three weeks later, for on November 1, 2015, Erdoğan's AKP won a landslide victory in the parliamentary elections, regaining the parliamentary majority it had lost five months earlier in the June 2015 general election. The results of this snap election called in August came as a surprise, with critics charging that government attacks on independent media and journalists by AKP supporters all but silenced the opposition. The election took place amid security concerns following the collapse of cease-fire negotiations with the PKK in July, resulting in a renewal of the Kurdish separatist conflict in which nearly 150 security personnel had lost their lives. Critics accused the government of deliberately sparking the conflict with the Kurds in order to win back votes it had lost to the MHP in June and decrease the turnout in the areas of the rising Kurdish HDP.

On November 24, 2015, Turkish fighters shot down a Russian Sukhoi Su-24 bomber. The Turks claimed that it had violated their airspace and that the Russian pilot had been warned. The Russians denied this. Washington supported Ankara's version. Russian president Vladimir Putin said the shoot-down would have "serious consequences." Russia then deployed S-400 antiaircraft missiles to its Hmeymim air base in Syria. These missiles have a range of some 155 miles, and the Turkish border is less than 30 miles distant. Putin also imposed economic sanctions on Turkey, including a ban on tourist travel there.

Terrorism continued to be a major threat in Turkey. Seeking to answer complaints by foreign governments that it was not doing enough to prevent ISIS access to its territory and the transit of recruits from Turkey to Syria, Turkey began a crackdown on ISIS. On January 12, 2016, an explosion rocked Sultanahmet Square in Istanbul, killing at least 10 people (8 of them Germans) and wounding 15 others. ISIS claimed responsibility. Then on March 19 a suicide bomber, reportedly also linked to ISIS, killed 4 people and wounded at least 36 others in a busy Istanbul shopping district. The dead included 2 Israelis and 2 Americans. Erdoğan continues his efforts to concentrate power in his own hands and crack down on press freedoms and critics of his government. He is also actively seeking a new constitution that would give the president ultimate authority. In May 2016 Erdoğan forced out his handpicked premier, Davutoglu, reportedly because he was upset over the international attention Davutoglu had received in negotiating a pact regarding the numerous refugees from Syria and other Middle Eastern trouble spots making their way through Turkey to other European nations.

In late June, Turkey reestablished diplomatic relations with both the Soviet Union and Israel. Then on June 28, three suicide bombers armed with automatic weapons and wearing suicide vests attacked Ataturk International Airport, Europe's third-busiest airport, in Istanbul, killing 42 people and wounding 239. The government blamed ISIS, which had called for such attacks during the Muslim holy month of Ramadan.

Many Turks resent the phobia expressed by many Americans and West Europeans toward their country's Muslim identity and what they perceive as a lack of support for Ankara's efforts to stamp out the Kurdish threat. Certainly Turkey continues to cast a watchful eye on the future of Iraq and Syria. Because Turkey is so important geopolitically, the rest of the world will watch it as well.

Timeline

1853–1856	The Crimean War occurs, with Britain, France, and Sardinia-Piedmont supporting the Ottoman Empire against Russian territorial aspirations.
1877–1878	In the Russo-Turkish War, Russia allies with the Ottoman principalities of Romania, Bulgaria, Serbia, and Montenegro to defeat Ottoman forces. Russia gains territory in the Caucasus, the principalities become independent, and Bulgaria becomes a principality. Austria-Hungary is allowed to occupy Bosnia and Herzegovina, and Great Britain secures Cyprus.
1908	Turkish reformers of the Committee of Union and Progress (CUP), part of the Young Turk movement, convince Sultan Abdul Hamid II (r. 1876–1909) to restore the parliament.
Apr 27, 1909	The CUP deposes Sultan Abdul Hamid II and replaces him with his younger brother, Mehmed V.
Sep 29, 1911	Italy declares war on the Ottoman Empire to secure Tripoli (present-day Libya).
Oct 8, 1912	Encouraged by the Italian success, Montenegro, Bulgaria, Serbia, and Greece begin the First Balkan War in order to secure Ottoman territory in Europe.
Oct 18, 1912	In the Treaty of Lausanne, Italy secures sovereignty over Libya.
Oct 28–Nov 3, 1912	The Bulgarians defeat the Ottomans in the Battle of Lulé Burgas.
Nov 16–18, 1912	The Serbs defeat the Ottomans in the Battle of Monastir (Bitola).
Jan 23, 1913	With Sultan Mehmed V discredited by the steady stream of Ottoman military reverses, the CUP mounts a coup d'état.
May 30, 1913	The Treaty of London ends the First Balkan War. The Ottoman Empire cedes the vast majority of its territory in Europe.
Jun 29, 1913	The Second Balkan War begins when the victors in the First Balkan War begin quarreling among themselves. The war pits Greece, Serbia, Romania, Montenegro, and the Ottoman Empire against Bulgaria, the chief territorial beneficiary in the first conflict.

Aug 10, 2013	The Treaty of Bucharest brings to an end the Second Balkan War. Bulgaria loses considerable territory to Greece and Serbia, and the Ottoman Empire recovers Adrianople.
Dec 1913	A German military mission arrives in Istanbul to help reorganize the Ottoman Army.
Aug 2, 1914	Ottoman leaders sign a secret alliance with Germany and the next day mobilize their military.
Oct 28, 1914	The former German battle cruiser *Goeben* and destroyer *Breslau*, given to Turkey but still under German command, attack Russian ports and shipping in the Black Sea.
Nov 4, 1914	Russia declares war on the Ottoman Empire.
Nov 14, 1914	Mehmed V proclaims jihad (holy war) against the Entente powers.
Dec 17, 1914	The Turkish Third Army commences offensive operations against the Russians in Caucasia.
Dec 22, 1914– Jan 17, 1915	The Turkish Third Army suffers a major defeat at the hands of the Russians in the Battle of Sariklamish.
Apr 1915	The Ottoman First and Third Armies contain the Entente landing at Gallipoli.
Apr 1915–1917	Some 1.5 million Armenians perish in the forced desert relocation known as the Armenian Massacre and, controversially, as the Armenian Genocide.
Apr 29, 1916	The Ottomans secure a major military victory at Kut in Mesopotamia when an entire Indian Army division surrenders to the Ottoman Sixth Army.
1917–1918	Aided by the British, Arabs of the Hejaz revolt against the Ottomans, greatly aiding British military efforts.
Oct 30, 1918	The Armistice of Mudros ends Ottoman participation in World War I.
Nov 15, 1918	The Ottoman Empire unofficially ends when Sultan Mehmed VI establishes a new government controlled by Greek and British troops. Considerable numbers of Allied troops then arrive. Turkish nationalists in eastern Anatolia, led by Generals Mustafa Kemal and Kazim Karabekir, affirm the unity of Turkish territory and deny that the Allies have occupation rights. The nationalists secure some aid from Bolshevik Russia.
May 15, 1919	Greek forces occupy Smyrna (Izmir).
May 19, 1919	Beginning of the Turkish War of Independence (1919–1923). Turkish nationalist forces resist the Greeks on the Western Front.

In the east, fighting occurs between the Turkish nationalists and the Armenians.

Sep 4–11, 1919　An assembly of representatives of the Turkish National Movement from all the Anatolia provinces meet at Sivas in east-central Turkey.

Mar 16, 1920　British troops seize government buildings in Istanbul and set up a pro-Allied cabinet.

Jun 22, 1920　Greek forces advance from Smyrna to help enforce the terms of the impending peace treaty with the empire and soon seize the major cities in western Anatolia and Adrianople in Thrace. In the east an Armenian attack collapses near Erzurum, and the Turks then force the Armenians to sue for peace, reducing Armenia to the province of Erivan.

Aug 10, 1920　The Ottoman government is forced to sign the punitive Treaty of Sèvres, which limits Ottoman control largely to Anatolia.

Mar 16, 1921　Turkish nationalists sign a treaty with Bolshevik Russia delimiting the border in the east and securing additional military assistance.

Mar 23, 1921　The Greeks open an offensive toward Ankara.

Aug 23–Sep 16, 1921　The Turks are successful in a series of engagements known as the Battle of the Sakarya across a 120-mile front.

Aug 18, 1922　British efforts to negotiate an end to the war through a partial revision of the Treaty of Sèvres having failed, the Turks take the offensive, routing the Greeks and driving them back to the coast.

Oct 11, 1922　An armistice is concluded, and peace talks open in November.

Jul 24, 1923　The Treaty of Lausanne brings to an end the Greco-Turkish War. Although the Turks agree to relinquish all prewar non-Turkish territory in the Middle East and lose almost all the offshore islands in the Aegean and the Mediterranean, the Greeks depart Anatolia, no reparations are paid, and there are no legal restrictions on the Turkish government.

Oct 29, 1923　The Republic of Turkey is formally established under the presidency of Mustafa Kemal, known as Kemal Ataturk. Determined to make his country a modern, secular state, Ataturk embarks on an ambitious reform program.

Jun 18, 1941　The consequences of World War I still fresh, Turkey resists pressure from both sides to join World War II. With the Germans controlling the Balkans, however, the Turks sign a treaty with Berlin granting Germany economic concessions.

Feb 23, 1945　Turkey declares war on Germany in order to secure membership in the United Nations.

Mar 12, 1947	With the Soviet Union applying tremendous pressure on Turkey to secure the two northeastern Turkish provinces of Kars and Ardahan and demanding a share of control over defense of the Turkish Straits, U.S. president Harry S. Truman issues what becomes known as the Truman Doctrine, which brings aid to both Turkey and Greece.
1950–1953	Turkish force participate in the Korean War as part of the United Nations Command.
Feb 18, 1952	Turkey joins the North Atlantic Treaty Organization.
1955–1979	Turkey is a member of the U.S.-sponsored Baghdad Pact.
May 27, 1960	Turkish Army officers seize power in a coup d'état but restore the administrative process to civilians in October 1961.
Mar 12, 1971	Amid worsening domestic strife, the Turkish Army again takes power in a coup d'état but relinquishes it in 1973.
Jul 20, 1974	Heightened tensions between Greece and Turkey over Cyprus almost bring war. A coup d'état on the island on July 15, 1974, by Greeks bent on securing the union of Cyprus with Greece brings a Turkish military invasion of Cyprus on this date and a subsequent land grab and proclamation of the Turkish Republic of Northern Cyprus. The standoff on Cyprus continues.
Nov 27, 1978	Abdullah Öcalan establishes the Partiya Karkerên Kurdistan (Kurdistan Workers' Party, PKK). Espousing a Marxist ideology, the PKK seeks an end to constraints on Kurdish culture and supports Kurdish autonomy.
Sep 12, 1980	The Turkish Army again seizes power but restores democratic rule three years later.
1984	The PKK commences an insurgency in southern Turkey, attacking Turkish government institutions and military installations.
Mid-1990s	The PKK initiates a series of suicide bombings, a majority of which are carried out by women.
Aug 1990–Feb 1991	Turkey is a member of the international coalition that expels Iraqi forces from Kuwait in the Persian Gulf War.
Mar 1995	In Operation STEEL CURTAIN, the Turkish Army sends 35,000 troops into the Kurdish zone of northern Iraq in an effort to trap guerrillas and halt PKK cross-border raids from Iraq.
Feb 15, 1999	Turkish commandos seize PKK leader Öcalan in Kenya. Brought to trial, he is condemned to death, but widespread demonstrations and international pressure lead to the sentence being commuted to life imprisonment.

Oct 2001   Following the terrorist attacks on the United States of September 11, 2001, Ankara extends airspace and refueling rights for the U.S.-led coalition operating against Afghanistan's Taliban regime in October 2001 and the next year sends troops to join the International Security Assistance Force–Afghanistan.

Feb 2008   Turkish forces mount an incursion into northern Iraq. Perhaps 550 PPK fighters are killed in the fighting.

2009–2011   Peace talks take place in Oslo between the Turkish government and the PKK but are unsuccessful.

2011–2013   Recep Tayyip Erdoğan, founder and leader of the Justice and Development Party (AKP) and prime minister of Turkey during 2003–2014, purges the Turkish military leadership. Hundreds of military officers are accused of conspiring against the government and are sentenced to prison, as are some members of parliament and journalists.

Mar 15, 2011 Beginning of the Syrian Civil War, with the government of Syrian president Bashar al-Assad seeking to crush a movement demanding political change. The Turkish government aligns itself squarely against Assad and calls for his removal.

Jan 2013   The Turkish government enters into peace talks with Öcalan, and the PKK leader calls for a cease-fire, which ensues in April.

Aug 28, 2014 Erdoğan assumes office as president of Turkey.

Oct 12, 2014 Erdoğan agrees to grant U.S. and other coalition forces aircraft basing rights in southern Turkey to attack Islamic State of Iraq and Syria (ISIS) targets.

Feb 19, 2015 Turkey and the United States sign an agreement to train and arm a limited number of Syrian rebels at a base in Kirsehir, Turkey.

Jul 20, 2015 An ISIS suicide bombing kills more than 30 Kurdish activists in the southern Turkish town of Suruc. The PKK blames the government for not preventing the attack and, coupled with the failure of the Turkish government to aid Kurds fighting ISIS at Kobani just across the border in Syria, declares the cease-fire at an end.

Jul 22, 2015 A PKK-linked car bombing kills two Turkish soldiers. Turkey retaliates with air strikes against PKK camps in northern Iraq and ISIS militants in Syria and also rounds up alleged supporters from both groups. On July 28, Erdoğan announces an end to the peace process.

Aug 28, 2015 The Turkish Air Force carries out its first air strikes as part of the coalition against ISIS in Syria.

Oct 10, 2015	Two powerful bombs explode near the main train station in Ankara, targeting a peace rally. In the deadliest terrorist attack in Turkish history, 103 people are killed, and some 400 others are injured. The explosions occur during a gathering of some 14,000 people for a peace march at noon. The demonstrators include members of the Kurdish-based People's Democratic Party, with the demonstrators calling for an end to the renewed conflict between the government and the PKK.
Nov 1, 2015	Erdoğan's AKP wins a landslide victory in national parliamentary elections, regaining the parliamentary majority it had lost five months earlier in the June 2015 general election.
Nov 24, 2015	Turkish fighters shoot down a Russian Sukhoi Su-24 bomber that the government claims had violated Turkish airspace. (The Turks had previously downed several Syrian aircraft in similar circumstances.) The two crewmen eject safely but are captured, and one is killed on the ground by Turkmen fighting the Syrian government (the other is rescued). Accusing the Turks of a deliberate provocation, Russian president Vladimir Putin sends antiaircraft missiles to a Russian base in Syria and institutes economic retaliation against Turkey.
Jan 12, 2016	An explosion in Sultanahmet Square in Istanbul kills at least 10 people (8 of them Germans) and wounds 15 others. ISIS claims responsibility.
Feb 17, 2016	A car bomb explodes in Ankara, killing 28 people and injuring 61 others. The blast is linked to the People's Protection Units, the military wing of the Kurdish Democratic Union Party, a PKK offshoot. The Turkish military retaliates with air strikes in northern Iraq targeting the PKK.
Mar 19, 2016	A suicide bomber, reportedly also linked to ISIS, kills 4 people and wounds at least 36 others in a busy shopping district in Istanbul.
Mar 13, 2016	Another blast occurs in Ankara, killing 37 people and wounding 125. Turkish aircraft retaliate with air strikes against alleged PKK bases in northern Iraq, although subsequently the Kurdish Freedom Falcons, another PKK offshoot, claims responsibility.
Jun 29, 2016	Three suicide bombers with automatic weapons and explosive vests attack Istanbul Ataturk Airport, killing 42 people and wounding 239. The government blames ISIS, which had called for such attacks during the Muslim holy month of Ramadan.

Further Reading

Barkey, Henri J., ed. *Reluctant Neighbor: Turkey's Role in the Middle East.* Washington, DC: U.S. Institute of Peace, 1996.

Butler, Daniel Allen. *Shadow of the Sultan's Realm: The Destruction of the Ottoman Empire and the Creation of the Modern Middle East.* Dulles, VA: Potomac Books, 2011.

Carkoglu, Ali, and William Hale, eds. *The Politics of Modern Turkey.* London: Taylor and Francis, 2008.

Deringil, Selim. *Turkish Foreign Policy during the Second World War.* New York: Cambridge University Press, 1989.

Finkel, Caroline. *Osman's Dream: The History of the Ottoman Empire.* New York: Basic Books, 2007.

Fromkin, David. *A Peace to End All Peace: The Fall of the Ottoman Empire and the Creation of the Modern Middle East.* Lakewood, WA: Owl Books, 2001.

Howard, Douglas Arthur. *The History of Turkey.* Westport, CT: Greenwood, 2001.

Karpat, H. Kemal. *Turkey's Foreign Policy in Transition, 1950–1974.* Leiden: E. J. Brill, 1975.

Lewis, Bernard. *The Emergence of Modern Turkey.* 3rd ed. New York: Oxford University Press, 2002.

Macfie, A. L. *The End of the Ottoman Empire, 1918–1923.* London: Longman, 1998.

Mango, Amdrew. *Ataturk: The Biography of the Founder of Modern Turkey.* New York: Penguin, 2002.

Mavkovsky, Alan, ed. *Turkey's New World: Changing Dynamics in Turkish Foreign Policy.* Washington, DC: Washington Institute for Near East Policy, 2000.

McCarthy, Justin. *The Ottoman Turks.* London: Longman, 1997.

Metz, Helen Chapin. *Turkey: A Country Study.* Washington, DC: Federal Research Division, Library of Congress, U.S. Government Printing Office, 1996.

Millman, Brock. *The Ill-Made Alliance: Anglo-Turkish Relations, 1934–1940.* Montreal: McGill-Queen's University Press, 1998.

Natali, Denise. *The Kurds and the State.* Syracuse, NY: Syracuse University Press, 2005.

Palmer, Alan. *The Decline and Fall of the Ottoman Empire.* London: Murray, 1992.

Robins, Philip. *Turkey and the Middle East.* New York: Council on Foreign Relations Press, 1991.

Shaw, Stanford J., and Ezel Kural Shaw. *History of the Ottoman Empire and Modern Turkey.* 2 vols. Cambridge: Cambridge University Press, 1977.

Tahiri, Hussein. *The Structure of Kurdish Society and the Struggle for a Kurdish State.* Costa Mesa, CA: Mazda Publications, 2007.

Turfan, M. Naim. *The Rise of the Young Turks: Politics, the Military and Ottoman Collapse.* New York: I. B. Tauris, 2000.

Weisband, Edward. *Turkish Foreign Policy, 1943–1945: Small State Diplomacy and Great Power Politics.* Princeton, NJ: Princeton University Press, 1973.

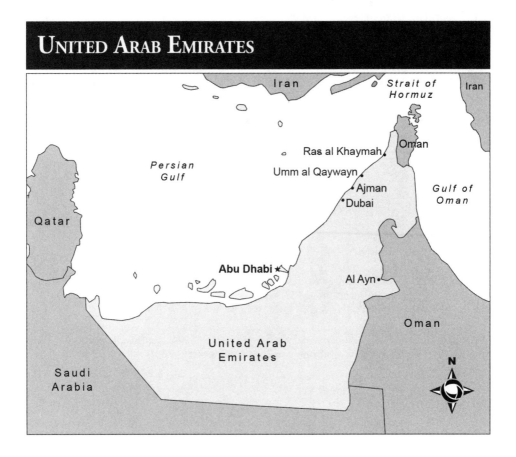

United Arab Emirates

Spencer C. Tucker and Wyndham E. Whynot

The United Arab Emirates (UAE) is located on the Persian Gulf along the southeastern end of the Arabian Peninsula. It is bordered by the Persian Gulf to the north, Oman to the east, and Saudi Arabia to the south and west. Known as the Trucial States until 1971, the UAE is a federation of seven emirates: Abu Dhabi, Ajman, Fujayrah, Sharjah, Dubai, Ras Khaymah, and Umm Qaiwain. The UAE comprises 32,278 square miles in area, just slightly larger than the U.S. state of South Carolina.

In 2016 the UAE had a population of some 9.267 million. Dubai is the most populous of the emirates, with nearly 36 percent of the total. About 50 percent of the UAE population is South Asian in ethnicity (including many Pakistanis, Indians, and Sri Lankans), 42 percent are Amirati Arabs and Iranians, and 8 percent are others. Islam is the official religion and is practiced by some 96 percent of the population; the remaining 4 percent practice Hinduism, Buddhism, and varying denominations of Christianity. Owing to its considerable oil reserves, the UAE is a prosperous and relatively wealthy nation, making it a significant draw for foreigners from other parts of the region.

Politics in the UAE are tightly controlled by the ruling sheikhs, and there are no political parties. The presidency and the post of prime minister are both hereditary positions, and members of the Supreme Council and the Council of Ministers are chosen by the leaders of the seven emirates.

Islam was established as the religion of the region in 630 CE. The Persian Gulf was a major trade route with India and China and attracted the Portuguese and then the Dutch and the British. Extensive piratical activity with attacks on merchant trade with India brought British military intervention in 1809 and again in 1819. In 1820 Britain and a number of local rulers signed a treaty to combat piracy. This and later agreements led to the term of the Trucial States, which defined the status of the coastal emirates. Another treaty with the British was signed in 1843.

Beginning in 1853, Great Britain forced the separate emirates of the area to sign treaties to prevent conflicts between them, reduce piracy in the Persian Gulf, and eliminate participation in the slave trade. During March 6–8, 1892, the British and the emirates signed another treaty that tightened the bonds between the two. As with treaties entered into by the British with other Persian Gulf principalities, the sheikhs agreed not to cede territory to any other nation or enter into commercial arrangements or other venues of exchange with foreign governments without the consent of the British government. In return, the British pledged to protect the emirates from outside aggression.

In 1952, the sheikhs formed the Trucial States Council. The tribal nature of society and the lack of drawn borders produced frequent territorial disputes, which were settled either through mediation or on occasion by force. To keep the peace, the British established a military formation known first as the Trucial Oman Levies, then the Trucial Oman Scouts.

Oil was discovered in drilling off Abu Dhabi in 1958, and oil exports began four years later. Subsequent oil revenues led Abu Dhabi ruler Zayed bin Sultan al-Nahyan to undertake a massive public works program. When Dubai's oil exports commenced in 1969, its ruler, Sheikh Rashid bin Saeed al-Maktoum, began the construction of modern-day Dubai.

The independence of India and Pakistan in 1947 greatly reduced British interest in controlling the Persian Gulf region. Britain also could no longer afford the expense. Therefore, on January 24, 1968, British prime minister Harold Wilson announced his government's decision to let the treaties with the emirates lapse in three years. This was reaffirmed in March 1971 by Prime Minister Edward Heath. Sufficiently worried about the ensuing threat from more powerful neighboring states, Abu Dhabi ruler Sheikh Zayed bin Sultan al-Nahyan offered to pay the full costs of keeping the British armed forces in the emirates if London would reconsider, but the Labour government refused. That the threat to the emirates was real

Recruits for the Trucial Oman Scouts march in Manama, Bahrain, in 1971. (AP Photo/Horst Faas)

was apparent when Iran seized by force the Tunb Islands and Saudi Arabia claimed territory in Abu Dhabi. In July 1971, six of the emirate rulers met in Dubai and there agreed to establish a union. In September, however, Qatar reversed course and declined to join.

With the expiration of the British treaty, the emirates became fully independent on December 1, 1971. The rulers of Abu Dhabi and Dubai formed a union of their two emirates, then drafted a constitution and called for the rulers of the other emirates to join. On December 2, 1971, four other emirates agreed to form the UAE. Bahrain and Qatar declined, while Ras al-Khaimah joined in early 1972. Meanwhile, the Trucial Oman Scouts became the Union Defence Force upon the formation of the UAE.

With the formation of the UAE, the Federal National Council was created, a consultative body appointed by the seven rulers. A permanent component of the country's governing structure, it includes the Supreme Council, the president, the cabinet, and the judiciary. The council is composed of 40 members—8 each from Abu Dhabi and Dubai, 6 each from Sharjah and Ras Al Khaimah, and 4 each from Ajman, Umm Al Quwain and Fujairah.

The UAE joined the Arab League in 1971. In May 1981, the UAE was a founding member of the Gulf Cooperation Council. In January 1982, prompted by the perceived threats of the Islamic Republic of Iran, the ongoing Iran-Iraq War, and the Soviet-Afghan War, the UAE joined Saudi Arabia, Bahrain, Kuwait, Oman, and Qatar in establishing a joint military command structure and integrated air defense system.

During the Iran-Iraq War (1980–1988) the UAE staked out a studiously ambivalent position toward the conflict. This was partly because its government sought to eschew entanglements with foreign powers but also because the nation profited handsomely from the war. UAE oil revenues rose dramatically as those of Iran and Iraq flagged. In late July 1990, however, when Iraqi forces were threatening to move against Kuwait, the UAE was among the first nations to recommend joint military action to deter Iraqi aggression. Indeed, the week prior to the August 2, 1990, Iraqi invasion of Kuwait, the air forces of the United States and the UAE engaged in a joint air-refueling exercise meant as a warning to Iraqi president Saddam Hussein.

Since its formation in 1971, the UAE has maintained generally good relations with the West and in particular the United States. The UAE contributed several hundred troops to the coalition effort in the 1991 Persian Gulf War, provided air support, and permitted U.S. military aircraft flying from its airfields to bomb Iraqi positions. By mid-1991 the UAE had given or pledged as much as $6 billion to foreign nations that had waged the war against Iraq. Six UAE soldiers were killed during the Persian Gulf War.

The UAE was one of only three nations to recognize the Taliban government of Afghanistan, the others being Pakistan and Saudi Arabia. The UAE has eyed Iran with trepidation since the 1979 revolution there brought a fundamentalist Islamic republic to power. Relations between the two nations have remained tense, abetted by disputes over control of several islands in the Persian Gulf. In the hopes of securing these islands, the UAE joined Kuwait and Saudi Arabia in providing considerable financial support to Iraq during the Iran-Iraq War (1980–1988). With Iran repeatedly threatening Israel and Western nations with the prospect of closing the strait at the mouth of the Persian Gulf, in July 2012 the UAE opened an overland oil pipeline, bypassing the Strait of Hormuz.

Following the September 11, 2001, terrorist attacks against the United States, the UAE sharply condemned such violence and has been a steady and reliable partner in the global war on terror. In the immediate aftermath of the attacks, the UAE promptly severed diplomatic ties with the ruling Taliban government in Afghanistan.

UAE armed forces, although still small in number, are equipped with some of the most modern weapon systems available. The United States, France, and Great Britain are the principal suppliers. In contrast to most other Arab states, the UAE permitted U.S. and coalition troops access to its military facilities to prosecute the Iraq War beginning in 2003. The UAE also contributed as many as 20,000 troops to protect Kuwait in the event that Iraqi forces moved against that country at the beginning of the war. However, as the war dragged on, UAE support for it waned, and the government condemned the conflict.

In March 2011, the UAE agreed to join the North Atlantic Treaty Organization's enforcement of a no-fly zone over Libya with a contribution of a dozen aircraft. The UAE and Egypt are close allies and military partners, with both opposing political Islam. In late August 2014 UAE and Egyptian aircraft carried out air strikes against Islamist-allied militias battling for control of Tripoli, Libya.

A member of the coalition formed to eradicate the radical Islamic State of Iraq and Syria (ISIS), the UAE in late September sent aircraft to join those of Saudi Arabia and the United States in attacking ISIS targets in Iraq and Syria. The UAE aircraft were led by Major Mariam al-Mansouri, the first female UAE fighter pilot.

In 2015, UAE forces participated in the Saudi Arabian–led military intervention in Yemen against the Iran-backed Houthi rebels. On September 4, 2015, at least 50 soldiers from the UAE and Bahrain were killed in the Marib area of central Yemen.

Timeline

630	Islam is established in the eastern Persian Gulf region.
1809, 1819	Piratical activity brings British military interventions.
1820	Britain and a number of local rulers sign a treaty to combat piracy along the Persian Gulf coast. This and later agreements lead to the term "Trucial States."
1843	The British and the Trucial States sign a new treaty to prevent conflicts between them, reduce piracy in the Persian Gulf, and eliminate the slave trade.
Mar 6–8, 1892	A new treaty between the British government and the emirates tightens the bonds between the two. The sheikhs agree not to cede territory to any other nation or enter into commercial arrangements

or other venues of exchange with foreign governments without the consent of the British government. In return, the British pledge to protect the emirates from outside aggression.

1951   To maintain order, the British establish a paramilitary force in the emirates known as the Trucial Oman Levies, renamed the Trucial Oman Scouts in 1956.

1952   The sheikhs form the Trucial States Council.

1958   Oil is discovered in drilling off Abu Dhabi. The resultant considerable oil revenues bring improvements in infrastructure and the standard of living.

Jan 24, 1968   British prime minister Harold Wilson announces his government's decision to let the treaties with the emirates lapse in three years.

Jul 18, 1971   Six sheikhs meet at Dubai and there agree to establish the United Arab Emirates (UAE) before the announced departure of the British late this year.

Sep 3, 1971   Qatar reverses course and declines to join the proposed union.

Dec 1, 1971   The emirates become fully independent.

Dec 2, 1971   Six of the emirates establish the UAE. Bahrain and Qatar decline to join. The Trucial Oman Scouts become the Union Defence Force.

Feb 11, 1972   Ras al-Khaimah joins the UAE, bringing its membership to seven states. The consultative 40-member Federal National Council is appoined by the seven rulers.

Jan 26, 1982   The UAE joins Saudi Arabia, Bahrain, Kuwait, Oman, and Qatar in establishing a joint military command structure and integrated air defense system. This is prompted by the perceived threats of the Islamic Republic of Iran, the ongoing Iran-Iraq War, and the Soviet-Afghan War.

Jan 1991   The UAE is among the first to urge collective military action against the Iraqi occupation of Kuwait. The UAE contributes several hundred troops to the U.S.-led coalition in the Persian Gulf War and also provides airfields for U.S. aircraft taking part in the conflict.

Mar 2003   In contrast to most other Arab states, the UAE permits U.S. and coalition troops access to its military facilities to prosecute the invasion of Iraq. The UAE also contributes as many as 20,000 troops to protect Kuwait in the event that Iraqi forces should move against that country at the beginning of the war. Ultimately UAE support for the war ends, and the government condemns the conflict.

Mar–Oct 2011   UAE aircraft participate in the North Atlantic Treaty Organization's enforcement of a no-fly zone over Libya with a contribution of a dozen aircraft.

Mar 14, 2011   The UAE announces its support for Saudi Arabia's military intervention in Bahrain on behalf of the Bahraini government following weeks of demonstrations.

Aug 25, 2014   Twice during the past week, UAE and Egyptian aircraft carry out air strikes against Islamist-allied militias battling for control of Tripoli, Libya.

Sep 23, 2014   The UAE joins other Arab coalition states and the United States in air strikes against the radical Islamic State of Iraq and Syria (ISIS).

Mar 26, 2015   The UAE contributes 30 aircraft to a Saudi Arabia–led military intervention in Yemen against Shia Islam Houthi rebels backed by Iran.

Sep 4, 2015   At least 50 UAE and Bahraini soldiers die in a Houthi rebel rocket attack in central Yemen.

Further Reading

Abd Allah, Muhammad Mursi, and Muhammad Morsy Abdullah. *The United Arab Emirates: A Modern History.* New York: Barnes and Noble, 1978.

Congressional Quarterly. *The Middle East.* 10th ed. Washington, DC: CQ Press, 2005.

Davidson, Christopher M. *The United Arab Emirates: A Study in Survival.* Boulder, CO: Lynne Rienner, 2005.

Morton, Michael Quentin. *Keepers of the Golden Shore: A History of the United Arab Emirates.* London: Reaktion Books, 2016.

Ochsenwald, William, and Sydney Nettleton Fisher. *The Middle East: A History.* 6th ed. New York: McGraw-Hill, 2004.

Zahlan, Rosemarie Said. *The Origins of the United Arab Emirates: A Political and Social History of the Trucial States.* London: Routledge, 2016.

YEMEN

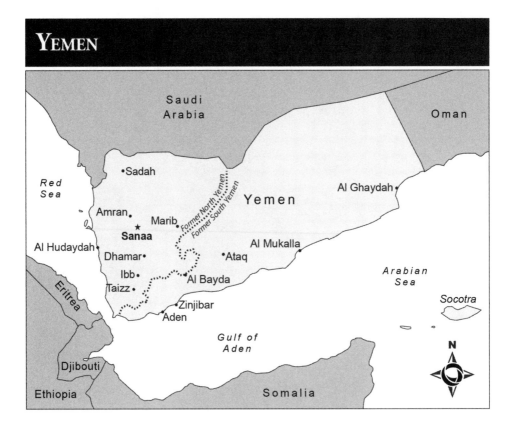

Saudi
Arabia

Oman

•Sadah

Red
Sea

Al Ghaydah•

Amran.

Marib•

Yemen

Former North Yemen

★

Former South Yemen

Sanaa

Al Hudaydah•

Dhamar•

Al Mukalla•

Ibb•

•Ataq

Arabian
Sea

Taizz•

Al Bayda•

Eritrea

Socotra

•Zinjibar

Aden•

Gulf of
Aden

Djibouti

Ethiopia

Somalia

N

Yemen

Paul G. Pierpaoli Jr. and Spencer C. Tucker

Yemen, officially known as the Republic of Yemen, is located in West Asia in the southern part of the Arabian Peninsula. Yemen comprises 203,850 square miles, about halfway in size between the U.S. states of California and Texas, and its territory includes some 200 islands. Yemen is bordered by Saudi Arabia to the north, Oman to the east, the Arabian Sea and the Gulf of Aden to the south, and the Red Sea to the west. Yemen's coastline stretches for about 1,200 miles. Not far off the western and southern coasts of the country lie the East African nations of Eritrea, Djibouti, and Somalia.

Yemen is the poorest country in the Arab world and has been identified by the international community as both a developing country and a failed state. The country's population in 2016 was some 27.428 million. Yemen's normal capital and largest city is Sana'a, but with the civil war now in progress the capital of the internationally recognized government has been temporarily relocated to the port city of Aden.

Yemen is of Arab ethnicity and is overwhelmingly Muslim. There is a sharp religious divide. About 52 percent of the nation's Muslims are Sunnis, and 48 percent are Shias. The Sunnis live principally in southern and southeastern Yemen, while the Shias are in the north. Yemen has one of the world's highest birth rates. Indeed, some 46 percent of the population are age 14 and younger, and fewer than 3 percent are older than 65. The median age is 16. Yemen's legal system is a mix of Islamic law, Turkish law (a holdover from Ottoman Empire rule), English common law, and local tribal dictates. Nevertheless, Islamic law almost always takes precedence.

Recorded human habitation in the region can be traced as far back as the ninth century BCE. Yemen's location on the Red Sea and the Gulf of Aden have made it an important crossroads and center for East-West trade as well as that from Asia to Africa. Christianity arrived in the fourth century CE, but in the seventh century Muslim caliphs began to exert their influence across the region. They gradually gave way to dynastic imams who retained the caliph's theocratic government until the modern era. Egyptian caliphs also held sway in Yemen. The Ottoman Empire controlled some or most of Yemen sporadically between the 1500s and 1918, when that empire collapsed with its defeat in World War I (1914–1918). Ottoman influence was the most pronounced in North Yemen; in South Yemen imams tended to be in control, although they were usually overseen to some extent by authorities in Constantinople (Istanbul).

The British came to be influential in South Yemen. They were anxious to secure a coal depot in the southern Arabian Peninsula to service their steamers plying the route to India. After a British merchant ship went down off the coast of Aden and was subsequently plundered, the British East India Company sent a warship commanded by Captain Stafford Haines to demand compensation. When this was rejected, Haines bombarded the port of Aden and on January 19, 1839, sent men ashore to take possession. The British then reached agreement with the sultan of Lahej for an annual payment for the port. That November some 5,000 tribesmen tried to retake Aden but were repulsed; perhaps 200 were slain.

To secure their position, the British concluded treaties with the tribes surrounding Aden that guaranteed their independence in return for a pledge that they would not conclude any treaties with another foreign government. Aden soon became a major entrepôt. Known as the Aden Settlement until 1937, when it was detached from administration by India, Aden and its harbor were the only areas under full British sovereignty. Together with some offshore islands, it was known as Aden Province (1932–1937), the Crown Colony of Aden (1937–1963), and the State of Aden (1963–1967).

As noted, North Yemen secured its independence in 1918 as a consequence of World War I. The new state was known as the Mutawakkilite Kingdom of Yemen from 1918 to 1962, the Yemen Arab Republic during 1962–1990, and the People's Republic of Yemen during 1967–1990. The two Yemeni states united in 1990 to form the Republic of Yemen.

Before 1962, the ruling imams in the Kingdom of Yemen pursued an isolationist foreign policy, although it did have commercial and cultural ties with Saudi Arabia. In the late 1950s the Chinese and Soviets attempted to lure the Kingdom of Yemen into their orbit with technological missions, and by the early 1960s North Yemen has become dependent on Egypt for financial and technical support.

Civil war broke out in the Kingdom of Yemen in 1962. The immediate catalyst was the death of Ahmad bin Yahya Hamidaddin in September 1962. Ahmad had been the ruling imam in the region since 1948 and had established there a thoroughly repressive regime. Although he harbored visions of uniting all of Yemen under his rule, he was unable to garner sufficient support to end British rule in the south. In 1955 Ahmad had fended off a coup attempt instigated by two of his brothers and disgruntled army officers.

To bolster his position, in April 1956 Ahmad entered into a formal military pact with Egypt and Saudi Arabia that placed Yemeni military forces under a unified command structure. That same year he also named his son, Muhammad al-Badr, as crown prince and heir apparent and established formal ties with the Soviet Union. In 1960 Ahmad left North Yemen to seek medical treatment. In his absence, al-Badr began to carry out several reform measures that his father had promised to implement but that had gone unfulfilled. Outraged by this, Ahmad promptly reversed the measures when he returned home. This, however, hardly endeared him to his subjects, and several weeks of civil unrest ensued, which the government crushed with a heavy hand.

Ahmad died on September 19, 1962, and al-Badr became imam. One of his first official acts was to grant a blanket amnesty to all political prisoners. This step did not long stave off discord. Indeed, on September 27 in the capital city of Sana'a, Abdullah al-Sallal, commander of the royal guard who had just been appointed to that post by al-Badr, launched a coup supported by half a dozen tanks and some artillery and declared himself president of the "Free Yemen Republic."

The rebels easily seized key locations in Sana'a, including the radio station and armory. They also moved against the Al-Bashaer Palace. The Imamate Guard refused to surrender, and fighting occurred, with the defenders surrendering the next day. The coup, however, brought on full-blown civil war. Meanwhile, an insurgency was in progress in South Yemen.

Al-Badr escaped to the northern reaches of the kingdom, where he received support from royalist tribes. He also secured support from the conservative monarchy of Saudi Arabia that bordered Yemen on the north. Al-Sallal received military assistance from Egypt. As early as October 5 an Egyptian battalion had been deployed to act as a personal guard for al-Sallal. Egyptian president Gamal Abdel Nasser, reeling from the breakup of the United Arab Republic of Egypt and Syria, hoped to recoup his prestige in the Arab world as well as deliver a rebuff to Egypt's rival Saudi Arabia. In undertaking this step, Nasser ignored repeated warnings by Ahmed Abu-Zeid, former Egyptian ambassador to the Kingdom of Yemen, that the country lacked a sense of nationhood, that no combat troops should be sent there, and that any aid should be limited to equipment and financial support. Nasser also failed to appreciate the depth of anger in Saudi Arabia regarding any Egyptian

Soldiers in turbans celebrate the overthrow of Imam Muhammad Al-Badr in Sana'a, southern Yemen, on October 9, 1962. The banner bears an image of Brigadier General Abdullah as-Sallal, leader of the revolt and head of the new military regime. (AP Photo)

intervention, which the Saudi royal family saw as a direct challenge to its hegemony over Yemen and the other Persian Gulf states.

Nasser soon discovered that many more troops would be required than initially thought. Egyptian numbers steadily increased, to a maximum of 55,000 men in late 1965. By the mid-1960s the royalists had also secured assistance from Iraq, Jordan, Pakistan, Iran, and Britain as well as covert assistance from Israel, while the Soviet Union and several other communist bloc nations joined Egypt in supporting the republicans' side. The conflict developed along Cold War lines, with the United States and other Western powers tending to support the royalists. On several occasions the United Nations (UN) attempted to mediate an end to the bloodshed, but the regional and international dynamics of the struggle worked against this.

Egyptian forces initially performed poorly. A paucity of maps, unfamiliarity with the terrain, and lack of knowledge of local conditions all impeded effectiveness. The Saudis did not have this problem, as they and the North Yemeni tribes were closely related. In January 1964, royalist forces laid siege to Sana'a.

Egyptian air strikes within Saudi territory on Najran and Jizan—staging areas for the royalist forces—almost led to war between Egypt and Saudi Arabia. U.S. President John F. Kennedy then supplied air defense systems and U.S. aircraft to help defend the kingdom if need be.

Although Egyptian tactics gradually improved, including extensive use of aircraft in a ground-support role, the war became a stalemated low-intensity conflict and a great drain on the Egyptian treasury and military. Indeed, the presence in Yemen of so many well-trained Egyptian troops and much equipment was keenly felt in the June 1967 Six-Day War. Egypt's ignominious defeat in that conflict forced Nasser to begin withdrawing his troops from Yemen. That same year the British withdrew from South Yemen.

The withdrawal of all foreign troops led to an agreement on April 14, 1970, whereby Saudi Arabia recognized the republican government of Yemen in return for the inclusion of royalists in several key government posts. There was, however, no role for al-Badr, for the agreement stipulated that he and his family leave the country. Al-Badr lived in Britain until his death in 1996. The eight-year-long conflict had claimed some 100,000–150,000 lives and had an immense adverse economic effect.

Meanwhile, fighting had broken out in South Yemen on October 14, 1963. Known in Britain as the Aden Emergency, it pitted the British and local sheikhs against two leftist nationalist groups: the Front for the Liberation of Occupied South Yemen (FLOSY) and the National Liberation Front (NLF). The British government announced in July 1964 its decision to grant independence to the Federation of South Arabia with the intention of maintaining its military base at Aden, but the ongoing insurgency and additional British military retrenchment led London to announce on November 2, 1967, that it was withdrawing all military forces from east of Suez. The British opened talks in Geneva with the NLF and signed with it an independence agreement, in effect abandoning the local sheikhdoms and emirates of the Federation of South Arabia with which Britain had protection agreements.

South Yemen became independent as the People's Republic of Southern Yemen on November 30, 1967, and the NLF gradually securing control. Following several unsuccessful coups in 1968, on June 22, 1969, a radical Marxist wing of the NLF seized power, and on December 1, 1970, Yemen became the People's Democratic Republic of Yemen (PDRY). All political parties were forced into the NLF, which was then renamed the Yemeni Socialist Party (YSP), the only legal political party.

The PDRY soon established close ties with the Soviet Union, the People's Republic of China, and other communist states as well as the Palestine Liberation Organization. It also acquired arms and training for its military from the communist bloc countries, while the Soviet Union secured access to PDRY naval facilities. The PDRY also aided rebels in Dhofar fighting the government of Oman and engaged in hostilities with Saudi Arabia during November 26–December 5, 1969, when there was fierce fighting between Yemeni and Saudi Arabian forces over the disputed Al Wadeiah oasis, which ended with the Saudis in firm control.

During the transition, several hundred thousand Yemenis from the south fled to North Yemen, overwhelming that nation's inadequate resources. Animosity between the two Yemeni states ebbed and flowed and led to sporadic fighting that would endure for two decades.

Heavy fighting occurred in 1972. The fighting ended in a cease-fire and negotiations under the auspices of the Arab League and a decision that the two Yemeni states would eventually be joined. On October 11, 1977, Yemen Arab Republic president Ibrahim al-Hamdi and the vice president, his brother Colonel Abdullah Mohammed al-Hamdi, were assassinated, probably to prevent talks with South Yemen regarding union. The new president, Ahmad al-Ghasmi, lasted only eight months. On June 24, 1978, he was killed by a bomb planted in the briefcase of the South Yemen ambassador, who also died in the blast. A three-man military council briefly assumed power. Then on June 25 in South Yemen, PDRY president Salem Rubaya Ali, suspected of wanting to reduce ties with the Soviet Union and improve relations with Saudi Arabia and the United States, was overthrown and later executed.

On July 18, 1978, Ali Abdallah Saleh became president of the Yemen Arab Republic. The next year fighting resumed between the two states, bringing renewed efforts for unification. During February 24–26, 1979, and May 1–June 1, 1980, there was more fighting.

Much more bloodshed occurred in the brief South Yemen Civil War of January–February 1986. On January 13, gunmen loyal to President Ali Nasser Muhammad al-Hasani killed several of his political opponents at a cabinet meeting in Aden. Fighting immediately began in Aden between Ali Nasser's supporters and those loyal to former president Abdul Fattah Ismail. Thousands died, among them Ismail. Ali Nasser was ousted on January 25. Some 60,000 people, including Ali Nasser and his supporters, fled into North Yemen. Much of the city of Aden was in ruins.

Finally in 1990, the governments of the two Yemeni states reached agreement and on May 22 established the Republic of Yemen. The constitution of the new state called for a popularly elected president and a prime minister appointed by the president. The executive branch was to share power with a bicameral legislature.

Saleh became the first president, with the vice president being Ali Salem al-Beidh, the general secretary of the YSP in South Yemen.

The new government opposed non-Arab military intervention in the region. After Iraq invaded and annexed Kuwait in August 1990, Yemen, then a member of the UN Security Council, abstained from a number of votes condemning Iraq and voted against the resolution authorizing use of force. The government of Saudi Arabia was especially upset at this stance and expelled some 800,000 Yemenis, creating staggering unemployment and an economic crisis.

Following food riots in major towns in 1992, a new coalition government was formed. In August 1993, however, al-Beidh returned to Aden, declaring his refusal to participate in the government until "marginalization" of the south was addressed. Negotiations occurred, and on February 20, 1994, an accord was signed in Amman, Jordan. However, the accord failed to resolve differences, and the armed forces of both north and south, having never been integrated, mobilized for war. The brief Yemeni Civil War of May–June 1994 saw the defeat of the southern forces backing secession and the flight abroad of many YSP leaders and other southern secessionists.

As the Yemeni government struggled with high inflation, excessive spending, and corruption on a vast scale, a new threat arose in Islamic militants. Indeed, at least three different types of Islamic militants have waged a persistent low-level insurgency, which the government has been unable to curtail. The kidnapping of foreigners remained an intractable problem.

On December 29, 1992, terrorists associated with the Al-Qaeda Islamic terrorist organization carried out what many consider to be the first Al-Qaeda attack on the United States, detonating bombs at two different tourist hotels in an apparent effort to kill U.S. marines staying there. The United States had been using Aden as a base to support its operations in Somalia. The blast killed two and wounded seven, but none of these were Americans. Shortly thereafter, however, Washington ordered U.S. military personnel from Yemen, and Al-Qaeda claimed this as a victory.

A more devastating attack occurred on October 12, 2000, again reportedly planned by Al-Qaeda, with the bombing of the U.S. Navy destroyer *Cole* while it rode at anchor in Aden Harbor. The blast killed 17 U.S. sailors, wounded 39 other soldiers, and badly damaged their ship. The attack also strained U.S.-Yemeni relations for several years.

On September 17, 2008, a least 16 people were killed in an attack on the heavily fortified U.S. embassy compound in Sana'a by terrorists wearing uniforms identifying them as Yemeni security personnel and riding in cars painted to resemble police vehicles but filled with explosives. The attackers failed to penetrate the gate, and a short but intense gun battle followed the blasts. The 16 dead included 6 guards, 4 civilians, and 6 terrorists. Islamic Jihad of Yemen claimed responsibility.

In August 2009, Houthi rebels in northwestern Yemen broke a yearlong ceasefire to renew warfare against the Yemeni government. The minority Houthis (officially known as Ansar Allah) are a revivalist Zaydi (Shia) Islamist sect. They had commenced warfare in 2004. On September 27 the Yemeni Army turned back a rebel offensive on the northern city of Sa'dah near the border with Saudi Arabia,

The Attack on USS *Cole*

On October 12, 2000, the U.S. Navy destroyer *Cole* (DDG-67) was in the Yemeni port of Aden for a refueling stop. At 11:18 a.m. local time, two suicide bombers in a small harbor skiff pulled alongside the anchored ship. There was no outward sign of hostile intent, and the *Cole* crew members assumed that the skiff probably belonged to the Yemeni harbor services. The bombers detonated explosives, and the ensuing shaped charge tore a gaping hole in the ship's side, killing 17 sailors and injuring 39 others. Both bombers also died in the blast.

The *Cole* was saved and subsequently repaired in the United States at a cost of more than $240 million and returned to service. The Al-Qaeda terrorist organization was determined to have been responsible. In late September 2004 Yemen sentenced two men to death for their participation, while four others received 5–10 years in jail. The bombing of the *Cole* was the first time a modern U.S. warship had been successfully targeted by terrorists.

and in early November Saudi Arabian forces retook control of the strategic mountain area known as the Jebel Dukhan on the Saudi-Yemeni border that had been seized by Houthi rebels a week earlier. The fighting raised the threat of a proxy war between Iran, supporting its coreligionist Houthis, and Saudi Arabia, supporting the Sunni-dominated Yemeni government. The Houthis are also strongly anti-American and anti–Saudi Arabian.

At the same time Al-Qaeda in the Arabian Peninsula (AQAP) began activities in Yemen. Established in 2009, it soon demonstrated why it is widely recognized as the most dangerous of the Al-Qaeda–affiliated organizations. AQAP launched a number of terrorist plots directed against the United States, including a December 25, 2009, attempt by a Nigerian, Umar Farouk Abdulmultallab, to blow up a Detroit-bound U.S. airliner. The Unites States responded with a series of drone strikes that killed a number of AQAP senior members.

On February 11, 2010, the Yemeni government agreed to a cease-fire with Houthi rebels, but the country was plunged into a new crisis in January 2011 during the so-called Arab Spring that swept much of the Arab world. Demonstrations began in Independence Square of the capital city protesting endemic poverty, high unemployment, and pervasive corruption (Saleh's presidency was widely characterized as a "kleptocracy"). Critics also condemned Saleh's plan to amend the constitution so as to eliminate the presidential term limit, in effect making him president for life. Saleh was also clearly grooming his eldest son Ahmed Saleh, commander of the Republican Guard, to succeed him. Saleh announced on February 1 that he would not run for reelection when his term ended in 2013, but opposition leaders called this insufficient and called for protests to continue. By mid-February there were clashes with security forces. Having secured the support of at least 11 tribal sheiks, on February 27 Saleh vowed to remain in power and to resist with "every drop of his blood." On March 19 he instituted a government crackdown in Sana'a resulting in the destruction of the demonstrators' makeshift encampments; hundreds of people were injured, and 46 were killed. Meanwhile, protestors had seized control of Dar Saad and Taiz in southern Yemen in what was easily the greatest challenge to Saleh's 32-year-rule.

On March 21, three prominent Yemeni Army commanders defected and called for an end to Saleh's rule. Massive demonstrations occurred in Sana'a, despite Saleh's declared state of emergency. Saleh's forceful actions led Washington to end its support for its longtime ally. On June 3, Saleh was badly injured in a rocket attack on a mosque in his compound in Sana'a; two days later he flew to Saudi Arabia for medical treatment.

Saleh returned to Yemen on September 23. This brought fighting and the risk of all-out civil war, but on November 23 in an arrangement worked out by the United States and the Gulf Cooperation Council, Saleh agreed to resign. Under the terms of the agreement Saleh was to step aside within 30 days, handing over power to Vice President Abd Rabbuh Mansur Hadi. Presidential elections would then follow. The deal also gave Saleh immunity from prosecution. Saleh departed as arranged, and on February 24 in a one-person race Hadi was elected president.

On March 18, 2012, the National Dialogue Conference began meeting to try to resolve the major issues dividing Yemen. AQAP remained active, and on May 12 an AQAP suicide bomber in Sana'a killed at least 90 soldiers and wounded another 222 as the men were rehearsing for a parade.

Iran also upped its support for the Houthi rebels. On January 28, 2013, Yemeni authorities, acting on information provided by the United States, intercepted a 130-foot dhow that was transporting weapons to Yemen. These included 10 heat-seeking antiaircraft missiles of Chinese manufacture as well as explosives, shells, rocket-propelled grenades, and equipment for making bombs. The Yemeni government claimed that the weapons had been shipped from Iran and were intended for the Houthi rebels.

In January 2014, the National Dialogue Conference extended Hadi's term for another year. U.S. aid increased, and on April 21, 2014, the Yemeni government announced that it had killed at least 65 AQAP members in a joint operation with the United States. According to one report, U.S. drone and air strikes in Yemen had to date killed an estimated 753 to 965 people; the large majority were militants, but at least 81 had been identified as civilians. Meanwhile Saleh, now in exile, had allied with the Houthis.

On September 21, 2014, the Houthis seized control of Sana'a, and Hadi fled. The Houthis then organized a "unity government" of various factions. Hadi and his prime minister and cabinet all resigned on January 22, 2015. This came only one day after an apparent power-sharing arrangement with the Houthis, who had nonetheless stripped Hadi of his powers. The UN, the United States, and the Gulf states, however, refused to recognize the new regime and characterized its seizure of power as a coup d'état. The UN Security Council voted unanimously to demand that Shiite rebels immediately relinquish control of Yemen's government. A number of Arab countries now pressed for military intervention to reverse what they characterized as an illegitimate seizure of power. Meanwhile on February 21, Hadi took back his resignation and from Aden declared that he was still the legitimate president. With Shana'a still under rebel control, Hadi proclaimed Aden to be Yemen's "temporary capital."

On March 20, 2015, two suicide bombers attacked two mosques in Aden, killing 137 people and wounding 357 in the deadliest assault yet targeting Shiites. An affiliate of the Sunni extremist Islamic State of Iraq and Syria claimed responsibility.

Saudi officials regarded the Yemeni situation as a major security threat, given their long border with Yemen and being home to some 1 million people of Yemeni descent. Saudi Arabia has also found itself locked in an intense geopolitical struggle with Iran. On March 26, Saudi Arabia and its regional allies openly entered the Yemeni Civil War, launching air strikes against the Houthis now besieging Aden. The coalition included Saudi Arabia, the United Arab Emirates (UAE), Bahrain, Kuwait, Qatar, Jordan, Morocco, and Sudan. The U.S. government announced its support and provided logistical and intelligence support.

A widened conflict in Yemen posed risks for global oil supplies. Tankers from Arab producers such as Saudi Arabia, the UAE, Kuwait, and Iraq pass Yemen's coastlines via the narrow 25-mile-wide strait between Yemen and Djibouti and the Strait of Hormuz between Saudi Arabia and Iran in the Gulf of Aden in order to transit the Red Sea and the Suez Canal to Europe. Thus, Brent Crude oil prices shot up nearly 6 percent upon news of the operation.

Despite the Saudi intervention and a week of intense air strikes, on April 1, with Hadi safely in Saud Arabia, Houthi rebels and their allies supported by tanks pushed into central Aden. Heavy coalition bombing continued, and apparently many Yemeni turned against the Saudis and the United States for having furnished the weaponry and munitions.

On April 14, the UN Security Council voted to impose an arms embargo on the Houthis. The resolution passed 14 to 0, with Russia abstaining. The Russians had been pressing for a ban on air strikes to let in humanitarian assistance, but the Gulf states had opposed this. On April 20, Washington ordered the U.S. Navy aircraft carrier *Theodore Roosevelt* to join other American warships off Yemen to intercept Iranian vessels that might be transporting weapons to the Houthis. U.S. drone strikes against AQAP also continued. These did not deter AQAP, however. On December 1, 2015, hundreds of AQAP fighters took control of the major cities of Zinjbare and Jaaar.

Additional proof that Iran was supplying the Houthis was provided in the March 5, 2016, seizure by an Australian Navy ship of a small stateless fishing vessel well off the coast of Oman, identified as having sailed from Iran with arms destined for Yemen by way of Somalia. The seized weapons included nearly 2,000 AK-47 assault rifles and 100 rocket-propelled grenades.

Ground combat continued, and on April 24, 2016, Yemeni government forces scored a significant victory. Supported by Saudi and UAE special forces, they secured control of AQAP's main stronghold of the port city of Mukalla and the surrounding coastal area, which AQAP had held for a year. Saudi Arabia claimed that more than 800 AQAP militants had been killed, although journalists on the spot disputed that number and claimed that AQAP fighters had merely withdrawn.

Yemen remains in difficult straits. The country has been devastated by war. Its economy is also reeling, with the important agricultural sector hard hit by periodic droughts. Coffee production, once a mainstay of northern Yemeni crops, has fallen off dramatically. Yemen does have significant oil deposits, but these are not of the same quality as Persian Gulf oil and so have not brought in substantial profit. Yemen does have major natural gas reserves, but these remains underdeveloped. Even if the civil war were to be ended tomorrow, future development would be very difficult.

Timeline

600s	Muslim caliphs extend their influence across the Arabian Peninsula.
1500s–1918	The Ottoman Empire controls most of present-day Yemen.
Jan 1839	The British East India Company establishes control over the South Yemen port of Aden. The British subsequently conclude treaties with the surrounding tribes that guarantee their independence in return for a pledge that they will not conclude treaties with any other foreign government. Soon the British create a formal colony that incorporates Aden and South Yemen. Known as the Aden Settlement (1939–1937), Aden and its harbor is the only area under full British sovereignty. Together with some offshore islands, it is known as the Province of Aden (1932–1937), the Crown Colony of Aden (1937–1963), and finally the State of Aden (1963–1967).
1914–1918	World War I sees the Ottoman Empire at war with Britain.
1918	North Yemen becomes independent on the defeat of the Ottoman Empire. It is known as the Mutawakkilite Kingdom of Yemen until 1962.
1937	Aden is detached administratively from India and becomes the Colony of Aden, a British crown colony under British control to 1967.
Apr 21, 1956	The Kingdom of Yemen concludes a formal military pact with Egypt and Saudi Arabia.
Sep 19, 1962	Imam Ahmad bin Yahya Hamidaddin, ruler of the Mutawakkilite Kingdom of Yemen, dies and is succeeded by his son, Crown Prince Muhammad al-Badr.
Sep 27, 1962	Abdullah al-Sallal leads a coup d'état in Sana'a and proclaims the "Free Yemen Republic." Full-blown civil war ensues, with al-Badr escaping into far northern Yemen, where he is aided by Saudi Arabia, while al-Sallal is supported by Egypt. Ultimately the royalists have assistance from Iraq, Jordan, Pakistan, Iran, and Britain

as well as covert assistance from Israel, while the Soviet Union and several other communist bloc nations support the republican side.

Jan 18, 1963   Aden and much of the protectorate are joined to form the State of Aden.

Oct 14, 1963   The armed conflict known as the Aden Emergency begins, pitting the British and local sheikhs against two leftist nationalist groups, the Front for the Liberation of Occupied South Yemen and the National Liberation Front (NLF).

Jul 1964   The British government announces its decision to grant independence to the Federation of South Arabia with the intention of maintaining its military base at Aden.

Nov 2, 1967   The British government announces that it will be withdrawing all military forces from east of Suez.

Nov 30, 1967   Having opened talks in Geneva with the NLF, the British sign an independence agreement, in effect abandoning the local sheikhdoms and emirates of the Federation of South Arabia with which it had protection agreements. On this date the south becomes independent as the People's Republic of Southern Yemen (PRSY).

1969   Both sides in the Yemen Civil War agree to the necessity to withdraw all foreign troops.

Jun 22, 1969   A radical Marxist wing of the NLF seizes power in South Yemen.

Nov 26–Dec 5, 1969   Fierce fighting occurs between the PRSY and Saudi Arabian forces over the disputed Al Wadeiah oasis but ends with the Saudis in firm control.

Apr 14, 1970   In a peace agreement, Saudi Arabia recognizes the Yemen Arab Republic in return for the inclusion of royalists in several key government posts. Al-Badr, however, goes into exile in Britain.

Dec 1, 1970   The PRSY becomes the People's Democratic Republic of Yemen (PDRY), a one-part state that establishes close ties with the communist bloc countries.

1972   Heavy fighting occurs between the two Yemeni states. It ends in a cease-fire and negotiations under the Arab League and a decision that the two Yemeni states will eventually be joined.

Oct 11, 1977   Yemen Arab Republic president Ibrahim al-Hamdi and two others are assassinated, probably to prevent talks with South Yemen over a union of the two countries.

Jun 24, 1978   New Yemen Arab Republic president Ahmad al-Ghasmi is assassinated. A three-man military council briefly assumes power.

Jun 25, 1978	PDRY president Salem Rubaya Ali, suspected of wanting to reduce ties with the Soviet Union and improve relations with Saudi Arabia and the United States, is overthrown and later executed.
Jul 18, 1978	Ali Abdallah Saleh becomes president of the Yemen Arab Republic.
1979	Fighting between the two Yemeni states occurs in February and May.
Jan–Feb 1986	Thousands of people are killed, and some 60,000 others, including President Ali Nasser Muhammad al-Hasani, flee into North Yemen as a consequence of the brief South Yemen Civil War that reduces much of Aden to ruins.
May 22, 1990	Leaders of the two Yemeni states reach agreement and on this date establish the Republic of Yemen. Saleh becomes the first president, with his vice president being Ali Salem al-Beidh, secretary-general of the Yemeni Socialist Party in South Yemen.
Aug 1990	Following the Iraqi invasion and absorption of Kuwait, Yemen, then a member of the United Nations Security Council, abstains from a number of key votes condemning Iraq and votes against the resolution that authorizes use of force. Saudi Arabia then expels some 800,000 Yemenis, creating staggering unemployment and an economic crisis in Yemen.
Dec 29, 1992	Terrorists associated with Al-Qaeda carry out what many consider the first Al-Qaeda attack on the United States, detonating bombs at two different tourist hotels in an apparent effort to kill U.S. military personnel staying there while in support of operations in Somali. Although two people are killed, none are Americans. Shortly thereafter, however, the United States removes its forces from Yemen.
Aug 1993	Internal discord leads al-Beidh to return to Aden, declaring that he will not participate in the government until "marginalization" of the south is addressed.
Feb 20, 1994	An accord is signed in Amman, Jordan, by the various Yemeni political factions.
May–Jun 1994	The Amman agreement having failed, Yemen falls into a brief civil war. It ends in the defeat of the southern forces supporting secession and the flight abroad of many Yemeni Socialist Party leaders and other southern secessionists.
Oct 12, 2000	In an attack planned by Al-Qaeda, 2 suicide bombers detonate a large explosive devise aboard a small coastal craft next to the U.S. Navy destroyer *Cole* in Aden Harbor. The blast kills 17 U.S. sailors,

wounds 39, and badly damages their ship. U.S.-Yemeni relations are badly strained.

Sep 17, 2008   At least 16 people die in an attack on the heavily fortified U.S. embassy compound in Sana'a. Sixteen people are killed, including 6 guards, 4 civilians, and 6 terrorists. Islamic Jihad of Yemen claims responsibility.

Aug 2009   Houthi rebels in northwestern Yemen end a yearlong cease-fire and renew warfare against the Yemeni government. The minority Houthis (officially known as Ansar Allah) are a revivalist Zaydi (Shia) Islamist movement that had commenced warfare in 2004.

Nov 2009   Saudi Arabian forces retake control of the strategic mountain area of the Jebel Dukhan on the Saudi-Yemeni border that had been seized by Houthi rebels. Iran is now supporting the coreligionist Shia Houthis, and Saudi Arabia is supporting the Sunni-dominated Yemeni government.

Dec 25, 2009   Established in 2009, Al-Qaeda in the Arabian Peninsula (AQAP) will launch a number of terrorist plots against the United States. Among these is an attempt of this date to blow up a Detroit-bound U.S. airliner. The Unites States responds with drone strikes that kill a number of AQAP senior members.

Feb 11, 2010   The Yemeni government enters into a cease-fire agreement with the Houthi rebels.

Jan 2011   Yemen is swept up in the events of the so-call Arab Spring, with much of the Arab world demanding democratic change. Demonstrations occur in Sana'a protesting the chronic poverty, high unemployment, and endemic corruption of Saleh's regime, which has held power since 1978.

Mar 19, 2011   Antigovernment demonstrations continue, and there are clashes between the protestors and security forces. Saleh vows that he will remain in power and on this date orders a government crackdown that brings the deaths of 46 people and injuries to many more.

Mar 21, 2011   Three prominent Yemeni Army commanders defect and call for an end to Saleh's rule. Massive demonstrations occur in Sana'a, despite Saleh's declared state of emergency.

Jun 3, 2011   Saleh is badly injured in a rocket attack on his compound in Sana'a and two days later flies to Saudi Arabia for medical treatment.

Sep 23, 2011   Saleh returns to Yemen. His return brings fighting and the risk of all-out civil war.

Nov 23, 2011   Saleh agrees to an arrangement worked out by the United States and the states of the Gulf Cooperation Council whereby he will step aside within 30 days and hand power to Vice President Abd Rabbuh Mansur Hadi. Presidential elections will follow within 90 days. The deal also gives Saleh immunity from prosecution.

Feb 24, 2012   Hadi is elected president of Yemen.

May 22, 2012   An AQAP suicide bomber kills at least 90 soldiers and wounds 222 others in Sana'a as the men are rehearsing for a parade.

Jan 28, 2013   Yemeni government authorities intercept a dhow transporting weapons to Yemen. The Yemeni government claims that the shipment had originated in Iran and was intended for the Houthi rebels.

Apr 21, 2014   The Yemeni government announces that it has killed at least 65 AQAP members in a joint operation with the United States.

Sep 21, 2014   Houthi rebels, now supported by Saleh, seize control of Sana'a, and President Hadi flees. The United Nations (UN), the United States, and neighboring Persian Gulf states, however, refuse to recognize the new regime and characterize this as a coup d'état. The UN Security Council then votes unanimously to demand that the Houthi rebels relinquish control.

Feb 21, 2015   Hadi proclaims himself still president and Aden as the temporary capital of Yemen.

Mar 20, 2015   Two suicide bombers attack two mosques in Aden, killing 137 people and wounding 357. This attack targeting Shiites is by an affiliate of the Islamic State of Iraq and Syria, a Sunni Islamist extremist organization.

Mar 26, 2015   Saudi Arabia and other allied Arab states enter the Yemeni Civil War openly, launching air strikes against the Houthis now besieging Aden. Yemen has now became the center of a proxy war, with Iran backing the Houthis, Saudi Arabia and the other Sunni states supporting president Hadi, and the U.S. government providing logistical and intelligence support.

Apr 1, 2015   Despite Saudi intervention and intense air strikes, Houthi rebels supported by tanks push into central Aden. Hadi is now in Saudi Arabia.

Apr 14, 2015   The UN Security Council imposes an arms embargo on the Houthis.

Dec 1, 2015   Taking advantage of the chaos occasioned by the civil war, hundreds of AQAP fighters seize control of the major cities of Zinjbare and Jaaar.

Mar 5, 2016   An Australian Navy ship seizes a small stateless fishing vessel well off the coast of Oman, identified as having sailed from Iran with a sizable cargo of nearly 2,000 assault rifles and 100 rocket-propelled grenades intended for the Houthi rebels in Yemen by way of Somalia.

Apr 25, 2016   Saudi Arabia claims that more than 800 Al-Qaeda militants have been killed in an offensive by Yemeni government forces supported by Saudi and United Arab Emirates special forces in the group's main stronghold, the port city of Mukalla.

Further Reading

Clark, Victoria. *Yemen: Dancing on the Heads of Snakes*. New Haven, CT: Yale University Press, 2010.

Day, Stephen W. *Regionalism and Rebellion in Yemen*. Cambridge: Cambridge University Press, 2012.

Dresch, Paul. *A History of Modern Yemen*. New York: Cambridge University Press, 2001.

Fraihat, Ibrahim. *Unfinished Revolutions: Yemen, Libya, and Tunisia after the Arab Spring*. New Haven, CT: Yale University Press, 2016.

Johnson, Gregory D. *The Last Refuge: Yemen, al-Qaeda, and America's War in Arabia*. New York: Norton, 2014.

Jones, Clive. *Britain and the Yemen Civil War*. London: Sussex Academic, 2004.

Mackintosh-Smith, Tim. *Yemen: The Unknown Arabia*. New York: Overlook, 2014.

Pridham, Brian. *Contemporary Yemen: Politics and Historical Background*. London: Palgrave Macmillan, 1984.

Rabi, Uzi. *Yemen: Revolution, Civil War and Unification*. London: I. B. Tauris, 2014.

Walker, Jonathan. *Aden Insurgency: The Savage War in Yemen, 1962–67*. Barnsley, UK: Pen and Sword Military, 2014.

Primary Documents

1. Declaration of the First Zionist Congress, Basel, Switzerland, August 1897

Introduction

The First Zionist Congress was held in Basel, Switzerland, in August 1897. Summoned by Theodor Herzl, the leading proponent and publicist of a separate Jewish state, it gathered in the Basel Municipal Casino's Concert Hall for three days, August 29–31, 1897. Around 200 delegates from 17 countries attended. Sixty-nine of these represented specific Zionist organizations, and the remainder had been invited in their personal capacity. The congress established the World Zionist Organization (WZO), electing Herzl as its first president. Its objectives, as stated in the declaration of the congress, were to encourage settlement and the creation of a national Jewish homeland in the territory of Palestine and to foster cooperation among all Jews. The WZO became the most prominent group working for the establishment of a Jewish state. For the first five years the Zionist congresses met annually, and from 1903 until 1939 they met every two years. The WZO provided the focal point and institutional underpinning for the Zionist movement, conducting extensive lobbying and propaganda campaigns and coordinating Zionist efforts to assist beleaguered Jews and win a Jewish national homeland. Many wealthier and more conservative Jews, however, regarded it with some distrust, considering its membership and campaigns overly radical and extreme and fearing that its activities would discredit well-established Jewish communities in states where they had won acceptance as a respected minority.

Primary Document

The aim of Zionism is to create for the Jewish people a home in Palestine secured by public law. The Congress contemplates the following means to the attainment of this end:

1. The promotion, on suitable lines, of the colonization of Palestine by Jewish agricultural and industrial workers.
2. The organization and binding together of the whole of Jewry by means of appropriate institutions, local and international, in accordance with the laws of each country.
3. The strengthening and fostering of Jewish national sentiment and consciousness.
4. Preparatory steps towards obtaining government consent, where necessary, to the attainment of the aim of Zionism.

Source: First Zionist Congress, Basel, Switzerland, August 31, 1897, *Jewish Chronicle*, September 3, 1897, 13.

2. The Sykes-Picot Agreement: Sir Edward Grey to Paul Cambon, May 15–16, 1916

Introduction

As Turkish power crumbled in the Middle East, British and French officials reached a tentative agreement as to how to divide influence within that region between their two nations. On May 9, 1916, Paul Cambon, the French foreign minister, wrote to British foreign secretary Sir Edward Grey formally proposing a disposition of the Middle East between France and Britain, along lines already agreed upon by junior French and British diplomats in the area. Sir Edward Grey replied, first briefly and then at greater length.

Primary Document

Sir Edward Grey to Paul Cambon, May 15, 1916

I shall have the honour to reply fully in a further note to your Excellency's note of the 9th instant, relative to the creation of an Arab State, but I should meanwhile be grateful if your Excellency could assure me that in those regions which, under the conditions recorded in that communication, become entirely French, or in which French interests are recognised as predominant, any existing British concessions, rights of navigation or development, and the rights and privileges of any British religious, scholastic, or medical institutions will be maintained.

His Majesty's Government are, of course, ready to give a reciprocal assurance in regard to the British area.

Sir Edward Grey to Paul Cambon, May 16, 1916

I have the honour to acknowledge the receipt of your Excellency's note of the 9th instant, stating that the French Government accept the limits of a future Arab State, or Confederation of States, and of those parts of Syria where French interests predominate, together with certain conditions attached thereto, such as they result from recent discussions in London and Petrograd on the subject.

I have the honour to inform your Excellency in reply that the acceptance of the whole project, as it now stands, will involve the abdication of considerable British interests, but, since His Majesty's Government recognise the advantage to the general cause of the Allies entailed in producing a more favourable internal political situation in Turkey, they are ready to accept the arrangement now arrived at, provided that the co-operation of the Arabs is secured, and that the Arabs fulfil the conditions and obtain the towns of Homs, Hama, Damascus, and Aleppo.

It is accordingly understood between the French and British Governments—

1. That France and Great Britain are prepared to recognize and protect an independent Arab State or a Confederation of Arab States in the areas (A) and (B) marked on the annexed map [not included in this printing], under the suzerainty of an Arab chief. That in area (A) France, and in area (B) Great Britain, shall have priority of right of enterprise and local loans. That in area (A) France, and in area (B) Great Britain, shall alone supply advisers or foreign functionaries at the request of the Arab State or Confederation of Arab States.

2. That in the blue area France, and in the red area Great Britain, shall be allowed to establish such direct or indirect administration or control as they desire and as they may think fit to arrange with the Arab State or Confederation of Arab States.

3. That in the brown area there shall be established an international administration, the form of which is to be decided upon after consultation with Russia, and subsequently in consultation with the other Allies, and the representatives of the Shereef of Mecca.

4. That Great Britain be accorded (1) the ports of Haifa and Acre, (2) guarantee of a given supply of water from the Tigris and Euphrates in area (A) for area (B). His Majesty's Government, on their part, undertake that they will at no time enter into negotiations for the cession of Cyprus to any third Power without the previous consent of the French Government.

5. That Alexandretta shall be a free port as regards the trade of the British Empire, and that there shall be no discrimination in port charges or facilities as regards British shipping and British goods; that there shall be freedom of transit for British goods through Alexandretta and by railway through the blue area, whether those goods are intended for or originate in the red area, or (B) area, or area (A); and there shall be no discrimination, direct or indirect, against British goods on any railway or against British goods or ships at any port serving the areas mentioned.

That Haifa shall be a free port as regards the trade of France, her dominions and protectorates, and there shall be no discrimination in port charges or facilities as regards French shipping and French goods. There shall be freedom of transit for French goods through Haifa and by the British railway through the brown area, whether those goods are intended for or originate in the blue area, area (A), or area (B), and there shall be no discrimination, direct or indirect, against French goods on any railway, or against French goods or ships at any port serving the areas mentioned.

6. That in area (A) the Baghdad Railway shall not be extended southwards beyond Mosul, and in area (B) northwards beyond Samarra, until a railway connecting Baghdad with Aleppo via the Euphrates Valley has been completed, and then only with the concurrence of the two Governments.

7. That Great Britain has the right to build, administer, and be sole owner of a railway connecting Haifa with area (B), and shall have a perpetual right to transport troops along such a line at all times.

It is to be understood by both Governments that this railway is to facilitate the connexion of Baghdad with Haifa by rail, and it is further understood that, if the engineering difficulties and expense entailed by keeping this connecting line in the brown area only make the project unfeasible, that the French Government shall be prepared to consider that the line in question may also traverse the polygon Banias-Keis Marib-Salkhab Tell Otsda-Mesmie before reaching area (B).

8. For a period of twenty years the existing Turkish customs tariff shall remain in force throughout the whole of the blue and red areas, as well as in areas (A) and (B), and no increase in the rates of duty or conversion from ad valorem to specific rates shall be made except by agreement between the two Powers.

There shall be no interior customs barriers between any of the above-mentioned areas. The customs duties leviable on goods destined for the interior shall be collected at the port of entry and handed over to the administration of the area of destination.

9. It shall be agreed that the French Government will at no time enter into any negotiations for the cession of their rights and will not cede such rights in the blue area to any third Power, except the Arab State or Confederation of Arab States, without the previous agreement of His Majesty's Government, who, on their part, will give a similar undertaking to the French Government regarding the red area.

10. The British and French Governments, as the protectors of the Arab State, shall agree that they will not themselves acquire and will not consent to a third Power acquiring territorial possessions in the Arabian peninsula, nor consent to a third Power installing a naval base either on the east coast, or on the islands, of the Red Sea. This, however, shall not prevent such adjustment of the Aden frontier as may be necessary in consequence of recent Turkish aggression.

11. The negotiations with the Arabs as to the boundaries of the Arab State or Confederation of Arab States shall be continued through the same channel as heretofore on behalf of the two Powers.

12. It is agreed that measures to control the importation of arms into the Arab territories will be considered by the two Governments.

I have further the honour to state that, in order to make the agreement complete, His Majesty's Government are proposing to the Russian Government to exchange notes analogous to those exchanged by the latter and your Excellency's Government on the 26th April last. Copies of these notes will be communicated to your Excellency as soon as exchanged.

I would also venture to remind your Excellency that the conclusion of the present agreement raises, for practical consideration, the question of the claims of Italy to a share in any partition or rearrangement of Turkey in Asia, as formulated in article 9 of the agreement of the 26th April, 1915, between Italy and the Allies.

His Majesty's Government further consider that the Japanese Government should be informed of the arrangement now concluded.

Source: British Documents on Foreign Affairs: Reports and Papers from the Foreign Office Confidential Print; Series H: The First World War, 1914–1918, Vol. 2 (Bethesda, MD: University Publications of America, 1989), 326–327.

3. The Balfour Declaration: British Foreign Secretary Arthur J. Balfour to Lord Rothschild, November 2, 1917

Introduction

On November 2, 1917, British foreign secretary Arthur James Balfour wrote an official letter to Lord Rothschild, a leading British Zionist figure. Although its terms were somewhat ambivalent, this brief communication offered Jews a homeland in Palestine, a development that eventually led to the creation of the State of Israel in 1948. Correctly or not, Sharif Hussein ibn Ali of Mecca, a British ally in revolt against Turkey, believed that he too had been promised this territory.

Primary Document

I have much pleasure in conveying to you, on behalf of His Majesty's Government, the following declaration of sympathy with Jewish Zionist aspirations which has been submitted to, and approved by, the Cabinet.

"His Majesty's Government view with favour the establishment in Palestine of a national home for the Jewish people, and will use their best endeavours to facilitate the achievement of this object, it being clearly understood that nothing shall be done which may prejudice the civil and religious rights of existing non-Jewish communities in Palestine, or the rights and political status enjoyed by Jews in any other country."

I should be grateful if you would bring this declaration to the knowledge of the Zionist Federation.

Source: "Balfour Declaration 1918," The Avalon Project, http://avalon.law.yale.edu/20th_century/balfour.asp.

4. United Nations Security Council, Resolution Adopted at Its 30th Meeting, April 4, 1946

Introduction

Negotiations between Soviet and Iranian diplomats over the presence of Soviet forces in Iran continued for several months in early 1946. On March 26, 1946, Andrei Gromyko, the Soviet representative to the United Nations (UN), reported to the UN Security Council that the two countries had reached agreement on the evacuation of Soviet forces, which had begun on March 2 and, he anticipated, would be completed within the next five to six weeks. On March 29 U.S. secretary of state James F. Byrnes introduced a Security Council resolution welcoming this development and in particular the fact that Soviet withdrawal was not connected to negotiations on other subjects, namely oil concessions in Iran, then in progress between Iranian and Soviet officials. The resolution recognized that logistical considerations made it difficult, if not impossible, to speed up by much the scheduled timetable for withdrawals and expressed the hope that the continued presence of some Soviet troops would not be used to pressure Iran in other ongoing negotiations. So long as the Soviet Union continued to remove its forces as anticipated, the Security Council therefore decided to defer any further discussion of the situation in Iran until May 6. The 11-member Security Council passed this resolution with 9 affirmative votes and 1 abstention, while the Soviet representative absented himself and therefore could not vote.

Primary Document

The Security Council,

Taking note of the Statements by the Iranian representative that the Iranian appeal to the Council arises from the presence of USSR troops in Iran and their continued presence there beyond the date stipulated for their withdrawal in the Tri-partite Treaty of 29 January 1942,

Taking note of the reply dated 3 April of the Government of the Union of Soviet Socialist Republics and the Iranian Government pursuant to the request of the Secretary-General for information as to the state of the negotiations between the two Governments and as to whether the withdrawal of USSR troops from Iran is conditional upon agreement on other subjects,

And in particular taking note of and relying upon the assurances of the USSR Government that the withdrawal of USSR troops from Iran has already commenced; that it is the intention of the USSR Government expects rapidly as possible; that the USSR Government expects the withdrawal of all USSR troops from the whole of Iran to be completed within five or six weeks; and that the proposals under negotiation between the Iranian Government and the USSR Government "are not connected with the withdrawal of USSR troops",

Being solicitous to avoid any possibility of the presence of USSR troops in Iran being used to influence the course of the negotiations between the Governments of Iran and the USSR,

Recognizing that the withdrawal of all USSR troops from the whole of Iran cannot be completed in a substantially shorter period of time than that within which the USSR Government has declared it to be its intention to complete such withdrawal,

Resolves that the Council defer further proceedings on the Iranian appeal until 6 May, at which time the USSR Government and the Iranian Government are requested to report to the Council whether the withdrawal of all USSR troops from the whole of Iran has been completed and at which time the Council shall consider what, if any, further proceedings on the Iranian appeal are required,

Provided, however, that if in the meantime either the USSR Government or the Iranian Government or any member of the Security Council reports to the Secretary-General any developments which may retard or threaten to retard the prompt withdrawal of USSR troops from Iran, in accordance with the assurances of the USSR to the Council, the Secretary-General shall immediately call to the attention of the Council such reports, which shall be considered as the first item on the agenda.

Source: UN Security Council, *Resolution 3 (1946) of 4 April 1946,* 4 April 1946, S/RES/3 (1946). © 1946. Reprinted with the permission of the United Nations.

5. U.S. Recognition of Israel, May 14, 1948

Introduction

Between the world wars hundreds of thousands of Jews immigrated to Palestine, where the local Arab community deeply resented their presence. After World War II Zionists, often citing the deaths of 6 million European Jews at the hands of Adolf Hitler's Germany, again took up the cause of an independent Jewish state. Against the advice of Secretary of State George Marshall, who feared that creating such an entity would permanently alienate Arab countries throughout the oil-rich Middle East, President Harry S. Truman supported its creation in the former British mandate. Truman, an avid reader of history, had a romantic respect for the Jewish people's dedication to the restoration of the ancient state of Israel and also felt that they deserved compensation for their wartime sufferings. As soon as the State of Israel came into existence, Truman recognized it. Israel was immediately confronted by a military attack from its Arab neighbors. Both the United States and the Soviet Union, which had also recognized the new state, sent massive arms shipments as they competed for its allegiance. Caught between the passionate support that American Jews accorded Israel and their fear of further alienating resentful and oil-rich Arab states, whose anger might propel them toward the Soviets, in 1948 U.S. officials launched the first of many successive and still continuing efforts to negotiate a lasting Middle East peace settlement between Arabs and Israelis. Meanwhile, the powerful domestic Jewish lobby ensured that the small beleaguered Israeli state quickly became a virtual U.S. client and the single-largest recipient of U.S. military and economic aid.

Primary Document

Text of Letter from the Agent of the Provisional Government of Israel to the President of the U.S.

[Released to the Press by the White House on May 15]

My Dear Mr. President:

I have the honor to notify you that the state of Israel has been proclaimed as an independent republic within frontiers approved by the General Assembly of the United Nations in its Resolution of November 29, 1947, and that a provisional government has been charged to assume the rights and duties of government for preserving law and order within the boundaries of Israel, for defending the state against external aggression, and for discharging the obligations of Israel to the other nations of the world in accordance with international law. The Act of Independence will become effective at one minute after six o'clock on the evening of 14 May 1948, Washington time.

With full knowledge of the deep bond of sympathy which has existed and has been strengthened over the past thirty years between the Government of the United States and the Jewish people of Palestine, I have been authorized by the provisional government of the new state to tender this message and to express the hope that your government will recognize and will welcome Israel into the community of nations.

Very respectfully yours,

Eliahu Epstein
Agent, Provisional Government of Israel

Statement by President Truman [Released to the press by the White House May 14]

This Government has been informed that a Jewish state has been proclaimed in Palestine, and recognition has been requested by the provisional government thereof.

The United States recognizes the provisional government as the *de facto* authority of the new State of Israel.

> Source: "Israel Proclaimed as an Independent Republic,"
> *Department of State Bulletin* 18(464) (1948): 673.

6. Egyptian Law Nationalizing the Suez Canal Company [Excerpt], July 26, 1956

Introduction

One of the major reasons that Britain had taken over the administration of Egypt in the 1880s was to protect the then strategically and commercially vital Suez Canal waterway linking the Persian Gulf to the Mediterranean Sea. Ownership of this was vested in the Suez Canal Company, owned by the British and French governments, although the Egyptian government controlled access to the canal. The nationalist Egyptian government that came to power in 1952 found foreign ownership of the commercially valuable canal and its revenues a constant irritant. Even before then, use and operation of the canal had become internationally controversial. From the date of Israel's creation in 1948, Egypt had denied the use of the canal not just to Israeli vessels but also to ships bearing goods bound for Israel on the grounds that since Israel and Egypt—even after the 1949 armistice—were formally at war, the normal stipulations of free navigation by all nations did not apply. In September 1951 the United Nations Security Council passed Resolution 95 demanding that Egypt permit passage through the canal of Israeli ships and goods bound for Israel, a demand that successive Egyptian governments simply ignored. Under Gamal Abdel Nasser, who took power in 1954, demands that ownership of the canal and its revenues pass from the Suez Canal Company to the Egyptian government intensified and by early 1956 were reaching a crisis point. On the symbolically significant fourth anniversary of the Egyptian revolution, just a few days after Britain, the United States, and the World Bank withdrew their pledged funding for the construction of the Aswan High Dam, a project that Nasser regarded as inextricably linked to Egypt's international prestige, Nasser responded by seizing the physical property and administration of the Suez Canal and taking over not just its operation but all its revenues. Several other Arab neighboring states immediately applauded his audacity in facing up to what they considered neocolonial exploitation, and Nasser became a hero to nationalist movements around the world.

Primary Document

ARTICLE 1

The International Company of the Suez Maritime Canal (Egyptian Joint Stock Company) is hereby nationalized. Its assets and liabilities revert to the State and the councils and committees at present responsible for its administration are dissolved.

The shareholders and holders of founders' shares will be compensated for the stock and shares which they own on the basis of their closing price on the Paris Bourse immediately preceding the date on which this law enters into force.

Payment of this compensation will be made when all the assets of the nationalized company have been fully handed over to the State.

ARTICLE 2

The administration of traffic services through the Suez Canal will be carried out by an independent body with the legal status of a corporation; it will be attached to the Ministry of Commerce. An order of the President of the Republic will fix the composition of this body and the payment to be made to its members. This body will have full powers necessary for controlling this service and will not be subject to administrative routine and regulations. . . .

ARTICLE 3

The funds of the nationalized company and its rights in Egypt and abroad are hereby frozen. Banks, institutions and private persons are forbidden to dispose of these assets in any way, to pay out any sum whatever or to meet claims for payment without previous sanction by the body envisaged in Article 2. . . .

ARTICLE 5

Any breach of the terms of Article 3 will be punished with imprisonment and a fine equal to three times the value of the sum involved. Any breach of the terms of Article 4 will be punished with imprisonment; the offender will, in addition, be deprived of any right to a gratuity, pension or compensation. . . .

Source: D. C. Watt, *Documents on the Suez Crisis: 26 July to 6 November 1956* (London: Royal Institute of International Affairs, 1957).

7. Abba Eban, Knesset Statement [Excerpt], May 13, 1969

Introduction

Speaking to the United Nations (UN) in the fall of 1968, Abba Eban was noncommittal as to which if any portions of the territories Israel intended to retain of those it had occupied during the Six-Day War. Addressing the Knesset (Israeli parliament) the following May, he was more forthright, listing three places that Israel considered vital to its interests. Even in these cases, however, some ambiguity remained, since Eban did not state that Israel intended to annex them outright. Instead, he called for Israel's "permanent presence at Sharm el-Sheikh," which could, for example, mean merely full or partial control or occupation; "a unified Jerusalem," under whose formal administration or sovereignty he declined to state; and the denial of the Golan Heights to Syria. While his statement may well have appeased hawks within the Knesset, in practice the ambiguities it contained left the foreign minister and his country substantial room to maneuver.

Primary Document

Three demands which Israel will not waive are a permanent presence at Sharm el-Sheikh, a unified Jerusalem despite concessions to Jordan over the Holy Places, and a Golan Heights for ever out of Syrian hands.

Source: Jerusalem Post, May 14, 1969.

8. United Nations Security Council Resolution 338, October 22, 1973

Introduction

As both sides in the Yom Kippur War decided to agree to a cease-fire, the United Nations (UN) Security Council passed a resolution ordering the cessation of hostilities within

12 hours. In addition, the UN called on all parties to begin peace negotiations using as a basis the earlier UN Security Council Resolution 242, which called on the Arab states to recognize Israel's existence and make lasting peace with that country in exchange for the return of most of the territories Israel had taken in both wars. The resolution also urged solving the Palestinian refugee issue and the internationalization of the city of Jerusalem. In July 1974 the Palestine Liberation Organization once again rejected Resolution 242. The resolution would nonetheless form the basis of protracted subsequent efforts to negotiate an Arab-Israeli peace settlement. Meanwhile, all states involved would be in the future decidedly more cautious in launching full-scale war. Israel later undertook two brief invasions of Lebanon, but these were relatively small operations. Arab states never again mounted major invasions of Israel, relying instead on diplomacy to regain the territories they had lost. In addition, over the next three decades the focus of the Arab-Israeli question increasingly switched to securing the Palestinian refugees a state of their own.

Primary Document

The Security Council,

1. *Calls upon* all parties to the present fighting to cease all firing and terminate all military activity immediately, no later than 12 hours after the moment of the adoption of this decision, in the positions they now occupy;

2. *Calls upon* all parties concerned to start immediately after the cease-fire the implementation of Security Council Resolution 242 (1967) in all of its parts;

3. *Decides* that, immediately and concurrently with the cease-fire, negotiations shall start between the parties concerned under appropriate auspices aimed at establishing a just and durable peace in the Middle East.

> *Source:* United Nations Security Council Official Records, S.C. Res. 338, October 22, 1973. © 1973. Reprinted with the permission of the United Nations.

9. Egypt-Israel Peace Treaty, March 26, 1979

Introduction

In the face of fierce Arab League and Palestine Liberation Organization (PLO) opposition, the Camp David Peace Treaty, also known as the Egypt-Israel Peace Treaty, was signed in 1979 as an outcome of the 1978 Camp David Summit Conference that brought leaders from Israel and Egypt to U.S. president Jimmy Carter's Camp David retreat. During the 13-day conference, a framework for peace between Israel and Egypt was negotiated and formally agreed upon. The treaty ended the state of war between Egypt and Israel and established a fixed boundary between the two, setting aside the status of the Gaza Strip—home to numerous Palestine refugees—for future resolution. The two states also opened full diplomatic relations, exchanging ambassadors. In accordance with the treaty, the following year Israel returned most of the Sinai Peninsula to Egypt, a process completed in 1982. The treaty contained no references to Israel's earlier suggestions that Palestinian Arabs in the Gaza Strip and the West Bank would be granted a substantial degree of autonomy, although talks on the issue began in May 1979, with Egyptian president Anwar Sadat urging the Israeli government to allow Palestinians in the occupied territories political freedoms far more extensive than those that Israeli officials were prepared to accord them. Western leaders and commentators greeted the treaty with enormous enthusiasm. Even relatively hard-line Israeli leaders, such as former prime minister Golda Meir, welcomed it, stating that it would ensure that their grandchildren could live in peace. Carter and others hoped that the peace treaty would prove to be a preliminary step to the subsequent negotiation of similar agreements between Israel and other Arab states, breaking the logjam blocking the conclusion of lasting Middle East peace settlements. In practice, fellow Arab states boycotted Egypt for making peace with Israel. In October 1981, moreover, Muslim extremist gunmen who resented the peace treaty assassinated Sadat, chief Egyptian architect of the Camp David Accords, while he was watching a military parade in Cairo, a discouraging omen for any Arab leader who might be tempted to emulate Sadat's efforts for peace.

Primary Document

PREAMBLE

The Government of the Arab Republic of Egypt and the Government of the State of Israel; Convinced of the urgent necessity of the establishment of a just, comprehensive and lasting peace in the Middle East in accordance with Security Council Resolution 242 and Resolution 338; Reaffirming their adherence to the 'Framework for Peace in the Middle East Agreed at Camp David,' dated September 17, 1978. . . . Agree to the following provisions:

ARTICLE I

1. The state of war between the Parties will be terminated and peace will be established between them upon the exchange of instruments of ratification of this Treaty.

2. Israel will withdraw all its armed forces and civilians from the Sinai behind the international boundary between Egypt and mandated Palestine . . . and Egypt will resume the exercise of its full sovereignty over the Sinai.

3. Upon completion of the interim withdrawal . . . the Parties will establish normal and friendly relations. . . .

ARTICLE II

The permanent boundary between Egypt and Israel is the recognized international boundary between Egypt and the former mandated territory of Palestine . . . without prejudice to the issue of the Gaza Strip. . . .

ARTICLE IV

1. In order to provide maximum security for both Parties on the basis of reciprocity, agreed security arrangements will be established including limited force zones in Egyptian and Israeli territory, and United Nations forces and observers . . . and other security arrangements the Parties may agree upon. . . .

ARTICLE V

1. Ships of Israel, and cargoes destined for or coming from Israel, shall enjoy the right of free passage through the Suez Canal and its approaches through the Gulf of Suez and the Mediterranean Sea. . . . Israeli nationals, vessels and cargoes, as well as persons, vessels and cargoes destined for or coming from Israel, shall be accorded non-discriminatory treatment in all matters connected with usage of the canal.

2. The Parties consider the Strait of Tiran and the Gulf of Aqaba to be international waterways open to all nations for unimpeded and nonsuspendable freedom of navigation and overflight. The Parties will respect each other's right to navigation and overflight for access to either country through the Strait of Tiran and the Gulf of Aqaba.

[Annex I describes the details of Israeli withdrawal from the Sinai Peninsula over a three-year period. It also establishes several zones in the Sinai and surrounding territory in Egypt and Israel and the restricted distribution of military forces in these areas, including the distribution of United Nations forces.]

[Annex II is a map of the Sinai Peninsula and the agreed upon boundary between Egypt and Israel.]

[Annex III sets the terms for the normalization of relations between Egypt and Israel in regard to diplomacy, economics and trade, culture, the freedom of movement of the citizens of each nation, transportation and communication, human rights, and territorial waters.]

Source: "Treaty of Peace between the Arab Republic of Egypt and the State of Israel," Department of State Bulletin 79(2026) (1979): 3–14.

10. U.S. Department of State, Statement on Afghanistan, December 26, 1979

Introduction

The American response to the 1979 Christmas Day Soviet military intervention in Afghanistan was swift. Within a few hours, the U.S. State Department issued an official statement deploring the new scale of Soviet involvement in the affairs of that country.

State Department spokesman Hodding Carter III read news correspondents a statement describing how Soviet transport planes had made more than 150 flights into Kabul on December 25 and 26. He also mentioned signs that at least five divisions of Soviet troops had massed on the border with Afghanistan and appeared ready to enter the country. The U.S. government strongly condemned this "blatant military interference into the internal affairs of an independent sovereign state." Carter also told newsmen that the United States was making strong direct representations on the subject to Soviet officials.

Primary Document

On December 25–26, there was a large-scale Soviet airlift into Kabul International Airport, perhaps involving over 150 flights. The aircraft include both large transports (AN-22s) and smaller transports (AN-12s). Several hundred Soviet troops have been seen at the Kabul airport and various kinds of field equipment have been flown in. I cannot give you an estimate of numbers.

The Soviet military buildup north of the Afghan border is continuing, and we now have indications that there are the equivalent of five divisions in Soviet areas adjacent to Afghanistan. It appears that the Soviets are crossing a new threshold in their military deployments into Afghanistan. We believe that members of the international community should condemn such blatant military interference into the internal affairs of an independent sovereign state. We are making our views known directly to the Soviets.

Source: U.S. Department of State, *American Foreign Policy, 1977–1980*
(Washington, DC: Department of State, 1983), 809.

11. Department of State, Daily Press Briefing on U.S. Policy toward the Iran-Iraq War and toward Exports to Iraq, May 14, 1982

Introduction

In September 1980 war broke out in the Persian Gulf region when Iran invaded Iraq. Saddam Hussein, who became president of Iraq in 1979 and had largely controlled its government since around 1969, saw the weakness of the Iranian military in the aftermath of the 1979 Iranian Revolution as an opportunity to make Iraq the predominant power in the region. He was motivated in part by long-standing disputes with Iran over control of the Shatt al-Arab waterway, only temporarily resolved in 1975 when the two states signed the Algiers Accord dividing their jurisdiction over the channel along a line running through its center. Hussein now claimed that Iraq should control the entire waterway, up to its Iranian shore. In addition, he resented the encouragement that Iran's new Shiite Muslim ruler, Ayatollah Ruhollah Khomeini, whom Saddam had expelled from Iraq in 1978, gave to Iraqi Shiites in efforts to rise up against his own regime and assassinate members of his cabinet. On September 23 Iraqi forces marched across the Shatt al-Arab waterway into southwestern Iraq, the beginning of eight years of war between the two

*countries. Officially, as U.S. State Department spokesmen reiterated in repeated state-
ments during those years, the United States remained neutral in this conflict, affirming its
support for the "independence and territorial integrity" of both states involved and stating
its hopes for the negotiation of an immediate peaceful cease-fire. In practice, for several
years the United States welcomed Iran's preoccupation with a lengthy and bloody conflict.
In February 1982 the U.S. government also removed Iraq from a list of countries subject
to antiterrorism controls, restrictions that had previously prevented Iraq from purchasing
American armaments. The administration of U.S. president Ronald Reagan successfully
resisted congressional efforts to restore Iran to that list. Iran, by contrast, remained subject to American antiterrorist export controls, a clear disadvantage to Iran in the ongoing
hostilities.*

Primary Document

Q. [D]o you have any position on the new developments in the Iran-Iraq war?

A. I don't really have anything on any new developments. I could reiterate for
you, though, our attitude towards it which I think might be appropriate as this all
progresses.

U.S. policy with regard to the Iran-Iraq war has been clear and consistent since
the outbreak of the hostilities 20 months ago. The policy enunciated when Iraqi
forces entered Iran remains our policy today. The United States supports the independence and territorial integrity of both Iran and Iraq as well as the other states
in the region. In keeping with our policy worldwide, we oppose the seizure of territory by force. We see the continuation of the war, as we have repeatedly said, as
a danger to the peace and security of all nations in the Gulf region and we have
therefore consistently supported an immediate cease-fire and a negotiated settlement. We have maintained a firm policy of not approving the sale or transfer of
American military equipment and supplies to either belligerent, and we have welcomed constructive international efforts to bring an end to the war on the basis
of each state's respect for the territorial integrity of its neighbors and each state's
freedom from external coercion.

Q. Is there a new turn in the war now that has changed your attitude?
A. No. Our policy remains consistent on this.

Q. Do you have any comment on the action by the House Foreign Affairs Committee
refusing to take Iraq off this list of terrorism-banned countries?
A. Yes, I do have something on that. Let me address the amendment as a whole as
it was adopted yesterday.

The amendment would impose the controls that were removed by the administration in February. The decisions to remove Iraq from the terrorism list, to exempt
civil aircraft for civil airlines from controls for antiterrorism purposes and to adjust
the controls for South Africa were made after a lengthy review which is required
annually. The review took into account the compatibility of the controls with U.S.

foreign policy objectives, the reaction of other countries to the controls, and the likely effect of continuing controls on U.S. export performance. All is required by the Export Administration Act.

We oppose the restrictions the amendment would impose. Fixing controls by legislation reduces our flexibility to respond to changes in the international arena and to insure that export controls further our foreign policy objectives as is required by the Export Administration Act itself. Changing course at this time will also confuse foreign governments and call into question the credibility of the United States as a reliable supplier.

Source: U.S. Department of State, *American Foreign Policy: Current Documents, 1982*
(Washington, DC: Department of State, 1985), 783–784.

12. Israel's Assumptions with Regard to the Baker Peace Plan, November 5, 1989

Introduction

Israeli prime minister Yitzhak Shamir was less than responsive to U.S. secretary of state James A. Baker's efforts to persuade Israel to negotiate directly with Palestinian representatives over projected Palestinian elections in the occupied territories. The Israeli government took several weeks to reply and then stated that it would talk only with Palestinian residents of the occupied territories. The Israeli statement specifically excluded negotiations with the Palestine Liberation Organization (PLO) and also, by implication, meant that Palestinians living in disputed East Jerusalem as well as those who resided in other countries would not be eligible to participate. Moreover, to make such assurances doubly sure, Israel would have to approve the membership of the Palestinian delegation in advance. Israel also demanded that the talks be limited strictly to the issue of elections, that the United States agree in advance to support Israel's position on the membership of delegations to these talks, and that Israel only be committed to attend one such meetings whose "results will determine if the talks will continue." The intransigent Israeli response to Baker's proposal, after PLO leader Yasser Arafat had made substantial concessions on direct PLO involvement in these talks, undermined Arafat's credibility within his own organization. Radical critics argued that he had gained nothing by abandoning the principle that the PLO was the only body that could represent the Palestinians.

Primary Document

a. The dialogue will begin after the composition of a list of Palestinian Arabs, residents of Judea, Samaria and Gaza, acceptable to Israel.

b. Israel will not negotiate with the PLO.

c. The substantive issues of the dialogue will be the election process in the territories, in a manner consistent with the outline included in the peace initiative of the Government of Israel.

d. The U.S. will publicly support the above Israeli positions and will stand by Israel in the event that another party to the dialogue deviates from what has been agreed upon.

e. The U.S. and Egypt will declare their support for the principles of the Camp David Accords, which are the foundation of the Israeli peace initiative, including the stages of negotiations and their substance.

f. The first meeting will take place in Cairo. The next step will be considered according to the results of the first meeting.

Source: "108 Cabinet Decision on the Five-Point Plan of Secretary Baker—5 November 1989," Israel Ministry of Foreign Affairs, http://mfa.gov.il/MFA /ForeignPolicy/MFADocuments/Yearbook8/Pages/108%20Cabinet%20 Decision%20on%20the%20Five-Point%20Plan%20of%20Sec.aspx.

13. President George H. W. Bush, Announcement of the Deployment of U.S. Armed Forces to Saudi Arabia for Operation DESERT SHIELD, August 8, 1990 [Excerpt]

Introduction

U.S. president George H. W. Bush responded quickly to the Iraqi takeover of Kuwait. American leaders feared that this was only an opening move in a systematic campaign by Iraqi president Saddam Hussein to make his country the dominant power in the Middle East and that the neighboring oil-rich but small and militarily weak kingdom of Saudi Arabia, a U.S. ally, would be his next target. In an address to the American people six days after Hussein's forces invaded Kuwait, Bush made it clear that the United States would not tolerate such actions and explained his policy toward Iraq and Kuwait. Drawing analogies with the 1930s when European leaders had failed to stand up to aggressive actions by fascist Germany and Italy, he warned that the United States would not yield to Hussein's demands or abandon its allies in the Middle East. Bush called for "the immediate, unconditional, and complete withdrawal of all Iraqi forces from Kuwait" and the removal of the "puppet government" Hussein had installed there. Bush described the broad economic sanctions that the United Nations, at U.S. insistence, had already imposed upon Iraq. He stated that the U.S. government would do all in its power to ensure that these sanctions were effective. Perhaps most important, however, he announced that additional American military forces, including a large airpower component, were being deployed in Saudi Arabia that day to safeguard that kingdom against potential aggression by Hussein. Bush's address marked the first step in the process that less than six months later would lead to a full-scale U.S. war to expel Iraq from Kuwait.

Primary Document

In the life of a nation we're called upon to define who we are and what we believe. Sometimes these choices are not easy. But today as President, I ask for your support in a decision I've made to stand up for what's right and condemn what's wrong, all in the cause of peace.

At my direction, elements of the 82nd Airborne Division as well as key units of the United States Air Force are arriving today to take up key defensive positions in Saudi Arabia. I took this action to assist the Saudi Arabian Government in the defense of its home-land. No one commits America's armed forces to a dangerous mission lightly, but after perhaps unparalleled international consultation and exhausting every alternative, it became necessary to take this action. Let me tell you why.

Less than a week ago, in the early morning hours of August 2nd, Iraqi armed forces, without provocation or warning, invaded a peaceful Kuwait. Facing negligible resistance from its much smaller neighbor, Iraq's tanks stormed in blitzkrieg fashion through Kuwait in a few short hours. With more than 100,000 troops, along with tanks, artillery, and surface-to-surface missiles, Iraq now occupies Kuwait. This aggression came just hours after Saddam Hussein specifically assured numerous countries in the area that there would be no invasion. There is no justification whatsoever for this outrageous and brutal act of aggression.

A puppet regime imposed from the outside is unacceptable. The acquisition of territory by force is unacceptable. No one, friend or foe, should doubt our desire for peace; and no one should underestimate our determination to confront aggression.

Four simple principles guide our policy. First, we seek the immediate, unconditional, and complete withdrawal of all Iraqi forces from Kuwait. Second, Kuwait's legitimate government must be restored to replace the puppet regime. And third, my administration, as has been the case with every President from President Roosevelt to President Reagan, is committed to the security and stability of the Persian Gulf. And fourth, I am determined to protect the lives of American citizens abroad.

Immediately after the Iraqi invasion, I ordered an embargo of all trade with Iraq and, together with many other nations, announced sanctions that both freeze all Iraqi assets in this country and protected Kuwait's assets. The stakes are high. Iraq is already a rich and powerful country that possesses the world's second largest reserves of oil and over a million men under arms. It's the fourth largest military in the world. Our country now imports nearly half the oil it consumes and could face a major threat to its economic independence. Much of the world is even more dependent upon imported oil and is even more vulnerable to Iraqi threats.

We succeeded in the struggle for freedom in Europe because we and our allies remain stalwart. Keeping the peace in the Middle East will require no less. We're beginning a new era. This era can be full of promise, an age of freedom, a time of peace for all peoples. But if history teaches us anything, it is that we must resist aggression or it will destroy our freedoms. Appeasement does not work. As was the case in the 1930s, we see in Saddam Hussein an aggressive dictator threatening his neighbors. Only 14 days ago, Saddam Hussein promised his friends he would not invade Kuwait. And 4 days ago, he promised the world he would withdraw. And twice we have seen what his promises mean: His promises mean nothing.

In the last few days, I've spoken with political leaders from the Middle East, Europe, Asia, and the Americas; and I've met with Prime Minister Thatcher, [Canadian] Prime Minister [Brian] Mulroney, and NATO Secretary General [Manfred] Woerner. And all agree that Iraq cannot be allowed to benefit from its invasion of Kuwait.

We agree that this is not an American problem or a European problem or a Middle East problem; it is the world's problem. And that's why, soon after the Iraqi invasion, the United Nations Security Council, without dissent, condemned Iraq, calling for the immediate and unconditional withdrawal of its troops from Kuwait. The Arab world, through both the Arab League and the Gulf Cooperation Council, courageously announced its opposition to Iraqi aggression. Japan, the United Kingdom, and France, and other governments around the world have imposed severe sanctions. The Soviet Union and China ended all arms sales to Iraq.

And this past Monday, the United Nations Security Council approved for the first time in 23 years mandatory sanctions under Chapter VII of the United Nations Charter. These sanctions, now enshrined in international law, have the potential for denying Iraq the fruits of aggression while sharply limiting its ability to either import or export anything of value, especially oil.

I pledge here today that the United States will do its part to see that these sanctions are effective and to induce Iraq to withdraw without delay from Kuwait.

But we must recognize that Iraq may not stop using force to advance its ambitions. Iraq has massed an enormous war machine on the Saudi border capable of initiating hostilities with little or no additional preparation. Given the Iraqi Government's history of aggression against its own citizens as well as its neighbors, to assume Iraq will not attack again would be unwise and unrealistic.

And therefore, after consulting with King Fahd, I sent Secretary of Defense Dick Cheney to discuss cooperative measures we could take. Following those meetings, the Saudi Government requested our help, and I responded to that request by ordering U.S. air and ground forces to deploy to the Kingdom of Saudi Arabia.

Let me be clear: The sovereign independence of Saudi Arabia is of vital interest to the United States. This decision, which I shared with the Congressional leadership, grows out of the longstanding friendship and security relationship between the United States and Saudi Arabia. U.S. forces will work together with those of Saudi Arabia and other nations to preserve the integrity of Saudi Arabia and to deter further Iraqi aggression. Through their presence, as well as through training and exercises, these multinational forces will enhance the overall capability of Saudi armed forces to defend the Kingdom.

I want to be clear about what we are doing and why. America does not seek conflict, nor do we seek to chart the destiny of other nations. But America will stand by her friends. The mission of our troops is wholly defensive. Hopefully, they will not be needed long. They will not initiate hostilities, but they will defend themselves, the Kingdom of Saudi Arabia, and other friends in the Persian Gulf. . . .

Source: George H. W. Bush, *Public Papers of the Presidents of the United States: George Bush, 1990,* Book 2 (Washington, DC: U.S. Government Printing Office, 1991), 1107–1108.

14. President George H. W. Bush, "The New World Order," Address before a Joint Session of Congress on the Cessation of the Persian Gulf Conflict, March 6, 1991 [Excerpts]

Introduction

The ending of the Cold War meant that the guiding principle of American foreign policy could no longer, as it had been for over four decades, be the strategy of containment of communism. Addressing Congress shortly after the Persian Gulf War had ended, a triumphant George H. W. Bush promised aid to the Middle East. He then proclaimed that the ending of the Cold War had made it possible for the United Nations (UN) to function as its founders had originally intended so that there was a "very real prospect of a new world order." This, Bush stated, would be "A world in which freedom and respect for human rights find a home among all nations." He urged Congress to take swift and decisive action on economic problems, pollution, and crime to enable the country to fill its historic mission of implementing that new world order. Bush's speech was somewhat vague as to precisely what the new world order would encompass or how it would be organized. Critics charged that he envisaged that the United States could use its unrivaled military and economic might to dominate the new world order in its own interests. Somewhat cynically, many also felt that American commitment to maintaining such a new world order would be selective and that the United States had only intervened against Iraq because that country had menaced the security of two major U.S. allies, Israel and Saudi Arabia, and also threatened continuing supplies of Middle Eastern oil to the United States.

Primary Document

Tonight, I come to this House to speak about the world—the world after war. The recent challenge could not have been clearer. Saddam Hussein was the villain; Kuwait, the victim. To the aid of this small country came nations from North America and Europe, from Asia and South America, from Africa and the Arab world, all united against aggression. Our uncommon coalition must now work in common purpose: to forge a future that should never again be held hostage to the darker side of human nature.

Tonight in Iraq, Saddam walks amidst ruin. His war machine is crushed. His ability to threaten mass destruction is itself destroyed. His people have been lied to, denied the truth. And when his defeated legions come home, all Iraqis will see and feel the havoc he has wrought. And this I promise you: For all that Saddam has done to his own people, to the Kuwaitis, and to the entire world, Saddam and those around him are accountable.

All of us grieve for the victims of war, for the people of Kuwait and the suffering that scars the soul of that proud nation. We grieve for all our fallen soldiers and their families, for all the innocents caught up in this conflict. And, yes, we grieve for the people of Iraq, a people who have never been our enemy. My hope is that one day we will once again welcome them as friends into the community of nations. Our commitment to peace in the Middle East does not end with the liberation of Kuwait. So, tonight let me outline four key challenges to be met.

First, we must work together to create shared security arrangements in the region. Our friends and allies in the Middle East recognize that they will bear the bulk of the responsibility for regional security. But we want them to know that just as we stood with them to repel aggression, so now America stands ready to work with them to secure the peace. This does not mean stationing U.S. ground forces in the Arabian Peninsula, but it does mean American participation in joint exercises involving both air and ground forces. It means maintaining a capable U.S. naval presence in the region, just as we have for over 40 years. Let it be clear: Our vital national interests depend on a stable and secure Gulf.

Second, we must act to control the proliferation of weapons of mass destruction and the missiles used to deliver them. It would be tragic if the nations of the Middle East and Persian Gulf were now, in the wake of war, to embark on a new arms race. Iraq requires special vigilance. Until Iraq convinces the world of its peaceful intentions—that its leaders will not use new revenues to rearm and rebuild its menacing war machine—Iraq must not have access to the instruments of war.

And third, we must work to create new opportunities for peace and stability in the Middle East. On the night I announced Operation Desert Storm, I expressed my hope that out of the horrors of war might come new momentum for peace. We've learned in the modern age geography cannot guarantee security, and security does not come from military power alone.

All of us know the depth of bitterness that has made the dispute between Israel and its neighbors so painful and intractable. Yet, in the conflict just concluded, Israel and many of the Arab States have for the first time found themselves confronting the same aggressor. By now, it should be plain to all parties that peacemaking in the Middle East requires compromise. At the same time, peace brings real benefits to everyone. We must do all that we can to close the gap between Israel and the Arab States—and between Israelis and Palestinians. The tactics of terror lead absolutely nowhere. There can be no substitute for diplomacy.

A comprehensive peace must be grounded in United Nations Security Council Resolutions 242 and 338 and the principle of territory for peace. This principle must be elaborated to provide for Israel's security and recognition and at the same time for legitimate Palestinian political rights. Anything else would fail the twin test of fairness and security. The time has come to put an end to Arab-Israeli conflict.

The war with Iraq is over. The quest for solutions to the problems in Lebanon, in the Arab-Israeli dispute, and in the Gulf must go forward with new vigor and determination. And I guarantee you: No one will work harder for a stable peace in the region than we will.

Fourth, we must foster economic development for the sake of peace and progress. The Persian Gulf and Middle East form a region rich in natural resources with a wealth of untapped human potential. Resources once squandered on military might must be redirected to more peaceful ends. We are already addressing the immediate economic consequences of Iraq's aggression. Now, the challenge is to reach higher, to foster economic freedom and prosperity for all the people of the region.

By meeting these four challenges we can build a framework for peace. I've asked Secretary of State Baker to go to the Middle East to begin the process. He will go to listen, to probe, to offer suggestions—to advance the search for peace and stability. I've also asked him to raise the plight of the hostages held in Lebanon. We have not forgotten them, and we will not forget them.

To all the challenges that confront this region of the world there is no single solution, no solely American answer. But we can make a difference. America will work tirelessly as a catalyst for positive change.

But we cannot lead a new world abroad if, at home, it's politics as usual on American defense and diplomacy. It's time to turn away from the temptation to protect unneeded weapons systems and obsolete bases. It's time to put an end to micromanagement of foreign and security assistance programs—micromanagement that humiliates our friends and allies and hamstrings our diplomacy. It's time to rise above the parochial and the pork barrel, to do what is necessary, what's right, and what will enable this nation to play the leadership role required of us.

The consequences of the conflict in the Gulf reach far beyond the confines of the Middle East. Twice before in this century, an entire world was convulsed by war. Twice this century, out of the horrors of war hope emerged for enduring peace. Twice before, those hopes proved to be a distant dream, beyond the grasp of man. Until now, the world we've known has been a world divided—a world of barbed wire and concrete block, conflict, and cold war.

Now, we can see a new world coming into view. A world in which there is the very real prospect of a new world order. In the words of Winston Churchill, a world order in which "the principles of justice and fair play protect the weak against the strong. . . ." A world where the United Nations, freed from cold war stalemate, is poised to fulfill the historic vision of its founders. A world in which freedom and respect for human rights find a home among all nations. The Gulf war put this new world to its first test. And my fellow Americans, we passed that test.

For the sake of our principles, for the sake of the Kuwaiti people, we stood our ground. Because the world would not look the other way, Ambassador al-Sabah, tonight Kuwait is free. And we're very happy about that.

Tonight, as our troops begin to come home, let us recognize that the hard work of freedom still calls us forward. We've learned the hard lessons of history. The victory over Iraq was not waged as "a war to end all wars." Even the new world order cannot guarantee an era of perpetual peace. But enduring peace must be our mission. Our success in the Gulf will shape not only the new world order we seek but our mission here at home. . . .

We went halfway around the world to do what is moral and just and right. We fought hard and, with others, we won the war.

We lifted the yoke of aggression and tyranny from a small country that many Americans had never even heard of, and we ask nothing in return.

We're coming home now—proud, confident, heads high. There is much that we must do, at home and abroad. And we will do it. We are Americans.

May God bless this great nation, the United States of America.

Source: George H. W. Bush, *Public Papers of the Presidents of the United States: George Bush, 1991,* Book 1 (Washington, DC: U.S. Government Printing Office, 1992), 218–222.

15. Brent Scowcroft, "Don't Attack Saddam," August 15, 2002

Introduction

Republicans from the administration of President George H. W. Bush, who had chosen in late February 1991 not to invade Iraq in an effort to overthrow President Saddam Hussein, were often uncomfortable with the growing enthusiasm that his son's administration displayed for war against Iraq. In August 2002 Brent Scowcroft, the elder Bush's national security adviser who had coauthored a foreign policy memoir with the former president, published an article in the conservative Wall Street Journal *urging caution. Scowcroft admitted that Hussein was a "thoroughly evil" and brutal dictator, enamored of military force, who had in the past made war on his neighbors, and Scowcroft bluntly stated that "We will all be better off when he is gone." In Scowcroft's opinion, however, Hussein did not seek to attack the United States directly, only to "dominate the Persian Gulf, to control oil from the region, or both." His differences with the United States derived from the fact that it blocked these ambitions. Hussein was unlikely to supply weapons to terrorist organizations he could not control, especially since such action was likely to bring the wrath of the United States down upon him. Scowcroft argued that while it might at some stage be desirable to bring about Hussein's overthrow, this would "undoubtedly be very expensive," and for some time to come the war on terror ought to be the first priority for the United States. Invading Iraq would likely prove to be a major diversion from this objective, one that would make other states less willing to cooperate in the war against terror and might well destabilize other Middle Eastern regimes. Many Arab states would also resent such action, perceiving it as a deliberate downgrading of attempts to resolve the Israeli-Palestinian conflict. Successes in prosecuting the war against terror and reaching an Israeli-Palestinian settlement would, by contrast, ultimately facilitate international support for efforts to drive Hussein from power. Scowcroft's warning received considerable publicity, but the very fact that he chose to make his case in the media, not behind closed doors as a trusted confidential adviser, was evidence that President George W. Bush and officials close to him did not wish to hear Snowcroft's message and proposed to ignore it.*

Primary Document

"Don't Attack Saddam—It Would Undermine Our Anti-terror Efforts"
By Brent Scowcroft

Our nation is presently engaged in a debate about whether to launch a war against Iraq. Leaks of various strategies for an attack on Iraq appear with regularity. The Bush administration vows regime change, but states that no decision has been made whether, much less when, to launch an invasion.

It is beyond dispute that Saddam Hussein is a menace. He terrorizes and brutalizes his own people. He has launched war on two of his neighbors. He devotes enormous effort to rebuilding his military forces and equipping them with weapons of mass destruction. We will all be better off when he is gone.

That said, we need to think through this issue very carefully. We need to analyze the relationship between Iraq and our other pressing priorities—notably the war on terrorism—as well as the best strategy and tactics available were we to move to change the regime in Baghdad.

Saddam's strategic objective appears to be to dominate the Persian Gulf, to control oil from the region, or both. That clearly poses a real threat to key U.S. interests. But there is scant evidence to tie Saddam to terrorist organizations, and even less to the September 11 attacks. Indeed Saddam's goals have little in common with the terrorists who threaten us, and there is little incentive for him to make common cause with them.

He is unlikely to risk his investment in weapons of mass destruction, much less his country, by handing such weapons to terrorists who would use them for their own purposes and leave Baghdad as the return address. Threatening to use these weapons for blackmail—much less their actual use—would open him and his entire regime to a devastating response by the U.S. While Saddam is thoroughly evil, he is above all a power-hungry survivor.

Saddam is a familiar dictatorial aggressor, with traditional goals for his aggression. There is little evidence to indicate that the United States itself is an object of his aggression. Rather, Saddam's problem with the U.S. appears to be that we stand in the way of his ambitions. He seeks weapons of mass destruction not to arm terrorists, but to deter us from intervening to block his aggressive designs.

Given Saddam's aggressive regional ambitions, as well as his ruthlessness and unpredictability, it may at some point be wise to remove him from power. Whether and when that point should come ought to depend on overall U.S. national security priorities. Our pre-eminent security priority—underscored repeatedly by the president—is the war on terrorism. An attack on Iraq at this time would seriously jeopardize, if not destroy, the global counter-terrorist campaign we have undertaken.

The United States could certainly defeat the Iraqi military and destroy Saddam's regime. But it would not be a cakewalk. On the contrary, it undoubtedly would be very expensive—with serious consequences for the U.S. and global economy—and could as well be bloody. In fact, Saddam would be likely to conclude he had nothing left to lose, leading him to unleash whatever weapons of mass destruction he possesses.

Israel would have to expect to be the first casualty, as in 1991 when Saddam sought to bring Israel into the Gulf conflict. This time, using weapons of mass destruction, he might succeed, provoking Israel to respond, perhaps with nuclear weapons, unleashing an Armageddon in the Middle East. Finally, if we are to achieve our strategic objectives in Iraq, a military campaign very likely would have to be followed by a large-scale, long-term military occupation.

But the central point is that any campaign against Iraq, whatever the strategy, cost and risks, is certain to divert us for some indefinite period from our war on terrorism. Worse, there is a virtual consensus in the world against an attack on Iraq at this time. So long as that sentiment persists, it would require the U.S. to pursue a virtual go-it-alone strategy against Iraq, making any military operations correspondingly more difficult and expensive. The most serious cost, however, would be to the war on terrorism. Ignoring that clear sentiment would result in a serious degradation in international cooperation with us against terrorism. And make no mistake, we simply cannot win that war without enthusiastic international cooperation, especially on intelligence.

Possibly the most dire consequences would be the effect in the region. The shared view in the region is that Iraq is principally an obsession of the U.S. The obsession of the region, however, is the Israeli-Palestinian conflict. If we were seen to be turning our backs on that bitter conflict—which the region, rightly or wrongly, perceives to be clearly within our power to resolve—in order to go after Iraq, there would be an explosion of outrage against us. We would be seen as ignoring a key interest of the Muslim world in order to satisfy what is seen to be a narrow American interest.

Even without Israeli involvement, the results could well destabilize Arab regimes in the region, ironically facilitating one of Saddam's strategic objectives. At a minimum, it would stifle any cooperation on terrorism, and could even swell the ranks of the terrorists. Conversely, the more progress we make in the war on terrorism, and the more we are seen to be committed to resolving the Israel-Palestinian issue, the greater will be the international support for going after Saddam.

If we are truly serious about the war on terrorism, it must remain our top priority. However, should Saddam Hussein be found to be clearly implicated in the events of September 11, that could make him a key counterterrorist target, rather than a competing priority, and significantly shift world opinion toward support for regime change.

In any event, we should be pressing the United Nations Security Council to insist on an effective no-notice inspection regime for Iraq—anytime, anywhere, no permission required. On this point, senior administration officials have opined that Saddam Hussein would never agree to such an inspection regime. But if he did, inspections would serve to keep him off balance and under close observation, even if all his weapons of mass destruction capabilities were not uncovered. And if he refused, his rejection could provide the persuasive casus belli which many claim we do not now have. Compelling evidence that Saddam had acquired nuclear-weapons capability could have a similar effect.

In sum, if we will act in full awareness of the intimate interrelationship of the key issues in the region, keeping counterterrorism as our foremost priority, there is much potential for success across the entire range of our security interests—including Iraq. If we reject a comprehensive perspective, however, we put at risk our campaign against terrorism as well as stability and security in a vital region of the world.

Source: U.S. Congress, *Congressional Record,* 107th Cong., 2nd sess., 2002, 7763–7764.

16. President George W. Bush, Address to the Nation on Iraq, March 17, 2003

Introduction

With Anglo-American efforts to obtain a United Nations (UN) Security Council mandate for war against Iraq deadlocked, on March 17, 2003, U.S. president George W. Bush announced to the American people his administration's decision to use force against Iraq. Once more he stated that Iraq possessed biological and chemical weapons of mass destruction and was developing a nuclear capability, which made it a threat already to the United States, one that would only grow in the future and that within a few years would be far more menacing. Bush also claimed that Iraq provided sanctuary, funding, and safe haven to terrorist organizations, including Al-Qaeda. The UN, Bush rather provocatively claimed, had failed to meet its responsibility to deal with President Saddam Hussein of Iraq, but the United States and its coalition of allies would do so. Bush told Hussein that only if he and his sons left Iraq within 48 hours could war be avoided. Bush appealed to the Iraqi military to abandon Hussein and offer no resistance to invading coalition forces. Bush also warned Iraqi officials against destroying the country's oil industry, "a source of wealth that belongs to the Iraqi people," and to disobey any orders instructing them to utilize weapons of mass destruction against the invaders or their own people. The U.S. president promised the Iraqi people that once Hussein and his followers had been ousted, they themselves would enjoy the benefits of democracy and "set an example to all the Middle East of a vital and peaceful and self-governing nation." Although Bush claimed that his country had no feasible alternative except war, his administration had clearly sought this conflict despite much international opposition. Major demonstrations in protest took place around the world, although in the United States early polls showed public support for Bush's policies on Iraq peaking at more than 70 percent in the war's early days, and even former critics of the intervention tended to mute their misgivings and rally around their country's armed forces.

Primary Document

My fellow citizens, events in Iraq have now reached the final days of decision. For more than a decade, the United States and other nations have pursued patient and honorable efforts to disarm the Iraqi regime without war. That regime pledged to reveal and destroy all its weapons of mass destruction as a condition for ending the Persian Gulf war in 1991.

Since then, the world has engaged in 12 years of diplomacy. We have passed more than a dozen resolutions in the United Nations Security Council. We have sent hundreds of weapons inspectors to oversee the disarmament of Iraq. Our good faith has not been returned.

The Iraqi regime has used diplomacy as a ploy to gain time and advantage. It has uniformly defied Security Council resolutions demanding full disarmament. Over the years, U.N. weapon inspectors have been threatened by Iraqi officials, electronically bugged, and systematically deceived. Peaceful efforts to disarm the Iraqi regime have failed again and again because we are not dealing with peaceful men.

Intelligence gathered by this and other governments leaves no doubt that the Iraq regime continues to possess and conceal some of the most lethal weapons ever devised. This regime has already used weapons of mass destruction against Iraq's neighbors and against Iraq's people.

The regime has a history of reckless aggression in the Middle East. It has a deep hatred of America and our friends. And it has aided, trained, and harbored terrorists, including operatives of Al Qaida.

The danger is clear: Using chemical, biological or, one day, nuclear weapons obtained with the help of Iraq, the terrorists could fulfill their stated ambitions and kill thousands or hundreds of thousands of innocent people in our country or any other.

The United States and other nations did nothing to deserve or invite this threat. But we will do everything to defeat it. Instead of drifting along toward tragedy, we will set a course toward safety. Before the day of horror can come, before it is too late to act, this danger will be removed.

The United States of America has the sovereign authority to use force in assuring its own national security. That duty falls to me as Commander in Chief, by the oath I have sworn, by the oath I will keep.

Recognizing the threat to our country, the United States Congress voted overwhelmingly last year to support the use of force against Iraq. America tried to work with the United Nations to address this threat because we wanted to resolve the issue peacefully. We believe in the mission of the United Nations. One reason the U.N. was founded after the Second World War was to confront aggressive dictators actively and early, before they can attack the innocent and destroy the peace.

In the case of Iraq, the Security Council did act in the early 1990s. Under Resolutions 678 and 687, both still in effect, the United States and our allies are authorized to use force in ridding Iraq of weapons of mass destruction. This is not a question of authority. It is a question of will.

Last September, I went to the U.N. General Assembly and urged the nations of the world to unite and bring an end to this danger. On November 8th, the Security Council unanimously passed Resolution 1441, finding Iraq in material breach of its obligations and vowing serious consequences if Iraq did not fully and immediately disarm.

Today, no nation can possibly claim that Iraq has disarmed, and it will not disarm so long as Saddam Hussein holds power. For the last 4 1/2 months, the United States and our allies have worked within the Security Council to enforce that Council's longstanding demands. Yet, some permanent members of the Security Council have publicly announced they will veto any resolution that compels the disarmament of Iraq. These governments share our assessment of the danger but not our resolve to meet it.

Many nations, however, do have the resolve and fortitude to act against this threat to peace, and a broad coalition is now gathering to enforce the just demands of the world. The United Nations Security Council has not lived up to its responsibilities, so we will rise to ours.

In recent days, some governments in the Middle East have been doing their part. They have delivered public and private messages urging the dictator to leave Iraq, so that disarmament can proceed peacefully. He has thus far refused.

All the decades of deceit and cruelty have now reached an end. Saddam Hussein and his sons must leave Iraq within 48 hours. Their refusal to do so will result in military conflict, commenced at a time of our choosing. For their own safety, all foreign nationals, including journalists and inspectors, should leave Iraq immediately.

Many Iraqis can hear me tonight in a translated radio broadcast, and I have a message for them: If we must begin a military campaign, it will be directed against the lawless men who rule your country and not against you. As our coalition takes away their power, we will deliver the food and medicine you need. We will tear down the apparatus of terror, and we will help you to build a new Iraq that is prosperous and free. In a free Iraq, there will be no more wars of aggression against your neighbors, no more poison factories, no more executions of dissidents, no more torture chambers and rape rooms. The tyrant will soon be gone. The day of your liberation is near.

It is too late for Saddam Hussein to remain in power. It is not too late for the Iraqi military to act with honor and protect your country by permitting the peaceful entry of coalition forces to eliminate weapons of mass destruction. Our forces will give Iraqi military units clear instructions on actions they can take to avoid being attacked and destroyed. I urge every member of the Iraqi military and intelligence services: If war comes, do not fight for a dying regime that is not worth your own life.

And all Iraqi military and civilian personnel should listen carefully to this warning: In any conflict, your fate will depend on your actions. Do not destroy oil wells, a source of wealth that belongs to the Iraqi people. Do not obey any command to use weapons of mass destruction against anyone, including the Iraqi people. War crimes will be prosecuted. War criminals will be punished. And it will be no defense to say, "I was just following orders."

Should Saddam Hussein choose confrontation, the American people can know that every measure has been taken to avoid war and every measure will be taken to win it. Americans understand the costs of conflict because we have paid them in the past. War has no certainty, except the certainty of sacrifice. Yet, the only way to reduce the harm and duration of war is to apply the full force and might of our military, and we are prepared to do so.

If Saddam Hussein attempts to cling to power, he will remain a deadly foe until the end. In desperation, he and terrorist groups might try to conduct terrorist operations against the American people and our friends. These attacks are not inevitable. They are, however, possible. And this very fact underscores the reason we cannot live under the threat of blackmail. The terrorist threat to America and the world will be diminished the moment that Saddam Hussein is disarmed.

Our Government is on heightened watch against these dangers. Just as we are preparing to ensure victory in Iraq, we are taking further actions to protect our homeland. In recent days, American authorities have expelled from the country certain individuals with ties to Iraqi intelligence services. Among other measures, I have directed additional security of our airports and increased Coast Guard patrols of major seaports. The Department of Home-land Security is working closely with the Nation's Governors to increase armed security at critical facilities across America.

Should enemies strike our country, they would be attempting to shift our attention with panic and weaken our morale with fear. In this, they would fail. No act of theirs can alter the course or shake the resolve of this country. We are a peaceful people. Yet we're not a fragile people, and we will not be intimidated by thugs and killers. If our enemies dare to strike us, they and all who have aided them will face fearful consequences.

We are now acting because the risks of inaction would be far greater. In 1 year, or 5 years, the power of Iraq to inflict harm on all free nations would be multiplied many times over. With these capabilities, Saddam Hussein and his terrorist allies could choose the moment of deadly conflict when they are strongest. We choose to meet that threat now, where it arises, before it can appear suddenly in our skies and cities.

The cause of peace requires all free nations to recognize new and undeniable realities. In the 20th century, some chose to appease murderous dictators, whose threats were allowed to grow into genocide and global war. In this century, when evil men plot chemical, biological, and nuclear terror, a policy of appeasement could bring destruction of a kind never before seen on this Earth.

Terrorists and terror states do not reveal these threats with fair notice, in formal declarations. And responding to such enemies only after they have struck first is not self-defense; it is suicide. The security of the world requires disarming Saddam Hussein now.

As we enforce the just demands of the world, we will also honor the deepest commitments of our country. Unlike Saddam Hussein, we believe the Iraqi people are deserving and capable of human liberty. And when the dictator has departed, they can set an example to all the Middle East of a vital and peaceful and self-governing nation.

The United States, with other countries, will work to advance liberty and peace in that region. Our goal will not be achieved overnight, but it can come over time. The power and appeal of human liberty is felt in every life and every land. And the greatest power of freedom is to overcome hatred and violence and turn the creative gifts of men and women to the pursuits of peace.

That is the future we choose. Free nations have a duty to defend our people by uniting against the violent. And tonight, as we have done before, America and our allies accept that responsibility.

Source: George W. Bush, *Public Papers of the Presidents of the United States: George Bush, 2003,* Book 1 (Washington, DC: U.S. Government Printing Office, 2003), 277–280.

17. White House Press Statement on Lifting of Sanctions on Libya, September 20, 2004

Introduction

American military success in invading Iraq and removing President Saddam Hussein from power made other longtime opponents of the United States exceptionally nervous. For more than 30 years since taking power in Libya in 1969 as head of a radical Islamic regime, Colonel Muammar Gaddafi had headed an Arab regime militantly hostile toward the United States. He had been a dedicated supporter of extremist elements within the Palestine Liberation Organization, which took refuge in Tripoli, Libya's capital, after its

1982 expulsion from Beirut, and had financed and provided asylum to other terrorist groups, especially the Abu Nidal organization that launched spectacular assaults on Israel and the West. The United States broke diplomatic relations with Libya in 1980, and in 1981 and again in 1986 U.S. president Ronald Reagan ordered heavy airstrikes against Libya in retaliation for specific terrorist operations. For decades, the two states remained on deeply antagonistic terms. In late 2003, however, Gaddafi responded to Saddam Hussein's downfall by moving to improve Libya's relationship with the United States. Libya agreed to end its program to develop weapons of mass destruction, including measures to enrich uranium to fuel nuclear armaments; open all its weapons facilities to international inspection; and destroy all suspect materials or hand them over to the United Nations. Gaddafi also agreed not to facilitate efforts to acquire weapons of mass destruction in countries whose proliferation efforts were the subject of international concern. In addition, he agreed to renounce his support for terrorist activities and pay compensation to the families of victims of Pan Am Flight 103, which exploded over Lockerbie, Scotland, in December 1988, killing 270 people, an episode for which Libya accepted responsibility. President George W. Bush's administration rewarded Gaddafi in September 2004 by ending the state of U.S. national emergency against Libya in place since 1986 and removing a wide range of economic sanctions on that country. U.S. trade with Libya was now permitted, as were direct air flights, and U.S. commerce with Libya was now eligible for funding from U.S. government programs to finance foreign trade. The Bush administration hinted that if Libya made more progress on such issues as human rights, further concessions might follow. As the icy atmosphere of U.S.-Libyan dealings slowly thawed, in May 2006 the United States and Libya resumed full diplomatic relations. It was no secret that by this juncture the Bush administration hoped that this demonstration of the potential for even a longtime enemy to normalize its relations with the United States by renouncing efforts to develop weapons of mass destruction might induce Iran to cease its program to enrich uranium and acquire nuclear armaments.

Primary Document

THE WHITE HOUSE Office of the Press Secretary
September 20, 2004
STATEMENT BY THE PRESS SECRETARY

Today, the United States has reached another milestone in the President's effort to combat the proliferation of weapons of mass destruction and the means of their delivery. Over the last nine months, Libya has worked with international organizations and the United States and United Kingdom to eliminate its WMD and longer-range missile programs in a transparent and verifiable manner. Libya's efforts open the path to better relations with the United States and other free nations.

These accomplishments are significant. Libya facilitated the removal of all significant elements of its declared nuclear weapons program, signed the IAEA Additional Protocol, began a process of converting the Rabta facility to a pharmaceutical plant, destroyed chemical munitions and secured chemical agents for destruction under international supervision, declared its chemical agents to the Organization for the

Prevention of Chemical Weapons, eliminated its Scud-C missile force, and agreed to eliminate its Scud-B missiles. Libya turned over nuclear weapons documentation, removed highly enriched uranium for its research reactor and equipment for uranium enrichment, allowed international personnel site access, and pledged to halt all military trade with countries of proliferation concern. Revelations by Libya greatly aided the international community's effort to understand and cripple the global black market in the world's most dangerous technologies.

Libya has also agreed to an ongoing trilateral arrangement in which the United States, the United Kingdom and Libya will address any other WMD-related issues as well as to further projects for mutual cooperation such as redirection of Libyan WMD personnel. The progress in US-Libyan relations reflects the cooperation and support exhibited by Libyan officials and experts over the last nine months. As a result, concerns over weapons of mass destruction no longer pose a barrier to the normalization of US-Libyan relations.

At the beginning of this process, the President committed to respond to concrete Libyan actions in good faith, noting that Libya "can regain a secure and respected place among the nations and, over time, better relations with the United States." In recognition of these achievements and our assessment that Libya has continued to meet the standard it set on December 19 to eliminate WMD and MTCR-class missiles and other developments, the President has:

— Terminated the national emergency declared in 1986 under the International Emergency Economic Powers Act (IEEPA), and revoked related Executive Orders. This rescinds the remaining economic sanctions under IEEPA and ends the need for Treasury Department licences for trade with Libya. It also permits direct air service and regular charter flights, subject to standard safety and other regulatory requirements. This action also unblocks assets belonging to Libyan and non-Libyan entities that were frozen when the national emergency was imposed.

— Adopted, as a general policy, the strategy of providing a level playing field for US business in Libya through the use of U.S. Government programs such as those administered by the Departments of Agriculture and Commerce, the Export-Import Bank, Overseas Private Insurance Corporation, and Trade Development Agency, as well as to waive the prohibitions on the availability of foreign tax credits. This policy will be furthered through the use of statutory waiver authorities where necessary and in some cases through proposed legislative relief from sanctions that would otherwise stand in the way.

As a result, we expect the families of the victims of Pan Am 103 to receive over $1 billion in additional compensation from Libya. The determination and courage of the Pan Am 103 families, in almost sixteen years of efforts to hold Libya accountable before the world, contributed greatly to efforts to secure an agreement under which Libya agreed to end all its WMD programs and pledged to end all connections with terrorism.

In conjunction with U.S. action to unblock frozen assets, with respect to the remaining cases brought against it by U.S. victims of terrorism Libya has reaffirmed to us that it has a policy and practice of carrying out agreed settlements and responding in good faith to legal cases brought against it, including court judgments and arbitral awards. We expect Libya to honor this commitment.

The US will continue its dialogue with Libya on human rights, political and economic modernization, and regional political developments. We welcome Libya's engagement with Amnesty International. We also share the European Community's concern over the plight of the Bulgarian medics. Diplomatic engagement and cooperation in education, health care, and scientific training can build the foundation for stronger relations. The United States supports Libya's efforts to reap the benefits of engagement, including prosperity and security for its citizens. As the President stated in December, 2003, "Should Libya pursue internal reform, America will be ready to help its people to build a more free and prosperous country." None of today's actions change Libya's status as a State Sponsor of Terrorism. We remain seriously concerned by the allegations of Libyan involvement in an assassination plot against Crown Prince Abdullah of Saudi Arabia and we have raised our concerns with the Libyan government. These concerns must be addressed. We welcome Libya's formal renunciation of terrorism and Libyan support in the global war against terrorism, but we must establish confidence that Libya has made a strategic decision that is being carried out in practice by all Libyan agencies and officials.

> *Source:* "Statement by the Press Secretary," September 20, 2004, National Archives, http://georgewbush-whitehouse.archives.gov/news/releases/2004/09/20040920-8.html.

18. President Obama on Military Operations against ISIS, September 10, 2014

Introduction

On the evening of September 10, 2014, President Barack Obama addressed the American people in a nationally televised speech. The subject of the address covered American and allied responses to the growing threat of the Islamic State of Iraq and Syria (ISIS), which for more than a year had been conducting a campaign of terror in large swaths of Iraq and Syria. ISIS threatened the viability of the Iraqi government and also threatened to plunge civil war–torn Syria into even more chaos. Moreover, ISIS had begun a campaign of publicly beheading prisoners, including several Westerners, to induce even more terror. The Obama administration had already begun limited bombing raids against ISIS in Iraq and had dispatched several hundred military advisers to aid the Iraqi government. The September 10 speech let Americans and the world know that the United States, in conjunction with a broad coalition of both Islamic and non-Islamic nations, would step up efforts to combat ISIS and ultimately destroy it. Obama announced the extension of U.S. bombing into Syria but warned that the war against ISIS might take many months, if not years.

Primary Document

My fellow Americans, tonight I want to speak to you about what the United States will do with our friends and allies to degrade and ultimately destroy the terrorist group known as ISIL.

As Commander-in-Chief, my highest priority is the security of the American people. Over the last several years, we have consistently taken the fight to terrorists who threaten our country. We took out Osama bin Laden and much of al Qaeda's leadership in Afghanistan and Pakistan. We've targeted al Qaeda's affiliate in Yemen, and recently eliminated the top commander of its affiliate in Somalia. We've done so while bringing more than 140,000 American troops home from Iraq, and drawing down our forces in Afghanistan, where our combat mission will end later this year. Thanks to our military and counterterrorism professionals, America is safer.

Still, we continue to face a terrorist threat. We can't erase every trace of evil from the world, and small groups of killers have the capacity to do great harm. That was the case before 9/11, and that remains true today. And that's why we must remain vigilant as threats emerge. At this moment, the greatest threats come from the Middle East and North Africa, where radical groups exploit grievances for their own gain. And one of those groups is ISIL—which calls itself the "Islamic State."

Now let's make two things clear: ISIL is not "Islamic." No religion condones the killing of innocents. And the vast majority of ISIL's victims have been Muslim. And ISIL is certainly not a state. It was formerly al Qaeda's affiliate in Iraq, and has taken advantage of sectarian strife and Syria's civil war to gain territory on both sides of the Iraq-Syrian border. It is recognized by no government, nor by the people it subjugates. ISIL is a terrorist organization, pure and simple. And it has no vision other than the slaughter of all who stand in its way.

In a region that has known so much bloodshed, these terrorists are unique in their brutality. They execute captured prisoners. They kill children. They enslave, rape, and force women into marriage. They threatened a religious minority with genocide. And in acts of barbarism, they took the lives of two American journalists—Jim Foley and Steven Sotloff.

So ISIL poses a threat to the people of Iraq and Syria, and the broader Middle East—including American citizens, personnel and facilities. If left unchecked, these terrorists could pose a growing threat beyond that region, including to the United States. While we have not yet detected specific plotting against our homeland, ISIL leaders have threatened America and our allies. Our Intelligence Community believes that thousands of foreigners—including Europeans and some Americans—have joined them in Syria and Iraq. Trained and battle-hardened, these fighters could try to return to their home countries and carry out deadly attacks.

I know many Americans are concerned about these threats. Tonight, I want you to know that the United States of America is meeting them with strength and resolve. Last month, I ordered our military to take targeted action against ISIL to stop its advances. Since then, we've conducted more than 150 successful airstrikes in Iraq. These strikes have protected American personnel and facilities, killed ISIL fighters, destroyed weapons, and given space for Iraqi and Kurdish forces to reclaim key territory. These strikes have also helped save the lives of thousands of innocent men, women and children.

But this is not our fight alone. American power can make a decisive difference, but we cannot do for Iraqis what they must do for themselves, nor can we take the place of Arab partners in securing their region. And that's why I've insisted that additional U.S. action depended upon Iraqis forming an inclusive government, which they have now done in recent days. So tonight, with a new Iraqi government in place, and following consultations with allies abroad and Congress at home, I can announce that America will lead a broad coalition to roll back this terrorist threat.

Our objective is clear: We will degrade, and ultimately destroy, ISIL through a comprehensive and sustained counterterrorism strategy.

First, we will conduct a systematic campaign of airstrikes against these terrorists. Working with the Iraqi government, we will expand our efforts beyond protecting our own people and humanitarian missions, so that we're hitting ISIL targets as Iraqi forces go on offense. Moreover, I have made it clear that we will hunt down terrorists who threaten our country, wherever they are. That means I will not hesitate to take action against ISIL in Syria, as well as Iraq. This is a core principle of my presidency: If you threaten America, you will find no safe haven.

Second, we will increase our support to forces fighting these terrorists on the ground. In June, I deployed several hundred American servicemembers to Iraq to assess how we can best support Iraqi security forces. Now that those teams have completed their work—and Iraq has formed a government—we will send an additional 475 servicemembers to Iraq. As I have said before, these American forces will not have a combat mission—we will not get dragged into another ground war in Iraq. But they are needed to support Iraqi and Kurdish forces with training, intelligence and equipment. We'll also support Iraq's efforts to stand up National Guard Units to help Sunni communities secure their own freedom from ISIL's control.

Across the border, in Syria, we have ramped up our military assistance to the Syrian opposition. Tonight, I call on Congress again to give us additional authorities and resources to train and equip these fighters. In the fight against ISIL, we cannot rely on an Assad regime that terrorizes its own people—a regime that will never regain the legitimacy it has lost. Instead, we must strengthen the opposition as the best counterweight to extremists like ISIL, while pursuing the political solution necessary to solve Syria's crisis once and for all.

Third, we will continue to draw on our substantial counterterrorism capabilities to prevent ISIL attacks. Working with our partners, we will redouble our efforts to cut off its funding; improve our intelligence; strengthen our defenses; counter its warped ideology; and stem the flow of foreign fighters into and out of the Middle East. And in two weeks, I will chair a meeting of the U.N. Security Council to further mobilize the international community around this effort.

Fourth, we will continue to provide humanitarian assistance to innocent civilians who have been displaced by this terrorist organization. This includes Sunni and Shia Muslims who are at grave risk, as well as tens of thousands of Christians and other religious minorities. We cannot allow these communities to be driven from their ancient homelands.

So this is our strategy. And in each of these four parts of our strategy, America will be joined by a broad coalition of partners. Already, allies are flying planes with us over Iraq; sending arms and assistance to Iraqi security forces and the Syrian opposition; sharing intelligence; and providing billions of dollars in humanitarian aid. Secretary Kerry was in Iraq today meeting with the new government and supporting their efforts to promote unity. And in the coming days he will travel across the Middle East and Europe to enlist more partners in this fight, especially Arab nations who can help mobilize Sunni communities in Iraq and Syria, to drive these terrorists from their lands. This is American leadership at its best: We stand with people who fight for their own freedom, and we rally other nations on behalf of our common security and common humanity.

My administration has also secured bipartisan support for this approach here at home. I have the authority to address the threat from ISIL, but I believe we are strongest as a nation when the President and Congress work together. So I welcome congressional support for this effort in order to show the world that Americans are united in confronting this danger.

Now, it will take time to eradicate a cancer like ISIL. And any time we take military action, there are risks involved—especially to the servicemen and women who carry out these missions. But I want the American people to understand how this effort will be different from the wars in Iraq and Afghanistan. It will not involve American combat troops fighting on foreign soil. This counterterrorism campaign will be waged through a steady, relentless effort to take out ISIL wherever they exist, using our air power and our support for partner forces on the ground. This strategy of taking out terrorists who threaten us, while supporting partners on the front lines, is one that we have successfully pursued in Yemen and Somalia for years. And it is consistent with the approach I outlined earlier this year: to use force against anyone who threatens America's core interests, but to mobilize partners wherever possible to address broader challenges to international order.

My fellow Americans, we live in a time of great change. Tomorrow marks 13 years since our country was attacked. Next week marks six years since our economy suffered its worst setback since the Great Depression. Yet despite these shocks, through the pain we have felt and the grueling work required to bounce back, America is better positioned today to seize the future than any other nation on Earth.

Our technology companies and universities are unmatched. Our manufacturing and auto industries are thriving. Energy independence is closer than it's been in decades. For all the work that remains, our businesses are in the longest uninterrupted stretch of job creation in our history. Despite all the divisions and discord within our democracy, I see the grit and determination and common goodness of the American people every single day—and that makes me more confident than ever about our country's future.

Abroad, American leadership is the one constant in an uncertain world. It is America that has the capacity and the will to mobilize the world against terrorists. It is America that has rallied the world against Russian aggression, and in support of the Ukrainian peoples' right to determine their own destiny. It is America—our scientists, our doctors, our know-how—that can help contain and cure the outbreak of Ebola. It is America that helped remove and destroy Syria's declared chemical weapons so that they can't pose a threat to the Syrian people or the world again. And it is America that is helping Muslim communities around the world not just in the fight against terrorism, but in the fight for opportunity, and tolerance, and a more hopeful future.

America, our endless blessings bestow an enduring burden. But as Americans, we welcome our responsibility to lead. From Europe to Asia, from the far reaches of Africa to war-torn capitals of the Middle East, we stand for freedom, for justice, for dignity. These are values that have guided our nation since its founding.

Tonight, I ask for your support in carrying that leadership forward. I do so as a Commander-in-Chief who could not be prouder of our men and women in uniform—pilots who bravely fly in the face of danger above the Middle East, and servicemembers who support our partners on the ground.

When we helped prevent the massacre of civilians trapped on a distant mountain, here's what one of them said: "We owe our American friends our lives. Our children will always remember that there was someone who felt our struggle and made a long journey to protect innocent people."

That is the difference we make in the world. And our own safety, our own security, depends upon our willingness to do what it takes to defend this nation and uphold the values that we stand for—timeless ideals that will endure long after those who offer only hate and destruction have been vanquished from the Earth.

May God bless our troops, and may God bless the United States of America.

Source: "Statement by the President on ISIL," The White House Office of the Press Secretary, September 10, 2014, http://www.whitehouse.gov/the-press-office/2014/09/10/statement-president-isil-1.

Contributors

Dr. Elena Andreeva
Assistant Professor
Department of History
Virginia Military Institute

Dr. Stefan M. Brooks
Assistant Professor of Political
Science
Lindsey Wilson College

Dr. William T. Dean III
Associate Professor
Air Command and Staff College

Dr. Benedict Edward DeDominicis
Associate Professor of Political Science
American University in Bulgaria

Dr. Louis A. DiMarco
Associate Professor
Department of Military History
U.S. Army Command & General
Staff College
Fort Leavenworth, Kansas

Dr. Timothy L. Francis
Branch Director
Naval Historical Center
Washington, D.C.

Dr. Elun A. Gabriel
Associate Professor
Department Chair, History
St. Lawrence University

Dr. Brent M. Geary
Ohio University

Dr. Laura J. Hilton
Associate Professor and Chair
Department of History
Muskingum University

Dr. Jack Vahram Kalpakian
Associate Professor of International
Studies
Al Akhawayn University, Morocco

Dr. Sedat Cem Karadeli
Assistant Professor
Cankaya University, Turkey

Robert S. Kiely
Independent Scholar

Dr. Arne Kislenko
Associate Professor of History
Ryerson University, Canada

Keith A. Leitich
Independent Scholar

Dr. Lucian N. Leustean
Senior Lecturer
Political Science and International
Relations
Aston University, England

Adam B. Lowther
Independent Scholar

Dr. James B. McNabb
Professor
Department of Social Science
American University of Iraq, Sulaimani

Larissa Mihalisko
Political Officer, Afghanistan
U.S. State Department

Dr. Jerry D. Morelock
Colonel
U.S. Army, Retired
Editor in Chief, *Armchair General*
Magazine

Gregory Wayne Morgan
Independent Scholar

Dr. Paul G. Pierpaoli Jr.
Fellow
Military History, ABC-CLIO, Inc.

Mark M. Sanders
Head of Reference
Joyner Library–East Carolina University

Dr. Daniel E. Spector
Independent Scholar

Dr. Spencer C. Tucker
Senior Fellow
Military History, ABC-CLIO, Inc.

Dr. Bruce Vandervort
Professor of History
Virginia Military Institute

Dr. William E. Watson
Professor of History and Chair
History Department
Immaculata University

Dr. Wyndham E. Whynot
Assistant Professor of History
Livingstone College

Dr. Sherifa Zuhur
Visiting Scholar
Center for Middle Eastern
Studies
University of California,
Berkeley

Index

About the Editor

Spencer C. Tucker, PhD, has been senior fellow in military history at ABC-CLIO since 2003. He is the author or editor of more than 60 books and encyclopedias, many of which have won prestigious awards. Tucker's last academic position before his retirement from teaching was the John Biggs Chair in Military History at the Virginia Military Institute in Lexington. He has been a Fulbright scholar, a visiting research associate at the Smithsonian Institution, and, as a U.S. Army captain, an intelligence analyst in the Pentagon. His recently published works include *Wars That Changed History: 50 of the World's Greatest Conflicts; U.S. Conflict in the 21st Century: Afghanistan War, Iraq War, and the War on Terror;* and the award-winning *World War II: The Definitive Encyclopedia and Document Collection,* all published by ABC-CLIO.